AN ESSAY CONCERNING

HUMAN UNDERSTANDING

BY

JOHN LOCKE

COLLATED AND ANNOTATED, WITH

PROLEGOMENA, BIOGRAPHICAL, CRITICAL, AND HISTORICAL

BY

ALEXANDER CAMPBELL FRASER

IN TWO VOLUMES

VOL. I

DOVER PUBLICATIONS, INC.
NEW YORK • NEW YORK

Published in Canada by General Publishing Company, Ltd., 30 Lesmill Road, Don Mills, Toronto, Ontario.

Published in the United Kingdom by Constable and Company, Ltd., 10 Orange Street, London WC 2.

This new Dover edition first published in 1959 is an unabridged and unaltered republication of the First Edition. It is published through special arrangement with Oxford University Press.

International Standard Book Number: 0-486-20530-4

Library of Congress Catalog Card Number: 59-3771

Manufactured in the United States of America
Dover Publications, Inc.
180 Varick Street
New York, N. Y. 10014

Although increased leisure, gained more than two years ago, by release from the public duties of the Edinburgh lecture-room, may have hardly compensated for abatement of strength in the evening of life, I have gladly devoted a portion of that strength to this labour of love in connexion with Locke; in succession to the development of the philosophy of Berkeley in which I was before engaged. In each undertaking I have been encouraged by the countenance of the illustrious University, associated with the historic memories of many centuries, which has not forgotten that Oxford was the academic home of Locke, and the chosen retreat of the old age of Berkeley.

I desire in particular to thank the Delegates, the Secretaries, and the other officials of the Clarendon Press for their kindness, in the course of those critical reconstructions of Berkeley and Locke, during the last twenty-five years.

I am indebted to Professor Andrew Seth, my distinguished successor in the University of Edinburgh, for reading the proofs of the greater part of the present work, and for valuable suggestions.

In the preparation of the Index I have had the able assistance of Mr. Henry Barker.

A. C. F.

GORTON HOUSE, HAWTHORNDEN, MID-LOTHIAN :
February 9, 1894.

CONTENTS

OF

THE FIRST VOLUME

———◆———

PROLEGOMENA,

BIOGRAPHICAL, CRITICAL, AND HISTORICAL.

(C.) HISTORICAL.

AN ESSAY CONCERNING HUMANE UNDERSTANDING,

IN FOUR BOOKS,

BY JOHN LOCKE.

BOOK I.

NEITHER PRINCIPLES NOR IDEAS ARE INNATE.

BOOK II.

OF IDEAS.

Contents.

ERRATA

Page 65², *for* § 70 *read* § 72
  ,,   113¹, line 5, *for* This *read* Now
  ,,   155, *insert* § 5 *opposite marginal analysis.*
  ,,   156, *insert* § 6 *opposite marginal analysis.*
  ,,   192¹, *for* initiating *read* irritating *in quotation from Prof. Huxley.*
  ,,   219, line 2, *for* ch. 4 *read* ch. 5
  ,,   241¹, line 17, *insert* not *before* impossible
  ,,   260², line 22, *for* former *read* latter
  ,,   308¹, *for* ' *Inquiry,* sect. vi.' *read* ' *Inquiry,* sect. vii.'
  ,,   315¹, line 6, *insert full stop after* motives
Ch. xxvii, in the numbering of the §§, numbers 10 and 11 are repeated.

PROLEGOMENA

BIOGRAPHICAL, CRITICAL, AND HISTORICAL

——•••——

PRELIMINARY.

EDITIONS AND INTERPRETATIONS OF LOCKE'S ESSAY.

FEW books in the literature of philosophy have so widely represented the spirit of the age and country in which they appeared, or have so influenced opinion afterwards, as Locke's *Essay concerning Human Understanding*. The art of education, political thought, theology, and philosophy, especially in Britain, France, and America, long bore the stamp of the *Essay*, or of reaction against it, to an extent that is not explained by the comprehensiveness of Locke's thought, or by the force of his genius.

Historical Influence of the Essay.

In the fourteen years that elapsed between its first appearance in 1690 and its author's death, the *Essay* passed through four editions, followed by more than forty in the course of last century, and by many since, besides abridgments, and translations into Latin and French. From the first the book was the subject of criticism, and the occasion of controversy. Opposite interpretations have been put upon its doctrines by its innumerable critics, from Stillingfleet and Leibniz in Locke's lifetime; Condillac with the French Encyclopaedists, and Reid with his followers in Scotland, in last century; to

Editions and versions.

Coleridge, Cousin, and Green, who treat the *Essay* as an incoherent expression of sensuous empiricism, or Webb and Tagart, with some recent German critics, who lay stress on its recognition of intuitive reason.

Critics of
the *Essay*. For a long time the *Essay* has been named more than it has been studied. Even historians of philosophy have dealt with it largely at second hand; without that candid comparison of parts with the spirit and design of the whole, which is necessary in the case of a book that deals with philosophy in the inexact language of common life; and also without sufficient allowance for the fact that it was composed by a man of affairs, who discussed questions appropriated by abstract philosophy with a view to the immediate interests of human life, as his occasional employment, in an unphilosophical age.

Commen-
taries of
Lee and
Leibniz. It has been remarked as curious that there should be no collated and annotated edition of this English philosophical classic, notwithstanding the successive changes introduced in the four English editions published under Locke's eye, and the prolonged controversial discussion of the *Essay*. It is true that even before Locke's death it was made the subject of elaborate comment, by Henry Lee, rector of Tichmarsh in Northamptonshire, in his *Anti-Scepticism: or Notes upon each chapter of Mr. Locke's Essay, with an explication of all the particulars of which he treats, and in the same order.* Of this work Stewart remarks, that the strictures, ' often acute and sometimes just, are marked throughout with a fairness and candour rarely to be met with in controversial writers'; and, according to the judgment of Sir James Mackintosh, Lee 'has stated the question of innate ideas more fully than Shaftesbury, or even Leibniz.' A more celebrated commentary on the *Essay* was that of Leibniz, in his posthumous *Nouveaux Essais sur l'Entendement Humain*, written before Locke died, but not published till 1765. In the inconvenient form of dialogue, the doctrines of the *Essay* are here discussed chapter by chapter, between the interlocutors, in the eclectic spirit which thus appears in the opening sentences of the preface:—'The *Essay on the Understanding*,' he says, ' by an illustrious Englishman, being one of the most

beautiful and esteemed works of the time, I have resolved
to make Remarks on it, because, having myself long
meditated upon this subject, and upon most of the matters
touched upon in the *Essay*, I have thought that it afforded
a good opportunity for putting forth my own thoughts
about them, under the title of *New Essays on the Understanding;* and that I might secure a favourable reception
for my thoughts, by presenting them in such good company.
I have hoped also that I might be able to profit by the
work of this author, not only in the way of relieving my
own labour (since it is easier to follow the thread of an
able author than to elaborate anew,) but also by adding
something to what he has done, which is less formidable
than to make an independent beginning ; and I think I
have cleared up some difficulties which he left unin-
vestigated.   It is true that I often differ from him ; but, so
far from denying the merit of famous writers, one bears
testimony to it, by frankly making known in what, and
why, one differs from their opinions ; because we ought
to prefer reason to even their authority on questions
of importance.   In fact, although the author of the *Essay*
says a thousand things of which I approve, our systems
are widely different.   His has more relation to Aristotle,
and mine to Plato ; while we both diverge in many ways
from those illustrious ancients.   Also the author of the
Essay adapts his style more to the general reader than I
pretend to do, for I am obliged occasionally to be more
acroamatical and abstract.'   This last consideration Lee
presses more strongly than Leibniz, when he mentions
'a natural elegancy of style ; an unaffected beauty in his
expressions ; and a just proportion and tuneable cadence
in all his periods' as, 'above all,' the qualities which
brought Locke's *Essay* into popularity—a judgment which
readers may regard as an exaggeration of its literary
merits.

Among more recent criticisms of the *Essay* the most
celebrated are contained in Cousin's *Ecole Sensualiste :
Système de Locke* (1829), according to Sir William Hamilton
'the most important work on Locke since the *Nouveaux
Essais* of Leibniz ' ; and in the Introduction to the philo-

Cousin and
Green.

sophical works of David Hume, by the late Mr. Green, who, notwithstanding the anachronism, has subjected the *Essay* to the canons of Neo-Hegelian dialectic.

The present work. The present work is meant partly as homage to its author's historical importance, as a chief factor in the development of modern philosophy during the last two centuries. It is also intended to recall to a study of Locke those who, interested in the philosophical and theological problems of this age, are apt to be dominated too exclusively by its spirit and maxims. They may thus study the problems in a fresher, although cruder, form than they have now assumed, through the controversies of the intervening period. The text has been prepared after collation with the four editions published when Locke was alive, and also with the French version of Coste, done under Locke's supervision. The successive changes are bracketed, many of them significant, especially those which express his oscillation of opinion about 'power' in moral agency, in Bk. II. ch. xxi. The archaic orthography of the original title—*Essay concerning Humane Understanding*—is retained on the title-page of the *Essay*, but is exchanged in the body of the work for the modern form. On the same principle (with reluctance) I have retained the 'it is' and 'has' of the best posthumous editions, instead of the ''tis' and (occasionally) 'hath' of the early folios. I have also reduced the superabundant italics and capitals of the early editions, retaining only what may remind readers that the book is not the work of a contemporary. The sectional analyses have been removed from the body of the text to the margin, occasionally corrected and enlarged, and new ones annexed to sections where they were wanting. The annotations might have been multiplied indefinitely; for almost every question in metaphysical philosophy and theology, as well as in philosophical physics, is suggested by the text, as well as innumerable references to the *Essay* in the literature of the last two centuries. The annotations offered are for the most part intended to keep the point of view and leading purpose of the *Essay* steadily before the reader; and the references are mostly to the works of Locke's contemporaries, and his immediate predecessors and successors. Occasional side-glances show recent phases of philosophical or theological thought, to which the development through controversy of what was latent in the *Essay* may have contributed. The corresponding portions of the *Nouveaux Essais* are often quoted, in the interest of the contrast, and of the speculative insight of the German philosopher. In the Prolegomena Locke's individuality, and the circumstances by which it was modified are presented in their relation to the *Essay*; this is followed by constructive criticism of the *Essay* itself, as a 'historical plain' account of a knowledge that, being finite and human, is at last determined by faith; and in the end attention is invited to two opposite directions into which the *Essay* helped to divert the main current of philosophical thought, in Berkeley and in Hume. The portrait of Locke presented in this work is reproduced from the picture in Christ Church, so long Locke's home.

(*A*.) BIOGRAPHICAL.

I. WHAT GAVE RISE TO THE ESSAY (1670).

Locke's personality a key to the interpretation of his Essay.

To interpret the *Essay* one must remember the personality of Locke and the circumstances of his life, for the book is in a singular degree the reflex of its author. It has been well said that all Locke's published writings, including even the *Essay*, were 'occasional,' being intended to overcome prevailing obstacles to civil, religious, and intellectual liberty. The seventy-two years of his life coincide at first with some of the stormiest and most momentous in the history of England, and then with the compromise and peaceful settlement in which he bore an influential part. The *Essay* itself was the issue of an accident, and in preparing it he was throughout moved by the sober moral purpose that animated his life.

A memorable meeting of 'five or six friends.'

Here is his own explanation of the way in which, when nearly forty years of age, he engaged in the intellectual enterprise that occupied him at intervals until he had entered on his fifty-eighth year :—' Were it fit to trouble thee with the history of this *Essay*, I should tell thee that five or six friends meeting at my chamber, and discoursing on a subject very remote from this, found themselves quickly at a stand, by the difficulties that arose on every side. After we had a while puzzled ourselves, without coming any nearer a resolution of those doubts which per-plexed us, it came into my thoughts that we took a wrong course ; and that before we set ourselves upon inquiries of that nature, it was necessary to examine our own abilities, and see what objects our understandings were or were not fitted to deal with. This I proposed to the company, who all readily assented ; and thereupon it was agreed that this should be our first inquiry. Some hasty, undigested thoughts, on a subject I had never before considered, which I set down against our next meeting, gave the first entrance into this Discourse; which, having been thus begun by chance, was continued by entreaty; written by incoherent parcels; and, after long intervals of neglect, resumed again, as my humour and occasions permitted; and at last, in a retirement, where an attendance on my health gave me leisure, it was brought into that order thou now seest it.' Locke does not mention the subject which, on this memorable occasion, puzzled the assembled friends, and led him to make an inquiry into the constitution and limits of human knowledge the chief work of his life. But we are not left quite in the dark. James Tyrrell, one of the party, not unknown afterwards as a political and historical writer, has recorded it, in a manuscript note on the margin of his copy of the *Essay*, now in the British Museum. The difficulties, according to this record, arose in the course of a discussion about the 'principles of morality and revealed religion.' This subject is indeed not far removed from the theory of human knowledge, which inevitably mixes itself up with all profound ethical and religious thought; and Locke's undertaking was thus associated from the first with the mysteries of existence of which religion promises a practical solution.

At the time of this fruitful reunion Locke was living in London, in the house of the first Earl of Shaftesbury, as his confidential secretary and friend, a sharer in the public work of the most remarkable statesman in the reign of Charles the Second. How came it about that now, in middle life, in the vortex of politics, this man of affairs entered a region that is occupied for the most part by those who devote their lives exclusively to abstract speculation? A summary retrospect of the preceding history of Locke's mind may help to explain how Lord Shaftesbury's secretary became the author of the *Essay concerning Human Understanding*.

Locke's circumstances when this meeting took place.

II. PREPARATION FOR THE ESSAY: LOCKE'S
EARLY LIFE IN SOMERSET, OXFORD,
AND LONDON. (1632–70.)

Locke's
birth and
boyhood
in a Puri-
tan family.

Information about Locke's early history is scanty. That he was the elder of two sons, in a respectable Somersetshire family, of Roundhead and Puritan sympathies—that he was born on August 29, 1632, at Wrington, under the shadow of the Mendip hills—that his boyhood was spent at Beluton, the rural home which he afterwards inherited from his father, a short distance from the little market town of Pensford, in the fertile valley of the Chew, six miles south-east from Bristol, and ten west from Bath—that his mother was several years older than his father, 'pious and affectionate,' whose early death left her sons in childhood without a mother's care—that his father, a small country attorney, 'kept his eldest son, when he was a boy, in much awe and at a distance, but relaxing still by degrees of that severity as he grew up to be a man, till he, being become capable of it, lived with him as a friend till his death,' when that son was almost thirty years of age—that the home training at Beluton must have been often interrupted, inasmuch as the father joined the army of the Parliament, in which, after two years' service, he rose to be captain, and in the end so suffered in those troubled times that he left a reduced estate to his son:—these are the chief recorded incidents of the boyhood of John Locke. We see a slender and delicate youth, living through the turbulent drama in which his father was for a time an actor. As Locke wrote in the year of the Restoration: 'I had no sooner perceived myself in the world but I found myself in a storm, which has lasted almost hitherto.' The Parliamentary patrons of the father found a place for the boy, when he was fourteen, on the foundation of Westminster School. He spent six years at Westminster. Little that is significant has been recorded about his Westminster life, unless the absence in the scanty record of signs of that genius for scholarship and literature which marked South and Dryden, who were among his schoolfellows. It was in those Westminster

years that the assembly of Puritan divines was debating
Calvinistic theology in the Jerusalem Chamber ; and in one
of the years Locke may have witnessed the tragedy at
Whitehall in which the Puritan revolution culminated.

In 1652 Locke gained a scholarship at Christ Church
and for fifteen years Oxford was his home. The picture
now becomes more distinct. We see him in Cromwellian
Oxford, 'under a fanatical tutor,' as Anthony Wood tells us,
Cromwell Chancellor of the University, with John Owen, the
famous Puritan divine and apostle of a political toleration
of religious differences, Dean of Christ Church and Vice-
Chancellor. The idea of toleration professed by Owen
and the Independents was probably not without influence
on the young scholar from Westminster. But his hereditary
sympathy with the Puritans seems to have abated at Christ
Church, as a consequence of the 'storm,' and in the larger
experience which opened at Oxford. He discovered that
'what was called general freedom was general bondage;
and that the popular asserters of liberty were the greatest
engrossers of it too, and not unjustly called its keepers.'
It was true that even in Cromwellian Oxford the Aristotle
of the Schoolmen still determined the studies of the place,
which were uncongenial to Locke, because 'perplexed with
obscure terms and useless questions.' He thus early showed
his love for facts rather than abstractions, and preferred
intercourse with persons to intercourse with books. 'I have
often heard him say,' Lady Masham reports, 'that he had
small satisfaction in his Oxford studies, as finding very
little light brought thereby to his understanding; that he
became discontented with his manner of life, and wished that
his father had rather designed him for anything else than
what he was there destined to.' He sought the company
of pleasant and witty men, whom he delighted to meet,
and 'in conversation and correspondence much of his
time was then spent.' Anthony Wood, one of his college
contemporaries, representing the spirit of the past, afterwards described 'John Locke of Christ Church, now a noted
writer,' as in his undergraduate days 'a man of turbulent
spirit, clamorous and discontented. While the rest of our
club took notes deferentially from the mouth of the master,

Locke at
Oxford dis-
satisfied.

the said Locke scorned to do so, but was ever prating and troublesome.' Nevertheless, in 1658 he took his master's degree, on the same day as Joseph Glanvill, who was akin to him in zeal for intellectual liberty, and author afterwards of the *Vanity of Dogmatising* and the *Scepsis Scientifica*, works probably not without influence upon the *Essay.*

Awakened to intellectual life by Descartes.

The year of the Restoration was an important one in Locke's history. It left him senior student and tutor in Christ Church. Soon after, by the death of his father, he came into possession of the little property of Beluton. He was thus in circumstances suited to independent study. The modern disposition to free inquiry was finding its way into Oxford, although it was not recommended in the colleges; and self-education was thus encouraged in a strong personality. The chief philosophical works of Descartes had appeared nearly twenty years before, and were awakening intellect in the universities of Europe. The *Human Nature* and *Leviathan* of Hobbes, and the *Syntagma Philosophicum* of Gassendi followed, during Locke's undergraduate years. He was never a great reader, at least of philosophical books: he disclaims intimacy with the works of Hobbes, and is silent about Gassendi. But he was strongly attracted to Descartes. ' The first books, as Mr. Locke has told me,' Lady Masham writes, ' which gave him a relish of philosophical things were those of Descartes. He was rejoiced in reading these, because, though he very often differed in opinion from this writer, yet he found that what he said was very intelligible; from whence he was encouraged to think that his not having understood others had possibly not proceeded from a defect in his understanding.' Descartes, often named in Locke's letters to Stillingfleet, probably influenced him more than any metaphysical philosopher, not only by his analytic intrepidity, but by his introspective method. He may have suggested the very question about human knowledge and its limits which led to the *Essay*—a question which Descartes says that any man who loves truth must examine once at least in his life; since the adequate investigation of it comprehends all intellectual method, and the organon of human knowledge; nothing being more absurd than to argue about the mysteries of the universe without consideration of the relative competency of the mind of man.

The religious temper, nourished in Locke by his education among the English dissenters, when Calvinistic theology was in the ascendant, suggested an ecclesiastical career. This was not favoured, however, by his growing sympathy with free inquiry, in reaction against scholastic studies, and against the fanaticism of which he had accused 'the popular asserters of liberty.' Experimental research became fashionable in England after the Restoration. This opened a field more congenial to Locke. The Royal Society was founded in 1660 at Oxford. Wallis and Wilkins, afterwards Boyle and Wren, at Oxford, with Barrow and Newton, at Cambridge, were helping to make investigation of nature take the place of the 'vermiculate' questions of medieval philosophy. About 1664 the young Student of Christ Church was busied in chemical experiments, and meteorological observations, and soon after in the study of medicine. Before 1666 he was engaged in a sort of amateur practice in Oxford. Although he never took a doctor's degree, he was in later life familiarly known among his friends as 'Doctor Locke.' Medicine did not long absorb one whose temperament inclined him to a variety of interests. Besides, he inherited a delicate constitution, unfavourable to practice as a physician, and all his life he had to offer a prudent resistance to chronic consumption and asthma. But to the end he was fond of the art of healing, and was ready on occasion to give friendly medical advice.

Imbibing the spirit, and adopting the methods of experimental inquiry, in the study of medicine.

Locke early applied himself to questions of social polity, as well as to medicine. The constitution of society, the relations of Church and State, and above all the right and duty of political toleration of religious differences, were revolved in his thoughts in those Oxford years; always in sympathy with individual freedom, and in a spirit of prudential utilitarianism. His commonplace-books between his twenty-eighth and thirty-fourth year prove this. Among them a fragment on the 'Roman Commonwealth,' and another headed 'Sacerdos,' show how soon the idea of liberty, civil and religious, was in process of formation in his

Investigating questions of social polity.

mind ; and how he looked at sacerdotalism as 'the one widespread perversion of the original simplicity of Christianity.' But the most remarkable revelation of those early Oxford years is in an ' Essay concerning Toleration,' found among his papers. It anticipates principles on behalf of which Locke published elaborate arguments in after years, when toleration became his social ideal. This juvenile essay is partly a plea for promoting a comprehensive national church, by restoring Christianity to its original simplicity, and thus removing occasion for nonconformity ; and partly a vindication of civil and ecclesiastical liberty, on the ground that it is foolish to employ persecution as a means for producing reasonable beliefs.

Engaged for some months in diplomatic service.

Locke's interest in the body politic was not merely academical, even in those early Oxford years. Unexpectedly we find the medical experiments interrupted, in the winter of 1665, by an engagement of some months in diplomatic service, at the court of the elector of Brandenburg, as secretary to Sir Walter Vane. This introduced him to life out of England and to business, but could hardly have been meant as a first step in a diplomatic career ; for after his return to Oxford, in February 1666, he declined to go to Spain, as secretary of the embassy—'pulled both ways by divers considerations,' before he finally resolved. This aptly expresses Locke's state of mind in these Christ Church years—pulled different ways by divers tastes and ready sympathies, but as yet without obviously deep, decided, and persistent intellectual purpose—Descartes, amateur medical experiments, theological problems, social problems, intercourse with men in public affairs, each in turn.

An accident at last carried him to London and determined his career.

An unexpected circumstance carried him into the political world of London, in his thirty-fifth year, so that for sixteen years of middle life his home was chiefly there, ' in the society of great wits and ambitious politicians,' a man of affairs and of the world, without much undisturbed leisure. All this came about through a meeting with Lord Ashley, soon after the celebrated first Earl of Shaftesbury, due to the accidental absence of Dr. Thomas, the physician for whose advice that statesman was visiting Oxford.

Dr. Thomas had entrusted his friend Locke one day with
the care of his patient, and the intercourse thus brought
about between the versatile statesman and the Christ
Church student, with his many-sided interests, ripened into
friendship. 'Soon after, my lord, returning to London,
desired Mr. Locke that from that time he would look upon
his house as his own house, and that he would let him see
him there in London as soon as he could.' So we are
told by Lady Masham. Accordingly, in 1667, Christ Church
was exchanged for 'Exeter House in the Strand,' and
Locke became *factotum* of the most striking political person-
age in the reign of Charles the Second.

The scientific inquirer was now brought into the society
of Halifax and Buckingham, amongst the politicians;
and was also encouraged in experiments, medical and
meteorological, by intercourse, amongst physicians and
experimentalists, with Sydenham and Boyle. Sydenham's
admiration was strongly expressed :—'You know,' he says,
in the dedication to Mapleton of his *Methodus curandi
Febres* (1676), 'you know how thoroughly my method is
approved of by an intimate and common friend of ours,
and one who has closely and exhaustively examined the
subject—I mean Mr. John Locke; a man whom, in the
acuteness of his intellect, in the steadiness of his judgment,
and in the simplicity, that is, in the excellence of his
manners, I confidently declare to have, amongst the men
of our own time, few equals and no superior.' Locke's
intimacy with Boyle was not less close, and the friendship
with this illustrious chemist was unbroken till his death
in 1691, when Locke, addicted to kindred pursuits, edited
Boyle's *General History of the Air*. Locke's intimates
when Exeter House was his London home were chiefly
physicists and politicians. We do not see him much in
the society of men of letters or moral philosophers. There
is no trace of intimacy with his former schoolfellow Dryden,
from whom he was separated by politics, or with the
illustrious poet of the Puritans, then far advanced in life.
He met Evelyn occasionally, but there is no report of
acquaintance with Temple or with Bentley. Age as well
as politics may have separated him from Hobbes, who

Locke's
London
surround-
ings.

spent most of his time after the Restoration in London. It is not without meaning that Locke's favourite preacher during this London life was Benjamin Whichcote, vicar of St. Lawrence Jewry from 1668 till 1683, a clerical moralist and latitudinarian churchman of the Cambridge School, modest, tolerant, and reasonable in an eminent degree.

The famous reunion. It seems to have been in the winter of 1670, after Locke had lived for three or four years in his London home at Exeter House, that the meeting of the 'five or six friends' took place which has made his name famous, and that converted the amateur physician, and shy student of human life, now the secretary and friend of the intriguing politician, into the author of the *Essay concerning Human Understanding*.

The bent of his thoughts in London. Locke's commonplace-books during those first years in London throw some light on the condition of mind in which the *Essay* was undertaken. A fragment, *De Arte Medica*, dated in 1668, amongst his papers, reveals earnest search for truth, and dependence on experience for detecting it, as in sentences like these :—' He that in physics shall lay down fundamental questions, and from thence, drawing consequences and raising disputes, shall reduce medicine into the regular form of a science, *totum, teres, atque rotundum*, has indeed done something to enlarge the art of talking, and perhaps laid a foundation for endless disputes : but if he hopes to bring men by such a *system* to the knowledge of the infirmities of their own bodies, or the constitution, changes, and history of diseases, with the safe and discreet way of their cure, he takes much what a like course with him that should walk up and down in a thick wood, outgrown with briars and thorns, with a design to take a view and draw a map of the country. True knowledge grew first in the world by experience and rational observations ; but proud man, not content with the knowledge he was capable of, and which was useful to him, would needs penetrate into the hidden causes of things, lay down principles, and establish maxims to himself about the operations of nature, and then vainly expect that nature, or in truth God, should proceed according to those laws which *his* maxims had prescribed to him ; whereas his narrow and weak faculties

could reach no further than the observation and memory
of some few facts produced by visible external causes, but
in a way utterly beyond the reach of his apprehension;—
it being perhaps no absurdity to think that this great and
curious fabric of the world, the workmanship of the
Almighty, cannot be perfectly comprehended by any
understanding but His that made it.   Man, still affecting
something of Deity, laboured by his imagination to supply
what his observation and experience failed him in ; and
when he could not discover (by experience) the principles,
causes and methods of nature's workmanship, he would
needs fashion all these out of his own thought, and make
a world to himself, framed and governed by his own
intelligence.   This vanity spread itself into many useful
parts of natural philosophy ; and by how much the more it
seemed subtle, sublime, and learned, by so much the more
it proved pernicious and hurtful, by hindering the growth
of practical knowledge.'   It was with this modest ideal of
human knowledge, and sense of the dependence of our ideas
of things on our experience of what things are, and not on
innate resources of our own, that Locke proposed—by an
' historical ' or matter-of-fact examination of what ' human
understanding ' is fit to compass, when it tries to understand existing things—to guard men against unwarranted
assumptions and verbal abstractions, made to do duty for
a real knowledge of the actual attributes and powers of
things.   We see how he suspected abstract maxims and
empty phrases, the offspring of a vain conceit of innate
knowledge, and was thus led to insist on the dependence of
human understanding upon experience, in our inquiries into
the qualities and behaviour of the substances, material or
spiritual, that constitute the universe.   The record of his
thoughts about the time when the *Essay* was projected
shows also a disposition to look to prudent action as the
chief end of intellectual exertion ; to clip the wings of
speculation ; and to disparage, as idle amusement, knowledge that is pursued for its own sake only, and without
regard to its efficacy in making human life happier.

III. PREPARATION OF THE ESSAY: IN LONDON, FRANCE, AND HOLLAND. (1670–89.)

The first
draft of the
Essay.

Locke tells his readers 'that when he first put pen to
paper,' in fulfilment of his promise to the assembled friends,
he 'thought that all he should have to say on the matter
would be contained on one sheet of paper,' but that 'the
further he went the larger prospect he had,' till, in the
course of years, the work gradually 'grew to the bulk it
now appears in.' The 'hasty, undigested thoughts,' which
he 'set down against the next meeting,' were perhaps contained in the following sentences, found among his manuscripts:—'*Sic cogitavit, de Intellectu Humano, Johannes
Locke, anno* 1671. *Intellectus humanus, cum cognitionis
certitudine et assensûs firmitate.* First, I imagine that all
knowledge is founded on, and ultimately derives itself from
Sense, or something analogous to it; and may be called
Sensation. Which is done by our senses, conversant about
particular objects, which gives us the simple ideas or images
of things; and thus we come to have ideas of light and
heat, hard and soft; which are nothing but the reviving
again in our mind the imaginations which these objects,
when they affected our senses, caused in us—whether by
motion or otherwise, it matters not here to consider: and
thus we do observe and conceive light or heat, yellow or
blue, sweet or bitter: and therefore I think that those
things which we call *sensible qualities* are the simplest ideas
we have, and the first objects of the understanding.'—The
inquiry in which Locke now engaged, of which this interesting fragment was probably the beginning, was pursued in
the 'historical' or matter-of-fact way he had become accustomed to in his investigation of natural phenomena, or, as
we should now say, in the scientific spirit and method;
but with introspective, not external, observation, as the
investigating faculty. He turned to the study of a human
understanding as to a manifested living reality—a fact
among other facts—the supreme fact indeed—the fact of facts,
which illuminated all other facts, by bringing them into the
light of conscious life—but still itself presented in expe-

rience, and therefore to be studied in its temporal relations, according to the 'historical plain method'; not dealt with *a priori* as an abstraction [1]. Our human understanding of the universe, and the extent to which intelligence can with us penetrate into reality, was for Locke a concrete problem, that had to be determined in a well-considered experience of the actual behaviour of the human mind. It was the knowledge of things that *men* are capable of, and its source; not any theory of a knowledge more comprehensive than the human; not an *a priori* criticism either of infinite knowledge, or of the metaphysical essences of things, that Locke undertook to present—at a point too of extreme opposition to the blind obedience to human authority, which spoiled the medieval ideal of intellectual system, verbally consistent with itself, but deduced as it seemed only from definitions of words. Independence of books and tradition was the new ideal : all in the individualistic temper favoured in England, where, as Hume remarks, 'the great liberty and independence which every man enjoys, allows him to display the manners peculiar to himself; so that the English of any people in the universe have the least of a national character, unless this very singularity may pass for such.'

'Intervals of neglect' must have often interrupted this inquiry into the limits of a human understanding of the universe, in the five years that immediately followed the memorable reunion in 1670. Early in 1672, Lord Ashley, risen in Court favour for a time, was created Earl of Shaftesbury. In the same year he became head of the Board of Trade and Lord Chancellor. This brought Locke into closer relation with public affairs, and in the following year he was advanced to the Board of Trade secretaryship. Its records illustrate the diligence, prudence, and methodical administration of the secretary—not without repeated signs of his weak health: the asthma from which he suffered much in middle life, and more afterwards, was a trouble during that life in London amidst official cares. The fall of Shaftesbury in 1675 enabled his secretary to retire to

A retreat to France for health and study.

---

[1] See *Essay*, 'Introduction,' § 2.

France, where he lived for nearly four years, seeking health and engaged in studying 'human understanding,' partly at Paris, chiefly at Montpellier, in a seclusion to which he had been long a stranger.   In France, for the first time, his daily history may be traced in the circumstantial record of a journal, as well as in commonplace-books, which disclose vigilant observation of the society and political institutions of France, and interest in its natural curiosities ; lucid intelligence, but no trace of sentiment or historic imagination.   The most significant particulars are those which present the *Essay* in process of formation.   At Montpellier he was busied for months in revising and expanding materials which seem to have accumulated in the busy years of official life in London.   At Montpellier Thomas Herbert, afterwards the accomplished seventh Earl of Pembroke and patron of Berkeley, to whom both Locke's *Essay* and Berkeley's *Principles* were dedicated, was his neighbour; with him, then and after, he was much in friendly intimacy. But it is remarkable that his social intercourse in France was with physicians, naturalists, jurists, and travellers ; not much, if at all, with metaphysicians.   Yet that was the brilliant period of French speculative thought, represented by Nicole, Arnauld, and Malebranche ; Leibniz coming into view in Germany, and when Spinoza was withdrawn by death in Holland.   It does not appear that Locke met Malebranche, unless one may infer the contrary from the personal regard for the French philosopher that is expressed in a letter to Molyneux.   He translated the *Essais* of Nicole soon after his return to England, and later on he criticised Malebranche.   Bernier, the expositor of the mechanical philosophy of Gassendi, is mentioned amongst Locke's occasional associates.

Progress of the *Essay* at Montpellier.

It is difficult to say how far the *Essay* had advanced when its author returned to London, and to Lord Shaftesbury, in April, 1679.   Although he wrote to his friend Thoynard, a few weeks after he got there, that his ' book was completed,' he added, that he 'thought too well of it to let it then go out of his hands.'   It was kept there for ten other years, for more mature consideration, the additions and transformations the occasion of much correspondence with friends in the interval. The current of his thoughts now becomes more distinctly seen in his journals. The scientific rather than the metaphysical habit of mind—the movement of events as determined by their secondary causes, and dealt with on the 'historical plain method,' according to calculations of probability—is what we are in contact with in these records. The method of experimental medicine; observation of 'what is,' not ultimate inquiry 'why it is,' is prevalent. The aptness of a human understanding to misconduct itself haunts him. He sees men ready to put empty sounds in place of lucid ideas; to suppose that they have ideas when they have none, or distinct ideas when their ideas are obscure and confused; blind submission to authority, without seeing for themselves; abstract maxims, and unwarranted assumptions, apt to exclude real events and experience; intellectual vanity in quest of solutions of unsoluble mysteries of existence, with oversight of man's appointed state of intellectual mediocrity, and of the fact that a human understanding is 'disproportionate to the infinite extent of things'; men unconsciously and fruitlessly assuming that they had overcome the disproportion; escaping the pain which submission to facts as they are imposes, by keeping in circulation words void of ideas, and by building on assumptions about the realities of the universe that had no support in well-considered experience. He sees too that it is only by having ideas to connect with our words that we are in a capacity for having any knowledge of the substances to which the words relate, or even for forming probable presumptions about the behaviour of things; so that the first step to knowledge of anything in the world is to admit the actual ideas in which the world reveals itself to our senses. Of what sorts then are those ideas of ours, and how do they come to be our own? In what cases are they complete? in what must they remain for ever incomplete and obscure, or at the most capable of carrying the understanding only into the region of probabilities? To mitigate the various diseases of a human understanding; especially to abate its vain pretensions; its indolent surrender of itself to maxims imposed by human authority, or by its own prejudices; and to explode the empty verbalism that passes under the name of knowledge—all with intent to promote useful intellectual exercise in the daily life of experience, not to solve purely speculative problems of knowing and being—was plainly prominent in Locke's view, when the *Essay* was in process of formation in studious seclusion in France.

Return to England and fall of Shaftesbury.

Locke passed through a troubled life in England in the next four years. He resumed his old relations with Shaftesbury. During his absence his patron had been imprisoned in the Tower. He was now restored to favour for a few months, during which Locke was overwhelmed with official work. A time of plots and counterplots followed. England seemed about to plunge into another civil war. In 1681 Shaftesbury was again in the Tower, charged with treason, acquitted, and welcomed back with popular enthusiasm, to use his liberty in support of the Duke of Monmouth, with the zeal of a partisan, contrary to the prudent counsel of Locke. The arrest of Monmouth in the end of 1682 paralyzed Shaftesbury, who escaped to Holland, and died at Amsterdam early in the following year.

Course of his thoughts in the four disturbed years that followed his return.

' Intervals of neglect,' and ' incoherent parcels' of the *Essay* must have abounded in these four troubled years, which were spent by Locke first with his hands full in Shaftesbury's service in London, then with his patron at his country seat of St. Giles, again with his friend Tyrrell in Oxfordshire, or at Christ Church, or with the Shaftesbury family, as the guardian of ' Mr. Anthony,' afterwards the author of the *Characteristics*. The news of ' my lord's death' in Holland was followed by Locke's appearance as one of the mourners at St. Giles. In 1683 he was under a cloud ; suspected and watched as the friend of the exiled statesman, although there is presumptive evidence that he had no part in the intrigues. In 1682 Prideaux had reported from Oxford that ' John Locke was living there a very cunning, unintelligible life, being two days in town and three out, and no one knows where he goes, or when he goes, or when he returns.' The year after, the Dean of Christ Church ' confidently affirms that there is not any one in the college, however familiar with him, who has heard him speak a word against, or so much as concerning the government ; and although very frequently, both in public and in private, discourses have been purposely introduced to the disparagement of his master, the Earl of Shaftesbury, his party and designs, he could never be provoked to take any notice, or discover in word or look the least concern ; so that I believe there is not in the world such a master of taciturnity and passion. He has here a physician's place, which frees him from the exercise of the college.' The history of his studies in the four years, spent chiefly in London and Oxford, that followed his return from France, may be traced faintly in his journals. They recall the early medical years at Oxford more than the speculations about human understanding at Montpellier. Indifferent health and official life had interrupted the practice of medicine. But soon after the return from France we find records of patients in town and country, and the intercourse with Sydenham was resumed. At the same time problems of social polity, and the conflict of parties in England, encouraged continued consideration of the relations of Church and State, the difference between civil and ecclesiastical power, and the duty of compromise, civil toleration, and ecclesiastical comprehension. He is loyal to the national church, but with 'a heart truly charitable to all pious and sincere Christians,' and so indifferent to questions of theological controversy that no organized religious community can lay an exclusive claim to him ; but with a gravitation to the national church of England, as that in which the freedom of thought he supremely loved could best be found. There are signs now and then that the *Essay* was not forgotten. Its essence and spirit appear in the following sentences, for instance, written in 1681 :—'All general knowledge is founded only upon true ideas, and so far as we have these we are capable of demonstration, or certain knowledge : for he that hath the true idea of a circle or triangle is capable of knowing any demonstration concerning these figures ; but if he have not the true idea of a scalenus, he cannot *know* anything concerning it, though he may have some confused or imperfect *opinion* ; but this is belief, and not knowledge. And the mind being capable of thus knowing moral things as well as figures, I cannot but think

Morality as well as Mathematics capable of demonstration, if men would employ their understanding to think more about it, and not give themselves up to the lazy traditional way of talking one after another. The knowledge of natural bodies and their operations, on the other hand, reaching little further than bare matter of fact, without our having perfect ideas of the ways and manners they are produced, or the concurrent causes they depend on; and also the well management of public or private affairs, depending upon the various and unknown interests, humours, and capacity of men, and not upon any settled ideas of things—it follows that Physics, Polity, and Prudence are not capable of demonstration; but a man is principally helped in them by the history of matter of fact, and a sagacity in inquiring into probable causes, and finding out an analogy in their operations and effects. Knowledge then depends upon right and true ideas: opinion upon history and matter of fact. Hence it comes to pass that our general knowledges are *aeternae veritates*, and depend not upon the existence or accidents of things; for the truths of mathematics and morality are certain, whether men make true mathematical figures, or suit their actions to the rules of morality, or no. For that the three angles of a triangle are equal to two right ones is infallibly true, whether there be any such figure as a triangle actually existing in the world or no. And it is true that it is every one's duty to be just, whether there be any such thing as a just man in the world or no. But whether this particular course in public or in private affairs will succeed well; whether rhubarb will purge, or quinquena cure an ague, is known only by experience: and therefore is but probability, grounded on experience or analogical reasoning, but is no certain knowledge or demonstration.' Human understanding, in short, cannot rise above the practical certainty of probability in any of its conclusions regarding the behaviour of the actual substances that compose the universe, or reach absolute certainty as to any general propositions regarding their laws. Unconditionally certain knowledge is confined to the abstract relations of our own mind-created abstractions; it cannot be extended to the causal relations of concrete things, which are all independent of our will. The *Essay* must have been well thought out when the last-quoted sentences were written. The 'survey of the extent of human knowledge' was now taking the form of a survey of human ideas, on the ground that unless we have ideas of things there is nothing for the mind to know, and therefore no knowledge.

Locke's correspondence during this time of political turmoil shows a growing intimacy (through their common friends the Clarkes of Chipley in Somerset) with the wife, the son, and the daughter[1] of Cudworth, the Cambridge Platonist and philosophical theologian of the Anglican Church in the seventeenth century. Cudworth was then a recluse at Cambridge. His *Intellectual System of the Universe* had appeared in 1678, when Locke was in France. But members of the Cudworth family now figure in his life, and were associated with him to the end. The association would be philosophically interesting if the influence of Cudworth and of Cambridge rationalism could be traced in the *Essay*. Direct evidence of this is scanty, and the idealising genius and learning of Cudworth had little in common with the 'ideism' and individualism of Locke. There is no record of personal intercourse between them, and the *Intellectual System* is only once named in Locke's writings—in the *Thoughts on Education*, published in 1693. There, in referring to 'systems of natural philosophy'; to 'that of Descartes' as 'the one which is most in fashion'; and to 'the modern Corpuscularians' as those who 'talk in most things more intelligibly than the Peripatetics,'—he advises any one 'who would look further back, and acquaint himself with the opinions of the ancients,' to 'consult Dr. Cudworth's *Intellectual System* ; wherein that very learned author hath, with such acuteness and judgment, collected and explained the opinions of the Greek philosophers, that what principles they built on, and what were the chief hypotheses that divided them, is better to be seen in him than anywhere else that I know' (§ 193). This was written when Locke was an inmate in the family of Lady Masham, the daughter of Cudworth. From Whichcote, another representative of the same school, if not from Culverwell, Locke probably borrowed

The Cudworth family and the Cambridge Platonists.

---

[1] Afterwards Lady Masham.

the metaphor of 'the candle of the Lord,' to signify reason, especially in its intuition of self-evident principles, on which Locke 'founds all certainty,' and as to which he tells Stillingfleet that 'whether they come into view of the mind earlier or later, this is true of them, that they are all known by their native evidences.' Fowler, afterwards Bishop of Gloucester, another Cambridge latitudinarian, was one of Locke's intimates. In his ideas of ecclesiastical toleration, and of the relation of religion to reason, Locke had more in common with the Cambridge thinkers than with any other ecclesiastical contemporaries. But their direct influence in the formation of the *Essay* is probably overrated by Dr. von Hertling, in his elaborate volume, *John Locke und die Schule von Cambridge* (1893). He suggests that Locke's juvenile empiricism may have been modified by the Idealism of Cambridge when the *Essay* was approaching completion, as an explanation of the more distinct recognition of intellectual elements of knowledge in the last book of the *Essay*, as well as of the seeming inconsistency of that book with the preceding books. It might be interesting to speculate upon the consequences to philosophy, in England and in Europe, if Locke had spent his academical life at Cambridge instead of Oxford, and had breathed its atmosphere of Platonism, instead of pursuing physical experiments at Oxford, when Oxford was giving birth to its Royal Society. In that case the *Essay* might have been pervaded by a higher conception of the capacities of man than that which its author is apt to find in the common sense of ordinary human intelligence.

Locke in Holland.

In the end of 1683 Locke reappears, now a voluntary exile in Holland, then the asylum in Europe for those who failed to find civil and religious liberty in their native country. Earlier in the century Descartes made it his retreat for solitary thought, and Spinoza was living at Amsterdam six years before Locke found a home there. Holland was his refuge for more than five years after the gloomy autumn of 1683 in England. This was 'the retirement in which attendance on his health gave him leisure,' so that the *Essay* was there 'brought into that order' in which its readers received it on its first appearance. Locke told

Lady Masham that 'in Holland, enjoying better health than he had for a long time done in England, or even in the fine air of Montpellier, he had full leisure to prosecute his thoughts on the subject of Human Understanding; a work,' she adds, 'which in all probability he would never have finished had he continued in England.' Curiosity and his health made him at first move from place to place, but in the winter of 1684 he settled at Utrecht for study, 'with all the books and other luggage that I brought from England'—not to live undisturbed even in this retirement. He was watched by the authorities in England, where the Dean of Christ Church, Dr. Fell, in this same year deprived him of his Studentship and home at Christ Church, in obedience to the King's command. For the Secretary of State—'given to understand that one Mr. Locke, who belonged to the Earl of Shaftesbury, has upon several occasions behaved himself very factiously and undutifully to the government, is a Student of Christ Church'—desired 'in the King's name, that the Dean would have him removed from being a Student.' Lady Masham adds that she heard from a friend of the Dean, 'that nothing had ever happened which had troubled him more than what he had been obliged to do against Mr. Locke, for whom he ever had a sincere respect, and whom he believed to be of as irreproachable manners and inoffensive conversation as was in the world.'

In Holland Locke found a friend in Philip von Limborch, lucid and learned, the leader of liberal theology in Holland, successor of Episcopius as Remonstrant professor, and the friend of Cudworth, Whichcote, and More. The copious correspondence of Locke with Limborch, during the rest of Locke's life, is an important revelation of his mind: it helped to develope in both the correspondents the principle of religious liberty, and a perception of the reasonableness of Christianity in its original simplicity. In a letter to Limborch, Lady Masham remarks that 'Mr. Locke was born and had finished his studies at a time when Calvinism was in fashion in England. But these doctrines,' she adds, 'had come to be little thought of before I came into the world [1];

Limborch and liberal theology.

---

[1] Lady Masham was born in 1659.

and Mr. Locke used to speak of the opinions I had been accustomed to at Cambridge, even among the clergy there, as something new and strange to him. As during some years before he went to Holland, he had very little in common with our ecclesiastics, I imagine that the sentiments that he found in vogue amongst you in Holland pleased him far more, and seemed to him far more reasonable, than anything that he used to hear from English theologians.' In Locke rationalising theology was still united with a remainder of his inherited Puritanism, and always with aversion to the sacerdotal form of Christianity, to which he was not naturally attracted by historic sentiment or imagination, although it too has sustained many saints and martyrs in the history of Christendom.

Le Clerc and Locke's beginning of authorship.

Le Clerc was another of his Dutch friends, then the youthful representative of letters and philosophy in the College of the Remonstrants, who had two years before withdrawn from Geneva and Calvinism into the milder ecclesiastical atmosphere of Holland. The friendship with Le Clerc is associated with Locke's first appearance as an author. The *Bibliothèque Universelle*, commenced in 1686, under Le Clerc's auspices, soon became the chief literary periodical of its time in Europe. Locke was induced to provide some of the articles. Although he was now in his fifty-fifth year, and afterwards a voluminous author, these occasional essays were his first contributions to literature. ' It is a very odd thing '—he had so written to Lord Pembroke a few months before—' that I did get the reputation of no small writer without having done anything for it ; for I think two or three verses of mine, published without my name to them, have not gained me that reputation. Bating these, I do solemnly protest in the presence of God that I am not the author, not only of any libel, but not any pamphlet or treatise whatever, good, bad, or indifferent.' The ' verses ' had appeared in a volume in praise of Cromwell, brought out by Dr. John Owen in 1654, in which Locke and other Oxford men figured. As one might expect, those by Locke contain no poetry. His tardiness as an author is significant. It agrees with the intellectual sobriety and caution that belong to his character, and is a contrast to the impetuous ardour which hurried Spinoza, Berkeley, and Hume to present to the world in youth their bolder and more comprehensive speculations. The last of Locke's articles in the *Bibliothèque* was an 'epitome' in French of the forthcoming *Essay*. It appeared in January 1688.

He was then living at Rotterdam. The scene soon changed. The course of English politics was now opening a way for his return to his native country. In Holland he had found friends among the English refugees, especially Burnet, afterwards Bishop of Salisbury, and Mordaunt, the famous Earl of Peterborough, with whom Berkeley travelled in Italy a quarter of a century later. Locke was known in Holland also to William of Orange. William landed at Torbay in November 1688 : Locke followed in February, 1689, in the fleet which carried the princess to Greenwich. The political struggle of half a century was then consummated in the compromise of the Revolution settlement, of which Locke, now rising into popular fame, became the intellectual representative and philosophical defender.

His return to England.

IV. PUBLICATION OF THE ESSAY : LONDON. (1689-91.)

Locke was busy in authorship after his return to England. According to Lady Masham, 'he continued for more than two years after the Revolution much in London, enjoying all the pleasure there that any one can find, who, after being long in a manner banished from his country, unexpectedly returning to it, was himself more generally esteemed and respected than ever he was before. If he had any dissatisfaction in this time, it could only be, I suppose, from the ill success now and then of our public affairs ; for his private circumstances were as happy, I believe, as he wished them. But of all the contentments that he then received there was none greater than that of spending one day every week with my Lord Pembroke, in a conversation undisturbed by such as could not bear a part in the best entertainment of rational minds—free discourse concerning useful truths. His old enemy, the town air, did indeed sometimes make war upon his lungs ; but the kindness of the now Earl of Peter-

Two years in London.

borough and his lady afforded him pleasing accommodation on these occasions, at a house of theirs at Parsons Green, advantaged with a delightful garden, which was what Mr. Locke always took pleasure in.' Those two years in London were spent in hired apartments, in the house of ' Mrs. Smithsby, Dorset Court, Channel Row, Westminster.' On the plea of health, in the month after his return from Holland, he declined the post of ambassador to Brandenburg, contented with a modest Commissionership of Appeals, as an official recognition by the new government.

Pioneers of the *Essay*.

Locke now worked diligently through the press, in the interest of individual liberty—religious, civil, and intellectual. An *Epistola de Tolerantia*, written in Holland, addressed to Limborch, published anonymously at Gouda, in 1689, a few weeks after he landed in England, and translated into English in the following summer by William Popple, vindicated freedom of opinion in religion. The English Revolution, as well as principles of social economy and jurisprudence which anticipated Hume and Adam Smith, and were in advance of Grotius and Puffendorf, were defended in his anonymous *Treatise on Government*, also written in Holland, which came out early in the following year.

Publication of the *Essay* in March 1690.

These two were pioneers of the *Essay concerning Human Understanding*, which at last issued from the press in March 1690. It proposed a way of escape from the bondage of too easily credited maxims that were supposed to be ' innate,' and warned against words, either empty or ambiguous, maintained by the 'blind credulity' of the multitude, or to sustain rash excursions of philosophers ' into the vast ocean of being'; without due regard to the limits of experience that are imposed upon a human understanding, when man seeks to know the qualities and powers of existing things. The *Essay* was the first work of Locke's that was not anonymous, and for prudential or other reasons he resumed the veil in most of those that followed. His correspondence with Limborch and Le Clerc in 1689 shows him in all that year busied in carrying the *Essay* through the press. We are told that he got £30 for the copyright, about the same sum as Kant

received, ninety-one years after, for the philosophical complement of the *Essay*—the *Kritik of Pure Reason.*

V. LOCKE AT OATES: CONTEMPORARY CRITICS OF THE ESSAY. (1691–1704.)

The *Epistola de Tolerantia*, followed, in October 1690,
by a *Second Letter on Toleration*—the *Treatise on Government*—and the *Essay concerning Human Understanding*,
made up Locke's literary outcome while he was living in
Dorset Court, in the two years after his return from Holland, that is up to his fifty-ninth year.   They express convictions gradually formed by observation of the collisions of
his contemporaries with the adversaries of the free exercise
of reason in experience.   His bodily ailments had latterly
increased in London.   It was early in 1691 that the home
of his old age, the brightest of his homes, opened to receive
him.   This was the retired manor house of Oates in Essex,
between Ongar and Harlow, the country seat of Sir Francis
Masham.   Lady Masham, married when Locke was in
Holland, was the accomplished daughter of Cudworth, who
died three years before Locke went to live at Oates.   In the
course of the two years spent at Dorset Court, as Lady
Masham told Le Clerc, Locke had, ' by some considerably
long visits to Oates, made trial of the air of the place, which
is some twenty miles from London, and he thought none
would be more suitable for him.   His company could not
but be very desirable for us, and he had all the assurance
we could give him of being always welcome ; but to make
him easy in living with us, it was necessary he should do
so on his own terms, which Sir Francis at last assenting to,
he then believed himself at home with us, and resolved, if
it pleased God, here to end his days—which he did.'   At
Oates he lived in the bosom of the Masham family, which
included Lady Masham's mother[1], and a step-daughter,
Esther Masham, a bright girl then about sixteen, who
became Locke's favourite companion in the simple pleasures
of country life.   The idyllic picture of his fourteen
remaining years presents as much domestic happiness and
literary labour as was consistent with declining health.

The Manor House at Oates and the Mashams.

---

[1] Dr. Cudworth died in 1688.

Life at Oates was varied by occasional visits to London, particularly in 1696 and the four following years, when, as a Commissioner of the Board of Trade, with an income of £1000 a year, he became again involved in official cares. One relaxation was the society of visitors who were attracted to Oates by its illustrious inmate—Newton, once and again, on his way to or from Cambridge, Molyneux from Dublin, Fowler, the latitudinarian Bishop of Gloucester, and the free-thinking Anthony Collins, then a young Essex squire.

Other philosophical work, occasioned by the Essay.

Work in the study was resumed with characteristic industry and method as soon as Locke was settled at Oates, latterly assisted by M. Coste as amanuensis. What he had published in the two preceding years, especially the *Essay*, soon involved him in controversies which lasted with intervals to the end of his life. New editions of the *Essay*, the second in 1694, followed by the third and fourth in 1695 and 1700, with important changes and new chapters in the second and fourth ; adverse criticism of the *Essay* by Norris, Thomas Burnet, Lowde, Sherlock, Sergeant, Leibniz, and Lee ; the famous controversy with Stilling-fleet ; the posthumous tractate on the *Conduct of the Understanding*, originally meant to form a chapter in the *Essay* ; the *Examination of Malebranche*, and the *Remarks on Norris*, both posthumous—formed the philosophical work at Oates, in these fourteen years, along with constant correspondence, especially with Molyneux, Limborch, and latterly Anthony Collins. The correspondence between Locke and Molyneux throws light on many parts of the *Essay*. It arose incidentally. In December 1692 a book reached Locke at Oates, presented by its author, William Molyneux, an eminent young member of Trinity College, Dublin. It was entitled *Dioptrica Nova*. In its preface Molyneux wrote, with reference to logic, that 'to none do we owe more for a greater advancement of this part of philosophy than to the incomparable Mr. Locke, who in his *Essay concerning Human Understanding*, hath rectified more received mistakes, and delivered more profound truths, established on experience and observation, for the direction of man's mind in the prosecution of knowledge, than are to be met with

in all the volumes of all the ancients. He has clearly over-
thrown all those metaphysical whimsies which infected
men's brains with a spice of madness, whereby they feigned
a knowledge when they had none, by making a noise with
sounds, without clear and distinct significations.' The
arrival of the *Dioptrica Nova* at Oates was the beginning
of an affectionate interchange of thoughts between its
author and the author of the *Essay*, about projected
improvements in the successive editions of the *Essay*, and
other common intellectual interests, which was continued
till the unexpected death of Molyneux, in October 1698,
a few weeks after his visit to Oates. Through him the
Essay made way in Dublin, as it had made way at Oxford,
with the help of Wynne's *Abridgment*, published in 1696.

The *Essay* rapidly attained a wide popularity, unpre-
cedented in the case of an elaborate philosophical treatise,
but explained by a relation of the book to life and action
that could be readily appreciated by persons unaccustomed
to metaphysical speculation. It was translated under
Locke's eye into French by M. Coste, his literary assistant.
The French version appeared soon after the fourth English
edition of the *Essay*, and has itself passed through several
editions. A Latin version followed in 1701.

Popularity of the Essay.

Locke's correspondence with Bishop Stillingfleet takes its
place among the memorable controversies of the philosophical world. It arose in this way:—Toland, the Irish Pan-
theist, in his *Christianity not Mysterious*, had exaggerated
some doctrines in the *Essay*, and then adopted them thus
exaggerated as premises of his own. In the autumn of
1696, Bishop Stillingfleet, a learned ecclesiastic more than
a philosophical reasoner, in a *Vindication of the Trinity*,
made some reflections upon Locke's *Essay*, for not leaving
room for the mysteries that are involved in the Christian
revelation. Locke replied, early in the next year, in
a *Letter* of 227 pages, defending his ideas of substance
and causality, as well as of nominal and real essences.
Stillingfleet's rejoinder appeared in May. It was followed by
a *Reply* or *Second Letter* from Locke, in August, nearly as
long as the first, in which he insists on the wide meaning
in which the term *idea* is used in the *Essay*, and shows how

Contro-versy with Stilling-fleet.

'the greatest part of a book treating of the Understanding must be taken up in considering ideas'; denies that he has placed the certainty of knowledge exclusively in ideas that are 'clear and distinct,' inasmuch as we may have knowledge of some relations of ideas that are in all other respects obscure and mysterious; and then returns to our ideas of 'substances,' of 'natures' or 'essences,' and of essences 'real and nominal.' The Bishop answered this in 1698. Locke's elaborate *Reply* was delayed till 1699. In it he pursues, with immense expenditure of vigorous reasoning and irony, the many ramifications of the controversy, 'wherein, besides other incident matters, what his lordship has said concerning certainty by reason, certainty by ideas, and certainty by faith; the resurrection of the same body; the immateriality of the soul; the inconsistency of Mr. Locke's notions with the articles of the Christian faith, and their tendency to sceptism (*sic*) is examined.' The death of Stillingfleet in the same year ended this trial of intellectual strength.

Other adverse Critics of the *Essay*.

Norris.

The *Essay* had encountered criticism almost as soon as it appeared. Its collision with received maxims, in the form of an assault on 'innate ideas and principles,' shocked those who had been accustomed to defer to authority, and to feed their minds on abstractions. In 1690 John Norris, afterwards a successor of George Herbert as Rector of Bemerton, an English mystic, the friend of Henry More and of Lady Masham, and a disciple of Malebranche, published *Cursory Reflections upon a Book called an Essay concerning Human Understanding*. He blames Locke, in this tract, 'for setting himself to prove that there are no innate or natural principles,' and for then 'inconsistently' granting that 'there are self-evident propositions to which we give ready assent' as soon as they are understood, while he still denies that the assent is 'universal,' on the ground that it is not consciously given in many cases; 'it being a contradiction to assert,' so Locke argued, 'that there can be any truths imprinted on the soul of which the soul is unconscious.' This brochure of Norris is interesting for a recognition thus early, by an English writer, of the implication of latent or unconscious reason in human experience,

analogous to the 'unperceived perception' of Leibniz, so
important in the part it plays in modern thought. Sherlock, _{Sherlock.}
afterwards Bishop of London, was another adversary. He
uttered a *caveat* against any book that rejects 'connate
ideas or inbred notions.' On this Locke expressed himself
with unusual asperity, in a letter to Molyneux (February 22,
1697):—'A man of no small name, as you know Dr. Sherlock is, has been pleased to declare against my doctrine of
no innate ideas, from the pulpit in the Temple; and as
I have been told charged it with little less than atheism.
Though the doctor be a great man, yet that would not
much fright me, because I am told that he is not always
obstinate against opinions which he has condemned, more
publicly than in an harangue to a Sunday's auditory; but
that it is possible he may be firm here, because it is also
said, he never quits his aversion to any tenet he has once
declared against, till change of times, bringing change of
interest, and fashionable opinions, open his eyes and his
heart, and then he kindly embraces what before deserved
his aversion and censure.' Sherlock's objections to the
Essay may be found in the 'Digression concerning Connate
Ideas and Inbred Knowledge,' which forms the second
chapter of his *Discourse concerning the Happiness of good
men, and punishment of the wicked in the next world* (1704).
Some of the current objections to theological and philo- _{Thomas}
sophical postulates in the *Essay* found expression in two _{Burnet.}
tracts, in 1697, by Thomas Burnet, the eccentric author
of the *Sacred Theory of the Earth*. To the doubts and
difficulties of Burnet, in the first of these, Locke curtly
replied, in an appendix to his *Second Letter* to Stillingfleet.
Burnet's rejoinder to this was left unnoticed by Locke,
whose contemptuous silence drew forth an angry Third
Letter in 1699 from Burnet, in which he complained that
he had not yet received 'the favour of an answer.' 'You
ruffled over the first in a domineering answer,' he says,
'without giving any satisfaction to its contents, but the
second being more full and explicit, I was in hopes you
would have been more concerned to answer, to answer them
calmly and like a philosopher.' Locke still treated his
antagonist as unworthy of public notice, but was so far

moved that in the solitude of his study at Oates he filled
the liberal margins of Burnet's pamphlet with counter
criticisms in his own handwriting. The annotated tract
fell into the hands of the late eminent Dr. Noah Porter,
some years ago, when part of the contents of Locke's
library was dispersed, and he has given an account of this
interesting memorial of the past, 'holographic from Locke's
own hand,' in *Marginalia Lockeana*, contributed to the
New Englander and Yale Review for July 1887. The
marginal criticisms are there presented—'pointed and
spirited, expressing his own positions in brief statements
that are often corrections of, or antagonistic to, those of
his critic. Now and then they are more clear and explicit
than the corresponding statements of the *Essay*.' Conscience, innate ideas and principles, the possibility of
cogitation in matter, and free will, are the topics on which
Locke here explains his meaning, removes objections, and
introduces distinctions. Thus where Burnet asks whether
the author of the *Essay* 'allows any powers to be innate to
mankind,' Locke notes on the margin :—' I think noe body
but this author who ever read my book could doubt that
I spoke only of innate *ideas*; for my subject was the understanding, and not of innate *powers*.' Of ideas there must
be a conscious understanding, that is to say, so that innate
Sergeant. potentiality was irrelevant to his design. Some curious
animadversions upon the *Essay* also appeared in 1697, in
a volume of 460 pages, entitled *Solid Philosophy asserted
against the Fancies of the Ideists*. The author was John
Sergeant (*alias* Smith), who had deserted the Church of
England for the Church of Rome, and had published in
1665 *Rational Discourses on the Rule of Faith*, answered
by Tillotson. 'Those who have in their minds only
similitudes or *ideas*, and only discourse of them,' says
Sergeant, 'which ideas are not the things themselves, do
build their discoveries upon nothing. They have no solid
knowledge.' 'Mr. Sergeant, a Popish priest,' Locke writes
to Molyneux, 'whom you must needs have heard of, has
bestowed a thick octavo upon my *Essay*, and Mr. Norris
I hear is (again) writing hard against it.' (This of Norris
appeared in Part II of his *Theory of the Ideal or Intelligible*

World, published in 1704.) 'Shall I not be quite slain, think you, amongst so many notable combatants, and the Lord knows how many more to come? . . . I do not wonder at the confusedness of Sergeant's notions, or that they should be unintelligible to me ; I should have much more admired had they been otherwise: I expect nothing from Mr. Sergeant but what is abstruse in the highest degree.' What Leibniz thought of the *Essay* was told to Locke Leibniz. by Molyneux, in a transcript of 'reflections' addressed by Leibniz to Mr. Burnet of Kermnay, in Aberdeenshire, in 1697. They anticipate some of the objections of the *Nouveaux Essais*, a work which was in preparation when Locke died, but was held back till 1765. Locke made light of the somewhat adverse criticisms of the German eclectic. 'You and I,' he writes to Molyneux, 'agree pretty well concerning the man ; and this sort of fiddling makes me hardly avoid thinking that he is not that very great man that has been talked of him.' Of the objections in Broughton's *Psychologia* (1703) Locke 'thinks not by what Brough- he has read to trouble himself to look further into him.' ton. The elaborate *Anti-scepticism* of Lee he classes with other Lee. books 'which, though they make a noise against me, at last state the question so as to leave no contradiction to my *Essay*.' Lee had charged the *Lssay* with scepticism by implication. He had argued that 'in the case of particular propositions, whether affirmative or negative, there can be no certainty, in the way of ideas only, so much as of the existence of those things which are the subjects and predicates of these propositions: if you suppose the real existence of anything out of the mind itself, then you go beyond your ideas ; for they are wholly in the mind, as the things themselves are without it, and therefore have no connexion in nature with each other.' 'Besides,' he continues, 'if you *suppose* the real existence of things out of the mind itself, then you are led inevitably to *suppose* also the truth of your senses and other faculties, and of all those common maxims in which all that have their senses are agreed; and thus you run upon the wall of *preconcessa* and *praecognita*, on which the idealist [e.g. Locke] will tell you human nature has been split, and has occasioned all those errors with which the intellectual world is now infected. On the other hand, if you will *not suppose* (as all men in their wits suppose without proof) the real existence of things without us, but will be for proving it ; then you'll fail again : for if you prove the real existence of one thing from another, then that second will need the like proof of its existence from a third, and that third from a fourth, and so on *in infinitum.* Hence those ideal principles must involve us in an endless scepticism.' In this interesting anticipation of fundamental positions of Buffier and Reid, Locke 'sees no contradiction to the doctrine of the *Essay.*' Lee further argues 'that there are no such things in the mind of man as he [Locke] calls simple ideas,' for that all actual ideas are complex; also that 'there are no such things as general abstract ideas [i. e. abstract images] in the mind.'

Meantime the *Essay* did not lack defenders. Among others was Mr. Samuel Bold, rector of Steeple in Dorsetshire, who had been in prison before the Revolution, for his *Plea for Moderation* and his liberal ideas of government. In 1699 he produced *Some Considerations on the Principal Objections which have been published against Mr. Locke's Essay of Humane Understanding.* The 'objections' redargued are two—(1) That Locke's definition of knowledge, as perception of the agreement or disagreement of ideas, is, particularly in the case of self-evident propositions, both untrue, and dangerous to religion, and (2) that it is impossible for us to know that God cannot endow systems of atoms with power to feel and think. There can be no way, Bold argues, by which the truth of self-evident propositions can be known except by *perceiving their self-evidence* ; and so far from such propositions 'having any opposition to the way of ideas, neither their truth can be known, nor any use be made of them, without ideas,' i.e. without understanding what the propositions mean. As to matter, in the form of a human organism having power to think joined to it—to deny this, he says, would be to deny the divine omnipotence ; and, inasmuch as the *Essay* allows (Bk. IV, ch. iii) that it involves an absolute contradiction to suppose 'Matter, which is evidently in its own nature void of

Defence of the Essay by Samuel Bold.

sense and thought,' to be the Supreme Being, so atheistic materialism cannot on this ground be alleged against it.

Although Locke took no public notice of Norris's *Reflections*, when they appeared in 1690, later on, at Oates, he prepared *Remarks on some of Mr. Norris's books, wherein he asserts P. Malebranche's opinion of seeing all things in God.* The *Remarks* were included among Locke's posthumous works. Locke maintains that to explain perception of sensible things as perception of divine ideas, is to lose our own power and personality in God's, and with this our moral responsibility. 'This,' he sarcastically adds, 'is the hypothesis that clears doubts, but brings us at last to the religion of Hobbes and Spinoza ; by resolving all, even the thoughts and will of men, into an irresistible fatal necessity.' No one, he insists, can explain perception. It must be accepted as an inexplicable fact. 'Wherein this change called perception consists is, for aught I can see, unknown to one side as well as the other ; only the one have the ingenuity to confess their ignorance, and the other pretend to be knowing.'

Locke's 'Remarks on Norris.'

Another posthumous philosophical work, done also in the seclusion of Oates, was an *Examination of Malebranche's Opinion of seeing all things in God,* in which the same theory of knowledge is dealt with more fully than in the few pages on Norris. It was at first meant to make an additional chapter in the fourth edition of the *Essay*; but he changed his purpose, he tells Molyneux, 'because I like not controversies, and have a personal kindness for the author'; it was left unfinished, 'lest I should be tempted by anybody to print it.' It exposed to Locke's satisfaction the 'vanity and unintelligibleness' of that mystical way of 'explaining human understanding,' and its inconsistency with 'the experience that any man may make on himself, or of the children he converses with, wherein he may note the *gradual steps* that we all make in knowledge.' He insists simply upon the fact that *we do have perception or knowledge* : he is indifferent to hypotheses that pretend to *explain* what seems to him essentially inexplicable. The organic motions that accompany the mental state of sense-perception may, he suggests, be explained

His 'Examination of Malebranche.'

'by the motions of particles of matter coming from bodies and striking on our organs.' But this is motion in the organism, mechanically explained by motions outside the organism, which throws no light on the origin or validity of the perception that accompanies or follows the motion. Motion is the merely physical condition, without which we could not rise into the percipient state, in consistency with the ordinary laws of nature that regulate our embodied conscious life. The rise of any perception in a human understanding is scientifically 'incomprehensible'; it 'can only be resolved into the good pleasure of God.' 'How,' Locke asks, 'can any one know, on Malebranche's explanation, that there is any such real being as the sun? Did he ever see *the sun itself*? No; but, on occasion of the presence of the sun to his eyes, he has seen *the idea of the sun in God*. How then does he know that there *is* a sun? What need is there that God should make a sun only that one might see its idea in Him, when this might as well be done without any real sun at all.' Locke here approaches the new question about the abstract reality of things of sense, apart from the living perceptions of any percipient, afterwards raised by Berkeley. To call our perceptions 'modifications' of the mind, or to say that 'ideas' are 'modifications,' Locke argues, does not at all help; for it only substitutes one name for another name, without adding to our insight of what perception is, or how it is caused. All we are justified in saying is, that in point of fact 'there is some alteration in the mind, when we think of something that we were not thinking of a moment before. What Malebranche says of universal reason, whereof all men partake, seems to me nothing new, but is only the power we find all men have to perceive the relations that are between ideas ; and therefore if an intelligent being at one end of the world, and another at the other end, will consider twice two and four together, they *cannot but* find them equal. God knows (at once) all these relations, and so His knowledge is infinite; but individual men are able only to discover more or less of them gradually, as they apply their minds. If he means that this universal reason, whereof men partake, is the reason of God, I can by no means assent : for I think we cannot say God reasons at all, for he has at once a view of all things ; but reason [he means reasoning] is a laborious and gradual progress in the knowledge of things. . . . I should think it presumptuous to suppose that I should partake in God's knowledge ; there being some proportion between mine and another man's understanding, but none between mine and God's.' All this sheds light on many passages in the *Essay*, in its recognition of the ultimate incomprehensibility by us of our own finite and transitory perceptions, and of God's infinite knowledge ; so that human philosophy can offer no theory of either, much less explain the one by means of the other.

New editions of the *Essay*, and the part he took in the controversies to which it gave rise, do not nearly exhaust Locke's work in his study at Oates. An elaborate *Third Letter on Toleration,* in reply to the criticisms of Proast and others, appeared in 1692 ; *Thoughts concerning Education,* in the summer of the following year ; besides three politico-economical tracts on *Money,* its interest, and the coinage, in 1691 and 1695, show versatility of taste, and acute thought. A common-sense defence of the *Reasonableness of Christianity as delivered in the Scriptures* was the chief work of 1695. It was followed by a *Vindication of the Reasonableness of Christianity from Mr. Edwards's Reflections,* a few months later, and by a *Second Vindication* in 1697. This more theological departure was connected with the proposals for wider ecclesiastical comprehension within the national Church, made in many quarters, in connexion with the Revolution settlement. Locke's sense of the reasonableness of religious unity in the nation, and in Christendom, made him desire to show how simple essential Christianity is, and to try to induce Christians to agree to differ about all beyond this. Accordingly, in the spirit of the *Essay,* he laboured to recal religion from the verbal wrangling of theologians, which had disturbed Christian unity, to the original elements of the faith. This was followed by some excursions in biblical criticism, in his last years, the fruits of which appeared posthumously as *A Paraphrase and Notes on certain Epistles of St. Paul; to which is prefixed an Essay for the understanding of St. Paul's Epistles*

Other works of Locke.

by consulting St. Paul himself. Here the scientific spirit and method of the *Essay* were applied to the interpretation of the literature which the Puritans who surrounded his boyhood had taught him to reverence as infallible. 'The holy Scripture,' he declares, 'is to me, and always will be, the constant guide of my assent; and I shall always hearken to it, as containing infallible truth relating to things of the highest concernment. And I wish I could say there are no mysteries in it: I acknowledge there are to me, and I fear always will be. But where I want the evidence of things, there yet is ground enough for me to believe, because God has said it: and I shall presently condemn and quit any opinion of mine, as soon as I am shown that it is contrary to any revelation in the holy scripture [1].' But the same sense of the need for founding all his beliefs on a perception of their reasonableness followed him in his biblical exegesis;—the same determination to get rid of unwarranted assumptions and to escape from the bondage of empty or ambiguous words. He discarded the exegetical methods of the Puritans, and resisted their disposition to interpret texts apart from contexts, or to read spiritual meanings dogmatically into texts, overlooking the circumstances in which the words were written, and their relation to the age and country in which they were produced. He was among the first in Europe to anticipate the spirit of modern criticism ; putting himself in the place of the writer, he tried to conceive the main design of the whole, and thus to evolve its rational meaning. But it was to the dry light of the understanding, judging according to prudential common sense, that Locke was ready to appeal, when, dissatisfied with 'systems of divinity,' he betook himself to 'the sole reading of the scriptures, for the understanding the Christian religion.' This is the foundation of his vindication and interpretation of Christianity, as well as of the remarks on miracles in the *Discourse* on that subject, written in 1702. The teachers as well as the assailants of Christianity, in the eighteenth century, alike appealed to the *Essay*, as their logical standard, and tested Christian belief by 'external and internal evidences' of the sort which satisfied

[1] 'Postscript' to first *Letter* to Stillingfleet.

Locke. His own faith, sincere and intelligent, is more represented in the prudential morality and religion that prevailed in England in the century after his death, than in that deeper faith, rooted in the divine life revealed in the soul of man, which is found in More, Cudworth, and Leighton, in the age preceding Locke, and, since Locke, in Berkeley and William Law, or in Coleridge and Schleiermacher.

After 1700 Locke was gathering himself up for the end in the repose of the family life at Oates. In that year the Commission at the Board of Trade was resigned, and he ceased to send his writings to the press. Adverse criticism, and the official discouragement of the *Essay* at Oxford, he took 'rather as a recommendation of the book'; so he wrote to Anthony Collins, adding that 'when you and I next meet we shall be merry on the subject.' One attack only moved him. In 1704 his old antagonist Jonas Proast revived their controversy. Locke in consequence began a *Fourth Letter on Toleration.* The few pages preserved in the posthumous volume, ending in an unfinished sentence, exhausted his strength. Thus religious liberty, which had so much occupied his thoughts at Oxford forty years before, and had been a ruling idea in the interval, was still dominant at Oates in the last year of his life. All that summer of 1704 he continued to decline, notwithstanding the watchful care of Lady Masham and her step-daughter Esther. On the 28th of October he passed away ; according to his dying words, 'in sincere communion with the whole Church of Christ, by whatever names Christ's followers call themselves.' His tomb may be seen beside the parish church of High Laver, a mile from Oates, bearing a Latin inscription prepared by his own hand. Lely and Kneller have made us familiar with his pensive and refined expression. His writings, according to the memorial on his tomb, reveal ' what sort of man he was ':—*Siste Viator. Hic juxta situs est JOHANNES LOCKE. Si qualis fuerit rogas, mediocritate sua contentum se vixisse respondet. Literis innutritus eousque tantum profecit, ut veritati unice litaret. Hoc ex scriptis illius disce; quae quod de eo reliquum est majori fide tibi exhibebunt quam epitaphii suspecta elogia.*

The last years of his life.

Virtutes, si quas habuit, minores sane quam quas sibi laudi tibi in exemplum proponeret. Vitia una sepeliantur. Morum exemplum si quaeras in Evangelio habes : vitiorum utinam nusquam : mortalitatis certe (quod prosit) hic et ubique. Natum Anno Dom. 1632, _Aug._ 29°. _Mortuum Anno Dom._ 1704, _Oct._ 28. _Memorat haec tabula, brevi et ipsa interitura_[1]. So the inscription runs. The writings of no philosopher are more distinctly stamped with the marks of the character and mind of their author than the _Essay_ and other works of Locke.

Post-humous Works.

The Commentaries on St. Paul were given to the world soon after Locke's death. In 1706 the volume of post-humous works appeared, which contains :—(1) _A Discourse of Miracles,_ (2) _A Fourth Letter on Toleration,_ (3) _An Examination of Malebranche's Opinion of seeing all things in God,_ (4) _The Conduct of the Understanding,_ (5) _Memoirs relating to the Life of Anthony, First Earl of Shaftesbury,_ (6) _Some Familiar Letters between Mr. Locke and several of his Friends_—including chiefly the correspondence with Limborch and Molyneux. This was followed in 1720 by another volume, edited by Des Maizeaux, including :— (1) _The Fundamental Constitutions of Carolina,_ (2) _A Letter from a Person of Quality giving an account of the Debates in the House of Lords in April and May_ 1675, (3) _Remarks on some of Mr. Norris's books, wherein he asserts Father Malebranche's Opinion of our seeing all things in God,_ (4) _Elements of Natural Philosophy,_ (5) _Some Thoughts concerning Reading and Study for a Gentleman,_ (6) _Rules of a Society which met once a week for their improvement in useful Knowledge, and for the promotion of Christian Truth and Charity,_ (7) _Letters to Anthony Collins, Samuel Bold and others._ Other writings, much in harmony with Locke's taste and studies, but not sufficiently authenticated, have been published under his name, in particular :—(1) _An Intro-ductory Discourse to Churchill's Collection of Voyages_ (1704)—

---

[1] So _Essay,_ Bk. II. ch. x. § 5 :— ' The ideas, as well as children, of our youth often die before us : and our minds represent to us those tombs to which we are approaching ; where, though the brass and marble remain, yet the inscriptions are effaced by time, and the imagery moulders away.'

many passages in the *Essay* and elsewhere show his fondness for books of travels. (2) *Observations upon the Growth and Culture of Vines and Olives,* written in 1679 and published in 1766, is said to be a result of observations during his retreat in France. (3) *The History of our Saviour Jesus Christ related in the words of Scripture* (1706), and (4) *Select Moral Books of the Old Testament and Apocrypha paraphrased* (1716), resemble Locke in subject and tone.

The *Éloge historique de feu M. Locke,* by Le Clerc, which appeared in the *Bibliothèque Choisie,* in 1705, has been the foundation of later biographies. Le Clerc found his materials during personal intercourse with Locke in Holland ; in his own and Limborch's correspondence with him afterwards ; in a letter from the third Lord Shaftesbury (author of the *Characteristics*) ; and in the interesting letter, already referred to, received by him from Lady Masham. A letter by M. Coste, Locke's amanuensis and translator of the French version of the *Essay,* gives a few additional particulars. Long after, in 1830, Lord King, the lineal descendant of Locke's cousin and executor, Lord Chancellor King, produced a *Life of John Locke, with Extracts from his Correspondence, Journals, and Commonplace Books* ; and in 1876 Mr. Fox Bourne's *Life of John Locke* added important documents and incidents, collected with much care and industry. Dr. Fowler's *Locke* (1880), in 'English Men of Letters,' and my own *Locke* (1890), in Blackwood's 'Philosophical Classics,' are intended to present the author of the *Essay* in his place in literature and in philosophy.

Biographies of Locke.

(*B.*) EXPOSITORY AND CRITICAL.

I. KNOWLEDGE: STRUCTURE OF THE ESSAY.

The main
design of
the Essay.

'You have done me and my book a great honour'—
so Locke writes, a few months before his death, to
Anthony Collins—'for having bestowed so much of your
thoughts upon it. You have a comprehensive knowledge
of it, and do not stick in the incidents, which I find many
people do; which whether true or false make nothing to
the main design of the *Essay*; that lies in a little compass.'
The fault Locke finds with those early interpreters has
beset most of their successors. They 'stick in the incidents,' and fail to comprehend the main design, for which
the structure of the *Essay*, 'written by incoherent parcels,'
may be an excuse. One turns to the 'Introduction' to
discover the design. Locke there proposes a modest
inquiry into the relation between 'human understanding'
and the realities of existence; with a view to determine the
limits of a human knowledge of what exists; and also the
foundation of that assent to probability through which men
are able to supplement their necessarily narrow knowledge.
The office of the *Essay* is put with more exactness in
Locke's *Second Letter* to Stillingfleet:—'If I have done
anything new [in the *Essay*], it has been to describe to
others, more particularly than has been done before, what
it is their minds do when they perform the action that they
call knowing.' To find, in the 'historical, plain method'
of investigating actual facts, pursued introspectively, under
what conditions *knowledge* becomes a fact in the individual
consciousness of *man*; to what extent a human understanding can penetrate and compass reality; how man falls
short of omniscience, without being reduced to nescience;
and on what ground our 'broken' knowledge may be
assisted by a reasonable faith in probabilities—all this is
within the compass of the *Essay*, according to its proposed
design. It is concerned with an understanding of things

that, being human, is somehow intermediate between omniscience and sense, participating in both.

The *Essay* was the first deliberate attempt, in modern philosophy, to engage in what might now be called epistemological inquiry, but mixed up by Locke with questions logical, psychological, and ontological; all subordinated in his design to 'what may be of use to us, in our present state,' and to 'our concerns as human beings[1].' Locke inaugurated the modern epistemological era, characteristic of philosophy in the eighteenth century, which culminated in Kant—the reaction against medieval dogmatism of authority, and against the abstract ontology of Spinoza and physiological materialism of Hobbes, in the seventeenth century, which last involve questions that Locke expressly avoids. 'I shall not meddle with the physical consideration of the mind,' he tells us at the outset[2], 'or trouble myself to examine wherein its essence consists [i. e. whether its substance is material or spiritual], or by what motions of our [animal] spirits, or alterations of our bodies, we come to have . . . ideas in our understandings; and whether these ideas do, in their formation, any or all of them, depend on matter or not.' *A mixed epistemological inquiry.*

The abstract demonstrations of Spinoza, and even the physiological psychology of Hobbes, were foreign to the modest introspection of the *Essay*. Locke warns his *Its modest forecast.*

---

[1] Molyneux, in one of his letters (Dec. 22, 1692), suggests that it is difficult to place the *Essay* in any of the recognised philosophical sciences (a tribute to its independent individuality), and that it might succeed better if its contents could be elaborated into a system of 'logic and metaphysics' by its author. To which Locke replies (Jan. 20, 1693):— 'That which you propose of turning my *Essay* into a body of logic and metaphysics, accommodated to the usual forms, though I thank you very kindly for it, and plainly see in it the care you have of the education of young scholars, yet I feel I shall scarce find time to do it. Besides that, if you have, in this book of mine, what you think the matter of these two *sciences*, or what you will call them, I like the method it is in better than that of the schools,' &c. In return Molyneux 'is fully convinced by the arguments you give me, for not turning your book into the scholastic form of logic and metaphysics; and I had no other reason to advise the other, but merely to get it promoted the easier in our [Dublin] university; one of the businesses of which place is to learn according to the old forms.' (March 2, 1693.)

[2] Introduction, § 2.

readers [1] 'not to expect undeniable cogent demonstrations'
of the conclusions which he maintains; and 'professes
no more than to lay down, candidly and freely, his own
conjectures, concerning a subject lying somewhat in the
dark, without any other design than an unbiassed inquiry
into truth.' It is no dialectical deduction of what knowledge in the abstract *must be* that he promises, but a matter-
of-fact account of what seem to be the resources of
human understanding, for comprehending the attributes
and powers of the material and spiritual substances that
actually exist, in a so-called science that, instead of
omniscience, is not raised far above sense. 'If by this
inquiry into the nature of the [human] understanding,
I can discover the powers thereof: how far they reach: to
what things they are in any degree proportionate: and
where they fail us—I suppose it may be of use to prevail
with the busy mind of man to be more cautious in meddling
with things exceeding its comprehension; to stop when it
is at the utmost extent of its tether; and to sit down in
a quiet ignorance of those things which, upon examination,
are found to be beyond the reach of our capacities. . . . For
I thought that the first step towards satisfying several
inquiries the mind of man was very apt to run into, was,
to take a view of our own understanding, examine our own
powers, and see to what things they were adapted. Till that
was done I suspected we began at the wrong   l, and in
vain sought for satisfaction in a quiet and sur possession
of truths that most concerned us, whilst we let loose our
thoughts into the vast ocean of Being; as if all that
boundless extent were the natural and undoubted possession of *our* understandings.' The 'truths which concern
us,' he insists, are those which determine human character,
not satisfaction of merely speculative curiosity. 'Our
business here is not to know all things, but those which
concern our conduct. If we can find out those measures
whereby a rational creature, put in that state in which
man is in this world, may and ought to govern his opinions,
and actions depending thereon, we need not to be troubled
that some other things escape our knowledge.' He thus

[1] Bk. I. ch. iii. § 25.

prepares us for finding that man's knowledge of the qualities and behaviour of existing realities, is of the intermediate sort—neither nescience nor omniscience, but, if one may use the word, *fiduscience*, or science that is at last a reasonable faith, in lack of omniscience. Things are what they are, and not other things than they are ; why therefore should we allow ourselves to be deceived regarding the possible extent of our knowledge, or regarding anything else ? This is Locke's attitude.

An answer of genuine worth for human purposes to the questions about Knowledge, is what is sought for throughout the *Essay*. So one naturally turns first to its definition of Knowledge. This comes out at the beginning of the Fourth, not, as might have been expected, at the beginning of the First Book. In fact the Fourth Book is in some respects more in its place when treated as the first, with the other three as a supplement ; and there is some ground for the conjecture that, in preparing this ' Discourse, written by incoherent parcels,' the investigations proper to the Fourth Book were those which engaged Locke at the outset, and that those now appropriated to the other three were entered on, when his conception of his enterprise became more comprehensive. To the end he recognised faults in the structure of the *Essay*, but pleaded age and want of leisure as an excuse for not reducing and reconstructing it. This need not now hinder an expositor from passing at once from the ' Introduction ' to the part of the *Essay* where the elements that are essential to human knowledge are distinguished from one another. The lines of inquiry in the rest of the *Essay* are then seen to radiate from the definition of knowledge as a centre.

Its analysis of human knowledge is in the Fourth Book.

Human knowledge, it there appears [1], is ' perception ' of ' connexion or repugnancy, of agreement or disagreement,' between ' ideas.' The unit of knowledge is thus a mental proposition, not an idea. It is a judgment, in the ordinary meaning of that term, but not exactly in Locke's restricted meaning ; for in the *Essay* 'judgment ' means 'presumption ' or ' assent,' founded on probability—not a perceived absolute certainty—of connexion or repugnance between ideas ; and

The four Books of the Essay in their mutual relation.

[1] Bk. IV. ch. i. § 1 ; cf. Bk. II. ch. xxi. § 5.

thus excludes the intellectual necessity which is essential to Locke's idea of 'knowledge,' when he employs that term (which he does not always do) with a rigorous meaning [1]. Proposition—spontaneous or reflective, mental or verbal—being thus the unit of knowledge, it follows that no one of the elements essential to knowledge can, *per se*, constitute knowledge. Ideas are presupposed in knowledge; and it also presupposes relations of connexion or repugnance between ideas; as well as a living perception of those relations. But not one of those three elements, abstracted from the other two, makes knowledge. Without 'ideas' mental propositions are empty and barren; without relations of connexion or repugnance ideas are unintelligible—the propositions have no copulas; without a living perception knowledge is dead or unconscious. The *Essay*, in its four Books, is throughout concerned with these three, logically separable, but actually inseparable, elements. The Second and Third Books deal especially with ideas and their verbal signs; the First Book with abstract principles, in refutation of the hypothesis that some of them are 'innate'; the Fourth Book, in its first thirteen chapters, describes the various perceptions of relations between ideas that, immediately or by demonstrated implication, are self-evident, thus offering an analytical description of human knowledge; the remaining chapters deal with the reasonable probabilities of presumptive faith, which, in lack of omniscience, do duty for knowledge, in a human understanding.

II. IDEAS, THE FIRST ELEMENT IN KNOWLEDGE.

The phenomena presented by external and internal realities, whether received, retained, or elaborated, are called 'ideas' by Locke.

'Idea' is the most obtrusive and significant word in Locke's *Essay*, which has been charged with 'inventing a new way of knowing—by means of ideas.' The word could not but occur often in an inquiry about knowledge, when idea means what Locke makes it mean. For an idea in the *Essay* signifies the particular object immediately known, or of which there is consciousness, in any act of understanding. The particular phenomena of outward things, when they are actually presented in sense, or of our own minds when

[1] See Bk. IV. ch. xiv. § 4.

we are self-conscious; the phenomena when represented in the particular mental images of memory, or of plastic imagination; and also the phenomena when, in our 'abstract notions,' they are viewed universally, or as appearances 'such as more than one particular thing can correspond with and be represented by'—all alike are 'ideas' in Locke's meaning of idea. 'Whatever it is which the mind can be employed about in thinking,' Locke tells us (Introduction, § 8) is what is meant by an idea in the *Essay*; and as every one is assured that when he knows he is conscious of *something*, he thinks it is unnecessary to prove that men have ideas, or to raise subtle questions about how realities that are independent of the particular ideas of individual men can be manifested in and through their ideas. The withdrawal of all ideas would plainly make knowledge impossible, because there would then be nothing for us to know; so, although ideas *per se* are not knowledge, but only abstractions considered apart from the living knowledge to which they are essential, yet there can be no actual knowledge when there are no ideas of any sort before the mind. Our knowledge of reality may be said, accordingly, to originate in, and depend upon, our ideas of what the particular reality is by which it is manifested to our understandings [1]. 'My new way of

---

[1] Locke's 'ideas' must be divested of Platonic connotation. He uses the term in at least as wide a meaning as Descartes had sanctioned. 'Par le nom d'idée,' Descartes says, in answer to Hobbes, ' il veut seulement qu'on intime ici *les images des choses matérielles dépeintes en la phantasie corporelle*; et cela étant supposé, il lui est aisé de montrer qu'on ne peut avoir propre et véritable idée de Dieu ni d'un ange; mais j'ai souvent averti, et principalement en celui-là même, *que je prends le nom d'idée pour tout ce qui est conçu immédiatement par l'esprit*; en sorte que, lorsque je veux et que je crains, parceque je conçois en même temps que je veux et que je crains, ce vouloir et cette crainte sont mis par moi en nombre des idées; et je me suis servi de ce mot, parcequ'il était déjà communément reçu par les philosophes pour signifier les formes des conceptions de l'entendement divin, encore que nous ne reconnoissions en Dieu aucune fantasie ou imagination corporelle.' The objections of Hobbes and Descartes' replies are determined by this primary difference between ideas as [sensuous] *images*, and ideas as unimaginable concepts that are nevertheless capable of being reasoned about. Gassendi denied anything to be an idea but what was imagined; and Locke says that all ideas are particular, and that particular ideas become general only by being taken

knowing *by means of ideas,*' Locke writes to Stillingfleet [1], 'may in the full latitude comprehend my whole
Essay; because, treating of the understanding, which
is nothing but the faculty of thinking, I could not well
treat of that faculty without considering the immediate
objects of the mind in thinking, which I call *ideas.* And
therefore I guess it will not be considered strange that the
greatest part of my book has been taken up in considering:—
what these objects of the mind in thinking are; whence
they come; what use the mind makes of them in its
several ways of thinking; and what are the outward marks
whereby it signifies them to others, or records them for its
own use. And this in short is my way by ideas, that
which your lordship calls my *new* way by ideas; which, my
lord, if it be new, is but a new history of an old thing.'
The 'new way of ideas,' which he was alleged to have 'invented,' is, and ever will be, Locke says, ' the same with the
old way of speaking intelligibly.' We must have ideas of
things, or in other words things must manifest themselves
to us in some sorts of ways, so that we may perceive what
they are. That what exists must make some appearance
or idea of itself, is a condition indispensable to the conversion of *reality* into *conscious knowledge,* in a finite
mind. In the case of mental propositions expressed in
words, this only implies that the terms of the proposition
must be significant and not idealess terms: idealess terms
are empty sounds that have no significant relation to the
understanding.

All human
ideas
originate
either in
what is
presented
to the
senses, or
in reflec-
tion upon
what we
are con-
scious of.

According to Locke, (1) extended things around us, and
(2) the mental operations of which we are conscious, are
the two sources back to which may be traced all the ideas
that can enter into any propositions about things, true or
false, spontaneous or reflective, that a *human* understanding can entertain. All significant assertions or denials that
are possible to human beings must involve, either ideas of
outward things that have been presented in our senses,

representatively, as generic images.
Descartes often asked Gassendi and
Hobbes to remember that he meant
by *idea* whatever was conceived by
the understanding, even *though not*

*capable of being represented in imagin-
ation.* Thus we imagine a (particular)
triangle, but cannot imagine, and yet
can reason about, a figure of 1000 sides.

[1] *Second Letter,* p. 72.

or else ideas of actual 'operations' of our own minds. These are Locke's two sorts of 'simple ideas.' Into these the *Essay*[1] makes all the 'complex ideas' we have, whether concrete ideas of things, or ideas in abstraction from things, at last resolve themselves. They are all gradually given in an experience of two sorts of substances—substances outside ourselves, and reflective experience of one's individual substance or self.

That we are born in complete ignorance of all things around us, and of ourselves too, and so without any ideas at all of what they or we are; that our matured ideas of things are the slow accumulation of a gradual and always imperfect experience, in which things around us show themselves to us only 'in part,' and in which we show only 'in part' our conscious selves to ourselves; that no human intelligence has a knowledge of any thing prior to the rise of its phenomena or ideas in the senses—is the burden of Locke's famous argument against innate ideas and innate principles, that fills up the First Book. All the ideas that we have and can have about existences must have been experienced in one or other of these ways, as far as their elementary constituents are concerned : otherwise the words supposed to have meanings are only empty sounds. *We are all born in ignorance of the universe of realities in which we now find ourselves.*

But while all our ideas are thus virtually, either qualities of outward things, of the several sorts presented in our senses, or else spiritual operations in which we are self-conscious; and while as to ideas of aught beyond these two sorts all human beings are in a condition like that of those who have been born blind, in relation to colours, there is nevertheless a sense in which, according to the *Essay*, men *can* 'invent' ideas. For we can not only retain, but we can also elaborate, in numberless ways, the simple or unanalysable appearances of things that were presented to our senses and in consciousness. This arbitrary elaboration to which men can subject the ideas they involuntarily receive, explains the new forms which ideas take in our imagination, as well as in the comprehensive conceptions of abstract science and philosophy. Human understanding can abstract and generalise ideas, in ways different from their *Human understanding can elaborate the original simple or unanalysable ideas in new creations of its own.*

[1] See Bk. II. ch. i. §§ 1-5.

groupings and aggregations in the involuntary experience of sense. This is illustrated in our (often erroneous) general- isations of substances, under supposed special relations of cause and effect. Human ideas, moreover, are originally per- ceived in complexity[1]; although all their complexities may be analysed either into qualities and powers of matter, or into spiritual operations, as their ultimate constituents. But our ideas, whether simple or complex, are 'every one of them particular existences; so that the perception of the agreement or disagreement of *our particular ideas* is the whole and utmost of all our knowledge. *Universality is but accidental to it*; and consists in this, that "the particular ideas about which it is are such as more than one particular thing *can* correspond with and be represented by"[2].'

Locke's simple ideas are not know- ledge, but one ele- ment in know- ledge. It has been a common charge against the *Essay* that it makes a bare apprehension of *simple ideas* the primary form of human *knowledge*, so that knowledge *begins* in simple ideas. On the contrary, by Locke's definition of knowledge, there can be no knowledge at all until an idea is perceived in its relation to another idea. The simple phenomena in which substances originally manifest them- selves are only *unanalysable elements* of the complex ideas that form our ordinary consciousness; and ideas, whether simple or complex, are in themselves only *elements* in knowledge, not knowledge. Certainty of knowledge, or even presumption of probability, is added to mere idea. A mere idea, Locke reiterates, can be neither true nor false, certain nor uncertain, self-evident nor demonstrable. 'Nothing is truer,' he tells Stillingfleet, 'than that it is *not* the idea that makes us certain, without reason, or without the understanding'; although 'it is as true, that it is not reason, it is not the understanding, that makes us certain without ideas. Nor is it *one idea by itself* that in any case makes us certain.' (Second Letter.) And where, he asks, 'do I anywhere speak of self-evident *ideas*; self-evidence belonging not to ideas, but to those *propositions* of which it is impossible for the mind to suppose the contrary.' The opposite view would make it possible to express know- ledge through a *term* only, whereas it requires a proposition

---

[1] See Bk. II. chh. ii. § 1; v i. §§ 7–9.   [2] Bk. IV. ch. xvii. § 8.

to express it. Hence Locke makes mental proposition the irreducible *atom* of knowledge. Ideas simple or complex, particular or universal, are *incognisable*, by the definition of knowledge given in the *Essay*, except so far as they are in a *perceived relation* to something that is predicated of them, predicated too with an intuitive assurance of the certainty of the relation. Knowledge thus begins in mental proposition; and all propositions that represent it, whether particular or universal, are (ultimately) intuitively known[1]. Locke nowhere says that knowledge can be really reached merely by compounding simple ideas, independently of those other elements. Ideas remain mere ideas, until they are perceived under relation, with an absolute assurance of the certainty of the relation.

The simple ideas, or unanalysable phenomena, in which things of sense and our own conscious spirits originally present themselves, are introduced into new relations through the elaborative activity of the individual understanding. They may thus be put together, or separated, in ways altogether different from those in which they were originally presented to the individual, in his senses or by reflection—elaborated in ways, it may be, in which they are never actually found in their original manifestation. They are in that case abstracted from the original experience; they are not given directly as manifestations of outward substances, or of our own spiritual substance, in sensation and reflection: they are 'invented by the understanding.' In this way, through those 'inventions of our understanding,' error often enters into our mental propositions. *(Our complex ideas inventions of human understanding.)*

The 'complex ideas' thus 'invented by the understanding' are of three sorts, according to the *Essay*. They are either ideas of the *modes* (simple or mixed) of substances, which 'contain not in them the idea of their subsistence by themselves, but only as dependent on or affections of individual substances, and so are considered in abstraction from substances'; or they are ideas of *substances* in their different sorts, that is to say, of 'distinct particular things, bodies or spirits,' that are supposed to be 'capable of subsistency independently'; or they are ideas of *relations* between *(Three sorts of complex or invented ideas.)*

[1] See Bk. IV. ch. ii. §§ 1–8.

modes, or between substances. The innumerable ideas thus 'invented by the human understanding,' as distinguished from the aggregates of simple ideas that are actually presented in the senses and in reflex consciousness, are referred by Locke to those three classes—ideas of Modes, Substances, and Relations [1]. Our 'invented' ideas of the different sorts of individual substances are central and supreme, among complex or invented ideas. But the *Essay* describes in the first place our invented ideas of Modes, perhaps for the reason suggested in one of Locke's letters to Mr. Samuel Bold:—' I agree with you,' he says, 'that the ideas of the modes and actions of substances are usually in our minds *before* the idea of *substance* itself: but in this I differ from you, that I do not think the ideas of the operations of things are antecedent to the ideas of their *existence* ; for they must exist before they can in any way affect us, or make us sensible of their operations, and we must suppose them to be before they operate' (May 16, 1699). Accordingly, the chapter on ' Power' is one of those in which 'modes' of ideas, 'simple and mixed,' are described. We are further told that their ' powers' make up a great part of the complex ideas of the different sorts of substances that human understandings invent, and so their supposed powers make up the 'nominal essences' to which particular substances are referred by the inventive understanding.

Our invented ideas of sorts of substances inadequate to, often inconsistent with, the real qualities of the substances.

Our 'invented ideas' of the different sorts of substances, material and spiritual, including God ; of their modes and powers; and of their mathematical, causal and moral relations, do not necessarily, or perhaps ever, attain to the essential ideas of them which constitute science proper. The complex ideas of things which men form are founded on superficial relations, and do not reach the centre of things. And they are often *idola* of the human mind, as Bacon would say, out of harmony with the Ideas of the Divine Mind.

In none of them can human understanding become in-

But do we, Locke virtually asks in this connexion, do we in the case of any of the 'invented ideas,' find that human understanding can ever rise into ideas that are independent of all the manifestations of themselves that external things

[1] Bk. II. ch. xii.

and our minds present, in our primary experience? Do
any of *our* complex ideas of modes, of substances in their
different kinds, or of relations, contain simple ideas that
are not modifications, or combinations, or correlations of
the primary data of external and internal sense? A great
part of the Second Book may be regarded as Locke's
reasoned answer to the question. From the thirteenth to
the end of the twenty-eighth chapter, he is as it were
offering a series of 'crucial instances,' in support of his
main thesis—the dependence of all our ideas on experience, without which our words must be barren and empty.
He is trying to show that even our sublimest imaginations, whether of modes, substances, or relations, must be
capable of being individualised, in terms either of phenomena
that are presented in the senses, or of operations of our self-
conscious spirits. Take our ' invented ideas ' of the infinite
in quantity, he virtually says,—whether a quantity of extension, or duration, or number; our ideas of power, active
or passive ; our ideas of any of the different sorts of substances ; our ideas of causal connexion ; our ideas of moral
relations. If none of *these* 'invented ideas' can transcend the
simple and inexplicable phenomena of real existence that
are originally given in our twofold experience; if even they
are all modifications, aggregations, and correlations of those
phenomena only—then we may conclude confidently that
it is unnecessary to suppose that men bring ideas of things
with them into the world before they have any experience ;
ideas that are independent of verification ; that are ours by
nature, not needing to become ours through the gradual
exercise of our understanding among the data of external
and internal sense. We are thus taught the lesson, that
man is not, like God, originally intelligent of the whole
universe of realities, or even of any part of it, but that our
intellectual office is discharged in a sphere intermediate
between the nescience of mere sense and divine omniscience,
so that each man becomes possessed of reality, whether in
knowledge or in probability, only gradually and ' in part.'

Here arises Locke's difficulty. If all our ideas, whether
of the realities or the unrealities of existence, can be
resolved into unanalysable phenomena, which happened

[margin note, top:] dependent of the simple or unanalys-able data of ex-perience.

[margin note, bottom:] Crucial instances of ideas which

might
seem to be
thus inde-
pendent.

to be presented either in our senses or in reflection, how comes it about that we have some complex ideas that refuse to be treated as arbitrary inventions of *our* understanding, but that, when they rise into consciousness, seem to be revelations of a higher understanding? Whatever we see, touch, hear, taste, or smell, is limited, rounded, transitory—finite in a word : the mental operations of which each man is conscious are also all changing and finite. Yet we find that we have, and are obliged by something in us to have, an idea of Immensity, or infinite space, that *refuses to submit to bounds*; also an idea of Duration, unbeginning and unending, *that cannot be completed*; for Immensity and Eternity are surely not meaningless words. Yet we have never seen or touched infinite space, nor reached through reflection an unbeginning and unending duration. Why, moreover, are we obliged to recognise inevitable *inadequacy* in *our* deepest and truest ideas of different sorts of substances; and why especially have we to form that 'obscure' general idea of substance, a vague 'something,' which Locke confesses that he finds involved in all the invented ideas we form of particular sorts of substances? We find too, in the heart of our ideas of the changes that are presented in experience, an idea of causal connexion between phenomena, which we are somehow obliged to have. Now this idea, alike in its infinite regress and in its infinite progress, is at the last *incomplete*, incapable of being satisfied by any possible multiplication of particular causes that are in turn effects : every change makes us think of its cause, and that cause in turn of *its* cause, and so on in an endless series, of which series we must have some sort of idea, unless the word 'cause' is a meaningless word. In all these words—immensity, eternity, substance, cause—does the meaning involve nothing more than can be reduced either to qualities of things presented to the senses, or to states in which our mind has consciously operated? If the ideas we have 'are truly every one of them particular existences,' must not these and other like supposed fundamental conceptions, be empty or idealess abstractions? Those just mentioned are crucial instances, which Locke brings in evidence of his main position—that all our

invented or complex ideas may be reduced to finite phenomena, originally given, either in our senses, or in reflection
upon our own mental operations. Locke's treatment of these
ideas is characteristic of his point of view, which is apt to
keep out of sight ultimate necessities of reason.

Take our idea of the Immensity within which our bodies Ideas of
are conceived to exist; or of the Duration, unbeginning Immensity and
and unending, within which our little lives, between birth Eternity,
and death, are conceived to be contained. Locke sees that or the
the words Immensity and Eternity are not meaningless. supposed infinite in
The one idea is apt to arise in connexion with the pre- Quantity.
sented ideas of sight and touch, but is itself neither seen
nor touched ; the other is blended with, but is more than, the
changing ideas whether of sensation or reflection. Something in reason hinders us from putting any limit to either
space or duration. ' I would fain meet with any thinking
man,' Locke grants, 'that *can in his thoughts set any bounds*
to space more than he can to duration.' Thus, by implication, he acknowledges, in our ideas of Immensity and
Eternity, what resists the restraint of finite imagination.
This *endless obligation to add* is not found in any simple
idea, or groups of simple ideas, as changing data of sensation
or reflection. It is an intellectual necessity, not a contingent manifestation of existence in sense. Locke, with
characteristic fidelity to facts, recognises the fact, that
human understanding ' cannot set bounds to space or to
duration,' but without taking this as evidence of the inadequacy of the hypothesis which makes all human ideas finite
or particular. He does not ask *why* we are obliged to add
without limit, and to divide without limit, when we try in
vain to reduce to the finitude of the imaginable our ultimate
thoughts of space and duration, and are thus involved in the
attempt to make a contradictory image of an unimaginable
quantity. When we try to imagine immensity, or unbeginning and unending duration, we usually suppose, he says, an
idea that is in its nature imaginable, and perhaps imagined,
in an imagination other than human, e. g. millions of miles
multiplied by millions, or millions of years multiplied by
millions. This expansion, however, does not explain *the
mental obligation always to continue expanding, without*

exhausting what we expand, or *to continue dividing, without reaching the indivisible* ; nor the thought we have that, after going ever so far, in expanding or subdividing, we are *as far from the unquantifiable Infinite as we were at the beginning of the process.* For it only describes, in the historic plain method, the process in which a human understanding is obliged to recognise what Locke calls 'an idea which lies in obscurity, and has all the indeterminate confusion of a negative idea.'

Idea of substance, abstracted from our complex ideas of particular sorts of substances.

Another crucial test is in what Locke calls 'the general idea of substance,' as distinct from complex ideas of particular substances, 'invented by us,' that are always inadequate to reality, and in which men are often misled. Here too, in his fidelity to facts, he accepts an intellectual obligation that surely cannot be literally regarded as a 'particular idea' of the senses, or of reflection. An arbitrary aggregate of sense-presented phenomena, without a 'material substance'; or of conscious states and acts, without a 'spiritual substance' on which they respectively depend, and of which they may be predicated, is, he finds, 'inconceivable.' It is like an adjective without its substantive ; and in fact the presupposition of substantives corresponding to their adjectives expresses, in another way, this mental obligation to *substantiate* simple ideas in all concrete experience. Locke allows the obligation, but complains that this ultimate idea of *substance in the abstract* is 'obscure'; that we cannot have it from our senses, or in our experience of our own mental operations: although both the ideas of the senses and the ideas of reflection somehow give rise to this 'uncertain supposition of something we know not what,' by which simple ideas of existence are 'supported,' and which is involved in all our complex ideas of anything that really exists. But when he tried to represent this abstract but indispensable 'something,' in an idea-image, he was baffled, as he was when he tried to complete the idea-image of Immensity and Eternity. It was an endless unimaginable regress. If one asks *what* the substance is to which the colour he sees, or the sound he hears, is to be attributed, and is told that it is the aggregated atoms of which the coloured or sonorous object consists, *this* indeed gives a particular idea that is representable in imagination ; but then it is inadequate, for one is mentally obliged to ask in turn, what *their* substance is, and if he gets in reply only another idea of sense, he has to repeat the question ; and so on without end—as long as the understanding is confined within the limits of sensuous imagination. 'He is in a difficulty like that of the Indian,' Locke says, ' who, after explaining that the world rested on an elephant, which in its turn was supported by a broad-backed tortoise, could at last only suppose the tortoise to rest on *something—I know not what.*' We can neither think, i. e. image, nor refrain from thinking, i. e. presupposing, the meaning that is connoted by the abstract term substance, as distinguished from the ' invented ideas ' of particular sorts of substances, which form their nominal essences. *Why* we are in the mental predicament of neither being able to image an abstract substance, nor to refrain from presupposing substance, in everything that we have an idea of as existing, Locke does not ask. It does not seem to occur to him that this mental predicament itself calls for consideration, since it cannot be resolved into the contingent advent of aggregates of simple ideas, in the senses and in reflection. After all, is not Locke's perplexity about the abstract idea of substance an example of that very misleading influence of abstractions against which the *Essay* so often warns us ? His ' general idea of substance ' is an impossible one —a something that makes *no* manifestation of itself, that is concealed, not revealed ' in part,' in the simple ideas that might properly be regarded as manifestations (so far) of what it is. The substance is partially revealed in our complex idea of it : the complete complex idea, involving omniscience, is unattainable in a human understanding. In perceiving its phenomena we necessarily so far perceive the substance, inadequate as the complex conception so found must be, in an understanding that at the most is able to receive only a few of the simple ideas or phenomena that existing substances *can* present.

Another example of inadequacy in Locke's account of those metaphysical ideas is found in what he says of *causality* and *power*. The idea of *a* change involves the idea of

Ideas of causality and power, abstracted

from our
ideas of
the actual
causes and
effects.

a cause, by a necessity which something in the constitution
of understanding imposes on us ; although the idea that
this particular change is caused by *that particular substance*
is the issue of custom or experience. Causality in the
abstract, which Locke leaves almost untouched, seems to be
a necessity of immanent or innate reason : what is chiefly
looked to in the *Essay* is the manner in which ideas of
particular causal connexions are formed—the powers, active
and passive, of the substances that exist. When he is
pressed by Stillingfleet, indeed, he falls back on the abstract
and universal principle of causality—that 'whatever has
a beginning must have a cause'—as 'a true principle of
reason, which we come to know by perceiving that the idea
of beginning to be is *necessarily connected* with the idea of
some operation ; and the idea of operation with that of
something operating, which we call a cause.' This abstract
necessity for *a* particular cause for *every* particular change
—like the abstract necessity for Immensity, or Eternity,
or Substance—carries the mind into thoughts that are unimaginable and mysterious. It confines us to the mysterious
alternative, on the one hand, of a necessarily endless regress
of finite causes that are in turn effects, and a necessarily
endless progress of finite effects that are in turn causes,
under the mechanical idea of *nature* ; or, on the other
hand, of free or originating causality, typified in responsible agents, and implied in an ideal of *moral* order that
transcends the mechanism of nature.

Crucial
instances
of the ex-
periential
origin of
all our
ideas.

Immensity, Eternity, Substantiality, and Causality are
examples of the complex ideas offered in the *Essay* as
a fortiori proof of the truth of its leading proposition,
—that *all* our ideas of actual and conceived realities are
gradually gathered in experiences of external and internal
reality, and that none of them are independent of this
experience, in the way Locke supposed that what he called
'innate ideas,' were meant to be. For the *Essay* dismisses
'innate ideas' by two sorts of arguments. In the Second
Book their advocates are virtually challenged to name
any idea in a human understanding that may not be
referred to finite data of experience—those of Immensity,
Eternity, Substance, and Causality being chosen as those

least likely to submit to the analysis. In the First Book, on the other hand, it is argued that the ideas which are reckoned as innate by some—the ideas of identity, of substance, and of God, for example—must depend upon each man's experience ; because some are never conscious of them at all ; nor are any conscious of them in infancy, as they must have been if they were in their minds at birth, seeing that an idea cannot be ' in the mind ' without the mind being conscious of it. For an 'innate idea' is with Locke an idea consciously possessed, independently of any experience, and without any need for an active exercise of the understanding among the data of experience in order to its attainment. ' Whatever idea is in the mind, the mind must be conscious of.' This too is the drift of his argument, at the beginning of the Second Book [1], against the hypothesis that the mind is *always* having ideas, e. g. during sleep, which for the most part seems to be a dreamless state. An idea that in Locke's sense is innate must be in the consciousness of all—infants, savages, and idiots. Of course it is easy for him to show that no ideas can be mentioned that answer this condition. The abstract ideas of immensity and eternity, of substance and cause, infants and savages are not conscious of ; and as for the idea of God, whole nations are destitute of it, while it appears in innumerable different forms in the minds of those who are familiar with the name. Therefore even those ideas are not innate ; and if not even those, *a fortiori,* none others can be so.

It is difficult to find any one who would have denied this ; or to tell who was chiefly in Locke's mind, in the famous assault on ' innate ideas,' that is carried on all along the line in the *Essay.* Lord Herbert alone is named [2]. Locke's familiarity with Descartes, as well as some of the arguments employed, suggest that he too was in view. But by an innate idea Descartes means something antecedent to all experience, potential in the constitution of the understanding, and not necessarily in consciousness—argued on the ground that the individual ideas contingently given in experience cannot fully explain ideas that are universal. This means

Innate ideas and their defenders.

[1] Ch. i. §§ 9–18.   [2] Bk. II. ch. ii. §§ 15–19.

that the mind has innate *faculty* for universal ideas. That only this sort of innateness was intended, Descartes expressly says, in explaining his meaning to Regius, who had insisted that innateness of idea was not needed to solve the phenomena, innateness of faculty being enough. As to which Descartes says—'Regius appears to differ from me merely in words; for when he says that the mind has no need of ideas that are innate, and meantime grants that we all have an innate faculty for thinking them, he asserts, in effect, what I myself hold, although he rejects it in words. For I have never said or thought that the mind has ideas that are innate, in any other sense than that it has a faculty for thinking such ideas.'

What made Locke dread the hypothesis that some of our ideas are 'innate'? Locke was so exclusively set upon the banishment of all words that are empty of ideas, that he had no patience with a theory which seemed to shelter 'ideas' that might never enter consciousness at all—ideas that seemed above the need of verification by experience. His point of view was too practical for an adequate appreciation of universal ideas, or necessities of thought, in the ultimate interpretation of the universe. He was too little read in the literature of philosophy to do full justice to those who, from Plato onwards, have recognised implicates in our physical and moral experience that deeply concern the ultimate destiny of man, and the reality of the universe. 'Innate,' as his pupil the third Lord Shaftesbury observes, 'innate is a word Mr. Locke poorly plays on. The right word, though less used, is *connatural*. For what has birth, or the progress of the fœtus, to do in this case'? The question, that is to say, is not as to the *time* when persons first become conscious of certain ideas that are of universal extent in their application. The true question is, as Shaftesbury puts it, 'whether the constitution of man be not such that, *being adult and grown up*, the ideas of order, and administration of a God, will not *infallibly and necessarily spring up in consciousness*'—if the man does justice, one may add, to all the elements that are 'innate' in his constitution. Locke himself would hardly deny this. 'That there are certain propositions,' we find him acknowledging, 'which, though the soul from the beginning, when a man is born, does not know, yet, by assistance from the outward senses, and the help of some previous cultivation, it may afterwards come either self-evidently, or with a demonstrable necessity, to know the truth of, is no more than what I have affirmed in my First Book[1].' What Locke cared for was the conscious possession, and practical application of ideas by the individual; not their unconscious immanence, either subjectively in human understanding, or objectively in the universe. This appears in his reply to Thomas Burnet, who meets the objection founded on unconsciousness of ideas that are credited with innateness, by an analogy, urging that it is no sufficient argument that there is no sun in the firmament, because his light is obscured in cloudy days, or does not appear in foggy regions. To which Locke's answer is, that 'though the sun be in the heaven, those yet are in the dark, who do not guide their steps by it, and show that his light is not innate in *them.*' On the whole, one does not find that Locke meant to deny that men may rise into consciousness of conceptions that, when risen, are felt to be imposed by an intellectual necessity; and also that some of those conceptions cannot be comprehended fully in sensuous imagination: what he meant to deny was, that such ideas are the *conscious* possession of all human beings, at all ages, and in all stages of mental development; so that they do not need either the contingent data of experience, or activity in our understanding, to enable us to individualise them in imagination. But he hardly saw the importance to man of a due regard to these elements of immanent reason, as distinguished from what is directly contributed in the shifting phenomena of experience. He was moved, too, by his assumption, that 'nothing can be in the mind of which the mind is not conscious,' to the neglect of the now acknowledged fact—that in the living consciousness of an individual there may arise only a part of what human understanding contains, by logical implication, in its essential constitution.

The ideas of the *Essay* are 'all of them particular existences,' in themselves: they are considered in their Abstract or general ideas.

[1] Preface to Second Edition of the *Essay.*

'universality' when it is believed that 'more than one particular thing' can be represented by the idea, which then becomes an 'abstract complex idea.' It is only when the mind refers any of its particular or general ideas to what is 'extraneous to them' that, as elements of knowledge, they become 'capable of being called true or false; because the mind, in such a reference, makes a tacit supposition of their conformity to that thing[1].' This *reference* is the essential factor in knowledge. As Locke puts it[2], the mind 'finding that if it should proceed by, and dwell upon only particular things, its progress would be very slow, and its work endless; therefore, to shorten its way to knowledge, and make each perception more comprehensive, the first thing it does is to bind them into bundles, and rank them into sorts, that what knowledge it gets of any of them, it may thereby with assurance extend to all of that sort, and so advance by larger steps in knowledge. This is the reason why we collect things under comprehensive ideas, with names annexed to them—into genera and species, i. e. into kinds and sorts.' The part which this sort of abstraction enables the particular ideas that undergo it to play in the constitution of human knowledge, and the dependence of the 'abstract ideas' upon words, gave rise to the Third Book of the *Essay*, which is concerned with Words, as the organism of ideas when ideas are considered as universals.

Locke's abstract idea of a triangle.

The language of the *Essay* about abstract (i. e. general) ideas is apt to be misunderstood. They are spoken of as 'fictions and contrivances of the mind, that carry difficulty with them.' 'Does it not,' Locke asks, 'require some pains and skill to form the general idea of a triangle; for it must be neither oblique nor rectangle; neither equilateral, equicrural, nor scalenon; but all and none of these at once? It is something imperfect, that cannot exist; an idea wherein some parts of different and inconsistent [particular] ideas are put together' (Bk. IV. ch. vii. § 9). This paradoxical statement, along with inadequate apprehension of the difference between sensuous images and notions of the understanding, was the occasion of Berkeley's objections

[1] See Bk. II. ch. xxxii. §§ 1–3.   [2] Bk. II. ch. xxxii. § 6.

to the abstract ideas of the *Essay*, in the Introduction to the *Principles of Human Knowledge.* Abstract notions, as such, cannot be 'particular ideas,' and cannot be presented in sense, or represented in imagination. What Locke seems to mean is, that the concept, e. g. of a triangle, *may* be individualised, or exemplified as a particular idea, in *any one* of many possible applications—oblique, equilateral, &c.—all of which it is potentially, but none of them actually, save when it is exemplified in that one. Only thus can 'abstract ideas' be presented in sense, or represented in imagination.

According to his account of 'ideas' and their particularity, and apart from their office as factors in knowledge, Locke is more properly an *ideist* or phenomenalist than an Idealist, our ideas being with him originally the particular phenomena in which real existences immediately present themselves in human experience.

Locke's ideism.

III. CONNEXION OR REPUGNANCY OF IDEAS, A SECOND ELEMENT IN KNOWLEDGE.

Knowledge, according to Locke, is concerned with the ideas, or particular manifestations, which existence presents to us. Now to get knowledge out of ideas implies that ideas are related to one another, and so are interpretable; for knowledge is mental assertion or denial, and this presupposes relations of 'connexion and agreement, or disagreement or repugnancy' as the foundation of assertion or denial. In short, an implied copula is distinctive of all proposition, mental or verbal, spontaneous or reflective.

Knowledge implies the interpretability of ideas.

Locke, accordingly, proceeds to inquire what sorts of knowable relations there are amongst ideas; whether these all come within the range of *human* knowledge; and if not, why not? He finds that the 'connexions or agreements and disagreements or repugnancies' between the ideas or phenomena of existence, which constitute our real and our imaginary worlds, are of four sorts. As thus[1]:—'To

Four sorts of relations between ideas.

---

[1] Bk. IV. ch. i. § 3. See also ch. iii. *passim.*

understand wherein this agreement or disagreement consists, I think we may reduce it all to these four sorts:—
(1) Identity or diversity. (2) Relation. (3) Coexistence,
or necessary connexion. (4) Real existence.' He adds
that 'though identity and coexistence are truly nothing
but relations, yet they are such peculiar ways of agreement or disagreement of our ideas that they deserve to
be considered as distinct heads, and not under relation
in general '—the second sort. This seems to imply that
perception of 'real existence' in and through means of
our ideas—the fourth sort of connexion—is other than
perception of relation between ideas, in the way the other
three preceding sorts are ;—although knowledge of 'real
existence,' like the other sorts of knowledge, takes the
form of proposition, with implied 'connexion' between two
ideas—'real existence' being therein predicated of the
subject, which is thereby brought within the sphere of
reality, in the mind's regard. Look a little at each sort.

Identity and diversity as knowable relations of ideas.

Take first Identity and Diversity. It is impossible to
have any ideas at all without perceiving that an idea is
what it is, and that one idea is not another idea. This is
the fundamental relation of all ideas, which in its ultimate
form of abstraction appears, in logic, as the two correlative
principles of identity and non-contradiction. It is so universally necessary that without a perception of it there
could be no knowledge of any sort ; so that, in having any
ideas, *this* relation, at any rate, is implied, ideas 'being'
universally and eternally known to be not the same, 'and
so being' universally and constantly denied of one another.
And this *negative* relation, the one in which knowledge
is fully coextensive with ideas, opens the way to positive
knowledge ; because unless it is presupposed ideas are
uninterpretable, there being no ideas to interpret.

Abstract relations in general between ideas, e. g. in pure mathematics.

Again, there are innumerable positive relations of ideas,
particular and universal, which arise when ideas are considered in abstraction from the contingencies of time and
change. Those abstract relations belong to them as such,
and Locke accordingly regards them as relations proper.
Pure mathematics and abstract ethics exemplify this second
category of the knowable.

Further, there are innumerable positive relations of ideas that arise out of their simultaneous and successive appearances, in the constant flux of which the sensible world and our own minds are the scenes. This third sort of knowable relation among ideas is described in the *Essay* as that of their 'co-existence or non-existence in the same subject.' It implies that they are supposed to be complex ideas in particular substances, material or spiritual, and not, as in the preceding case, abstracted from conditions of time.

Lastly, there is the agreement or repugnance of ideas with the 'real existence' of the particular substance which they then manifest to us. This is illustrated in all propositions, mental and verbal, spontaneous and reflective, in which 'real existence' is affirmed or denied.

Within these four sorts of agreement or disagreement of ideas, according to the *Essay*, lies all the knowledge we have, or are capable of. For all assertions that can be made concerning any idea presented in experience are—that it is, or is not the same with some other idea ; that it has this or that abstract, e. g. mathematical or moral, relation with some other idea ; that it does or does not always coexist with some other idea in the same individual substance ; or that it has real existence, independent of any momentary perception. Thus 'blue is not yellow' is an example of the relation of diversity ; 'two triangles upon equal bases between two parallels are equal' is an example of abstract relation ; 'iron is susceptible of magnetical impressions' illustrates coexistence of ideas ; 'I exist,' 'things around me exist,' 'God exists,' are assertions of real existence. Pure logic reflects scientifically the first of these sorts of 'connexion and disagreement,' in their ultimate abstraction, as applicable to all ideas. The abstract sciences of mathematics and ethics, and also reasonings that deal only with arbitrary definitions of words, exemplify the second sort. Experiential inquiries into the laws of natural ideas or phenomena, under the presuppositions of physical causality, aim at the discovery of relations of the third sort. The fundamental propositions which affirm the ultimate realities of existence, constitute the fourth sort of connexion or repugnance of ideas.

IV. PERCEPTION, A THIRD ELEMENT IN
KNOWLEDGE.

Know-
ledge dis-
tinguished
from
judgment
of prob-
ability.

In the views which the mind finds itself obliged or able to take of the connexions and repugnances amongst ideas, or of the interpretation to be put upon them, Locke finds a difference. There is the *perceived absolute certainty* which is essential to knowledge, and the *presumption*, or *judgment of probability*, on which after all human life turns. In knowledge or science proper we 'certainly perceive, and are undoubtedly satisfied of the agreement or disagreement of any ideas.' In judgments of probability, which are often practically certain, we affirm or deny ideas of one another, when their unconditionally certain agreement or disagreement is not perceived, but only presumed. Our knowledge extends only as far as we are conscious of an intellectual insight of necessary relation between the subject and the predicate of the mental proposition in which the knowledge rises into consciousness.

Know-
ledge
proper is
essentially
intuitive,
or self-
evident,
according
to the
Essay.

This 'perception' or insight Locke describes as fundamentally intuitive ; the relation is perceived 'at once, as the eye perceives light, only by being directed to it.' The unconditional certainty we have that 'white is not black' ; that 'a circle is not a triangle' ; that 'three are more than two, or equal to one and two,' are examples of this intuitive perception. It does not need the medium of reasoning, and it is the utmost certainty that human understanding is capable of, or that one can even suppose possible in any intelligent being. Intuitive knowledge, according to the *Essay*, is 'irresistible,' and, like bright sunshine, forces itself immediately to be perceived as soon as ever the mind turns its view that way : it leaves no room for hesitation, doubt, or examination, but the mind is presently filled with the clear light of it. 'It is on this intuition that depends all the certainty and evidence of all our knowledge ; which certainty every one finds to be so great, that he cannot imagine, and therefore cannot require, a greater : for a man cannot conceive himself capable of a greater certainty that to know [i.e. perceive intuitively] that any idea in his mind is such

as he perceives it to be ; and that two ideas, wherein he
perceives a difference, are different, and not precisely the
same. He that demands a greater certainty than this,
demands he knows not what, and shows only that he has
a mind to be a sceptic without being able to be so.' (Bk. IV.
ch. ii. § 1.) Thus, while Locke, in treating of ideas *per se,*
in the Second Book, makes human knowledge depend
upon our getting particular ideas of things, through external and internal experience, without the aid of any
ideas that are ' innate ' or prior to ' all experience,'—in the
Fourth Book he represents intuition, or self-evidence, as
not less essential than experience ; for on it, he says,
' depends all the certainty and evidence of all our knowledge.' In this recognition of the second of these two
cardinal constituents of knowledge, Locke agrees with his
favourite Hooker, who says that ' to make nothing *evident
of itself* unto man's understanding were to take away the
possibility of knowing anything '; and that ' herein that of
Theophrastus is true—they that seek a reason of all things
do utterly overthrow reason.'

But while human knowledge is fundamentally intuitive, Demon-
according to the *Essay,* the percipient act in it is not in stration
involves
all instances a *direct* intuition. In the finite human under- a series of
standing the range of direct intuition is narrow. In many intuitions.
human acts of knowing, the known relation between the
two ideas is not perceived ' at first sight.' It needs intermediate ideas, or the chain of intuited relations which
constitutes *demonstration.* Thus, while the axioms of
geometry are known by a direct intuition, the great body
of geometrical truths has to be demonstrated : it is reached
in the form of intellectually necessary conclusions, not of
truths that are evident at once. In a demonstrated conclusion the absolute certainty of knowledge is not immediately forced upon the understanding : it is reached
gradually, in a series of steps, adapted to that weakness
which obliges man to have recourse to reasoning. But all
reasoning that is properly demonstrative is, as it were,
saturated with intuition ; each step is taken in the light
of intuition ; and we march towards the conclusion in
a series of self-evident steps. Demonstration is intuition

or self-evidence *accommodated to a finite intelligence*; and it is required in that larger portion of his knowledge in which man cannot at once enter into the perfect intellectual light of direct insight. In omniscience all is intuitively known, and then demonstration and reasoning of any sort is superfluous.

We have knowledge in all actual sensation, which is sense-perception.

In the same matter-of-fact 'historical' way, Locke finds yet another class of examples of that perception of complete certainty to which he restricts the term knowledge. In them the certainty is less luminous than in intuition proper, or even than in demonstration. One has it when he is obliged, as he always is, to regard the ideas presented in sensation as manifestations of the real existence of *something* outside the sensations, and outside the subject of them. Whatever may be the best way of expressing the relation between this 'something,' its sensuous manifestations, and our acts or states of sense-perception—Locke finds himself conscious of absolute certainty, that the simple ideas of sensation *are* its manifestations, to and in his understanding. This evidence, as every one finds, 'forbids doubting.' 'For I ask any one,' he continues, 'whether he is not invincibly conscious to himself of a different perception, when he looks on the sun by day, and only thinks on it at night; when he actually tastes wormwood, or smells a rose, or only thinks of that savour and odour? We as plainly find the difference there is between an idea *revived in our minds* by our own memory, and *its actual coming into our minds by the senses*, as we do between any two ideas. This certainty is as great as our happiness and misery, beyond which we have no concernment to know or be [1].' In this 'sensitive knowledge,' as Locke calls it, or sense-perception, according to later terminology, we have, he insists, a third instance of human knowledge;—less luminously revealed than demonstrated knowledge, still less luminous than when we have an immediate intuition of self-evident connexion between ideas, but withal different in kind from all fallible presumptions of probability. Of this sensuous perception, awakened in us only when our organs of sense are actually affected, the *Essay* declines to attempt an explanation.

---

[1] Bk. IV. chh. ii. § 14; xi. §§ 1-10.

It only announces the inexplicable fact, and refers it to the 'will of God.' The organic accompaniments of the percipient act, Locke suggests, are not out of the reach of explanation, on the ground that motion is the mechanical cause of motion ; so that motion, and contact with extra-organic moving bodies, *may* account mechanically for motions within our corporeal organs: we thus learn indeed to distinguish ' our own bodies ' from all the rest of the solid and extended world. But the irresistible perception of the external reality of sense-received ideas remains an inexplicable mystery. Perception is not from the thing known but from the percipient. Outward things do not *make* living knowledge.

V. HUMAN KNOWLEDGE OF REAL EXISTENCES: SELF, GOD, AND OUTWARD THINGS.

Is human understanding actually, or at least virtually, in possession, to any extent, of the absolute certainty that is able to resist all sceptical questioning ; and if so, in which of the four sorts of ' perceived ' ' agreement or repugnancy ' between ' ideas ' to which Locke, by his definition, confines the term knowledge, is this certainty to be attained by him? Are there any mental propositions—particular or universal—which it is impossible for a human mind seriously and practically to hold in suspense, inasmuch as they are intuitively or demonstrably certain? Or is man confined, in all his interpretations of all his ideas, in all their relations, logical, mathematical, physical, and metaphysical, to hypothetical presumptions of probability—to propositions that are only provisionally true, because subject to the flux of experience, and because therein dependent on agents that are imperfectly known? The Fourth Book of the *Essay*, in the chapters which treat of the extent and reality of human knowledge [1], contains Locke's answer to these questions. Again inverting his order of procedure, let us consider first, how far he recognises this absolute certainty in the mental propositions, either particular or universal, in which ' real existence ' is affirmed.

As to which of those four sorts of knowable connexion can a human understanding attain to knowledge ?

First, Knowledge of real existences.

[1] Bk. IV, especially chh. iv, ix, x, xi.

Two sorts of real existences are presupposed, at the opening of the *Essay*, and throughout.

The *Essay* starts, even in the Second Book, with the presupposition of two 'real existences,' to one or other of which all the simple ideas of men are assumed to be originally referable. The growth of our experience accordingly consists in the increased variety of simple and complex ideas gradually attributed to those two sorts of realities. Whence, he asks, has the mind of man the ideas that constitute the distinctive element in each concrete example of knowledge, and that form men's conceptions of what the realities are? 'Our observation,' he replies[1], 'employed either about external objects, or about the operations of our own minds, is what supplies the understanding with all its attainable materials of positive knowledge.' Here 'external sensible objects,' and 'our own minds,' are presupposed to exist, and to become gradually clothed with qualities, through an experience of the simple ideas in which they make themselves known in sense. Afterwards, in the Fourth Book, the two presupposed realities are offered as examples of the unconditionally certain knowledge of real existences that is within reach even of a human understanding.

Connexion of abstracted ideas, without any irresistible assurance of real existence, is a 'castle in the air.'

With an element of reality, ideas must be implicated from the first; otherwise it could never enter into them. Locke himself sees that 'connexion and repugnance' of abstracted ideas is construction of 'castles in the air.' 'If it be true that all knowledge lies only in perception of the agreement or disagreement of our own ideas,' he supposes a critic to say, 'the visions of an enthusiast, and the reasonings of a sober man will be equally certain. It is no matter how *things* are; so a man can observe but the agreement of *his own imaginations*, and talk conformably, it is all truth, all certainty. Such castles in the air will be as strongholds of truth as the demonstrations of Euclid. Of what use is all this fine knowledge of men's own imaginations to a man that inquires after the reality of things? It matters not what men's fancies are: it is the knowledge of things only that is to be prized—things as they really are.' To all which Locke replies, 'that if our knowledge of our ideas terminate in them, and reach no further, where

[1] Bk. II. ch. i. § 1.

there is something further intended, our most serious thoughts will be of little more use than the reveries of a crazy brain. But I hope,' he adds, 'to make it plain, that this way of certainty, by the knowledge of our own ideas, goes a little further than bare imagination[1].' We must see whether he makes it plain.

The test offered in the *Essay* of our possession of at least a subjective certainty that 'actual and real existence agrees to an idea' is, the irresistible assurance of reality, of which we are conscious, or at least may become conscious. 'Wherever we are sure that our ideas agree with the reality of things, there is certain *real* knowledge. Of which agreement of our ideas with the reality of things, having given the marks, I think I have shown whence certainty, real certainty, consists; which, whatever it was to others, was, I confess, to me, heretofore, one of those desiderata which I found great want of[2].' Adopting this test of the legitimate employment of the term 'real existence,' as a predicate in our mental assertions, Locke finds that in the original reception of *all* our simple ideas, we are 'sure,' actually or by implication, that the received ideas 'agree with,' manifest, or signify, at least 'our own existence.' We are also sure that many of our simple ideas 'agree with,' manifest, or reveal, the real existence of 'some external sensible object.' All our ideas thus originally involve an irresistible assurance of reality: when we have them we are obliged to presuppose something more permanent than the momentary consciousness, and that is therefore independent of that momentary consciousness. Locke does not much trouble himself with the puzzle of *how* we can determine 'agreement' of 'ideas' with 'reality,' without first having the real existence presented to us *apart from all ideas of it.* This question Reid and other critics have pressed, when they ask whether Locke's supposition does not imply either a contradiction, or a double consciousness, i. e. a consciousness of our own ideas, and also a knowledge of *reality apart from all ideas,* with which to compare our own ideas, and so discern their agreement with it.

Locke's test of the certainty of real existence found in the irresistible intuitive assurance of which we are conscious.

[1] Bk. IV. ch. iv. §§ 1, 2.   [2] Bk. IV. ch. iv. § 18.

Our simple ideas, in the process of being received, carry with them this irresistible assurance.

Locke asks indeed, 'how the mind, when it perceives nothing but its own ideas, can *know* that they agree with things themselves?' 'This,' he says, 'though it seems not to want difficulty,' yet we have perfect assurance that 'all our *simple ideas*' agree with the idea of reality[1]. Something in the mind obliges us to predicate reality of *them*, for we cannot but have irresistible certainty, when they arise, that they are manifesting to us what things really are, to the extent, and in those relations, which our condition requires. This he thinks is enough of real knowledge for all practical purposes. It enables us to regulate our conduct in harmony with the realities of existence, and with the system of relations which goes to constitute reality, and to distinguish what is real from what is illusory.

The intuitive assurance each man has of the reality of 'his own existence.'

The one intuitive assurance of reality that Locke finds *all* our ideas charged with is, assurance of 'our own existence,' made known in 'the operations of which we are conscious,' as well as those which supply us with simple ideas of reflection. He puts it thus[2]:—'As for our own existence we perceive it so plainly and so certainly that it neither needs nor is capable of any proof. For nothing can be more evident to us than our own existence : I think, I reason, I feel pleasure and pain ; can any of these be more evident to me than my own existence? If I doubt of all other things, that very doubt makes me perceive my own existence. . . . Experience then convinces us that we have an intuitive knowledge of our own existence, and an internal infallible perception that we are.' In short there cannot be any consciousness of any sort of idea without an implied assurance of the truth of the mental proposition —'I really exist.'

Ulterior questions involved in this certainty, of which Locke says nothing.

Locke does not pause to ask what is meant by either the subject or the predicate in this proposition ; or what is the source of the ideas signified by 'I,' and by 'real existence.' 'Existence,' he indeed tells us, in the Second Book[3], is an idea 'suggested to the understanding by every object without, and every idea within'; but nothing is said of the nature and origin of the idea signified by *real*, although 'real knowledge' is distinguished from what is merely

---

[1] See Bk. IV. ch. iv. §§ 3, 4.   [2] See Bk. IV. ch. ix. § 3.
[3] Bk. II. ch. vii. § 7.

'certain' (e. g. in Bk. IV. ch. iv. § 18). Then what is meant by '*my own* existence,' and by the personal pronoun 'I'? Is any idea associated with a personal pronoun? It is not mentioned in the *Essay* among the simple ideas either of sensation or of reflection. Finding that it could not be individualised in a sensuous image, and yet could not be dismissed as a meaningless term, Berkeley called its meaning a *notion* instead of an *idea*[1]. Hume, dismissing all words as meaningless when the supposed meaning could not be resolved into a particular impression of sense—a simple idea of sense, as Locke would say—and finding that he could never thus 'catch himself' at any time 'without a perception,' nor light upon anything but a momentary perception, to answer to the personal pronoun I—added, that if any one thinks he has a different notion of *himself* than as a momentary perception, 'I must confess I can reason no longer with him: he may perhaps perceive something *simple and continued*, which he calls *himself*; though I am certain there is no such principle in me.' Nor does Locke explain whether by ' my own existence'—of which he assumes that we must all have 'an internal infallible perception'—he intends only an existence that lasts during the consciousness of each moment, or one which includes a past self, given in memory, through which the present consciousness is identified with an imperfectly remembered past. The chapter on 'Personal Identity,' in the Second Book, as well as the chapters on 'our complex ideas of Substances,' and on our idea of ' Power,' especially ' the active power we find in ourselves,' may be compared with what is said in the Fourth Book about our intuitive knowledge of 'our own existence,' as aids to the discovery of what Locke means. The treatment of the subject in the *Essay* shows his disposition to avoid speculative questions and the ultimate mysteries, and to remain contented with the point of view that satisfies ordinary minds.

While this intuitive certainty of ' our own existence ' is Locke's signal instance of a proposition concerning reality which we are mentally obliged to receive at once, with an

---

[1] 'In Berkeley,' as Reid says, 'the most important objects are known without *ideas*.'

existence
of 'other
things.'

undoubting certainty, he finds, in the eleventh chapter of
the Fourth Book, another example of knowledge of reality,
in the irresistible 'assurance all men have' of the 'real
existence' of 'other things,' at those moments when, 'by
actually operating upon our senses, they make themselves
perceived by us.' For it is to their present actual operation
upon the organs of sense that he says our knowledge of
things around us is limited. So when 'outward things'
are absent from our senses—distant or future—they cannot
be 'known' to exist really: their existence is then only
'presumed,' with more or less probability. When I am
actually looking at the sun, I 'know' that it really exists;
when I only think of it at night, and then expect its
reappearance in the morning, this, he would say, is only
a probable judgment that it exists, although it amounts
to practical certainty.

Ulterior
questions
involved
in this
certainty
of which
Locke says
nothing.

When Locke finds, by applying his own criterion of
reality, that something real, outside of 'our own existence,'
is manifested to us, as immanent, so to speak, in our actual
sensations and sense-ideas, he does not tell us whether it is
equally and alike manifested in *all* our 'sensations.' The
eleventh chapter of the Fourth Book should therefore be
compared with the eighth chapter of the Second Book,
in which certain simple ideas, or qualities, of matter are
signalised, as 'primary' or 'real,' 'inseparable from body,
in what state soever it be,' and 'such as sense finds in every
particle of matter which has bulk enough to be perceived.'
Ideas of this sort are there said to be 'in the external
things themselves,'—in whatever mysterious way the perceived can be said to exist in the percipient, and yet be
a quality of the perceived. But when Locke is dealing,
in the Fourth Book, with our irresistible assurance of
the existence of 'whatever is actually operating upon our
senses,' he does not refer to what he had said in the Second
Book, about the 'primary qualities' of things. In the
light of what was there said about these 'essential qualities'
of matter, this 'something operating upon our senses' must
be *something solid and extended*, and must be construable
in terms of *motion*[1]. Neither does he try to remove the

---

[1] Cf. Bk. IV. ch. iv. § 4.

obvious difficulty involved in the apparent conversion of molecular movements into simple ideas. He seems how-ever to regard them as only correlatives that are not causally convertible. Then as to 'operation,'—what *sort* of causality and power does operation here connote? Else-where [1] he hesitates to include 'active power' in our complex idea of any material substance—'material sub-stances being not perhaps so truly active powers as our hasty thoughts are apt to represent them.' The world of solid moveable things, in the momentary revelations of themselves which they make, during our experience of actual sensations, would thus be an *occasion* rather than the *active cause* of our 'perceptions' of 'real existence'; and with Berkeley we should look for the needed active power in the Supreme Power in the universe.

It should be noted that Locke seems to say that those sense-perceptions of outward things also involve a simultaneous revelation of the reality of the existence of the Ego. 'It is for want of reflection,' he says, 'that we are apt to think that our senses show us nothing but material things. Every act of sensation, when duly considered, gives us an equal view of *both* parts of nature—the corporeal and spiritual. For, whilst I know, by seeing or hearing, that there is some corporeal being without me—the object of that sensation, I do more certainly know that there is some spiritual being within me that sees and hears [2].' This approaches the estimate of sense-perception given by Reid and Hamilton. 'Every conception of self neces-sarily involves a conception of not-self: every perception of what is different from me, implies a recognition of the percipient subject, in contradistinction from the object perceived. In one act of knowledge indeed the object is the prominent element; in another the subject; but there is none in which either is known out of relation to the other [3].' But the language of the *Essay* is not always thus.

A duality of some sort, in real existence as it appears in human experience, is thus, according to the *Essay*,

A simulta-neous reve-lation of the Ego and the non-Ego, in sense-percep-tion.

A demon-strative certainty

---

[1] See Bk. II. ch. xxi. § 2 ; also ch. xxiii. § 28. Hume seems to overlook this, in *Inquiry*, Note D.

[2] Bk. II. ch. xxiii. § 15.

[3] Hamilton's *Discussions*, p. 51.

of the real existence of God, or the Eternal Mind, maintained in the *Essay.*

originally given, in an irresistible assurance, which can be awakened in all men, of the real existence of the Ego, and also of something outside the Ego, of which each Ego has the sense-ideas in which this 'something' manifests its real existence. But Locke finds further (Bk. IV. ch. x) that experience of the real is not satisfied with an unexplained duality, in which each factor is finite and dependent. 'Though God has given us no innate ideas of Himself,' so that thus individuals, and even whole nations, may remain without an idea of God, yet He has so 'furnished us with faculties, that we cannot want a clear proof that He exists' as long as we carry *ourselves* about us. Each man knows intuitively that he himself exists, and that he has not existed always; it is therefore 'unavoidable for all rational creatures to conclude, that something has existed from eternity; this being of all absurdities the greatest, to imagine, that pure nothing, the perfect negation and absence of all beings, should ever produce any real existence.' I cannot myself be this eternal Something, seeing that my own existence had a beginning; and whatever had a beginning must have been produced by something else, and also must have got all that now belongs to its real existence from another being. Further, I am a thinking being: therefore the something that eternally exists, the source of my existence, must think; it being 'as impossible that what is wholly void of knowledge, and operating blindly, and without any perception, should produce a knowing being as I am, as it is impossible that a triangle should make itself three angles bigger than two right ones.' That God really exists is therefore 'the most obvious truth that reason [reasoning] discovers,' and its evidence is 'equal to mathematical certainty'; although 'it requires thought and attention, and the mind must apply itself to a regular deduction of it from some part of our intuitive knowledge, else we shall be as ignorant of this as of other propositions, which are in themselves capable of clear demonstration'; seeing that none of them are 'innate,' inasmuch as individual men can remain ignorant of them. This 'eternal Something' may be called 'eternal Mind,' because practically known as Mind, or so known, 'as far as is necessary to the true end of our being, and the great concernment of our happiness'; yet only in this relative sense after all, according to one of Locke's last letters to Anthony Collins, in which he says—'Though I call the thinking faculty in me, *mind*, I cannot, because of that name, equal it in anything to that eternal and incomprehensible Being, which, for want of right and distinct conceptions, is called *Mind* also, or the eternal Mind.' (June 29, 1704.)

These last words express a deeper sense of the mystery that is involved in our idea of the ultimate reality than appears in the *Essay*; but with what looks like an insufficient perception of the inadequacy of reasoning to infer, on the basis of an experience of *finite* beings, the actual existence of the *Infinite* Mind in whom alone we can have an absolute trust. Unless the conclusion is presupposed in the premisses, Locke's 'demonstration' breaks down. The assumption that perfect Reason is immanent and active in the universe, seems to be a presupposition needed for the satisfaction of the human spirit, in its fully developed condition, and for the interpretation of our 'simple ideas' of the finite realities ; but the cosmological proof, of which Locke's 'mathematically certain demonstration' is a modification, is, when taken by itself, an eminent example of circular reasoning. Moreover the 'God' of the *Essay* seems to be conceived as one among an innumerable aggregate of individual substances, each really existing, that make up the universe of reality, forming its *minima intelligibilia*. If God is supposed only as a self-centred individual, the unity of reality disappears in an aggregate of separated substances. This is surely an inadequate apprehension of the absolute *uniqueness* of Deity, as the single being, not comprehended under any species or genus, and so incapable of being classed with finite substances.

Ulterior questions involved in this 'demonstrable' certainty of God's existence, which Locke does not discuss.

In Locke's 'demonstration' of the existence of God, the universality and necessity of the causal principle is *tacitly* presupposed, although, in the analysis of the complex idea of causality (Bk. II. ch. xxvi. § 1) its contents were referred exclusively to 'observation of the constant vicissi-

Locke's demonstration of God's existence presupposes the

universal-
ity and
necessity
of the
causal
principle.

tude of things.' Now this analysis could only explain
concrete instances and special laws of causality, not the
necessary and universal relation assumed in this demonstration. It is characteristic of the analysis of ideas in the
Essay to look only to concrete embodiments of fundamental
conceptions, in disregard of the absolute universality and
necessity on which nevertheless Locke's argumentative
theism depends. And so it came to pass that what was
dogmatically assumed in the *Essay*, in working out
a theological conception of the universe, but without
critical vindication of the validity of the assumption, was
afterwards explained away by Hume, who could find no
ground for presupposing the applicability of the causal
principle to immensities and eternities ; and who concluded that the only objects of legitimate demonstration
must lie within the purely abstract ideas of 'quantity and
number.' 'These,' Hume says, 'may safely, I think, be
pronounced the *only* proper objects of knowledge and
demonstration.' As for demonstrations about the Supreme
Power, and the Final Purpose of the universe, ' our line
is too short to fathom such immense abysses,' which open
when we apply it in this way to subjects that lie beyond
the contingencies of experience. And unless the universal
reason in which we share implies that we are living and
having our being in a reality that must be active moral
reason at last, surely, the whole becomes, as here with
Hume, 'a riddle, an enigma, an inexplicable mystery.'

The three
ultimate
realities in
their
mutual
relations.

On the whole, according to Locke, a merely human
knowledge of what really exists is confined to the intuitive
knowledge we all have of our own existence, as far back
as memory can go ; the sensitive knowledge or perception
we all have of the real existence of things 'outside' of
ourselves, when we are actually sentient; and the demon-
strative certainty we may all have of the eternal reality of
' what, from want of right and distinct conceptions is called
Mind, or the eternal Mind.' So, in treating of our ideas of
substance and identity, in the Second Book [1], he finds that
'we have the ideas of but three sorts of substances:—(1) God.
(2) Finite intelligences. (3) Bodies. God is without begin-

[1] Bk. II. ch. xxvii. § 2.

ning, eternal, unalterable, and everywhere, and therefore concerning his identity there can be no doubt. Finite spirits
have each had its determined time and place of beginning
to exist; the relation to that time and place will always
determine to each of them its identity as long as it exists.
The same will hold of every particle of matter, to which no
addition or subtraction of matter being made, it is the same.
For, though these three sorts of substances, as we term them,
do not exclude one another out of the same place, yet we
cannot conceive but that they must necessarily, each of them,
exclude any of the same kind out of the same place, or else
there could be no such distinction of substances one from
another.' Locke's disposition to conceive the universe of
reality mechanically, appears in this application of relations
of ' place' to all the ' three sorts of substances.' He suggests,
however, that the word ' substance,' when applied to finite
beings, corporeal or spiritual, which are not absolutely self-
subsistent or complete in themselves, is not to be used in the
same meaning as when it is applied to the Supreme Mind.

Are not Locke's three realities tacitly assumed by *These*
all men, as immanent in experience from the first, in *three*
a faith which becomes at last human reason in its *realities*
highest form? If not, could they have any claim to *assumed*
recognition afterwards; and are not all the three uncon- *by men,*
sciously presupposed in human life and action, even when *even when*
one or other of them is denied in speculation? For *words.*
the sceptic is found, in word and action, to bear witness
to an irresistible primary faith in himself, in things,
and in God. The history of philosophy, in its deepest
meaning, is the history of human endeavour to determine
the complex conceptions of self, and external nature, and
God that issue from the deepest and truest interpretation
of the realities which rise into perception in external
and internal sense. The daily employment of the personal
pronoun ' I,' and the application of the words which imply
an individual responsibility of persons for their own actions,
as worthy of praise or blame, carry a *latent* assurance
of his own existence all through the experience of the
speculative doubter; even while, like Hume, he asks in

vain for an idea-image of an abstract Ego. Life and action also spontaneously reveal a latent faith in something outside each individual personality, that is real enough to be at least a medium of intercourse between persons, and the occasion too of each person's consciousness of his own personality being awakened in him. As to the supreme and ultimate reality, the scientific agnostic, who professes ignorance of the existence of God, does himself, as an experimental inquirer, presuppose immanence of natural order, and, to that extent, of God, in the physical universe, without which it could not be reasoned about. For the atheistic hypothesis—which logically implies that experience is ultimately a physical as well as moral chaos, without reason in the heart of things, to be the final appeal in all inquiries ; and which thus empties the universe of all natural and moral government, and therefore of all natural as well as moral law—is a self-contradictory hypothesis, belied by every reasonable action in our lives : trust even in natural law is faith in God in its germ. Mere Egoism, atheistic Materialism, and Pantheism, are each philosophical exaggerations of one or other of the three final realities, to the apparent exclusion of the other two ; which still unconsciously govern, in diminished strength, the life and experience even of those who suppose that they have got rid of them by philosophical reasoning. It thus appears that the spirit in man, unconsciously if not reflectively, presupposes the antithesis which distinguishes each person from the external world with which his senses and actions bring him into contact and collision ; and also presupposes God, in the physical order, and in the ideals of duty, which make science and morality possible.

VI. HUMAN KNOWLEDGE OF IDEAS, AS COEXISTING ATTRIBUTES AND POWERS OF REAL EXISTENCES.

The narrow extent of human knowledge regarding things and persons.

Thus, according to the *Essay*, human knowledge of what really exists is narrow. It comprehends only, (1) the existence of the knower, as a 'thinking substance,' manifested to himself in the operations of which he is momentarily conscious, and also in those for which he trusts his memory, and thus recognises his own continuous reality as a person ;

(2) the actual existence of (solid and extended) substances, outside each person, while they do, or when they did, present simple ideas through sense, of which he is percipient—because he is somehow unable to doubt that 'such collections of simple ideas as we observe, or have observed, by our senses to be united together, do really exist together'; and (3) the existence of 'a most powerful and most knowing Being, whose eternal existence is demonstrable with an evidence equal to mathematical certainty.' The existence of 'the infinite and incomprehensible Being, which, for want of right and distinct conceptions, is called mind, or the Eternal Mind'; 'our own existence,' coextensively with our present and remembered self-conscious life; and the existence of 'things outside of us,' coextensively with the actual and remembered sensations which they occasion in us, exhaust, according to the *Essay*, the knowledge of realities that is possible to a human understanding. With the unique exception of the 'Eternal Mind,' all (or nearly all) that is not actually presenting itself, in our momentary self-consciousnesses and in our sensations, or that is not remembered as having done so, is not knowable by man. We are thus debarred from absolute certitude, with regard to the attributes and behaviour of any of at least the finite substances in existence, including our own 'thinking substance,' save and except what may be given in present perceptions and in memory. The temporal history, past and future, of all substances that neither are nor have been present in his sensations, and the history, past and future, of his own thinking substance, outside his present and remembered consciousness of its states, supremely important as this history is to his welfare, is outside possible knowledge; it can only be matter of probability; so that human life thus turns at last on faith in probabilities, in all our intercourse with things and persons. The universe, in the most practical of all its relations to the life of man, namely, as a sphere of innumerable activities, or the subject of innumerable changes, which determine our pleasures and pains, is withdrawn from the intuitive and demonstrative certainty in which man can share.

We are
dependent
on the con-
tingencies
of experi-
ence, for
our under-
standing
of the
actual
qualities
and beha-
viour of
things and
persons.

This is what Locke implies when he asserts that our
knowledge of the simple ideas, that is to say the attributes
and powers, that 'coexist' in the individual substances of
which the universe of reality is comprised, is 'very short,
though in this consists the greatest and most material
part of knowledge concerning substances.' For 'our [com-
plex] ideas of the species of substances being, as I have
showed, nothing but a certain collection of simple ideas
[found by sense to be] united in one subject, and so
coexisting together ; e.g. our idea of *flame* is a body hot,
luminous, and moving upward : of *gold*, body heavy in
a certain degree, yellow, malleable, and fusible ;—these, or
some such *complex ideas* as these, in men's minds, do these
two *names* of the different substances, flame and gold, stand
for. When we would know anything further concerning these,
or any other sort of substances, what do we inquire but
what *other* qualities or powers these substances have or
have not ? Which is nothing else but to know what other
simple ideas do or do not coexist with those that make up
that complex idea [i. e. our present complex idea of that
species of substance]. This, how weighty and considerable
a part soever of human science, is yet very narrow, and
scarce any at all. The reason whereof is, that the
simple ideas whereof *our* complex ideas of substances
are made up are, for the most part, such as carry with
them no visible *necessary* connexion or inconsistency with
any other simple ideas, whose existence with them we
would inform ourselves about[1].' In short, so far as
human knowledge of the substances that compose the
real universe goes, any simple idea, i. e. any quality or
power, may *a priori* consist with any other in that substance.
We cannot show demonstratively that, because this quality
is found in a substance, that other *must* also belong to it.
The reason for this limitation of our knowledge of the
constitution of substances, and so of the laws of coexistence
and succession illustrated in the changes to which they
are subject, is—the dependence of all human understanding
upon the contingencies of human experience, and the impossibility of building absolutely certain knowledge upon

[1] Bk. IV. ch. iii. §§ 9, 10.

inexperienced conditions about which one is uncertain. We are at the mercy of a narrow experience, and of imperfectly known agents, which transcend our experience, in our most important relations to the material substances which present themselves to our senses, and to the spiritual substance that is presented in reflection.

It follows from this, that men can have no absolute certainty, i. e. no strictly scientific knowledge, of the truth or falsehood of any *general* proposition regarding matters of fact; for assertions about the qualities and powers of substances are by implication always general : also that all particular assertions that would not be certain if they were made general, are assertions concerning real existence ; 'they declaring only the *accidental* union or separation of ideas [qualities] in things now existing, which in their abstract natures have no known *necessary* union or repugnancy[1].' This implies that a human understanding, incapable of omniscience, can know certainly only the existence of finite things, and of their qualities and powers, so far as these are, or have been, momentarily presented to the senses, or in self-consciousness. Science, or complete knowledge of things really existing, transcends the faculties and experience of man. This is the favourite conclusion of the *Essay*, reiterated in many forms, and at different points of view, but with illustrations drawn almost exclusively from substances in the universe of matter. 'I am apt to doubt that, how far soever human industry may advance useful and experimental philosophy in physical things, scientifical will still be out of our reach; because we want perfect and adequate [complex] ideas of those very bodies [material substances] that are nearest to us, and most under our command[2].' That is to say, we may have presumptions of probability, about the behaviour of the substances amidst which we live, that may sometimes amount to practical certainty ; but we cannot have the unconditional certainty that is essential to what Locke intends by 'knowledge[3].'

Hence no science of Nature, or the actual cosmical order, within reach of a human understanding.

---

[1] Bk IV. ch. ix. § 1.
[2] Bk. IV. ch. iii. § 26.
[3] As Bacon profoundly says— '*Ex parte scimus,* and to have the form of a total where there is but matter for a part, cannot be without supplies by supposition and presumption.' (*Advancement,* Bk. II.)

The real or primary, and the imputed or secondary qualities of sensible things.

In this connexion the *Essay* has much to say about the 'qualities,' and 'active or passive powers' of external bodies, a subject discussed in the eighth chapter of the Second Book, and often returned to afterwards. By far the greater part of their qualities and powers are, it is argued, 'no more the likeness of something existing without us than the names that stand for them are the likeness of our ideas, which yet upon hearing they are apt to excite in us[1].' This immense aggregate of interesting qualities we can only 'impute' to bodies, thereby meaning that those bodies to which they are imputed are the occasions of sensations in us; and therefore the ideas we have of them are not ideas which can be predicated of the bodies themselves, in the way that the real or primary qualities can. We can no more suppose that the taste or the fragrance we attribute to an orange, exists in the orange itself, in the way it does in our simple ideas, than we can suppose the pain of a wound existing in the knife that inflicts it. The imputed qualities are those that make bodies interesting to us, but they are all our own sensations, not direct manifestations of the bodies themselves. The only qualities that really exist in body, as given in our simple ideas, and that are predicable of *it* and not of *us*, are 'those we are obliged to suppose utterly inseparable from it, in what state soever it be; such as *sense* constantly finds in every particle of matter which has bulk enough to be perceived, and the *mind* finds inseparable from every particle of matter, though less than to make itself singly be perceived by *our* senses[2].' Our ideas of those 'real or primary qualities' resemble what is in the body, and are indeed virtually identical with what is in it; as far as a passing percept can be identical with what exists independently of any particular perception of an individual.

Matter to be interpretable in terms of molecular motion.

Now the only real qualities thus predicable by us of outward things are, *extension, solidity* and *mobility*, in their modes. Bodies accordingly seem to be revealed to us as essentially *atomic* or *molecular* in constitution, so that all their 'real' or 'primary' qualities might be interpreted in terms of motion. Their innumerable 'imputed or secondary'

[1] Bk. II. ch. viii. § 7.　　　　[2] Bk. II. ch. viii. § 9.

qualities, full of human interest, as well as their 'power' to change the simple ideas or phenomena that are presented by other bodies, are conditioned by, and must be scientifically interpreted in terms of, the size, figure, and motion of the constituent molecules in each of them ; unless, indeed, they depend, Locke adds, upon something else in them, more mysterious, and that wholly transcends all human ideas. Now, even if we adopt the hypothesis that the entire behaviour of each substance in the material world *is* interpretable in terms of molecular motion—an hypothesis, not an absolute certainty—Locke still urges that unless man can discover of what sorts the ultimate constituent atoms in a substance actually are, and also the sorts of sensation which the various possible modes of atoms naturally occasion in a sentient being, there can be no absolutely certain prevision of its behaviour, or of the changes in other substances which may follow changes in that substance.

Thus, according to the *Essay*, the absolute certainties that are within man's reach, about the world of 'outside things,' cannot extend beyond the real or primary qualities of the individual things that are, or that have been, present in his sensations. We must remain scientifically ignorant of the manner in which the constituent atoms in each thing began to exist; how ultimately they have assumed their present collocations ; or what future changes are latent, according to the order of the universe, in their imperfectly perceived collocations ; and latent too in other imperfectly known agents that might modify the customary course of external nature. So Locke concludes that 'for a human understanding there can be no *science* of natural bodies.' Our so-called natural science is only a mass of 'presumptions'; often indeed practically certain, as when we 'presume' that the sun will rise to-morrow, but which in no instance can reach the unconditional certainty that is independent of incalculable agencies. Every 'previsional' inference of change in the universe is therefore in this sense a leap in the dark. The reason for denying absolute certainty as to what phenomena in nature must coexist with other phenomena is so important and significant in Locke's

We cannot interpret our sensations. in terms of molecular motion, with absolute certainty.

philosophy that it is best put in his own words, in one of the many passages in the *Essay* in which it finds expression. Take the following [1] :—

This doc-
trine as
expressed
in the
Essay.

' The ideas that our complex ones of [material] substances are made up of, and about which our knowledge concerning substances is most employed, are those of their secondary qualities [and powers]; which depending all, as has been shown, upon the primary [real] qualities of their minute and insensible parts; *or, if not upon them, upon something yet more remote from our comprehension* ;—it is impossible we should know which have a *necessary* union or in-consistency with one another: for, not knowing the root they spring from [i. e. their *real* essence], not knowing, that is to say, what size, figure, and texture of parts they are on which depend, and from which result, those qualities which make *our* complex idea, e. g. of gold, it is impossible we should know what other qualities result from, or are in-compatible with, the same constitution of the insensible parts of gold; and so consequently must always coexist with that complex idea *we* have of it, or else are incon-sistent with it. But besides this our ignorance of the primary qualities of the insensible parts of bodies [i. e. of their imperceptible molecules], on which [hypothetically] depend all their secondary qualities . . . there is no [by us] discoverable connexion between any secondary quality and those primary qualities that it [hypothetically] depends on. That the size, figure, and motion of one body should cause a change in the size, figure, and motion of another body [no power by us unknown, natural or supernatural, inter-posing] is not beyond our conception : the separation of the parts of one body upon the intrusion of another; the change from rest to motion upon impulse—these and the like seem to have some [necessary?] *connexion* one with another. . . . But our minds not being able to discover any *connexion* betwixt these primary qualities of bodies, and the sensations that are produced in us by them, *we* can never be able to establish certain and undoubted rules of the consequence or coexistence of any secondary qualities, even though we could discover the size, figure,

[1] Bk. IV. ch. iii. §§ 11-13, 25.

and motion of those invisible parts which immediately produce them. .... Insensible corpuscles, being the active parts of matter, and the great instruments of nature, on which depend not only all their secondary qualities, but also most of their natural operations, our want of precise, distinct ideas of their primary qualities keeps us in an incurable ignorance of what we desire to know about them. I doubt not but, if we could discover the figure, size, texture, and motion of the minute constituent parts of any two bodies, we should know, *without trial,* several of their operations upon one another, as we do now the properties of a square or triangle. Did we know the mechanical affections of the particles of rhubarb, hemlock, opium, and a man, as a watchmaker does those of a watch, whereby it performs its operations, ... we should be able to tell beforehand that rhubarb will purge, hemlock kill, and opium make a man sleep. ... But whilst we are destitute of senses acute enough to discover the minute particles of bodies, and to give us ideas of their mechanical affections, we must be content to be ignorant of their properties and ways of operation; nor can we be assured about them any further than some few trials we make are able to reach. But whether they will succeed again another time, we cannot be certain. This hinders our certain knowledge of universal truths concerning natural bodies.'

Locke, like Socrates, thus advocates what Professor Huxley calls a kind of 'inverse agnosticism,' in concluding that for man physical problems are beyond the reach of the absolute certainty which belongs to science, while much in ethics and natural theology admits of demonstration. Scientific prevision of natural phenomena, and all human applications of the principle of physical causality to the changes in nature, are therefore expressions of our faith in probability, not of an intuition of what is intellectually necessary. Absolute certainty about distant changes, and future changes, in nature is not to be attained. The constant lesson of the *Essay* is that reasonable probability, not unconditional certainty, is what man's limited understanding of the universe of change is confined to, in all his intellectual intercourse with

The Essay teaches agnosticism in physics, and unconditional certainty in pure ethics, and natural theology.

ever-fluctuating nature. Within this sphere, objections to competing hypotheses have to be 'balanced,' and often wisdom more than logical subtlety is needed to conduct to right conclusions. This is the sphere characteristic of an understanding that has to play a part intermediate between mere sense and omniscience : for mere sense cannot calculate probabilities, and omniscience, which always sees all in each, leaves no room for probability and faith. But man, sharing at once in animal sense and divine reason, is obliged to hazard expectations and inductive guesses, which nevertheless, through his participation in divine reason, may be more than mere 'leaps in the dark.' Something like this is perhaps implied in the chapters on presumption of probability, in the Fourth Book of the *Essay*[1]. It is Locke's answer to the question which he proposed to his friends at the memorable reunion, nearly twenty years before the answer was matured and given to the world.

The 'created universe' of the *Essay* consists ultimately of atoms and egos, with their respective powers, passive or active.

The atomic hypothesis[2], in the way now explained, governs the conclusions of the *Essay*, with regard to the limits of a human knowledge of 'outward things.' The substances that constitute the material world are supposed to be aggregates of *atoms*, in correlation, through sense, with sentient and thinking *Egos*. The universe consists of these two sorts of substances—solid, extended and moveable molecules (or else something yet more remote from our comprehension), and self-conscious Egos. These are all interrelated, as causes or effects ; for their respective 'powers,' active or passive, 'make up a great part, if not the whole,' of our complex ideas of existing substances. 'He has the perfectest idea of any particular [sort of] substance, who has gathered and put together most of those simple ideas which do exist in it ; among which are to be reckoned its active powers and passive capacities.' (Bk. II. ch. xxiii. § 7.) Locke's individual substances are centres of the active and passive powers, to which their simple ideas may be referred. In this respect they resemble the *monads* of Leibniz, appercipient and percipient.

---

[1] Bk. IV. chh. xiv–xx.

[2] The difficulty of determining between the counter-hypotheses of *extended* and *unextended* parts, as the ultimate constituents of bodies, does not seem to occur to Locke.

One of the most significant suggestions in the *Essay*, in
this connexion, is in a passage where Locke indulges more
than he usually does in metaphysical speculation. He had
explained how customary experience, that like changes
are always in sequence to like antecedents, somehow gives
rise to a general idea of capacity in things for being
changed, and of active power to originate changes, as characteristic of substances (Bk. II. ch. xxi. § 1). Elsewhere he
treats the idea which thus arises as an intellectual necessity,
unconditioned and universal in its application, so that we
are obliged to infer, with mathematical certainty, the 'real
existence' of Eternal Mind. Like Aristotle, he also distinguishes power, as either passive and active—power to
be an effect, and power to originate an effect. Now of
active or originative power Locke finds no trace in outward
things—only perennial flux—capacity of continual change ;
he finds God revealed as the original source, never as the
passive subject, of changes ; he sees man intermediate
between these extremes, yet in a measure participating in
both. He suggests, accordingly, that 'matter is probably
destitute of active power, as its author, God, is truly above
all passive power ; and that the intermediate state of
created spirits may be that alone in which beings exist that
are endowed at once with active and passive power. 'Since
active powers make so great a part of our complex ideas of
natural substances ; and I mention them as such according
to common apprehension ;—yet they, being not perhaps so
truly *active* powers as our hasty thoughts are apt to represent them, I judge it not amiss, by this intimation, to direct
our minds to the consideration of God and spirits, for the
clearest idea of active power.' (Bk. II. ch. xxi. § 2 ; see also
ch. xxiii. § 28.) Locke's 'intimation' that the language of
'active power' is applied by him to solid and moveable substances according to popular usage only—'because our hasty
thoughts so represent them'—must not be forgotten in
interpreting passages in the *Essay* which refer simple ideas
of qualities of matter to the 'powers' of outward things ; or
in which 'body, by reason of the constitution of its primary
qualities,' is said to be '*able to produce*' such change in
another body as to make *it* '*operate* on our senses' differently

*Power
either
passive
or active.
Material
substances
wholly
passive ;
God
wholly
active ; and
finite
spiritual
substances
both
active and
passive.*

from what it did before,—so that the sun for example 'has power to make wax white, and fire to make lead fluid,' for 'these are usually called powers' (Bk. II. ch. viii. § 23); and also such statements as that a man comes to perceive the existence of any outward thing 'only when, *by actually operating upon him, it makes itself perceived by him*,' or that 'perceptions are *produced in us by exterior causes* affecting our senses' (Bk. IV. ch. xi. §§ 1, 4, &c.). Locke's disposition, after Descartes, to see active power only in spirits is one of his unconscious approaches to an ultimately spiritual conception of all the activities of the universe, akin to that afterwards advocated by Berkeley. By making 'matter only passive,' and referring its apparent actions to divine activity, it harmonises with the conception of divine immanence in nature, and of nature and natural law being throughout supernaturally active.

The chapters on our ideas of Power, Personal Identity, and Substances, may be compared.

The chapter on our idea of 'Power,' in the Second Book, contains an analysis of this complex idea which refers it to our experience of the voluntary activity of egos or thinking beings, responsible for their activities. It may be read in connexion with the chapter on 'Personal Identity' in the same Book, which deals with the idea of separate personality, connecting present with past feelings and thoughts, all which, through faith in memory, we are obliged to regard as exclusively 'our own.' Accordingly, although a sensuous image of a continuously identical abstract ego is impossible, the personal pronoun 'I' is not meaningless, but rather an inevitable intelligible implicate in all that we say and do [1]. The chapter on 'our complex ideas of Substances,' material and spiritual, should be compared with the one on 'Power,' and also with that on the idea of Identity in persons.

The obligation in moral reason to attribute a self-originated activity to morally re-

Here one may ask, what Locke found in his experience of his own voluntary activity, that made him refer our ideas of active power exclusively to this source; and that also suggested the impotence, in themselves, of the solid, moveable things which compose the material world? Why am 'I' conceived to be 'active,' while the changes in the cosmic

[1] Berkeley accordingly gives it a separate name, and says that we have a *notion*, not a (sensuous) *idea*, of it.

phenomena are the passive subjects of a power that does not properly belong to the visible and tangible things which present the changes? Moreover, what is meant by the 'activity' with which 'I' and other spiritual agents are credited? It cannot be said that Locke's famous chapter on 'Power' offers distinct and coherent answers to those questions; and he was himself dissatisfied with his results, even after the transformations to which this chapter was subjected, in the editions of the *Essay* that were brought out under his care. Yet our answers to such questions determine for us, whether our ultimate conception of the universe is moral and spiritual, or only non-moral and physical:—whether it resolves man into a physical organism, and his supposed 'actions' into issues of natural laws, to the exclusion of personal responsibility; or, on the contrary, makes us reject, as inadequate to the implicates of spiritual experience and the necessities of moral reason, the exclusively physical conception, on the ground that, although many of our mental states are dependent upon the inherited organism, we are also obliged to recognise, as our own creation, all those acts or states for which we are justly accountable. The second alternative may be held, even while it is allowed that *our* inevitable ignorance of the exact line which separates *nature in men* from *moral or immoral agency of man in nature*, requires, in each case, a large exercise of charity, when we, in our intermediate sphere of finite experience, judge the overt acts of other men.

The self-originated power of spiritual agents, that is presupposed in their moral responsibility, is, in the *Essay*, subordinated to the mechanical causality by which our interpretations of the cosmic successions of phenomena are regulated; and thus the freedom of man's voluntary agency is regarded, not as self-contained power to determine one's own volition, but merely as freedom of the volition, when it has been determined according to cosmic law, from interference by other causes that would hinder its intended consequences. The *uniqueness* of an *immoral will*, in the mechanism of nature, seems to be inadequately recognised by Locke, owing to an inadequate recognition of what is implied in all agency that is morally responsible. It is

sponsible agents.

Inadequately recognised in the *Essay*.

in acknowledging his own responsibility that man recognises, that *he* must be an agent who creates his own actions, and who, so far as he is this, must be *free* from the Power that regulates the mechanical order of natural causality. In the activity for which he is personally accountable, he finds the only example of real originative activity that is given in human experience, and in virtue of it he finds himself sharing in a higher order than the mechanical. Freedom from the chain of cosmic causality—i.e. of an unbeginning and unending, and therefore ultimately unimaginable and mysterious, natural succession—is indeed reached in its fullness, when a man does what he ought to do—when he realises the moral ideal. But this right determination, this harmony of human action with moral reason, presupposes a power in a finite agent also to act immorally or irrationally, and, by so acting, power even to destroy his free agency. Then, as a mere animal, he has lost his proper personality, and become only a part of the natural system of mechanically regulated phenomena, because he has lost the moral power needed for the fulfilment of the highest law of his being. The intermediate place of man in the ordered universe, is seen in this conflict between the natural or externally determined, and the supernatural or spiritual, in his *action*, not less than in the limitation of his *knowledge* to what is intermediate between mere sense and divine omniscience.

The final outcome as to man's knowledge of the simple ideas that coexist in substances.

That the universe of realities—alike in its sensuous or natural, and in its spiritual or supernatural revelations of itself—must throughout be ultimately the expression of perfect order and purpose, is presupposed in every exercise of our reason about physical and moral events. A complete intuition of the Divine Ideal, including the rational harmony of the natural order or physical government, in subordination to the spiritual order or moral government, is presumably confined to the Eternal Mind; yet even human understanding may see no reason for asserting that the supposition of this universal harmony is self-contradictory. This is acknowledged in his own way by Locke, in one of his letters to Molyneux (Jan. 20, 1693):—'I own freely to you the weakness of my understanding: though it be unquestionable, that there is omnipotence and omniscience in God ; and though I cannot have a clearer perception of anything, than that I am free—yet I cannot make freedom in man consistent with omnipotence and omniscience in God ; though I am as fully persuaded of *both* as of any truths I most firmly assent to. And therefore I have long since given off the consideration of this question, resolving all into this short conclusion :—that if it be possible for God to make a free agent, then man is free ; though I see not the way of it.' This is one way of expressing the mystery of immoral or irrational agency, within the divine or perfect system—moral disorder within the universal order—the moral government, which presupposes freedom, combined with the mechanical government, in which all events, including human actions, are passive examples of natural laws. The theological idea of the universe, as ultimately the orderly manifestation of rational purpose, but in ways that human understanding cannot elaborate in their infinite detail; and the merely physical idea of it, as purposeless causal mechanism—both lead our limited understanding at last into mystery. Reason surely finds the reasonable alternative in that mystery which satisfies the divine spirit in man, without necessarily contradicting the scientific understanding, which limits its judgments to the laws of sense.

What Locke teaches about the necessary narrowness of man's knowledge of the attributes and the powers of substances, or, in his own language, about 'simple ideas' in the 'coexistences' implied in the connotations of their class names, is seen, at another point of view, in the many passages of the *Essay*, especially in the Third Book, in which it is argued that a human understanding can be concerned only with 'nominal,' not with the 'real,' *essences* of individual substances [1]. 'Nominal essences' are those 'abstract' or general ideas of substances that men form for themselves : conformity to such ideas, on the part of real substances, when it is found by experience to exist, gives the conforming substances a right to the name appropriated

Nominal and real Essences.

---

[1] An edition of the Third Book of the *Essay*, with useful annotations, was published in 1881 by Mr. Ryland, of St. John's College, Cambridge.

to the 'abstract idea,' which the name thus connotes.
Having that conformity, and having the nominal essence,
mean the same thing. 'To be a man, or of the species
man, and to have a right to the name man is the same
thing. Since nothing can be a man [in our regard], or
have a right [according to our conceptions] to the name man,
but what has a conformity to the abstract idea the name
man stands for in our mind ; nor anything be a man, or
have a right to the species man, but what has the essence
of that species [i. e. its nominal essence] ;—it follows that
the abstract idea for which the name stands, and the
[nominal] essence of the species is one and the same.' It
also follows, that the different essences of the different
sorts of substances are 'inventions of the human understanding' ; and the 'sorts,' created thus by our minds, are
applied to actual things, according as the cap prepared by
the inventors is found to fit. Take away the abstract idea
according to which *we* sort individual substances, and which
we attribute, as nominal essence, to objects in which attributes
are found corresponding to our connotation of the name,
and 'our thought of anything essential to them instantly
vanishes.' We have no idea of their essence, except in an
abstract idea that may be applicable to them, or that seems
to be exemplified in them. It is impossible that anything
deeper than the complex idea connoted by our class name
should determine *for us* the species of substances ; and this
idea of ours is what Locke calls a 'nominal essence.' 'Why
do we say, "This is a horse, and that a mule; this is
an animal, and that an herb?" How comes any particular
thing to be of this or that *sort*, but because it has that
nominal essence ; or, which is all one, agrees to that abstract
idea that name is annexed to?' Hence 'our ranking and
distinguishing natural substances into species consists in the
nominal essences the mind [of man] makes, and not in the
real essences to be found in the things themselves. It is
evident that we sort and name substances by their nominal,
and not by their real, essences. And these nominal essences
are made by the mind [of man] and not by nature ; for
were they nature's workmanship, they could not be so
various and different in several men as experience tells us

they are [1].' *Nature*, in short, makes particular things, which differ in their molecular or other ultimate constitution—that is, in the real essences that make them be the particular things that they actually are; *men* connect with names their own abstract ideas, which they 'invent,' and they apply those names to particular substances that seem to correspond to abstract ideas or *nominal* essences thus formed by themselves, although the ideas must fall short of the deeper reality which belongs to the (by us) undiscoverable *real* essences. In those comparatively superficial 'inventions' of men consists, Locke would say, the whole business of genus and species—so far as a human understanding can be concerned with it.

We are ignorant of that molecular constitution of each body, which, as containing its real essence, makes each be the individual body that it is; we are ignorant too of the ultimate constitution of self-conscious persons, and must not take for granted, Locke thinks, that consciousness cannot be among the attributes that coexist in matter, at least in certain material substances, such as the human organism. According to the *Essay*, the real essences of bodies, hidden in the primary qualities of their atomic constitution, outside human experience, cannot be made the principle according to which things are classed by men, or the ground of their scientific inferences. But men can form abstract notions, associate their notions with names, apply the names to things, and evolve logical conclusions in which the significant names are the terms, thus constructing 'sciences' that may be only verbal. Inasmuch as the real essence—that which makes each individual thing be the thing it really is—is hidden from human observation, the nominal essences that we are obliged to make our reasonings about things turn upon, and which connote only superficial qualities of the particular substances to which they are applied, afford no sufficient foundation for the absolute certainty that alone is entitled to be called knowledge. So-called 'science' of nature must thus be for ever, in a human understanding, provisional and hypothetical. It is progressive just so far as the nominal essences made by men approximate to the

The real essences of particular substances, bodies or spirits.

---
[1] See Bk. III. ch. vi.

real essences that are hid from man's view by inexorable conditions, imposed upon every human inquirer into the ultimate causes of the changes which material substances are always undergoing. The 'essences' with which man can be concerned are all of his own construction, and, as Bacon says, fall far short of the subtlety of nature. In regard to the natural universe of coexistences and changes, human understanding, according to Locke, is confined to judgments of probability, and must operate within what is at best a sphere of faith and hope, not of knowledge or absolute certainty.

Nature is supernatural.

If Locke had thought out what is implied in his own idea of active power being properly spiritual, he might perhaps have seen that, through the eternal and universal presence of the divine activity in the cosmical system, God and nature are not mutually exclusive; that the contemporaneous and successive 'coexistences' of the changing ideas or phenomena, in which nature presents itself, are all signs and revelations of the supreme Reason and Will that eternally maintains this orderly system; according to laws, and for ends, that are only imperfectly comprehensible, in any knowledge of the realities that, like the human, is necessarily incomplete. Nature would thus be conceived as (so far) an incarnation of God. But Locke's point of view in the *Essay* always gives prominence to the external conditions under which knowledge and faith arise in a human understanding. It thus overlooks the innate spiritual reason that forms their background, and that is presupposed in the very laws according to which changes are physically regulated; and also in the 'real essences,' or individual 'natures,' with which things are charged, and by which their individualities are so determined as that each is what it is.

VII. HUMAN KNOWLEDGE OF IDEAS IN THEIR ABSTRACT RELATIONS.

Knowledge of abstract maxims.

So much for Locke's account of the knowableness, by a human understanding, of mental propositions in which the agreement or disagreement of the ideas concerns, either 'real existences,' manifested in their simple ideas, or 'coexistence' of ideas, as qualities or powers of different sorts of substances. See next what the *Essay* teaches about the other two sorts of 'agreement or disagreement' of ideas —relation proper, and identity with diversity—in which the ideas are abstracted from real substances and their changes, and are viewed without respect to conditions of time and place, or to what happens in an experience of the concrete universe. Although propositions concerned with 'coexistences,' i. e. which present human interpretations of matters of fact, have not got absolute certainty—are tentative, though it may be progressive, hypotheses, that gradually approximate to ultimate truth—Locke finds that the case is different with purely abstract assertions that are independent of the contingencies of time and sense.

The relations of the ideas that are abstracted from par- *Illustrated* ticular substances, and liberated from bondage to the changes *in pure* of sense, are, according to the *Essay*, the only ones in which a *mathe-* human understanding can reach *general* propositions that are *in abstract* unconditionally certain. The reason of this is, that a human *ethics.* understanding is the sole creator and preserver of the abstract ideas which enter into such propositions. In this way the assertions which they involve escape interference on the part of the powers, imperfectly calculable by the narrow experience of man, that determine the coexistences and sequences in nature. Those relations of our abstract ideas, as they form 'the largest field of our knowledge, so it is hard to determine how far it may extend ; because the advances that are made in this part of our knowledge, depending on our sagacity in finding intermediate ideas that may show the relations and habitudes of ideas whose coexistence [in nature] is not considered, it is hard matter to tell when we are at an end in such discoveries.' (Bk. IV. ch. iii. § 18.) Accordingly, there is a prospect of indefinite advancement in pure mathematics, Locke's signal example of this sort of knowledge. But abstract ideas of quantity are not his only examples of the absolute certainty of abstract knowledge. 'The [abstract] idea of a Supreme Being, infinite in power, goodness and wisdom, whose workman-ship we are, and on whom we depend, and the [abstract] idea of ourselves as rational beings, being such as are clear in us, would, I suppose, if duly considered and pursued, afford such foundations of our duty, and rules of action, as might place [abstract] morality among the sciences capable of demonstration : wherein I doubt not but, from self-evident propositions, by necessary consequences, as incontestable as those in mathematics, the measures of right and wrong [in the abstract] might be made out. "Where there is no property there is no injustice," is a proposition as certain as any demonstration in Euclid ; for the idea of *property* being [by definition] a right to anything, and the idea to which the name *injustice* is given being [by definition] an invasion or violation of that right, it is evident that these ideas, being thus established [by our definitions], and these names annexed to them, I can *as certainly know* this proposition to be true as I know that a triangle has three angles equal to two right ones.' (Bk. IV. ch. iii. § 18.)

Does Locke recognise, in any abstract propositions, synthetic as well as analytic necessity ?

Pure mathematics and abstract ethics are Locke's examples of absolute certainty in general propositions. But here it is not easy to determine whether he means, that the certainty depends in all such cases upon men's arbitrary definitions of the names which enter into their reasonings, as those who allege that Locke is an empirical Nominalist would say that he does ; or whether he intends to leave room for *a priori* intellectual necessities, involved in the abstract conceptions, with the Conceptualists ; or even with the Realists sees in them necessities of reason that, inasmuch as reason is innate in the nature of things, makes things fit to be reasoned about. It seems that Locke tacitly allows that even a human understanding becomes aware of abstract relations of ideas that are independent of the arbitrary definitions of men. ' In *some* of our ideas,' he says, ' there are certain relations, habitudes, and connexions, *so visibly included in the relation of the ideas themselves*, that we cannot conceive them separable from them *by any power whatsoever* ; and in these only we are capable of certain and real knowledge. Thus the idea of a right-angled triangle *necessarily* carries with it an equality of its angles to two right ones. Nor can we conceive this relation of these two ideas to be possibly mutable, or to depend on any arbitrary power, which of choice made it thus, and could make it otherwise.' (Bk. IV. ch. iii. § 29.) Such relations of ideas are therefore seen by us to be 'eternal and immutable'; in contrast with all relations of 'coexistence' in particular substances, as well as with relations that depend on our arbitrary definitions. At the same time, mathematical and moral propositions, so Locke implies, are *at first* perceived by us to be thus necessarily true, not in their most general form, but only in one or other of their particular embodiments; and they are actually true only when there are individual things or persons really existing that correspond to the general idea. The abstract proposition thus constitutes what might be called an *a priori* knowledge of what, in that respect, the actual things *must be, on the hypothesis that they really exist in nature.* The eternity and immutability of the abstract 'maxims' of mathematics and of ethics, with all that is logically implied in them, is steadily maintained in the *Essay.* With reference to the abstract principles of morals, he says, in reply to Lowde, that if this critic 'had been at the pains to reflect on what I have said, he would have seen what I think of the eternal and immutable nature of right and wrong, and what I call virtue and vice; and if he had observed that, in the place he quotes, I only report, as matters of fact, what other men call virtue and vice, he would not have found it liable to any great exception.' When asked, 'Why a man should keep his word or his contract?' Locke answers, 'Truth, and keeping of faith, belong to men as men, and not only as members of society; nor can custom serve in place of reason [1].'

Although the *Essay* does not expressly include the relation of Causality among those 'connexions of ideas' that are intellectually, and therefore universally necessary, Locke virtually takes this for granted, in his 'demonstration' of the existence of the Eternal Mind. This proceeds on the assumption, as he tells Stillingfleet, that the proposition —'everything that has a beginning must have a cause'— is 'a true principle of reason, or a *general* proposition that is certainly true.' So too with the correlative idea of substance: that the simple ideas or appearances presented

He tacitly recognises the necessity of the abstract principles of Causality and Substance, and of the abstract postulates of reasoning.

---

[1] *Marginalia Lockeana.*

in the senses and in self-consciousness *must* be referred, as qualities, to substances, is implied in the treatment of simple ideas throughout the *Essay*. And the abstract principle of all analytical and verbal logic, that our ideas *must not* contradict one another, is, above all, according to Locke, independent of proof from experience ; although, apart from sense-experience, like other abstract maxims, it does not actually rise into consciousness. ' He would be thought void of common sense,' the *Essay* tells us [1], 'who asked, on the one side, or on the other, went about to give a reason, Why it is impossible for the same thing to be and not to be. It carries its own light and evidence with it, and needs no other proof: he that understands the terms assents to it for its own sake, or else nothing will ever be able to prevail with him to do it.' All those different sorts of abstract principles are tacitly treated in the *Essay* as principles of universal reason, accepted in the faith of 'common sense,' but without adequate criticism of their nature and origin. To reject them, or to subordinate them to the contingencies of sense, would be as inconsistent with Locke's account of human knowledge, as it would be to say that he denies that experience is the source of all assertions about qualities and powers that men attribute to particular substances.

Abstract maxims and syllogistic forms.

Notwithstanding this virtual acknowledgment, that abstract ' maxims ' which are incapable of proof, because above proof, are presupposed by implication in our interpretations of simple ideas, Locke looks with suspicion on maxims. He suspects them, because they have been credited with an innateness not consistent (in his idea of innateness) with the fact that they are consciously held, in their abstract form, only by a few persons, after prolonged exercise of their understandings among data of experience ; and also because he thinks they do not add to our knowledge of things.[2]. He insists that self-evident maxims need not be innate, merely because they are seen to be self-evidently true when we *do* become conscious of them ; and he argues that the abstract forms of syllogism, and the laws of formal logic, add nothing to our knowledge of

[1] Bk. I. ch. ii. § 4.   [2] See Bk. IV. chh. vii, viii, xvii.

facts. No abstract maxims, how self-evident soever they may be, 'can help one to an acquaintance with ethics, or instruct us in the practice of morality.' We may amuse ourselves for ever with such self-evident propositions, or with a series of demonstrated propositions, self-evidently their consequences, in syllogistic forms, without adding at all to our practical acquaintance with the material and spiritual substances that exist. 'It is but like a monkey shifting his oyster from the one hand to the other ; and had he had words, might no doubt have said " oyster in right hand is subject, oyster in left hand is predicate," and so might have made a self-evident proposition of " oyster is oyster " ; and yet with all this not have been one whit wiser or more knowing.' (Bk. IV. ch. viii. §§ 1–3.) So too syllogism cannot, he argues, increase real knowledge : its premisses always implicitly contain its conclusions. It can be used as a criterion merely of argumentative consistency—which indeed, one may add, is all that its philosophical advocates claim for it. Locke rejects it as a source of real knowledge, on the ground that without experience it is impossible to interpret the actual order of nature; and also that 'no pro- position can be said to be in the mind of which the mind is unconscious.' The highest office of syllogistic logic is, to evolve the forms according to which men (in general un- conscious of the form) make patent to themselves and others propositions that were logically implied in their assumed knowledge.

With his eye exclusively fixed upon experience, as the supreme condition of any true interpretation of the world of realities, Locke is apt to underestimate the human im- portance of those abstract intellectual necessities. Must not any finite understanding of the actual world presuppose principles—by most persons held unconsciously—which form the rational construction of experience, through which the individual is connected with the universal—the finite and temporal with the eternal and divine? Is not man's power of penetrating into what was before unknown dependent on those necessary implicates, alike of the consti- tution of his own knowing mind, and of the universal system of things which he seeks to know? Suspicion of

Self- evident maxims are not innate.

a claim to too wide a range of absolute certainties on the part of human understanding, founded upon an innate possession of self-evident abstract maxims, and a deep conviction that in our scientific inductions we cannot rise above practical certainties of probability, roused Locke to his celebrated assault upon ' innate principles,' in the First Book of the *Essay*. With him their *innateness* consists in their being principles that are so born with each man that he is conscious of them even in their abstract forms at birth, and this without exercising his understanding in experience. But that is a meaning of innateness which makes Locke's objections irrelevant, and puts him at cross-purposes with those who, from Plato onwards, have argued for the inadequacy of the mere phenomena presented in experience to explain even sense-perception itself. The ambiguity and irrelevancy of Locke's negative conclusion was shown by the earliest critic of the *Essay*, John Norris, in his later remarks[1] upon its most prominent doctrine :—' I say as to the principle from which Mr. Locke derives our ideas, that if by having our ideas from our senses, his meaning be,— that sensible objects do send or convey ideas of themselves to our minds by the mediation of the senses ; if this be what he means (*as indeed I once thought*, and the rather because he expresses himself much after the same manner as the schools do, whose known meaning this is, according to that maxim quoted by Aquinas from Aristotle's "Metaphysics "—*Principium nostrae cogitationis est a sensu*,) then it appears, by the whole tendency of this Discourse, that he has derived our ideas from a false original. But if his meaning be, *as perhaps it may*, (for indeed his way of expressing himself, upon this occasion, is not so clear but that one may pardonably mistake him) — that sensible objects do, by the impression which they make upon our outward senses, serve to excite ideas in our minds, so that we are beholding to them as the *occasions* of our having such ideas : I say, if this be all that he means by pretending to make Sense the original and source of our ideas, I think

[1] See Norris's *Essay towards the Theory of the Ideal or Intelligible World*, vol. ii. p. 371, which appeared in 1704, fourteen years after his *Cursory Reflections* on the *Essay*.

there is nothing either so dangerous, or so extraordinary in it, but that we may, without scruple, in a great measure allow it to him. For though ideas do not come from objects, as any genuine *issue* or *production* of theirs, nor are so much as the *causal* result of any of their impressions; yet there is no absurdity in supposing that the Author of Nature may establish a connexion between certain sensible impressions and certain *ideas*, as well as between such impressions and certain *sensations*. Nay we find by experience it is so in fact.'

It is against the innateness of ideas, when ideas mean abstract notions, that Locke argues in the First Book : in the Second Book 'ideas' mean ultimately particular impressions of external or internal sense. Universality is 'accidental' to ideas, according to Locke; in respect that an individual mind may, or may not, become aware, that any of the 'particular ideas' which enter into knowledge 'are such as more than one particular thing in nature corresponds with and is represented by.' But the *abstract* intellectual necessity of what may or may not arise actually in the individual consciousness, cannot be disposed of in the 'historical method.' Locke easily shows the absurdity of supposing that all infants are philosophers ; but in thus restricting his view to the process according to which knowledge happens to rise in consciousness, he neglects important elements, found consciously only in the educated mind, yet tacitly supposed in the validity of the process through which the contingent suggests what is necessary, and on which morality and religion depend. There is an inadequate appreciation in the *Essay* of the human importance that may belong to concepts, in respect of their universality and necessity, and thus its range of speculative interest is confined. Locke's inclination to look at abstract ideas only in their concrete applications, makes him indifferent to principles that are independent of the changes presented by things, in the experience of particular persons ; and that are independent too of the imperfectly known agencies by which changes are determined : yet it is on *principles* that faith, which is human reason in its highest form, finally steadies itself. He is so much moved by the desire to recall dog-

Why Locke objected to ' innate principles.'

matists, and concept-mongers, to 'particular ideas' given in experience, that the *Essay* takes no sufficient account of the psychical fact,—that human experience tacitly involves concepts and principles that are logically independent of accidents in the history of any individual consciousness. For, in the spirit of his 'historical plain method,' it is conscious realisation of them by individual minds, and patient exercise of individual understanding with a view to this realisation, that he wants to substitute for the indolence which tempts men to dispense with reflection, and to assume principles blindly on authority.   He thought he saw in 'innate principles' what 'eased the lazy from the pains of search, and stopped the inquiry of the doubtful concerning all that was once styled innate . . . which was to take men off from the use of their own reason and judgment, and put them on believing and taking upon trust, without further examination . . . Whereas had they examined the ways whereby [individual] men come to the knowledge of universal truths, they would have found them to result, in the minds of men, from the being of things themselves when duly considered ; and that they were discovered by the application of those faculties that were fitted by nature to receive and judge of them, when duly employed about them [1].' But when *innateness* means immanence of reason in the constitution of the universe and of man, which needs active exercise of mind for its awakening into life in a human mind, it no longer appears, as it did to Locke, to be an obstacle to the freest exercise of human understanding among the phenomena presented in experience.

The really philosophical question about innateness.   The philosophical yet human question that underlies Locke's irrelevant argument is not touched in the *Essay*. It is not a question about an event, or succession of events, in the early history of each human mind: it is about the necessary constitution and implicates of a *matured* human experience of reality.   The term *a priori*, in this connexion, has no such reference to time as Locke supposed.   It no more means, that all men enter life conscious of certain highly abstract principles or categories of know-

---

[1] See Bk. I. ch. iii. § 24 ; also Bk. IV. chh. vii, viii.

ledge, which they *afterwards* make concrete in receiving data through experience, than Locke himself means, that an idea or phenomenon of sense, in its ultimate simplicity, is the earliest example of *knowledge* in the consciousness of each man. Each of these hypotheses admits of easy refutation. That knowledge itself cannot be resolved into simple ideas or sensations, although it is evoked in sensation, has been shown, at various points of view, from Plato to Kant and Hegel. Otherwise there could be no unconditional certainty for man, as the possibility of demonstration proves that there is; no categorical imperative of morality, although immutable morality shows the contrary; and no faith, although daily life as well as science reposes in faith.

This latent apriority of abstract principles to the data of experience—simple ideas of external and internal sense— is as insufficiently recognised in the hypothesis of inherited aptitudes, which biology since Locke has brought into vogue, as it was in the *Essay*, where the history of individual consciousness was alone taken into account. Dogmas or prejudices, as well as scientific discoveries of the past, are unconsciously born with us; but this 'historical' fact does not explain the contents of the matured reason and conscience, nor supply an answer to the self-contradictory question, '*Why* reason is reasonable?' The critical analysis of reason has no direct reference to time and the succession of events, either in the history of the individual, or in that of the human race. *Inherited principles.*

Locke overlooks the part played by ultimate abstract principles and moral ideals, in constituting the validity of human knowledge, and in regulating our interpretations of events, as well as our estimate of the final purpose of the changes through which we and things around us are passing. For the *Essay* is throughout an attempt to show that our understanding, but for the simple ideas or attributes of things presented in experience, must be barren, and that the presented ideas can be interpreted only gradually, in a progressive experience; so that, without experience, an idealess understanding is 'like a closet wholly shut out from light,' ignorant of all that it concerns man to know about the *Locke's dread of abstract maxims.*

properties and powers of surrounding things, and about his own thinking substance. The background of the whole—the fundamental abstractions of space and immensity, duration and eternity, infinity, substance and personality, power and causality, eternal and immutable duty—is looked at only in and through the finite ideas or phenomena in which those abstractions receive concrete expression ; not in the light of the necessity of the abstract principles themselves to the rational reality of the universe. In this way it was easy to show, as in the Second Book, that even the complex ideas there taken as 'crucial instances,' when individualised in the sensuous imagination, may be resolved into unanalysable manifestations of realities presented either in the senses or in reflection. For without these, the abstract universals remain, for us, immanent and unconscious ; they cannot rise into consciousness without being blended with the simple ideas which they then enable us to interpret.

VIII. FAITH INSTEAD OF OMNISCIENCE.

Relation between the abstract presuppositions of intellectual and moral reason, and our presuppositions of probability.

How are the abstract certainties that belong to the known relations of our fundamental conceptions connected with the practical certainties of probability which regulate human life,—in our judgments regarding the causal connexions and behaviour of 'particular substances,' material and spiritual, which compose the universe of finite realities ? Locke does not discuss this question, although it underlies the *Essay*, especially in those parts of the Fourth Book where connexions of 'co-existence,' and faith in judgments of probability are considered. He finds that the unconditional certainty, which alone he dignifies with the name of 'knowledge' or 'science,' is within reach of a human understanding, only to the extent of each man being able to know:—(1) his own existence as a thinking being; (2) the present and past existence of outward things that are or were actually presented in his sensations ; and (3) the eternal reality of the Supreme Mind. He also finds absolute certainty in relations of ideas, particular and universal, when the ideas are abstracted from change and temporal relations, and thus from dependence upon the imperfectly known powers that are constantly at work in the universe. These abstract relations are illustrated in pure mathematics and in pure ethics, and (so his theistic demonstration implies) also in the abstract principle of causality; all which relations can be predicated only hypothetically in our assertions about the concrete things that are contingently presented in actual experience [1].

What then of the sphere of knowable relations that is in a manner intermediate between our knowledge of the three primal realities, and our knowledge of the abstract relations which are tacitly assumed in the *Essay* to be necessities of speculative or moral reason, latent in the ultimate nature of things, as well as in the human understanding? It is to this intermediate sphere that all the qualities and powers that 'coexist' in substances belong, forming the ever-changing world of bodies and spirits, all mutually related ; and within this sphere, according to the *Essay*, 'the greatest and most material part of knowledge concerning substances' lies ;—that which shows how each existing substance is related practically to other substances. Locke finds that the unconditional certainty which belongs to knowledge is here unattainable by a human understanding. The attainment would involve omniscience ; and man, neither omniscient nor wholly nescient, must, in all this, fall back upon 'faith ventures,' or presumptions of probability. In his interpretations of the ever-changing phenomena of things and persons, he must be satisfied, as his only attainable ideal, with what are at last hypothetical judgments, although some of them are practically certain. After disposing, in the first thirteen chapters of the Fourth Book, of the three certainties of real existence, and the many certainties of abstract thought—two categories which, according to the *Essay*, exhaust human 'knowledge,' the remainder of the Book deals with human understanding in its chief practical office—forming in faith presumptions of probability, about the attributes and powers that

Propositions of probability belong to the sphere that is intermediate between knowledge of the three primary realities and knowledge of the abstract presuppositions of reason.

[1] Knowledge, as Origen says, is the only thing which creatures have that is in its own nature firm and absolute. In this only they have infallibility; without possessing which, to some extent, nothing at all could be proved absolutely.

coexist in substances. Now this implies that *faith* is the deepest form of man's intellectual intercourse with the universe of reality, as presented in the transient manifestations which reality makes of itself in sense, during this short life, between two eternities.

The *Essay* does not carry us far into a theory of probable judgments. What Locke calls presumption, or undemonstrable proposition, to which 'assent' is given, comprehends all inductions, whether more or less complete. It is curious that while he refuses to such propositions the name of knowledge or science, it is among propositions that rest upon inductive comparison and verification that experimental inquirers now profess to find man's highest attainable certainty; and this notwithstanding the unproved hypotheses that are involved even in scientific 'verification.' Locke does not inquire into the ultimate grounds of inductive proof. Yet one might naturally look for this, in a work on human understanding which made its appearance in the age and country of Bacon. The defect was noticed by Bishop Butler, the philosophical theologian of the school of Locke. In explaining[1] how, in his *Analogy*, he did not intend any 'inquiry into the nature, the foundation, and the measure of probability; or whence it proceeds that *likeness* should beget that presumptive opinion and full conviction which the human mind is found to receive from it, and which it does naturally produce in each one,'—Butler adds, that 'this is a part of logic which has not yet been thoroughly considered, little having in this way been attempted by those who have treated of our intellectual powers and the exercise of them[2].' Probable evidence, he goes on to say, 'affords but an imperfect kind of information, and is to be considered only as relative to beings of limited capacities. For nothing which is the possible object of knowledge, whether past, present, or future, can be probable to Infinite Intelligence; since it cannot but be discovered absolutely as it is in itself, certainly true or certainly false.' In omniscience, in short, there is no room

The *Essay* does not propose a philosophical theory of judgments of probability or co-existence.

---

[1] *Analogy*—Introduction.

[2] As we shall see, this was afterwards attempted by Hume, as the chief problem in his *Inquiry concerning Human Understanding*.

for probability, and therefore no room for the faith which is at the root of all human interpretations of the phenomena presented by real existences in experience. But for man, with his limited experience, and correspondingly narrow intelligence, faith in the necessities of causal and moral reason, which is faith in God, is the highest form of human reason, in its dealings either with the actual mechanism of nature, or with the history and destiny of man.

A reader of the *Essay* is apt to ask, how the faith that is at the root of our judgments of probability, which look so much like leaps in the dark, can be after all justified by reason, the final court of appeal? How can the understanding satisfy itself, in interpretations of the phenomena of things that carry our judgments into the distant and the future, nay even to the eternal and infinite? Locke contributes little to the controversy between scepticism and faith in this form. In the *Essay* 'faith' usually means assent to biblical revelations of God that are commonly called supernatural or miraculous; but no question is asked about the philosophical meaning of supernaturality or miraculousness. The sort of faith which the *Essay*[1] recognizes, 'as absolutely determines our mind,' it tells us, 'and as perfectly excludes all wavering, as our knowledge itself does; and we may as well doubt of our own being as we can whether any revelation of God be true. Only we must be sure that it be a divine revelation, and that we understand it right: else we shall expose ourselves to all the extravagancy of enthusiasm.' After this is secured, faith becomes 'assent founded on the highest reason.' Dread of 'enthusiasm[2],' and a consequent disposition to look for the criteria of real revelation among external things of sense, predisposed Locke to take physical miracles as the chief test for distinguishing what is truly divine from illusions of this enthusiasm. To rest 'contented with fancy and sentiment,' without support from facts presented to the senses, was with him a sure sign of the absence of love for intellectual truth. 'This sort of confidence that one is right is commonly a sign that one is wrong.' And Locke sees the supernatural in

(margin note: Our judgments of probability are rooted in our faith in the ultimate rationality and morality of the universe.)

---

[1] Bk. IV. ch. xvi. § 14.　　　　[2] Bk. IV. ch. xix.

extraordinary events in external nature rather than in what is moral and spiritual.

Miracles, according to Locke.

Yet in the *Discourse of Miracles*, as well as now and then in the *Essay*, the argument suggests that the ultimate foundation of any revelation of God must be transferred not only from unreasoned dogmas, and from enthusiasm, which he always warned against, but also from physical miracles merely as such, in order to be rested on the response which the alleged revelation meets with in the moral reason. 'A miracle,' Locke says[1], 'is a sensible operation, which, being above the comprehension of the spectator, and in *his* opinion contrary to the established connexion of nature, is taken by him to be divine.' This seems to imply that physical miracles, if they do occur, cannot in themselves be *anomic*—that no manifestation in external nature can be really irrational and purposeless—although human understanding and experience are too limited to enable *man* to articulate scientifically, in all their applications to the 'coexistences' in nature, the intellectual and moral principles that contain the final explanation of *all* phenomena, whether called natural or miraculous. Man must repose in the reasonable trust, that the Supreme Ideal is on the whole and finally reasonable. Philosophical faith is the conviction that the universe of finite realities cannot be absolutely in contradiction to the intellectual and moral reason, which is God immanent in nature and in man, and which is revealed in the physical and moral order. Events that are incomprehensible under the mechanical laws discoverable by human understanding, may, as relative miracles, serve the purpose of awakening the religious consciousness, otherwise latent, not only in the lower or non-moral way in which it is awakened even in our faith in natural order, on which mechanical science rests, but also in the deeper faith, in moral and spiritual order, which regulates religious thought in its further development. The history of man's interpretations of external nature, under mechanical categories, as well as of the increasing command of things that he obtains by obedience to the natural order, is a history of faith in God, as the constantly immanent power; so that

---

[1] *Discourse of Miracles*, § I.

even *scientific* agnosticism itself is, so far, *unconscious* recognition of the divine order or God. Must not any revelation that is more specially called 'supernatural' be the complement, or further development, of this revelation in external nature; sustained by faith, not merely in the non-moral order, but in the supremacy of the moral and spiritual order, i.e. by faith in God, as the constantly active moral reason?

Locke's faith in the Christian revelation of God, and, through this, in a deeper and fuller meaning of the three final realities, rests at last on his sense of the moral excellence of Christianity, when it is interpreted in its original simplicity, and received in connexion with the miracle of the resurrection. The spiritual response, not anomic and purposeless miracle, makes him accept as reasonable a life of faith in God morally personified in Christ. 'Even in those books which have the greatest proof of revelation from God, and the attestation of miracles to confirm their being so, the miracles,' he says, 'are to be judged by the doctrine, not the doctrine by the miracles.' The resurrection, merely as a physical miracle, cannot be a spiritual revelation, or other in kind than an uncommon manifestation of the immanent power that is revealed in all natural order; although it may be apt, by its uncommonness, to arouse attention to the personality and inner life of the subject of the change. Faith in God is faith in the ultimate rationality and morality of the power continually operative and supreme in the universe. This faith justifies regard for inductively gathered laws, as trustworthy in their applications, through the assurance that understanding in us cannot be finally put to confusion by nature. Atheism is the opposite despair; the Nescience which, in thoroughgoing consistency, is bound to withdraw even its physical faith in the ordinary expectations of daily life, and also in the interpretations and verifications of natural science; not to speak of the higher faith, in the final tendency of the whole, in its relation to self-conscious moral agents, in and through whom the universe exemplifies actuality and purpose.

Faith—in this large or philosophical meaning—sustained by the abstract necessities of intellectual and moral reason

The basis of Locke's faith in the Christian revelation of God.

Faith in
its larger
meaning
is the
character-
istic of an
intelli-
gence that
is inter-
mediate
between
Sensuous
Feeling
and Om-
niscience.

that are eternally and universally active in God, and
that must be embodied in all revelations of God, either in
external nature or in spiritual history, whether looked
at on their natural or their supernatural side — thus
becomes the foundation and inspiring source of our interpretations of the attributes and powers of any of the finite
substances presented in human experience, and of any of
the temporal manifestations which they make of themselves,
in what Locke calls 'agreements of coexistence.' Human
life, sensuous and spiritual, accordingly reposes on the
absolute reasonableness and goodness of the Power that
is supreme. If the Christian conception of the universe is
found to give the fullest satisfaction to what is highest in
man, bringing all the complex elements of his constitution
into harmony with the realities of existence, *then*, even
without omniscience, man may vindicate his faith in it.
If his intelligence could be put to confusion by *this* experience, he must be living and moving and having his being
in an illusory 'reality'—in a universe that, because insane
and immoral, is absolutely incalculable, and therefore unfit
to be reasoned about, since experience of it puts understanding to confusion, in sceptical or pessimist despair. Yet in
all our actions and scientific previsions, as well as in the
more comprehensive interpretations of existence implied
in religious thought, we rest at last in the faith that law or
order *is* supreme ; although *we* cannot naturally articulate the infinite reality in all its details, or 'perceive' all
finite realities in all their causal and moral relations to one
another and to the supreme Power. For this faith is just
recognition of the universal truth, that one is really living,
not in a physical and moral chaos, but in a physical and
moral cosmos ; notwithstanding that one is unable to compass all the parts, in the omniscience that sees each part in
its causal relations to every other. The philosophical faith
that regulates human understanding, in the education of
an intelligence that is intermediate between nescience and
omniscience, presupposes that the universe, in its temporal
'coexistences' and changes, is *somehow* the expression of
perfect reason ; although this reason cannot be so applied,
in an understanding of limited experience, as that man can

have prevision of all changes, or even unconditionally certain prevision of any particular change; the course even of 'verified' laws being always open to modification by as yet unknown agents. When we advance beyond the immediate data of the senses, we are always making faith and hope ventures about the particular event; but in absolute certainty of the supremacy of the intellectual and moral order, or divine immanence, in all. Our inferences, in propositions of 'coexistence,' would be leaps wholly 'in the dark,' but for the faith that they all somehow consist with the abstract intellectual and moral order on which what is best and highest in man is obliged at last to rest. This large faith thus becomes reason in its highest human form, and may be in a way the final solution of the difficulties 'concerning morality and revealed religion' which are said to have first suggested the *Essay concerning Human Understanding.*

(C.) HISTORICAL.

I. THE ESSAY AS IN BERKELEY: SPIRITUAL PHILOSOPHY.

Locke's
Essay in
Dublin.

Chiefly through the influence of William Molyneux, the *Essay concerning Human Understanding* was introduced soon after it appeared into the course of study at Trinity College, Dublin. About the time of Locke's death the new methods of Bacon and Descartes, in their application to the invisible facts and events presented in our conscious intelligence, were, through the *Essay*, producing a reaction in Dublin against the traditions and abstract logic of the schools. Then and there the new philosophy found a critical yet sympathetic response in the mind of George Berkeley, who entered Trinity College in 1700, fresh from his native valley of the Nore, full of inquisitive enthusiasm. It was in Ireland, through Berkeley, that the English philosophy of Locke was first developed and modified, in a manner so signal as to possess historical significance. The problems that were only latent in it took root in a mind more subtle and less given to compromise than Locke's, of wider and acuter speculative grasp, while less endowed with prudential common sense. About a year after Locke's death, Berkeley was the leading member of an academical society that met weekly for promoting inquiries into the facts of external nature and life, according to the methods of Boyle and Newton in physics, and of Locke in human understanding. The *Essay* was above all the subject of debate and free criticism.

Berkeley's
College
Common-
place
Book.

A remarkable revelation of Berkeley's state of mind in 1705, and in the two years following, is contained in his college 'Commonplace Book' of queries and occasional thoughts, in logic, ontology, and ethics [1]. The startling inspiration of a new philosophical principle runs through

[1] See my *Collected Works* of Berkeley, vol. iv. pp. 419-501.

its pages, suggested by the *Essay*, with much in which this Commonplace Book is at variance. The 'new principle' rose out of meditation upon the meaning of the word 'real,' especially when applied to 'outward things.' That Locke had overlooked the nature and origin of this idea, in his famous analysis of human ideas, was borne in upon Berkeley in his study of the *Essay*. His own explanation of the meaning of reality when it is affirmed of 'outward things,' was destined to encounter the ridicule of the multitude, always apt to put words in place of thoughts, and to take outward things for the only type of what is real, without troubling themselves to ask what reality means. Whatever is real—all Locke's three final realities—Berkeley began to see, must depend for their actual reality on conscious mind. Withdraw from existence all living perception, and then the unperceiving and unperceived things supposed to remain necessarily lose all their attributes and powers; for the universe can be *actual*, only in and through active or self-conscious mind. Existence of any sort is not conceivable without living perceptions and volitions. Existence *is* perceiving and willing, or else being perceived and willed. The term 'real existence' is not intelligible otherwise. Actual things are therefore 'ideas,' or dependent on mind for their actuality. Ignorance of this, Berkeley takes to be the chief source of all scepticism and folly, all the contradictory and inexplicable puzzling absurdities that have in all ages been a reproach to human reason. If, he says, in this and some other things 'I differ from a philosopher that I profess to admire [Locke], it is for that very thing on account of which I admire him, namely, the love of truth.' Berkeley anticipates one great bar to the reception of his new world-transforming principle in the very evil which the *Essay* of Locke was mainly directed against— man's disposition to abuse words to the perversion and even the paralysis of thought. True philosophical principles are perpetually concealed by the 'mist and veil of words.'

Berkeley, charged with this new philosophical conception of what reality means, issued from his 'obscure corner,' as he calls it, to become a leader in European philosophy, in immediate succession to Locke. His governing conception was unintelligible to his contemporaries, and to generations of his successors. He had himself only an imperfect appreciation of what it implied. In his old age it was so modified that it led him to reverse the nominalistic empiricism which was at first suggested to his uncompromising intelligence by Locke's *Essay*.

Metaphysical negation prominent in Berkeley's juvenile treatises.

Within ten years after Locke's death three treatises, in which the 'new principle' was explained and vindicated, negatively more than on its constructive side, were given by Berkeley to the world. That outward things cannot be actual or real, out of all relation to any knowing mind—that they must otherwise be unsubstantial and impotent, is their more obvious outcome. The way in which percipient mind sustains reality, and the philosophical formulas in which this office of intelligence may receive ultimate expression, were left in the background; while the polemic against 'abstract ideas,' with which the new conception of real existence was introduced, even exaggerated the depreciation of abstract universals in the *Essay*.

Three doctrines in the *Essay* which led to Berkeley's new conception of the material world.

Berkeley's 'new principle,' which makes all actual reality depend on percipient or conscious mind, is suggested by three doctrines that are conspicuous in the *Essay*:—(1) Its reference of all secondary or imputed qualities of 'outward things' to sentient mind. (2) Its repeated hints that 'pure matter is only passive,' active power being attributed exclusively to 'created spirits' like ourselves, and to 'God.' (3) Its tendency to separate material substances from the simple ideas in which their qualities are manifested; along with the occasionally implied assumption, that our own self-conscious personality is more immediately revealed than the things of sense—'no one of the things the mind contemplates, *besides itself*, being *present* to the understanding[1].' Let us look at each of these.

The dependence of the secondary, or imputed, qualities

(1) The *imputed* qualities of matter Locke had argued must all be referred to sentient minds; apart from them they are meaningless: matter *per se* must be interpreted exclusively in terms of solid extension and motion, which alone are its essential, real, or original qualities. But

---

[1] Bk. IV. ch. xxi. § 4.

all the qualities in which matter manifests itself, or in which it can be supposed to manifest itself, Berkeley argues, are equally dependent for their actuality upon conscious mind : so 'matter,' stripped of all its qualities, by the subtraction of all percipient mind, must be an empty abstraction—one of those meaningless words against which Locke had protested. Therefore its real existence must be the existence, in us and other percipient beings, of a certain order of ideas or phenomena—namely, those of which we and they are conscious in actual seeing and touching; ideas which possess marks that plainly distinguish them from 'unreal' fancies. It is of no importance to say, as Locke does, that our primary ideas of matter are 'copies or resemblances' of an 'unthinking' substance; for an idea can be only like another idea, and ideas obviously all depend upon percipient minds : besides, it is impossible to have ideas of solid atoms in motion without also imputing to them some of the qualities that are called secondary. In short, the very phenomena presented in sense, primary as well as secondary, are themselves the 'outward things': we call them *real*, partly because they appear involuntarily, as far as each of us is concerned ; partly because they are more vivid than our unreal fancies are ; and partly too because they are elements in that universal order, on which our pleasures and pains, and all the interests of human life, are found to depend. *[of matter upon sentient mind.]*

(2) For us 'outward things' are in this way constantly undergoing annihilation and re-creation. They are in a perpetual flux; but then it is flux in a cosmical system, which the immutable principle of causality obliges us to refer to Eternal Mind as its sustaining and supreme cause; because mind is the only active power of which we have any idea, or rather any 'notion.' The constant activity and supremacy of Mind is the only possible explanation of the natural order on which human life depends, and which all scientific interpretation of natural phenomena, all expectation or prevision, presupposes. Hence the presence of reason or order in the coexistences and successions of sensuous phenomena; the real or sense ideas of which things are composed are practically the same for all minds; *[That pure matter is only passive, and that all active power in the universe must be referred to mind.]*

ideas of sense can in this way be calculated upon ; they may be used as sense-symbols through which finite spirits can communicate with one another ; and collectively they embody a divine language in which God is constantly addressing men. The essential as well as the imputed qualities of ' outward things,' therefore, exist ' in mind,' i.e. dependent on perception ; not, as they were supposed to do, as modes or attributes of unperceived and unperceiving substances, which must all be impotent, and can have no independent subsistence.

That our own mind is present to our understanding in a way that outward substances are not, so that we have a notion, but not an idea of it.

(3) But as to the personal or substantial existence of *thinking* beings, on the contrary, this, Berkeley argues, is not open to the objection to which unthinking substance is open, that it involves a manifest repugnance and inconsistency. ' That ideas should exist in what doth not perceive, or be produced by what doth not act, *is* repugnant. But it is no repugnancy to say that a perceiving thing should be the subject of ideas, or an active thing the cause of them. I have a *notion* of spirit, though I have not, strictly speaking, an *idea*[1] of it. I know and am conscious of my own being. But I am not in like manner conscious either of the existence or essence of Matter.' There is therefore ' no parity of case' between a material and a spiritual substance. As Locke had said, ' none of the things the mind contemplates, *besides itself,* are present to the understanding.'

Berkeley's philosophy in middle life.

In Berkeley's Latin tract, *De Motu,* published sixteen years after Locke's death, this exclusive activity of mind or spirit is the special conclusion argued for ; and twelve years later the ' outward world' of merely sensible realities appears transformed into a system of sensible and significant effects, emptied of all efficient causality, in Berkeley's *Alciphron.* With more emphasis he now insists, that the connexion of real ideas, or actual sense-phenomena, according to natural laws, ' does not imply the relation of cause and effect, but only of a mark or sign with the thing signified.' This proposition might be taken for the motto of Berkeley's philosophical work in middle life ; in which external nature appears as an infinite sense-symbolism, constantly sustained

---

[1] ' idea,' i.e. a sensuous image, as distinguished from an unrepresentable *notion*, which is not meaningless nevertheless.

and directed in all its changes, according to the divinely imposed order.

In old age Berkeley was employed less in the elimination of independence and active power from our conceptions of 'outward things'; more in reconstruction, through the supernatural and eternal Mind, to which all reality and power, except that implied in the dependent existence yet responsible agency of finite moral beings, is referred by him. In the aphoristic thoughts of *Siris*, he approaches absolute Idealism by making sense absolutely subordinate to constructive reason.   The crude nominalism derived from the *ideism* and 'nominal essences' of Locke is exchanged for Platonic Realism or Idealism. All so-called *causes* or *powers* in external nature are interpreted as only orderly phenomenal *effects* of Divine power.   The universe is a unity, in and through the causal chain, which leads up, in an order of development, to the active Reason that is supreme and pervading.   Take the following utterances :—
'Nothing mechanical either is or really can be a cause. . .
Strictly sense knows nothing. . . Sense is reason immersed and plunged into matter, as Cudworth says. . . Sense and experience acquaint us only with the course and analogy of appearances, or natural effects: thought, reason, and intellect introduce us into the knowledge of their causes.   The [abstract] principles of science are neither objects of sense nor of imagination: and intellect and reason are alone the sure guides of truth. . . Sense at first besets and overbears the mind. We look no further than to it for realities and causes; till Intellect begins to dawn, and casts a ray on this shadowy scene. We then perceive the true principles, and those that before seemed to be the whole of being, upon taking an intellectual view, are seen to be but phantoms. . . Plato held original ideas in the mind ; that is *notions*, such as never were nor can be in the sense. Mind is not a *tabula rasa*, as some hold. There are properly no *ideas* or passive objects in the mind but what were derived from sense; but there are also besides these her own acts or operations, as *notions*. . . There runs a chain [of rational order] through the whole system of things, in which the meanest things are connected with the

Its development in old age, in *Siris*, in which ideas or phenomena of Sense are subordinate to Reason.

highest.   A divine force or influence permeates the entire universe. . . Plotinus represents God as order; Aristotle as law. . . Comprehending God and the creatures in one general *notion*, we may say that all together make one Universe, or τὸ πᾶν.   But if we should say that all things thus make one God, this would indeed be an erroneous notion of God, but would not amount to Atheism, as long as Mind or Intellect was admitted to be the governing part.'   'Our constant endeavour,' he concludes, 'should be to rise into and recover this "lost region of light."'   Theology and philosophy 'gently unbind the ligaments that chain the soul down to the earth and assist her flight towards the Sovereign Good.'

Siris and the *Essay*.
  Thus in *Siris* 'propositions of real existence,' which Locke vaguely accepts as the intuitive starting-point of human knowledge, but without asking what their 'reality' means, are interpreted by Berkeley in the light of fundamental conceptions, which necessarily connect all actual reality with percipient and active mind; 'propositions of co-existence' are recognised as attempts, often futile, to express relations of physical causality in what is really a system of sense-signs, maintained by the perpetual activity of the Supreme Reason in which we live and have our being;— the sense-symbolism awakening in its human interpreters dormant principles of reason (which Locke unconsciously acknowledges in his abstract 'propositions of relation') that unite all to God, the perfect active Reason.   Yet this conception of the universe, as reason-charged, and with all its activities fundamentally activities of Mind, is not in *Siris* regarded as the issue of man's omniscience, or man's power to solve the problems of 'propositions of co-existence,' in the way the 'eternal geometer,' supposed by Leibniz, could solve them.   That in this mortal state we must be modestly satisfied with transient 'glimpses' of the universal laws, and imperfect forecasts of their actual exemplifications in the concrete facts and events in the history of nature and of man, is its final lesson.   'Human souls in this low situation, bordering on mere animal life, bear the weight and see through the dusk of a gross atmosphere, gathered from wrong judgments daily passed, false opinions daily

learned, and early habits of an older date than either judgment or opinion. Through such a medium the sharpest eye cannot see clearly. And if by some extraordinary effort the mind should surmount this dusky region, and snatch a glimpse of pure light, she is soon drawn backwards, and depressed by the heaviness of the animal nature to which she is chained. And if again she chanceth, amidst the agitation of wild fancies and strong affections, to spring upwards, a second relapse speedily succeeds into this region of darkness and dreams.' The particular *ideism* or phenomenalism of the *Essay*, its assertion of the impotence of matter, and its occasional assumption that our own mind is present to itself in a way that 'outward things' are not, is in *Siris* transformed into this universal active Idealism, expressed naturally in a sense-symbolism that is imperfectly interpretable by man. *Siris*, or the spiritual philosophy into which Locke was transformed in Berkeley, was as a whole unintelligible to the Anglo-Saxon mind in the century in which Berkeley lived. It finds a more congenial reception now, in a generation accustomed to the larger philosophical conceptions of Hegel and Lotze, and which has cast its eye back upon the history of human thought struggling with ultimate problems, in a way to which Locke with his 'historical plain method' was a stranger. The fragments of ancient and medieval speculation that are scattered through *Siris* suggest an appreciation of previous thought, of which there is no trace in the *Essay*. For it must always be remembered that with Locke 'historical' method is simply the method that recognises actual facts or events —contingent phenomena, when men essay to interpret realities, whether outward things or human understandings; and 'the action that we call knowing' is itself, in his view, an act or event presented in human experience. The historical learning deposited in books, Locke held in small esteem. *Antiquitas sæculi, juventus mundi*, expressed his deep-rooted conviction, as well as Bacon's. As for the history of philosophic thought being itself the intellectual system of the universe, in its course of gradual development in human understanding, this idea was foreign to him, and to the age he belonged to.

II. THE ESSAY AS IN DAVID HUME: PHILOSOPHICAL NESCIENCE.

Locke in
Hume.

    The spiritual philosophy of Berkeley in Ireland was thus a development in one direction of elements latent in Locke's *Essay*. The next succeeding evolution of philosophy in these islands, of historical importance, occurred in Scotland, in an opposite direction. Hume's *Treatise of Human Nature*, and his *Inquiry concerning Human Understanding*, were published half a century after the *Essay*; the one some years before, and the other rather later than *Siris*. Locke's *Essay* was the new philosophical influence at work at Edinburgh in Hume's youth, and the negative side of Berkeley's new conception of the world of the senses was engaging attention there and then, as a sceptical paradox[1]. Hume awoke into intellectual life in this atmosphere, with a natural disposition to doubt, and to apply sceptical paradox to the prevailing philosophy, as he found it in Locke's *Essay*. His agnostic criticism emptied the *Essay* of most of its fundamental elements, and in particular banished the 'propositions of real existence' that Locke took as presupposed in all 'knowledge by means of ideas[2].'

---

[1] In Hume's youth, when he was a student in Edinburgh, a Society of young men was formed for discussing Berkeley's conception of the material world, and for correspondence with him. (See my *Life and Letters of Berkeley*, p. 224.) That Hume was influenced by the *destructive*, to the exclusion of the *constructive*, aspect of Berkeley's religious theory of the universe appears, when he says that 'the writings of that very ingenious author [Berkeley] form the best lessons of scepticism which are to be found either among the ancient or modern philosophers, Bayle not excepted. . . That all his arguments, though otherwise intended, are merely sceptical, appears from this —*that they admit of no answer, and produce no conviction.*' (Hume's *Inquiry concerning Human Understanding*, Note N.)

[2] Hume's references to Locke are not complimentary. Take the following :—'The fame of Cicero flourishes, but that of Aristotle is utterly decayed. La Bruyere passes the seas, and maintains his reputation ; but the glory of Malebranche is confined to his own nation and to his own age. And Addison perhaps will be read with pleasure when Locke shall be entirely forgotten.' (*Inquiry*, Sect. I.) 'Locke was betrayed by the Schoolmen into this question [about innate ideas]; who, making use of undefined terms, draw out their disputes to a tedious length, without ever touching the point in question. A like ambiguity and circumlocution seem to run through

According to the historians of philosophy and philosophical critics, including Green, the latest and most elaborate of Hume's critics, the nescience of the *Treatise* and the *Inquiry* is a legitimate *reductio ad absurdum* of the account of human knowledge in the *Essay*; for knowledge begins, Locke is made to say, in ' simple ideas,' or sensations taken in isolation, and is thus emptied at the beginning of all reality. Mere phenomena, in which what is real is in no way manifested—simple ideas that are ideas of nothing—can never of course become real knowledge of anything. Unless knowledge begins in propositions of real existence, propositions of real existence can never enter into it. It can never rise out of the momentary sense-consciousnesses that are called (not simple ideas but) 'impressions' by Hume. These may ' coexist,' but in relations which may be capricious, and which may in the end put understanding to confusion : the whole looks hollow and evanescent—'a riddle, an enigma, an inexplicable mystery' —an experience emptied of all absolute certainties. The unexplained background of real substances, material and spiritual, presupposed in the *Essay*, and actually manifested to us, according to Locke, in our simple ideas or phenomena of ' real existences,' disappears, when the sensuous ideas, abstracted from realities, are made the sole elements and measure of what is called human knowledge. A supposed knowledge that is the issue of unconnected phenomena— momentary impressions—can be nothing more than a finite and transitory impression.

Measured by this test, Locke's three ultimate existences all become meaningless. For there is no idea or sensuous

Is the Nescience of Hume the re-ductio ad absurdum of the Essay?

---

that philosopher's reasonings, on this as well as most other subjects.' (*Inquiry,* Note A.) 'As to Sprot, Locke, and even Temple, they know too little of the rules of art to be esteemed elegant writers. . . Men in this country have been so much occupied in the great disputes of religion, politics, and philosophy, that they had no relish for the seemingly minute observations of grammar and criticism. And though this turn must have improved our talent of reasoning, it must be confessed that, even in those sciences, we have not any standard book which we can transmit to posterity. The utmost we have to boast of are a few essays towards a more just philosophy.' (Hume's *Essays*—' Of the Original Contract.')

image of something simple and continued, corresponding to the personal pronoun 'I'; the personal pronoun can therefore apply only to the particular perception of each moment: this sweeps away the mental assertion of their own real continued existence which Locke and Berkeley find accompanying *all* their particular ideas. 'Outward things' are equally transitory: when the 'impressions' or *momentary* sense-perceptions are withdrawn, no *permanent* impression remains behind: so Locke's assertions of the real existence of outward things can legitimately retain no permanent realities in their meaning. As for the mathematically certain 'demonstration' of Eternal Mind, and the constant presence of reason in what is thus the divine language of sense, Hume finds no 'impression' (simple idea) corresponding to this supposed reality, and concludes that 'our line is too short to fathom such immense abysses [1].' There can be no agreements or disagreements of the impossible ideas to which the meaningless term 'real existence' is applied ; so that this sort of proposition, which plays so great a part in the *Essay*, is superfluous and illusory. It follows that, with knowledge thus eviscerated, matter-of-fact propositions of 'coexistence' have no ground in reason. Whatever is, might be different. No negation of a fact can involve a contradiction. If we reason *a priori*, anything is able to produce anything—if indeed we are still to speak of 'production.' 'The falling of a pebble may, for aught we know, extinguish the sun, or the wish of a man control the planets in their orbits [2].' Propositions that are 'intuitively or demonstratively certain' may perhaps still be found among the abstract relations of ideas, as in 'our abstract reasoning concerning quantity or number' ; but these must always be divorced from, and empty of concrete reality, and in the end such abstract reasonings even are involved in insurmountable contradictions.

But what about propositions of 'coexistence,' in which, according to Locke, we attribute powers and qualities to particular substances, and which thus involve the causal relations of substances? Hume's *Inquiry* is an attempt to save *them* from the wreck, for the practical purposes

---

[1] *Inquiry*, section vii.　　　　[2] *Inquiry*, section xii. pt. 3.

of human life. 'Human knowledge' becomes throughout a probable presumption, and all human propositions that are concrete are converted into hypothetical ones. It remains to explain how this is done.

If all the elements of experience are only momentary consciousnesses, in the form of transitory simple ideas or impressions, there can be no 'uniting principle' for connecting one simple idea or impression with another. Yet without this there cannot be even the semblance of knowledge or proposition; for as long as phenomena rise in absolute isolation they are unintelligible. It is in this predicament that Hume at last finds himself in contemplating knowledge. At the end of his review of 'human understanding' in the *Treatise*, the three fundamental realities, including even the reality supposed to be signified by the personal pronoun 'I,' are dissolved in meaninglessness—the synthetic principles implied in the fundamental conceptions of abstract thought are reduced to self-contradiction—all assertion and all denial on all subjects paralysed—'simple ideas' the only residuum. 'I am affrighted and confounded,' is his confession, 'with that forlorn solitude in which I am placed by my philosophy, and fancy myself some strange uncouth monster, who, not being able to mingle and unite in society, has been expelled all human converse, and left utterly abandoned and disconsolate . . . The intense view of these manifold contradictions and imperfections in human reason has so wrought upon me, and heated my brain, that I am ready to reject all belief and reasoning, and can look upon no opinion even as more probable or likely than another. Where am I or what? From what causes do I derive my existence, and to what condition shall I return? Whose favour shall I court, and whose anger must I dread? What beings surround me? and on whom have I any influence, or who have any influence on me? I am confounded with all these questions.' Yet the very expression of these questions, the use of the personal pronoun 'I,' the term 'surrounding beings,' and the pervading causal presuppositions, all bring back, by implication, the three realities of knowledge, the discharge of which had reduced the divine cosmos to this chaos of simple ideas or impressions,

Hume's predicament, when the simple idea is taken as the only accepted element in knowledge.

—phenomena in which no realities are manifested. The words dismissed as meaningless already call out for philosophical recognition.

Thus 'bereft of reason,' by the supposed meaninglessness of some of the propositions in which reason ultimately consists, and the self-contradictoriness of others, Hume, in his philosophical nescience, turns to 'feeling' as a reconstructive influence. He finds that some ideas of 'impressions' include 'a strong propensity to consider objects *strongly* in that view in which they appear,' which causes us to receive the 'enlivened ideas' of the absent impressions in memory, as 'true pictures of past perceptions.' The *remembered* existence of *absent* impressions is accordingly accepted as probable; not on ground of reason, but as the issue of this 'strong propensity.' But what of the absent that is unremembered—past, distant, or future, roughly represented by Locke's propositions of 'coexistence'? What of our understanding or belief of absent phenomena that are neither actually perceived nor remembered? We are here brought to Hume's 'sceptical *solution* of sceptical doubts,' which, with its applications, may be said to form the problem of the *Inquiry*. This problem is thus put by himself:—' The contrary of every matter of fact [proposition of coexistence] is still possible; because it can never imply a contradiction. That the sun will not rise to-morrow is no less intelligible a proposition, and implies no more contradiction, than the affirmation that it will rise. We should in vain therefore attempt to *demonstrate* its falsehood. . . It may therefore be a subject worthy of curiosity, to inquire, What is the nature of that evidence which assures us of any real existence and matter of fact *beyond the present testimony of our senses, and the records of our memory*? This part of philosophy, it is observable, has been little cultivated either by the ancients or the moderns.' The solution which Hume offers of this, the central philosophical problem of his *Inquiry*, is—the 'strong propensity' which causes expectations of the reappearance of the past in the future ; so that propositions of coexistence among phenomena are held together by the habit generated by the (inexplicable) 'custom' of certain 'simple ideas,' as Locke would call them—or 'impressions' in the language of Hume—to 'coexist.' Without ground in necessities of reason, there is somehow gradually formed a *blind* disposition to treat 'impressions' as units in an ordered system, consisting of customary, or as men call them 'natural' sequences. Here there is a bar to all further inquiry. Deeper than this, all is darkness—nowhere any absolute foundation on which to rest in reasonable trust. All that is supposed below this, or around this, is illusion. The past custom of coexistence among impressions is the highest object of trust. Blind Custom takes the place of God. What has been, we have to suppose will be. The only constructive principles are the customary sequences of the simple ideas that appear in sense. Is this adequate to the facts? Are there not other presuppositions, some of them tacitly made by Hume himself, which as much admit of justification as those that are expressly recognised even in this thin and hollow construction, which still tacitly proceeds upon the three fundamental realities *attenuated*, even after it has professed to dissolve them all in isolated impressions?

Association of impressions, followed by a corresponding association of the representative ideas, was for Hume the sole synthetic principle, if this accident can be called a principle, of human understanding. 'Association' then became the supreme rule of English psychology—in Hartley, Priestley, the Mills; now with Mr. Herbert Spencer expanded, through recognition of heredity, and under a larger philosophical conception, into the evolutionary principle of all cosmical change; also in the French 'ideology' of Condillac and the *Aufklärung*, in last century, and since in the *Philosophie Positive* of Comte. By Locke, on the contrary, 'association,' as illustrated in the 'history' of ideas, is introduced[1], not as the ultimate explanation of human understanding, but as an explanation of many of its illusions and prejudices; whereas Hume, and his English and French successors, bring in custom or association to explain all 'assurance of any real existence and matter of fact, beyond the present testimony of the senses, and the records of memory,' if not even the very testimony of sense and memory itself.

[1] Bk. II. ch. xxxiii.

The spiritual philosophy of Berkeley and the philosophical nescience of Hume—opposite issues of the *Essay* of Locke—are types of the two antithetical modes of treating the eternal problem of the universe and our knowledge of it, that have appeared, in various phases, in all ages of philosophical activity. They are distinguished by what is after all a difference of degree in the depth to which thinkers go in their interpretations; this determined by the degree in which reason and will, the supernatural elements in man, along with reverential faith, are awakened in the interpreter. Is man justified in interpreting the universe spiritually at last, as well as sensually at first; or is a positive conception, under associations of mechanical causality, all that is legitimate: and if this last, is even this, or indeed any, interpretation at all, philosophically competent? To describe the answers since given, in the line of Berkeley, on the one hand, and in the line of Hume on the other, would be to present a history of modern religious and philosophical thought; and it might illustrate the sentiment of Bacon, ' that a little philosophy inclineth Man's mind to atheism, but depth in philosophy bringeth men's minds about to religion.'

AN ESSAY

CONCERNING

HUMANE UNDERSTANDING

IN FOUR BOOKS

[¹ WRITTEN BY

JOHN LOCKE, GENT.]

[² As thou knowest not what is the way of the Spirit, nor how the bones do grow in the womb of her that is with child: even so thou knowest not the works of God, who maketh all things.—ECCLES. XI. 5.]

Quam bellum est velle confiteri potius nescire quod nescias, quam ista effutientem nauseare, atque ipsum sibi displicere.—CIC. DE NATUR. DEOR. l. i.

LONDON

Printed by Eliz. Holt, for Thomas Basset, at the George in Fleet Street, near St. Dunstan's Church.

MDCXC

—

¹ Added in second edition.   ² Added in fourth edition.

TO THE RIGHT HONOURABLE

THOMAS, EARL OF PEMBROKE AND MONTGOMERY,

BARON HERBERT OF CARDIFF

LORD ROSS, OF KENDAL, PAR, FITZHUGH, MARMION, ST. QUINTIN, AND SHURLAND;
LORD PRESIDENT OF HIS MAJESTY'S MOST HONOURABLE PRIVY COUNCIL;
AND LORD LIEUTENANT OF THE COUNTY OF WILTS, AND OF SOUTH WALES[1].

MY LORD,

THIS Treatise, which is grown up under your lordship's eye, and has ventured into the world by your order, does now, by a natural kind of right, come to your lordship for that protection which you several years since promised it[2]. It is not that I think any name, how great soever, set at the beginning of a book, will be able to cover the faults that are to be found in it. Things in print must stand and fall by their own worth, or the reader's fancy. But there being nothing more to be desired for truth than a fair unprejudiced hearing, nobody is more likely to procure me that than your lordship, who are allowed to have got so intimate an acquaintance with her, in

---

[1] Thomas Herbert, eighth Earl of Pembroke (1656–1733), the patron and friend of Locke, and also of Berkeley, who, twenty years afterwards, dedicated his *Principles of Human Knowledge* to that ' ornament and support of learning.' In his day Pembroke filled high offices of state, the representative of an illustrious family, of whom Lord Herbert of Cherbury, the metaphysician, and his brother George Herbert the poet, were members. He was president of the Royal Society in 1690, when Locke's *Essay* was dedicated to him ' in token of kind offices done in evil times.'

[2] About 1676 Locke and Pembroke (then Mr. Herbert) were intimate at Montpellier, Locke's retreat for study at that time, and where he completed the first draft of the *Essay*. Afterwards till the end of his life, ' Mr. Herbert ' and ' Lord Pembroke ' often appear in Locke's letters.

her more retired recesses. Your lordship is known to have so far
advanced your speculations in the most abstract and general knowledge of things, beyond the ordinary reach or common methods, that
your allowance and approbation of the design of this Treatise will at
least preserve it from being condemned without reading, and will
prevail to have those parts a little weighed, which might otherwise
perhaps be thought to deserve no consideration, for being somewhat
out of the common road. The imputation of Novelty is a terrible
charge amongst those who judge of men's heads, as they do of their
perukes, by the fashion, and can allow none to be right but the
received doctrines. Truth scarce ever yet carried it by vote anywhere at its first appearance : new opinions are always suspected,
and usually opposed, without any other reason but because they are
not already common [1]. But truth, like gold, is not the less so for
being newly brought out of the mine. It is trial and examination
must give it price, and not any antique fashion ; and though it be
not yet current by the public stamp, yet it may, for all that, be as old
as nature, and is certainly not the less genuine. Your lordship can
give great and convincing instances of this, whenever you please to
oblige the public with some of those large and comprehensive discoveries you have made of truths hitherto unknown, unless to some
few, from whom your lordship has been pleased not wholly to
conceal them. This alone were a sufficient reason, were there no
other, why I should dedicate this *Essay* to your lordship ; and its
having some little correspondence with some parts of that nobler

---

[1] Locke is conscious that he is
making a new departure in the *Essay*.
Its novelty is here assumed, and was
at once recognised by Molyneux and
other enthusiastic readers when it appeared, though now less apparent. Its
own influence has since converted
much in its spirit and doctrine into
commonplace. Its novel assault on
innate ideas and *a priori* theorising
was Locke's way of leading the great
modern revolt against blind authority
and empty verbalism. Stillingfleet
charges him with inventing a 'new
way of certainty by means of ideas,
instead of the old way of certainty by
means of reason.' Lee, in *Anti-Scepticism*, complains that the *Essay* is 'writ
throughout in a kind of new language.'
The inductive, yet introspective psychology of Locke was also a 'novelty,'
in contrast both to the verbal reasonings of the schools, and to the empirical
materialism of Hobbes and Gassendi.
But the originality of the *Essay* is
mainly due to its being a genuine revelation of the powerful individuality
of its author.

and vast system of the sciences your lordship has made so new, exact, and instructive a draught of, I think it glory enough, if your lordship permit me to boast, that here and there I have fallen into some thoughts not wholly different from yours [1]. If your lordship think fit that, by your encouragement, this should appear in the world, I hope it may be a reason, some time or other, to lead your lordship further; and you will allow me to say, that you here give the world an earnest of something that, if they can bear with this, will be truly worth their expectation. This, my lord, shows what a present I here make to your lordship; just such as the poor man does to his rich and great neighbour, by whom the basket of flowers or fruit is not ill taken, though he has more plenty of his own growth, and in much greater perfection. Worthless things receive a value when they are made the offerings of respect, esteem, and gratitude: these you have given me so mighty and peculiar reasons to have, in the highest degree, for your lordship, that if they can add a price to what they go along with, proportionable to their own greatness, I can with confidence brag, I here make your lordship the richest present you ever received. This I am sure, I am under the greatest obligations to seek all occasions to acknowledge a long train of favours I have received from your lordship; favours, though great and important in themselves, yet made much more so by the forwardness, concern, and kindness, and other obliging circumstances, that never failed to accompany them. To all this you are pleased to add that which gives yet more weight and relish to all the rest: you vouchsafe to continue me in some degrees of your esteem, and allow me a place in your good thoughts, I had almost said friendship. This, my lord, your words and actions so constantly show on all occasions, even to others when I am absent, that it is not vanity in me to mention what everybody knows: but it would be want of good manners not to acknowledge what so many are witnesses of, and every day tell me I am indebted to your lordship for. I wish they could as easily assist my gratitude, as

---

[1] Allowance must be made for the customary exaggeration of dedications in Locke's time.

they convince me of the great and growing engagements it has to your lordship. This I am sure, I should write of the *Understanding* without having any, if I were not extremely [1] sensible of them, and did not lay hold on this opportunity to testify to the world how much I am obliged to be, and how much I am,

MY LORD,

Your Lordship's most humble and most obedient servant,

JOHN LOCKE.

[[2] DORSET COURT,
24th of May, 1689.]

---

[1] 'Certainly,' in first edition.

[2] The place and date were added in the fourth edition. When Locke returned from Holland, in February 1689, after five years of exile there, he settled in apartments at Mrs. Smithsby's in Dorset Court, Channel Row, Westminster, which was his home till he removed to Oates in Essex in the spring of 1691. The Dedication is dated nearly a year before the *Essay* was published. Dorset Court lay between Channel (now Cannon) Row and the Thames. According to Strype, it was 'a handsome open place, containing but six houses, large and well built, fit for gentry to dwell in, of which those towards the Thames have gardens towards the water side very pleasant.' They were built on the site of Dorset House, a few years before Locke came to live in one of them. Dorset Court was demolished towards the end of last century, and the place is now partly occupied by the building of the Civil Service Commission.

THE

EPISTLE TO THE READER[1].

READER,

I HAVE put into thy hands what has been the diversion of
some of my idle and heavy hours. If it has the good luck to
prove so of any of thine, and thou hast but half so much
pleasure in reading as I had in writing it, thou wilt as little
think thy money, as I do my pains, ill bestowed. Mistake
not this for a commendation of my work; nor conclude,
because I was pleased with the doing of it, that therefore
I am fondly taken with it now it is done. He that hawks at
larks and sparrows has no less sport, though a much less
considerable quarry, than he that flies at nobler game: and
he is little acquainted with the subject of this treatise—the
UNDERSTANDING [2]—who does not know that, as it is the most
elevated faculty of the soul, so it is employed with a greater
and more constant delight than any of the other. Its searches
after truth are a sort of hawking and hunting, wherein the
very pursuit makes a great part of the pleasure [3]. Every step

[1] Locke, in defending himself against
his critics, refers to this 'Epistle,' for an
explanation of his design in the *Essay*,
and of the circumstances which suggested it.

[2] The distinction between 'Understanding' with its hypothetical judgments, finite and relative, and 'Reason'
with its immediate and absolute insight
of primary truth and ultimate ends, in
which intelligence culminates, was
foreign to Locke. He means by
'Human Understanding' the intelligence of man in its various degrees of
development as related to its objects
immediate and remote.

[3] So Pascal in the *Pensées* —' Nous
ne cherchons jamais les choses, mais
la recherche des choses.' The analogy
of the chase is not original to Locke.
Philosophical finality is inconsistent
with a human intelligence and finite
experience; which presupposes an
endless assimilation and application of
the infinite thought in which the intelligibility of things consists—a progress
through continuous striving to evolve
the reason that is latent in each of us
in harmony with the Reason that is
manifested in the universe of nature
and spirit.

the mind takes in its progress towards Knowledge makes some discovery, which is not only new, but the best too, for the time at least[1].

For the understanding, like the eye[2], judging of objects only by its own sight, cannot but be pleased with what it discovers, having less regret for what has escaped it, because it is unknown. Thus he who has raised himself above the alms-basket, and, not content to live lazily on scraps of begged opinions, sets his own thoughts on work, to find and follow truth, will (whatever he lights on) not miss the hunter's satisfaction; every moment of his pursuit will reward his pains with some delight; and he will have reason to think his time not ill spent, even when he cannot much boast of any great acquisition.

This, Reader, is the entertainment of those who let loose their own thoughts, and follow them in writing; which thou oughtest not to envy them, since they afford thee an opportunity of the like diversion, if thou wilt make use of thy own thoughts in reading. It is to them, if they are thy own, that I refer myself: but if they are taken upon trust from others, it is no great matter what they are; they are not following truth, but some meaner consideration; and it is not worth while to be concerned what he says or thinks, who says or thinks only as he is directed by another[3]. If thou judgest for thyself I know thou wilt judge candidly, and then I shall not be harmed or offended, whatever be thy censure. For though it be certain that there is nothing in this Treatise of the truth whereof I am not fully persuaded, yet I consider

---

[1] A recognition of the tentative and provisional character of man's interpretations of the universe, whether philosophic or merely scientific; each leading on to others, deeper and truer, in an endless evolution of thought.

[2] This analogy between the eye and the understanding is a favourite one with Locke.

[3] Locke's dominant passion was for seeing and interpreting things for himself, as they really are—unmodified by fancy, or sentiment, or authority, and for getting others to see and interpret them for themselves too. Cf. Bk. IV. ch. xix. § 1. Unlike Plato and Bacon, Locke has little eye for the beautiful; he suspects imagination, and dreads the errors to which abstract speculation about reality is exposed.

myself as liable to mistakes as I can think thee, and know that this book must stand or fall with thee, not by any opinion I have of it, but thy own. If thou findest little in it new or instructive to thee, thou art not to blame me for it. It was not meant for those that had already mastered this subject, and made a thorough acquaintance with their own understandings; but for my own information, and the satisfaction of a few friends, who acknowledged themselves not to have sufficiently considered it.

Were it fit to trouble thee with the history of this *Essay*, I should tell thee, that five or six friends meeting at my chamber[1], and discoursing on a subject very remote from this[2], found themselves quickly at a stand, by the difficulties that rose on every side. After we had awhile puzzled ourselves, without coming any nearer a resolution of those doubts which perplexed us, it came into my thoughts that we took a wrong course; and that before we set ourselves upon inquiries of that nature, it was necessary to examine our own abilities, and see what *objects*[3] our understandings were, or were not, fitted to deal with. This I proposed to the company, who all readily assented; and thereupon it was agreed that this should be our first inquiry. Some hasty and undigested thoughts, on a subject I had never before considered, which I set down against our next meeting, gave the first entrance

---

[1] Locke was always fond of reunions or clubs of this sort. We find him helping to form them at Oxford, in London, in Holland. This memorable one belongs to the time when his home was with Lord Ashley (Shaftesbury), in Exeter House in London. The incident here recorded probably occurred in the winter of 1670–71, when he was in his 39th year.

[2] According to his friend James Tyrrell, who was at the 'meeting,' the 'difficulties' arose in discussing the 'principles of morality and revealed religion.' This is recorded in a manuscript note in his copy of the *Essay* now in the British Museum. Tyrrell (1642–

1718), son of Sir T. Tyrrell of Shotover, near Oxford, and grandson of Abp. Usher, a lifelong friend of Locke, became known as the author of a 'History of England,' and of works in political philosophy. He published an abridgement of Cumberland's *De Legibus Naturae*.

[3] 'What objects' — i. e., in the favourite phraseology of the *Essay*, what *ideas* men are capable of having; and what *relations* among their ideas they are able to determine, either with absolute certainty, or with more or less probability. Not the 'vast ocean of Being' but the limited intellectual experience of man, is what Locke asked his friends to contemplate.

into this Discourse ; which having been thus begun by chance, was continued by intreaty ; written by incoherent parcels ; and after long intervals of neglect, resumed again, as my humour or occasions permitted[1] ; and at last, in a retirement where an attendance on my health gave me leisure[2], it was brought into that order thou now seest it.

This discontinued way of writing may have occasioned, besides others, two contrary faults, viz., that too little and too much may be said in it. If thou findest anything wanting, I shall be glad that what I have written gives thee any desire that I should have gone further[3]. If it seems too much to thee, thou must blame the subject ; for when I put pen to paper, I thought all I should have to say on this matter would have been contained in one sheet of paper ; but the further I went the larger prospect I had ; new discoveries led me still on, and so it grew insensibly to the bulk it now appears in. I will not deny, but possibly it might be reduced to a narrower compass than it is, and that some parts of it might be contracted, the way it has been writ in, by catches, and many long intervals of interruption, being apt to cause some repetitions. But to confess the truth, I am now too lazy, or too busy, to make it shorter[4].

[1] This helps to explain verbal and other inconsistencies, repetitions, and defects of arrangement complained of in the *Essay*.

[2] In Holland, where Locke completed the *Essay*, during his retirement there in 1683-89. Yet in June 1679, soon after he left Montpellier, he says in a letter to Thoynard, ' I think too well of my book, *which is completed*, to let it go out of my hands.' So he kept it, recast it, and corresponded about it with his friends, for ten other years.

[3] Locke's hope has been fulfilled. The strong unspeculative common sense, which was his congenial element, with the consequent inadequacy and incoherence of his philosophical outcome, has so stimulated thought, through controversy and otherwise, that the history of philosophy since the *Essay* appeared, may be said to be a history of the criticism to which it has given rise, and of the new points of view to which it has thus conducted. Plato and Plotinus, Spinoza and Hegel would be inaccessible to Locke, and yet he has unconsciously led into their problems.

[4] The 'prolixity' of the *Essay* and its repetitions are obvious to the reader. In preparing the second edition he thus apologises to his Dublin friend Molyneux : ' You will find, by my Epistle to the Reader, that I was not insensible of the fault I committed by being too long upon some points ; and the repetitions that by my way of writing I had got into, I let it pass with, but not without advice so to do.

I am not ignorant how little I herein consult my own reputation, when I knowingly let it go with a fault, so apt to disgust the most judicious, who are always the nicest readers. But they who know sloth is apt to content itself with any excuse, will pardon me if mine has prevailed on me, where I think I have a very good one. I will not therefore allege in my defence, that the same notion, having different respects, may be convenient or necessary to prove or illustrate several parts of the same discourse, and that so it has happened in many parts of this: but waiving that, I shall frankly avow that I have sometimes dwelt long upon the same argument, and expressed it different ways, with a quite different design. I pretend not to publish this *Essay* for the information of men of large thoughts and quick apprehensions ; to such masters of knowledge I profess myself a scholar, and therefore warn them beforehand not to expect anything here, but what, being spun out of my own coarse thoughts, is fitted to men of my own size, to whom, perhaps, it will not be unacceptable that I have taken some pains to make plain and familiar to their thoughts some truths which established prejudice, or the abstractedness of the ideas themselves, might render difficult. Some objects had need be turned on every side ; and when the notion is new, as I confess some of these are to me; or out of the ordinary road, as I suspect they will appear to others, it is not one simple view of it that will

But now that my notions are got into the world, and have in some measure bustled through the opposition and difficulty they were like to meet with from the received opinion, and that prepossession which might hinder them from being understood upon a short proposal; I ask you whether it would not be better now to pare off, in a second edition, a great part of that which cannot but appear superfluous to an intelligent and attentive reader.' (September 20, 1692.) ' I never quarrelled with a book for being too prolix,' replied Molyneux, 'especially where the prolixity is pleasant, and tends to the illustration of the matter in hand, as I am sure yours always does. And after I received your letter I communicated the contents thereof to two very ingenious persons here, and at the same time I sent them your book, desiring them to examine it strictly, and to find out and note whatever might be changed, added, or subtracted. After a diligent perusal, they agreed with me in the conclusion, that the work in all its parts was so wonderfully curious and instructive that they would not venture to alter anything in it.' (December 22, 1692.) And so the ' repetitions' were left untouched.

gain it admittance into every understanding, or fix it there with a clear and lasting impression. There are few, I believe, who have not observed in themselves or others, that what in one way of proposing was very obscure, another way of expressing it has made very clear and intelligible ; though afterwards the mind found little difference in the phrases, and wondered why one failed to be understood more than the other. But everything does not hit alike upon every man's imagination. We have our understandings no less different than our palates ; and he that thinks the same truth shall be equally relished by every one in the same dress, may as well hope to feast every one with the same sort of cookery : the meat may be the same, and the nourishment good, yet every one not be able to receive it with that seasoning ; and it must be dressed another way, if you will have it go down with some, even of strong constitutions. The truth is, those who advised me to publish it, advised me, for this reason, to publish it as it is : and since I have been brought to let it go abroad, I desire it should be understood by whoever gives himself the pains to read it. I have so little affection to be in print [1], that if I were not flattered this *Essay* might be of some use to others, as I think it has been to me, I should have confined it to the view of some friends, who gave the first occasion to it. My appearing therefore in print being on purpose to be as useful as I may, I think it necessary to make what I have to say as easy and intelligible to all sorts of readers as I can [2]. And I had much rather the speculative

---

[1] Locke did not appear as an author till 1686, when he was 54, and then only as an anonymous contributor to Le Clerc's *Bibliothèque universelle.*

[2] The result has not been according to the intention. Locke's endeavour to accommodate his *Essay* to all sorts of readers has made it perhaps the most difficult of modern philosophical classics to reduce to luminous and consecutive thought. The desire to avoid scholastic terms, combined with vacillation and want of precise connotation in the use of some of the most important words, have made the *Essay* the puzzle of commentators and critics. The reader, labouring after the meaning, must not ' stick in the incidents,' as Locke complained to Collins that critics often did, but must strive to take a comprehensive view of the work in its main design, which he says ' lies in a little compass' (*Letter*, 21 March, 1704).

and quick-sighted should complain of my being in some parts tedious, than that any one, not accustomed to abstract speculations, or prepossessed with different notions, should mistake or not comprehend my meaning.

It will possibly be censured as a great piece of vanity or insolence in me, to pretend to instruct this our knowing age ; it amounting to little less, when I own, that I publish this *Essay* with hopes it may be useful to others. But, if it may be permitted to speak freely of those who with a feigned modesty condemn as useless what they themselves write, methinks it savours much more of vanity or insolence to publish a book for any other end ; and he fails very much of that respect he owes the public, who prints, and consequently expects men should read, that wherein he intends not they should meet with anything of use to themselves or others : and should nothing else be found allowable in this Treatise, yet my design will not cease to be so ; and the goodness of my intention ought to be some excuse for the worthlessness of my present. It is that chiefly which secures me from the fear of censure, which I expect not to escape more than better writers. Men's principles, notions, and relishes are so different, that it is hard to find a book which pleases or displeases all men. I acknowledge the age we live in is not the least knowing, and therefore not the most easy to be satisfied. If I have not the good luck to please, yet nobody ought to be offended with me. I plainly tell all my readers, except half a dozen[1], this Treatise was not at first intended for them ; and therefore they need not be at the trouble to be of that number. But yet if any one thinks fit to be angry and rail at it, he may do it securely, for I shall find some better way of spending my time than in such kind of conversation[2]. I shall always have the satisfaction to have aimed sincerely at truth and usefulness, though in one of the meanest

[1] The 'half dozen' friends whose 'difficulties' suggested the *Essay*.

[2] Locke's celebrated controversy with Stillingfleet (1697-99) shows that he had to modify this resolution.

ways. The commonwealth of learning is not at this time without master-builders, whose mighty designs, in advancing the sciences, will leave lasting monuments to the admiration of posterity : but every one must not hope to be a Boyle [1] or a Sydenham [2]; and in an age that produces such masters as the great Huygenius [3] and the incomparable Mr. Newton [4], with some others of that strain, it is ambition enough to be employed as an under-labourer in clearing the ground a little, and removing some of the rubbish that lies in the way to knowledge [5];—which certainly had been very much more advanced in the world, if the endeavours of ingenious and industrious men had not been much cumbered with the learned but frivolous use of uncouth, affected, or unintelligible terms, introduced into the sciences, and there made an art of, to that degree that Philosophy, which is nothing but the true knowledge of things [6], was thought unfit or incapable to be brought into well-bred company and polite conversation. Vague and insignificant forms of speech, and abuse of language, have so long passed for mysteries of science ; and hard and misapplied words, with little or no meaning, have, by prescription, such a right to be mistaken for deep learning and height of speculation, that it will not be easy to persuade either those who speak or those who hear them, that they are but the covers of ignorance, and hindrance of true knowledge. To break in upon the sanctuary of vanity and ignorance will be, I suppose, some service to human understanding ; though

---

[1] Robert Boyle (1626-91), son of the first Earl of Cork, founder of the 'Boyle Lectures,' which were inaugurated by Dr. Samuel Clarke's *Demonstration of the Being and Attributes of God.* Boyle was a friend of Locke, who edited his *History of the Air,* and added meteorological observations of his own.

[2] Thomas Sydenham (1624-89), one of the greatest names in the history of medicine, intimate with Locke and Boyle.

[3] Christian Huygens (1629-93), the

Dutch mathematician and physicist.

[4] 'Sir Isaac' in 1705,—the year after Locke's death.

[5] The 'master-builders' whom he names all worked by way of observation and generalisation of facts. Locke represents himself as 'an under labourer, clearing the ground' for further advance in the interpretation of nature, by like methods.

[6] 'Philosophy is nothing else but the study of wisdom and truth.' (Berkeley, *Principles,* Introd. Sect. 1.)

so few are apt to think they deceive or are deceived in the use of words; or that the language of the sect they are of has any faults in it which ought to be examined or corrected, that I hope I shall be pardoned if I have in the Third Book dwelt long on this subject, and endeavoured to make it so plain, that neither the inveterateness of the mischief, nor the prevalency of the fashion, shall be any excuse for those who will not take care about the meaning of their own words, and will not suffer the significancy of their expressions to be inquired into [1].

I have been told that a short Epitome of this Treatise, which was printed in 1688 [2], was by some condemned without reading, because *innate ideas* were denied in it; they too hastily concluding, that if innate ideas were not supposed, there would be little left either of the notion or proof of spirits. If any one take the like offence at the entrance of this Treatise, I shall desire him to read it through; and then I hope he will be convinced, that the taking away false foundations is not to the prejudice but advantage of truth, which is never injured or endangered so much as when mixed with, or built on, falsehood [3].

---

[1] It is curious that vagueness and vacillation in the use of words should be the chief defect of the *Essay* itself, which so aptly illustrates what Sir James Mackintosh says of the inadequacy of the words of ordinary language for the delicate purposes of philosophy. Cf. Berkeley on the abuse of words, *Principles*, Introd. Sect. 18-25.

[2] This Epitome appeared in Le Clerc's French version. It was published in the *Bibliothèque universelle* (Amsterdam, January, 1688, more than two years before the *Essay*), with this heading—'Extrait d'un livre Anglais, qui n'est pas encore publié, intitulé: Essai Philosophique concernant l'Entendement, où l'on montre quelle est l'étendue de nos connaissances certaines, et la manière dont nous y parvenons.

Communiqué par Monsieur Locke.' It fills more than ninety pages of Le Clerc's celebrated journal.

[3] The following paragraph in the *first* edition is omitted in the later ones that appeared in Locke's lifetime, in which the summaries are printed in the margin, at the suggestion of Molyneux:—'One thing more I must advertise my reader of, and that is, that the summary of each section is printed [in the text] in italic characters; whereby the reader may find the contents almost as well as if it had been printed in the margin by the side, if a little allowance be made for the grammatical construction, which in the text itself could not always be so ordered as to make perfect propositions, which yet by the words printed in italic may be easily guessed at.'

In the Second Edition [1] I added as followeth :—

The bookseller will not forgive me if I say nothing of this New Edition, which he has promised, by the correctness of it, shall make amends for the many faults committed in the former [2]. He desires too, that it should be known that it has one whole new chapter concerning *Identity* [3], and many additions and amendments in other places. These I must inform my reader are not all new matter, but most of them either further confirmation of what I had said, or explications, to prevent others being mistaken in the sense of what was formerly printed, and not any variation in me from it.

I must only except the alterations I have made in Book II. chap. xxi.

What I had there written concerning Liberty and the Will, I thought deserved as accurate a view as I am capable of ; those subjects having in all ages exercised the learned part of the world with questions and difficulties, that have not a little perplexed morality and divinity, those parts of knowledge that men are most concerned to be clear in. Upon a closer inspection into the working of men's minds, and a stricter examination of those motives and views they are turned by, I have found reason somewhat to alter the thoughts I formerly had concerning that which gives the last determination to the Will in all voluntary actions. This I cannot forbear to acknowledge to the world with as much freedom and readiness as I at first published what then seemed to me to be right ; thinking myself more concerned to quit and renounce any opinion of my own, than oppose that of another, when truth appears against it. For it is truth alone I seek [4], and that will always be welcome to me, when or from whencesoever it comes.

---

[1] Published ' with large additions,' in May 1694. The preparation of it occupied much of the two preceding years at Oates. See his correspondence during these years with Molyneux.

[2] Locke regrets, in his correspondence with Molyneux, the numerous *errata* found in the first edition.

[3] Bk. II. ch. xxvii.

[4] See Bk. I. ch. iii. § 23 ; Bk. IV. ch. v ; xix. § 1.

But what forwardness soever I have to resign any opinion I have, or to recede from anything I have writ, upon the first evidence of any error in it ; yet this I must own, that I have not had the good luck to receive any light from those exceptions I have met with in print against any part of my book, nor have, from anything that has been urged against it, found reason to alter my sense in any of the points that have been questioned. Whether the subject I have in hand requires often more thought and attention than cursory readers, at least such as are prepossessed, are willing to allow; or whether any obscurity in my expressions casts a cloud over it, and these notions are made difficult to others' apprehensions in my way of treating them ; so it is, that my meaning, I find, is often mistaken, and I have not the good luck to be everywhere rightly understood [1].

[Of this the ingenious author [2] of the *Discourse Concerning the Nature of Man* has given me a late instance, to mention no other. For the civility of his expressions, and the candour that belongs to his order, forbid me to think that he would have closed his Preface with an insinuation, as if in what I had said, Book II. ch. xxvii, concerning the third rule which men refer their actions to, I went about to make virtue vice and vice virtue, unless he had mistaken my meaning; which he could not have done if he had given himself the trouble to consider what the argument was I was then upon, and what was the chief design of that chapter, plainly enough set down in the fourth section and those following. For I was there not laying down moral rules, but showing the original and nature of moral ideas, and enumerating the rules men make use of in moral relations, whether these rules were true or false : and pursuant thereto I tell what is everywhere called virtue and vice ; which 'alters not the nature of things,' though men generally do judge of

---

[1] Locke's letters are full of complaints that his meaning in the *Essay* is misapprehended by his critics.

[2] Mr. Lowde. This and the four following bracketed paragraphs are omitted in the posthumous editions.

and denominate their actions according to the esteem and fashion of the place and sect they are of.

If he had been at the pains to reflect on what I had said, Bk. I. ch. ii.[1] sect. 18, and Bk. II. ch. xxviii.[1] sect. 13, 14, 15 and 20, he would have known what I think of the eternal and unalterable nature of right and wrong, and what I call virtue and vice. And if he had observed that in the place he quotes I only report as a matter of fact what *others* call virtue and vice, he would not have found it liable to any great exception. For I think I am not much out in saying that one of the rules made use of in the world for a ground or measure of a moral relation is—that esteem and reputation which several sorts of actions find variously in the several societies of men, according to which they are there called virtues or vices. And whatever authority the learned Mr. Lowde places in his *Old English Dictionary*, I daresay it nowhere tells him (if I should appeal to it) that the same action is not in credit, called and counted a virtue, in one place, which, being in disrepute, passes for and under the name of vice in another. The taking notice that men bestow the names of 'virtue' and 'vice' according to this rule of Reputation is all I have done, or can be laid to my charge to have done, towards the making vice virtue or virtue vice. But the good man does well, and as becomes his calling, to be watchful in such points, and to take the alarm even at expressions, which, standing alone by themselves, might sound ill and be suspected.

'Tis to this zeal, allowable in his function, that I forgive his citing as he does these words of mine (ch. xxviii.[1] sect. 11): 'Even the exhortations of inspired teachers have not feared to appeal to common repute, Philip. iv. 8;' without taking notice of those immediately preceding, which introduce them, and run thus: 'Whereby even in the corruption of manners, the true boundaries of the law of nature, which ought to be the rule of virtue and vice, were pretty well preserved. So that even the exhortations of inspired teachers,' &c. By which

---

[1] The references are to the chapters as numbered in this edition.

words, and the rest of that section, it is plain that I brought
that passage of St. Paul, not to prove that the general measure
of what men called virtue and vice throughout the world was,
the reputation and fashion of each particular society within
itself; but to show that, though it were so, yet, for reasons
I there give, men, in that way of denominating their actions,
did not for the most part much stray from the Law of Nature;
which is that standing and unalterable rule by which they
ought to judge of the moral rectitude and gravity of their
actions, and accordingly denominate them virtues or vices.
Had Mr. Lowde considered this, he would have found it little
to his purpose to have quoted this passage in a sense I used
it not; and would I imagine have spared the application he
subjoins to it, as not very necessary. But I hope this Second
Edition will give him satisfaction on the point, and that this
matter is now so expressed as to show him there was no
cause for scruple.

Though I am forced to differ from him in these apprehensions he has expressed, in the latter end of his preface, concerning what I had said about virtue and vice, yet we are
better agreed than he thinks in what he says in his third
chapter (p. 78) concerning 'natural inscription and innate
notions.' I shall not deny him the privilege he claims (p. 52),
to state the question as he pleases, especially when he states
it so as to leave nothing in it contrary to what I have said.
For, according to him, 'innate notions, being conditional things,
depending upon the concurrence of several other circumstances
in order to the soul's exerting them,' all that he says for 'innate,
imprinted, impressed notions' (for of innate *ideas* he says
nothing at all), amounts at last only to this—that there are
certain propositions which, though the soul from the beginning,
or when a man is born, does not know, yet 'by assistance from
the outward senses, and the help of some previous cultivation,'
it may *afterwards* come certainly to know the truth of; which
is no more than what I have affirmed in my First Book. For
I suppose by the 'soul's exerting them,' he means its beginning

to know them ; or else the soul's ' exerting of notions ' will be to me a very unintelligible expression ; and I think at best is a very unfit one in this, it misleading men's thoughts by an insinuation, as if these notions were in the mind before the ' soul exerts them,' i. e. before they are known ;—whereas truly before they are known, there is nothing of them in the mind but a capacity to know them, when the ' concurrence of those circumstances,' which this ingenious author thinks necessary ' in order to the soul's exerting them,' brings them into our knowledge.

P. 52 I find him express it thus : ' These natural notions are not so imprinted upon the soul as that they naturally and necessarily exert themselves (even in children and idiots) without any assistance from the outward senses, or without the help of some previous cultivation.'   Here, he says, they ' exert themselves,' as p. 78, that the ' soul exerts them.'   When he has explained to himself or others what he means by ' the soul's exerting innate notions,' or their ' exerting themselves ;' and what that ' previous cultivation and circumstances ' in order to their being exerted are—he will I suppose find there is so little of controversy between him and me on the point, bating that he calls that ' exerting of notions ' which I in a more vulgar style call ' knowing,' that I have reason to think he brought in my name on this occasion only out of the pleasure he has to speak civilly of me ; which I must gratefully acknowledge he has done everywhere he mentions me, not without conferring on me, as some others have done, a title I have no right to.]

[[1] There are so many instances of this [2], that I think it justice to my reader and myself to conclude, that either my book is plainly enough written to be rightly understood by those who peruse it with that attention and indifferency [3], which every one who will give himself the pains to read ought to employ in reading ; or else that I have written mine so obscurely that

---

[1] This paragraph first appears in the posthumous editions.

[2] ' this,' i. e. misapprehension.

[3] ' indifferency' i.e. freedom from bias.

it is in vain to go about to mend it. Whichever of these be the truth, it is myself only am affected thereby; and therefore I shall be far from troubling my reader with what I think might be said in answer to those several objections I have met with, to passages here and there of my book; since I persuade myself that he who thinks them of moment enough to be concerned whether they are true or false, will be able to see that what is said is either not well founded, or else not contrary to my doctrine, when I and my opposer come both to be well understood.]

If any other authors, careful that none of their good thoughts should be lost, have published their censures of my *Essay*, with this honour done to it, that they will not suffer it to be an essay, I leave it to the public to value the obligation they have to their critical pens, and shall not waste my reader's time in so idle or ill-natured an employment of mine, as to lessen the satisfaction any one has in himself, or gives to others, in so hasty a confutation of what I have written[1].

The booksellers preparing for the Fourth Edition[2] of my *Essay*, gave me notice of it, that I might, if I had leisure, make any additions or alterations I should think fit. Whereupon I thought it convenient to advertise the reader, that besides several corrections I had made here and there, there

---

[1] The following paragraph, which appeared in the Second Edition, is omitted in the Fourth:—

'Besides what is already mentioned, this Second Edition has the summaries of the several sections not only printed as before in a table by themselves, but in the margin too. And at the end there is now an Index added. These two, with a great number of short additions, amendments and alterations, are advantages of this Edition which the bookseller hopes will make it sell. As to the larger additions and alterations, I have obliged him, and he has promised me to print them by them-selves, so that the former Edition may not be wholly lost to those who have it, but by the inserting in their proper places the passages that will be re-printed alone, to that purpose, the former book may be made as little defective as is possible.'

[2] The last which appeared in Locke's lifetime. In it this and the five follow-ing paragraphs were added to the 'Epistle.' It was published in the end of 1699, dated 1700, 'with large additions.' The third edition, which was only a reprint of the second, ap-peared in 1695.

was one alteration which it was necessary to mention, because it ran through the whole book, and is of consequence to be rightly understood. What I thereupon said was this :—

Clear and *distinct ideas* are terms which, though familiar and frequent in men's mouths, I have reason to think every one who uses does not perfectly understand. And possibly 'tis but here and there one who gives himself the trouble to consider them so far as to know what he himself or others precisely mean by them. I have therefore in most places chose to put *determinate* or *determined*, instead of *clear* and *distinct*, as more likely to direct men's thoughts to my meaning in this matter. By those denominations, I mean some object in the mind, and consequently determined, i. e. such as it is there seen and perceived to be. This, I think, may fitly be called a determinate or determined idea, when such as it is at any time objectively in the mind, and so determined there, it is annexed, and without variation determined, to a name or articulate sound, which is to be steadily the sign of that very same object of the mind, or determinate idea [1].

To explain this a little more particularly. By *determinate*, when applied to a simple idea, I mean that simple appearance which the mind has in its view, or perceives in itself, when that idea is said to be in it : by *determined*, when applied to a complex idea, I mean such an one as consists of a determinate number of certain simple or less complex ideas, joined in such a proportion and situation as the mind has before its view, and sees in itself, when that idea is present in it, or should be present in it, when a man gives a name to it. I say *should* be, because it is not every one, nor perhaps any one, who is so careful of his language as to use no word till

[1] That Locke made certainty in all cases depend upon the possession of clear and distinct, or ' determinate,' ideas, about that of which we are certain, was a proposition which Stillingfleet charged him with maintaining.

This Locke emphatically disavows, and maintains that in some instances we have determined ideas of *relations* among ideas that otherwise are obscure and mysterious.

he views in his mind the precise determined idea which he resolves to make it the sign of. The want of this is the cause of no small obscurity and confusion in men's thoughts and discourses.

I know there are not words enough in any language to answer all the variety of ideas that enter into men's discourses and reasonings. But this hinders not but that when any one uses any term, he may have in his mind a determined idea, which he makes it the sign of, and to which he should keep it steadily annexed during that present discourse. Where he does not, or cannot do this, he in vain pretends to clear or distinct ideas: it is plain his are not so; and therefore there can be expected nothing but obscurity and confusion, where such terms are made use of which have not such a precise determination.

Upon this ground I have thought determined ideas a way of speaking less liable to mistakes, than clear and distinct [1] : and where men have got such determined ideas of all that they reason, inquire, or argue about, they will find a great part of their doubts and disputes at an end; the greatest part of the questions and controversies that perplex mankind depending on the doubtful and uncertain use of words, or (which is the same) indetermined ideas, which they are made to stand for. I have made choice of these terms to signify, (1) Some immediate object of the mind, which it perceives and has before it, distinct from the sound it uses as a sign of it. (2) That this idea, thus determined, i. e. which the mind has in itself, and knows, and sees there, be determined without any change to that name, and that name determined to that precise idea. If men had such determined ideas in their inquiries and discourses, they would both discern how

---

[1] Locke has not been generally followed in this 'alteration.' He seems not to have known the *De Cognitione*, &c., of Leibniz, inserted in the *Acta* of Leipsic in 1684, in which ideas are carefully distinguished, as clear and obscure, distinct and confused. 'Determination' is commonly applied by logicians to the process by which the content or comprehension of a notion is increased—by which it is concreted.

far their own inquiries and discourses went, and avoid the greatest part of the disputes and wranglings they have with others [1].

Besides this, the bookseller will think it necessary I should advertise the reader that there is an addition of two chapters wholly new ; the one of the *Association of Ideas*, the other of *Enthusiasm*. These, with some other larger additions never before printed, he has engaged to print by themselves, after the same manner, and for the same purpose, as was done when this *Essay* had the second impression.

In the Sixth Edition there is very little added or altered. The greatest part of what is new is contained in the twenty-first chapter of the second book, which any one, if he thinks it worth while, may, with a very little labour, transcribe into the margin of the former edition [2].

[1] So in Berkeley's *Principles*, Introd. §§ 18–25.

[2] The Sixth Edition, issued in 1706, two years after Locke's death, with these two sentences appended to the 'Epistle,' contains a few slight additions and alterations. Most of them had appeared in Coste's French Version of the *Essay*,—prepared at Oates under Locke's eye. 'The author being present,' says Le Clerc, 'he corrected several places in the original, that he might make them more plain.' Coste was Locke's amanuensis, and lived with him at Oates for some years till his death.

ESSAY

CONCERNING

HUMAN UNDERSTANDING.

INTRODUCTION [1].

INTROD.

An Inquiry
into the
Under-
standing
pleasant
and useful.

1. SINCE it is the *understanding* [2] that sets man above the rest of sensible beings, and gives him all the advantage and dominion which he has over them [3]; it is certainly a subject, even for its nobleness, worth our labour to inquire into. The understanding, like the eye, whilst it makes us see and perceive all other things, takes no notice of itself; and it requires art and pains to set it at a distance and make it its own object [4]. But whatever be the difficulties that lie in the way of this inquiry; whatever it be that keeps us so much in the dark to ourselves; sure I am that all the light we can let in upon our minds, all the acquaintance we can make with our

---

[1] I follow Coste's French Version in separating the 'Introduction' from the First Book, an arrangement more expressive of its relation to the *Essay* than that adopted in the other editions.

[2] 'The understanding' with Locke is that in man which enables him to have ideas; and to form intuitive, demonstrable, and probable propositions about what exists. It represents man in his ultimate relations to truth and error. Cf. note on p. 7.

[3] 'Scientia et potentia humana in idem coincidunt'—as Bacon puts it, *Nov. Org.* i. aph. 3.

[4] Locke assumes that 'human understanding' can be investigated as one among the other 'objects' which present themselves in the universe; but with this signal peculiarity, that it is itself the factor of knowledge; and also an object that is apprehended, not by any of the five senses, but introspectively, and therefore with difficulty, because all men are in early life accustomed to confine their attention to external objects, so that in introspection or reflection they have to resist habit.

INTROD.
—•+•—

own understandings, will not only be very pleasant, but bring us great advantage, in directing our thoughts in the search of other things[1].

Design.

2. This, therefore, being my purpose—to inquire into the original, certainty, and extent of *human knowledge*[2], together with the grounds and degrees of *belief, opinion,* and *assent*[2] ;— I shall not at present meddle with the physical consideration[3] of the mind ; or trouble myself to examine wherein its essence[4] consists ; or by what motions of our spirits[5] or alterations of our bodies we come to have any *sensation*[6] by our organs, or any *ideas*[6] in our understandings ; and whether those ideas[6] do in their formation, any or all of them, depend on matter or not[7]. These are speculations which, however

---

[1] 'All the sciences,' says Hume, 'have a relation to human nature, and are in some measure dependent on the science of Man; since they all lie under the cognizance ("understanding") of men, and are judged by their powers and faculties' (*Treatise of Human Nature,* Introduction). Human understanding, in short, is the common element in all the sciences.

[2] In Locke's use of words, *knowledge* usually means what is absolutely certain ; *judgment, belief, opinion,* and *assent,* on the contrary, refer to the sphere of probability, including all degrees from moral certainty down to the faintest likelihood. By the ambiguous term 'original' of knowledge he means the time and circumstances in which men begin to be percipient, and the sources from which a human understanding gradually derives its knowledge of facts.

'Physical consideration,' i. e. study of the understanding as expressed in terms of the physical organism, instead of by introspective consciousness of its actual operations.

[4] Its 'essence,' i. e. whether the real essence of mind in man is material or spiritual—whether God has endowed the human organism with self-con-

sciousness, or has given to each man a spiritual substance.

[5] 'Spirits'—the animal spirits which some ancient philosophers, and Des Cartes among the moderns, adduced in explanation of external perception, memory, and sensuous imagination.

[6] He connects 'sensations' with the organism, which must be observed by the senses ; 'ideas' with the understanding, which must be studied through self-consciousness. Cf. Bk. II. ch. i. § 23, on *sensation,* and Introd. § 8, on *idea.*

[7] He thus declines both, not only ontology, but also physiological psychology, of which Hobbes had given an example, and thus isolates the 'human understanding' from its organic relations, treating it as non-natural, at the point of view of physiological materialists. It were to be wished, Stewart remarks, that Locke had adhered more to this resolution. If he had done so, he would have been less disposed to seek the explanation of experience in organic functions, which themselves need to be explained, than in the ultimate constitution of reason— in the supernatural in man and in the universe.

curious and entertaining, I shall decline, as lying out of my way in the design I am now upon. It shall suffice to my present purpose, to consider the discerning faculties of a man, as they are employed about the objects [1] which they have to do with. And I shall imagine I have not wholly misemployed myself in the thoughts I shall have on this occasion, if, in this historical, plain method [2], I can give any account of the ways whereby our understandings come to attain those notions of things we have [3]; and can set down any measures of the certainty of our knowledge [4]; or the grounds of those persuasions [5] which are to be found amongst men, so various, different, and wholly contradictory; and yet asserted somewhere or other with such assurance and confidence, that he that shall take a view of the opinions of mankind, observe their opposition, and at the same time consider the fondness and devotion wherewith they are embraced, the resolution and eagerness wherewith they are maintained, may perhaps have reason to suspect, that either there is no such thing as truth at all, or that mankind hath no sufficient means to attain a certain knowledge of it [6].

3. It is therefore worth while to search out the bounds between opinion and knowledge; and examine by what measures, in things whereof we have no certain knowledge, we ought to regulate our assent and moderate our persuasion [7]. In order whereunto I shall pursue this following method :—

---

[1] 'Objects,' i. e. *ideas*, in Locke's language. It is not a critical analysis of the ultimate constitution of knowledge —an abstract epistemology—that he has in view, any more than it is an interpretation of human understanding in terms of its organism. It begins with an inquiry into the ideas or phenomena which provide material for the human understanding.

[2] This assumes that human understanding in its ultimate relations to its objects *can* be dealt with adequately when it is examined as an aggregate of phenomena, a succession of invisible events, to which the 'historical plain method' is applicable. 'Historical,'—

the method of observing what happens in time, in contrast to logical analysis of what is abstracted from time and place.

[3] See Bk. II.

[4] See Bk. IV. ch. i–xiii.

[5] See Bk. IV. ch. xiv–xx.

[6] Yet the motive spirit of the *Essay* is to disintegrate prejudices, not reaction against scepticism—to encourage free thought rather than constructive philosophy and conservation of belief. If Hume had preceded instead of following Locke, the latter might have looked at his subject more from the conservative point of view of Reid.

[7] This is the special subject of the Fourth Book.

First, I shall inquire into the original of those *ideas*, notions, or whatever else you please to call them, which a man observes, and is conscious to himself he has in his mind ; and the ways whereby the understanding comes to be furnished with them [1].

Secondly, I shall endeavour to show what *knowledge* the understanding hath by those ideas; and the certainty, evidence, and extent of it [2].

Thirdly, I shall make some inquiry into the nature and grounds of *faith* or *opinion* : whereby I mean that assent which we give to any proposition as true, of whose truth yet we have no certain knowledge.   And here we shall have occasion to examine the reasons and degrees of *assent* [3].

Useful to
know the
Extent of
our Com-
prehen-
sion.

4. If by this inquiry into the nature of the understanding, I can discover the powers thereof; how far they reach ; to what things they are in any degree proportionate [4] ; and where they fail us, I suppose it may be of use to prevail with the busy mind of man to be more cautious in meddling with things exceeding its comprehension ; to stop when it is at the utmost extent of its tether; and to sit down in a quiet ignorance of those things which, upon examination, are found to be beyond the reach of our capacities.   We should not then perhaps be so forward, out of an affectation of an universal knowledge, to raise questions, and perplex ourselves and others with disputes

[1] The subject of the Second Book, and negatively of the First.

[2] The basis and boundary of human 'knowledge,' or absolute certainty, is examined in the first thirteen chapters of the Fourth Book.

[3] 'Assent,' in its degrees of probability, from moral certainty down to the faintest presumption, is considered in the fourteenth and following chapters of the Fourth Book.   This Book is thus the culmination of the whole inquiry ; yet it has been left in the background by most critics of the *Essay*, who, with Cousin, assume that for Locke the study of the 'understanding' is the study of man's 'ideas,' or Idealogy ; instead of a study of man's 'intellectual 'perceptions' and probable 'presumptions,' concerning the *relations* of his ideas,—in which perceptions and presumptions alone, according to Locke, knowledge and probability consist.   His design, thus announced, is so far analogous to Kant's, although it is a history of the presented data, not a critical analysis of the rational constitution, of human understanding. Whether the work designed and executed by Locke should be called 'Logic,' or 'Metaphysics,' is a question, touched by Locke himself, in his correspondence with Molyneux.

[4] That human knowledge is neither Omniscience nor Nescience, but must, in all instances of it, be somewhere intermediate between the two, is the central lesson of the *Essay*.

about things to which our understandings are not suited ; and
of which we cannot frame in our minds any clear or distinct
perceptions, or whereof (as it has perhaps too often happened)
we have not any notions at all. If we can find out how far
the understanding can extend its view; how far it has faculties
to attain certainty ; and in what cases it can only judge and
guess, we may learn to content ourselves with what is attainable by us in this state.

5. For though the comprehension of our understandings
comes exceeding short of the vast extent of things, yet we
shall have cause enough to magnify the bountiful Author of
our being, for that proportion and degree of knowledge he has
bestowed on us, so far above all the rest of the inhabitants
of this our mansion [1]. Men have reason to be well satisfied
with what God hath thought fit for them, since he hath given
them (as St. Peter says) πάντα πρὸς ζωὴν καὶ εὐσέβειαν, whatsoever is necessary for the conveniences of life and information
of virtue ; and has put within the reach of their discovery, the
comfortable provision for this life, and the way that leads
to a better. How short soever their knowledge may come of
an universal or perfect comprehension of whatsoever is, it yet
secures their great concernments, that they have light enough
to lead them to the knowledge of their Maker, and the sight
of their own duties. Men may find matter sufficient to busy
their heads, and employ their hands with variety, delight,
and satisfaction, if they will not boldly quarrel with their
own constitution, and throw away the blessings their hands
are filled with, because they are not big enough to grasp
everything. We shall not have much reason to complain of
the narrowness of our minds, if we will but employ them
about what may be of use to us ; for of that they are
very capable. And it will be an unpardonable, as well as
childish peevishness, if we undervalue the advantages of our

---

[1] Locke always takes for granted
that an understanding of what exists
is in some degree possible for man,
varying in each individual according to
his intellectual development and oppor-
tunities of experience; while in all it
is an incomplete understanding, because dependent upon incomplete,
though it may be progressive, experience.

INTROD.
—◆◆—
knowledge, and neglect to improve it to the ends for which it was given us, because there are some things that are set out of the reach of it. It will be no excuse to an idle and untoward servant, who would not attend his business by candle light, to plead that he had not broad sunshine. The Candle that is set up in us[1] shines bright enough for all our purposes. The discoveries we can make with this ought to satisfy us; and we shall then use our understandings right, when we entertain all objects in that way and proportion[2] that they are suited to our faculties, and upon those grounds they are capable of being proposed to us ; and not peremptorily or intemperately require demonstration, and demand certainty, where probability only is to be had, and which is sufficient to govern all our concernments. If we will disbelieve everything, because we cannot certainly know all things, we shall do muchwhat as wisely as he who would not use his legs, but sit still and perish, because he had no wings to fly[3].

Knowledge of our Capacity a Cure of Scepticism and Idleness.
6. When we know our own strength, we shall the better know what to undertake with hopes of success ; and when we have well surveyed the *powers* of our own minds, and made some estimate what we may expect from them, we shall not be inclined either to sit still, and not set our thoughts on work at all, in despair of knowing anything ; nor on the other side, question everything, and disclaim all knowledge, because some things are not to be understood[3]. It is of great use to the sailor to know the length of his line, though

---

[1] 'The Spirit of man is the candle of the Lord' (Prov. xx. 27). This metaphor of the 'candle,' for the light of intuitive reason, is familiar to Whichcote, Locke's favourite preacher; also to Culverwell, who says that 'God hath breathed into all the sons of men reasonable souls, which may serve as so many candles to enlighten and direct them' (*Light of Nature*, p. 29), thus making the expression equivalent to the light of reason in human experience. It suggests the share of divine or universal reason, that is latent in man—as distinguished from the Supreme Reason, immanent to the universe—resplendent in what is self-evident, and in what is demonstrable ; glimmering through the transitory phenomena of sense in what is probable, where we have to grope our way.

[2] Here 'proportion' implies that man is not, and cannot become, omniscient, although each man may be progressively conquering the real for himself.

[3] Cf. *Conduct of Understanding*, § 39, on 'those who despond at the first difficulty.'

he cannot with it fathom all the depths of the ocean. It is
well he knows that it is long enough to reach the bottom, at
such places as are necessary to direct his voyage, and caution
him against running upon shoals that may ruin him. Our
business here is not to know all things, but those which
concern our conduct[1]. If we can find out those measures,
whereby a rational creature, put in that state in which man
is in this world, may and ought to govern his opinions, and
actions depending thereon, we need not to be troubled that
some other things escape our knowledge.

7. This was that which gave the first rise to this *Essay*
concerning the understanding. For I thought that the first
step towards satisfying several inquiries the mind of man was
very apt to run into, was, to take a survey of our own understandings, examine our own powers, and see to what things
they were adapted. Till that was done I suspected we
began at the wrong end, and in vain sought for satisfaction
in a quiet and sure possession of truths that most concerned
us, whilst we let loose our thoughts into the vast ocean of
Being; as if all that boundless extent were the natural
and undoubted possession of our understandings, wherein
there was nothing exempt from its decisions, or that escaped
its comprehension. Thus men, extending their inquiries
beyond their capacities, and letting their thoughts wander
into those depths where they can find no sure footing, it is no
wonder that they raise questions and multiply disputes, which,
never coming to any clear resolution, are proper only to continue and increase their doubts, and to confirm them at last in
perfect scepticism[2]. Whereas, were the capacities of our
understandings well considered, the extent of our knowledge
once discovered, and the horizon found which sets the bounds

---

[1] This might be the motto of the *Essay*, and the watchword of English philosophy, which characteristically seeks to keep in direct relation to life and conduct.

[2] We must remember that Locke's study of the constitution and reality of human knowledge, and of probability, is not in reaction against scepticism.

It is in reaction against irrationally imposed authority, empty verbalism, and neglect to educate and exercise individual judgment, and is meant to encourage by doubt the disintegration of traditional systems. That Locke lived before Hume, while Reid and Kant lived after him, is important to the interpreter of Locke.

INTROD.

between the enlightened and dark parts of things; between what is and what is not comprehensible by us, men would perhaps with less scruple acquiesce in the avowed ignorance of the one, and employ their thoughts and discourse with more advantage and satisfaction in the other [1].

What Idea stands for.

8. Thus much I thought necessary to say concerning the occasion of this Inquiry into human Understanding. But, before I proceed on to what I have thought on this subject, I must here in the entrance beg pardon of my reader for the frequent use of the word *idea*, which he will find in the following treatise. It being that term which, I think, serves best to stand for whatsoever is the *object* of the understanding when a man thinks, I have used it to express whatever is meant by *phantasm, notion, species,* or *whatever it is which the mind can be employed about in thinking* ; and I could not avoid frequently using it [2].

[1] It has been well said, that this passage expresses the inmost thought of Locke, and that ' in it may be found the key to his thoughts on all subjects.' Without being omniscient, man may be able to discover that he cannot know the universe fully—that his science, dependent on a limited experience, must always fall short of the intellectual ideal.

[2] *Idea* is thus, with Locke, a term of most comprehensive generality, embracing all that is in any way immediately apprehensible by the mind of man,—whether as a datum of external or internal sense, a sensuous image, or an individualized product of generalizing thought. It is difficult to find an adequate synonym, but perhaps *phenomenon* would be the nearest. Locke's first task is to analyse the complex ideas, or aggregated phenomena, which occupy the mind, into their simple or irreducible elements, showing how they arise in consciousness, and what modifications they undergo. Perceptions in sense, imaginations or phantasms, and abstract conceptions or notions, are all species of the Lockian idea; which must not be confounded with the supersensible archetypes called ideas by Plato, with Kant's transcendent ideas of Reason, or with the absolute idea of Hegel. Locke's *idea*, moreover, instead of being synonymous with *knowledge*, is contrasted with it, though among others, Mr. J. S. Mill confounds them (*Logic*, Bk. I, ch. vi. § 3). Ideas or phenomena are an indispensable *element* in knowledge : knowledge itself is the intuition or perception of their relations. Without this intuition or perception ideas are blind ; although by abstraction they may be considered apart from their relations in knowledge, in the way Locke considers them in the second books of the *Essay* ; or ordinary logic, in distinguishing concepts or terms from judgments or propositions. Locke explains and defends what he intends by this watchword of the *Essay*, in his controversy with Stillingfleet, by whom he was blamed for introducing a

I presume it will be easily granted me, that there are such *ideas* in men's minds : every one is conscious of them in himself; and men's words and actions will satisfy him that they are in others.

Our first inquiry then shall be,—how they come into the mind [1].

' new way of ideas.' ' Having thoughts and having ideas,' he says, 'with me mean the same thing; and as every one who uses words *intelligibly* is *conscious* of having ideas, the existence of ideas in the mind may reasonably be taken for granted.' In reply to Stillingfleet's taunt about reaching certainties and probabilities 'by ideas' being ' a new way of *not* doing so,' he says, that to have ideas only implies that we must have some meaning in any proposition which we entertain, whether the proposition be true or false. ' The new way of *ideas*,' he says, ' and the old way of *speaking intelligibly* was always, and will ever be, the same.' The objection to 'ideas' he takes to be a dispute about words ; but if any should prefer to say that *notions*—rather than ideas—are presupposed in all certainties and probabilities, he says that his only objection to this would be, that 'notion' is commonly used in a narrower application than the all-comprehensive meaning which he wants to express —' notion' being commonly confined to that class of ideas which he calls 'mixed modes.' ' I think it will not *sound* altogether so well to say, the *notion* of red, or the *notion* of a horse, as the *idea* of red or the *idea* of horse; but if any one thinks it will, I contend not ; I have no fondness for, nor antipathy to, any particular articulate sounds' (*Reply*, p. 69). To have an idea of anything is to perceive, or to imagine, to conceive it; to have no idea of it is, not to perceive, imagine, or conceive it at all. Locke speaks of ideas not only as ' objects' but as 'perceptions,' implying that in all cases an idea or phenomenon is, *as such*, dependent on a person being conscious of it. Whatever the mind is conscious of is an idea. Either its intrinsic reality, or its correspondence with objective reality, introduces considerations foreign to ideas considered in themselves, which is the point of view in the Second Book. Locke's ideas, moreover, whether simple or aggregated, are 'truly every one of them particular existences ; universality being but accidental to them, and consisting only on this, that the particular ideas about which it is are such as more than one particular thing can be represented by' (Bk. IV, ch. xvii. § 8).—*Phantasm, notion, species* are, with Locke, not co-extensive with, but subordinate to *idea*.— Cf. Descartes in his use of the term ' idea'; also Berkeley's distinction between *idea*, which he confines to sensuous presentation or representation, and *notion*, or meaning which cannot be sensuously represented ; and Hume's distinction of *impression*, or what is presented in sense, and *idea*, or what is represented in imagination.

[1] ' How they come into the mind,' i.e. under what conditions, and when, a human mind *becomes conscious, or* ' *thinks*,' *of anything*.

BOOK I

NEITHER PRINCIPLES NOR IDEAS ARE
INNATE

SYNOPSIS OF THE FIRST BOOK.

————•••————

THE First Book of the *Essay* is meant to open the way to Locke's account of the origin and history of human ideas, and the certain knowledge and probable presumptions to which they give rise,—by showing that men are *born* ignorant of everything. This is argued for on the grounds, (1) that there are no propositions, either speculative or practical, which are consciously received as true by every human being at birth; nor (2) even by all in whom reason is developed; (3) that to suppose aught to be innate in the mind, of which that mind is unconscious, involves a contradiction; (4) that although knowledge, when formed, is found to involve self-evident principles, their self-evidence does not prove (rather disproves) their innateness; and (5) that the hypothesis of their innateness is unnecessary, as the actual steps to knowledge and assent can be proved not to depend on our being born with a consciousness of the meaning and truth of any alleged innate principles. Moreover there could be no innate principles without innate ideas; but our ideas of identity, quantity, substance, and (above all) God, which (if any) must be innate, are plainly dependent on experience. The supposition of innate principles, thus at variance with facts and superfluous, has come into vogue because it ' eases the lazy from the pains of search,' and stops inquiry concerning all that is thus accepted, so that it becomes ' the principle of principles, that innate principles must not be questioned.'

CHAPTER I.

NO INNATE SPECULATIVE PRINCIPLES.

1. IT is an established opinion amongst some men[1], that there are in the understanding certain *innate principles*; some primary notions, κοιναὶ ἔννοιαι, characters, as it were stamped upon the mind of man; which the soul receives in its very first being, and brings into the world with it[2]. It would be

CHAP. I.
—♦—
The way shown
how we come by any

---

[1] Locke does not name the 'men' of 'innate principles' whose 'opinion' he proceeds to criticise; nor does he quote their words in evidence of what *they* intended by the opinion. He says (ch. ii. § 15) that after he had argued out objections to the 'established opinion,' his attention was directed to the arguments in its defence in the *De Veritate* of Lord Herbert, which thereupon he proceeds to controvert. From the first, Descartes, with whose writings he was early familiar, was probably in his view. According to Descartes there are three sources of ideas : ' Entre ces idées, *les unes semblent être nées avec moi* ; les autres être étrangères et venir de dehors; et les autres être faites et inventées par moi-même.' (*Méd.* iii. 7.) But even the 'idées nées avec moi' of Descartes were not regarded by him as in consciousness until 'experience' had evoked them from latency—a position which Locke's argument always fails to reach. Though Locke nowhere names More, Hale, or Cudworth, he might have found expressions of theirs which, on a superficial view, appear to countenance the *sort* of innateness which he attributes to the 'established opinion.' See Hume's *Inquiry concerning Human Understand-*

ing, in Note A, on 'innate ideas,' and Locke's 'loose sense of the word idea.'

[2] The impossibility of resolving the intellectual necessities, which govern and constitute knowledge and existence, into transitory data of sense ; or of explaining, by means of nature and its evolutions, the spiritual elements in human experience, which connect man with the supernatural, the infinite, the divine—has suggested that those elements, presupposed by experience, must have been *innate*, or born with the mind; thus potentially belonging to it, antecedently to all acquired knowledge. This hypothesis has found expression in many forms ; and it has waxed or waned, as the spiritual or the sensuous was most developed in the consciousness of the philosopher or of the age. Locke assails it in its crudest form, in which it is countenanced by no eminent advocate; according to which the ideas and principles which ultimately constitute knowledge are supposed to be held *consciously*, from birth, or even before it, in every human mind, being thus 'stamped' on us from the beginning, and 'brought into the world' with us. It is easy to refute this ; for it can be shown that there are no principles of which all men are aware as soon

CHAP. I.

——

Know-
ledge,
sufficient
to prove it
not innate.

sufficient to convince unprejudiced readers of the falseness of this supposition, if I should only show (as I hope I shall in the following parts of this Discourse) how men, barely by the use of their natural faculties [1], may attain to all the knowledge they have, without the help of any innate impressions ; and may arrive at certainty, without any such original notions or principles. For I imagine any one will easily grant that it would be impertinent to suppose the ideas of colours innate in a creature to whom God hath given sight, and a power to receive them by the eyes from external objects : and no less unreasonable would it be to attribute several truths to the impressions of nature, and innate characters, when we may observe in ourselves faculties fit to attain as easy and certain knowledge of them as if they were originally imprinted on the mind.

But because a man is not permitted without censure to follow his own thoughts in the search of truth, when they lead him ever so little out of the common road [2], I shall set down the reasons that made me doubt of the truth of that opinion, as an excuse for my mistake, if I be in one ; which I leave to be considered by those who, with me, dispose them-selves to embrace truth wherever they find it.

General
Assent the
great
Argument.

2. There is nothing more commonly [3] taken for granted than that there are certain *principles*, both *speculative* and *practical*, (for they speak of both), universally agreed upon by all mankind : which therefore, they argue, must needs be

as they are born, or even in which all mankind are agreed when they are adult. That data of experience are needed, to awaken what must otherwise be the slumbering poten-tialities of man's spiritual being ; and that human knowledge is the issue of sense when sense is combined with latent intellect, is an interpretation of the 'established opinion,' which Locke does not fairly contemplate.

[1] Locke recognises the *innateness* of 'faculties' in calling them 'natural'; but without examining whether any, and if so what, ideas and judgments

are (consciously or unconsciously) presupposed in a rational exercise of the innate faculties.

[2] 'Originally imprinted,' and which therefore, he concludes, must have been present consciously from the first, before our faculties were exer-cised in experience.

[3] This dogma of the conscious in-nateness of certain principles, or 'maxims,' is represented as the 'common road'; departure from which seems to Locke to give his *Essay* that air of 'novelty' to which he so often refers.

the constant impressions[1] which the souls of men receive in
their first beings, and which they bring into the world with
them, as necessarily and really as they do any of their
inherent faculties.

3. This argument, drawn from universal consent, has this Universal Consent proves nothing innate.
misfortune in it, that if it were true in matter of fact, that
there were certain truths wherein all mankind agreed, it
would not prove them innate, if there can be any other way
shown how men may come to that universal agreement, in
the things they do consent in, which I presume may be
done[2].

4. But, which is worse, this argument of universal consent, 'What is, is,' and 'It is impossible for the same Thing to be and not to be,' not universally assented to.
which is made use of to prove innate principles, seems to me
a demonstration that there are none such: because there are
none to which all mankind give an universal assent. I shall
begin with the speculative, and instance in those magnified
principles of demonstration, 'Whatsoever is, is,' and 'It is
impossible for the same thing to be and not to be'; which,
of all others, I think have the most allowed title to innate[3].

[1] 'Constant impressions,' i. e. of which there is a conscious impression in all human beings from birth, and about which all, even infants and idiots, are agreed.

[2] Conscious consent on the part of every human being cannot be alleged on behalf of any abstract principle, as Locke is easily able to show. There is no proposition which some one has not been found to deny. A better criterion of the supernatural or divine, in man and in the universe, than this of 'universal consent,' which Locke makes so much of, is found, when it is shown,—that the full and adequate exercise of our faculties in experience necessarily presupposes principles of which the mass of mankind may be only dimly conscious, or wholly unconscious. Locke ignores the main issue; and when he explains his meaning is found nearer than he supposes to those who hold the innateness of reason in experience.

He acknowledges innateness of faculty. Also that knowledge involves and is based upon what is self-evident is a prominent lesson of the Fourth Book. 'That there can be any knowledge without self-evident propositions,' he assures Stillingfleet that he is so far from denying, 'that I am accused by your lordship for requiring more such in demonstration than you think necessary' (*Third Letter*, p. 264). 'I contend for the usefulness and necessity of self-evident propositions in all certainty, whether of intuition or demonstration' (p. 286). 'I make self-evident propositions necessary to certainty, and found all knowledge or certainty in them' (p. 340).

[3] These two, called by logicians the principles of *identity* and of *contradiction*, are again treated of in Bk. IV. ch. vii, where his distinction between *consciousness of them at birth*, which he denies, and the *gradual discovery*

CHAP. I.

—+—

These have so settled a reputation of maxims universally received, that it will no doubt be thought strange if any one should seem to question it. But yet I take liberty to say, that these propositions are so far from having an universal assent, that there are a great part of mankind to whom they are not so much as known.

Not on the Mind naturally imprinted, because not known to Children, Idiots, &c.

5. For, first, it is evident, that all children and idiots have not the least apprehension or thought of them. And the want of that is enough to destroy that universal assent [1] which must needs be the necessary concomitant of all innate truths: it seeming to me near a contradiction to say, that there are truths imprinted on the soul, which it perceives or understands not: imprinting, if it signify anything, being nothing else but the making certain truths to be perceived. For to imprint anything on the mind without the mind's perceiving it, seems to me hardly intelligible. If therefore children and idiots have souls, have minds, with those impressions upon them, *they* must unavoidably perceive them, and necessarily know and assent to these truths; which since they do not, it is evident that there are no such impressions. For if they are not notions naturally imprinted, how can they be innate? and if they are notions imprinted, how can they be unknown? To say a notion is imprinted on the mind, and yet at the same time to say, that the mind is ignorant of it, and never yet took notice of it, is to make this impression nothing. No proposition can be said to be in the mind which it never yet knew, which it was never yet conscious of [2]. For if any one may, then, by the same

of their self-evidence, which he recognises, is illustrated. The second of the two is the axiom of axioms with Aristotle, itself indemonstrable because presupposed in all proof.

[1] 'Assent,' i. e. actual or conscious, not potential or unconscious, although the whole question turns upon the latter. In Bk. IV. he confines 'assent' to judgments of probability exclusively, thus contrasting it with 'knowledge' or absolute certainty.

[2] The argument in this section assumes that ideas cannot be held mentally in a latent or unconscious state, that there cannot be impressions made on the mind without accompanying consciousness of them, a mental impression and a consciousness of it being regarded as identical. That there may be *conditions,* implied in the constitution of reason, to which our ideas, when they do emerge in consciousness, must conform, by necessity of reason, is a conception foreign to his view. Locke argues that no idea can be said to be 'in the mind' of which that mind is not either actually

reason, all propositions that are true, and the mind is capable
ever of assenting to, may be said to be in the mind, and to be
imprinted : since, if any one can be said to be in the mind,
which it never yet knew, it must be only because it is capable
of knowing it; and so the mind is of all truths it ever shall
know. Nay, thus truths may be imprinted on the mind
which it never did, nor ever shall know ; for a man may live
long, and die at last in ignorance of many truths which his
mind was capable of knowing[1], and that with certainty. So
that if the capacity of knowing be the natural impression
contended for, all the truths a man ever comes to know will,
by this account, be every one of them innate; and this great
point will amount to no more, but only to a very improper
way of speaking; which, whilst it pretends to assert the
contrary, says nothing different from those who deny innate
principles. For nobody, I think, ever denied that the mind
was capable of knowing several truths. The capacity, they
say, is innate ; the knowledge acquired. But then to what
end such contest for certain innate maxims? If truths can
be imprinted on the understanding without being perceived,
I can see no difference there can be between any truths the
mind is *capable* of knowing in respect of their original : they
must all be innate or all adventitious : in vain shall a man go
about to distinguish them[2]. He therefore that talks of
innate notions in the understanding, cannot (if he intend
thereby any distinct sort of truths) mean such truths to be in
the understanding as it never perceived, and is yet wholly
ignorant of. For if these words 'to be in the understanding'
have any propriety, they signify to be understood. So that
to be in the understanding, and not to be understood ; to be
in the mind and never to be perceived, is all one as to say

percipient, or through memory capable
of becoming percipient.

[1] Locke never asks, as Kant afterwards did, what this 'capacity,' which
he allows to be latent or innate, necessarily implies.

[2] Not so; if the primitive necessities
which constitute reason in us and in
the universe can be distinguished by
marks from the empirical generalisations of sense, and from generalised
sense data. Not so; if there are ideas
(concepts) which, by an intellectual
necessity, on certain occasions in experience, form themselves in us, without our forming them by tentative
generalisation. The question still remains—What does a capability of
having experience imply?

CHAP. I. anything is and is not in the mind or understanding. If therefore these two propositions, 'Whatsoever is, is,' and ' It is impossible for the same thing to be and not to be,' are by nature imprinted, children cannot be ignorant of them: infants, and all that have souls, must necessarily have them in their understandings, know the truth of them, and assent to it [1].

That men know them when they come to the Use of Reason answered.

6. To avoid this, it is usually answered, that all men know and assent to them, *when they come to the use of reason* [2]; and this is enough to prove them innate. I answer:

7. Doubtful expressions, that have scarce any signification, go for clear reasons to those who, being prepossessed, take not the pains to examine even what they themselves say. For, to apply this answer with any tolerable sense to our present purpose, it must signify one of these two things: either that as soon as men come to the use of reason these supposed native inscriptions come to be known and observed by them; or else, that the use and exercise of men's reason, assists them in the discovery of these principles, and certainly makes them known to them.

If Reason discovered them, that would not prove them innate.

8. If they mean, that by the use of reason men may discover these principles, and that this is sufficient to prove them innate; their way of arguing will stand thus, viz. that whatever truths reason can certainly discover to us, and make us firmly assent to, those are all naturally imprinted on the mind; since that universal assent, which is made the mark of them, amounts to no more but this,—that by the use of reason we are capable to come to a certain knowledge [3] of and assent to them; and, by this means, there will be no

[1] Universal consent may mean that any who do think such propositions intelligently *must* think them in one and the same way; not that every human being does in fact think them with conscious intelligence. In any other meaning universal consent could be no criterion of reason being innate or latent in us, and in the universe; for there are no propositions to which all human beings, including infants, give conscious consent.

[2] Locke often uses 'reason' for reasoning; so here he means, when they come to the conscious use of the deductive faculty, which elicits previously unknown propositions from those already known.

[3] 'Knowledge' and 'assent,' here used convertibly, are in Bk. IV distinguished emphatically—self-evidence and demonstrable evidence constituting knowledge, while assent is determined by weighing probabilities.

difference between the maxims of the mathematicians, and theorems they deduce from them : all must be equally allowed innate [1]; they being all discoveries made by the use of reason, and truths that a rational creature may certainly come to know, if he apply his thoughts rightly that way.

9. But how can these men think the use of reason necessary to discover principles that are supposed innate, when reason (if we may believe them) is nothing else but the faculty of deducing unknown truths from principles or propositions that are already known? That certainly can never be thought innate which we have need of reason to discover ; unless, as I have said, we will have all the certain truths that reason ever teaches us, to be innate [2]. We may as well think the use of reason necessary to make our eyes discover visible objects, as that there should be need of reason, or the exercise thereof, to make the understanding see what is originally engraven on it, and cannot be in the understanding before it be perceived by it. So that to make reason discover those truths thus imprinted, is to say, that the use of reason discovers to a man what he knew before: and if men have those innate impressed truths originally, and before the use of reason, and yet are always ignorant of them till they come to the use of reason, it is in effect to say, that men know and know them not at the same time [3].

It is false that Reason discovers them.

10. It will here perhaps be said that mathematical demonstrations, and other truths that are not innate, are not assented to as soon as proposed, wherein they are distinguished from these maxims and other innate truths. I shall have occasion

No use made of reasoning in the discovery of these two maxims.

---

[1] As Leibniz held, who argued that all arithmetic and all geometry are virtually innate, and may (with effort) be found in the mind ; as Plato showed when he made Socrates oblige a child to admit abstract truths without telling him anything. The innate knowledge of Plato and Leibniz is characterised, not by its independence of, and priority to, mental development in the individual, but by its intuited necessity and universality *after* it has been awakened into consciousness, in the exercise of intuitive and discursive reason.

[2] Not so ; if the criterion of innateness is sought, not in the process, but in the intellectual characteristics of the product.

[3] The unconscious presence of principles which can be proved (by philosophical analysis) to be virtually presupposed in our certainties, and even in our assent to probability, is here overlooked.

to speak of assent upon the first proposing, more particularly by and by. I shall here only, and that very readily, allow, that these maxims and mathematical demonstrations are in this different : that the one have need of reason, using of proofs, to make them out and to gain our assent ; but the other, as soon as understood, are, without any the least reasoning, embraced and assented to[1]. But I withal beg leave to observe, that it lays open the weakness of this subterfuge, which requires the use of reason[2] for the discovery of these general truths : since it must be confessed that in their discovery there is no use made of reasoning at all. And I think those who give this answer will not be forward to affirm that the knowledge of this maxim, ' That it is impossible for the same thing to be and not to be,' is a deduction of our reason. For this would be to destroy that bounty of nature they seem so fond of, whilst they make the knowledge of those principles to depend on the labour of our thoughts. For all reasoning[3] is search, and casting about, and requires pains and application. And how can it with any tolerable sense be supposed, that what was imprinted by nature, as the foundation and guide of our reason, should need the use of reason to discover it ?

And if there were this would prove them not innate.

11. Those who will take the pains to reflect with a little attention on the operations of the understanding, will find that this ready assent of the mind to[4] some truths, depends not, either on native inscription, or the use of reason, but on a faculty of the mind quite distinct from both of them, as we shall see hereafter[5]. Reason, therefore, having nothing to do

[1] That is, they are self-evidently true, but not what Locke means by innate ; for he here argues that self-evidence in a principle is no proof of its innateness.

[2] ' Reason,' i. e. reasoning, which is not needed for discovering the truth of self-evident mathematical axioms.

[3] On the contrary, philosophical reasoning and analysis are needed for quickening into distinct consciousness, in their abstract form, those conscious principles of reason which are logically presupposed in all reasoning and infer-

ence. This must in the nature of the case be posterior, not anterior, to the exercise of intellect in experience.

[4] Rather *intellectual necessity to perceive*, of which only the developed intelligence becomes conscious. 'Assent' here again used for rational perception, instead of the presumed probability to which the term is confined in Bk. IV.

[5] Cf. Bk. IV. ch. ii. § 1 ; ch. vii. § 19 ; ch. xvii. §§ 14, 17, in which the truths referred to are shown to be ' perceived at first sight, by bare intuition,' as soon as the mind, sufficiently educated to per-

in procuring our assent to these maxims, if by saying, that 'men know and assent to them, when they come to the use of reason,' be meant, that the use of reason assists us in the knowledge of these maxims, it is utterly false; and were it true, would prove them not to be innate.

12. If by knowing and assenting to them 'when we come to the use of reason,' be meant, that this is the time when they come to be taken notice of by the mind[1]; and that as soon as children come to the use of reason, they come also to know and assent to these maxims; this also is false and frivolous. First, it is false; because it is evident these maxims are not in the mind so early as the use of reason; and therefore the coming to the use of reason is falsely assigned as the time of their discovery. How many instances of the use of reason may we observe in children, a long time before they have any knowledge of this maxim, 'That it is impossible for the same thing to be and not to be?' And a great part of illiterate people and savages pass many years, even of their rational age, without ever thinking on this and the like general propositions. I grant, men come not to the knowledge of these general and more abstract truths, which are thought innate, till they come to the use of reason; and I add, nor then neither. Which is so, because, till after they come to the use of reason, those general abstract ideas are not framed in the mind, about which those general maxims are, which are mistaken for innate principles, but are indeed discoveries made and verities introduced and brought into the mind by the same way, and discovered by the same steps, as several other propositions, which nobody was ever so extravagant as to suppose innate[2]. This I hope to make

---

ceive them, 'turns its view that way.' Truths thus *intuited* (not inferred) are there presented by Locke as the foundation of 'all the certainty and evidence of all our knowledge'—as 'known by a superior and higher evidence than reasoning,' and generalisation by calculated experiments. They are at first apprehended as embodied in concrete instances, and then in their abstract expression.

[1] That is, if their being 'innate' means, as with Locke it does, that we were all born with a conscious knowledge of them, and in their abstract expression too; his own fundamental principle being, that we are born destitute of all knowledge and belief, so that his task is, to show how we gradually acquire more or less of both.

[2] Though it is only gradually, and by dint of abstract thinking, that the

CHAP. I.
—◆—

plain in the sequel of this Discourse. I allow therefore, a necessity that men should come to the use of reason before they get the knowledge of those general truths; but deny that men's coming to the use of reason is the time of their discovery.

By this they are not distinguished from other knowable Truths.

13. In the mean time it is observable, that this saying, that men know and assent to these maxims 'when they come to the use of reason,' amounts in reality of fact to no more but this,—that they are never known nor taken notice of before the use of reason, but may possibly be assented to some time after, during a man's life; but when is uncertain. And so may all other knowable truths, as well as these; which therefore have no advantage nor distinction from others by this note of being known when we come to the use of reason[1]; nor are thereby proved to be innate, but quite the contrary.

If coming to the Use of Reason

14. But, secondly, were it true that the precise time of their being known and assented to[2] were, when men come to

conscious apprehension of those abstract axioms of identity and contradiction is reached, in the individual mind,—yet when one does realise them, it is with a sense of their absolute intellectual necessity, which is wanting in the case of tentative inductions from experience. And this it is that makes them be regarded as somehow innate in the reason that is also innate in things, thus making real inference, deductive and inductive, possible.

[1] Their 'note' is *not* properly alleged to consist in their becoming known as soon as one comes to the use of reason; for they are to be tested by the fact that, as soon as there is consciousness of them, there is an involved perception of their *absolute* necessity,—in contrast to the *conditional* 'necessity' of generalisations which depend merely upon the custom of experience.

[2] Throughout this whole argument it is forgotten that in this matter the question of interest in philosophy is

not one of *time* at all,—not of *when* individuals become aware of what, if apprehended, is seen to be self-evidently true. The philosophical question about innateness, as Shaftesbury well puts it, really is—'whether the constitution of man be such that, *being adult and grown up*,' certain ideas do not '*infallibly and necessarily* spring up in consciousness.' And Locke grants this when he replies,—that 'there *are* certain propositions which, *though the soul from the beginning, when a man is born, does not* [consciously] *know*, yet, by assistance from the outward senses, and the help of some previous cultivation, it may *afterwards come self-evidently, or with a demonstrable necessity, to know the truth of*, is no more than what I have affirmed in my First Book.' Innateness, as argued by Locke, means original *conscious* possession of such truths, without the laborious intellectual effort that must be put forth before they are recognised in their philosophical abstraction.

CHAP. I.

—••—

were the
Time of
their Dis-
covery, it
would not
prove them
innate.

the use of reason; neither would that prove them innate. This way of arguing is as frivolous as the supposition itself is false. For, by what kind of logic will it appear that any notion is originally by nature imprinted in the mind in its first constitution, because it comes first to be observed and assented to when a faculty of the mind, which has quite a distinct province, begins to exert itself? And therefore the coming to the use of speech, if it were supposed the time that these maxims are first assented to, (which it may be with as much truth as the time when men come to the use of reason,) would be as good a proof that they were innate, as to say they are innate because men assent to them when they come to the use of reason. I agree then with these men of innate principles, that there is no knowledge of these general and self-evident maxims [1] in the mind, till it comes to the exercise of reason: but I deny that the coming to the use of reason is the precise time when they are first taken notice of; and if that were the precise time, I deny that it would prove them innate. All that can with any truth be meant by this proposition, that men 'assent to them when they come to the use of reason,' is no more but this,—that the making of general abstract ideas, and the understanding of general names, being a concomitant of the rational faculty, and growing up with it, children commonly get not those general ideas, nor learn the names that stand for them, till, having for a good while exercised their reason about familiar and more particular ideas, they are, by their ordinary discourse and actions with others, acknowledged to be capable of rational conversation [2]. If assenting to these maxims, when

---

It is the need for this effort that he wants to show. He is really arguing, throughout the First Book, for the exercise of individual judgment, and against blind submission to dogmas. Hume hardly sees this when he pronounces the discussion 'frivolous, if by innate Locke meant contemporary to our birth; nor is it worth while to inquire *at what time thinking begins*, whether before, at, or after our birth.' (*Inquiry*, Note A.)

[1] He still refers indefinitely to 'these men of innate principles.' Here, too, the very maxims that are denied to be 'innate' are expressly called 'self-evident.'

[2] The axioms of identity and contradiction, which Locke takes as his examples of speculative principles alleged to be consciously innate, are of all others the most abstract, and therefore among the latest, to be recognised by the mind, which must nevertheless

CHAP. I.   men come to the use of reason, can be true in any other
——   sense, I desire it may be shown; or at least, how in this, or
any other sense, it proves them innate.

The Steps   15. The senses at first let in *particular* ideas, and furnish
by which   the yet empty cabinet[1], and the mind by degrees growing
the Mind

have always virtually assumed their
truth. It is this *unconscious assumption* that his opponents offer, as evidence of the principles named being
' universally' assented to,—in a potential or implied assent.

[1] In this and the two following
sentences Locke anticipates his own
account, in the Second Book, of the
origin and elaboration of *ideas*, which
' are all at first particular,' their
generalisations being moreover only
' accidental.' The ' empty cabinet '
represents the mind before its latent
faculties have been quickened into
exercise in experience. The ' sheet
of blank paper' and the 'waxed tablet'
are misleading metaphors, which, after
Aristotle and others, he elsewhere employs. In his endeavour to emphasise
the difference between the continuous
effort involved in the formation of
human knowledge, and the perfect
knowledge eternally present in the
Supreme Mind,—thus enforcing his
favourite lesson of an active private
judgment in man,—he fails to see that
to attribute to human knowledge innate
elements, and also data of experience, is not contradictory, since all
knowledge may involve *both* elements.
But Locke might have unconsciously in
view what his favourite Hooker thus expresses :—' In the matter of knowledge
there is between the angels of God
and the children of men this difference :—angels already have full and
complete knowledge in the highest
degree that can be imparted to them ;
men, if we view them in their spring,
are at first without understanding or
knowledge at all. Nevertheless, from
this utter vacuity, *they grow by degrees*,
till they come at length to be even as

the angels themselves are. That which
agreeth to the one *now*, the other shall
attain unto *in the end*; they are not so
far disjoined and severed but that they
come at length to meet. The soul of
man being therefore *at the first as a
book wherein nothing is, and yet all
things may be imprinted*, we are to
search by what steps and degrees it
riseth into perfection of knowledge'
(*Eccles. Polit.* Bk. I. § 6). Leibniz
takes the analogy of the marble to
illustrate the latent presence in experience of ideas and principles which
are influential without being recognised :—' Je me suis servi aussi de la
comparaison d'une pierre de marbre
qui a des veines plutôt que d'une pierre
de marbre tout unie ou de tablettes
vides, c'est-à-dire de ce qui s'appelle
tabula rasa chez les philosophes. Car
si l'âme ressemblait à ces tablettes
vides, les vérités seraient en nous
comme la figure d'Hercule est dans
un marbre *quand le marbre est tout à
fait indifférent à recevoir ou cette figure
ou quelque autre*. Mais s'il y avait des
veines dans la pierre qui marquassent
*la figure d'Hercule préférablement à
d'autres figures*, cette pierre y serait
plus déterminée, et *Hercule y serait
comme inné en quelque façon*, quoiqu'il
fallût du *travail pour decouvrir ces veines,
et pour les nettoyer par la polissure, en
retranchant ce qui les empêche de
paraître*. C'est ainsi que les idées et
les vérités nous sont innées, comme
des inclinations, des dispositions, des
habitudes, ou des virtualités na-
turelles, et non pas comme des actions ;
quoique ces virtualités soient toujours
accompagnées de quelques actions,
souvent insensibles, qui y répondent.'
(*Nouveaux Essais*, Avant Propos.)

familiar with some of them, they are lodged in the memory, and names got to them. Afterwards, the mind proceeding further, abstracts them, and by degrees learns the use of general names [1]. In this manner the mind comes to be furnished with ideas and language, the *materials* about which to exercise its discursive faculty. And the use of reason becomes daily more visible, as these materials that give it employment increase [2]. But though the having of general ideas and the use of general words and reason usually grow together, yet I see not how this any way proves them innate. The knowledge of some truths, I confess, is very early in the mind; but in a way that shows them not to be innate. For, if we will observe, we shall find it still to be about ideas, not innate, but acquired; it being about those first which are imprinted by external things, with which infants have earliest to do, which make the most frequent impressions on their senses [3]. In ideas thus got, the mind discovers that some agree and others differ, probably as soon as it has any use of memory; as soon as it is able to retain and perceive distinct ideas. But whether it be then or no, this is certain, it does so long before it has the use of words; or comes to that which we commonly call ' the use of reason.' For a child knows as certainly before it can speak the difference between the ideas of sweet and bitter (i.e. that sweet is not bitter), as it knows afterwards (when it comes to speak) that wormwood and sugarplums are not the same thing [4].

[1] The process of human experience is here described as presenting three stages—perception or acquisition, retention, and elaboration of its material.

[2] But the intellectual authority of a principle when evolved does not depend upon its natural genesis or evolution. That a judgment should arise in one's consciousness *under natural law* does not disprove its intrinsic necessity and universality, which reflective analysis may detect after it has thus arisen.

[3] ' Les idées qui viennent des sens,' says Leibniz, ' sont confuses, et les vérités qui en dépendent le sont aussi, au moins en partie ; au lieu que les idées intellectuelles, et les vérités qui en dépendent sont distinctes, et ni les unes ni les autres n'ont point leur origine des sens ; quoiqu'il soit vrai que nous n'y penserions jamais sans les sens.' (*Nouv. Ess.* I. i.)

[4] That ' sweet is not bitter' involves recognition, in data of sense, of the abstract principle, that it is impossible for the same thing to be and not to be ' at the same time.' It is true that this concrete embodiment of it in a particular example is more evident to an uneducated mind than the highly abstract maxim or axiom which

Chap. I.

⟶

Assent to supposed innate truths depends on having clear and distinct ideas of what their terms mean, and not on their innateness.

16. A child knows not that three and four are equal to seven, till he comes to be able to count seven, and has got the name and idea of equality; and then, upon explaining those words, he presently assents to, or rather perceives the truth of that proposition. But neither does he then readily assent because it is an innate truth, nor was his assent wanting till then because he wanted the use of reason; but the truth of it appears to him as soon as he has settled in his mind the clear and distinct ideas that these names stand for. And then he knows the truth of that proposition upon the same grounds and by the same means, that he knew before that a rod and a cherry are not the same thing; and upon the same grounds also that he may come to know afterwards 'That it is impossible for the same thing to be and not to be,' as shall be more fully shown hereafter[1]. So that the later it is before any one comes to have those general ideas about which those maxims are; or to know the signification of those general terms that stand for them; or to put together in his mind the ideas they stand for; the later also will it be before he comes to assent to those maxims;—whose terms, with the ideas they stand for, being no more innate than those of a cat or a weasel, he must stay till time and observation have acquainted him with them; and then he will be in a capacity to know the truth of these maxims, upon the first occasion that shall make him put together those ideas in his mind[2], and observe whether they agree or disagree, according as is expressed in those propositions. And therefore it is that a man knows that eighteen and nineteen are equal to thirty-seven, by the same self-evidence that he knows one and two to be equal to three: yet a child knows this not so soon as the other; not for want of the use of reason, but because the ideas the words eighteen,

the embodiment logically presupposes, when its principle remains unexpressed in words or in consciousness, like an unexpressed premiss in ordinary reasoning.

[1] In Bk. IV. ch. ii. § 1, and ch. vii. § 9, as well as in other places, the need of time, and the active continuous exercise of our faculties, as con-

ditions indispensable to a conscious intuition of the self-evidence of these and other truths, are insisted on.

[2] They are thus distinguished from inductive generalisations, which presuppose calculated observations, and after all are only probabilities that may be modified by unexpected conditions.

nineteen, and thirty-seven stand for, are not so soon got, as CHAP. I.
those which are signified by one, two, and three [1].

17. This evasion therefore of general assent when men come Assenting
to the use of reason, failing as it does, and leaving no difference - as soon as
proposed
between those supposed innate and other truths that are after- and under-
wards acquired and learnt, men have endeavoured to secure an proves
stood,
universal assent to those they call maxims [3], by saying, they them not
innate.
are generally assented to as soon as proposed, and the terms
they are proposed in understood: seeing all men, even children,
as soon as they hear and understand the terms, assent to these
propositions, they think it is sufficient to prove them innate.
For, since men never fail after they have once understood the
words, to acknowledge them for undoubted truths, they would
infer, that certainly these propositions were first lodged in the
understanding, which, without any teaching, the mind, at the
very first proposal immediately closes with and assents to, and
after that never doubts again.

18. In answer to this, I demand whether ready assent given If such an
to a proposition, upon first hearing and understanding the Assent be
a Mark of
terms, be a certain mark of an innate principle [4]? If it be not, Innate,
such a general assent is in vain urged as a proof of them: if then
'that one
it be said that it is a mark of innate, they must then allow all and two
such propositions to be innate which are generally assented are equal
to as soon as heard, whereby they will find themselves plenti- that Sweet-
to three,
fully stored with innate principles. For upon the same ground, Bitterness is not

---

[1] And until the 'ideas' are got, the
judgments into which they enter cannot be formed; while, on the other
hand, *mere idea* (as the term is understood by Locke) cannot be regarded
as knowledge, as long as it is viewed
in abstraction from *judgment*, which
is the unit of knowledge and belief.

[2] No 'difference' in the time at
which the individual consciously recognises and accepts them. But this
is quite consistent with difference in the
intellectual character of the acceptance,
in each case when it does take place,
as Locke allows in the next sentence.

[3] Cf. Bk. IV. ch. vii.

[4] In what follows there is still failure
to distinguish between the later philosophical analysis, in which the mind
consciously discerns, as necessarily
true, abstract principles which are
logically presupposed in knowledge
and assent, and the earlier unconscious proceeding upon those
principles. Also we must distinguish
between the innumerable concrete examples in which self-evident truths
are embodied, and the abstract philosophical expression of the same
truths.

CHAP. I.

ness,' and a thousand the like, must be innate.

viz. of assent at first hearing and understanding the terms, that men would have those maxims pass for innate, they must also admit several propositions about numbers to be innate; and thus, that one and two are equal to three, that two and two are equal to four, and a multitude of other the like propositions in numbers, that everybody assents to at first hearing and understanding the terms, must have a place amongst these innate axioms. Nor is this the prerogative of numbers alone, and propositions made about several of them; but even natural philosophy, and all the other sciences, afford propositions which are sure to meet with assent as soon as they are understood. That 'two bodies cannot be in the same place' is a truth that nobody any more sticks at than at these maxims, that 'it is impossible for the same thing to be and not to be,' that 'white is not black,' that 'a square is not a circle,' that 'bitterness is not sweetness[1].' These and a million of such other propositions, as many at least as we have distinct ideas of, every man in his wits, at first hearing, and knowing what the names stand for, must necessarily assent to[2]. If these men will be true to their own rule, and have assent at first hearing and understanding the terms to be a mark of innate, they must allow not only as many innate propositions as men have distinct ideas, but as many as men can make propositions wherein different ideas are denied one of another. Since every proposition wherein one different idea is denied of another, will as certainly find assent at first hearing and understanding the terms as this general one, 'It is impossible

[1] The proposition, *the sweet is not the bitter*, is not innate, says Leibniz, according to the proper meaning of the term innate truth. 'Car les sentiments de *doux* et de l'*amer* viennent des sens externes. Ainsi c'est un conclusion *melée* (*hybrida conclusio*), ou l'axiome est appliqué à une vérité sensible' (*Nouv. Ess.*).

[2] Again, he contrasts self-evident maxims with empirical generalisations, while denying that the former are 'innate,' because, on the one hand, not patent in the consciousness of all,

and, on the other hand, incapable of being latent, inasmuch as for the mind to possess an idea or a principle of which it is unconscious is assumed to be a contradiction in terms. Here Leibniz asks, why, since acquired knowledge may, as Locke acknowledges, be latent in *memory*,—why may not nature have in like manner included in the primary constitution of the mind ideas on which the constitution of knowledge necessarily depends? For a reference to memory cf. ch. iii. § 20.

for the same thing to be and not to be,' or that which is the
foundation of it. and is the easier understood of the two,
' The same is not different' ; by which account they will have
legions of innate propositions of this one sort, without men-
tioning any other [1]. But, since no proposition can be innate
unless the *ideas* about which it is be innate, this will be to
suppose all our ideas of colours, sounds, tastes, figure, &c.,
innate, than which there cannot be anything more opposite
to reason and experience [2]. Universal and ready assent upon
hearing and understanding the terms is, I grant, a mark of
self-evidence ; but self-evidence, depending not on innate
impressions, but on something else, (as we shall show hereafter [3],) belongs to several propositions which nobody was yet
so extravagant as to pretend to be innate.

19. Nor let it be said, that those more particular self-evident
propositions, which are assented to at first hearing, as that
' one and two are equal to three,' that ' green is not red,' &c.,
are received as the consequences of those more universal propositions which are looked on as innate principles; since any
one, who will but take the pains to observe what passes in the
understanding, will certainly find that these, and the like
less general propositions, are certainly known, and firmly
assented to by those who are utterly ignorant of those
more general maxims ; and so, being earlier in the mind
than those (as they are called) first [4] principles, cannot owe

[margin note: Such less general Propositions known before these universal Maxims.]

---

[1] As Leibniz says, all arithmetic and
all geometry are virtually innate or in
the mind.

[2] There is.here again confusion of
the perceived truth of an intellectual
principle in its most abstract form, and
perception of the truth of propositions
which ultimately depend upon it, as
well as perception of its variable and
contingent embodiments. This is
further exaggerated by Hume, when
he asserts that, ' if innate be equivalent
to natural, then *all* the perceptions
and ideas of the mind must be allowed
to be innate' (*Inquiry*, Note A)—at
least if this be taken in the sense
Hume seems to intend.

[3] Cf. Bk. IV. ch. ii. § 1, &c. Again,
so far from identifying them in a
common condemnation, he contrasts
' innate' and ' self-evident '—rejecting
innateness of knowledge, because 'we
are all born ignorant of everything';
and arguing for self-evidence, as that on
which all the certainty of all our knowledge ultimately depends, and which,
in the intellectually awakened mind, is
' perceived' as the eye perceives light,
only by being directed towards it.

[4] But they are not 'first' because
soonest apprehended by the individual
mind, but because presupposed in the
nature of things, or in reason, and so
first in logical order.

One and
one equal
to Two,
&c., not
general
nor useful
answered.

to them the assent wherewith they are received at first hearing [1].

20. If it be said, that these propositions, viz. 'two and two are equal to four,' 'red is not blue,' &c., are not general maxims, nor of any great use, I answer, that makes nothing to the argument of universal assent upon hearing and understanding. For, if that be the certain mark of innate, whatever proposition can be found that receives general assent as soon as heard and understood, that must be admitted for an innate proposition, as well as this maxim, 'That it is impossible for the same thing to be and not to be,' they being upon this ground equal. And as to the difference of being more general, that makes this maxim more remote from being innate [2]; those general and abstract ideas being more strangers to our first apprehensions than those of more particular self-evident propositions ; and therefore it is longer before they are admitted and assented to by the growing [3] understanding. And as to the usefulness of these magnified maxims, that perhaps will not be found so great as is generally conceived, when it comes in its due place to be more fully considered [4].

These
Maxims
not being
known
sometimes
till pro-
posed,

21. But we have not yet done with 'assenting to propositions at first hearing and understanding their terms.' It is fit we first take notice that this, instead of being a mark that they are innate, is a proof of the contrary ; since it supposes that several, who understand and know other things, are ignorant

[1] Notwithstanding, the 'more general' are *so* presupposed logically in the less general and particular propositions, that the former (though often only latent or unconsciously held) could not be denied without involving denial of the latter. We rest on them as we rest on suppressed sumptions in enthymemes, in which the force of the conclusion is determined by what is suppressed or latent.

[2] In Locke's meaning of innateness or apriority.

[3] That a human understanding of the innate, or of any part of it, must be a growth,—the issue of labour and a tentative experience, and that

none of it is born with us, is the lesson intended by Locke in this controversy against innate ideas and principles.

[4] See Bk. IV. ch. vii. The reason of the less general truths is found in the more abstract, and in that sense the more simple, which, as Leibniz puts it, are in us virtually and before all apperception. Yet they form the soul and tissue of our knowledge, being as necessary to it as the muscles and sinews are for walking, though we may not actually think of either, and do not distinguish them by abstraction till we have become philosophical.

of these principles till they are proposed to them ; and that Chap. I.
one may be unacquainted with these truths till he hears them
from others. For, if they were innate, what need they be pro- proves
them not
posed in order to gaining assent, when, by being in the under- innate.
standing, by a natural and original impression, (if there were
any such,) they could not but be known before? Or doth the
proposing them print them clearer in the mind than nature
did ? If so, then the consequence will be, that a man knows
them better after he has been thus taught them than he did
before. Whence it will follow that these principles may be
made more evident to us by others' teaching [1] than nature has
made them by impression : which will ill agree with the opinion
of innate principles, and give but little authority to them ; but,
on the contrary, makes them unfit to be the foundations of
all our other knowledge; as they are pretended to be. This
cannot be denied, that men grow first acquainted with many
of these self-evident truths upon their being proposed : but it
is clear that whosoever does so, finds in himself that he then
begins to know a proposition, which he knew not before, and
which from thenceforth he never questions; not because it
was innate, but because the consideration of the nature of the
things contained in those words would not suffer him to think
otherwise [2], how, or whensoever he is brought to reflect on
them. [[3] And if whatever is assented to at first hearing and
understanding the terms must pass for an innate principle,
every well-grounded observation, drawn from particulars into
a general rule [4], must be innate. When yet it is certain that

---

[1] 'Assent when proposed' is here interpreted, assent on the ground of proposal by a person, i. e. deference to human authority, instead of rational insight by the person himself. This introduces a new and irrelevant question, about the rationale of authority. The question is, whether, when such judgments are *anyhow* brought into our consciousness, the supposition of their being false must not be seen by us to be necessarily absurd.

[2] Truths intellectually necessary or self-evident are here again opposed to innate truths, which Locke supposes

we must all be conscious of when we are born, if they are innate.

[3] Added in Second Edition.

[4] That is, every empirical generalisation formed by a sufficient induction, which Locke strongly distinguishes in Bk. IV. from self-evident and demonstrated truths. But is the *conditional* necessity which constrains an educated man to accept the law of gravitation of the same sort as the *absolute* intellectual necessity which constrains an educated man to accept the abstract principle of non-contradiction or of causality?

CHAP. I.

not all, but only sagacious heads, light at first on these observations, and reduce them into general propositions: not innate, but collected from a preceding acquaintance and reflection on particular instances. These, when observing men have made them, unobserving men, when they are proposed to them, cannot refuse their assent to.]

Implicitly known before proposing, signifies that the Mind is capable of understanding them, or else signifies nothing.

22. If it be said, the understanding hath an *implicit* knowledge of these principles, but not an *explicit*, before this first hearing (as they must who will say 'that they are in the understanding before they are known,') it will be hard to conceive what is meant by a principle imprinted on the understanding implicitly, unless it be this,—that the mind is capable of understanding and assenting firmly to such propositions. And thus all mathematical demonstrations, as well as first principles, must be received as native impressions on the mind; which I fear they will scarce allow them to be, who find it harder to demonstrate a proposition than assent to it when demonstrated. And few mathematicians will be forward to believe, that all the diagrams they have drawn were but copies of those innate characters which nature had engraven [1] upon their minds.

The Argument of assenting on first hearing, is upon a false supposition of no precedent teaching.

23. There is, I fear, this further weakness in the foregoing argument, which would persuade us that therefore those maxims are to be thought innate, which men admit at first hearing; because they assent to propositions which they are not taught, nor do receive from the force of any argument or demonstration, but a bare explication or understanding of the terms. Under which there seems to me to lie this fallacy, that men are supposed not to be taught nor to learn anything *de novo*; when, in truth, they are taught, and do learn something they were ignorant of before. For, first, it is evident that they have learned the terms, and their signification; neither of which was born with them. But this is not all the acquired knowledge in the case: the ideas themselves, about which the proposition is, are not born with them, no more

---

[1] That is, 'had engraven' *consciously at birth*, which no one worth arguing against would maintain. Cf. Bk. IV. ch. ii. § 7, on the *intuitive* evidence of *each step* in every mathematical or other demonstration. Locke himself argues in Bk. IV. for the perceived intellectual necessity of all mathematical truths, and of the existence of God,— or as we should say, their latent 'innateness.'

than their names, but got afterwards. So that in all propositions that are assented to at first hearing, the terms of the proposition, their standing for such ideas, and the ideas themselves that they stand for, being neither of them innate, I would fain know what there is remaining in such propositions that is innate. For I would gladly have any one name that proposition whose terms or ideas were either of them innate. We *by degrees* get ideas and names, and *learn* their appropriated connexion one with another; and then to propositions made in such terms, whose signification we have learnt, and wherein the agreement or disagreement we can perceive in our ideas when put together is expressed, we at first hearing assent; though to other propositions, in themselves as certain and evident, but which are concerning ideas not so soon or so easily got, we are at the same time no way capable of assenting. For, though a child quickly assents to this proposition, 'That an apple is not fire,' when by familiar acquaintance he has got the ideas of those two different things distinctly imprinted on his mind, and has learnt that the names apple and fire stand for them; yet it will be some years after, perhaps, before the same child will assent to this proposition, ' That it is impossible for the same thing to be and not to be'; because that, though perhaps the words are as easy to be learnt, yet the signification of them being more large, comprehensive, and abstract than of the names annexed to those sensible things the child hath to do with, it is longer before he learns their precise meaning, and it requires more time plainly to form in his mind those general ideas they stand for. Till that be done, you will in vain endeavour to make any child assent to a proposition made up of such general terms; but as soon as ever he has got those ideas, and learned their names, he forwardly closes with the one as well as the other of the forementioned propositions: and with both for the same reason; viz. because he finds the ideas he has in his mind to agree or disagree, according as the words standing for them are affirmed or denied one of another in the proposition. But if propositions be brought to him in words which stand for ideas he has not yet in his mind, to such propositions, however evidently true or false in themselves, he affords

CHAP. I. neither assent nor dissent, but is ignorant. For words being but empty sounds, any further than they are signs of our ideas, we cannot but assent to them as they correspond to those ideas we have, but no further than that. But the showing by what steps and ways knowledge comes into our minds; and the grounds of several degrees of assent, being the business of the following Discourse, it may suffice to have only touched on it here, as one reason that made me doubt of those innate principles [1].

Not innate because not universally assented to.

24. To conclude this argument of universal consent, I agree with these defenders of innate principles,—that if they are innate, they must needs have universal assent [2]. For that a truth should be innate and yet not assented to, is to me as unintelligible as for a man to know a truth and be ignorant of it at the same time [3]. But then, by these men's own confession, they cannot be innate; since they are not assented to by those who understand not the terms; nor by a great part of those who do understand them, but have yet never heard nor thought of those propositions; which, I think, is at least one half of mankind. But were the number far less, it would be enough to destroy universal assent, and thereby show these propositions not to be innate, if children alone were ignorant of them [4].

[1] Here and elsewhere Locke persists in taking for granted, that the 'innateness' of ideas and of knowledge is being maintained by his adversaries in a sense that is inconsistent with much that is innate being consciously apprehended only late in life, progressing by steps, and in all cases dependently upon development of the mind, and accumulation of experience. The 'steps and ways' of knowledge, and the 'grounds of assent,' described in the sequel, need not have been thus put in antagonism to the ultimate principles for which the philosopher seeks (the only innateness worth discussing), though Locke, in his controversial temper, presented them in the light of contradictories.

[2] But it is a 'universal assent' that needs to be elicited and verified by a philosophical analysis of our complex experience.

[3] *Conscious* assent, as he reiterates, is with him of the essence of innateness, and must be given by all (including infants) to all principles, however abstract, for which innateness can be claimed. It is easy, on this assumption, to show, either that there are no innate principles, or that, if there are, it is superfluous to vindicate their truth,—as, *ex hypothesi*, every human being from birth is, and must be, conscious that they are true.

[4] Not if 'innate' means *necessarily latent* in an experience in which even children in a degree participate. Yet

Chap. I.

—✦—

These
Maxims
not the
first
known.

25. But that I may not be accused to argue from the thoughts of infants, which are unknown to us, and to conclude from what passes in their understandings before they express it; I say next, that these two general propositions are not the truths that first possess the minds of children, nor are antecedent to all acquired and adventitious notions: which, if they were innate, they must needs be. Whether we can determine it or no, it matters not, there is certainly a time when children begin to think, and their words and actions do assure us that they do so. When therefore they are capable of thought, of knowledge, of assent, can it rationally be supposed they can be ignorant of those notions that nature has imprinted, were there any such? Can it be imagined, with any appearance of reason, that they perceive the impressions from things without, and be at the same time ignorant of those characters which nature itself has taken care to stamp within? Can they receive and assent to adventitious notions, and be ignorant of those which are supposed woven into the very principles of their being, and imprinted there in indelible characters, to be the foundation and guide of all their acquired knowledge and future reasonings? This would be to make nature take pains to no purpose; or at least to write very ill; since its characters could not be read by those eyes which saw other things very well: and those are very ill supposed the clearest parts of truth, and the foundations of all our knowledge, which are not first known, and without which the undoubted knowledge of several other things may be had. The child certainly knows, that the nurse that feeds it is neither the cat it plays with, nor the blackmoor it is afraid of: that the wormseed or mustard it refuses, is not the apple or sugar it cries for: this it is certainly and undoubtedly assured of: but will any one say, it is by virtue of this principle, 'That it is impossible for the same thing to be and not to be,' that it so firmly assents to these and other parts of its knowledge? Or that the child has any notion or apprehension of that proposition at an age, wherein yet, it is plain, it knows a great many other truths? He that will say, children join in these general abstract speculations

Locke himself says that 'we are born free, *as we are born rational*,' not that we have the actual exercise of either.' (*Tr. of Govt.* II. § 61).

with their sucking-bottles and their rattles, may perhaps, with justice, be thought to have more passion and zeal for his opinion, but less sincerity and truth, than one of that age [1].

And so not innate.

26. Though therefore there be several general propositions that meet with constant and ready assent, as soon as proposed to men grown up, who have attained the use of more general and abstract ideas, and names standing for them; yet they not being to be found in those of tender years, who nevertheless know other things, they cannot pretend to universal assent of intelligent persons, and so by no means can be supposed innate;—it being impossible that any truth which is innate (if there were any such) should be unknown, at least to any one who knows anything else. Since, if they are innate truths, they must be innate thoughts: there being nothing a truth in the mind that it has never thought on [2]. Whereby it is evident, if there be any innate truths, they must necessarily be the first of any thought on; the first that appear [3].

Not innate, because they appear least, where what is innate shows itself clearest.

27. That the general maxims we are discoursing of are not known to children, idiots, and a great part of mankind, we have already sufficiently proved: whereby it is evident they have not an universal assent, nor are general impressions. But there is this further argument in it against their being innate: that these characters, if they were native and original impressions, should appear fairest and clearest in those persons in whom yet we find no footsteps of them; and it is, in my opinion, a strong presumption that they are not innate, since they are

---

[1] But the concrete judgments which children see the truth of could not be true *if* the abstract principles of identity and contradiction were false. They are therefore latent, and in that sense innate, in the concrete judgments;—and not useless either, for science would become chaos, and reasoning about what is real impossible, in the absence of some absolute principles of reason in us and in things.

[2] Again, Locke's controversial conception of innateness, as implying *conscious apprehension* of the principles and ideas which are needed to harmonize experience. The other sort of innate-ness seems unintelligible to him.

[3] This reasoning, as Leibniz shows, proves too much; for if all the truths on which experience depends must be present to the consciousness of each person, we should be deprived not only of those ultimate abstractions (which many have never actually realised in consciousness), but also of ideas of which we once thought, but have ceased to think; while, if truths are not necessarily conscious thoughts, but only natural aptitudes, there is no obstacle to our possessing some such of which we have never actually thought, and may never actually think.

least known to those in whom, if they were innate, they must needs exert themselves with most force and vigour. For children, idiots, savages [1], and illiterate people, being of all others the least corrupted by custom, or borrowed opinions ; learning and education having not cast their native thoughts into new moulds ; nor by superinducing foreign and studied doctrines, confounded those fair characters nature had written there ; one might reasonably imagine that in *their* minds these innate notions should lie open fairly to every one's view, as it is certain the thoughts of children do [2]. It might very well be expected that these principles should be perfectly known to naturals ; which being stamped immediately on the soul, (as these men suppose,) can have no dependence on the constitution or organs of the body, the only confessed difference between them and others. One would think, according to these men's principles, that all these native beams of light (were there any such) should, in those who have no reserves, no arts of concealment, shine out in their full lustre, and leave us in no more doubt of their being there, than we are of their love of pleasure and abhorrence of pain. But alas, amongst children, idiots, savages, and the grossly illiterate, what general maxims are to be found ? what universal principles of knowledge ? Their notions are few and narrow, borrowed only from those objects they have had most to do with, and which have made upon their senses the frequentest and strongest impressions. A child knows his nurse and his cradle, and by degrees the playthings of a little more advanced age ; and a young savage has, perhaps, his head filled with love and hunting,

[1] 'Savages': salvages, in the early editions, here and afterwards.

[2] The opposite conclusion follows when 'innate' is otherwise understood. Those principles which are latent in the mind of man, and in the nature of things, become patent in the consciousness of individuals, through reflex attention given to them. But 'infants, idiots, savages, and illiterate people' do not rise to this ; they direct any attention which they exert to their own bodies and the external world. The abstract truths of logic and of mathematics are, in a sense, in us, and in the nature of things,—because in apprehending them we apprehend their self-evidence ; yet we need exercise of the intellectual faculty to rise into this intuitive perception of their truth. Children may be less perverted from truth, by accidental association and the hardening of custom, than adults are, while they are nevertheless unfit, as philosophers, to realise the ultimate truths on which knowledge and life depend.

CHAP. I.
—◆◆—
according to the fashion of his tribe. But he that from a child untaught, or a wild inhabitant of the woods, will expect these abstract maxims and reputed principles of science, will, I fear, find himself mistaken. Such kind of general propositions are seldom mentioned in the huts of Indians : much less are they to be found in the thoughts of children, or any impressions of them on the minds of naturals. They are the language and business of the schools and academies of learned nations, accustomed to that sort of conversation or learning, where disputes are frequent ; these maxims being suited to artificial argumentation and useful for conviction, but not much conducing to the discovery of truth or advancement of knowledge[1]. But of their small use for the improvement of knowledge I shall have occasion to speak more at large, l. 4, c. 7 [2].

Recapitulation.
28. I know not how absurd this may seem to the masters of demonstration. And probably it will hardly go down with anybody at first hearing. I must therefore beg a little truce with prejudice, and the forbearance of censure, till I have been heard out in the sequel of this Discourse, being very willing to submit to better judgments. And since I impartially search after truth, I shall not be sorry to be convinced, that I have been too fond of my own notions ; which I confess we are all apt to be, when application and study have warmed our heads with them.

Upon the whole matter, I cannot see any ground to think these two speculative Maxims innate : since they are not universally assented to ; and the assent they so generally find is no other than what several propositions, not allowed to be innate, equally partake in with them : and since the assent that is given them is produced another way [3], and comes not from natural inscription, as I doubt not but to make appear

[1] The ultimate principles through which knowledge is harmonized, and seen in its universality, are *chronologically* not *first* principles but *last* principles—in the history alike of the individual mind and of the human race. And in both it is the history of approximation, not complete attainment. There can be no finality in human philosophy.

[2] Which treats of 'maxims,' or axioms.

[3] Through intuition, aided, more or less, by elaborative thinking, as explained in Bk. IV.

in the following Discourse. And if *these* 'first principles' of
knowledge and science are found not to be innate, no *other*
speculative maxims can (I suppose), with better right pretend
to be so [1].

---

[1] In refusing to start in speculation with abstract 'first' principles, or to allow that all men start with them, Locke seemed to himself to be leading away from the 'vast ocean of Being' into the familiar facts of ordinary experience. But philosophy, thus led, in the end raised its old questions in a new form, when it inquired with Kant as to the *foundation* of scientific experience, which Hegel saw in the divine essence of things,—the absolute Idea.

CHAPTER II.

NO INNATE PRACTICAL PRINCIPLES [1].

Chap. II.

—•—

No moral
Principles
so clear
and so
generally
received
as the
foremen-
tioned
speculative
Maxims.

1. IF those speculative Maxims, whereof we discoursed in the foregoing chapter, have not an actual universal assent from all mankind, as we there proved, it is much more visible concerning *practical* Principles, that they come short of an universal reception : and I think it will be hard to instance any one moral rule which can pretend to so general and ready an assent as, ' What is, is ' ; or to be so manifest a truth as this, that ' It is impossible for the same thing to be and not to be.' Whereby it is evident that they are further removed from a title to be innate ; and the doubt of their being native impressions on the mind is stronger against those moral principles than the other [2]. Not that it brings their truth at all in question. They are equally true, though not equally evident. Those speculative maxims carry their own evidence with them : but moral principles require reasoning and discourse, and some exercise of the mind, to discover the certainty of their truth. They lie not open as natural characters engraven on the mind ; which, if any such were, they must needs be visible by themselves, and by their own light be certain and known to everybody. But this is no derogation to their truth and certainty ; no more than it is to the truth or certainty of the three angles of a triangle being equal to two right ones : because it is not so evident as ' the whole is bigger than a part,'

---

[1] In this chapter Locke passes from the abstract principles of *speculative* knowledge—interesting to the philosophic few, to the principles of *morality and conduct*—more interesting to the mass of mankind. In this, as in the previous argument, when he concludes against innateness, he asserts self-evidence.

[2] It has been remarked that ' the argument for common sense,'—i. e. on behalf of the theoretical and practical principles latent in man—is of principal importance ' in reference to the practical principles.' The speculative axioms, ' from their converse being absolutely incogitable, sufficiently guard themselves.' (Hamilton's Reid, p. 754.)

nor so apt to be assented to at first hearing [1]. It may suffice CHAP. II.
that these moral rules are capable of demonstration [2]: and
therefore it is our own faults if we come not to a certain
knowledge of them. But the ignorance wherein many men
are of them, and the slowness of assent wherewith others receive them, are manifest proofs that they are not innate, and
such as offer themselves to their view without searching [3].

[1] Locke reiterates the difference between an 'innate' law, *consciously*
impressed upon the mind in its first
original, and an intellectual necessity
in the reason of things, which, although
at first ignorant of, we may realise in
its self-evidence, ' by the due application of our natural faculties.' In this
last category Locke himself puts 'the
eternal and unalterable nature of right
and wrong.'

[2] The *demonstrable* character of the
conclusions of abstract morality, determined by the eternity and immutability
of abstract ethical distinctions, was a
favourite speculation with Locke, which
Molyneux, in his correspondence, thus
urged him to develop into an ethical
system :—' One thing I must needs
insist on to you, which is, that you
would think of obliging the world
with a Treatise on Morals, drawn up
according to the hints you frequently
give in your *Essay* of their being demonstrable according to mathematical
method. This is most certainly true ;
but then the task must be undertaken
only by so clear and distinct a thinker
as you are, and there is nothing I
should more ardently wish for than to
see it.' (Molyneux to Locke, August,
1692.) Locke thus replies :—' Though
by the view I had of moral ideas, when
I was considering that subject, I thought
I saw that morality might be *demonstratively* made out, yet whether I am
able so to make it out is another question. Every one could not have demonstrated what Mr. Newton's book
hath shown to be demonstrable.'
' Good sir,' rejoins Molyneux, ' let me

renew my requests ; for believe me,
sir, 'twill be one of the most useful and
glorious undertakings that can employ
you. The touches you give in many
places of your book on this subject are
wonderfully curious. Be as large as
'tis possible on this subject, and by all
means let it be in English. He that
reads the 45th section on your 129th
page (1st ed., now Bk. II. ch. xxi.
§ 72) will be inflamed to read more of
the same kind from the same incomparable pen.' Locke in the end excused himself, on grounds of age and
health, from the formidable enterprise. ' The Gospel,' he adds, ' contains so perfect a body of Ethics that
reason may be excused from that inquiry, since she may find man's duty
clearer and easier in revelation than in
herself. This is the excuse of a man
who, having a sufficient rule of his
actions, is content therewith, and
thinks he may employ the little time
and strength he has in other researches
wherein he is more in the dark.'
Locke's thesis, that morality is as demonstrable as mathematics, is held by
Cumberland, *De Legibus Naturae*, ch.
i. §§ 7, 8 ; iv. § 4. See also Reid,
Essays on the Intellectual Powers, vii.
ch. 2.

[3] ' Without searching' suggests
Locke's moral purpose in this controversy against innateness—that it
tends to ' ease the lazy of the pains
of search,' and to leave the individual
the slave of prejudices, under cover
of their being ' innate principles,' given
at our birth, without trouble on our
part.

CHAP. II.
—✦—
Faith and
Justice not
owned as
Principles
by all Men.

2. Whether there be any such moral principles, wherein all men do agree, I appeal to any who have been but moderately conversant in the history of mankind, and looked abroad beyond the smoke of their own chimneys. Where is that practical truth that is universally received, without doubt or question, as it must be if innate[1]? *Justice*, and keeping of contracts, is that which most men seem to agree in[2]. This is a principle[3] which is thought to extend itself to the dens of thieves, and the confederacies of the greatest villains; and they who have gone furthest towards the putting off of humanity itself, keep faith and rules of justice one with another. I grant that outlaws themselves do this one amongst another: but it is without receiving these as the innate laws of nature. They practise them as rules of convenience within their own communities: but it is impossible to conceive that he embraces justice as a practical principle, who acts fairly with his fellow-highwayman, and at the same time plunders or kills the next honest man he meets with. Justice and truth are the common ties of society; and therefore even outlaws and robbers, who break with all the world besides, must keep faith and rules of equity amongst themselves; or else they cannot hold together. But will any one say, that those that live by fraud or rapine have innate principles of truth and justice which they allow and assent to?

Objection:
though
Men deny
them in

3. Perhaps it will be urged, that the tacit assent of their minds agrees to what their practice contradicts. I answer, first, I have always thought the actions of men the best

---

[1] That diversity of belief is greater in regard to fundamental principles of action than in the case of the abstract principles of identity and contradiction, does not prove want of self-evidence in the former, but only that owing to the greater complexity of practical principles, and their affinity with our passions, 'more pain of search' is needed to enable the individual to recognise the self-evidence that is latent.

[2] But might not all, by due development of their latent reason, be made to see the self-evident morality in-

volved in contract-keeping; thus showing that our mind is not originally like white paper, in the sense of being equally disposed to accept any propositions regarding conduct; and disproving the hypothesis that antecedent to human custom and constitution, or to special revelation, there was nothing absolutely good or bad?

[3] As put by Locke himself, 'it is every man's duty to be just, whether there is any such thing as a just man in the world or no.' (*Conduct of Understanding*, § 24.)

interpreters of their thoughts. But, since it is certain that Chap II.
most men's practices, and some men's open professions, have
either questioned or denied these principles, it is impossible
to establish an universal consent, (though we should look for
it only amongst grown men,) without which it is impossible
to conclude them innate. Secondly, it is very strange and
unreasonable to suppose innate practical principles, that
terminate only in contemplation. Practical principles, derived
from nature, are there for operation, and must produce
conformity of action, not barely speculative assent to their
truth, or else they are in vain distinguished from speculative
maxims. Nature, I confess, has put into man a desire of
happiness and an aversion to misery: these indeed are innate
practical principles [1] which (as practical principles ought) *do*
continue constantly to operate and influence all our actions
without ceasing: these may be observed in all persons and
all ages, steady and universal; but these are *inclinations of
the appetite* to good, not impressions of truth on the understanding. I deny not that there are natural tendencies
imprinted on the minds of men; and that from the very first
instances of sense and perception, there are some things that
are grateful and others unwelcome to them; some things that
they incline to and others that they fly: but this makes
nothing for innate characters on the mind, which are to be
the principles of knowledge regulating our practice. Such
natural impressions on the understanding are so far from
being confirmed hereby, that this is an argument against

their
Practice,
yet they
admit them
in their
Thoughts
answered.

---

[1] In our natural desire for the continuance and return of felt pleasure,
and our aversion from felt uneasiness,
—Locke finds an example of a tendency which he allows to be 'innate,'
because practically operative as soon
as there is any consciousness of either.
Whether this innate tendency is the
supreme motive of human action is
considered in the sequel (e. g. Bk. II.
ch. xxi). Moreover, men often mistake
or differ in their applications even of
this acknowledged innate tendency,
and in their estimates of remote as
compared with near and obvious rewards and punishments, but this difference of judgment is not inconsistent
with the innateness of the tendency.
'Men have a natural tendency to what
delights and from what pains them.
This universal observation has established past doubt. But that the soul
has such a tendency to what is morally
good and from evil has not fallen
under my observation, and therefore
I cannot grant it.' (MS. *Marginalia
Lockiana,* 1699.)

them; since, if there were certain characters imprinted by nature on the understanding, as the principles of knowledge, we could not but perceive them constantly operate in us and influence our knowledge, as we do those others on the will and appetite; which never cease to be the constant springs and motives of all our actions, to which we perpetually feel them strongly impelling us.

Moral Rules need a Proof, *ergo* not innate. 4. Another reason that makes me doubt of any innate practical principles is, that I think *there cannot any one moral rule be proposed whereof a man may not justly demand a reason* : which would be perfectly ridiculous and absurd if they were innate ; or so much as self-evident, which every innate principle must needs be, and not need any proof to ascertain its truth, nor want any reason to gain it approbation [1]. He would be thought void of common sense [2] who asked on the one side, or on the other side went to give a reason *why* 'it is impossible for the same thing to be and not to be.' It carries its own light and evidence with it, and needs no other proof : he that understands the terms assents to it for its own sake or else nothing will ever be able to prevail with him to do it. But should that most unshaken rule of morality and foundation of all social virtue, 'That one should do as he would be done unto,' be proposed to one

---

[1] All that was (in Locke's sense) 'innate' would also be self-evident; but what is self-evident is not therefore innate, if innate means consciously recognised at birth.

[2] The 'common sense,' or common reason, is here taken by Locke as the evidence and guarantee of the abstract logical axiom of contradiction. 'There is here,' says Hamilton, 'a confession, the importance of which has been observed neither by Locke nor his antagonists. Had Locke not . . . been led astray in the pursuit of an *ignis fatuus*—in his refutation of the Cartesian theory of Innate Ideas, which certainly as impugned by him neither Descartes nor the representatives of his school ever dreamt of holding—he would have seen that, in thus appealing to *common sense*, he was, in fact, surrendering his thesis — that all our knowledge is an educt from experience. For in admitting, as he here virtually does, that experience must ultimately ground its procedure on the laws of intellect, he admits that intellect contains principles of judgment on which experience, being dependent, cannot possibly be their precursor or their cause.' (Hamilton's Reid, pp. 784, 5.) This depends on whether Locke does or does not include in 'experience' *its own necessary presuppositions*, which are held unconsciously in ordinary experience, but which it is the office of speculative philosophy (neglected by Locke) to articulate into distinct consciousness.

who never heard of it before, but yet is of capacity to understand its meaning; might he not without any absurdity ask a
reason why? And were not he that proposed it bound to
make out the truth and reasonableness of it to him? Which
plainly shows it not to be innate; for if it were it could
neither want nor receive any proof; but must needs (at least
as soon as heard and understood) be received and assented
to as an unquestionable truth, which a man can by no means
doubt of. So that the truth of all these moral rules plainly
depends upon some other antecedent to them, and from which
they must be *deduced*[1]; which could not be if either they
were innate or so much as self-evident.

5. That men should keep their compacts is certainly a
great and undeniable rule in morality. But yet, if a Christian,
who has the view of happiness and misery in another life, be
asked why a man must keep his word, he will give this as a
reason :—Because God, who has the power of eternal life and
death, requires it of us[2]. But if a Hobbist be asked why?
he will answer :—Because the public requires it, and the
Leviathan will punish you if you do not[3]. And if one of the
old philosophers had been asked, he would have answered :—
Because it was dishonest, below the dignity of a man, and
opposite to virtue, the highest perfection of human nature, to
do otherwise.

Instance in keeping Compacts.

6. Hence naturally flows the great variety of opinions
concerning moral rules which are to be found among men,
according to the different sorts of happiness they have a
prospect of, or propose to themselves; which could not be if
practical principles were innate, and imprinted in our minds
immediately by the hand of God. I grant the existence of
God is so many ways manifest, and the obedience we owe

Virtue generally approved, not because innate, but because profitable.

[1] Deduction may be needed to
evolve that which is nevertheless virtually in us, and in the nature of
things, already.

[2] He looks here to the received
sanctions of conduct, rather than to the
immutability of moral law in the nature
of things. Reasoning resolves the self-
evident principles of morality into the
eternal and immutable nature of God;
but without legislative sanctions it fails
to guard conduct against the pressure
of the appetites.

[3] See Hobbes, *De Homine*, ch. 14.
This sarcastic reference is the only
express mention of Hobbes in the
Essay.

CHAP. II. him so congruous to the light of reason, that a great part of mankind give testimony to the law of nature: but yet I think it must be allowed that several moral rules may receive from mankind a very general approbation, without either knowing or admitting the true ground of morality; which can only be the will and law of a God, who sees men in the dark, has in his hand rewards and punishments, and power enough to call to account the proudest offender [1]. For, God having, by an inseparable connexion, joined virtue and public happiness together, and made the practice thereof necessary to the preservation of society, and visibly beneficial to all with whom the virtuous man has to do; it is no wonder that every one should not only allow, but recommend and magnify those rules to others, from whose observance of them he is sure to reap advantage to himself. He may, out of interest as well as conviction, cry up that for sacred, which, if once trampled on and profaned, he himself cannot be safe nor secure. This, though it takes nothing from the moral and eternal obligation which these rules evidently have [2], yet it shows that the outward acknowledgment men pay to them in their words proves not that they are innate principles: nay, it proves not so much as that men assent to them inwardly in their own minds, as the inviolable rules of their own practice; since we find that self-interest, and the conveniences of this life, make many men own an outward profession and approbation of them, whose actions sufficiently

[1] That a Christian, a Hobbist, and a Heathen should give different reasons for observing a moral rule does not disprove the obligation of that rule, antecedently to the intermediate principles on which they ground it. Locke is apt to rest content with premisses which are short of the ultimate ones for which the philosopher craves; but he recognises in many passages the conception of ethical law, eternal and divine, superior to custom and to the judgments of human conscience. ' Truth and keeping of faith,' he says, ' belong to men as men, and not merely as members of society.' (*Tr. of Government*, ii. 14.)

[2] Moral obligation, which is eternal and grounded on reason, is thus distinguished from the contingency of an individual recognition of, and conformity to, what is in itself thus obligatory. In what follows it only appears that men are not actually as good as they know they ought to be. His argument is, that immoral practice *without reproach of conscience* proves that the law transgressed cannot be innate, or consciously acknowledged by all.

prove that they very little consider the Lawgiver that pre- scribed these rules ; nor the hell that he has ordained for the punishment of those that transgress them.

7. For, if we will not in civility allow too much sincerity to the professions of most men, but think their actions to be the interpreters of their thoughts, we shall find that they have no such internal veneration for these rules, nor so full a persuasion of their certainty and obligation. The great principle of morality, 'To do as one would be done to,' is more com- mended than practised. But the breach of this rule cannot be a greater vice, than to teach others, that it is no moral rule, nor obligatory, would be thought madness, and contrary to that interest men sacrifice to, when they break it them- selves. Perhaps *conscience* will be urged as checking us for such breaches, and so the internal obligation and establish- ment of the rule be preserved.

Men's actions convince us, that the Rule of Virtue is not their internal Principle.

8. To which I answer, that I doubt not but, without being written on their hearts, many men may, by the same way that they come to the knowledge of other things, come to assent to several moral rules, and be convinced of their obligation. Others also may come to be of the same mind, from their education, company, and customs of their country ; which persuasion, however got, will serve to set conscience on work ; which is nothing else but [our own opinion or judgment of the moral rectitude or pravity of our own actions [1]] ; and if conscience be a proof of innate principles, contraries may be

Con- science no Proof of any innate Moral Rule.

---

[1] In first three editions—' Our own opinion of our own actions.' Locke's ' conscience ' is individual and variable, and thus distinguished from the ab- stract relations of eternal and immu- table morality. When Thomas Burnet asked him, ' What those laws are that we ought to obey, or how we can know them without revelation, unless you take in natural conscience for a distinction of good and evil, or another idea of God than what you have given us ?' he replied—' It is not conscience that *makes* the distinction of good and evil, conscience only judging of an action by *that which it takes to be* [eternal] rule of good and evil, acquits or condemns it. But where is it,' he asks, ' I so much as mention, much less assert, an *arbitrary* difference of good and evil ?' Again, ' I call not conscience practical principles. Pro- duce the place where I so represent it. He who confounds the judgment made with the rule or law upon which it is made may perhaps talk so. Conscience is not the law of nature, but judging by that which is (by it) taken to be the law.' (*Marginalia Lockiana.*)

CHAP. II. innate principles; since some men with the same bent of
conscience prosecute what others avoid [1].

Instances
of
Enormities
practised
without
Remorse.

9. But I cannot see how any men should ever transgress
those moral rules, with confidence and serenity, were they
innate, and stamped upon their minds.   View but an army at
the sacking of a town, and see what observation or sense of
moral principles, or what touch of conscience for all the
outrages they do.   Robberies, murders, rapes, are the sports
of men set at liberty from punishment and censure.   Have
there not been whole nations, and those of the most civilized
people, amongst whom the exposing their children, and leaving
them in the fields to perish by want or wild beasts has been
the practice ; as little condemned or scrupled as the begetting
them [2] ?   Do they not still, in some countries, put them into
the same graves with their mothers, if they die in childbirth ;
or despatch them, if a pretended astrologer declares them to
have unhappy stars?   And are there not places where, at
a certain age, they kill or expose their parents, without any
remorse at all [3]?   In a part of Asia, the sick, when their
case comes to be thought desperate, are carried out and laid
on the earth before they are dead ; and left there, exposed to
wind and weather, to perish without assistance or pity [4].

[1] If moral ideas or moral rules
(which are the moral principles I deny
to be innate) are innate, I say children
must actually know them as well as
men.   But if by moral principles you
mean a faculty to find out in time the
moral difference of actions—besides,
that this is an improper way of speaking, to call a power principles, I never
denied such a *power* to be innate, but
that which I denied was that any *idea*
or *connection of ideas* was innate.'
(*Marginalia Lockiana.*)   In what follows the fallibility of ' conscience,' as
a guide in concrete morality, or as
a spontaneous revelation of eternal
and immutable principles to the individual, is argued, from the various and
self-contradictory moral judgments of
men.

[2] The custom of infanticide has been
vindicated, on the ground that human
life is valuable, and its destruction
criminal, only after it has lasted long
enough to be possessed of self-conscious intelligence.

[3] Extreme old age was regarded as
a return of infancy.

[4] Gruber, apud Thevenot, part iv.
p. 13.   The reference here and elsewhere is to the collection of travels, in
two folios, entitled *Relations des divers
Voyages curieux*, par M. Melchisedec
Thevenot, of which some account is
given in the appendix to the ' History
of Navigation,' prefixed to Churchill's
Collection of Voyages (1704)—by some
attributed to Locke, and contained in
the 1812 edition of his Works, vol. x.
p. 357.

It is familiar among the Mingrelians, a people professing CHAP. II.
Christianity, to bury their children alive without scruple[1].
There are places where they eat their own children[2]. The
Caribbees were wont to geld their children, on purpose to fat
and eat them[3]. And Garcilasso de la Vega tells us of
a people in Peru which were wont to fat and eat the children
they got on their female captives, whom they kept as concu-
bines for that purpose, and when they were past breeding, the
mothers themselves were killed too and eaten[4]. The virtues
whereby the Tououpinambos believed they merited paradise,
were revenge, and eating abundance of their enemies. They
have not so much as a name for God[5], and have no religion,
no worship. The saints who are canonized amongst the
Turks, lead lives which one cannot with modesty relate. A
remarkable passage to this purpose, out of the voyage of
Baumgarten[6], which is a book not every day to be met with,
I shall set down at large, in the language it is published in.
Ibi (*sc. prope* Belbes *in* Ægypto) *vidimus sanctum unum
Saracenicum inter arenarum cumulos, ita ut ex utero matris
prodiit nudum sedentem. Mos est, ut didicimus, Mahometistis,
ut eos, qui amentes et sine ratione sunt, pro sanctis colant
et venerentur. Insuper et eos, qui cum diu vitam egerint
inquinatissimam, voluntariam demum pœnitentiam et pauper-
tatem, sanctitate venerandos deputant. Ejusmodi verò genus
hominum libertatem quandam effrenem habent, domos quos
volunt intrandi, edendi, bibendi, et quod majus est, concum-
bendi; ex quo concubitu, si proles secuta fuerit, sancta similiter
habetur. His ergo hominibus dum vivunt, magnos exhibent
honores; mortuis verò vel templa vel monumenta extruunt
amplissima, eosque contingere ac sepelire maximæ fortunæ
ducunt loco. Audivimus hæc dicta et dicenda per interpretem
à Mucrelo nostro. Insuper sanctum illum, quem eo loco vidimus, publicitus apprimè commendari, eum esse hominem sanctum,*

---

[1] Lambert apud Thevenot, p. 38.
[2] Vossius, *De Nili Origine*, c. 18, 19.
[3] P. Mart, Dec. 1.
[4] *Hist. des Incas*, l. i. c. 12.
[5] Lery, c. 16, 216, 231.
[6] A German nobleman, whose travels
in Egypt, Arabia, and Palestine in
1507 contain much information that at
the time was new and curious concerning the history, manners, and religion of these countries. His journal
of his travels, in Latin, was corrected
by Joseph Scaliger, and first appeared
in English in Churchill's *Collection.*

CHAP. II. *divinum ac integritate præcipuum; eo quod, nec fæminarum unquam esset, nec puerorum, sed tantummodo asellarum concubitor atque mularum.* (Peregr. Baumgarten, l. ii. c. 1. p. 73.) [[1] More of the same kind concerning these precious saints amongst the Turks may be seen in Pietro della Valle, in his letter of the 25th of January, 1616.]

Where then are those innate principles of justice, piety, gratitude, equity, chastity? Or where is that universal consent that assures us there are such inbred rules? Murders in duels, when fashion has made them honourable, are committed without remorse of conscience: nay, in many places innocence in this case is the greatest ignominy. And if we look abroad to take a view of men as they are, we shall find that they have remorse, in one place, for doing or omitting that which others, in another place, think they merit by.

Men have contrary practical Principles. 10. He that will carefully peruse the history of mankind, and look abroad into the several tribes of men, and with indifferency[2] survey their actions, will be able to satisfy himself, that there is scarce that principle of morality to be named, or rule of virtue to be thought on, (those only excepted that are absolutely necessary to hold society together, which commonly too are neglected betwixt distinct societies,) which is not, somewhere or other, slighted and condemned by the general fashion of whole societies of men, governed by practical opinions and rules of living quite opposite to others.

Whole Nations reject several Moral Rules. 11. Here perhaps it will be objected, that it is no argument that the rule is not known, because it is broken. I grant the objection good where men, though they transgress, yet disown not the law; where fear of shame, censure, or punishment carries the mark of some awe it has upon them. But it is impossible to conceive that a whole nation of men should all publicly reject and renounce what every one of them certainly and infallibly knew to be a law; for so they must who have it naturally imprinted on their minds. It is possible men may sometimes own rules of morality which in their private thoughts they do not believe to be true, only to keep them-

---

[1] Added in French version.   [2] 'With indifferency'—without bias.

selves in reputation and esteem amongst those who are persuaded of their obligation. But it is not to be imagined that a whole society of men should publicly and professedly disown and cast off a rule which they could not in their own minds but be infallibly certain was a law; nor be ignorant that all men they should have to do with knew it to be such: and therefore must every one of them apprehend from others all the contempt and abhorrence due to one who professes himself void of humanity: and one who, confounding the known and natural measures of right and wrong, cannot but be looked on as the professed enemy of their peace and happiness. Whatever practical principle is innate, cannot but be known to every one to be just and good. It is therefore little less than a contradiction to suppose, that whole nations of men should, both in their professions and practice, unanimously and universally give the lie to what, by the most invincible evidence, every one of them knew to be true, right, and good [1]. This is enough to satisfy us that no practical rule which is anywhere universally, and with public approbation or allowance, transgressed, can be supposed innate.—But I have something further to add in answer to this objection.

12. The breaking of a rule, say you, is no argument that it is unknown. I grant it: but the *generally allowed* breach of it anywhere, I say, is a proof that it is not innate. For example: let us take any of these rules, which, being the most obvious deductions of human reason, and conformable to the natural inclination of the greatest part of men, fewest people have had the impudence to deny or inconsideration to doubt of. If any can be thought to be naturally imprinted, none, I think, can have a fairer pretence to be innate than this: 'Parents, preserve and cherish your children.' When, therefore, you say that this is an innate rule, what do you mean? Either that it is an innate principle which upon all occasions excites and directs the actions of all men; or else, that it is a truth which all men have imprinted on their minds, and

The generally allowed breach of a rule proof that it is not innate.

---

[1] 'Whatever may be affirmed of the nature of any whole nation may likewise be affirmed of all mankind; as all the properties of bread are in a loaf, and also in a piece cut out of it.' (MS. note by Tyrrell in his copy of the *Essay.*)

which therefore they know and assent to.   But in neither of these senses is it innate.   *First,* that it is not a principle which influences all men's actions, is what I have proved by the examples before cited : nor need we seek so far as Mingrelia or Peru to find instances of such as neglect, abuse, nay, and destroy their children ; or look on it only as the more than brutality of some savage and barbarous nations, when we remember that it was a familiar and uncondemned practice amongst the Greeks and Romans to expose, without pity or remorse, their innocent infants.   *Secondly,* that it is an innate truth, known to all men, is also false.   For, ' Parents preserve your children,' is so far from an innate truth, that it is no truth at all : it being a command, and not a proposition, and so not capable of truth or falsehood.   To make it capable of being assented to as true, it must be reduced to some such proposition as this : ' It is the duty of parents to preserve their children.'   But what duty is, cannot be understood without a law ; nor a law be known or supposed without a lawmaker, or without reward and punishment ; so that it is impossible that this, or any other, practical principle should be innate, i. e. be imprinted on the mind as a duty, without supposing the ideas of God, of law, of obligation, of punishment, of a life after this, innate : for that punishment follows not in this life the breach of this rule, and consequently that it has not the force of a law in countries where the generally allowed practice runs counter to it, is in itself evident.   But these ideas (which must be all of them innate, if anything as a duty be so) are so far from being innate, that it is not every studious or thinking man, much less every one that is born, in whom they are to be found clear and distinct ; and that one of them, which of all others seems most likely to be innate, is not so, (I mean the idea of God,) I think, in the next chapter[1], will appear very evident to any considering man.

If men can be ignorant of what is   13. From what has been said, I think we may safely conclude, that whatever practical rule is in any place generally and with allowance broken, cannot be supposed innate ; it

[1] Ch. iii §§ 8–17.

being impossible that men should, without shame or fear,
confidently and serenely, break a rule which they could not
but evidently know that God had set up, and would certainly
punish the breach of, (which they must, if it were innate,) to
a degree to make it a very ill bargain to the transgressor.
Without such a knowledge as this, a man can never be certain
that anything is his duty. Ignorance or doubt of the law,
hopes to escape the knowledge or power of the law-maker, or
the like, may make men give way to a present appetite ; but
let any one see the fault, and the rod by it, and with the
transgression, a fire ready to punish it; a pleasure tempting,
and the hand of the Almighty visibly held up and prepared
to take vengeance, (for this must be the case where any duty
is imprinted on the mind,) and then tell me whether it be
possible for people with such a prospect, such a certain knowledge as this, wantonly, and without scruple, to offend against
a law which they carry about them in indelible characters,
and that stares them in the face whilst they are breaking it ?
Whether men, at the same time that they feel in themselves
the imprinted edicts of an Omnipotent Law-maker, can, with
assurance and gaiety, slight and trample underfoot his most
sacred injunctions ?　And lastly, whether it be possible that
whilst a man thus openly bids defiance to this innate law and
supreme Lawgiver, all the bystanders, yea, even the governors
and rulers of the people, full of the same sense both of the
law and Law-maker, should silently connive, without testi-
fying their dislike or laying the least blame on it ?　Principles
of actions indeed there are lodged in men's appetites ; but
these are so far from being innate moral principles, that if
they were left to their full swing they would carry men to
the overturning of all morality. Moral laws are set as a
curb and restraint to these exorbitant desires, which they
cannot be but by rewards and punishments that will over-
balance the satisfaction any one shall propose to himself in
the breach of the law. If, therefore, anything be imprinted
on the minds of all men as a law, all men must have a certain
and unavoidable knowledge that certain and unavoidable
punishment will attend the breach of it. For if men can be
ignorant or doubtful of what is innate, innate principles are

innate,
certainty
is not
described
by innate
principles.

CHAP. II.
insisted on, and urged to no purpose; truth and certainty (the things pretended) are not at all secured by them; but men are in the same uncertain floating estate with as without them. An evident indubitable knowledge of unavoidable punishment, great enough to make the transgression very uneligible, must accompany an innate law; unless with an innate law they can suppose an innate Gospel too. I would not here be mistaken, as if, because I deny an innate law, I thought there were none but positive laws. There is a great deal of difference between an innate law, and a law of nature; between something imprinted on our minds in their very original, and something that we, being ignorant of, may attain to the knowledge of, by the use and due application of our natural faculties. And I think they equally forsake the truth who, running into contrary extremes, either affirm an innate law, or deny that there is a law knowable by the light of nature, i.e. without the help of positive revelation[1].

Those who maintain innate practical Principles tell us not what they are.

14. The difference there is amongst men in their practical principles is so evident that I think I need say no more to evince, that it will be impossible to find any innate moral rules by this mark of general assent; and it is enough to make one suspect that the supposition of such innate principles is but an opinion taken up at pleasure; since those who talk so confidently of them are so sparing to tell us

[1] Thus Locke distinguishes 'innate law,' which he argues against, from the eternal and immutable moral law of nature, which he acknowledges (cf. Bk. II. ch. xxviii. §§ 7, 8, as in the successive editions of the *Essay*.) In a letter to Tyrrell (August 4, 1691, see Lord King's ' Life '), he tries to remove misunderstandings as to what he intended by ' the law of nature,' as part of the revealed *divine* law,—the consideration of which he regards as irrelevant, when he is 'not designing to treat of the [absolute and universal] grounds of true morality, which is necessary to true and perfect happiness,' but was only trying to show ' whence men had got their moral ideas, and what they were.' ' I only report as matters of fact *what others call virtue and vice*,' is his reply to Lowde's charge of 'subverting the eternal and immutable nature of moral distinctions.' The facts of human life may thus conceal the abstract laws with which they are at variance; for the eternal laws of morality do not put men under physical necessity actually to obey them, but only under moral obligation. Locke's admiration of Hooker may have influenced him in his recognition of 'that law which, as laid up in the bosom of God, they call eternal.' See *Eccles. Hist.* Bk. I. 3. Note how Locke contrasts 'innate ' and ' natural.'

which they are. This might with justice be expected from those men who lay stress upon this opinion; and it gives occasion to distrust either their knowledge or charity, who, declaring that God has imprinted on the minds of men the foundations of knowledge and the rules of living, are yet so little favourable to the information of their neighbours, or the quiet of mankind, as not to point out to them which they are, in the variety men are distracted with. But, in truth, were there any such innate principles there would be no need to teach them. Did men find such innate propositions stamped on their minds, they would easily be able to distinguish them from other truths that they afterwards learned and deduced from them ; and there would be nothing more easy than to know what, and how many, they were. There could be no more doubt about their number than there is about the number of our fingers ; and it is like then every system would be ready to give them us by tale. But since nobody, that I know, has ventured yet to give a catalogue of them, they cannot blame those who doubt of these innate principles ; since even they who require men to believe that there are such innate propositions, do not tell us what they are[1]. It is easy to foresee, that if different men of different sects should go about to give us a list of those innate practical principles, they would set down only such as suited their distinct hypotheses, and were fit to support the doctrines of their particular schools or churches ; a plain evidence that there are no such innate truths. Nay, a great part of men are so far from finding any such innate moral principles in themselves, that, by denying freedom to mankind, and thereby making men no other than bare machines, they take away not only innate, but all moral rules whatsoever, and leave not a possibility to believe any such, to those who cannot conceive

[1] To detect and to express in their abstract generality and harmony the principles in which the universe, and thus the sciences, are harmonised, is the ideal towards which philosophy is perpetually struggling ; although inadequate capacity and experience now, perhaps for ever, hinder the philosopher from attaining a clear and distinct understanding of the universe, in the full light of the reason according to which it is constituted. Nevertheless human intellect remains restless in the isolation of the special sciences, notwithstanding their relative lucidity.

how anything can be capable of a law that is not a free agent. And upon that ground they must necessarily reject all principles of virtue, who cannot put *morality* and *mechanism* together, which are not very easy to be reconciled or made consistent[1].

Lord
Herbert's
innate
Principles
examined.

15. When I had written this, being informed that my Lord Herbert had, in his book *De Veritate*[2], assigned these innate principles, I presently consulted him, hoping to find in a man of so great parts, something that might satisfy me in this point, and put an end to my inquiry. In his chapter *De Instinctu Naturali*, p. 72, ed. 1656, I met with these six marks of his *Notitiæ Communes*:—1. *Prioritas*. 2. *Independentia*. 3. *Universalitas*. 4. *Certitudo*. 5. *Necessitas*, i.e. as he explains it, *faciunt ad hominis conservationem*. 6. *Modus conformationis*, i.e. *Assensus nullâ interpositâ morâ*. And at the latter end of his little treatise *De Religione Laici*, he says this of these innate principles: *Adeo ut non uniuscujusvis religionis confinio arctentur quæ ubique vigent veritates. Sunt enim in ipsâ mente cælitus descriptæ, nullisque traditionibus, sive scriptis, sive non scriptis, obnoxiæ*, p. 3. And *Veritates nostræ catholicæ, quæ tanquam indubia Dei emata in foro interiori descriptæ.*

Thus, having given the marks[3] of the innate principles or

---

[1] In thus distinguishing 'morality' and 'mechanism' Locke recognises the inadequacy of a merely physical interpretation of morality, and leaves room for the supremacy of moral and spiritual reality over that reality which is only sensuous and physical.

[2] The *De Veritate, prout distinguitur a Revelatione, a Verisimili, a Possibili, et a Falso* of Lord Herbert of Cherbury (1581–1648), appeared in 1624, at Paris and London. To the third edition (London, 1645) are annexed two tractates—*De Causis Errorum* and *De Religione Laici*. The speculations of this remarkable thinker deserve the careful study of every critical reader of Locke's *Essay*, not only on account of this explicit reference to them, but as a significant phenomenon in the history of English philosophy. They had

before Locke attracted the attention of Descartes (*Œuvres*, ed. Par. viii. 138, 168), Gassendi (Op. iii. 411), and Culverwell in his *Light of Nature*. That Locke should have been thus ignorant of the *De Veritate* shows his comparative indifference to books, and to the philosophical opinions of others. Lord Herbert tried to place English Deism on a philosophical basis, as the universal religion, *constituted by the 'innate principles'* here mentioned, which seemed to him to make external or miraculous revelation superfluous. Yet miracles might be a means of evoking and consolidating spiritual ideas and principles otherwise latent in man, even on Lord Herbert's hypothesis.

[3] The 'universal consent,' of which Locke makes so much in this and the

common notions, and asserted their being imprinted on the CHAP. II.
minds of men by the hand of God, he proceeds to set them
down, and they are these[1]:—1. *Esse aliquod supremum numen.*
2. *Numen illud coli debere.* 3. *Virtutem cum pietate con-*
junctam optimam esse rationem cultûs divini. 4. *Resipiscendum*
esse à peccatis. 5. *Dari præmium vel pœnam post hanc vitam*
transactam. Though I allow these to be clear truths, and

preceding chapter, is thus not the only, nor indeed the chief, *test* which Lord Herbert proposes for distinguishing truths ultimate and absolute from the contingent data of experience; nor does he assume, regarding the former, that they are innate in the sense of being truths of which every human being is conscious at birth, or that they are then held otherwise than virtually. Leibniz made an advance here, in his proposed test of their existence, and his express recognition that they are at first, and may be always, only unconsciously held. Their test is with him *the intellectual necessity we find our-selves under to accept them as soon as they are perceived,* and *the intellectual im-possibility of supposing their contradic-tories.* Thus, that two parallel straight lines cannot enclose a space is *seen to be intellectually necessary*; the suppo-sition that they can enclose it is in-capable of being realised in thought, in the way that a suspension of the law of gravitation, or of any other natural law, might be conceived. And though this example may not have occurred in the conscious experience of some men, it can be shown, by analysis of what consciousness implies, to be in it *virtually.* 'Do all truths,' he asks, 'depend upon induction and experi-ence, or are there not some which have another foundation? The senses, although their data are needed for actual knowledge, are inadequate to account for all that knowledge implies; for the senses can only give ex-amples, that is particular or individual truths. Now the examples which verify

an inductive generalisation, however numerous, cannot show that it is *uni-versally necessary*; for we are not intel-lectually obliged to conceive that what has happened must always in like manner happen. ... That day follows night is seen not to be a necessary or eternal truth, when we consider that the earth and sun themselves (on which this succession depends) have no necessary existence, and that a time may come when the whole solar system will cease to exist—at least, in its present form. . . . The original proof of truths of reason comes from the necessities of reason, while other truths are dependent on what we happen to observe. How great soever may be the number of observed in-stances of an inductive generalisation, we can never be absolutely certain of its universality, unless we discern its intellectual necessity. The senses may verify generalisations, but cannot de-monstrate their eternal and uncon-ditional certainty.' (See *Nouveaux Essais*, Avant-Propos.) But while the 'innate' (not in Locke's sense) prin-ciples of *speculation* are thus guarded by their perceived necessity, 'innate' *moral* principles are those rather which only *good* men cannot reject.

[1] The five propositions which follow are offered by Lord Herbert, not as the result of an exhaustive analysis of the 'natural instincts,' or constituents of the Common Reason, but only as examples of those among them which constitute the catholic religion of mankind.

BOOK I.

CHAP. II.

such as, if rightly explained, a rational creature can hardly avoid giving his assent to, yet I think he is far from proving them innate impressions *in foro interiori descriptæ.* For I must take leave to observe :—

These five either not all, or more than all, if there are any.

16. First, that these five propositions are either not all, or more than all, those common notions written on our minds by the finger of God; if it were reasonable to believe any at all to be so written. Since there are other propositions which, even by his own rules, have as just a pretence to such an original, and may be as well admitted for innate principles, as at least some of these five he enumerates, viz. 'Do as thou wouldst be done unto.' And perhaps some hundreds of others, when well considered.

The supposed marks wanting.

17. Secondly, that all his marks are not to be found in each of his five propositions, viz. his first, second, and third marks agree perfectly to neither of them ; and the first, second, third, fourth, and sixth marks agree but ill to his third, fourth, and fifth propositions. For, besides that we are assured from history of many men, nay whole nations, who doubt or disbelieve some or all of them[1], I cannot see how the third, viz. 'That virtue joined with piety is the best worship of God,' can be an innate principle, when the name or sound *virtue,* is so hard to be understood ; liable to so much uncertainty in its signification ; and the thing it stands for so much contended about and difficult to be known[2]. And therefore this cannot be but a very uncertain rule of human practice, and serve but very little to the conduct of our lives, and is therefore very unfit to be assigned as an innate practical principle.

Of little use if they were innate.

18. For let us consider this proposition as to its meaning, (for it is the sense, and not sound, that is and must be the principle or common notion,) viz. 'Virtue is the best worship of God,' i. e. is most acceptable to him ; which, if virtue be

---

[1] As already remarked, Locke looks too much for express recognition, and overlooks indirect signs of the presence of unconscious or semi-conscious beliefs. He is besides uncritically credulous of reports, by travellers and others, even less critical than he was himself.

[2] This is his often repeated assumption,—that innate *principles* always presuppose innate *ideas*, inasmuch as they must be otherwise propositions containing meaningless terms. He grants that *connections* of ideas, after experience has given the ideas, may be seen to be necessary.

taken, as most commonly it is, for those actions which,
according to the different opinions of several countries, are accounted laudable, will be a proposition so far from being certain, that it will not be true. If virtue be taken for actions conformable to God's will, or to the rule prescribed by God—which is the true and only measure of virtue [¹when virtue is used to signify what is in its own nature right and good]—then this proposition, 'That virtue is the best worship of God,' will be most true and certain, but of very little use in human life: since it will amount to no more but this, viz. 'That God is pleased with the doing of what he commands';— which a man may certainly know to be true, without knowing *what it is* that God doth command; and so be as far from any rule or principle of his actions as he was before. And I think very few will take a proposition which amounts to no more than this, viz. 'That God is pleased with the doing of what he himself commands,' for an innate moral principle written on the minds of all men, (however true and certain it may be,) since it teaches so little². Whosoever does so will have reason to think hundreds of propositions innate principles; since there are many which have as good a title as this to be received for such, which nobody yet ever put into that rank of innate principles³.

19. Nor is the fourth proposition (viz. 'Men must repent of their sins') much more instructive, till what those actions are that are meant by sins be set down. For the word *peccata*, or sins, being put, as it usually is, to signify in general ill actions that will draw punishment upon the doers, what great principle of morality can that be to tell us we should be sorry, and cease to do that which will bring mischief upon us; without knowing what those particular actions are that will do so? Indeed this is a very true proposition, and fit to be

---

¹ Added in second edition.

² The 'emptiness' of the ultimate, and therefore highly abstract, princi- ples which are called 'innate' is one of his objections to their being recog- nised by a practical philosopher like himself. They cannot, *per se*, inform the mind of anything that happens.

³ Because a philosopher seeks for the most comprehensive categories of thought; but not primarily for all the conclusions that may be evolved from them, or that are determined by them, as applied presuppositions in concrete inferences.

inculcated on and received by those who are supposed to have been taught *what* actions in all kinds *are* sins: but neither this nor the former can be imagined to be innate principles; nor to be of any use if they were innate, unless the particular measures and bounds of all virtues and vices were engraven in men's minds, and were innate principles also, which I think is very much to be doubted. And therefore, I imagine, it will scarcely seem possible that God should engrave principles in men's minds, in words of uncertain signification, such as *virtues* and *sins*, which amongst different men stand for different things: nay, it cannot be supposed to be in words at all, which, being in most of these principles very general, names, cannot be understood but by knowing the particulars comprehended under them. And in the practical instances, the measures must be taken from the knowledge of the actions themselves, and the rules of them,—abstracted from words, and antecedent to the knowledge of names; which rules a man must know, what language soever he chance to learn, whether English or Japan, or if he should learn no language at all, or never should understand the use of words, as happens in the case of dumb and deaf men. When it shall be made out that men ignorant of words, or untaught by the laws and customs of their country, know that it is part of the worship of God, not to kill another man; not to know more women than one; not to procure abortion; not to expose their children; not to take from another what is his, though we want it ourselves, but on the contrary, relieve and supply his wants; and whenever we have done the contrary we ought to repent, be sorry, and resolve to do so no more;—when I say, all men shall be proved actually to know and allow all these and a thousand other such rules, all of which come under these two general words made use of above, viz. *virtutes et peccata*, virtues and sins, there will be more reason for admitting these and the like, for common notions and practical principles. Yet, after all, universal consent (were there any in moral principles) to truths [1], the knowledge whereof may be attained

---

[1] All truths, whether intellectually necessary or (for us) contingent, are reached by the exercise of our faculties in experience; and not antecedently to, but in dependence on, the presentation of data in external or internal sense.

otherwise, would scarce prove them to be innate; which is all
I contend for.

20. Nor will it be of much moment here to offer that very
ready but not very material answer, viz. that the innate
principles of morality may, by education, and custom, and the
general opinion of those amongst whom we converse, be
darkened, and at last quite worn out of the minds of men.
Which assertion of theirs, if true, quite takes away the argument of universal consent, by which this opinion of innate
principles is endeavoured to be proved; unless those men will
think it reasonable that their private persuasions, or that of
their party, should pass for universal consent;—a thing not
unfrequently done, when men, presuming themselves to be the
only masters of right reason, cast by the votes and opinions of
the rest of mankind as not worthy the reckoning.   And then
their argument stands thus :—' The principles which all mankind allow for true, are innate; those that men of right reason
admit, are the principles allowed by all mankind ; we, and
those of our mind, are men of reason ; therefore, we agreeing,
our principles are innate ' ;—which is a very pretty way of
arguing, and a short cut to infallibility.   For otherwise it
will be very hard to understand how there be some principles
which all men do acknowledge and agree in ; and yet there
are none of those principles which are not, by depraved custom
and ill education, blotted out of the minds of many men :
which is to say, that all men admit, but yet many men do
deny and dissent from them.   And indeed the supposition of
such first principles will serve us to very little purpose ; and
we shall be as much at a loss with as without them, if they
may, by any human power—such as the will of our teachers,
or opinions of our companions—be altered or lost in us : and
notwithstanding all this boast of first principles and innate
light, we shall be as much in the dark and uncertainty as if
there were no such thing at all : it being all one to have no
rule, and one that will warp any way ; or amongst various
and contrary rules, not to know which is the right.   But concerning innate principles, I desire these men to say, whether
they can or cannot, by education and custom, be blurred and
blotted out ; if they cannot, we must find them in all mankind

BOOK I.
—◆◆—
CHAP. II.
Objection,
Innate
Principles
may be
corrupted,
answered.

alike, and they must be clear in everybody; and if they may suffer variation from adventitious notions, we must then find them clearest and most perspicuous nearest the fountain, in children and illiterate people, who have received least impression from foreign opinions. Let them take which side they please, they will certainly find it inconsistent with visible matter of fact and daily observation [1].

Contrary
Principles
in the
World.

21. I easily grant that there are great numbers of opinions which, by men of different countries, educations, and tempers, are received and embraced as first and unquestionable principles; many whereof, both for their absurdity as well as oppositions to one another, it is impossible should be true [2]. But yet all those propositions, how remote soever from reason, are so sacred somewhere or other, that men even of good understanding in other matters, will sooner part with their

---

[1] This argument against 'innate principles for determining conduct' proceeds, like his previous arguments, upon Locke's interpretation of innateness, as involving *actual realisation in the consciousness of each individual from birth*. But a principle may be *potentially innate*, and only evoked in the consciousness of the few who are highly educated, morally and intellectually. To *awaken a response* in individuals to the principles on which human life reposes is the aim of the higher education. From Socrates onwards this has been recognised by teachers of religion and philosophy. These 'innate' elements are not consciously apprehended by all; some of them are always dormant in some persons, or are acted on without a philosophical intelligence of their meaning. 'Children and illiterate people' cannot have this intelligence. Moral principles may be vindicated on the ground that—operative in good men, though dormant in others—they ought not to be surrendered, unless they can be shown to contradict necessities of intellect. Note that Locke's point still is,—the time and way in which the individual becomes aware of the abstract principles of morality; not whether the moral constitution of things be not such that, *at the proper time, and under the natural conditions*, self-evident truths *must* shine forth in their self-evidence.

[2] It is granted even by Reid—an uncritical advocate of 'first principles' —that it cannot 'without great want of charity' be denied, that men who love truth may 'differ about first principles.' He argues, however, that nature has not left us destitute of means whereby the candid and honest part of mankind may be brought to unanimity when they happen to differ about first principles. Those principles 'which are really the dictates of common sense, and directly opposed to absurdities of opinion, will always, *from the constitution of human nature, support themselves*, and gain rather than lose ground among mankind. There are certain ways of reasoning about them by which those that are just and solid may be confirmed, and those that are false may be detected.' Some of those 'ways' Reid points out. See *Essays on Intellectual Powers*, VI. ch. iv.

lives, and whatever is dearest to them, than suffer themselves to doubt, or others to question, the truth of them.

BOOK I.
—••—
CHAP. II.
How men
commonly
come by
their
Principles.

22. This, however strange it may seem, is that which every day's experience confirms; and will not, perhaps, appear so wonderful, if we consider the ways and steps by which it is brought about; and how really it may come to pass, that doctrines that have been derived from no better original than the superstition of a nurse, or the authority of an old woman, may, by length of time and consent of neighbours, grow up to the dignity of *principles* in religion or morality. For such, who are careful (as they call it) to principle children well, (and few there be who have not a set of those principles for them, which they believe in,) instil into the unwary, and as yet unprejudiced, understanding, (for white paper[1] receives any characters,) those doctrines they would have them retain and profess. These being taught them as soon as they have any apprehension ; and still as they grow up confirmed to them, either by the open profession or tacit consent of all they have to do with ; or at least by those of whose wisdom, knowledge, and piety they have an opinion, who never suffer those propositions to be otherwise mentioned but as the basis and foundation on which they build their religion and manners, come, by these means, to have the reputation of unquestionable, self-evident, and innate truths[2].

23. To which we may add, that when men so instructed are grown up, and reflect on their own minds, they cannot find anything more ancient there than those opinions, which were taught them before their memory began to keep a register of their actions, or date the time when any new thing appeared to them ; and therefore make no scruple to conclude, that those propositions of whose knowledge they can find in themselves no original, were certainly the impress of God and nature upon their minds, and not taught them by any one else. These

Principles
supposed
innate
because
we do not
remember
when we
began to
hold them.

[1] The *tabula rasa* metaphor. It is apt to suggest that we are merely passive or receptive in the acquisition of experience ; and that experience is simple, and therefore incapable of critical analysis.

[2] But without *perception* of their intellectual necessity. Note here once more the motive of Locke's attack on innate principles—to explode prejudices, dispel empty phrases, and substitute rational insight for *blind* dependence on authority.

they entertain and submit to, as many do to their parents with veneration; not because it is natural; nor do children do it where they are not so taught; but because, having been always so educated, and having no remembrance of the beginning of this respect, they think it is natural.

How such
principles
come to
be held.

24. This will appear very likely, and almost unavoidable to come to pass, if we consider the nature of mankind and the constitution of human affairs; wherein most men cannot live without employing their time in the daily labours of their callings; nor be at quiet in their minds without *some* foundation or principle to rest their thoughts on[1]. There is scarcely any one so floating and superficial in his understanding, who hath not some reverenced propositions, which are to him the principles on which he bottoms his reasonings, and by which he judgeth of truth and falsehood, right and wrong; which some, wanting skill and leisure, and others the inclination, and some being taught that they ought not to examine, there are few to be found who are not exposed by their ignorance, laziness, education, or precipitancy, to *take them upon trust.*

Further
explained.

25. This is evidently the case of all children and young folk; and custom, a greater power than nature[2], seldom failing to make them worship for divine what she hath inured them to bow their minds and submit their understandings to, it is no wonder that grown men, either perplexed in the necessary affairs of life, or hot in the pursuit of pleasures, should *not* seriously sit down to examine their own tenets; especially when one of their principles is, that principles ought not to be questioned[3]. And had men leisure, parts, and will, who is there almost that dare shake the foundations of all his past thoughts and actions, and endure to bring upon himself the

[1] *The felt need for something fixed and persistent on which to rest,* in a continually changing and hazardous world, originated philosophy and sustains religion.

[2] Hume afterwards, like the Greek sceptics, sought to resolve all judgments about matters of fact into the natural issue of *custom,* thus making it the supreme (physical) cause in determining our sense of the true, the beautiful, and the good.

[3] Note the antithesis here between premisses accepted blindly, and that criticism of premisses which his argument against innate ideas and principles was meant to encourage. Cf. Bk. IV. ch. xx. § 2.

shame of having been a long time wholly in mistake and
error? Who is there hardy enough to contend with the
reproach which is everywhere prepared for those who dare
venture to dissent from the received opinions of their country
or party? And where is the man to be found that can
patiently prepare himself to bear the name of whimsical,
sceptical, or atheist; which he is sure to meet with, who does
in the least scruple any of the common opinions? And he
will be much more afraid to question those principles, when
he shall think them, as most men do, the standards set up by
God in his mind, to be the rule and touchstone of all other
opinions. And what can hinder him from thinking them
sacred, when he finds them the earliest of all his own thoughts,
and the most reverenced by others?

26. It is easy to imagine how, by these means, it comes to A worship of idols.
pass that men worship the idols that have been set up in
their minds[1]; grow fond of the notions they have been long
acquainted with there; and stamp the characters of divinity
upon absurdities and errors; become zealous votaries to bulls
and monkeys, and contend too, fight, and die in defence of
their opinions. *Dum solos credit habendos esse deos, quos ipse
colit.* For, since the reasoning faculties of the soul, which
are almost constantly, though not always warily nor wisely
employed, would not know how to move, for want of a foundation and footing, in most men, who through laziness or
avocation do not, or for want of time, or true helps, or for
other causes, cannot penetrate into the principles of knowledge, and trace truth to its fountain and original[2], it is natural
for them, and almost unavoidable, to take up with some

---

[1] A reference to the *idola* of Bacon,
—those phantoms of the human mind,
which we are apt to prefer to the
' ideas of the divine mind' that are
expressed in the laws of nature. ' Non
leve quiddam interest inter humanae
mentis *idola*, et divinae mentis ideas.'
Nov. Org. i. aph. 23. See relative notes
in Dr. Fowler's edition. This is one
of the few allusions to Bacon in the
Essay. His *idola*, as they are unreal
ideas and false principles, are *false*

gods; and we (so far) find the true
God in finding the genuine principles of physical and moral experience,
and (so far) worship God by living in
harmony with them.

[2] That is to say, indolent persons,
who live thus, cannot become philosophers: the genuine principles of
reason remain for them latent. They
are thus ready to accept spurious ones
in the form of their own prejudices.

borrowed principles; which being reputed and presumed to be the evident proofs of other things, are thought not to need any other proof themselves. Whoever shall receive any of these into his mind, and entertain them there with the reverence usually paid to principles, never venturing to examine them, but accustoming himself to believe them, because they are to be believed, may take up, from his education and the fashions of his country, any absurdity for innate principles; and by long poring on the same objects, so dim his sight as to take monsters lodged in his own brain for the images of the Deity, and the workmanship of his hands.

Principles must be examined.

27. By this progress, how many there are who arrive at principles which they believe innate may be easily observed, in the variety of opposite principles held and contended for by all sorts and degrees of men. And he that shall deny this to be the method wherein most men proceed to the assurance they have of the truth and evidence of their principles, will perhaps find it a hard matter any other way to account for the contrary tenets, which are firmly believed, confidently asserted, and which great numbers are ready at any time to seal with their blood. And, indeed, if it be the privilege of innate principles to be received upon their own authority, without examination[1], I know not what may not be believed, or how any one's principles can be questioned. If they may and ought to be examined and tried, I desire to know how first and innate principles can be tried; or at least it is reasonable to demand the *marks* and *characters* whereby the genuine innate principles may be distinguished from others: that so, amidst the great variety of pretenders, I may be kept from mistakes in so material a point as this. When this is done, I shall be ready to embrace such welcome and useful propositions; and till then I may with modesty doubt; since I fear universal consent, which is the only one produced, will scarcely prove

---

[1] It is the ready reception of 'customary' premises, without criticism of their claims in reason, which makes Locke pursue with so much moral intensity this otherwise tedious argument. Accordingly, in this and the seven preceding sections, he dwells on the difficulty and danger of mistake in the *process* through which self-evident truth is realised in its self-evidence, while he overlooks the intellectual necessity and universality of the *product*, when it has at last been reached, by dint of reflective energy.

a sufficient mark to direct my choice, and assure me of any
innate principles.

From what has been said, I think it past doubt, that there are no practical principles wherein all men agree ; and therefore none innate[1].

---

[1] Although a *conscious* 'universal agreement' is necessarily the test of innateness, in Locke's meaning of 'innate,' it is not the only, nor indeed a possible, test of *virtual* innateness. Cf. Leibniz, and Reid, *ut supra*; also Kant's test of principles that are not mere generalisations from contingent data, but derived to the mind from its own operation,—which he finds in our consciousness of their intellectual necessity and universality.

CHAPTER III.

OTHER CONSIDERATIONS CONCERNING INNATE PRINCIPLES, BOTH SPECULATIVE AND PRACTICAL.

BOOK I.

CHAP. III.

Principles not innate, unless their Ideas be innate.

1. HAD those who would persuade us that there are innate principles not taken them together in gross, but considered separately the parts out of which those propositions are made, they would not, perhaps, have been so forward to believe they were innate. Since, if the *ideas* which made up those truths were not, it was impossible that the *propositions* made up of them should be innate, or our knowledge of them be born with us. For, if the ideas be not innate, there was a time when the mind was without those principles ; and then they will not be innate, but be derived from some other original. For, where the ideas themselves are not, there can be no knowledge, no assent, no mental or verbal propositions about them[1].

Ideas, especially those belonging to Principles, not born with Children.

2. If we will attentively consider new-born children, we shall have little reason to think that they bring many ideas into the world with them. For, bating perhaps some faint ideas of hunger, and thirst, and warmth, and some pains, which they may have felt in the womb, there is not the least appearance of any settled ideas at all in them ; especially of *ideas*

---

[1] Intelligible *propositions*, in short, presuppose intelligible *terms*. The world had been perplexed, he implies, by being asked to believe propositions in which the terms were void of meaning. Hence Locke's hostility to innate propositions, as inconsistent with genuine insight, and with the consciousness which he assumes to be essential to an ' idea.' But, as one of his earliest critics remarks, ' we call ideas innate, not because we are born with an *actual notion* of all the particulars in our minds, but with a *natural facility to know them*, as soon as the things implied in the words that stand for them are presented to the understanding ; and a *natural and unavoidable determination to judge them true*, as soon as we know the things themselves, or the words by which they are signified to others.' (Lee, *Anti-Scepticism*, Bk. I. ch. iv.)

answering the terms which make up those universal propositions that are esteemed innate principles[1]. One may perceive how, by degrees, afterwards, ideas come into their minds ; and that they get no more, nor other, than what experience, and the observation of things that come in their way, furnish them with ; which might be enough to satisfy us that they are not original characters stamped on the mind.

3. ' It is impossible for the same thing to be,· and not to be,' is certainly (if there be any such) an innate *principle*. But can any one think, or will any one say, that 'impossibility' and 'identity' are two innate *ideas*? Are they such as all mankind have, and bring into the world with them? And are they those which are the first in children, and antecedent to all acquired ones? If they are innate, they must needs be so[1]. Hath a child an idea of impossibility and identity, before it has of white or black, sweet or bitter? And is. it from the knowledge of this principle that it concludes, that wormwood rubbed on the nipple hath not the same taste that it used to receive from thence? Is it the actual knowledge of *impossibile est idem esse, et non esse*, that makes a child distinguish between its mother and a stranger; or that makes it fond of the one and flee the other? Or does the mind regulate itself and its assent by ideas that it never yet had? Or the understanding draw conclusions from principles which it never yet knew or understood? The names *impossibility* and *identity* stand for two ideas, so far from being innate, or born with us, that I think it requires great care and attention to form them right in our understandings. They are so far from being brought into the world with us, so remote from the thoughts of infancy and childhood, that I believe, upon examination it will be found that many grown men want them[2].

[1] Although 'universal' propositions are *a priori* and ultimate *in rerum natura,* they are not *a priori* in the time of their conscious apprehension. Their apriority is not in time, but as conditions of the constitution of our experience of what is real, and therefore of the nature of things. The argument which runs through the First Book continually overlooks this distinction—especially in what follows.

[2] The human mind proceeds *towards* universal or 'first' principles rather than *from* them, in gradually becoming conscious of the logical and metaphysical conditions that in ordinary experience are unconsciously presupposed as necessary.

4. If *identity* (to instance that alone) be a native impression, and consequently so clear and obvious to us that we must needs know it even from our cradles, I would gladly be resolved by any one of seven, or seventy years old, whether a man, being a creature consisting of soul and body, be the same man when his body is changed? Whether Euphorbus and Pythagoras, having had the same soul, were the same men, though they lived several ages asunder[1]? Nay, whether the cock too, which had the same soul, were not the same with both of them[2]? Whereby, perhaps, it will appear that our idea of *sameness* is not so settled and clear as to deserve to be thought innate in us. For if those innate ideas are not clear and distinct, so as to be universally known and naturally agreed on, they cannot be subjects of universal and undoubted truths, but will be the unavoidable occasion of perpetual uncertainty. For, I suppose every one's idea of identity will not be the same that Pythagoras and thousands of his followers have. And which then shall be true? Which innate? Or are there two different ideas of identity, both innate?

5. Nor let any one think that the questions I have here proposed about the identity of man are bare empty speculations; which, if they were, would be enough to show, that there was in the understandings of men no innate idea of identity. He that shall with a little attention reflect on the resurrection, and consider that divine justice will bring to judgment, at the last day, the very same persons, to be happy or miserable in the other, who did well or ill in this life, will find it perhaps not easy to resolve with himself, what makes the same man, or wherein identity consists; and will not be forward to think he, and every one, even children themselves, have naturally a clear idea of it[3].

---

[1] The allusion is to the Pythagorean teaching about the transmigration of souls. Locke deals with the idea of 'identity' more fully under our complex ideas, Bk. II. ch. xxvii.

[2] The reference is to Lucian's satire of the Pythagorean metempsychosis.

[3] Locke puzzled himself about the meaning which should be expressed by the terms 'identity,' 'same,' &c. Cf. Bk. II. ch. xxvii. See Bp. Butler's *Dissertation on Personal Identity* (1736), and Perronet's *Vindication* (1738), for a criticism and a defence of Locke, whose idea of sameness in persons has continued to be matter of controversy since.

6. Let us examine that principle of mathematics, viz. *that the whole is bigger than a part.* This, I take it, is reckoned amongst innate principles. I am sure it has as good a title as any to be thought so ; which yet nobody can think it to be, when he considers [that] the ideas it comprehends in it, *whole* and *part*, are perfectly relative; but the positive ideas to which they properly and immediately belong are extension and number, of which alone whole and part are relations. So that if whole and part are innate ideas, extension and number must be so too; it being impossible to have an idea of a relation, without having any at all of the thing to which it belongs, and in which it is founded. Now, whether the minds of men have naturally imprinted on them the ideas of extension and number, I leave to be considered by those who are the patrons of innate principles[1].

7. That *God is to be worshipped*, is, without doubt, as great a truth as any that can enter into the mind of man, and deserves the first place amongst all practical principles. But yet it can by no means be thought innate, unless the ideas of *God* and *worship* are innate. That the idea the term worship stands for is not in the understanding of children, and a character stamped on the mind in its first original, I think will be easily granted, by any one that considers how few there be amongst grown men who have a clear and distinct notion of it. And, I suppose, there cannot be anything more ridiculous than to say, that children have this practical principle innate, ' That God is to be worshipped,' and yet that they know not what that worship of God is, which is their duty[2]. But to pass by this.

8. If any idea can be imagined innate, the idea of *God* may, of all others[3], for many reasons, be thought so ; since it is

---

[1] Locke would account, by means of sight and touch, for the rise in consciousness of the idea of ' extension ' in both of which senses concrete extensions are presented (Bk. II. ch. v); and for unity and ' number,' as modes ' suggested by every object of which we can be conscious' (Bk. II. ch. vii. § 7).

[2] Lord Herbert assumed it to be innate. We may be long unconscious of an idea which, when it does rise into consciousness, is perceived to be necessary and universal.

[3] That the idea of God is to be regarded as innate might be maintained on other grounds than those

hard to conceive how there should be innate moral principles, without an innate idea of a Deity. Without a notion of a law-maker, it is impossible to have a notion of a law, and an obligation to observe it. Besides the atheists taken notice of amongst the ancients [2], and left branded upon the records of history, hath not navigation discovered, in these later ages,

conceived by Locke, and in another sense of innateness than his. It is easy to show, as he does in the sequel, that the idea is obscured in many minds, and that it takes many unworthy forms. But if faith in God is virtually implied in the fundamental assumption of the constant supremacy of Order or Reason in the universe, to which man, as intelligent and responsible, responds,—then the existence of God is virtually, if unconsciously, assumed even in the faith in *physical order or natural law*, with the ideas and principles therein presupposed, on which all common life and science of nature depend—a faith which is the basis of natural religion; while faith in the ultimate supremacy of *spiritual order and moral purpose*, with their presupposed moral ideas, is the basis of spiritual or supernatural religion. Atheism is thus that negation of reason, in the universe and in us, which logically should become the speechless scepticism with which Plato deals. The necessary presuppositions of physical science, and still more the necessary presuppositions of morality, are virtually presuppositions of God's existence,—as the immanent ever active Reason that is at once the beginning and the end of philosophy as well as of religion. This whole question about innate, in the sense of presupposed absolute, principles, thus becomes the religious question in its ultimate intellectual form. But this is not Locke's point of view. With him the existence of God is a thesis to be proved; not a pre-

supposition, apart from which nothing else can be proved — the ultimate ground of any explanation of the phenomena of the universe into which we are born, and of us who are born into it.

For Locke's account of man's idea and knowledge of God, in addition to §§ 8–18 in this chapter, see Bk. II. ch. xv. §§ 2, 12; xxiii. §§ 21, 33-36; Bk. IV. ch. x; also Letter to Collins, June 29, 1704, as to how far we can interpret the universe ultimately in terms of human consciousness.

[2] Locke is apt to accept without criticism the crude reports of travellers, who were often unable to interpret the languages of the nations they described, and thus, with an uncharacteristic deference to authority, he maintains that whole nations exist to whom the ideas of God and a future life are strange. Yet while, on this ground, he here denies the innateness of these ideas, he elsewhere seeks to show that God's existence is demonstrable—'as certain as any conclusion in pure mathematics' (Bk. IV. ch. x). Moreover, he nowhere takes sufficient account of the very different degrees in which the complex idea of God is developed in different persons, and of the various phases assumed by this, the deepest and most comprehensive of all the presuppositions of our real experience. To presuppose the rationality of experience, as all reasoning about reality must do, is to presuppose the *immanent* existence or presence of God.

whole nations, at the bay of Soldania[1], in Brazil[2], [[3]in Boran-day,] and in the Caribbee islands, &c., amongst whom there was to be found no notion of a God, no religion? Nicholaus del Techo[4], *in Litèris ex Paraquaria, de Caiguarum Conversione,* has these words: *Reperi eam gentem nullum nomen habere quod Deum, et hominis animam significet; nulla sacra habet, nulla idola.* [[5]These are instances of nations where uncultivated nature has been left to itself, without the help of letters and discipline, and the improvements of arts and sciences. But there are others to be found who have enjoyed these in a very great measure, who yet, for want of a due application of their thoughts this way, want the idea and knowledge of God. It will, I doubt not, be a surprise to others, as it was to me, to find the Siamites of this number. But for this, let them consult the King of France's late envoy thither[6], who gives no better account of the Chinese themselves. And[7] if we will not believe La Loubère, the missionaries of China, even the Jesuits themselves, the great encomiasts of the Chinese, do all to a man agree, and will convince us, that the sect of the *literari,* or learned, keeping to the old religion of China, and the ruling party there, are all of them

---

[1] Roe, in Thevenot's *Relation de divers Voyages Curieux.* Sir Thomas Roe, a distinguished diplomatist, was King James's ambassador to the Great Mogul in 1614–18. The report of his experience there appeared in 1665, as an appendix to the translation of Pietro della Valle's travels, and again in Churchill's *Collection.* He died in 1644.

[2] Jo. de Lery, p. 16, who travelled in Brazil in the end of the sixteenth century, and wrote a history of that country.

[3] Added in fourth edition. Martinière $\frac{291}{342}$; Terry, *Voyage to the Mogul,* $\frac{17}{545}$ and $\frac{23}{545}$; Ovington $\frac{489}{808}$. (Ovington's *Voyage to Surat* in 1689.)

[4] Nicholas de Techo, a Jesuit missionary, who wrote an account of Paraguay and other countries in South America, where he lived for twenty-

five years. He reports many particulars of the customs of the savage Indians, in his Letters from Paraguay, and as to the conversion of the Indians of that South American province. See Churchill's *Collection,* vol. iv.

[5] This and the next three sentences added in *fourth* edition. Locke again trusts too much to the statements of strangers imperfectly acquainted with the native languages, ignorant too of the sciences of comparative religion and comparative philology, and thus apt to misinterpret the imperfectly developed and inarticulate beliefs of savages.

[6] La Loubère, *Du Royaume de Siam,* tom. i. c. 9, § 15; c. 20, §§ 4–22; c. 22, § 6, and c. 23. M. de la Loubère (1642–1729) was the envoy of Louis XIV to Siam in 1687.

[7] This and the next sentence added in Coste's French Version.

BOOK I.
CHAP. III.

atheists. Vid. Navarette[1], in the *Collection of Voyages*, vol. i., and *Historia Cultus Sinensium*.]   And perhaps, if we should with attention mind the lives and discourses of people not so far off, we should have too much reason to fear, that many, in more civilized countries, have no very strong and clear impressions of a Deity upon their minds, and that the complaints of atheism made from the pulpit are not without reason. And though only some profligate wretches own it too barefacedly now; yet perhaps we should hear more than we do of it from others, did not the fear of the magistrate's sword, or their neighbour's censure, tie up people's tongues; which, were the apprehensions of punishment or shame taken away, would as openly proclaim their atheism as their lives do[2].

The name of God not universal or obscure in meaning.

9. But had all mankind everywhere a notion of a God, (whereof yet history tells us the contrary,) it would not from thence follow, that the idea of him was innate. For, though no nation were to be found without a name, and some few

---

[1] A Dominican friar, sent in 1646 by his order as a missionary to the Philippine Islands, and afterwards to China, where he spent more than twenty years in the service of Christianity. His learned account of the Chinese, in Spanish, appears in a translation in Churchill's *Collection*.

[2] 'I think' (Locke afterwards says, in his *Third Letter* to Stillingfleet, p. 447), 'I think that the "universal consent" of mankind as to the being of a God amounts to thus much—that the vastly greater majority have, in all ages of the world, actually believed a God; that the majority of the remaining part have not actually disbelieved it; and consequently those who have actually opposed the belief of a God have truly been very few. . . . This is all the universal consent which truth of matter of fact will allow, and therefore all that can be made use of to prove a God. . . . But a consent of every man, even to a man, in all ages and countries, this would make it either no argument or an unnecessary one.

For, if anyone deny a God, such perfect universality of consent is destroyed; and if nobody does deny a God, what need of arguments to convince atheists? what need of arguments against a fault from which mankind are so wholly free? If you say (as I doubt not but you will) that they have had atheists in the world, then your lordship's "universal consent" reduces itself to only a great majority; and I have not said one word that does in the least invalidate *this* argument for a God. The argument I was upon there was, to show that the idea of God was not innate; and to my purpose this sufficed—if there were but a less number found who had no idea of God than your lordship will allow there have been of professed atheists; *for whatsoever is innate must be universal in the strictest sense; one exception is a sufficient proof against it.*'—This argument is good against the explicit, but not against the implicit innateness of the ideas of God and religion.—Locke elsewhere argues against toleration of atheists.

dark notions of him[1], yet that would not prove them to be natural impressions on the mind; no more than the names of fire, or the sun, heat, or number, do prove the ideas they stand for to be innate; because the names of those things, and the ideas of them, are so universally received and known amongst mankind. Nor, on the contrary, is the want of such a name, or the absence of such a notion out of men's minds, any argument against the being of a God; any more than it would be a proof that there was no loadstone in the world, because a great part of mankind had neither a notion of any such thing nor a name for it; or be any show of argument to prove that there are no distinct and various species of angels, or intelligent beings above us, because we have no ideas of such distinct species, or names for them. For, men being furnished with words, by the common language of their own countries, can scarce avoid having some kind of ideas of those things whose names those they converse with have occasion frequently to mention to them. And if they carry with it the notion of excellency, greatness, or something extraordinary; if apprehension and concernment accompany it; if the fear of absolute and irresistible power set it on upon the mind,— the idea is likely to sink the deeper, and spread the further; especially if it be such an idea as is agreeable to the common light of reason[2], and naturally deducible from every part of our knowledge, as that of a God is. For the visible marks of extraordinary wisdom and power appear so plainly in all the works of the creation, that a rational creature, who will but seriously reflect on them, cannot miss the discovery of a Deity. And the influence that the discovery of such a Being must necessarily have on the minds of all that have but once heard of it is so great, and carries such a weight of thought and communication with it, that it seems stranger to me that

---

[1] For the origin and constitution of the complex idea of God, see Bk. II. ch. xxiii. §§ 33–35. The idea is found in very various stages of development, and with Locke himself is external and mechanical, excluding immanence in the actuality of the world of experi-ence. It is the deistical idea, in short.

[2] 'Common light of reason' is else-where 'intuition' (Bk. IV. ch. ii. § 1), 'natural revelation' (Bk. IV. ch. xix. § 4), and 'the candle of the Lord set up by God Himself in men's minds' (ch. iii. 20).

BOOK I.
—++—
CHAP. III.

Ideas of God and idea of Fire.

a whole nation of men should be anywhere found so brutish as to want the notion of a God, than that they should be without any notion of numbers, or fire [1].

10. The name of God being once mentioned in any part of the world, to express a superior, powerful, wise, invisible Being, the suitableness of such a notion to the principles of common reason, and the interest men will always have to mention it often, must necessarily spread it far and wide; and continue it down to all generations: though yet the general reception of this name, and some imperfect and unsteady notions conveyed thereby to the unthinking part of mankind, prove not the idea to be innate; but only that they who made the discovery had made a right use of their reason, thought maturely of the causes of things, and traced them to their original; from whom other less considering people having once received so important a notion, it could not easily be lost again [2].

Idea of God not innate.

11. This is all could be inferred from the notion of a God, were it to be found universally in all the tribes of mankind, and generally acknowledged, by men grown to maturity in all countries. For the generality of the acknowledging of a God, as I imagine, is extended no further than that; which, if it be sufficient to prove the idea of God innate, will as well prove the idea of fire innate; since I think it may be truly said, that there is not a person in the world who has a notion of a God, who has not also the idea of fire. I doubt not but if a colony of young children should be placed in an island where no fire was, they would certainly neither have any notion of such

---

[1] Here and elsewhere he speaks of God as one object among many (fire, loadstone, &c.), rather than as unique, and incapable of being classed—the perfect ever-active Reason in which all finite persons live and have their being, but in a way that is somehow consistent with *their* individuality and moral freedom. 'Rien de plus beau,' says Leibniz, in reference to this section, 'et de plus à mon gré, que cette suite des pensées.' But he adds—'Je dirais seulement ici que l'auteur, parlant des plus simples lumières de la raison qui s'accordent avec l'idée de Dieu, et de

ce qui en découle naturellement, ne paraît guere s'éloigner de mon sens sur les vérités innées.' (*Nouv. Ess.* Liv. I. ch. iii.)

[2] Although the full presence of the complex idea of Deity in individuals presupposes their spiritual activity, it may, when it does arise, show *by its constitution* that it cannot be analysed into accidents of experience—that, on the contrary, it was a sustaining, organising faith, necessarily latent in the experience of those who were least conscious of it—manifest in a degree even in their habitual trust in natural order.

a thing, nor name for it, how generally soever it were received
and known in all the world besides; and perhaps too their
apprehensions would be as far removed from any name, or
notion, of a God[1], till some one amongst them had employed
his thoughts to inquire into the constitution and causes of
things, which would easily lead him to the notion of a God;
which having once taught to others, reason, and the natural
propensity of their own thoughts, would afterwards propagate,
and continue amongst them[2].

12. Indeed it is urged, that it is suitable to the goodness of
God, to imprint upon the minds of men characters and notions
of himself, and not to leave them in the dark and doubt in so
grand a concernment; and also, by that means, to secure to
himself the homage and veneration due from so intelligent a
creature as man; and therefore he has done it[3].

This argument, if it be of any force, will prove much more
than those who use it in this case expect from it. For, if we
may conclude that God hath done for men all that men shall
judge is best for them, because it is suitable to his goodness
so to do, it will prove, not only that God has imprinted on
the minds of men an idea of himself, but that he hath plainly
stamped there, in fair characters, all that men ought to know
or believe of him; all that they ought to do in obedience to

---

[1] But are the ideas of 'fire' and of 'God,' or supreme active Reason, when we do have them, alike, in being *intellectually necessary* to the philosophic conception of the universe? Are they equally implied in the logic of natural and moral experience? Locke himself recognises the difference, in holding as he does that the existence of God is as demonstrable as any conclusion in pure mathematics, which the existence of fire is not.

[2] The idea appears in degrees of development so various that the term 'God' suggests very different ideas in different ages and nations, as well as in individual minds in the same age or nation.

[3] The argument for the existence, if not for the complex idea, of God, founded on the 'common consent of mankind,'—the *consensus gentium* as the *vox naturae*, formulated in the *quod semper, quod ubique, quod ab omnibus*,—cannot claim the weight which might be due to the inevitable conscious conviction of every human being, children and adults, savages and philosophers; for in that case atheists and agnostics would be impossible phenomena, and arguments would be superseded. It can only claim the deference proper to convictions commonly experienced, in successive ages and various nations, to which Cicero and the Fathers of the Church appealed; and not even this if, as Reid puts it, 'we could show some prejudice as universal as that consent is, which might be the cause of it.'

his will; and that he hath given them a will and affections conformable to it. This, no doubt, every one will think better for men, than that they should, in the dark, grope after knowledge, as St. Paul tells us all nations did after God (Acts xvii. 27); than that their wills should clash with their understandings, and their appetites cross their duty. The Romanists say it is best for men, and so suitable to the goodness of God, that there should be an infallible judge of controversies on earth; and therefore there is one. And I, by the same reason, say it is better for men that every man himself should be infallible. I leave them to consider, whether, by the force of this argument, they shall think that every man *is* so. I think it a very good argument to say,—the infinitely wise God hath made it so; and therefore it is best. But it seems to me a little too much confidence of our own wisdom to say,—'I think it best; and therefore God hath made it so.' And in the matter in hand, it will be in vain to argue from such a topic, that God hath done so, when certain experience shows us that he hath not[1]. But the goodness of God hath not been wanting to men, without such original impressions of knowledge or ideas stamped on the mind; since he hath furnished man with those faculties[2] which will serve for the sufficient discovery of all things requisite to the end of such a being; and I doubt not but to show, that a man, by the right use of his natural abilities[2], may, without any innate principles, attain a knowledge of a God, and other things that concern him. God having endued man with those faculties of knowledge which he hath[2], was no more obliged by his goodness to plant those innate notions in his mind, than that, having given him reason, hands, and materials, he should build him bridges or houses,—which some people in the world, however of good parts, do either totally want, or are but ill provided of, as well as others are wholly without ideas of God and principles of morality, or at least have but very ill ones; the reason in both cases being, that they never employed their

---

[1] 'Things are what they are, and are not other things; why therefore should we desire to be deceived?'

[2] This so far recognises *potential* innateness, although it does not take account of the necessary rational implicates in the 'natural faculties,' manifested when they operate adequately.

parts, faculties, and powers industriously that way, but contented themselves with the opinions, fashions, and things of their country, as they found them, without looking any further. Had you or I been born at the Bay of Soldania, possibly our thoughts and notions had not exceeded those brutish ones of the Hottentots that inhabit there. And had the Virginia king Apochancana been educated in England, he had been perhaps as knowing a divine, and as good a mathematician as any in it; the difference between him and a more improved Englishman lying barely in this, that the exercise of his faculties was bounded within the ways, modes, and notions of his own country, and never directed to any other or further inquiries. And if he had not any idea of a God, it was only because he pursued not those thoughts that would have led him to it.

13. I grant that if there were any ideas to be found imprinted on the minds of men, we have reason to expect it should be the notion of his Maker, as a mark God set on his own workmanship, to mind man of his dependence and duty; and that herein should appear the first [1] instances of human knowledge. But how late is it before any such notion is discoverable in children? And when we find it there, how much more does it resemble the opinion and notion of the teacher, than represent the true God? He that shall observe in children the progress whereby their minds attain the knowledge they have, will think that the objects they do first and most familiarly converse with are those that make the first impressions on their understandings; nor will he find the least footsteps of any other. It is easy to take notice how their thoughts enlarge themselves, only as they come to be acquainted with a greater variety of sensible objects; to retain the ideas of them in their memories; and to get the skill to compound and enlarge them, and several ways put them together. How, by these means, they come to frame in their minds an idea men have of a Deity, I shall hereafter show [2].

Ideas of God various in different Men.

---

[1] That is, 'first' in time; not the apriority, in the very nature of experience and of things, which consists with late and imperfect manifestation in the individual mind, or with no manifestation at all in some minds.

[2] See Bk. II. ch. xxiii. §§ 33 36; Bk. IV. ch. x.

BOOK I.

Chap. III.

Contrary
and incon-
sistent
ideas of
God under
the same
name.

Gross
ideas of
God.

14. Can it be thought that the ideas men have of God are the characters and marks of himself, engraven in their minds by his own finger, when we see that, in the same country, under one and the same name, men have far different, nay often contrary and inconsistent ideas and conceptions of him? Their agreeing in a name, or sound, will scarce prove an innate notion of him.

15. What true or tolerable notion of a Deity could they have, who acknowledged and worshipped hundreds? Every deity that they owned above one was an infallible evidence of their ignorance of Him, and a proof that they had no true notion of God, where unity, infinity, and eternity were excluded. To which, if we add their gross conceptions of corporeity, expressed in their images and representations of their deities; the amours, marriages, copulations, lusts, quarrels, and other mean qualities attributed by them to their gods; we shall have little reason to think that the heathen world, i.e. the greatest part of mankind, had such ideas of God in their minds as he himself, out of care that they should not be mistaken about him, was author of. And this universality of consent, so much argued, if it prove any native impressions, it will be only this:—that God imprinted on the minds of all men speaking the same language, a *name* for himself, but not any *idea*; since those people who agreed in the name, had, at the same time, far different apprehensions about the thing signified. If they say that the variety of deities worshipped by the heathen world were but figurative ways of expressing the several attributes of that incomprehensible Being, or several parts of his providence, I answer: what they might be in the original I will not here inquire; but that they were so in the thoughts of the vulgar I think nobody will affirm. And he that will consult the voyage of the Bishop of Beryte[1], c. 13, (not to mention other testimonies,) will find that the theology of the Siamites professedly owns a plurality of gods: or, as the Abbé de Choisy more judiciously remarks in his *Journal du Voyage de Siam*[2], $\frac{107}{177}$, it consists properly in acknowledging no God at all.

---

[1] The Bishop of Berytus's land journey, through India, into Siam, written by a priest who went with him. See *Journal des Savans*, v. i. p. 591.

[2] In 1585-86.

BOOK I.

CHAP. III.

Idea of
God not
innate
although
wise men
of all
nations
come to
have it.

16. If it be said, that wise men of all nations came to have true conceptions of the unity and infinity of the Deity, I grant it. But then this,

First, excludes universality of consent in anything but the name; for those wise men being very few, perhaps one of a thousand, this universality[1] is very narrow.

Secondly, it seems to me plainly to prove, that the truest and best notions men have of God[2] were not imprinted, but acquired by thought and meditation, and a right use of their faculties[3]: since the wise and considerate men of the world, by a right and careful employment of their thoughts and reason, attained true notions in this as well as other things; whilst the lazy and inconsiderate part of men, making far the greater number, took up their notions by chance, from common tradition and vulgar conceptions, without much beating their heads about them. And if it be a reason to think the notion of God innate, because all wise men had it, virtue too must be thought innate ; for that also wise men have always had.

17. This was evidently the case of all Gentilism. Nor hath even amongst Jews, Christians, and Mahometans, who acknowledged but one God, this doctrine, and the care taken in those nations to teach men to have true notions of a God, prevailed so far as to make men to have the same and the true ideas of him. How many even amongst us, will be found upon inquiry to fancy him in the shape of a man sitting in heaven; and to have many other absurd and unfit conceptions of him? Christians as well as Turks have had whole sects owning and contending earnestly for it,—that the Deity was corporeal, and of human shape: and though we find few now amongst us who profess themselves *Anthropomorphites*, (though some I have met with that own it,) yet I believe he that will make it his business may find amongst the ignorant and uninstructed

Odd, low,
and pitiful
ideas of
God
common
among
men.

---

[1] That is, patent or conscious, not latent or unconscious, universality. The process of *making patent* may cost much reflective effort on the part of the individual theologian or philosopher.

[2] It is not the 'existence' of God, but the notions men have of the sort of being that exists under that name, that

he has here in view. It is the existence of a Supreme Mind that he elsewhere undertakes to 'demonstrate.' Bk. IV. ch. x.

[3] Locke's 'innate ideas' are supposed by him to have been originally 'imprinted' consciously in each man at birth, and so *not* 'acquired by the use of his faculties' in experience.

Christians many of that opinion. Talk but with country people, almost of any age, or young people almost of any condition, and you shall find that, though the name of God be frequently in their mouths, yet the notions they apply this name to are so odd, low, and pitiful, that nobody can imagine they were taught by a rational man ; much less that they were characters written by the finger of God himself. Nor do I see how it derogates more from the goodness of God, that he has given us minds unfurnished with these ideas of himself, than that he hath sent us into the world with bodies unclothed ; and that there is no art or skill born with us. For, being fitted with faculties to attain these, it is want of industry and consideration in us, and not of bounty in him, if we have them not. It is as certain that there is a God, as that the opposite angles made by the intersection of two straight lines are equal[1]. There was never any rational creature that set himself sincerely to examine the truth of these propositions that could fail to assent to them ; though yet it be past doubt that there are many men, who, having not applied their thoughts that way, are ignorant both of the one and the other. If any one think fit to call this (which is the utmost of its extent) *universal consent,* such an one I easily allow[2] ; but such an universal consent as this proves not the idea of God, any more than it does the idea of such angles, innate.

If the Idea of God be not innate, no other can be supposed innate. 18. Since then though the knowledge of a God be the most natural discovery of human reason, yet the idea of him is not innate, as I think is evident from what has been said ; I imagine there will be scarce any other idea found that can pretend to it. Since if God hath set any impression, any character, on the understanding of men, it is most reasonable to expect it should have been some clear and uniform idea of Himself ; as far as our weak capacities were capable to receive so incomprehensible and infinite an object. But our minds being at first void of that idea which we are most concerned

---

[1] While he thus acknowledges the mathematical certainty to which we may ultimately rise in our search after God, he rejects innateness in the knowledge and idea, because it is only after effort that we rise to it, and this effort is inconsistent with his idea of innateness.

[2] This is really a concession of 'innate principles' and 'universal consent,' in the only meaning of 'innateness' which needs to be considered.

to have, it is a strong presumption against all other innate
characters. I must own, as far as I can observe, I can find
none, and would be glad to be informed by any other.

19. I confess there is another idea which would be of
general use for mankind to have, as it is of general talk as if
they had it; and that is the idea of *substance*; which we
neither have nor can have by sensation or reflection[1]. If
nature took care to provide us any ideas, we might well expect
they should be such as by our own faculties we cannot procure
to ourselves; but we see, on the contrary, that since, by those
ways whereby other ideas are brought into our minds, this
is not, we have no such *clear* idea at all[2]; and therefore
signify nothing by the word *substance* but only an uncertain
supposition[3] of we know not what, i. e. of something whereof

---

[1] See Bk. II. ch. xiii §§ 17-20; ch.
xxiii. *passim*, for Locke's account of
our idea of substance, our ideas of
particular substances, and how those
ideas are formed.

[2] Stillingfleet, assuming that Locke
rested all certainty on ideas that are
'clear and distinct,' alleged that, in
denying that we have a 'clear' idea
of substance, he 'excludes the notion
out of rational discourse,'—a charge,
'which,' Locke replies, 'concerns not
me, for I lay not all foundation of
certainty as to matters of faith upon
clear and distinct ideas. . . . Of substance I do not say that we have any
clear or distinct idea; but barely that
we take it to be something, we know
not what.' (*Third Letter*, pp. 381, &c.)
In fact we can have no positive idea
of any substance abstracted from all its
phenomena: in its perceived phenomena the substance is partially manifested, and we can *say* of it that it
is so far what it is thus perceived
to be.

[3] 'Uncertain' may here mean a supposition that, taken abstractly, is vague
and obscure, although it is practically
equivalent to the grammatical rule that
an adjective presupposes a substan-

tive. 'There are multitudes of things,'
Stillingfleet objects, 'which we are
not able to conceive, and yet it is not
allowed us to *suppose* what we think
fit upon that account.' 'It does not
therefore follow,' Locke answers, 'that
we may not with certainty *suppose or
infer* that which is an undeniable consequence of such inability to conceive,
or repugnancy to our conceptions. . . .
Your lordship grounds the idea of
substance upon *reason*, or because it is
a repugnancy to our just conceptions
of things that modes or accidents
should subsist by themselves; and I
conclude the same thing. What the
difference of certainty is from a repugnancy to our conceptions, and
from our not being able to conceive, I
am not acute enough to discern.'
(*Third Letter*, pp. 375, &c.; also *First
Letter*, pp. 27, &c.) Locke offers no
proof of this repugnancy; nor can
any proof of it be given, if it is a
first principle. But he elsewhere
'agrees' with one of his correspondents, that 'the ideas of the modes
and actions (i. e. phenomena) of substances are usually in men's minds
before the idea of substance itself.'
(*Letter to Samuel Bold*, 15 May, 1699.)

BOOK I.

CHAP. III.

we have no [¹particular distinct positive] idea, which we take to be the *substratum*, or support, of those ideas we do know².

No Propositions can be innate, since no Ideas are innate.

20. Whatever then we talk of innate, either speculative or practical, principles, it may with as much probability be said, that a man hath £100 sterling in his pocket, and yet denied that he hath there either penny, shilling, crown, or other coin out of which the sum is to be made up ; as to think that certain *propositions* are innate when the *ideas* about which they are can by no means be supposed to be so³. The general reception and assent that is given doth not at all prove, that the ideas expressed in them are innate ; for in many cases, however the ideas came there, the assent to words expressing the agreement or disagreement of such ideas, will necessarily follow. Every one that hath a true idea of *God* and *worship*, will assent to this proposition, 'That God is to be worshipped,' when expressed in a language he understands ; and every rational man that hath not thought on it to-day, may be ready to assent to this proposition to-morrow ; and yet millions of men may be well supposed to want one or both

¹ Added in *fourth* edition, to meet objections of Stillingfleet.

² Regarded as a mere datum of sense, added to the other sense data which constitute the 'qualities' of a thing, 'substance ' would be a meaningless term ; and so ' by those ways whereby ideas are brought into our minds, this is not.' But he acknowledges elsewhere that an ' obscure' concept of substance (not an idea-image) is *necessarily* formed in the human mind. ' I never said,' he tells Stillingfleet, ' that (complex) ideas of relations, such as that of substance, come in as simple ideas of sensation or reflection. I never denied that the mind could form for itself ideas of relation, *and that it is obliged to do so.* . . . I conclude there *is* substance, *because we cannot conceive how qualities should subsist by themselves.* . . . Sensible qualities carry the supposition of substance along with

them, but not intromitted by the senses with them. . . . By carrying with them a supposition, I mean that sensible qualities *imply* a substratum to exist in.' (*Third Letter* to Stillingfleet.) Substance, in short, is the concrete permanent in changing phenomena : these are correlatives, neither intelligible without the other,—which Locke seems to imply, though his language is inadequate. When he denies that we have an idea of substance, he uses idea for mental *image*, and so in its anti-Platonic meaning.

³ That is to say, all propositions presuppose terms. But there may be an innate intellectual obligation to perceive relations among those ideas that are themselves data of experience, e. g. to recognise necessary causal relation between sense-given sequences. Connection of ideas might be thus innate, although the connected ideas are not.

those ideas to-day. For, if we will allow savages, and most country people, to have ideas of God and worship, (which conversation with them will not make one forward to believe,) yet I think few children can be supposed to have those ideas, which therefore they must begin to have some time or other; and then they will also begin to assent to that proposition, and make very little question of it ever after. But such an assent upon hearing, no more proves the *ideas* to be innate, than it does that one born blind (with cataracts which will be couched to-morrow) had the innate ideas of the sun, or light, or saffron, or yellow; because, when his sight is cleared, he will certainly assent to this proposition, 'That the sun is lucid, or that saffron is yellow.' And therefore, if such an assent upon hearing cannot prove the ideas innate, it can much less the *propositions* made up of those ideas[1]. If they have any innate ideas, I would be glad to be told what, and how many, they are.

[21.[2] To which let me add: if there be any innate ideas, any ideas in the mind which the mind does not actually think on, they must be lodged in the memory; and from thence must be brought into view by remembrance; i. e. must be known, when they are remembered, to have been perceptions in the mind before; unless remembrance can be without remembrance. For, to remember is to perceive anything with memory, or with a consciousness that it was perceived or known before. Without this, whatever idea comes into the mind is new, and not remembered; this consciousness of its having been in the mind before, being that which distinguishes remembering from all other ways of thinking. Whatever idea was never *perceived* by the mind was never in the mind. Whatever idea is in the mind, is, either an actual perception, or else, having been an actual perception, is so in the mind that, by the memory, it can be made an actual perception again[3]. Whenever there is

No innate Ideas in the Memory.

---

[1] This loses sight of the distinction between propositions which, after they emerge in consciousness, are seen to be eternally and absolutely, and those that seem to be only temporarily and conditionally true; to which last category Locke himself refers all proposi-

tions concerning matters of fact, except the existence of God.

[2] This section was added in the second edition.

[3] Here Locke grants that our acquired knowledge exists in a latent or unconscious state, during the intervals

the actual perception of any idea without memory, the idea appears perfectly new and unknown before to the understanding. Whenever the memory brings any idea into actual view, it is with a consciousness that it had been there before, and was not wholly a stranger to the mind[1]. Whether this be not so, I appeal to every one's observation. And then I desire an instance of an idea, pretended to be innate, which (before any impression of it by ways hereafter to be mentioned) any one could revive and remember, as an idea he had formerly known; without which consciousness of a former perception there is no remembrance; and whatever idea comes into the mind without *that* consciousness is not remembered, or comes not out of the memory, nor can be said to be in the mind before that appearance. For what is not either actually in view or in the memory, is in the mind no way at all, and is all one as if it had never been there[2]. Suppose a child had the use of his eyes till he knows and distinguishes colours; but then cataracts shut the windows, and he is forty or fifty years perfectly in the dark; and in that time perfectly loses all memory of the ideas of colours he once had. This was the case of a blind man I once talked with, who lost his sight by the small-pox when he was a child, and had no more notion of colours than one born blind. I ask whether any one can say this man had then any ideas of colours in his mind, any· more than one born blind? And I think nobody will say that either of them had in his mind any ideas of colours at all. His cataracts are couched, and then he has the ideas (which he remembers not) of colours, *de novo*, by his restored sight, conveyed to his mind, and that without any consciousness of a former acquaintance. And these now he can revive and call to mind in the dark. In this case all these ideas of colours.

---

in which it is not actually and consciously present. He gives no sufficient reason for confining latency to *acquired* knowledge, thus excluding latent reason, and apriority in the nature of things. Acquired ideas, he says, are either actual, i.e. conscious, perceptions, or latent power of memory to re-perceive.

[1] This suggests Plato's theory, that our knowledge of those truths which, when awakened in us, are *seen to be intellectually necessary*, is of the nature of *reminiscence*; though unaccompanied by the recognition of them as formerly ours of which we are conscious in ordinary memory.

[2] This is a dogmatic assumption.

which, when out of view, can be revived with a consciousness
of a former acquaintance, being thus in the memory, are said
to be in the mind. The use I make of this is,—that whatever
idea, being not actually in view, is in the mind, is there only
by being in the memory; and if it be not in the memory, it
is not in the mind; and if it be in the memory, it cannot by
the memory be brought into actual view without a perception
that it comes out of the memory; which is this, that it had
been known before, and is now remembered. If therefore
there be any innate ideas, they must be in the memory, or
else nowhere in the mind; and if they be in the memory,
they can be revived without any impression from without;
and whenever they are brought into the mind they are remembered, i.e. they bring with them a perception of their
not being wholly new to it. This being a constant and distinguishing difference between what is, and what is not in
the memory, or in the mind;—that what is not in the memory,
whenever it appears there, appears perfectly new and unknown
before; and what is in the memory, or in the mind, whenever
it is suggested by the memory, appears not to be new, but the
mind finds it in itself, and knows it was there before. By
this it may be tried whether there be any innate ideas in the
mind before impression from sensation or reflection. I would
fain meet with the man who, when he came to the use of
reason, or at any other time, remembered any of them;
and to whom, after he was born, they were never new. If
any one will say, there are ideas in the mind that are *not* in
the memory, I desire him to explain himself, and make what
he says intelligible[1].]

22. Besides what I have already said, there is another
reason why I doubt that neither these nor any other principles are innate. I that am fully persuaded that the infinitely wise God made all things in perfect wisdom, cannot
satisfy myself why he should be supposed to print upon the

*Principles
not innate,
because of
little use
or little
certainty.*

---

[1] What Locke had to disprove was
the alleged fact, that there are ideas
and principles contained in knowledge
which are seen on reflection to be
intellectually necessary to its constitution, and in this respect to be not
'wholly new,' while they are not recognised because formerly experienced,
as in memory, and are therefore to be
spoken of as 'reminiscences' only by
a metaphor.

BOOK I.
——
CHAP. III.

minds of men some universal principles; whereof those that are pretended innate, and concern *speculation*, are of no great use [1]; and those that concern *practice*, not self-evident [2]; and neither of them distinguishable [3] from some other truths not allowed to be innate. For, to what purpose should characters be graven on the mind by the finger of God, which are not clearer there than those which are afterwards introduced, or cannot be distinguished from them [3]? If any one thinks there are such innate ideas and propositions, which by their clearness and usefulness are distinguishable from all that is adventitious in the mind and acquired, it will not be a hard matter for him to tell us *which they are* [4]; and then every one will be a fit judge whether they be so or no. Since if there be such innate ideas and impressions, plainly different from all other perceptions and knowledge, every one will find it true in himself. Of the evidence of these supposed innate maxims, I have spoken already: of their usefulness I shall have occasion to speak more hereafter [5].

Difference of Men's Discoveries depends upon the different Application of

23. To conclude: some ideas forwardly offer themselves to all men's understanding; and some sorts of truths result from any ideas, as soon as the mind puts them into propositions [6]: other truths require a train of ideas placed in order, a due comparing of them, and deductions made with attention, before they can be discovered and assented to [7]. Some of

---

[1] Nature, as Leibniz remarks, has not *uselessly* given herself the trouble of impressing upon us innate principles; for without them there would be no means of arriving at actual knowledge in demonstration, or at the reason of facts, and we should have only animal experiences. We build on those (innate) general maxims as we do on a suppressed premiss when we reason in enthymeme, when it is always true that the force of the conclusion is determined by the latent premiss. There is latent principle, too, in all reasoning about the future. Why should the future resemble the past? Not because *it* has always done so; this would involve the contradic-

tion that the future is already past, while of the future, as such, we can never have had any experience.

[2] Incompletely evidenced, or merely probable, propositions are those with which human life is mainly concerned, according to Locke.

[3] On the *criteria* of the truths in question, see note 3, p. 80.

[4] It is the permanent task of philosophy to evolve them from the experience in which they are implicitly contained, and thus to reach a distinct consciousness of them in their organic unity.

[5] Bk. IV. ch. vii.

[6] Self-evident truths.

[7] It must never be forgotten that

the first sort, because of their general and easy reception, have
been mistaken for innate : but the truth is, ideas and notions are no more born with us than arts and sciences ; though some of them indeed offer themselves to our faculties more readily than others; and therefore are more generally received : though that too be according as the organs of our bodies and powers of our minds happen to be employed ; God having fitted men with faculties and means to discover, receive, and retain truths, according as they are employed. The great difference that is to be found in the notions of mankind is, from the different use they put their faculties to[1]. Whilst some (and those the most) taking things upon trust, misemploy their power of assent, by lazily enslaving their minds to the dictates and dominion of others, in doctrines which it is their duty carefully to examine, and not blindly, with an implicit faith, to swallow; others, employing their thoughts only about some few things, grow acquainted sufficiently with them, attain great degrees of knowledge in them, and are ignorant of all other, having never let their thoughts loose in the search of other inquiries[2]. Thus, that the three angles of a triangle are quite equal to two right ones is a truth

Locke's method is chronological— i.e. the historical method—that from the outset he waives the transcendent questions that refer to Being, and the ultimate principles presupposed in mental operations—that he assumes without criticism the possibility of an experience of what is real, and the premisses which are necessary for demonstrating the existence of God. It was by the counter assumption of ' innate ideas and principles '— not acquired in the methodical exercise of our faculties, but so introduced consciously into each mind at birth as to be independent of the circumstances and experience of individuals—that, as it seemed to him, men had been losing themselves 'in the ocean of Being,' instead of beginning tentatively at the other end, among the facts presented in experience.

[1] Locke dreads innateness—that is,

the sort of innateness which necessarily implies *consciousness of the innate* —because it is apt to supersede the exercise of our faculties. This the only innateness worth inquiring about has no such tendency, consciousness of the ' innate' elements in human knowledge depending upon the active exercise of the individual faculties ; and distinct recognition of them in their universal or philosophic form depending too upon the exercise of our *higher* faculties.

[2] In this sentence we find the moral of the prolonged argument of the First Book—to rouse men to active exercise of their higher faculties and thus to withdraw them from the idolatrous service of assumptions indolently taken upon trust, and engage them in the worship and service of the God who is truth.

as certain as anything can be, and I think more evident than many of those propositions that go for principles ; and yet there are millions, however expert in other things, who know not this at all, because they never set their thoughts on work about such angles. And he that certainly knows this proposition may yet be utterly ignorant of the truth of other propositions, in mathematics itself, which are as clear and evident as this ; because, in his search of those mathematical truths, he stopped his thoughts short and went not so far. The same may happen concerning the notions we have of the being of a Deity. For, though there be no truth which a man may more evidently make out to himself than the existence of a God, yet he that shall content himself with things as he finds them in this world, as they minister to his pleasures and passions, and not make inquiry a little further into their causes, ends, and admirable contrivances, and pursue the thoughts thereof with diligence and attention, may live long without any notion of such a Being. And if any person hath by talk put such a notion into his head, he may perhaps believe it ; but if he hath never examined it, his knowledge of it will be no perfecter than his, who having been told, that the three angles of a triangle are equal to two right ones, takes it upon trust, without examining the demonstration ; and may yield his assent as a probable opinion, but hath no knowledge of the truth of it ; which yet his faculties, if carefully employed, were able to make clear and evident to him. But this only, by the by, to show how much *our knowledge depends upon the right use of those powers nature hath bestowed upon us,* and how little upon *such innate principles as are in vain supposed to be in all mankind for their direction* ; which all men could not but know if they were there, or else they would be there to no purpose. [¹ And which since all men do not know, nor can distinguish from other adventitious truths, we may well conclude there are no such.]

Men must
think and
24. What censure doubting thus of innate principles may

---

¹ Added in second edition. Strictly interpreted, the words would imply that the philosophical analysis of the constitution of knowledge, in quest of the principles which afford the ultimate explanation of individual facts, is doomed to failure.

deserve from men, who will be apt to call it pulling up the old foundations of knowledge and certainty [1], I cannot tell;— I persuade myself at least that the way I have pursued, being conformable to truth, lays those foundations surer. This I am certain, I have not made it my business either to quit or follow any authority in the ensuing Discourse. Truth has been my only aim; and wherever that has appeared to lead, my thoughts have impartially followed, without minding whether the footsteps of any other lay that way or not. Not that I want a due respect to other men's opinions; but, after all, the greatest reverence is due to truth: and I hope it will not be thought arrogance to say, that perhaps we should make greater progress in the discovery of rational and contemplative knowledge, if we sought it in the fountain, *in the consideration of things themselves*; and made use rather of our own thoughts than other men's to find it. For I think we may as rationally hope to see with other men's eyes, as to know by other men's understandings. So much as we ourselves consider and comprehend of truth and reason, so much we possess of real and true knowledge. The floating of other men's opinions in our brains, makes us not one jot the more knowing, though they happen to be true. What in them was science, is in us but opiniatrety [2]; whilst we give up our assent only to reverend names, and do not, as they did, employ our own reason to understand those truths which gave them reputation. Aristotle was certainly a knowing man, but nobody ever thought him so because he blindly embraced, and confidently vented the opinions of another. And if the taking up of another's principles, without examining them, made not him a philosopher, I suppose it will hardly make anybody else so. In the sciences, every one has so much as he really knows and comprehends. What he believes only, and takes upon trust, are but shreds; which, however well in the whole piece, make no considerable addition to his stock

[1] 'The received maxims of all mankind, which used to be the touchstone by which to try truth, must, it seems, be tried themselves; and in the meantime are to be reckoned purely artificial, and wholly owing to the power-ful influence of custom and education.' (Lee, *Anti-Scepticism.*)

[2] 'Opinionatrety,' i. e. obstinate adherence to opinion. Occasionally used by Locke; also Brown, *Vulgar Errours*, Bk. VII. ch. ix.

who gathers them. Such borrowed wealth, like fairy money, though it were gold in the hand from which he received it, will be but leaves and dust when it comes to use.

25. When men have found some general propositions that could not be doubted of as soon as understood, it was, I know, a short and easy way to conclude them innate [1]. This being once received, it eased the lazy from the pains of search, and stopped the inquiry of the doubtful concerning all that was once styled innate [2]. And it was of no small advantage to those who affected to be masters and teachers, to make this the principle of principles,—*that principles must not be questioned.* For, having once established this tenet,—that there are innate principles, it put their followers upon a necessity of receiving *some* doctrines as such ; which was to take them off from the use of their own reason and judgment, and put them on believing and taking them upon trust without further examination : in which posture of blind credulity, they might be more easily governed by, and made useful to some sort of men, who had the skill and office to principle and guide them [3]. Nor is it a small power it gives one man over another, to have the authority to be the dictator of principles, and teacher of unquestionable truths ; and to make a man swallow that for an innate principle which may serve to his purpose who teacheth them [4]. Whereas had they

---

[1] Self-evident principles, he means to say, were falsely assumed to be ' innate,' or seen to be necessarily true *from birth by all men.* He deprecates this uncritical assumption of them, because it encourages laziness, and opens the door to innumerable prejudices, under the specious name of 'innate principles.' He protests against the indolence which thus blindly reposes on the opinions of the community, and which grudges the private judgment by which each man is detached from the community and becomes *himself.* This development of the individual, in isolation from the race, Locke exaggerates, making it an end in itself, instead of a means to the higher end of an improved or more

developed Common Reason. Cf. *Conduct of Understanding*, § 41.

[2] Hence Locke's hostility to them.

[3] ' Si le dessein de l'auteur est de conseiller qu'on *cherche les preuves* des vérités qui en peuvent recevoir sans distinguer si elles sont innées ou non, nous sommes entièrement d'accord ; et l'opinion des vérités innées, de la manière que je les prends, n'en doit détourner personne.' (Leibniz, *Nouv. Essais.*)

[4] This is another expression of the moral purpose of Locke's warfare with innateness of knowledge,—understood by him as knowledge got without personal exertion, and without the contact and suggestions of experience.

examined the ways whereby men came to the knowledge of many universal truths, they would have found them to result in the minds of men from the being of things themselves, when duly considered[1]; and that they were discovered by the application of those faculties that were fitted by nature to receive and judge of them, when duly employed about them.

26. To show *how* the understanding proceeds herein is the design of the following Discourse; which I shall proceed to when I have first premised, that hitherto,—to clear my way[2] to those foundations which I conceive are the only true ones, whereon to establish those notions we can have of our own knowledge,—it hath been necessary for me to give an account of the reasons I had to doubt of innate principles[3].

Conclusion.

[1] Not abstract reasonings about Being considered *a priori*,—which is to begin at the wrong end, and to 'lose ourselves in the vast ocean' of abstract ontology; but beginning at the other end, *a posteriori*, among the phenomena presented in perception, sensuous and spiritual, in which concrete beings are manifested in part, and may be gradually interpreted, to the extent that is necessary for us, as men sensuous and spiritual—this is the intellectual ideal of the *Essay*.

[2] The First Book is not part of Locke's positive explanation of Human Understanding. It does not appear in the abstract of the *Essay* published by Le Clerc. In this section he projects a transition from the deductive argument with which he opens, to 'experience and observation,' and an inductive interpretation of phenomena. But inductive interpretation involves unconscious presuppositions as well as deductive argument; and philosophy is the reflective organisation of the presuppositions of both, which are implied in all the phenomena of nature and spirit.

[3] 'In the First Book the author is very elaborate in the proof that there are no innate ideas, and consequently propositions, which are compounded of ideas—in order to remove the rubbish which encumbered the foundation on which he intended to erect his new scheme of knowledge. All which, I think, might have been saved, in the strict sense which *he* puts upon the word *innate; for therein surely he has no adversary*. For no one does, or at least can reasonably assert, that the minds of embryos, in the first moment after their creation or union to their organised bodies, are ready furnished with [conscious] ideas, or have any propositions or principles [consciously] implanted in them or stamped upon them; that is an idle supposition. Such expressions are to be understood figuratively, to signify that the ideas *owe their origin to the constitution of human nature, as it stands necessarily related to other parts of the universe.*' (Lee, *Anti-Scepticism*, Preface, p. 1.) Locke's determination to purge the human mind of its *idola*—to have a *tabula rasa* from which to start on the march of modern enlightenment—leads him in this First Book to attack what no one worth arguing with would care to defend; while his recognition of self-evident ultimate truth is a concession to the principle of innateness, which,

And since the arguments which are against them do, some of them, rise from common received opinions, I have been forced to take several things for granted; which is hardly avoidable to any one, whose task is to show the falsehood or improbability of any tenet;—it happening in controversial discourses as it does in assaulting of towns; where, if the ground be but firm whereon the batteries are erected, there is no further inquiry of whom it is borrowed, nor whom it belongs to, so it affords but a fit rise for the present purpose. But in the future part of this Discourse, designing to raise an edifice uniform and consistent with itself, as far as my own experience and observation will assist me, I hope to erect it on such a basis that I shall not need to shore it up with props and buttresses, leaning on borrowed or begged foundations: or at least, if mine prove a castle in the air, I will endeavour it shall be all of a piece and hang together. Wherein I warn the reader not to expect undeniable cogent demonstrations, unless I may be allowed the privilege, not seldom assumed by others, to take my principles for granted[1]; and then, I doubt not, but I can demonstrate too. All that I shall say for the principles I proceed on is, that I can only appeal to men's own unprejudiced experience and observation[2] whether they be true or not; and this is enough for a man who professes no more than to lay down candidly and freely his own conjectures, concerning a subject lying somewhat in the dark, without any other design than an unbiassed inquiry after truth.

if he had carried it out, might have brought him into harmony with its philosophical advocates.

[1] As little in the remaining, as in the preceding part of this Discourse, can he advance without presuppositions. The trustworthiness and supremacy of active Reason in the universe, and necessary implicates of Reason, are consciously or unconsciously assumed. Only complete sceptics surrender all principles, and then they become incapable of making any propositions.

[2] Yet Cousin regards the whole *Essay* as a gratuitous hypothesis, in which the facts presented by the human understanding are made to conform to a foregone theory or conclusion. According to Green and others, it is a mass of incoherent and mutually contradictory propositions; but Locke in this paragraph designs that, even if 'a castle in the air,' it should at least be 'an edifice uniform and consistent with itself,' 'all of a piece,' and that 'hangs together.'

BOOK II

_____

OF IDEAS

SYNOPSIS OF THE SECOND BOOK.

In the Second Book Locke offers what seems to him the true history of the ideas or phenomena in which the human understanding finds knowledge and probability, intending it to take the place of the 'established opinion,' controverted in the First Book,—that we are conscious at birth of certain regulating ideas and principles, which are thus independent of criticism and verification by experience. That all the simple ideas or phenomena of existence, with which the understanding of man can be concerned, are either, those presented in the five senses, which we refer to external things, or those presented in a reflex experience of our own mental operations,—is the counter thesis that is stated and illustrated in the first eleven chapters of the Second Book. That our most abstract ideas, how remote soever they may seem from data of sense or from operations of our own minds, are yet only such as our understanding frames to itself, by repeating, uniting, substantiating, and connecting ideas, received either from objects of sense or from its own operations about them, and thus by the active exercise of its faculties, is the theory of which chapters xii–xxviii contain the verification. It consists of 'a series of crucial instances,' intended to show that even in such complex ideas as those of *space, time, infinity, substance, power, identity,* and *morality,* which seem most remote from the original phenomena of experience, the understanding 'stirs not one jot beyond' those phenomena, by which, accordingly, our original ignorance of what exists is removed. The qualities of our simple and complex ideas,—as clear, distinct, adequate, and true, with their opposites, are illustrated in chapters xxix–xxxii. The Book concludes in chapter xxxiii with examples of mental 'association,' as an influence that is apt to mar the quality of our ideas, making them unfit to determine either knowledge or probability.

CHAPTER I.

OF IDEAS IN GENERAL, AND THEIR ORIGINAL.

1. EVERY man being conscious to himself that he thinks; and that which his mind is applied about whilst thinking being the *ideas* that are there [1], it is past doubt that men have in their minds several ideas,—such as are those expressed by the words *whiteness, hardness, sweetness, thinking, motion, man, elephant, army, drunkenness,* and others: it is in the first place then to be inquired, *How he comes by them?*

I know it is a received doctrine, that men have native ideas, and original characters, stamped upon their minds in their very first being. This opinion I have at large examined already; and, I suppose what I have said in the foregoing Book will be much more easily admitted, when I have shown whence the understanding may get all the ideas it has; and by what ways and degrees they may come into the mind;— for which I shall appeal to every one's own observation and experience.

2. Let us then suppose the mind to be, as we say, white paper [2], void of all characters, without any ideas:—How comes it to be furnished? Whence comes it by that vast store which the busy and boundless fancy of man has painted on it with an almost endless variety? Whence has it all the

---

[1] Cf. Introd. § 8. It must be remembered that 'ideas,' as treated of in the Second Book, are not regarded as *cognitions* (the subject reserved for the Fourth Book), but as phenomena considered in abstraction from affirmation and denial, truth and falsehood, as simple apprehensions in short. And he here asks, in the 'historical plain method,' under what conditions the phenomena of real existence begin to appear, and gradually multiply, in new combinations, in a human understanding?

[2] 'White paper' might suggest that we are originally void of ideas or appearances of which there is *consciousness*; but not necessarily void of *latent capacities* and *their intellectual implicates.* He means by the metaphor that we are all born ignorant of every thing.

BOOK II.
CHAP. I.

materials of reason and knowledge[1]? To this I answer, in one word, from EXPERIENCE[2]. In that all our knowledge is founded; and from that it ultimately derives itself. Our observation employed either, about external sensible objects, or about the internal operations of our minds perceived and reflected on by ourselves, is that which supplies our understandings with all the *materials* of thinking[3]. These two are the fountains[4] of knowledge, from whence all the ideas we have, or can naturally have, do spring.

The Objects of Sensation

3. First, our Senses, conversant about particular sensible objects, do convey into the mind several distinct perceptions[5]

---

[1] Assuming, then, that the human mind is at first ignorant of everything,—what, he asks, is the explanation of the state in which adult human understanding may now be found, with its often rich stores of varied and elaborated ideas?

[2] 'Experience.' The ambiguity of this term is a main source of the controversies which the *Essay* has occasioned. Locke did not see that *innateness* (in a different meaning) and *experience* are not contradictories, but are really two different ways of regarding the possessions of the understanding. 'Our attitude towards the philosophy of Experience must entirely depend upon the meaning we put into the term experience. . . . The point on which issue should be joined is,—the identification of Experience with *mere* sense. If we prove that this is not so, and that, on the contrary, mere sense is an abstraction, impossible *in rerum natura,* Experientialism is at once shorn of all its supposed terrors.' (Seth, *Scottish Philosophy,* pp. 142, 3.) What Locke argues for is, that, *in respect of the time of its manifestation in the conscious life of each man,* no knowledge that he possesses can *precede* awakening of intellectual life into (at first dim and imperfect) exercise through impressions on the senses. He thus makes our adult understand-

ing of things the issue of the exercise of the faculties in 'experience'; but he does not get in sight of Kant's question, or try to disengage the elements of reason through which a *scientific* or *intelligible* experience is itself possible, —the problem of the next great critique of a human understanding of the universe.

[3] But the '*materials* of thinking' presuppose, for their conversion into scientific experience, *intellectual conditions,* which conditions Locke either leaves in the background, or mixes up with the 'materials,' i. e. with those gradually accumulated data without which our notions would be empty, and our common terms meaningless.

[4] The *exordium* of knowledge, back to which the *contents* of all our concepts may be traced, and apart from which they would be empty; not its *origo,* or the elements in the intellectual products that are found, after critical analysis of its logical constitution. Locke means by 'origin,' 'exordium,' which alone has relation to his 'historical' method. The acquired contents of our real knowledge, he goes on to show, must be either ideas of the qualities of matter, or ideas of the operations of mind.

[5] Here *perception* is virtually equivalent to *idea*—but regarded from the point of view of the apprehensive act, not of the phenomena apprehended.

of things, according to those various ways wherein those objects do affect them. And thus we come by those *ideas* we have of *yellow, white, heat, cold, soft, hard, bitter, sweet,* and all those which we call sensible qualities; which when I say the senses convey into the mind, I mean, they from external[1] objects convey into the mind what produces there those perceptions. This great source of most of the ideas we have, depending wholly upon our senses, and derived by them to the understanding, I call SENSATION[2].

BOOK II.

CHAP. I.

one Source of Ideas.

4. Secondly, the other fountain from which experience furnisheth the understanding with ideas is,—the perception of the operations of our own mind within us, as it is employed about the ideas it has got;—which operations, when the soul comes to reflect on and consider, do furnish the understanding with another set of ideas, which could not be had from things without. And such are *perception, thinking, doubting, believing, reasoning, knowing, willing,* and all the different actings of our own minds;—which we being conscious of, and observing in ourselves, do from these receive into our understandings as distinct ideas as we do from bodies affecting our senses. This source[3] of ideas every man has wholly in himself; and though it be not sense, as having nothing to do with external objects, yet it is very like it, and might properly enough be called *internal sense*[4]. But as I call the other Sensation, so

The Operations of our Minds, the other Source of them.

For the three cognate meanings of 'perception' in the *Essay*, see ch. xxi. § 5, the second and third of these being those only which 'use allows us' to attribute to the 'understanding.' In its third meaning 'perception' plays a great part in the Fourth Book.

[1] 'External objects,' i. e. extra-organic objects.

[2] This is one of Locke's definitions of *sensation*, which he here treats as incapable of analysis—passive impression of extra-organic phenomena upon the organism. Cf. § 23; also ch. xix. § 1.

[3] These metaphorical terms, 'source,' 'fountain,' 'channel,' which he employs here and elsewhere, are ambiguous. Is their equivalent *exordium*

or *origo*? The former alone is properly within the scope of the 'historical plain method' of psychology: the critical analysis which finds intellectual necessities presupposed in the operations of mind belongs to metaphysical philosophy, to which Locke's historical method is inadequate, if 'reflection' is limited to *contingent ideas* of 'internal sense.'

[4] That Locke applies the term *sense* to 'perception of the operations of our own mind,' seems to confine 'reflection' to empirical apprehension of mental states. But his use of this term is not conclusive on the point. Reid and Hamilton, along with many other philosophers, call the *a priori* or

I call this REFLECTION, the ideas it affords being such only as the mind gets by reflecting on its own operations within itself. By reflection then, in the following part of this discourse, I would be understood to mean, that notice which the mind takes of its own operations, and the manner of them, by reason whereof there come to be ideas of these operations in the understanding[1]. These two, I say, viz. external material things, as the objects of SENSATION, and the operations of our own minds within, as the objects of REFLECTION[2], are to me the only originals from whence all our ideas take their beginnings. The term *operations* here I use in a large sense, as comprehending not barely the actions of the mind about its ideas, but some sort of passions arising sometimes from them, such as is the satisfaction or uneasiness arising from any thought.

'All our Ideas are of the one or the other of these.
5. The understanding seems to me not to have the least glimmering of any ideas which it doth not receive from one of these two. *External objects*[2] furnish the mind with the ideas of sensible qualities, which are all those different perceptions they produce in us; and *the mind*[2] furnishes the understanding with ideas of its own operations[3].

These, when we have taken a full survey of them, and their several modes, [4 combinations, and relations,] we shall find to contain all our whole stock of ideas; and that we have

---

Common Reason a sense—the ' Common Sense.'

[1] Whether *reflection* should be interpreted in the *Essay* empirically or intellectually, is a primary question for the interpreter, since on the answer depends whether it includes *reflex consciousness of reason proper*, with the judgments therein necessarily presupposed as conditions of our having more in experience than the momentary data. The alternative was not contemplated by Locke.

[2] He, here and throughout, presupposes ' external material things ' and ' our own minds,' as the causes of the phenomena (simple ideas) given in external and internal ' sense,' but without metaphysical discussion of the reason

of the assumption. This is (so far) inquired into in Bk. IV. ch. ix. and xi.

[3] So Bacon—'Homo, naturae minister et interpres, tantum facit et intelligit quantum de naturae ordine re vel mente observaverit.' (*Nov. Org.* Lib. I. Aph. I.) ' The distinction intended by *re vel mente*,' says Dr. Fowler, ' may be either between the observation of facts and the subsequent process of reflection on such observation, or between external and internal perception. According to either interpretation the passage will remind the reader of the main position in Locke's *Essay*, to which it might well serve as a motto.' (Fowler's *Nov. Org.* p. 188.)

[4] 'and the compositions made out of them'—in the first three editions.

nothing in our minds which did not come in one of these two ways. Let any one examine his own thoughts, and thoroughly search into his understanding; and then let him tell me, whether all the original ideas he has there, are any other than of the objects[1] of his senses, or of the operations of his mind, considered as objects of his reflection. And how great a mass of knowledge soever he imagines to be lodged there, he will, upon taking a strict view, see that he has not any idea in his mind but what one of these two have imprinted;—though perhaps, with infinite variety compounded and enlarged by the understanding, as we shall see hereafter [2].

6. He that attentively considers the state of a child, at his first coming into the world, will have little reason to think him stored with plenty of ideas[3], that are to be the matter of his future knowledge. It is *by degrees* he comes to be furnished with them. And though the ideas of obvious and familiar qualities imprint themselves before the memory begins to keep a register of time or order, yet it is often so late before some unusual qualities come in the way, that there are few men that cannot recollect the beginning of their acquaintance with them. And if it were worth while, no doubt a child might be so ordered as to have but a very few, even of the ordinary ideas, till he were grown up to a man. But all that are born into the world, being surrounded with bodies that perpetually and diversely affect them, variety of ideas, whether care be taken of it or not, are imprinted on the minds of children. Light and colours are busy at hand everywhere, when the eye is but open; sounds

Observable in Children.

---

[1] Leibniz grants that ideas are 'objects'—adding, 'pourvu que vous ajoutiez que c'est un objet immédiat interne, et que cet objet est une expression de la nature ou des qualités des choses. Si l'idée était la *forme* de la pensée, elle naîtrait et cesserait avec les pensées *actuelles* qui y répondent; mais en étant l'objet, elle pourra être antérieure et postérieure aux pensées.' (*Nouv. Essais*, Lib. II. i.) *The mind,* according to Leibniz, is its own immediate *internal* object; but only so far as

it contains (implicitly) 'ideas,' or what in intellect corresponds to things.

[2] See ch. xiii–xxviii. Does this limitation of our ultimate sources of experience make the *Essay* an expression of the materialistic formula,—' Every man counts as an animal; and *no man can count for more than an animal*'?

[3] 'Stored,' i.e. with phenomena of which there is consciousness—not *potentially* 'stored,' with conditions necessarily presupposed in the constitution of adult knowledge.

BOOK II.
Chap. I.

and some tangible qualities fail not to solicit their proper senses, and force an entrance to the mind ;—but yet, I think, it will be granted easily, that if a child were kept in a place where he never saw any other but black and white till he were a man, he would have no more ideas of scarlet or green, than he that from his childhood never tasted an oyster, or a pine-apple, has of those particular relishes.

Men are differently furnished with these, according to the different Objects they converse with.

7. Men then come to be furnished with fewer or more simple ideas from without, according as the objects they converse with afford greater or less variety ; and from the operations of their minds within, according as they more or less reflect on them. For, though he that contemplates the operations of his mind, cannot but have plain and clear ideas of them ; yet, unless he turn his thoughts that way, and considers them *attentively*, he will no more have clear and distinct ideas of all the operations of his mind, and all that may be observed therein, than he will have all the particular ideas of any landscape, or of the parts and motions of a clock, who will not turn his eyes to it, and with attention heed all the parts of it. The picture, or clock may be so placed, that they may come in his way every day ; but yet he will have but a confused idea of all the parts they are made up of, till he applies himself with attention, to consider them each in particular [1].

Ideas of Reflection later, because they need Attention.

8. And hence we see the reason why it is pretty late before most children get ideas of the operations of their own minds ; and some have not any very clear or perfect ideas of the greatest part of them all their lives. Because, though they pass there continually, yet, like floating visions, they make not deep impressions enough to leave in their mind clear, distinct, lasting ideas, till the understanding turns inward upon itself, reflects on its own operations, and makes them the objects of its own contemplation. Children [2 when they

[1] This may be interpreted consistently with the fact that, ideas and principles presupposed in mind and in real experience need intellectual *effort* to awaken them into consciousness. If so, it is not necessarily mere empiricism.

[2] In first edition—'at their first coming into the world seek particularly after nothing but what may ease their hunger or other pain, but take all other objects as they come; are generally pleased with all new ones that are not painful;'

come first into it, are surrounded with a world of new things, which, by a constant solicitation of their senses, draw the mind constantly to them ; forward to take notice of new, and apt to be delighted with the variety of changing objects. Thus the first years are usually employed and diverted in looking abroad. Men's business in them is to acquaint themselves with what is to be found without ;] and so growing up in a constant attention to outward sensations, seldom make any considerable reflection[1] on what passes within them, till they come to be of riper years ; and some scarce ever at all.

9. To ask, at what *time* a man has first any ideas, is to ask, when he begins to perceive ;—*having ideas*, and *perception*, being the same thing[2]. I know it is an opinion, that the soul always thinks, and that it has the actual perception of ideas

[1] 'This reflection ought to be distinguished from consciousness, with which it is too often confounded, even by Mr. Locke. All men are conscious of the operations of their own minds at all times while they are awake ; but there are few who reflect upon them, or make them objects of thought.' (Reid, *Intell. Powers*, I. v.)

[2] The argument against constant 'thinking,' or constant consciousness in the human soul, ' as long as it exists,' elaborated in this and the ten following sections, looks like a digression, interpolated without reason in the exposition of Locke's thesis—that all our original ideas are phenomena of sensation and reflection. It is really meant to clear the ground. An ' innate idea,' according to Locke, is an idea of which the soul is conscious *before the organs of sense have given rise to the normal conscious life within which the sphere of memory lies.* But if an abnormal consciousness, divorced from memory, occurs in sleep, and other intervals of the normal life, this affords an analogy in support of a similar state of the soul antecedent to

any presentation of data of experience, and to all acquired knowledge. To show that there is no ground for the conclusion that the soul is conscious during sleep, when divorced from memory and the normal life of the man, is to deprive the advocate of innateness (in Locke's sense of innate) of the support of an analogy. If *during later life* the soul cannot have ideas, or be conscious, out of connection with memory, the supposed fact of a forgotten consciousness in sleep cannot be pleaded in support of its having been conscious, alike out of connection with memory and with the man, *at or before birth.* Locke fears that, ' if the soul should think whilst the organs of the external senses cease from exercise, it should steal some ideas which it had not got in his honest way of sensation [and reflection] only.' (Lee, *Anti-Scepticism*, p. 44.) This discussion about the continuity of consciousness, in §§ 9-19, might have found its place in the First Book, to which the subject of potential, as distinguished from actual, intelligence is cognate.

BOOK II.

CHAP. I.

in itself constantly, as long as it exists; and that actual thinking is as inseparable from the soul as actual extension is from the body[1]; which if true, to inquire after the beginning of a man's ideas is the same as to inquire after the beginning of his soul. For, by this account, soul and its ideas, as body and its extension, will begin to exist both at the same time.

The Soul thinks not always; for this wants Proofs.

10. But whether the soul be supposed to exist antecedent to, or coeval with, or some time after the first rudiments of organization, or the beginnings of life in the body, I leave to be disputed by those who have better thought of that matter[2]. I confess myself to have one of those dull souls, that doth not perceive itself always to contemplate ideas; nor can conceive it any more necessary for the soul always to think, than for the body always to move: the perception of ideas being (as I conceive) to the soul, what motion is to the body; not its essence, but one of its operations. And therefore, though thinking be supposed never so much the proper action of the soul, yet it is not necessary to suppose that it should be always thinking, always in action. That, perhaps, is the privilege of the infinite Author and Preserver of all things, who 'never slumbers nor sleeps'; but is not competent to any finite being, at least not to the soul of man. We know certainly, by experience, that we *sometimes* think; and thence draw this infallible consequence,—that there is something in us that has a power to think. But whether that substance *perpetually* thinks or no, we can be no further assured than experience informs us. For, to say that actual thinking is

---

[1] The Cartesians are here immediately in view, with their *a priori* maxim as to the essence of the soul, according to which its very existence consists in *actual consciousness*, so that, if consciousness were interrupted, it would necessarily cease to exist. The inquiry which Locke here undertakes had been pursued apart from experience; at least, not by an appeal to facts. The Cartesians justified their position by arguing that that without which we can have no notion, and with which we have a distinct notion, of *spirit*, must be an *essential* attribute of spirit, and assume that this can be said only of 'thinking,' or being conscious.

[2] Locke confines his regard to 'soul' as manifested in the present life. He distrusts metaphysical inferences as to its existence *prior* to the birth of the body. Afterwards, on ground of supernatural revelation, he expresses faith in its existence *after* the dissolution of this body—questions these which concern metaphysical or theological philosophy, not scientific psychology.

essential to the soul, and inseparable from it, is to beg what is in question, and not to prove it by reason;—which is necessary to be done, if it be not a self-evident proposition [1] But whether this, 'That the soul always thinks,' be a self-evident proposition, that everybody assents to at first hearing, I appeal to mankind. [It [2] is doubted whether I thought at all last night or no. The question being about a matter of fact, it is begging it to bring, as a proof for it, an hypothesis, which is the very thing in dispute: by which way one may prove anything, and it is but supposing that all watches, whilst the balance beats, think, and it is sufficiently proved, and past doubt, that my watch thought all last night. But he that would not deceive himself, ought to build his hypothesis on matter of fact, and make it out by sensible experience, and not presume on matter of fact, because of his hypothesis, that is, because he supposes it to be so; which way of proving amounts to this, that I must necessarily think all last night, because another supposes I always think, though I myself cannot perceive that I always do so.

But men in love with their opinions may not only suppose what is in question, but allege wrong matter of fact. How else could any one make it an inference of mine, that a thing is not, because we are not sensible of it in our sleep? I do not say there is no *soul* in a man, because he is not sensible of it in his sleep; but I do say, he cannot *think* at any time, waking or sleeping, without being sensible of it. Our being sensible of it is not necessary to anything but to our thoughts; and to them it is; and to them it always will be necessary, till we can think without being conscious of it [3].]

---

[1] Another recognition of 'self-evident propositions,' while all intellectual innateness is argued against.

[2] The remainder of this section (within brackets) was added in the second edition.

[3] That there may be ideas without any consciousness of them—that thoughts of which the individual is unconscious may influence the individual—that principles may exist potentially, in the nature of things, explaining our experience of things—all this seems impossible to Locke. Yet, as Leibniz says, this is the knot of the main question of the *Essay*—'le nœud de l'affaire.' It is solved, he would say, by the hypothesis, that the individual mind and the universe of experience necessarily contain more thought than there can be a proper consciousness of, simultaneously, or even in succession, in

11. I grant that the soul, in a waking man, is never without thought, because it is the condition of being awake. But whether sleeping without dreaming be not an affection of the whole man, mind as well as body, may be worth a waking man's consideration ; it being hard to conceive that anything should think and not be conscious of it. If the soul doth think in a sleeping man without being conscious of it, I ask whether, during such thinking, it has any pleasure or pain, or be capable of happiness or misery? I am sure the man is not ; no more than the bed or earth he lies on. For to be happy or miserable without beng conscious of it, seems to me utterly inconsistent and impossible. Or if it be possible that the *soul* can, whilst the body is sleeping, have its thinking, enjoyments, and concerns, its pleasures or pain, apart, which the *man* is not conscious of nor partakes in [1],—it is certain that Socrates asleep and Socrates awake is not the same person ; but his soul when he sleeps, and Socrates the man, consisting of body and soul, when he is waking, are two persons : since waking Socrates has no knowledge of, or concernment for that happiness or misery of his soul, which it enjoys alone by itself whilst he sleeps, without perceiving anything of it ; no more than he has for the happiness or misery of a man in the Indies, whom he knows not. For, if we take wholly away all consciousness of our actions and sensations, especially of pleasure and pain, and the concernment that accompanies it, it will be hard to know wherein to place personal identity [2].

that mind. The latent stores of memory illustrate this, as even Locke acknowledges, ch. x. §§ 2, 7, 8, where he speaks of '*dormant*' ideas. Leibniz goes further, when he adds—'il reste quelque chose de *toutes* nos pensées passées, et aucune n'en saurait jamais être effacée entièrement.' But while he argues that no past ideas of which we have been conscious can ever be entirely effaced, he allows that most of them must be latent, while the rest are consciously held. That we have ideas of which we are unconscious, is the

principal argument against Locke in Norris's *Cursory Reflections* upon the *Essay*, published in 1690, a few months after the *Essay* appeared.

[1] This does not apply to potential thought, with its necessary implicates, into which actual consciousness does not enter—the perception as distinguished from the apperception of Leibniz—which may be the condition of the 'soul,' and the whole 'man' in a deep sleep.

[2] Cf. ch. xxvii. Locke holds that consciousness *constitutes* personal iden-

12. The soul, during sound sleep, thinks, say these men. BOOK II.
Whilst it thinks and perceives, it is capable certainly of those
of delight or trouble, as well as any other perceptions; and
it must necessarily be *conscious* of its own perceptions. But
it has all this apart: the sleeping *man*[1], it is plain, is
conscious of nothing of all this. Let us suppose, then, the
soul of Castor, while he is sleeping, retired from his body;
which is no impossible supposition for the men I have here
to do with, who so liberally allow life, without a thinking soul,
to all other animals[2]. These men cannot then judge it
impossible, or a contradiction, that the body should live
without the soul; nor that the soul should subsist and think,
or have perception, even perception of happiness or misery,
without the body. Let us then, I say, suppose the soul
of Castor separated during his sleep from his body, to
think apart. Let us suppose, too, that it chooses for its
scene of thinking the body of another man, v. g. Pollux,
who is sleeping without a soul. For, if Castor's soul can
think, whilst Castor is asleep, what Castor is never conscious
of, it is no matter what *place* it chooses to think in. We
have here, then, the bodies of two men with only one soul
between them, which we will suppose to sleep and wake
by turns; and the soul still thinking in the waking man,
whereof the sleeping man is never conscious, has never the

CHAP. I.
If a sleep-
ing Man
thinks
without
knowing
it, the
sleeping
and
waking
Man are
two
Persons.

tity, which he has to reconcile with
his argument here, that continuous
personality is consistent with intervals
of unconsciousness—in sleep, &c. But
Butler objects, as against Locke, that
'though consciousness of what is past
does *ascertain* our personal identity to
ourselves, yet to say that it *makes*
personal identity, or is necessary to
our being the same persons, is to say
that a person has not existed a single
moment, nor done one action, but what
he can remember. And we should
really think it self-evident, that consciousness of personal identity presupposes, and therefore cannot constitute, personal identity, any more than
knowledge in any other case can constitute the truth [reality] which it

presupposes.' (*Essay on Personal
Identity.*)

[1] The 'man' means the soul in union
with the body; 'soul,' *per se*, means
the source of consciousness as it exists
when the organs of external sense are
dormant. Locke's assumption,—that
either the soul or the man 'must
necessarily be *conscious* of the perceptions,' is not self-evident, any more
than the Cartesian supposition,—that if
consciousness is interrupted, there
must either be *no soul during the interruption*, or else the soul of man
is only *a special function of the human
body*, which disappears when the appropriate organs cease from exercise.

[2] According to the Cartesians animals are unconscious automatons.

least perception. I ask, then, whether Castor and Pollux, thus with only one soul between them, which thinks and perceives in one what the other is never conscious of, nor is concerned for, are not two as distinct *persons* as Castor and Hercules, or as Socrates and Plato were? And whether one of them might not be very happy, and the other very miserable?[1] Just by the same reason, they make the soul and the man two persons, who make the soul think apart what the man is not conscious of. For, I suppose nobody will make identity of persons to consist in the soul's being united to the very same numerical particles of matter. For if that be necessary to identity, it will be impossible, in that constant flux of the particles of our bodies, that any man should be the same person two days, or two moments, together.

Impossible to convince those that sleep without dreaming, that they think.   13. Thus, methinks, every drowsy nod shakes their doctrine, who teach that the soul is always thinking. Those, at least, who do at any time *sleep without dreaming*, can never be convinced that their thoughts are sometimes for four hours busy without their knowing of it; and if they are taken in the very act, waked in the middle of that sleeping contemplation, can give no manner of account of it.

That Men dream without remembering it, in vain urged.   14. It will perhaps be said,—That the soul thinks even in the soundest sleep, but the *memory* retains it not[2]. That the soul in a sleeping man should be this moment busy a thinking, and the next moment in a waking man not remember nor be able to recollect one jot of all those thoughts, is very hard to be conceived, and would need some better proof than bare assertion[3] to make it be believed. For who

---

[1] This whimsical illustration implies that the source of consciousness in man is a substance that is capable of acting apart from his body; and even of occupying the body of another man; which one might say it can no more be or do than one man can be actually conscious of the successive thoughts and feelings of another man.

[2] Locke's *first* argument for interrupted consciousness was,—that we cannot feel or think during sleep without being conscious of it *at the*

time. He now meets the objection, that we may have been conscious in sleep, but so slightly, or so rapidly, that when we awake we lose all memory of the consciousness.

[3] The phenomena of somnambulism have since been adduced, as evidence of the existence of intellectual activities wholly forgotten by the agent. The facts that persons suddenly awakened find themselves in a dream; also that dreams are often remembered only for a brief interval after awaking, and are

can without any more ado, but being barely told so, imagine that the greatest part of men do, during all their lives, for several hours every day, think of something, which if they were asked, even in the middle of these thoughts, they could remember nothing at all of? Most men, I think, pass a great part of their sleep without dreaming[1]. I once knew a man that was bred a scholar, and had no bad memory, who told me he had never dreamed in his life, till he had that fever he was then newly recovered of, which was about the five or six and twentieth year of his age. I suppose the world affords more such instances: at least every one's acquaintance will furnish him with examples enough of such as pass most of their nights without dreaming[2].

---

then irrecoverably lost, are offered as evidence of the abnormal action of memory during sleep. For experimental reasons for concluding, that the mind has been then and otherwise conscious of activities afterwards wholly lost, see Jouffroy, *Mélanges Philos.*— Du Sommeil ; Hamilton's *Lectures on Metaph.* xvii. But if remembered dreams occur only during the semi-conscious periods of falling asleep and of awaking, these experiments do not warrant the application of the inference to deep sleep. In this relation some curious facts, regarding unconsciousness in hysteria, are referred to in James's *Psychology*, ch. viii., suggesting occasions on which there is a disruption of the conscious life into separate consciousnesses, so that a part of the consciousness 'may sever its connection with other parts and yet continue to be.'

[1] Leibniz argues that we can never be without *perceptions*; but as he also maintains that perception may exist without *apperception* or consciousness, his position does not necessarily imply that we are never unconscious, or without dreams, even in deep sleep. Wolf adopts the views of Leibniz on this question, *Psychologia Rationalis*, § 59.

[2] This and what follows implies that *memory of dreams* is the *only* channel through which there could be evidence of continuous mental activity during sleep ; and also that the activity can never be an imperfect consciousness —both which assumptions may be disputed. The effects which semiconscious and unconscious perceptions leave behind them in the current of conscious life, rather than memory, afford the evidence on which, for example, Leibniz relies : ' Il y a mille marques qui font juger qu'il y a à tout moment une infinité de perceptions en nous, mais sans aperception et sans réflexion ; c'est-à-dire des changements dans l'âme même, dont nous ne nous apercevons pas, parce que ces impressions sont ou trop petites, et en trop grand nombre, ou trop unies, en sorte qu'elles n'ont rien d'assez distinguant à part ; mais jointes à d'autres elles ne laissent pas de faire leur effet et de se faire sentir dans l'assemblage au moins confusément.' (*Nouv. Ess.* Avant-Propos.) The phenomena of habit are then referred to as examples —e.g. unconscious perception of the motion of a mill or a waterfall, when we listened so long that the undulations at last induce perception without apperception ; or the noise of the sea, in hearing which we must have an unconscious perception of the noise of

15. To think often, and never to retain it so much as one moment, is a very useless sort of thinking ; and the soul, in such a state of thinking, does very little, if at all, excel that of a looking-glass, which constantly receives variety of images, or ideas, but retains none ; they disappear and vanish, and there remain no footsteps of them ; the looking-glass is never the better for such ideas, nor the soul for such thoughts. Perhaps it will be said, that in a waking *man* the materials of the body are employed, and made use of, in thinking ; and that the memory of thoughts is retained by the impressions that are made on the brain, and the traces there left after such thinking ; but that in the thinking of the *soul*, which is not perceived in a sleeping man, there the soul thinks apart, and making no use of the organs of the body, leaves no impressions on it, and consequently no memory of such thoughts. Not to mention again the absurdity of two distinct persons, which follows from this supposition, I answer, further,—That whatever ideas the mind can receive and contemplate without the help of the body, it is reasonable to conclude it can retain without the help of the body too ; or else the soul, or any separate spirit, will have but little advantage by thinking. If it has no memory of its own thoughts ; if it cannot lay them up for its own use, and be able to recall them upon occasion ; if it cannot reflect upon what is past, and make use of its former experiences, reasonings, and contemplations, to what purpose does it think ? They who make the soul a thinking thing, at this rate, will not make it a much more noble being than those do whom they condemn, for allowing it to be nothing but the subtilist parts of matter. Characters drawn on dust, that the first breath of wind effaces ; or impressions made on a heap of atoms, or animal spirits, are altogether as

each wave, which produces conscious perception of the *collective* sound— clear in the aggregate but confused in the parts—since we could not otherwise become conscious of the sound of a hundred thousand waves ; a hundred thousand nothings could not make something. Another explanation that has been suggested of this want of memory is, that in deep and seemingly dreamless sleep, and other abnormal states, while there is continuous consciousness, the successive states are so rapid that there can be no retention of them, under the ordinary conditions of memory.

useful, and render the subject as noble, as the thoughts of a soul that perish in thinking; that, once out of sight, are gone for ever, and leave no memory of themselves behind them. Nature never makes excellent things for mean or no uses: and it is hardly to be conceived that our infinitely wise Creator should make so admirable a faculty as the power of thinking, that faculty which comes nearest the excellency of his own incomprehensible being, to be so idly and uselessly employed, at least a fourth part of its time here, as to think constantly, without remembering any of those thoughts, without doing any good to itself or others, or being any way useful to any other part of the creation. If we will examine it, we shall not find, I suppose, the motion of dull and senseless matter, any where in the universe, made so little use of and so wholly thrown away [1].

16. It is true, we have sometimes instances of perception whilst we are asleep, and retain the memory of those thoughts: but how extravagant and incoherent for the most part they are; how little conformable to the perfection and order of a rational being, those who are acquainted with dreams need not be told. This I would willingly be satisfied in,—whether the soul, when it thinks thus apart, and as it were separate from the body [2], acts less rationally than when conjointly with it, or no. If its separate thoughts be less rational, then these men must say, that the soul owes the perfection of rational

---

[1] It might be held that, instead of being 'useless,' these unremembered, because semi-conscious and unconscious, perceptions have immense efficacy in the spiritual economy. ' Ces petites perceptions,' Leibniz argues, ' sont donc de plus grand efficace qu'on ne pense. Ce sont elles qui forment ce je ne sais quoi—ces goûts, ces images des qualités des sens, claires dans l'assemblage, mais confuses dans les parties ; ces impressions que les corps qui nous environnent font sur nous et qui enveloppent l'infini ; cette liaison que chaque être a avec tout le reste de l'univers. On peut même dire qu'en conséquence de ces petites perceptions

le présent est plein de l'avenir et chargé du passé, que tout est conspirant, et que dans la moindre des substances, des yeux aussi perçants que ceux de Dieu pourraient lire toute la suite des choses de l'univers.' *Nouv. Essais*, Avant-Propos. Other 'useful' consequences of 'unconscious perceptions' are suggested in the sequel.

[2] No reason is given for the assumption, that even in dreams the soul thinks apart from the body, for there is experimental evidence that dreams are conditioned by the organism ; though not equally with waking perception by the special organ of each sense.

thinking to the body : if it does not, it is a wonder that our dreams should be, for the most part, so frivolous and irrational ; and that the soul should retain none of its more rational soliloquies and meditations.

17. Those who so confidently tell us that the soul always actually thinks, I would they would also tell us, what those ideas are that are in the soul of a child, before or just at the union with the body, before it hath received any by sensation. The dreams of sleeping men are, as I take it, all made up of the waking man's ideas ; though for the most part oddly put together. It is strange, if the soul has ideas of its own that it derived not from sensation or reflection, (as it must have, if it thought before[1] it received any impressions from the body,) that it should never, in its private thinking, (so private, that the man himself perceives it not,) retain any of them the very moment it wakes out of them, and then make the man glad with new discoveries. Who can find it reason that the soul should, in its retirement during sleep, have so many hours' thoughts, and yet never light on any of those ideas it borrowed not from sensation or reflection ; or at least preserve the memory of none but such, which, being occasioned from the body, must needs be less natural to a spirit ? It is strange the soul should never once in a man's whole life recall over any of its pure native thoughts, and those ideas it had before it borrowed anything from the body ; never bring into the waking man's view any other ideas but what have a tang of the cask, and manifestly derive their original from that union[2]. If it always thinks, and so had ideas before it

[1] Here again the metaphysical constitution (*origo*) of adult knowledge is reduced to a question regarding the history of the growth of knowledge in the individual. But, as Shaftesbury long ago observed, ' the question is not about the time the ideas entered, but whether the constitution of man [and of knowledge] be such that . . . sooner or later (*no matter when*) the ideas of order, administration, and a God, for instance, will not *infallibly, inevitably, necessarily spring up*'—because involved in the rationality of things, and of our experience of their changes.

[2] The inadequacy of empiricism to express the facts and implicates of experience is maintained, not on the ground that it neglects ideas which the soul was *conscious of* before it borrowed anything from the body, but because the knowledge to which man afterwards ascends, in union with his body, involves elements which cannot be analysed into mere sensations and their accidental aggregates. The first steps of

was united, or before it received any from the body [1], it is not to be supposed but that during sleep it recollects its native ideas; and during that retirement from communicating with the body, whilst it thinks by itself, the ideas it is busied about should be, sometimes at least, those more natural and congenial ones which it had in itself, underived from the body, or its own operations about them: which, since the waking man never remembers, we must from this hypothesis conclude [either [2] that the soul remembers something that the man does not; or else that memory belongs only to such ideas as are derived from the body, or the mind's operations about them.]

18. I would be glad also to learn from these men who so confidently pronounce that the human soul, or, which is all one, that a man always thinks, how they come to know it; nay, how they come to know that they themselves think, when they themselves do not perceive it. This, I am afraid, is to be sure without proofs, and to know without perceiving. It is, I suspect, a confused notion, taken up to serve an hypothesis; and none of those clear truths, that either their own evidence forces us to admit, or common experience makes it impudence to deny. For the most that can be said of it is, that it is possible the soul may always think, but not always retain it in memory. And I say, it is as possible that the soul may not always think; and much more probable that it should sometimes not think, than that it should often think, and that a long while together, and not be conscious to itself, the next moment after, that it had thought [3].

the intellectual ascent, in the form of expectations of the future, illustrate this. It is a contradiction to say that the *ultimate reason of expectation* is,—our individual and inherited experience that the future resembles the past; for men never had, and never can have, any experience of the *future*.

[1] Locke thus sees, in the hypothesis that the soul 'always thinks,' a support to the hypothesis of 'innate ideas,' according to his interpretation of 'innateness.'

[2] In first edition — 'that memory belongs only to ideas derived from the body, and the operations of the mind about them; or else that the *soul* remembers something that the *man* does not.'

[3] The kind of evidence which Locke's opponents would adduce is referred to in preceding notes. It is either *a priori*, or inference from observation of the phenomena of consciousness, in our waking normal state. But is there after all evidence

BOOK II.

Chap. I.

That a
Man
should be
busy in
Thinking,
and yet
not retain
it the next
moment,
very im-
probable.

19. To suppose the soul to think, and the man not to perceive it, is, as has been said, to make two persons in one man[1]. And if one considers well these men's way of speaking, one should be led into a suspicion that they do so. For they who tell us that the *soul* always thinks, do never, that I remember, say that a *man* always thinks[2]. Can the soul think, and not the man? Or a man think, and not be conscious of it? This, perhaps, would be suspected of jargon in others. If they say the man thinks always, but is not always conscious of it, they may as well say his body is extended without having parts. For it is altogether as intelligible to say that a body is extended without parts, as that anything thinks without being conscious of it, or perceiving that it does so. They who talk thus may, with as much reason, if it be necessary to their hypothesis, say that a man is always hungry, but that he does not always feel it; whereas hunger consists in that very sensation, as thinking consists in being conscious that one thinks[3]. If they say that a man is always conscious to himself of thinking, I ask, How they know it? Consciousness is the perception of what passes in a man's own mind. Can another man perceive that I am conscious of anything, when I perceive it not myself? No man's knowledge here can go beyond his experience. Wake a man out of a sound sleep, and ask him what he was that moment thinking of. If he himself be conscious of nothing he then thought on, he must be a notable diviner of thoughts that can assure him that he was thinking. May he not, with more reason, assure him he was not asleep? This is something beyond philosophy; and it cannot be less than revelation, that discovers to another thoughts in my mind, when I can find none there myself. And they must needs have a penetrating sight who can certainly see that I

---

to justify a positive conclusion regarding this question, either in the form of *a priori* metaphysics, or *a posteriori* experiences?

[1] There are phenomena, observed since Locke wrote, which might suggest the supposition of this sort of double personality.

[2] What they might say is, that the conscious experience of the adult presents phenomena from which it may be inferred, that more was latent in it from the first than the subject of it was then conscious of.

[3] See previous notes.

think, when I cannot perceive it myself, and when I declare that I do not ; and yet can see that dogs or elephants do not think, when they give all the demonstration of it imaginable, except only telling us that they do so. This some may suspect to be a step beyond the Rosicrucians[1] ; it seeming easier to make one's self invisible to others, than to make another's thoughts visible to me, which are not visible to himself. But it is but defining the soul to be ' a substance that always thinks,' and the business is done. If such definition be of any authority, I know not what it can serve for but to make many men suspect that they have no souls at all; since they find a good part of their lives pass away without thinking. For no definitions that I know, no suppositions of any sect, are of force enough to destroy constânt experience ; and perhaps it is the affectation of knowing beyond what we perceive, that makes so much useless dispute and noise in the world[2].

20. I see no reason, therefore, to believe that the soul thinks before the senses have furnished it with ideas to think on[3] ; and as those are increased and retained, so it comes, by exercise, to improve its faculty of thinking in the several parts of it ; as well as, afterwards, by compounding those ideas, and reflecting on its own operations, it increases its stock, as well as facility in remembering, imagining, reasoning, and other modes of thinking[4].

No ideas but from Sensation and Reflection, evident, if we observe Children.

21. He that will suffer himself to be informed by observation and experience, and not make his own hypothesis the rule of nature, will find few signs of a soul accustomed to much thinking in a new-born child, and much fewer of any reasoning at all. And yet it is hard to imagine that the

State of a child in the mother's womb.

[1] The mystical society called *Rosicrucians*, with their secret symbols, was formed early in the seventeenth century. According to their doctrine, the four elements are inhabited by invisible spirits, with whom men may hold familiar intercourse on certain conditions.

[2] These objections fall if there is evidence, other than that of *present consciousness*, or *memory of past consciousness*, to show that men have been unconsciously, or semi-unconsciously, active (in sleep).

[3] ' We are born ignorant of everything.' (*Conduct of Understanding*, § 38.)

[4] This and what follows, to the end of the chapter, is history of the gradual growth of experience in the individual man—not critical analysis of the ultimate rational constitution of the growing experience.

BOOK II.
—◦—
CHAP. I.

rational soul should think so much, and not reason at all. And he that will consider that infants newly come into the world spend the greatest part of their time in sleep, and are seldom awake but when either hunger calls for the teat, or some pain (the most importunate of all sensations), or some other violent impression on the body, forces the mind to perceive and attend to it;—he, I say, who considers this, will perhaps find reason to imagine that a *fœtus* in the mother's womb differs not much from the state of a vegetable, but passes the greatest part of its time without perception or thought; doing very little but sleep in a place where it needs not seek for food, and is surrounded with liquor, always equally soft, and near of the same temper; where the eyes have no light, and the ears so shut up are not very susceptible of sounds; and where there is little or no variety, or change of objects, to move the senses [1].

The mind thinks in proportion to the matter it gets from experience to think about.

22. Follow a child from its birth, and observe the alterations that time makes, and you shall find, as the mind by the senses comes more and more to be furnished with ideas, it comes to be more and more awake; thinks more, the more it has matter to think on. After some time it begins to know the objects which, being most familiar with it, have made lasting impressions. Thus it comes by degrees to know the persons it daily converses with, and distinguishes them from strangers; which are instances and effects of its coming to retain and distinguish the ideas the senses convey to it. And so we may observe how the mind, *by degrees*, improves in these; and *advances* to the exercise of those other faculties of enlarging, compounding, and abstracting its ideas [2], and of

[1] It is easy thus to show that a child in its mother's womb is not consciously conversant with the abstract principles of the philosopher.

[2] According to Locke, men at first perceive and image individual objects. 'Our ideas every one of them are particular; universality is but accidental to them.' (Bk. IV. ch. xvii. § 8.) For the intellectual advance is from particular images to the intelligent use of common terms. In proportion as men accumulate particular ideas, they become less conscious of them, and more apprehensive of their concepts. *Idea* is here confined to what is representable in the sensuous or individualising imagination (φάντασμα); and, so understood, an *abstract* idea (διανόημα and νόημα) is an absurdity. Yet we find more than is presentable in the senses, and representable in imagination, in those abstract meanings which we are intellectually obliged

reasoning about them, and reflecting upon all these ; of which BOOK II.
I shall have occasion to speak more hereafter.

CHAP. I.

23. If it shall be demanded then, *when* a man *begins* to
have any ideas, I think the true answer is,—*when he first has*
any sensation. For, since there appear not to be any ideas in
the mind before the senses have conveyed any in, I conceive
that ideas in the understanding are coeval with *sensation* ;
which is such an impression or motion made in some part of
the body, as [*produces* [1] *some perception*] *in the understanding* [2].
[It [3] is about these impressions made on our senses by outward
objects that the mind seems *first* to employ itself, in such
operations as we call perception, remembering, consideration,
reasoning, &c.]

A man begins to have ideas when he first has sensation. What sensation is.

24. [In [4] time the mind comes to reflect on its own operations
about the ideas got by sensation, and thereby stores itself
with a new set of ideas, which I call ideas of reflection. These
are the impressions that are made on our senses by outward
objects that are extrinsical to the mind ; and its own operations, proceeding from powers intrinsical and proper to
itself, which, when reflected on by itself, become also
objects of its contemplation—are, as I have said, the original

The Original of all our Knowledge.

---

to entertain,—so ' obliged,' we must
presume, because reason is immanent
in what is real, and thus objective
as well as subjective.

[1] In first three editions—' makes it
be taken notice of.' ' Sensation ' is
here an affection of the *organism*, and
' perception ' the *mental apprehension*
which accompanies or follows it.

[2] This is one of Locke's definitions
of sensation, according to which it is
an *organic* affection which may be
manifested to the senses of an observer. In the next section he refers
to it as the receptive ' capacity of the
human *intellect*'; and in ch. xix. § 1
he describes it as ' the actual entrance
of any idea into the *understanding* by
the senses,' adding that ' the same idea,
when it recurs without the operation
of the like [extra-organic] object on
the external sensory, is *remembrance.*'

It may thus with Locke include what
has since been distinguished as sensuous feeling (sensation proper), and
the intellectual apprehension in sense
of solid extension in its various relations (perception proper).

[3] This sentence was introduced in
the French version.

[4] The first four editions, instead of
the sentences bracketed, read thus :—
' The impressions then that are made on
our senses by outward objects that are
extrinsical to the mind; and its own
operations about these impressions, reflected on by itself, as proper objects to
be contemplated by it, are, I conceive,
the original of all knowledge.' The two
sentences within brackets appear first
in the French version. The meaning
of the second is obscure, unless for
' These are the impressions,' we read,
' Thus the impressions &c.'

of all knowledge.] Thus the first capacity of human intellect is,—that the mind is fitted to receive the impressions made on it; either through the senses by outward objects, or by its own operations when it reflects on them [1]. This is the first step a man makes towards the discovery of anything, and the groundwork whereon to build all those notions which ever he shall have naturally in this world. All those sublime thoughts which tower above the clouds, and reach as high as heaven itself, take their rise and footing here: in all that great extent wherein the mind wanders, in those remote speculations it may seem to be elevated with, it stirs not one jot beyond those ideas which *sense* or *reflection* have offered for its contemplation [2].

In the Reception of simple Ideas, the Understanding is for the most part passive.

25. In this part the understanding is merely passive; and whether or no it will have these beginnings, and as it were materials of knowledge, is not in its own power [3]. For the objects of our senses do, many of them, obtrude their particular ideas upon our minds whether we will or not; and the operations of our minds will not let us be without, at least, some obscure notions of them [4]. No man can be wholly ignorant of what he does when he thinks. These simple ideas, when offered to the mind [5], the understanding

---

[1] That is to say, intelligence in the individual deals at first with concrete 'impressions,' and advances in the way of comprehending their more general, and at last their ultimate or philosophical relations. Whether in those ultimate relations Locke saw only generalisation by induction; or whether he recognised conditions necessarily embedded in all experience of reality, because necessities of the reason that is inherent in things, is the question to be settled in determining his philosophical position.

[2] Nothing, says Hume, is 'beyond the power of thought, except what implies an absolute contradiction.' But Locke here looks to the limits of the *materials*, contingently presented, with which human thought is concerned.

[3] This passivity, or *involuntariness*, is one of the marks by which external and internal perception are distinguished from plastic imagination. Mental images can be modified by our will, and are thus subject to our control; the data of sense, on the contrary, are independent of our will, as long as the objects are present to the senses; so that, in this respect, we are passive in the 'reception' of them. At another point of view than Locke's, we are active even in acquisition; for sense-perception itself necessarily involves some attention, and constructive activity of intelligence.

[4] In spontaneous self-consciousness, as distinguished from deliberate introspection.

[5] But he does not say that they are ever 'offered' *in their simplicity*—as

can no more refuse to have, nor alter when they are im-printed [1], nor blot them out and make new ones itself, than a mirror can refuse, alter, or obliterate the images or ideas which the objects set before it do therein produce. As the bodies that surround us do diversely affect our organs, the mind is forced to receive the impressions [2]; and cannot avoid the perception of those ideas that are annexed to them.

isolated sensations. Elsewhere he implies the contrary, when he mentions 'ideas that necessarily accompany' all our other ideas, e.g. those of 'existence,' 'duration,' and 'substance.'

[1] 'imprinted,' i.e. in all actual perception external and internal.

[2] 'Impressions.' This term was afterwards employed by Hume to designate 'all our more lively perceptions, when we hear, or see, or feel, or love, or hate, or desire, or will,' in contrast with 'idea,' which he applies only to the 'less lively' mental representations of preceding 'impressions,'—in memory and imagination (*Hume's Inquiry concerning Human Understanding*, Sect. II).

CHAPTER II.

OF SIMPLE IDEAS.

1. THE better to understand the nature, manner, and extent of our knowledge, one thing is carefully to be observed concerning the ideas we have ; and that is, that some of them are *simple* and some *complex*[1].

Though the qualities that affect our senses are, in the things themselves, so united and blended, that there is no separation, no distance between them; yet it is plain, the ideas they produce in the mind enter by the senses simple and unmixed. For, though the sight and touch often take in from the same object, at the same time, different ideas ;—as a man sees at once motion and colour ; the hand feels softness and warmth in the same piece of wax : yet the simple ideas thus united in the same subject, are as perfectly distinct[2] as those that come in by different senses. The coldness and

---

[1] In distinguishing *simple* from *complex* ideas Locke does not assert that the former are, or can be, received, or represented, *in their simplicity* ; nor does he deny that a ' simple' idea of sense, *as such*, is an abstraction from our actual experience. On the contrary, he tells us that simple ideas are received in groups or combinations in the senses ; and that some simple ideas (e.g. those of *existence, unity*, &c.) are ' necessary' concomitants of all other simple ideas (ch. vii. § 7). None of them, as it were, ' hang in the air alone.' And besides this recognition of the fact that simple ideas are received in complexity, in the contemporaneous activity of the several senses—though, by logical analysis of the percepts,

images, and concepts of which we are conscious, they may afterwards be considered apart—he also usually distinguishes mere *ideas*, both simple and complex, from *knowledge* and *assent*, into which they enter as elements, but which, *per se*, they cannot constitute. The additional elements involved in ' knowledge,' and in ' assent to probability,' are discussed in the Fourth Book. The simple and complex ideas of the Second Book are with Locke analogous to the 'simple apprehension' (considered apart from judgment) of logicians.

[2] That is, in themselves, either in virtue of spontaneous abstraction by the separate senses, or, by logical analysis of our concepts of things.

hardness which a man feels in a piece of ice being as distinct
ideas in the mind as the smell and whiteness of a lily; or
as the taste of sugar, and smell of a rose. And there is
nothing can be plainer to a man than the clear and distinct
perception he has of those simple ideas; which, being each in
itself uncompounded, contains in it nothing but *one uniform
appearance, or conception in the mind,* and is not distinguishable
into different ideas[1].

2. These simple ideas, the materials of all our knowledge,
are suggested and furnished to the mind only by those two
ways above mentioned, viz. sensation and reflection[2]. When
the understanding is once stored with these simple ideas, it
has the power to repeat, compare, and unite them, even to an
almost infinite variety, and so can make at pleasure new complex ideas[3]. But it is not in the power of the most exalted
wit, or enlarged understanding, by any quickness or variety of
thought, to *invent* or *frame* one new simple idea in the mind,
not taken in by the ways before mentioned: nor can any
force of the understanding *destroy* those that are there.
The dominion of man, in this little world of his own understanding being muchwhat the same as it is in the great
world of visible things; wherein his power, however managed
by art and skill, reaches no farther than to compound and
divide the materials that are made to his hand; but can do
nothing towards the making the least particle of new matter,
or destroying one atom of what is already in being. The
same inability will every one find in himself, who shall go
about to fashion in his understanding one simple idea, not
received in by his senses from external objects, or by reflection

---

[1] They are 'simple' in the sense of
being incapable of analysis, while all
complex ideas can be analysed.

[2] This sentence, in expressing the
leading principle in the Second Book,
distinguishes ideas as in some cases
'furnished' and in others 'suggested.'
The term 'suggested' was adopted
afterwards by Berkeley and Reid.
Its meaning in the *Essay* is illustrated
in the sequel, where ideas are described
which Locke refers to suggestion (e. g.

ch. iii. § 1; ch. vii. §§ 7-9).

[3] 'Complex ideas,' according to
Locke, are both 'made *for* us,' and
'made *by* us.' They are made *for* us
in the perceived union of qualities in
individual things; and more generally
in the invariable 'suggestion' e. g. of
the ideas of existence, unity, and power,
along with all that we can consciously
apprehend. They are made *by* us in
the voluntary constructions of plastic
imagination and of abstract thought.

BOOK II.
CHAP. II.

from the operations of his own mind about them. I would have any one try to fancy any taste which had never affected his palate; or frame the idea of a scent he had never smelt: and when he can do this, I will also conclude that a blind man hath ideas of colours, and a deaf man true distinct notions of sounds[1].

Only the qualities that affect the senses are imaginable.

3. This is the reason why—though we cannot believe it impossible to God to make a creature with other organs, and more ways to convey into the understanding the notice of corporeal things than those five, as they are usually counted, which he has given to man—yet I think it is not possible for any *man*[2] to imagine any other qualities in bodies, howsoever constituted, whereby they can be taken notice of, besides sounds, tastes, smells, visible and tangible qualities. And had mankind been made but with four senses, the qualities then which are the objects of the fifth sense had been as far from our notice, imagination, and conception, as now any belonging to a sixth, seventh, or eighth sense can possibly be ;—which, whether yet some other creatures, in some other parts of this vast and stupendous universe, may not have, will be a great presumption to deny. He that will not set himself proudly at the top of all things, but will consider the immensity of this fabric, and the great variety that is to be found in this little and inconsiderable part of it which he has to do with, may be apt to think that, in other mansions of it, there may be other and different intelligent beings, of whose faculties he has as little knowledge or apprehension as a worm shut up in one drawer of a cabinet hath of the senses or understanding of a man ; such variety and excellency being suitable to the wisdom and power of the Maker[3].   I

---

[1] Locke elsewhere insists that although he uses the word 'idea' often, in unfolding his 'way of knowledge through ideas,' i.e. on condition of having ideas,—he uses it to warn men against giving currency to empty words. 'The new way of *ideas*,' he tells Stillingfleet, 'and the old way of *speaking intelligibly* ever will be the same.' Apprehension of meaning (i.e. having idea) is necessarily implied in all knowledge and judgment, although simple apprehension of ideas, *per se*, is not knowledge.

[2] 'Any *man*,' i. e. any being with only man's limited number of senses.

[3] We have no reason *a priori* to deny the existence in other worlds of animated intelligences in whom *our* five senses are all wanting, but who may be endowed with five (or five hundred) *other* senses, to which their sensible

have here followed the common opinion of man's having but five senses; though, perhaps, there may be justly counted more [1];—but either supposition serves equally to my present purpose.

worlds correspond — thus presenting qualities to them all of which are unimaginable by human beings, and unperceived by us in our material world.

[1] Thus the sense of simple contact, the muscular sense, and the sense of temperature are now distinguished. Various classifications of the external senses have been proposed, from Aristotle downwards. The number is irrelevant to Locke's argument, which concludes that (whatever the number) man cannot speak or think intelligibly about any other qualities of things than those which are presented to *his* senses.

CHAPTER III.

OF SIMPLE IDEAS OF SENSE.

1. THE better to conceive the ideas we receive from sensation[1], it may not be amiss for us to consider them, in reference to the different ways whereby they make their approaches to our minds, and make themselves perceivable by us.

First, then, There are some which come into our minds *by one sense only*.

Secondly, There are others that convey themselves into the mind *by more senses than one*.

Thirdly, Others that are had from *reflection only*.

Fourthly, There are some that make themselves way, and are suggested to the mind *by all the ways of sensation and reflection*.

We shall consider them apart under these several heads.

There are some ideas which have admittance only through one sense, which is peculiarly adapted to receive them[2]. Thus light and colours, as white, red, yellow, blue; with their several degrees or shades and mixtures, as green, scarlet, purple, sea-green, and the rest, come in only by the eyes. All kinds of noises, sounds, and tones, only by the ears. The several tastes and smells, by the nose and palate. And if these organs, or the nerves which are the conduits to

---

[1] 'from sensation.' Unless reflection is regarded as itself a sense—'internal sense' (ch. i. § 4)—the words 'from sensation' are added by an oversight; for the division which follows comprehends *all* the 'simple ideas,' or pheno-menal atoms, of our experience.

[2] By 'ideas of one sense' he means those qualities (of things) which are perceived exclusively through one sort of bodily organ.

convey them from without to their audience in the brain,— the mind's presence-room (as I may so call it)—are any of them so disordered as not to perform their functions, they have no postern to be admitted by; no other way to bring themselves into view, and be perceived by the understanding[1].

The most considerable of those belonging to the touch[2], are heat and cold, and solidity: all the rest, consisting almost wholly in the sensible configuration, as smooth and rough; or else, more or less firm adhesion of the parts, as hard and soft, tough and brittle, are obvious enough[3].

2. I think it will be needless to enumerate all the particular simple ideas belonging to each sense. Nor indeed is it possible if we would; there being a great many more of them belonging to most of the senses than we have names for. The variety of smells, which are as many almost, if not more, than species of bodies in the world, do most of them want names. Sweet and stinking commonly serve our turn for these ideas, which in effect is little more than to call them pleasing or displeasing; though the smell of a rose and violet, both sweet, are certainly very distinct ideas. Nor are the different tastes, that by our palates we receive ideas of, much better provided with names. Sweet, bitter, sour, harsh, and salt are almost all the epithets we have to denominate that numberless variety of relishes, which are to be found distinct, not only in almost every sort of

Few simple Ideas have Names.

---

[1] This is a metaphorical way of describing the organic conditions on which our sense-perceptions are found in fact to depend.

[2] He includes under 'touch' what is now distinguished as muscular sense, locomotive sense, and the sense of temperature.

[3] Taste, smell, hearing, and sight have been compared to special languages; touch to a general language— all uniting in presenting the external universe for interpretation, at the human point of view. For, as already suggested, we may suppose the universe to be manifested to a sentient intelligence destitute of all our senses, and endowed with others, five or five hundred in number, and accordingly presenting qualities wholly unimaginable by man; or we may suppose the senses with which man is endowed indefinitely intensified, and thus charged with a superhuman intelligence. Even in our human experience the world undergoes transformation to each observer, in the ratio of his increased knowledge and intellectual power.

creatures, but in the different parts of the same plant, fruit, or animal. The same may be said of colours and sounds. I shall, therefore, in the account of simple ideas I am here giving, content myself to set down only such as are most material to our present purpose, or are in themselves less apt to be taken notice of though they are very frequently the ingredients of our complex ideas; amongst which, I think, I may well account solidity [1], which therefore I shall treat of in the next chapter.

[1] An exhaustive enumeration of the simple ideas, or unanalysable phenomena, of which man may be percipient in sense, is of course impossible. In the next chapter Locke signalises the one which plays the most important part among our complex ideas of bodies, especially as body is distinguished from pure space, and also in a criticism of the Cartesian analysis of matter.

CHAPTER IV.

IDEA OF SOLIDITY.

1. THE idea of *solidity* we receive by our touch: and it arises from the resistance which we find in body to the entrance of any other body into the place it possesses, till it has left it[1]. There is no idea which we receive more constantly from sensation than solidity. Whether we move or rest, in what posture soever we are, we always feel something under us that supports us, and hinders our further sinking downwards; and the bodies which we daily handle make us percieve that, whilst they remain between them, they do, by an insurmountable force, hinder the approach of the parts of our hands that press them. *That which thus hinders the approach of two bodies, when they are moved one towards another, I call solidity.* I will not dispute whether this acceptation of the word solid be nearer to its original signification than that which mathematicians use it in. It suffices that I think the common notion of solidity will allow, if not justify, this use of it; but if any one think it better to call it *impenetrability*, he has my consent. Only I have thought the term solidity the more proper to express this idea, not only because of its vulgar use in that sense, but also because it carries something more of positive in it than impenetrability; which is negative, and is perhaps more a

---

[1] At bottom we get our distinct idea of solidity, according to Leibniz, through reason; although 'touch' provides reason with something which shows that solidity exists in nature. (See *Nouv. Ess.* Liv. ii. ch. 5.) According to the *Essay*, the idea arises from the feeling of resistance, and the motor sensations that are included vaguely under 'touch'—'suggested' by, but distinguished from, this mere feeling. Cf. the various ways in which Locke describes the idea of solidity in this section; also in § 2 and in § 6; in which last he 'sends us to our senses' if we want to know what solidity means.

BOOK II. consequence of solidity, than solidity itself[1]. This, of all
CHAP. IV. other, seems the idea most intimately connected with, and
essential to body; so as nowhere else to be found or imagined,
but only in matter. And though our senses take no notice
of it, but in masses of matter, of a bulk sufficient to cause
a sensation in us: yet the mind, having once got this idea
from such grosser sensible bodies, traces it further, and considers it, as well as figure, in the minutest particle of matter
that can exist; and finds it inseparably inherent in body,
wherever or however modified.

Solidity
fills Space.
2. This is the idea which belongs to body, whereby we
conceive it to fill space. The idea of which filling of space
is,—that where we imagine any space taken up by a solid
substance, we conceive it so to possess it, that it excludes
all other solid substances; and will for ever hinder any
other two bodies, that move towards one another in a straight
line, from coming to touch one another, unless it removes
from between them in a line not parallel to that which they
move in[2]. This idea of it, the bodies which we ordinarily
handle sufficiently furnish us with.

[1] Solidity, here defined by Locke, and afterwards (ch. viii) included in his list of the primary or real qualities of matter, is an ambiguous term, used in various meanings—geometrical and physical. ' The term *solidity* denotes, besides the *absolute and necessary* property of occupying space, simply, and in its two phases of Extension and Impenetrability, also the *relative and contingent* qualities of the Dense, the Inert, the Heavy, and the Hard.' (Hamilton.) With Locke it means the impenetrability, or *ultimate incompressibility*, of matter—the impossibility by pressure of transforming an extended atom into something unextended. This impossibility is *assumed* to be permanent and absolute; but why thus assumed—whether on *a priori* or on experimental grounds—Locke does not inquire. At any rate, this necessary permanence is not a datum in the contingent experience of the sense of

touch, whether regarded as the sense of simple contact, or including sense of muscular resistance; for sense is transitory, not absolute, in its revelations, and an intellectual impossibility of supposing a body that is not incompressible would refer the ' perception ' to reason instead of sense. Moreover one can say that it is only as incompressible, because space-occupying, and obliged to resist the entrance of other bodies into *its* space, that what we call ' body ' can be judged by *us* to exist at all.

[2] This is to identify the idea of solidity, or the permanently and absolutely incompressible, with the idea of body, as something that is necessarily extended or space-occupying. In what follows Locke notes the distinction between the ' simple idea ' of the solid and incompressible, and the idea of *pure* (empty) extension (§§ 3, 5); and between each of these

3. This resistance, whereby it keeps other bodies out of the space which it possesses, is so great, that no force, how great soever, can surmount it. All the bodies in the world, pressing a drop of water on all sides, will never be able to overcome the resistance which it will make, soft as it is, to their approaching one another, till it be removed out of their way: whereby our idea of solidity is distinguished both from pure space, which is capable neither of resistance nor motion; and from the ordinary idea of hardness. For a man may conceive two bodies at a distance, so as they may approach one another, without touching or displacing any solid thing, till their superficies come to meet; whereby, I think, we have the clear idea of space without solidity. For (not to go so far as annihilation of any particular body) I ask, whether a man cannot have the idea of the motion of one single body alone, without any other succeeding immediately into its place? I think it is evident he can: the idea of motion in one body no more including the idea of motion in another, than the idea of a square figure in one body includes the idea of a square figure in another. I do not ask, whether bodies do so *exist*, that the motion of one body cannot really be without the motion of another. To determine this either way, is to beg the question for or against a *vacuum*. But my question is,—whether one cannot have the *idea* of one body moved, whilst others are at rest? And I think this no one will deny. If so, then the place it deserted gives us the idea of pure space without solidity; whereinto any other body may enter, without either resistance or protrusion of anything. When the sucker in a pump is drawn, the space it filled in the tube is certainly the same whether any other body follows the motion of the sucker or not: nor does it imply a contradiction that, upon the motion of one body, another that is only contiguous to it should not follow it. The necessity of such a motion is built only on the supposition that the world is full; but not on the distinct *ideas* of space and solidity, which are as different as resistance and not resistance, protrusion and not protrusion.

and the idea of *hardness*, i.e. resistance, *firm but variable*, on the part of an aggregate of atoms, to disintegration and change of figure (§§ 3, 4).

BOOK II.
Chap. IV.

From Hardness.

And that men have ideas of space without a body, their very disputes about a vacuum plainly demonstrate, as is shown in another place [1].

4. Solidity is hereby also differenced from hardness, in that solidity consists in repletion, and so an utter exclusion of other bodies out of the space it possesses: but hardness, in a firm cohesion of the parts of matter, making up masses of a sensible bulk, so that the whole does not easily change its figure. And indeed, hard and soft are names that we give to things only in relation to the constitutions of our own bodies; that being generally called hard by us, which will put us to pain sooner than change figure by the pressure of any part of our bodies; and that, on the contrary, soft, which changes the situation of its parts upon an easy and unpainful touch [2].

But this difficulty of changing the situation of the sensible parts amongst themselves, or of the figure of the whole, gives no more solidity to the hardest body in the world than to the softest; nor is an adamant one jot more solid than water. For, though the two flat sides of two pieces of marble will more easily approach each other, between which there is nothing but water or air, than if there be a diamond between them; yet it is not that the parts of the diamond are more solid than those of water, or resist more; but because the parts of water, being more easily separable from each other, they will, by a side motion, be more easily removed, and give way to the approach of the two pieces of marble. But if they could be kept from making place by that side motion, they would eternally [3] hinder the approach of these two pieces of marble, as much as the diamond; and it would be as impossible by any force to surmount their resistance, as to surmount the resistance of the parts of a diamond. The softest body in the world will as invincibly resist the

---

[1] Ch. xiii. §§ 21–23.

[2] In this the hardness is contrasted with the solidity, impenetrability, and compressibility of matter, which Locke takes to be not relative to our sensations but necessary to its existence.

[3] Mere sense, which, in strictness, is only of the present, cannot reveal what is eternally necessary, and so cannot reveal what Locke finds in the idea of solidity.

coming together of any other two bodies, if it be not put out of the way, but remain between them, as the hardest that can be found or imagined. He that shall fill a yielding soft body well with air or water, will quickly find its resistance[1]. And he that thinks that nothing but bodies that are hard can keep his hands from approaching one another, may be pleased to make a trial, with the air inclosed in a football. [The experiment[2], I have been told, was made at Florence, with a hollow globe of gold filled with water, and exactly closed ; which further shows the solidity of so soft a body as water. For the golden globe thus filled, being put into a press, which was driven by the extreme force of screws, the water made itself way through the pores of that very close metal, and finding no room for a nearer approach of its particles within, got to the outside, where it rose like a dew, and so fell in drops, before the sides of the globe could be made to yield to the violent compression of the engine that squeezed it.]

By this idea of solidity is the extension of body distinguished from the extension of space :—the extension of body being nothing but the cohesion or continuity of solid, separable, movable parts; and the extension of space[3], the continuity of unsolid, inseparable, and immovable parts. Upon the solidity of bodies also depend their mutual impulse, resistance, and protrusion. Of pure space then, and solidity, there are several (amongst which I confess myself one) who persuade themselves they have clear and distinct ideas ; and that they can think on space, without anything in it that resists or is protruded by body. This is the idea of pure space[4], which they think they have as clear as any idea they

---

[1] 'its existence,' i. e. its present solidity or incompressibility.

[2] This and the next sentence added in Second Edition.

[3] He speaks of the 'extension of space' as if extension was a quality of space, not a synonym for it, as he sometimes makes it, for he vacillates in his connotation of this and other words.

[4] 'Space in itself seems,' Locke wrote some years before, 'to be nothing but *a capacity or possibility for extended* beings, or bodies, to exist. . . . In truth it is *really nothing*, and signifies no more but a bare possibility that body may exist where now there is none . . . or if there be a necessity to suppose a being there, it must be God, whose being we thus suppose extended but not impenetrable . . . But when we speak of space in general—abstract and separate from all consideration of any body or any other being—it seems not then to be any real thing, but only

can have of the extension of body : the idea of the distance between the opposite parts of a concave superficies being equally as clear without as with the idea of any solid parts between : and on the other side, they persuade themselves that they have, distinct from that of pure space, the idea of *something that fills space,* that can be protruded by the impulse of other bodies, or resist their motion[1]. If there be others that have not these two ideas distinct, but confound them, and make but one of them, I know not how men, who have the same idea under different names, or different ideas under the same name, can in that case talk with one another ; any more than a man who, not being blind or deaf, has distinct ideas of the colour of scarlet and the sound of a trumpet, could discourse concerning scarlet colour with the blind man I mentioned in another place, who fancied that the idea of scarlet was like the sound of a trumpet.

What Solidity is.
If any one asks me, *What this solidity is,* I send him to his senses to inform him[2]. Let him put a flint or a football

the consideration of a bare possibility of body to exist. . . . For when one says, there is space for another world as big as this, it seems to me to be no more than [to say] there is no repugnancy why another world as big as this might not exist ; and in this sense space may be said to be infinite ;—and so in effect space, as antecedent to body, is in effect nothing—is not capable of greater or less, and not separable into parts . . . That which makes us so apt to mistake in this point I think is this— that having been all our lifetime accustomed to speak, and to hear others speak, of space, in phrases that import it to be a real thing, e. g. to occupy *so much* space, we come to be possessed with this prejudice that it is a real thing, and not a bare relation. . . . We are apt to think that it as really exists beyond the utmost extent of all bodies or finite beings, though there are no beings there to sustain it, as it does here [as a relation] amongst bodies. For, though it be true that the black lines drawn on a rule have the

relation one to another of an inch distance, they being real sensible things ; and though it be also true that I, having the idea of an inch, can imagine that length, without imagining body, as well as I can imagine figure, without imagining body ; yet it is no more true that there is any real distance in that which we call imaginary space, than that there is any real figure there.' (Locke's *Miscellaneous Papers* (1677–78), in Lord King's *Life,* vol. ii. pp. 175–85.)

[1] Do not these 'ideas' of pure space and of impenetrable or occupied space, in adults, involve more than the contingent and transitory data of the sense of simple contact and of muscular resistance ? If so, they are 'suggested' by something in intelligence, rather than received as either tactual or muscular feelings.

[2] That is to say, apart from data of the sense of touch, we could not put meaning into the term 'solidity.' (See *Third Letter* to Stillingfleet, p. 301.) If ' sense ' means *mere* feeling, a man's

between his hands, and then endeavour to join them, and he BOOK II.
will know. If he thinks this not a sufficient explication of CHAP. IV.
solidity, what it is, and wherein it consists; I promise to tell
him what it is, and wherein it consists, when he tells me
what thinking is, or wherein it consists; or explains to me
what extension or motion is, which perhaps seems much
easier. The simple ideas we have, are such as experience
teaches them us ; but if, beyond that, we endeavour by words
to make them clearer in the mind, we shall succeed no better
than if we went about to clear up the darkness of a blind
man's mind by talking; and to discourse into him the ideas of
light and colours. The reason of this I shall show in another
place[1].

senses can only inform him of his own transitory feeling of resistance; though, on occasion of this, intelligence may necessarily suggest the idea of an absolutely or permanently incompressible object. The knowledge one gets when a ball is placed within his hands involves ideas of the feeling, and also of the absolute impenetrability—each of which ideas may be considered in abstraction from the 'knowledge' to which they contribute. The ultimate or metaphysical meaning of solid existence thus transcends *mere* sense. Man needs more than 'his senses' to 'inform him what it is.'

[1] Bk. III. ch. ii.

CHAPTER V.

OF SIMPLE IDEAS OF DIVERS SENSES.

BOOK II.
⎯✦⎯
CHAP. V.
Ideas
received
both by
seeing and
touching. THE ideas we get by more than one sense are, of *space* or *extension*[1], *figure, rest,* and *motion.* For these make perceivable impressions, both on the eyes and touch; and we can receive and convey into our minds the ideas of the extension, figure, motion, and rest of bodies, both by seeing and feeling[2]. But having occasion to speak more at large of these in another place[3], I here only enumerate them.

[1] The ideas of *space, figure, motion,* and *rest,* which Locke refers to 'more than one' of the external senses, are, according to Leibniz, suggestions of the common sense (*sens commun*), due, that is to say, to the latent constitution of the mind itself; for they are ideas of pure understanding—although they have relation to what the senses present; and they are also capable of definition and demonstration—which 'simple ideas' are not. Along with *solidity* and *number,* they are what Locke afterwards calls the primary qualities of matter, in which bodies as they really exist are (in part) manifested to us; and they are by him regarded as sensuous data of touch and sight, with little attempt at either physiological or logical analysis of the conditions on which they depend.

Whether and how *extension* is a datum of sight, or of touch, or of both—whether it is involved in every 'sensation' as such, although more distinctly in some sorts than in others—whether the judgments to which the idea gives rise are contingent or necessary, analytical or synthetical, due to individual and inherited experience, or to the eternal constitution of intelligence,—are examples of relative questions since discussed which Locke hardly sees.

[2] 'Body is the only being capable of *distance between its own parts,* which is extension. . . . This plainly shows the difference of the words *extension,*—which is for distance, a part of the same body, or that which is considered as one body—and *space,* which is the distance between any two beings, *without the consideration of body interjacent.*' (Locke's *Miscell. Papers.*)

[3] Ch. xiii, xv.

CHAPTER VI.

OF SIMPLE IDEAS OF REFLECTION.

THE mind receiving the ideas mentioned in the foregoing chapters from without, when it turns its view inward upon itself, and observes its own actions about those ideas it has, takes from thence other ideas[1], which are as capable to be the objects of its contemplation as any of those it received from foreign things.

The two great and principal actions of the mind, which are most frequently considered, and which are so frequent that every one that pleases may take notice of them in himself, are these two:—

Perception[2], or *Thinking*; and
Volition, or *Willing*.

[The[3] power of thinking is called the *Understanding*, and the power of volition is called the *Will*; and these two powers or abilities in the mind are denominated faculties.]

Of some of the *modes* of these simple ideas of reflection, such as are *remembrance, discerning, reasoning, judging, knowledge, faith*, &c., I shall have occasion to speak hereafter[4].

---

[1] 'Other ideas,' i. e. the ideas we receive of the 'operations' which give meaning to the words that represent self-conscious life and activity in man and in the universe. Locke's 'reflection' is self-consciousness intensified, and different only in degree from the self-consciousness that is involved in sense-perception, and every conscious state as such. He is apt to treat Intellect and Will as merely finite phenomena.

[2] 'Perception' is of 'three sorts' according to Locke:—(1) perception of *ideas* (phenomena) in our minds, or simple apprehension; (2) perception of the *meanings* of words; and (3) perception of *connection* or *repugnancy* between ideas, — expressed by propositions. The last alone is equivalent to knowledge; and by use 'understanding' is limited to the second and third. See Bk. II. ch. xxi. § 5.

[3] In First Edition—'The power in the mind of producing these actions, we denominate faculties, and are called the *Understanding* and the *Will*.'

[4] See ch. x, xi; and Bk. IV. ch. xvii, xiv-xvi, i-xiii, xviii. In the Fourth Book, ' *reasoning, judging, knowledge*, and *faith* are viewed primarily as mental assertions or denials, which are either true or false; not as mere ideas which are neither. He says nothing here of what is contained in the idea (or *notion* as Berkeley afterwards called it) signified by the personal pronoun I, of its origin.

CHAPTER VII.

OF SIMPLE IDEAS OF BOTH SENSATION AND REFLECTION.

1. THERE be other simple ideas which convey themselves into the mind by all the ways of sensation and reflection, viz. *pleasure* or *delight*, and its opposite, *pain*, or *uneasiness* ; *power* ; *existence* ; *unity*.

2. Delight or uneasiness, one or other of them, join themselves to almost all our ideas both of sensation and reflection : and there is scarce any affection of our senses from without, any retired thought of our mind within, which is not able to produce in us pleasure or pain. By pleasure and pain, I would be understood to signify, whatsoever delights or molests us ; whether it arises from the thoughts of our minds, or anything operating on our bodies. For, whether we call it satisfaction, delight, pleasure, happiness, &c., on the one side, or uneasiness, trouble, pain, torment, anguish, misery, &c., on the other, they are still but different degrees of the same thing, and belong to the ideas of pleasure and pain, delight or uneasiness ; which are the names I shall most commonly use for those two sorts of ideas.

3. [1]The infinite wise Author of our being, having given us the power over several parts of our bodies, to move or keep them at rest as we think fit ; and also, by the motion of them,

---

[1] In this and the three following sections Locke digresses into consideration of the *final cause* of our pleasures and pains, although his primary object is to show that 'pleasure,' 'pain,' and correlative terms are not meaningless, but charged with ideas that are due either to impressions of external sense, or to the higher operations of the mind. While he represents pleasure or pain as the 'concomitants' of sensuous and spiritual experience, he offers no explanation of their variations in duration, intensity, and kind,—though the text implies that those variations are an index of the healthful action of our functions or the opposite.

to move ourselves and other contiguous bodies, in which consist all the actions of our body: having also given a power to
our minds, in several instances, to choose, amongst its ideas,
which it will think on, and to pursue the inquiry of this
or that subject with consideration and attention, to excite us
to these actions of thinking and motion that we are capable
of,—has been pleased to join to several thoughts, and several
sensations a perception of delight. If this were wholly separated from all our outward sensations, and inward thoughts,
we should have no reason to prefer one thought or action to
another; negligence to attention, or motion to rest. And so
we should neither stir our bodies, nor employ our minds, but
let our thoughts (if I may so call it) run adrift, without any
direction or design, and suffer the ideas of our minds, like
unregarded shadows, to make their appearances there, as it
happened, without attending to them. In which state man,
however furnished with the faculties of understanding and
will, would be a very idle, inactive creature, and pass his time
only in a lazy, lethargic dream. It has therefore pleased our
wise Creator to annex to several objects, and the ideas which
we receive from them, as also to several of our thoughts, a
concomitant pleasure, and that in several objects, to several
degrees, that those faculties which he had endowed us with
might not remain wholly idle and unemployed by us.

4. Pain has the same efficacy and use to set us on work *An end*
that pleasure has, we being as ready to employ our faculties *and use of*
to avoid that, as to pursue this[1]: only this is worth our con- *pain.*
sideration, that pain is often produced by the same objects
and ideas that produce pleasure in us. This their near conjunction, which makes us often feel pain in the sensations
where we expected pleasure, gives us new occasion of admiring
the wisdom and goodness of our Maker, who, designing the
preservation of our being, has annexed pain to the application of many things to our bodies, to warn us of the harm
that they will do, and as advices to withdraw from them.
But he, not designing our preservation barely, but the preservation of every part and organ in its perfection, hath in

---

[1] Ideas of pleasure and pain are   Locke; inasmuch as by them conduct
'our great concernment,' according to   is determined. See chh. xx and xxi.

many cases annexed pain to those very ideas which delight us. Thus heat, that is very agreeable to us in one degree, by a little greater increase of it proves no ordinary torment: and the most pleasant of all sensible objects, light itself, if there be too much of it, if increased beyond a due proportion to our eyes, causes a very painful sensation. Which is wisely and favourably so ordered by nature, that when any object does, by the vehemency of its operation, disorder the instruments of sensation, whose structures cannot but be very nice and delicate, we might, by the pain, be warned to withdraw, before the organ be quite put out of order, and so be unfitted for its proper function for the future. The consideration of those objects that produce it may well persuade us, that this is the end or use of pain. For, though great light be insufferable to our eyes, yet the highest degree of darkness does not at all disease them : because that, causing no disorderly motion in it, leaves that curious organ unarmed in its natural state. But yet excess of cold as well as heat pains us : because it is equally destructive to that temper which is necessary to the preservation of life, and the exercise of the several functions of the body, and which consists in a moderate degree of warmth ; or, if you please, a motion of the insensible parts of our bodies, confined within certain bounds.

Another end.

5. Beyond all this, we may find another reason why God hath scattered up and down several degrees of pleasure and pain, in all the things that environ and affect us ; and blended them together in almost all that our thoughts and senses have to do with ;—that we, finding imperfection, dissatisfaction, and want of complete happiness, in all the enjoyments which the creatures can afford us, might be led to seek it in the enjoyment of Him with whom there is fullness of joy, and at whose right hand are pleasures for evermore.

Goodness of God in annexing pleasure and pain to our other ideas.

6. Though what I have here said may not, perhaps, make the ideas of pleasure and pain clearer to us than our own experience does, which is the only way that we are capable of having them ; yet the consideration of the reason why they are annexed to so many other ideas, serving to give us due sentiments of the wisdom and goodness of the Sovereign Disposer of all things, may not be unsuitable to the main end

of these inquiries : the knowledge and veneration of him being BOOK II.
the chief end of all our thoughts, and the proper business of CHAP. VII.
all understandings.

7. *Existence* and *Unity* are two other ideas that are sug- Ideas of Existence and Unity.
gested to the understanding by every object without, and
every idea within. When ideas are in our minds, we consider
them as being actually there, as well as we consider things to
be actually without us ;—which is, that they exist, or have
existence [1]. And whatever we can consider as one thing,
whether a real being or idea, suggests to the understanding
the idea of unity.

8. *Power* also is another of those simple ideas which we Idea of Power.
receive from sensation and reflection. For, observing in ourselves that we do and can think, and that we can at pleasure
move several parts of our bodies which were at rest ; the
effects, also, that natural bodies are able to produce in one
another, occurring every moment to our senses,—we both
these ways get the idea of power [2].

9. Besides these there is another idea, which, though sug- Idea of Succession.
gested by our senses, yet is more constantly offered to us by
what passes in our minds ; and that is the idea of *succession*.

---

[1] 'Suggested' seems to imply more than that they are only sensuous pre-sentations. The idea that they exist, and the idea that they are numerable, accompany all our simple ideas, according to the text ; our ideas are there-fore complex in experience, although, by subsequent abstraction, the pheno-mena of which they consist may be reduced to simple elements. Locke does not examine enough the 'simple' idea of *existence* and its 'modes,' although, as Berkeley afterwards in-sisted, 'nothing is of more import-ance towards erecting a firm system of sound and real knowledge than to lay the beginning in a distinct ex-plication of *what is meant* by *thing, reality, existence.*' (*Principles*, § 89.) Berkeley's own problem was—to find 'what is meant' by the term *exist*, when it is applied to sensible things. 'Il me semble,' says Leibniz, 'que les *sens* ne sauraient nous convaincre de l'existence des choses sensibles, *sans le secours de la raison.* Ainsi, je croirais que la considération de l'exist-ence vient de la reflection.' In a letter to S. Bold ((16 May, 1699) Locke says, 'I do not think the ideas of the *operations* of things are *antecedent* to the ideas of their *existence* ; for … we must suppose them to be before they operate.' Hume argues that 'the idea of existence is the very same with the idea of what we conceive to be existent,' so that, 'when conjoined with the idea of any object, it makes no addition to it.' (*Treatise*, pt. ii. sect. vi.)

[2] Cf. ch. xxi. in which 'simple modes' of the simple idea of power are described.

For if we look immediately into ourselves, and reflect on what is observable there, we shall find our ideas always, whilst we are awake, or have any thought, passing in train, one going and another coming, without intermission[1].

Simple
Ideas the
materials
of all our
Know-
ledge.
10. These, if they are not all, are at least (as I think) the most considerable of those simple ideas which the mind has, and out of which is made all its other knowledge; all which it receives only by the two forementioned ways of sensation and reflection[2].

Nor let any one think these too narrow bounds for the capacious mind of man to expatiate in, which takes its flight further than the stars, and cannot be confined by the limits of the world; that extends its thoughts often even beyond the utmost expansion of Matter, and makes excursions into that incomprehensible Inane. I grant all this, but desire any one to assign any *simple idea* which is not received from one of those inlets before mentioned, or any *complex idea* not made out of those simple ones[3]. Nor will it be so strange to think these few simple ideas sufficient to employ the quickest thought, or largest capacity; and to furnish the materials of all that various knowledge, and more various fancies and opinions of all mankind, if we consider how many words may

[1] What exists is revealed to us in all concrete experience through change, and thus in constant connection with the idea of change or succession. The unchangeable is incapable of being experienced.

[2] That is to say, it is only gradually, through the phenomena presented by the senses, and in reflection, that our original ignorance of everything can be removed.

[3] According to the foregoing account of the origin (*exordium*) of human ideas, men are incapable of any ideas of what exists, except those which they receive in the simple or unanalysable appearances of external things and of their own spirits—presented in complexity in their concrete-experi-

ence, the appearances being blended always with ideas of their *existence, number, succession* or *change,* and of *power* in a substance; and all susceptible of elaboration, by plastic imagination, or in scientific and philosophic interpretations of the phenomena which originally appeared in external sense and in reflection. But should not those blended ideas be distinguished from the occasional phenomena of experience, by which they are 'suggested,' and which they 'always accompany,' inasmuch as they connect us with the infinite, and are presupposed in the Common Reason, that 'candle of the Lord,' which is lighted in man by the transitory phenomena of sense?

be made out of the various composition of twenty-four letters; BOOK II.
or if, going one step further, we will but reflect on the variety
of combinations that may be made with barely one of the CHAP. VII.
above-mentioned ideas, viz. number, whose stock is inexhaustible and truly infinite: and what a large and immense
field doth extension alone afford the mathematicians?

CHAPTER VIII.

SOME FURTHER CONSIDERATIONS CONCERNING OUR SIMPLE IDEAS OF SENSATION.

BOOK II.
—•—
CHAP. VIII.
Positive
Ideas from
privative
causes.

1. CONCERNING the simple ideas of Sensation, it is to be considered,—that whatsoever is so constituted in nature as to be able, by affecting our senses, to cause any perception in the mind, doth thereby produce in the understanding a simple idea [1]; which, whatever be the external cause of it, when it comes to be taken notice of by our discerning faculty, it is by the mind looked on and considered there to be a real positive idea in the understanding, as much as any other whatsoever; though, perhaps, the cause of it be but a privation of the subject.

Ideas in
the mind
distin-
guished
from that
in things
which
gives rise
to them.

2. Thus the ideas of heat and cold, light and darkness, white and black, motion and rest, are equally clear and positive ideas in the mind; though, perhaps, some of the causes which produce them are barely privations, in those subjects from whence our senses derive those ideas. These the understanding, in its view of them, considers all as distinct positive ideas, without taking notice of the causes that produce them: which is an inquiry not belonging to the idea, as it is in the understanding, but to the nature of the things existing without us. These are two very different things, and carefully to be distinguished; it being one thing to perceive and know the idea of white or black, and quite

---

[1] In other words, whatever makes the proper impression upon the appropriate sense organ is in consequence *perceived*, or gives rise to the corresponding sense idea, e. g. colour when the eye, or sound when the ear is the organ thus impressed. Now this perception, *as a mental state*, he argues, cannot in any case be a negation whatever its correlate may be in external nature. It is a positive idea.

another to examine what kind of particles they must be, and BOOK II how ranged in the superficies, to make any object appear white ⟶ or black. CHAP. VIII.

3. A painter or dyer who never inquired into their causes We may hath the ideas of white and black, and other colours, as have the clearly, perfectly, and distinctly in his understanding, and we are perhaps more distinctly, than the philosopher[1] who hath ignorant of busied himself in considering their natures, and thinks he physical knows how far either of them is, in its cause, positive or causes. privative; and the idea of black is no less positive in his mind than that of white, however the cause of that colour in the external object may be only a privation.

4. If it were the design of my present undertaking to Why a inquire into the natural causes and manner of perception[2], privative I should offer this as a reason why a privative cause might, nature in some cases at least, produce a positive idea; viz. that all may sensation being produced in us only by different degrees and a positive modes of motion in our animal spirits, variously agitated by idea. external objects, the abatement of any former motion must as necessarily produce a new sensation as the variation or increase of it; and so introduce a new idea, which depends only on a different motion of the animal spirits in that organ[3].

5. But whether this be so or not I will not here determine, Negative but appeal to every one's own experience, whether the shadow names of a man, though it consists of nothing but the absence of be mean- light (and the more the absence of light is, the more dis- ingless. cernible is the shadow) does not, when a man looks on it, cause as clear and positive idea in his mind, as a man himself,

---

[1] 'Philosopher,' i. e. the natural philosopher or physicist, whose province is invaded in this chapter, which is supplementary to the preceding account of the simple ideas presented in the senses.

[2] 'Natural causes and manner,' i. e. the organic conditions which accompany or precede reception of ideas in sense. Locke has already (Introd. § 2) declined to meddle with details of organic psychology, as foreign to what he proposed to inquire into and to his introspective method. English philosophy has retrograded since Locke, in as far as it has inclined to substitute observation of the nerves and their functions for reflex study of the invisible operations of the spirit of man.

[3] But in this example the physical cause (the organic condition) would still be positive— a (reduced) 'motion' in the 'animal spirits,' which were then supposed by physiologists to impart sense and motion to the body.

though covered over with clear sunshine? And the picture of a shadow is a positive thing. Indeed, we have negative names, [¹which stand not directly for positive ideas, but for their absence, such as *insipid, silence, nihil,* &c.; which words denote positive ideas, v. g. *taste, sound, being,* with a signification of their absence.]

6. And thus one may truly be said to see darkness². For, supposing a hole perfectly dark, from whence no light is reflected, it is certain one may see the figure of it, or it may be painted; or whether the ink I write with makes any other idea, is a question. The privative causes I have here assigned of positive ideas are according to the common opinion; but, in truth, it will be hard to determine whether there be really any ideas from a privative cause, till it be determined, whether rest be any more a privation than motion.

7. To discover the nature of our *ideas* the better, and to discourse of them intelligibly, it will be convenient to distinguish them *as they are ideas or perceptions in our minds;* and *as they are modifications of matter in the bodies that cause such perceptions in us:* that so we may not think (as perhaps usually is done) that they are exactly the images and resemblances of something inherent in the subject³; most of those of sensation being in the mind no more the likeness of something existing without us, than the names that stand for them are the likeness of our ideas, which yet upon hearing they are apt to excite in us⁴.

¹ In the first three editions—'to which there be no positive ideas; but they consist wholly in negation of some certain ideas, as *silence, invisible*; but these signify not any ideas in the mind but their absence.' The change in the text is meant to show that even negative names are not meaningless—not the empty sounds which it was a chief motive of the *Essay* to expel from language.

² With Milton we speak of 'darkness visible.'

³ 'Subject,' i. e. the substance perceived, which, in the case of bodies, he goes on to show, is not *directly* mani-

fested in most of the ideas or phenomena which we refer to it.

⁴ Without a previous enquiry as to the nature of our ideas of 'self' and of 'external things'; and without explaining how our ideas come to be regarded as 'qualities' of things, or how the idea of a quality of a thing originates,—Locke, in this chapter, supplements the preceding description of the simple ideas of sense, by distinguishing some of them as *direct manifestations* of bodies in their solid extension, while others are only *effects*, in our sensuous organism, or in extra-organic things, of 'powers' inherent

8. Whatsoever the mind perceives *in itself*, or is the immediate object of perception, thought, or understanding, that I call *idea* ; and the power to produce any idea in our mind, I call *quality* of the subject wherein that power is. Thus a snowball having the power to produce in us the ideas of white, cold, and round,—the power to produce those ideas in us, as they are in the snowball, I call qualities ; and as they are sensations or perceptions in our understandings, I call them ideas ; which *ideas,* if I speak of sometimes as in the things themselves, I would be understood to mean those qualities in the objects which produce them in us.

BOOK II.
CHAP. VIII.
Our Ideas and the Qualities of Bodies.

9. [¹ Qualities thus considered in bodies are,

First, such as are utterly inseparable from the body, in what state soever it be ;] and such as in all the alterations and changes it suffers, all the force can be used upon it, it constantly keeps ; and such as sense constantly finds in every particle of matter which has bulk enough to be perceived ; and the mind finds inseparable from every particle of matter, though less than to make itself singly be perceived by our senses : v.g. Take a grain of wheat, divide it into two parts ; each part has still solidity, extension, figure, and mobility : divide it again, and it retains still the same qualities ; and so divide it on, till the parts become insensible ² ; they must retain

Primary Qualities of Bodies.

in bodies. For he finds body discovering itself in sense in both these ways—in the phases of its own solid extension, and in the sensuous states which it occasions in sentient persons. The former he calls its *primary* or *real,* and the latter its *secondary* or *imputed* qualities. In the former, matter seems to be manifested to him as directly as his own mind is manifested to him, in his *ideas* of his own mental operations when he is conscious. In the latter, matter is indirectly manifested, in and through his ideas of the sensuous states to which it gives rise in himself.

¹ In the first three editions section 9 stands thus :—' Concerning these qualities we may, I think, observe these primary ones in bodies that produce simple ideas in us, viz. *solidity, extension, motion* or *rest, number,* and *figure.*' This sentence was omitted in the fourth edition, as well as the words, ' These, which I call *original* or *primary* qualities of body, are wholly inseparable from it,' which were at the beginning of what was § 10 (now § 9), instead of the words bracketted.

² Does the divisibility continue after the parts become insensible ' to us— *ad infinitum* ? The perplexities which are involved in an affirmative answer Berkeley boldly tried to relieve, by making the commencement of insensibility the terminus of the divisibility of extension and space, thus assuming that our idea of space involves nothing but what sense happens to give. See his *Principles,* §§ 123, &c.

BOOK II.
———
CHAP. VIII.

still each of them all those qualities. For division (which is all that a mill, or pestle, or any other body, does upon another, in reducing it to insensible parts) can never take away either solidity, extension, figure, or mobility from any body, but only makes two or more distinct separate masses of matter, of that which was but one before; all which distinct masses, reckoned as so many distinct bodies, after division, make a certain number. [¹ These I call *original* or *primary qualities* ² of body, which I think we may observe to produce simple ideas in us, viz. solidity, extension, figure, motion or rest, and number.

Secondary
Qualities
of Bodies.

10. *Secondly,* such qualities which in truth are nothing in the objects themselves but powers³ to produce various sensations in us by their primary qualities, i. e. by the bulk, figure, texture, and motion of their insensible parts⁴, as colours, sounds, tastes, &c. These I call *secondary qualities*². To these might be added a *third* sort, which are allowed to be barely powers⁵; though they are as much real qualities in

---

¹ This sentence and the following section were introduced in the *fourth* edition.

² The qualities of matter were distinguished under these names before Locke, by his friend Boyle, whose physical speculations may have suggested the subject of this chapter. See Boyle on the *Origin of Forms and Qualities* (Oxford, 1666).

³ The idea of *power*, as already noted (ch. vii. § 8), accompanies all our ideas both of sensation and reflection. But what is here meant by 'power'? Does it mean more than constant sequence; and can body, as such, be conceived as the active cause of any effect? The idea of 'power,' including this question, is the subject of ch. xxi.

⁴ He here (without proof) takes for granted that felt sensations, which give their only positive meaning to the so-called secondary qualities of things, are all physically caused by modifications of their *primary atoms*, under natural law, and may therefore be interpreted in terms of mathematics;

although he elsewhere allows that this is only hypothetical, and that the 'power' to which the sensations are due may lie in 'what is still more remote from our comprehension' (Bk. IV. ch. iii. § 11). Any way he postulates *something in extended things*, on which the relation to the felt sensations depends. Hence, as Boyle says—'if there were no sensitive beings in existence, bodies that are now the objects of our senses would be *dispositively* endowed with colours, tastes, &c.; but *actually* only with those more catholic affections, as figure, motion, texture, &c., which are called primary.' Both sorts of qualities are distinguished from 'ideas of reflection,' because regarded as either phenomena or effects of *external things*.

⁵ Have the things of sense *such* 'power,' either in the collocations and textures of their constituent atoms, or otherwise, as that any changes in our sensations, and in extended things, can be referred to *them*, as their ultimate and proper cause?

the subject as those which I, to comply with the common way of speaking, call qualities, but for distinction, secondary qualities. For the power in fire to produce a new colour, or consistency, in *wax* or *clay*,—by its primary qualities, is as much a quality in fire, as the power it has to produce in *me* a new idea or sensation of warmth or burning, which I felt not before,—by the same primary qualities, viz. the bulk, texture, and motion of its insensible parts.]

11. [[1] The next thing to be considered is, how bodies produce ideas in us; and that is manifestly by impulse, the only way which we can conceive bodies to operate in [2].]

12. If then [3] external objects be not united to our minds when they produce ideas therein; and yet we perceive these *original* qualities in such of them as singly fall under our senses, it is evident [4] that some motion must be thence con-

---

[1] In the first three editions this section stands thus—'The next thing to be considered is, how bodies operate one upon another; and that is manifestly by impulse, and nothing else. It being impossible to conceive that body should operate on *what it does not touch* (which is all one as to imagine it can operate where it is not), or when it does touch, operate any other way than by motion.' The change introduced in the fourth edition is in fulfilment of a promise to Stillingfleet:—'It is true I say that bodies operate *by impulse, and nothing else.* And so I thought when I wrote it; and can yet *conceive* no other way of operation. But I am since convinced by the judicious Mr. Newton's incomparable book, that it is too bold a presumption to limit God's power on this point by my narrow conceptions. The gravitation of matter towards matter, by ways inconceivable to me, is not only a demonstration that God can, if he pleases, put into bodies powers, and ways of operation, above what can be derived from our idea of body, or can be explained by what we know of matter, but is also an unquestionable

and everywhere visible instance that he has done so. And therefore, in the next edition of my book, I shall take care to have that passage rectified.' (*Reply to Second Letter* (1699), p. 468.) Cf. Bk. IV. ch. iii. § 6.

[2] Motion, he assumes, can itself produce nothing but motion; but how 'motion made in some part of the body produces some perception in the understanding' (ch. i. § 23) he does not profess to explain. He says elsewhere that 'it seems probable that in us ideas depend on, and are in some way or other the effect of, motion, since they are so fleeting; it being almost impossible to keep in our minds the same idea long together, unless when the object that produces it is present.' (*Remarks on Norris,* § 17.)

[3] The words which here follow in the first three editions—'bodies cannot operate at a distance, and'—are omitted in the *fourth* edition. Cf. § 18.

[4] 'Evident'—because bodies, he assumes, cannot otherwise than by continuity of motion occasion the motions in the organism on which our perceptions somehow depend.

tinued by our nerves, or animal spirits, by some parts of our bodies, to the brains or the seat of sensation, there to produce in our minds the particular ideas we have of them. And since the extension, figure, number, and motion of bodies of an observable bigness, may be perceived at a distance[1] by the sight, it is evident some singly imperceptible bodies must come from them to the eyes, and thereby convey to the brain some motion ; which produces these ideas which we have of them in us.

How secondary Qualities produce their ideas.

13. After the same manner that the ideas of these original qualities are produced in us, we may conceive that the ideas of *secondary* qualities are also produced, viz. by the operation of insensible particles[2] on our senses. For, it being manifest that there are bodies and good store of bodies, each whereof are so small, that we cannot by any of our senses discover either their bulk, figure, or motion,—as is evident in the particles of the air and water, and others extremely smaller than those ; perhaps as much smaller than the particles of air and water, as the particles of air and water are smaller than peas or hail-stones ;—let us suppose at present that the different motions and figures, bulk and number, of such particles, affecting the several organs of our senses, produce in us those different sensations[3] which we have from the colours and smells of bodies ; v. g. that a violet, by the impulse of such insensible particles of matter, of peculiar figures and bulks, and in different degrees and modifications of their motions[4], causes the ideas of the blue colour, and sweet scent of that flower to be produced in our minds. It being no more impossible to conceive that God[5] should annex

---

[1] This does not necessarily imply that the perception of distance in the line of sight is an immediate datum of the sense of sight.

[2] 'Insensible particles,' i. e. ultimate atoms, the existence of which he infers, although they are not perceptible by the senses of men.

[3] Does 'sensation' here mean only a physical impression, or motion induced in some part of the human *body*, as in ch. i. § 23?

[4] 'Motions'—here supposed to be

the mechanical cause, or natural occasion, of the sensations which we refer to extended things.

[5] Perception itself is thus scientifically inexplicable. The *perceptions*, as distinguished from the *organic impressions*, he refers not to motions, or laws of motion, but to the will of God, proceeding according to some (by us) unknown law : we perceive because God has somehow given us the power of perceiving.

such ideas to such motions, with which they have no simili-tude, than that he should annex the idea of pain to the motion of a piece of steel dividing our flesh, with which that idea hath no resemblance.

14. What I have said concerning colours and smells may be understood also of tastes and sounds, and other the like sensible qualities; which, whatever reality we by mistake attribute to them, are in truth nothing in the objects them-selves, but powers to produce various sensations in us; and depend on those primary qualities, viz. bulk, figure, texture, and motion of parts [¹as I have said].

They depend on the primary Qualities.

15. From whence I think it easy to draw this observa-tion,—that the ideas of primary qualities of bodies are resemblances of them, and their patterns do really exist in the bodies themselves², but the ideas produced in us by these secondary qualities have no resemblance² of them at all. There is nothing like² our ideas, existing in the bodies them-selves. They are, in the bodies we denominate from them, only a power to produce those sensations in us: and what is sweet, blue, or warm in idea, is but the certain bulk, figure, and motion of the insensible³ parts, in the bodies themselves, which we call so.

Ideas of primary Qualities are Resem-blances; of second-ary, not

16. Flame is denominated hot and light; snow, white and

Examples.

¹ ' and therefore I call them *Second-ary Qualities*'—in first three editions.

² This implies that what we are directly percipient of, i. e. the idea, be-longs, in the case of the real or primary qualities of sensible things, to the things themselves, being *body itself manifested*, so far as a percept *can* present what is extended. But what we are directly percipient of, i. e. the idea, in the case of the imputed or secondary qualities, is *our own felt sensations*, which can have no likeness to, or virtual identity with, any ap-pearance in which extended things themselves are presented. Berkeley afterwards argued, in opposition to this, that neither identity nor resem-blance is in either case possible; seeing that an idea, which is mental, can be like nothing but another idea, and so cannot represent the abstract un-ideal, unphenomenal ' matter' against which he contended; both sorts of qualities too being in their nature alike dependent on a sentient intelligence. Locke, less subtle, probably means, in his vague way, that the primary qualities are virtually the ideas we have of them, while of the other qualities there is nothing in the things that can be identified with what we feel. The alleged ' resemblance' in the former case is Locke's way of asserting the objective existence of the presented appearance or idea.

³ ' insensible'—yet supposed to be solid and moveable, or endowed with primary qualities.

cold; and manna, white and sweet, from the ideas they produce in us. Which qualities are commonly thought to be the same in those bodies that those ideas are in us, the one the perfect resemblance of the other, as they are in a mirror, and it would by most men be judged very extravagant if one should say otherwise. And yet he that will consider that the same fire that, at one distance produces in us the sensation of warmth, does, at a nearer approach, produce in us the far different sensation of pain [1], ought to bethink himself what reason he has to say—that this idea of warmth, which was produced in him by the fire, is *actually in the fire*; and his idea of pain, which the same fire produced in him the same way, is *not* in the fire. Why are whiteness and coldness in snow, and pain not, when it produces the one and the other idea in us [2]; and can do neither, but by the bulk, figure, number, and motion of its solid parts?

The ideas of the Primary alone really exist.

17. The particular bulk, number, figure, and motion of the parts of fire or snow are really in them,—whether any one's senses perceive them or no: and therefore they may be called *real* qualities, because they really exist in those bodies. But light, heat, whiteness, or coldness, are no more really in them than sickness or pain is in manna. Take away the sensation of them; let not the eyes see light or colours, nor the ears hear sounds; let the palate not taste, nor the nose smell, and all colours, tastes, odours, and sounds, *as they are such particular ideas*, vanish and cease, and are reduced to their causes, i. e. bulk, figure, and motion of parts [3].

---

[1] So in Hume's table argument.— (*Inquiry H. U.*, sect. xii. pt. i.)

[2] Berkeley makes this 'production in us' an example, not of final or even of properly efficient causality, but of 'sign and thing signified.' The motion said to cause heat, is not properly the *cause* of the sensation thus attributed to it, but is only the *sign* to forewarn of the sensations that are connected with such motions, according to the method of procedure established in nature by the supreme power of God.

[3] Because 'nothing can be *like* a sensation or idea, but a sensation or idea,' Berkeley argues against the *independent* or *substantial* existence of the sensible world; for the so-called *real* qualities must all disappear, when the 'ideas' of solidity, figure, and motion, cease to be perceived by any one, so that their *esse* is *percipi*. See the first *Dialogue between Hylas and Philonous*, which in effect argues, that the annihilation of *all* conscious and percipient life, in God and finite beings, would

18. A piece of manna of a sensible bulk is able to produce in us the idea of a round or square figure; and by being removed from one place to another, the idea of motion. This idea of motion represents it as it really is in manna moving: a circle or square are the same, whether in idea or existence, in the mind or in the manna. And this, both motion and figure, are really in the manna, whether we take notice of them or no [1] : this everybody is ready to agree to. Besides, manna, by the bulk, figure, texture, and motion of its parts, has a power to produce [2] the sensations of sickness, and sometimes of acute pains or gripings in us. That these ideas of sickness and pain are *not* in the manna, but effects of its operations on us, and are nowhere when we feel them not ; this also every one readily agrees to. And yet men are hardly to be brought to think that sweetness and whiteness are not really in manna ; which are but the effects of the operations of manna, by the motion, size, and figure of its particles, on the eyes and palate: as the pain and sickness caused by manna are confessedly nothing but the effects of its operations on the stomach and guts, by the size, motion, and figure of its insensible parts, (for by nothing else can a body operate, as has been proved): as if it could not operate on the eyes and palate, and thereby produce in the mind particular distinct ideas, which in itself it has not, as well as we allow it can operate on the guts and stomach, and thereby produce distinct ideas, which in itself it has not. These ideas, being all effects of the operations of manna on several parts of our bodies, by the size, figure, number, and

BOOK II.

CHAP. VIII.

The secondary exist in things only as modes of the primary.

render meaningless the 'primary or real,' equally with the secondary or imputed, qualities of things.

[1] This is Locke's *proof* that our ideas of real qualities ' resemble,' or are virtually 'identical with,' the objective qualities themselves. 'A circle or square are *the same* whether in idea or existence ; in the mind or in the manna.' He thus practically identifies the sensuous ideas or phenomena of figures and motions with actual figures and motions, in the things we see and touch; the ideas *perfectly* resembling the primary or real qualities, in what is thus an identity of similars. He follows what Hume calls ' a blind and powerful instinct,' which makes us suppose the very images presented by the senses to be virtually a presentation of the external things themselves.

[2] It signifies that the continuously active Divine Reason, immanent in things, is about to produce those ' sensations ' in us.

motion of its parts ;—why those produced by the eyes and palate should rather be thought to be really in the manna, than those produced by the stomach and guts ; or why the pain and sickness, ideas that are the effect of manna, should be thought to be nowhere when they are not felt ; and yet the sweetness and whiteness, effects of the same manna on other parts of the body, by ways equally as unknown, should be thought to exist in the manna, when they are not seen or tasted, would need some reason to explain [1].

Examples.
19. Let us consider the red and white colours in porphyry. Hinder light from striking on it, and its colours vanish; it no longer produces any such ideas in us : upon the return of light it produces these appearances on us again.   Can any one think any real alterations are made in the porphyry by the presence or absence of light; and that those ideas of whiteness and redness are really in porphryry in the light, when it is plain *it has no colour in the dark*?   It has, indeed, such a configuration of particles, both night and day, as are apt, by the rays of light rebounding from some parts of that hard stone, to produce in us the idea of redness, and from others the idea of whiteness ; but whiteness or redness are not in it at any time, but such a texture that hath the power to produce such a sensation in us [2].

20. Pound an almond, and the clear white colour will be altered into a dirty one, and the sweet taste into an oily one. What real alteration can the beating of the pestle make in any body, but an alteration of the texture of it [3]?

---

[1] Berkeley applies an analogous argument to the 'real' or primary qualities—thus melting *all* the appearances which Locke refers to permanent things into transitory felt sensations.

[2] Berkeley in like manner argues for the dependence of what is *solid* on percipient mind.   Let all conscious life or percipiency be suddenly extinguished, and the whole world of sensible things must therefore lose its actuality, which the return of self-conscious life would restore, as the entrance of light introduces variety of colours in a room that was colourless in the dark.

[3] Locke implies in many passages, that *all* the so-called 'powers' in sensible things may be resolved into motions and change of texture ; and that both when the 'effects' take the form of sensations in us, and of changes in the 'texture,' and there-fore in the appearance, of extra organic bodies. If so, and if one could know all the motions in the world, and all their laws of procedure, he could *predict* all the changes in things, and all our changes of sensa-

21. Ideas being thus distinguished and understood, we may BOOK II.
be able to give an account how the same water, at the same
time, may produce the idea of cold by one hand and of heat CHAP. VIII.
by the other [1] : whereas it is impossible that the same water, Explains how water
if those ideas were really in it, should at the same time be felt as cold by one
both hot and cold. For, if we imagine *warmth*, as it is in our hand may
hands, to be nothing but a certain sort and degree of motion be warm to the
in the minute particles of our nerves or animal spirits, we may other.
understand how it is possible that the same water may, at the
same time, produce the sensations of heat in one hand and
cold in the other; which yet *figure* never does, that never
producing the idea of a square by one hand which has produced the idea of a globe by another. But if the sensation
of heat and cold be nothing but the increase or diminution of
the motion of the minute parts of our bodies, caused by the
corpuscles of any other body, it is easy to be understood,
that if that motion be greater in one hand than in the other;
if a body be applied to the two hands, which has in its minute
particles a greater motion than in those of one of the hands,
and a less than in those of the other, it will increase the
motion of the one hand and lessen it in the other; and so
cause the different sensations of heat and cold that depend
thereon [2].

22. I have in what just goes before been engaged in phy- An ex-
sical inquiries a little further than perhaps I intended. But, cursion into
it being necessary to make the nature of sensation a little natural
understood ; and to make the difference between the *qualities* philo-sophy.
in bodies, and the *ideas* produced by them in the mind, to
be distinctly conceived, without which it were impossible to
discourse intelligibly of them;—I hope I shall be pardoned
this little excursion into natural philosophy [3] ; it being neces-

---

tion, and thus reach a perfect scientific
interpretation of nature. But as this
cannot be, demonstrable science of
nature transcends the experience and
intelligence of man.

[1] So Berkeley in his First Dialogue.
Hume's 'table argument' is analogous,
applied to the primary qualities.

[2] 'Depend'—as their *physical* causes,
or signs, which are not to be regarded
as ultimate or truly efficient causes of
the sensations.

[3] In Locke's *Elements of Natural
Philosophy*, matter is defined to be
'an *extended solid substance*, which,
being comprehended under distinct

sary in our present inquiry to distinguish the *primary* and *real* qualities of bodies, which are always in them (viz. solidity, extension, figure, number, and motion, or rest, and are sometimes perceived by us, viz. when the bodies they are in are big enough singly to be discerned), from those *secondary* and *imputed* qualities, which are but the powers of several combinations of those primary ones, when they operate without being distinctly discerned[1];—whereby we may also come to know what ideas are, and what are not, resemblances[2] of something really existing in the bodies we denominate from them.

Three
Sorts of
Qualities
in Bodies.
23. The qualities, then, that are in bodies, rightly considered, are of three sorts :—

First, The bulk, figure, number, situation, and motion or rest of their solid parts. Those are in them, whether we perceive them or not; and when they are of that size that we can discover them[3], we have by these an idea of the thing as it is in itself; as is plain in artificial things. These I call *primary qualities*.

Secondly, The power that is in any body, by reason of its insensible primary qualities[4], to operate after a peculiar

surfaces, makes so many particular distinct *bodies*'; and *motion* is said to be 'so well known by the sight and touch that to use words to give a clearer idea of it would be vain.'

[1] If the primary constitution *were* perceptible, the secondary qualities would, he argues, disappear. (Cf. Bk. II. ch. xxiii. § 11.)

[2] Locke's doctrine is objected to by Cousin, on the ground that we cannot speak of likeness between material and spiritual things, but only between material things among themselves. (*Histoire de la Philosophie*, 21me. leçon.) This seems to be a difference about words. Locke treats primary qualities as 'real,' or 'perfectly resembling the real,' and virtually 'the same'; but called ideas in the mind, at one point of view, phenomena presented by the thing, at another. Even Hamilton some-

times allows this : ' If we modify the obnoxious language of Locke, and instead of saying that the ideas or notions of the primary qualities *resemble*, merely assert that they *totally represent* their objects, that is, afford us such a knowledge of their nature as we should have were an immediate intuition of the extended reality in itself competent to man . . . Reid's doctrine and his would be found in perfect unison.' (Hamilton's *Reid*, p. 842.)

[3] That is, discover them by our senses, and not by supersensible inference.

[4] This 'reason' or explanation of the secondary qualities, and other 'powers' of things (assumed in this and the following sections) is elsewhere stated by Locke less confidently—as a probable hypothesis, which cannot be

manner on any of our senses, and thereby produce in *us* the different ideas of several colours, sounds, smells, tastes, &c. These are usually called *sensible qualities*[1].

Thirdly, The power that is in any body, by reason of the particular constitution of its primary qualities[1], to make such a change in the bulk, figure, texture, and motion of *another body*, as to make it operate on our senses differently from what it did before. Thus the sun has a power to make wax white, and fire to make lead fluid. [[2] These are usually called *powers*.]

The first of these, as has been said, I think may be properly called real, original, or primary qualities; because they are in the things themselves, whether they are perceived or not: and upon their different modifications it is that the secondary qualities[3] depend.

The other two are only powers to act differently upon other things: which powers result from the different modifications of those primary qualities.

24. But, though the two latter sorts of qualities are powers barely, and nothing but powers, relating to several other bodies, and resulting from the different modifications of the original qualities[4], yet they are generally otherwise thought of. For the *second* sort, viz. the powers to produce several ideas

The first areResemblances; the second thought to be Resemblances,

absolutely verified. They are supposed at any rate to be the 'constant effects' of *some* non-resembling cause in the extended solid. Cf. ch. xxx. § 2.

[1] Locke takes no special account, under either head, of the *roughness, smoothness, hardness, softness,* and *fluidity* of bodies, which Reid and others include among their real or primary qualities; although they are not, like space—occupancy necessarily implied in our positive conception of body. Hamilton calls them *secundoprimary*, as a mixture of the two.

[2] Added in *fourth* Edition.

[3] Distinguished by some as *qualities*

proper, in contrast with matter *quantified*, or under mathematical relations, in its so-called primary or real qualities. So Hobbes:—'Whatever *qualities* our senses make us think there are in the world, they be not *there*, but are seeming and apparitions only; the things that really are in the world without us are those *motions* by which these seemings are caused.' (*Human Nature*, ch. ii. § 10.) Not so Locke.

[4] Our felt sensations and all the other phenomena of sense, are thus referred by Locke at last to molecular activity—the various 'powers' of *atoms*,—in their varied combinations and motions,—as their *natural* cause.

BOOK II.
Chap. VIII.
but are
not; the
third
neither
are, nor
are
thought so.
in us, by our senses, are looked upon as real qualities in the things thus affecting us: but the *third* sort are called and esteemed barely powers. v. g. The idea of heat or light, which we receive by our eyes, or touch, from the sun, are commonly thought real qualities existing in the sun, and something more than mere powers in it. But when we consider the sun in reference to wax, which it melts or blanches, we look on the whiteness and softness produced in the wax, not as qualities in the sun, but effects produced by powers in it. Whereas, if rightly considered, these qualities of light and warmth, which are perceptions in me when I am warmed or enlightened by the sun, are no otherwise in the sun, than the changes made in the wax, when it is blanched or melted, are in the sun. They are all of them equally *powers in the sun, depending on its primary qualities* ; whereby it is able, in the one case, so to alter the bulk, figure, texture, or motion of some of the insensible parts of my eyes or hands, as thereby to produce in me the idea of light or heat ; and in the other, it is able so to alter the bulk, figure, texture, or motion of the insensible parts of the wax, as to make them fit to produce in me the distinct ideas of white and fluid.

Why the
secondary
are ordin-
arily taken
for real
Qualities,
and not for
bare
Powers.
25. The reason why the one are ordinarily taken for real qualities, and the other only for bare powers, seems to be, because the ideas we have of distinct colours, sounds, &c., containing nothing at all in them of bulk, figure, or motion, we are not apt to think them the effects of these primary qualities ; which appear not, to our senses, to operate in their production, and with which they have not any apparent congruity or conceivable connexion. Hence it is that we are so forward to imagine, that those ideas are the resemblances of something really existing in the objects themselves : since sensation discovers nothing of bulk, figure, or motion of parts in their production ; nor can reason show how bodies, *by their bulk, figure, and motion*, should produce in the mind the ideas of blue or yellow, &c. But, in the other case, in the operations of bodies changing the qualities one of another, we plainly discover that the quality produced hath commonly no resemblance with anything in the thing pro-

ducing it; wherefore we look on it as a bare effect of power [1]. For, through receiving the idea of heat or light from the sun, we are apt to think *it* is a perception and resemblance of such a quality in the sun; yet when we see wax, or a fair face, receive change of colour from the sun, we cannot imagine *that* to be the reception or resemblance of anything in the sun, because we find not those different colours in the sun itself. For, our senses being able to observe a likeness or unlikeness of sensible qualities in two different external objects, we forwardly enough conclude the production of any sensible quality in any subject to be an effect of bare power [2], and not the communication of any quality which was really in the efficient, when we find no such sensible quality in the thing that produced it. But our senses, not being able to discover any unlikeness between the idea produced in us, and the quality of the object producing it, we are apt to imagine that our ideas [3] are resemblances of something in the objects, and not the effects of certain powers placed in the modification of their primary qualities, with which primary qualities the ideas produced in us have no resemblance.

26. To conclude. Beside those before-mentioned primary qualities in bodies, viz. bulk, figure, extension, number, and motion of their solid parts; all the rest, whereby we take notice of bodies, and distinguish them one from another, are nothing else but several powers in them, depending on those primary qualities; whereby they are fitted, either by immediately operating on our bodies to produce several different ideas in us; or else, by operating on other bodies, so to change their primary qualities as to render them capable of producing ideas in us different from what before they did. The former of these, I think, may be called secondary qualities *immediately*

Secondary Qualities twofold: first, immediately perceivable; secondly, mediately perceivable.

---

[1] Here again Locke tends to resolve physical science into molecular physics, in which the successive changes in bodies are ultimately interpretable in terms of the constitution and behaviour of atoms.

[2] 'in any subject,' i. e. by one body in another body—'bare power,' i. e. there being no discernible *equivalence* between the 'cause' and its effects.

[3] 'our ideas,' i. e. of secondary or imputed qualities.

BOOK II.
CHAP. VIII.

perceivable: the latter, secondary qualities, *mediately perceivable* [1].

[1] Berkeley's famous question about the meaning of ' reality,' in its application to the world of sense, and the dependence or independence of sensible things upon sentient intelligence, arose naturally out of the analysis of the qualities and powers of matter presented in this chapter, which may be compared with ch. xxi., especially §§ 1-4; and ch. xxiii., especially §§ 7-13, on our ideas of ' power' and ' substance,' here silently presupposed.

CHAPTER IX.

OF PERCEPTION.

1. *Perception*[1], as it is the first faculty[2] of the mind exercised

about our ideas ; so it is the first and simplest idea we have
from reflection, and is by some called thinking in general.
Though thinking, in the propriety of the English tongue,
signifies that sort of operation in the mind about its ideas,
wherein the mind is active ; where it, with some degree of
voluntary attention, considers anything[3]. For in bare naked
perception, the mind is, for the most part, only passive ; and
what it perceives, it cannot avoid perceiving[4].

2. What perception is, every one will know better by
reflecting on what he does himself, when he sees, hears,
feels, &c., or thinks, than by any discourse of mine. Whoever
reflects on what passes in his own mind cannot miss it. And
if he does not reflect, all the words in the world cannot make
him have any notion of it.

3. This is certain, that whatever alterations are made in
the body, if they reach not the mind ; whatever impressions
are made on the outward parts, if they are not taken notice

---

[1] Cf. Bk. IV. ch. i. § 2, ch. iii. § 14,
&c. See also Bk. II. ch. xxi. § 5 for
three different meanings of 'perception' in the *Essay*.

[2] Locke accounts for cognitive life
by the assumption of 'faculties' inherent in self-conscious agents. This and
the two next chapters deal with facul·
ties, as a sort of appendix to 'simple
ideas of reflection,' treating both of the
faculties, and of the ideas we have of
them when we reflect.

[3] Locke, like most of his contemporaries, often uses 'thought' and
'thinking' in a wider meaning than is

now common among exact thinkers.

[4] The ideas or phenomena that are
actually present in sense, or in reflection, are not dependent on our *will* in
the way representations of imagination are. As Berkeley puts it :—'When
in broad daylight I open my eyes, it is
not in my power to choose whether
I shall see or no, or to determine what
particular objects shall present themselves to my view. And so, too, with
the acts or states of which I am conscious, which when they actually arise
I cannot help being conscious of
them.'

BOOK II.
—✛—
CHAP. IX.
notices the
organic im-
pression.

of within, there is no perception[1]. Fire may burn our bodies with no other effect than it does a billet, unless the motion be continued to the brain, and there the sense of heat, or idea of pain, be produced in the mind; wherein consists actual perception.

Impulse
on the
organ in-
sufficient.

4. How often may a man observe in himself, that whilst his mind is intently employed in the contemplation of some objects, and curiously surveying some ideas that are there, it takes no notice of impressions of sounding bodies made upon the organ of hearing, with the same alteration that uses to be for the producing the idea of sound? A sufficient impulse there may be on the organ; but it not reaching the observation of the mind, there follows no perception: and though the motion that uses to produce the idea of sound be made in the ear, yet no sound is heard. Want of sensation, in this case, is not through any defect in the organ, or that the man's ears are less affected than at other times when he does hear: but that which uses to produce the idea, though conveyed in by the usual organ, not being taken notice of in the understanding[2], and so imprinting no idea in the mind, there follows no sensation. So that wherever there is sense or perception, there some idea is actually produced, and present in the understanding.

Children,
though
they may
have Ideas
in the
Womb,
have none
innate.

5. Therefore I doubt not but children, by the exercise of their senses about objects that affect them in the womb, receive some few ideas before they are born[3], as the unavoidable effects, either of the bodies that environ them, or else of those wants or diseases they suffer; amongst which (if one may conjecture concerning things not very capable of examination) I think the ideas of hunger and warmth are

[1] Percipient and self-conscious life is thus contrasted with motion in bodies, although our perception is in this world conditioned by modes of cerebral motion, which are the occasions on which the spiritual processes arise. To ascertain more fully those organic conditions is scientifically interesting, and might be in a high degree useful, but the knowledge must always be philosophically inadequate.

[2] This virtually implies activity in the 'understanding,' and its active presence, as an element even in primary perception.

[3] Although acquired before birth, they would not be *innate*, in Locke's meaning of the term, if thus *acquired in an ante-natal sense experience.*

two : which probably are some of the first that children have, and which they scarce ever part with again.

6. But though it be reasonable to imagine that children receive some ideas before they come into the world, yet these simple ideas are far from those *innate principles* which some contend for, and we, above, have rejected. These here mentioned, being the effects of sensation, are only from some affections of the body, which happen to them there, and so depend on something exterior to the mind ; no otherwise differing in their manner of production from other ideas derived from sense, but only in the precedency of time. Whereas those innate principles are supposed to be quite of another nature, not coming into the mind by any accidental alterations in, or operations on the body [1] ; but, as it were, original characters impressed upon it, in the very first moment of its being and constitution.

7. As there are some ideas which we may reasonably suppose may be introduced into the minds of children in the womb, subservient to the necessities of their life and being there : so, after they are born, those ideas are the earliest imprinted which happen to be the sensible qualities which first occur to them ; amongst which light is not the least considerable, nor of the weakest efficacy. And how covetous the mind is to be furnished with all such ideas as have no pain accompanying them, may be a little guessed by what is observable in children new-born ; who always turn their eyes to that part from whence the light comes, lay them how you please. But the ideas that are most familiar at first, being various according to the divers circumstances of children's first entertainment in the world, the order wherein the several ideas come at first into the mind is very various, and uncertain also ; neither is it much material to know it.

8. We are further to consider concerning perception, that the ideas we receive by sensation are often, in grown people,

---

[1] Although our ideas are thus de-pendent on organic impressions, whe-ther after or before birth, so that no knowledge of things, in any man, can be *antecedent* to data of ' experience,' it still does not follow that all the ideas, which thus arise, can be fully analysed into the contingent impressions which called them forth.

BOOK II.

CHAP. IX.
Sensations
often
changed
by the
Judgment.

altered by the judgment, without our taking notice of it[1]. When we set before our eyes a round globe of any uniform colour, v. g. gold, alabaster, or jet, it is certain that the idea thereby imprinted on our mind is of a flat circle, variously shadowed, with several degrees of light and brightness coming to our eyes. But we having, by use, been accustomed to perceive what kind of appearance convex bodies are wont to make in us; what alterations are made in the reflections of light by the difference of the sensible figures of bodies;— the judgment presently, by an habitual custom, alters the appearances into their causes[2]. So that from that which is truly variety of shadow or colour, collecting the figure, it makes it pass for a mark of figure, and frames to itself the perception of a convex figure and an uniform colour; when the idea we receive from thence is only a plane variously coloured, as is evident in painting[3]. [4 To which purpose I shall here insert a problem of that very ingenious and studious promoter of real knowledge, the learned and worthy Mr. Molineux, which he was pleased to send me in a letter some months since[5]; and it is this:—'Suppose a man *born* blind, and now adult, and taught by his *touch* to distinguish

---

[1] This section gives Locke's account of the evolution of sense perceptions, in and through what Berkeley afterwards called 'suggestion'—with its latent judgment—the rise of our 'acquired' perceptions, in short. He here shows (by a subtle illustration) that nature, or inexplicable 'faculty,' does less, 'habit' or 'experience' more, in the production of our supposed direct 'perceptions' of things, than appears on the surface.

[2] i. e. the directly perceived signs into the indirectly perceived phenomena which they signify.

[3] 'Perspective, shading, giving relief, and colouring, are nothing else but copying the appearance which things make to the eye.' (Reid's *Inquiry*, ch. vi. § iii.)

[4] The rest of this section was added in the second Edition.

[5] We find among Locke's published correspondence a letter from Molyneux, dated March 2, 1693, in which the passage here quoted occurs, introduced as 'a jocose problem.' Berkeley refers to it in confirmation of his theory of the original invisibility of the 'real' distances, magnitudes, and figures of things, and especially of his antithesis of visible and tangible extension. (*Essay on Vision*, §§ 132, 133.) In the *Nouveaux Essais*, liv. ii. ch. ix, Leibniz disputes the alleged heterogeneity, as well as Locke's solution of this problem, and concludes that if the born-blind man had known beforehand, by touch only, that the cube and the globe were there, he could *at once*, when he recovered sight, distinguish them by reason, in combination with the sensuous data of touch; because otherwise a born-blind man could not learn the rudiments of geometry by touch only, as

between a cube and a sphere of the same metal, and nighly of the same bigness, so as to tell, when he felt one and the other, which is the cube, which the sphere. Suppose then the cube and sphere placed on a table, and the blind man be made to see: *quære*, whether *by his sight, before he touched them*, he could now distinguish and tell which is the globe, which the cube?' To which the acute and judicious proposer answers, 'Not. For, though he has obtained the experience of how a globe, how a cube affects his touch, yet he has not yet obtained the experience, that what affects his touch so or so, must affect his sight so or so; or that a protuberant angle in the cube, that pressed his hand unequally, shall appear to his eye as it does in the cube.'—I agree with this thinking gentleman, whom [1] I am proud to call my friend, in his answer to this problem; and am of opinion that the blind man, at first sight, would not be able with certainty to say which was the globe, which the cube, whilst he only saw them; though he could unerringly name them by his touch, and certainly distinguish them by the difference of their figures felt. This I have set down, and leave with my reader, as an occasion for him to consider how much he may be beholden to experience, improvement, and acquired notions [2], where he thinks he had not the least use of, or help from them. And the rather, because this observing gentleman further adds, that 'having, upon the occasion of my book, proposed this to divers very ingenious men, he hardly ever met with one

---

he is able to do. The *concept* of extension suggested by sight and by touch is the same, he implies, although there are no common *images* of them; which shows the need for distinguishing images of sense (*vorstellungen*) from abstract notions of the intellect.—On the 'geometry of visibles,' &c., see Reid's *Inquiry*, ch. v. sect. 9.

[1] In the second and third Editions the words—'though I have never had the happiness to see him,' follow,—omitted in the *fourth* edition, which appeared more than a year after Molyneux's visit to Locke at Oates in 1698.

[2] The acquired perceptions of sight afford unique illustrations of the large part which *habit* and *suggestion* play in the early stages of our intellectual development. This is all auxiliary to Locke's main thesis, that men are originally ignorant of everything, and dependent for all their ideas and knowledge of real existence on the gradual acquisitions of experience. But he fails to inquire into the ultimate *rationale* of the interpretations, progressively reached in science and in philosophy, of the presented ideas of sense.

BOOK II.
CHAP. IX.

This judgment apt to be mistaken for direct perception.

that at first gave the answer to it which he thinks true, till by hearing his reasons they were convinced.']

9. But this is not, I think, usual in any of our ideas, but those received by sight. Because sight, the most comprehensive of all our senses, conveying to our minds the ideas of light and colours, which are peculiar only to that sense; and also the far different ideas of space, figure, and motion[1], the several varieties whereof change the appearances of its proper object, viz. light and colours; we bring ourselves by use to judge of the one by the other. This, in many cases by a settled habit,—in things whereof we have frequent experience, is performed so constantly and so quick, that we take that for the perception of our sensation which is an idea formed by our judgment; so that one, viz. that of sensation, serves only to excite the other, and is scarce taken notice of itself;—as a man who reads or hears with attention and understanding, takes little notice of the characters or sounds, but of the ideas that are excited in him by them[2].

How, by Habit, ideas of Sensation are unconsciously

10. Nor need we wonder that this is done with so little notice, if we consider how quick the actions of the mind are performed. For, as itself is thought to take up no space[3], to have no extension; so its actions seem to require no time,

---

[1] 'Space or distance,' says Berkeley, commenting on this passage, 'is no otherwise the object of sight than of hearing. As for figure and extension, I leave it to any one that shall calmly attend to his own clear and distinct ideas, to decide whether he has any idea intromitted *immediately* by sight save only light and colours. In a strict sense I see nothing but light and colours, with their several shades and variations. . . . It must be owned indeed that, by the mediation of light and colours, far different ideas are *suggested* to my mind. But upon this score I see no reason why the sight should be thought more comprehensive than the hearing, which besides sounds, which are peculiar to that sense, doth, by their mediation, suggest not only space, figure, and motion,

but all other ideas whatsoever that can be signified by words.' (*Essay on Vision*, § 130.) The original perception of the eye is a vague apprehension of coloured surface only. The third dimension of space, with the real (tangible) sizes and figures of things, is gained through the habit of associating shades of colour, and modes of *tension* in the muscles of the eye, with modes of tactual, muscular, and motor experience; so that the eye gradually learns to judge of distance outwards, and of the relative distances of things. Educated sight is calculated foresight.

[2] So Reid on sensations as signs that are not noticed save in their significates.—*Inquiry*, ch. vi. §§ xxi-xxiii.

[3] Cf. ch. xxvii. § 2, on the 'place' of spirits.

but many of them seem to be crowded into an instant. I
speak this in comparison to the actions of the body. Any
one may easily observe this in his own thoughts, who will
take the pains to reflect on them. How, as it were in an
instant, do our minds, with one glance, see all the parts of
a demonstration, which may very well be called a long one, if
we consider the time it will require to put it into words, and
step by step show it another? Secondly, we shall not be so
much surprised that this is done in us with so little notice, if
we consider how the facility which we get of doing things,
by a custom of doing, makes them often pass in us without
our notice. Habits, especially such as are begun very early,
come at last to produce actions in us, which often escape our
observation. How frequently do we, in a day, cover our
eyes with our eyelids, without perceiving that we are at all
in the dark! Men that, by custom, have got the use of a
by-word, do almost in every sentence pronounce sounds
which, though taken notice of by others, they themselves
neither hear nor observe. And therefore it is not so strange,
that our mind should often change the idea of its sensation
into that of its judgment, and make one serve only to excite
the other, without our taking notice of it.

11. This faculty of perception seems to me to be, that
which puts the distinction betwixt the animal kingdom and
the inferior parts of nature. For, however vegetables have,
many of them, some degrees of motion, and upon the different
application of other bodies to them, do very briskly alter
their figures and motions, and so have obtained the name of
sensitive plants, from a motion which has some resemblance
to that which in animals follows upon sensation: yet I
suppose it is all bare *mechanism*; and no otherwise produced
than the turning of a wild oat-beard, by the insinuation of
the particles of moisture, or the shortening of a rope,
by the affusion of water. All which is done without any
sensation in the subject, or the having or receiving any
ideas.

12. Perception, I believe, is, in some degree, in all sorts of
animals; though in some possibly the avenues provided by

BOOK II.
CHAP. IX.

nature for the reception of sensations are so few, and the perception they are received with so obscure and dull[1], that it comes extremely short of the quickness and variety of sensation which is in other animals; but yet it is sufficient for, and wisely adapted to, the state and condition of that sort of animals who are thus made. So that the wisdom and goodness of the Maker plainly appear in all the parts of this stupendous fabric, and all the several degrees and ranks of creatures in it.

According to their condition.

13. We may, I think, from the make of an oyster or cockle, reasonably conclude that it has not so many, nor so quick senses as a man, or several other animals; nor if it had, would it, in that state and incapacity of transferring itself from one place to another, be bettered by them. What good would sight and hearing do to a creature that cannot move itself to or from the objects wherein at a distance it perceives good or evil? And would not quickness of sensation be an inconvenience to an animal that must lie still where chance has once placed it, and there receive the afflux of colder or warmer, clean or foul water, as it happens to come to it[2]?

Decay of perception in old age.

14. But yet I cannot but think there is some small dull perception, whereby they are distinguished from perfect insensibility. And that this may be so, we have plain instances, even in mankind itself. Take one in whom decrepit old age has blotted out the memory of his past knowledge, and clearly wiped out the ideas his mind was formerly stored with, and has, by destroying his sight, hearing, and smell quite, and his taste to a great degree, stopped up almost all the passages for new ones to enter; or if there be some of the inlets yet half open, the impressions made are scarcely perceived, or not at all retained. How far such an one (notwithstanding all that is boasted of innate principles) is in his knowledge and intellectual faculties above the condition of a cockle or an oyster, I leave to be con-

---

[1] According to Leibniz, brutes have only the confused, obscure, semi-conscious perceptions, which human beings also occasionally have.

[2] This suggests a development of special senses under evolutionary law.

sidered. And if a man had passed sixty years in such a state, as it is possible he might, as well as three days, I wonder what difference there would be, in any intellectual perfections, between him and the lowest degree of animals [1].

15. Perception then being the *first* step and degree towards knowledge, and the inlet of all the materials [2] of it; the fewer senses any man, as well as any other creature, hath; and the fewer and duller the impressions are that are made by them; and the duller the faculties are that are employed about them,—the more remote are they from that knowledge which is to be found in some men [3]. But this being in great variety of degrees (as may be perceived amongst men) cannot certainly be discovered in the several species of animals, much less in their particular individuals. It suffices me only to have remarked here,—that perception is the first operation of all our intellectual faculties, and the inlet of all knowledge [4] in our minds. And I am apt too to imagine, that it is perception, in the lowest degree of it, which puts the boundaries between animals and the inferior ranks of creatures. But this I mention only as my conjecture by the

---

[1] Still there is a *latent* difference, even when the mind is thus dormant, and universal truths are therefore out of sight. The spiritual faculties may *subside* without being effaced, though for a time overborne by sense, thus showing that a man is more than an organised body.

[2] 'materials'—otherwise called by Locke 'simple ideas'—but which he sometimes applies to organic impressions of whatever sort, which so stimulate 'the mind' as that ideas of things appear.

[3] The *Micromégas* of Voltaire suggests the illimitable variety of sense ideas which may be perceived by other orders of sentient beings, who may have more and other senses than ours; or perhaps be percipient without organs of sense at all, as men may

be in a higher life. 'It seems very easy to conceive the soul to exist in a separate state (i.e. divested from those limits and laws of motion and perception with which she is embarrassed here) and to exercise herself on new ideas, without the intervention of those tangible things we call *our bodies*. It is even very possible to conceive how the soul may have ideas of colour without an eye, or of sounds without an ear.' (Berkeley; *Life*, p. 181.) Why an organism and organs are the established conditions of perception in man is really the mystery.

[4] Of all knowledge, i. e. of all *contingently presented ideas*, in the utter absence of which there could be no actual knowledge of anything that really exists.

by ; it being indifferent to the matter in hand which way the learned shall determine of it [1].

[1] Although, in the preceding chapter, Locke seems to regard the reflex idea of 'perception' as 'simple,' its complexity has exercised philosophers in Britain and Germany, since the *Essay* appeared, more than any problem. In different aspects it has determined the speculations of Berkeley, Reid, and Kant. Here with Locke it is equivalent to 'the power' of acquiring 'simple ideas'; but with the questions suggested by 'externality' omitted,—referred for consideration to some extent in the Fourth Book (e. g. chh. ix. xi). Indeed with Locke perception of presented phenomena is throughout an inexplicable fact. 'Ideas,' he says,' it is certain I have, and God is the *original* cause of my having them ; *but how I come by them, how it is that I perceive, I confess I understand not.* . . Ideas are nothing but perceptions of the mind, annexed to certain motions of the body by the will of God, who hath ordered such perceptions to accompany such motions, *though we know not how they are produced*. . . . That which is said about objects exciting perceptions in us *by motion* does not fully explain how this is done. *In this I frankly confess my ignorance.*' (*Examination of Malebranche*, §§ 10-16, &c.) In short, perception—consciousness in every form—is to Locke inexplicable, and is accepted by him as a mysterious fact which science cannot resolve. Motion may mechanically explain other motion, but not the rise of perception. So too Prof. Huxley :—'How it is that anything so remarkable as a state of consciousness comes about as a result of initiating nervous tissue, is just as unaccountable as the appearance of the Djin, where Aladdin rubbed his lamp in the story, or as any other ultimate fact in nature.' (*Elementary Physiology*, p. 193.)

CHAPTER X.

OF RETENTION.

1. THE next faculty of the mind, whereby it makes a further progress towards knowledge, is that which I call *retention*; or the keeping of those simple ideas which from sensation or reflection it hath received. This is done two ways.

First, by keeping the idea which is brought into it, for some time [1] actually in view, which is called *contemplation*.

2. The other way of retention is, the power to revive again in our minds those ideas which, after imprinting, have disappeared, or have been as it were laid aside out of sight. And thus we do, when we conceive heat or light, yellow or sweet,—the object being removed. This is *memory* [2], which is as it were the storehouse [3] of our ideas. For, the narrow mind of man not being capable of having many ideas

---

[1] It is in and through 'retention' that we get the idea of *time*, and specially of time as past; without which, and therefore without memory in some degree, perception and consciousness in any form is impracticable. And perception of the present is always blended with conception of a past, if not also with anticipation of a future.

[2] Hobbes calls 'remembrance' a sixth sense—the other five senses 'taking notice of objects without us,' which 'notice' is 'our conception' (idea) of the object perceived. But we also so 'notice' the conceptions thus gained, as that, when they come again, 'we take notice *that it is again*.' (*Human Nature*, ch. iii. § 6.) Locke makes our reflex idea of the operation of memory, like that of perception, a 'simple idea of reflection,'—in each case overlooking their rational implicates, but not wholly their organic accompaniments.

[3] The 'wax tablet' and 'storehouse' metaphors do not help to explain memory as a mental act, and only illustrate the poverty of language for the expression of 'ideas of reflection.' At the same time observation shows that in the order of nature motions in the organism accompany the act of conservation. Memory as well as original sense perception is thus conditioned by organic impressions, under relations on which physiology has now thrown considerable light.

under view and consideration at once[1], it was necessary to have a repository, to lay up those ideas which, at another time, it might have use of. [[2]But, our *ideas* being nothing but actual perceptions in the mind, which cease to be anything when there is no perception[3] of them ; this laying up of our ideas in the repository of the memory signifies no more but this,—that the mind has a power[4] in many cases to revive perceptions which it has once had, with this additional perception annexed to them, that *it has had them before.* And in this sense it is that our ideas are said to be in our memories, when indeed they are actually nowhere ;—but only there is an ability in the mind[5] when it will to revive them again, and as it were paint them anew on itself, though some with more, some with less difficulty ; some more lively, and others more obscurely.] And thus it is, by the assistance of this faculty, that we are said to have all those ideas in our understandings which, though we do not actually contemplate, yet we *can* bring in sight, and make appear again, and be the objects of our thoughts, without the help of those sensible qualities which first imprinted them there.

Attention, Repetition, Pleasure and Pain, fix Ideas.

3. Attention[6] and repetition help much to the fixing any ideas in the memory. But those which naturally at first make the deepest and most lasting impressions, are those which are accompanied with pleasure or pain. The great business of the senses being, to make us take notice of what hurts or advantages the body, it is wisely ordered by nature, as has

[1] Cf. § 9.

[2] This and the next sentence were added in the second edition.

[3] Although the ideas are then 'actually nowhere,' in consciousness it has been suggested that 'the capability of being put into a mental state is itself something actual, and is, moreover, a different something when the state to be reproduced is different.' (See Ward's article, 'Psychology.')

[4] This potential and *unconscious* retention of what has been consciously perceived, favours by analogy recognition of 'innate' intellect (often in like manner potential and unconscious in the individual) as presupposed in, and a regulative condition of all experience.

[5] The 'rudiments of memory are involved in the *minimum* of consciousness. The first beginnings of it appear in that *minimum*, just as the first beginnings of perception do. The fact that the *minimum* of consciousness is difference, or change of feelings, is the ultimate explanation of memory as well as of single perceptions.' (Hodgson, *Philos. of Reflection*, i. p. 248.)

[6] Attention, as an element in the acquisition and retention of ideas, is

been shown, that pain should accompany the reception of BOOK II.
several ideas; which, supplying the place of consideration ⎯⎯
and reasoning in children, and acting quicker than considera- CHAP. X.
tion in grown men, makes both the old and young avoid
painful objects with that haste which is necessary for their
preservation; and in both settles in the memory a caution
for the future.

4. Concerning the several degrees of lasting, wherewith Ideas fade
ideas are imprinted on the memory, we may observe,—that in the
Memory.
some of them have been produced in the understanding by
an object affecting the senses once only, and no more than
once; [¹others, that have more than once offered themselves
to the senses, have yet been little taken notice of: the mind,
either heedless, as in children, or otherwise employed, as
in men intent only on one thing; not setting the stamp
deep into itself. And in some, where they are set on with
care and repeated impressions, either] through the temper
of the body, or some other fault, the memory is very weak.
In all these cases, ideas [²in the mind] quickly fade, and
often vanish quite out of the understanding, leaving no more
footsteps or remaining characters of themselves than shadows
do flying over fields of corn, and the mind is as void of them
as if they had never been there³.

5. Thus many of those ideas which were produced in the Causes of
minds of children, in the beginning of their sensation, (some oblivion.
of which perhaps, as of some pleasures and pains, were before
they were born, and others in their infancy,) if in the future

---

not overlooked by Locke. This is
not inconsistent with what he says
of the 'passivity' of the understanding
in perception. We cannot make that
white which is presented to sight as
black, or that square and soft which is
exhibited in sense as circular and hard,
but we can *concentrate* consciousness
upon any one of the many objects
which thus present themselves.

¹ In first edition:—'especially if
the mind, then otherwise employed,
took but little notice of it, and set not
on the stamp deep into itself; or else

when through the temper of the body,
or otherwise, the memory is very
weak, such ideas,' &c.

² Added in the second edition:—
'in the mind,' i.e. in the private
store-house of individual memory;
not ideas of external sense presented
to all.

³ That the range of *potential* memory
is much wider than that of *actual*
reproduction, *possible under ordinary
conditions*, is shown by well-attested
examples of abnormal resuscitation—
in dreams and cases of cerebral disease.

course of their lives they are not repeated again, are quite lost, without the least glimpse remaining of them. This may be observed in those who by some mischance have lost their sight when they were very young; in whom the ideas of colours having been but slightly taken notice of, and ceasing to be repeated, do quite wear out; so that some years after, there is no more notion nor memory of colours left in their minds, than in those of people born blind. The memory of some men, it is true, is very tenacious, even to a miracle. But yet there seems to be a constant decay [1] of all our ideas, even of those which are struck deepest, and in minds the most retentive; so that if they be not sometimes renewed, by repeated exercise of the senses, or reflection on those kinds of objects which at first occasioned them, the print wears out, and at last there remains nothing to be seen. Thus the ideas, as well as children, of our youth, often die before us: and our minds represent to us those tombs to which we are approaching; where, though the brass and marble remain, yet the inscriptions are effaced by time, and the imagery moulders away [2]. The pictures drawn in our minds are laid in fading colours; and if not sometimes refreshed, vanish and disappear. How much the constitution of our bodies [[3] and the make of our animal spirits] are concerned in this; and whether the temper of the brain makes this difference, that in some it retains the characters drawn on it like marble, in others like freestone, and in others little better than sand, I shall not here inquire; though it may seem probable that the constitution of the body does sometimes influence the memory, since we oftentimes find a disease quite strip the mind of all its ideas, and the flames of a fever in a few days calcine all

---

[1] Hobbes speaks of imagination and memory as 'decaying sense,' and describes 'remembrance' as 'nothing else but the missing of parts. To see at a great distance of place, and to remember at a great distance of time, is to have like conceptions of the thing; for there wanteth distinction of parts in both; the one conception being weak by operation at distance, the other by decay.' (*Human Nature,* ch. iii. § 7.)

[2] The imaginative sensibility that one often misses in Locke—attributed by Stewart, forgetful of Bunyan and Milton, to inherited puritanical austerity, is not wanting in this touching passage.

[3] Added in the fourth edition.

those images to dust and confusion, which seemed to be as
lasting as if graved in marble [1].

CHAP. X.
Constantly
repeated
Ideas can
scarce be
lost.

6. But concerning the ideas themselves, it is easy to remark, that those that are oftenest refreshed (amongst which are those that are conveyed into the mind by more ways than one) by a frequent return of the objects or actions that produce them, fix themselves best in the memory, and remain clearest and longest there ; and therefore those which are of the original qualities of bodies, viz. solidity, extension, figure, motion, and rest ; and those that almost constantly affect our bodies, as heat and cold ; and those which are the affections of all kinds of beings, as existence, duration, and number, which almost every object that affects our senses, every thought which employs our minds, bring along with them ;—these, I say, and the like ideas, are seldom quite lost, whilst the mind retains any ideas at all [2].

7. In this secondary perception [3], as I may so call it, or viewing again the ideas that are lodged in the memory, the mind is oftentimes more than barely passive ; the appearance of those dormant pictures depending sometimes on the *will* [4]. The mind very often sets itself on work in search of some hidden idea, and turns as it were the eye of the soul upon it ; though sometimes too they start up in our minds of their

In Re-
member-
ing, the
Mind is
often
active.

[1] The conscious act of memory presents what Locke calls a 'simple idea of reflection.' It is not a phenomenon presentable to the senses ; although in man, in this life, it is dependent upon organic conditions, regarding which recent physiological research has largely added to our useful knowledge, but without thereby affording more than a mechanical explanation of the invisible act itself. Mind may explain brain ; brain cannot explain memory. Why self-conscious life in man is embodied life at all is by us inexplicable.

[2] Whether any 'idea' of which a man has been conscious is ever *wholly* lost, so that it cannot revive, in this or in a future life, may be questioned. Some facts suggest that no conscious (or even unconscious) energy can be wholly obliterated. The act perishes, but not the 'habit.' Coleridge suggests that, in connection perhaps with a finer organism—a 'body celestial'— one's whole past life may be revived consciously ; and that this resuscitation may be that 'book of judgment' in which every idle word and deed is thus indelibly registered.

[3] 'Secondary perception'—instead of Hobbes's 'sixth sense.'

[4] This is *recollection* (the ἀνάμνησις as distinguished from the μνήμη of Aristotle), in which intelligent purpose *uses* associative law to recover what has been *partly* forgotten ; and in which the more numerous the associations, the easier the recollective act.

BOOK II.

CHAP. X.

own accord, and offer themselves to the understanding; and very often are roused and tumbled out of their dark cells into open daylight, by turbulent and tempestuous passions; our affections bringing ideas to our memory, which had otherwise lain quiet and unregarded. [[1] This further is to be observed, concerning ideas lodged in the memory, and upon occasion revived by the mind, that they are not only (as the word *revive* imports) none of them new ones, but also that the mind takes notice of them as of a former impression, and renews its acquaintance with them, as with ideas it had known before. So that though ideas formerly imprinted are not all constantly in view [2], yet in remembrance they are constantly known to be such as have been formerly imprinted; i. e. in view, and taken notice of before, by the understanding.]

Two defects in the Memory, Oblivion and Slowness.

8. Memory, in an intellectual creature, is necessary in the next degree to perception. It is of so great moment, that, where it is wanting, all the rest of our faculties are in a great measure useless [3]. And we in our thoughts, reasonings, and knowledge, could not proceed beyond present objects, were it not for the assistance of our memories; wherein there may be two defects:—

First, That it loses the idea quite, and so far it produces perfect ignorance. For, since we can know nothing further than we have the idea of it, when that is gone, we are in perfect ignorance [4].

Secondly, That it moves slowly, and retrieves not the ideas

---

[1] These two sentences were added in the second edition.

[2] Finite human memory, at its best, is revival *in fragments*, under associative laws, of a past experience, which man cannot keep *simultaneously, in its totality*, in consciousness.

[3] Without memory all our 'faculties' would be, not only 'in a great measure' but absolutely, useless.

[4] This 'perfect ignorance' may consist with continued *potential* knowledge, if memory is the issue of indelible modes of self-activity. On that hypothesis, 'oblivion,' rather than 're-membrance,' would have to be accounted for; as due to the gradual subsidence into semi-consciousness, and then into unconsciousness, of energies that are latent because superseded (within the necessarily limited capacity of a human consciousness) by new activities, but which are never absolutely annihilated. 'Ideas which remain long without being attended to have a natural tendency to drop out of consciousness.' (J. S. Mill.)

that it has, and are laid up in store, quick enough to serve

the mind upon occasion. This, if it be to a great degree, is stupidity ; and he who, through this default in his memory, has not the ideas that are really preserved there, ready at hand when need and occasion calls for them, were almost as good be without them quite, since they serve him to little purpose. The dull man, who loses the opportunity, whilst he is seeking in his mind for those ideas that should serve his turn, is not much more happy in his knowledge than one that is perfectly ignorant. It is the business therefore of the memory to furnish to the mind those dormant ideas [1] which it has present occasion for ; in the having them ready at hand on all occasions, consists that which we call invention, fancy, and quickness of parts [2].

9. [[3] These are defects we may observe in the memory of one man compared with another. There is another defect which we may conceive to be in the memory of man in general ;—compared with some superior created intellectual beings, which in this faculty may so far excel man, that they may have *constantly* in view the whole scene of all their former actions, wherein no one of the thoughts they have ever had may slip out of their sight. The omniscience of God, who knows all things, past, present, and to come, and to whom the thoughts of men's hearts always lie open, may satisfy us of the possibility of this. For who can doubt but God may communicate to those glorious spirits, his immediate attendants, any of his perfections ; in what proportions he pleases, as far as created finite beings can be capable? It is reported of that prodigy of parts, Monsieur Pascal, that till the decay of his health had impaired his memory, he forgot nothing of what he had done, read, or thought, in any part of

A defect which belongs to the memory of Man, as finite.

---

[1] 'Dormant ideas' imply latency or unconscious innateness. Throughout life, by far the greater part of the phenomena acquired in experience are thus dormant, yet more or less revivable.

[2] A good memory is (*a*) apt to receive, (*b*) tenacious in retention, and (*c*) ready to produce—under the associative laws. Association, psychical and organic, individual and inherited —is the mechanical explanation of memory.

[3] This interesting section was added in the second edition. It might be the text of an essay on a *human* understanding of the universe, as intermediate between Omniscience and the nescience of Sense.

BOOK II.
CHAP. X.

his rational age[1]. This is a privilege so little known to most men, that it seems almost incredible to those who, after the ordinary way, measure all others by themselves; but yet, when considered, may help us to enlarge our thoughts towards greater perfections of it, in superior ranks of spirits. For this of Monsieur Pascal was still with the narrowness that human minds are confined to here,—of having great variety of ideas only by succession, not all at once. Whereas the several degrees of angels may probably have larger views; and some of them be endowed with capacities able to retain together, and constantly set before them, as in one picture, all their past knowledge at once. This, we may conceive, would be no small advantage to the knowledge of a thinking man,—if all his past thoughts and reasonings could be *always* present to him[2]. And therefore we may suppose it one of those ways, wherein the knowledge of separate spirits may exceedingly surpass ours.]

Brutes have Memory.

10. This faculty of laying up and retaining the ideas that are brought into the mind, several other animals seem to have to a great degree, as well as man. For, to pass by other instances, birds learning of tunes, and the endeavours one may observe in them to hit the notes right, put it past doubt with me, that they have perception, and retain ideas in their memories, and use them for patterns. For it seems to me impossible that they should endeavour to conform their voices to notes (as it is plain they do) of which they had no ideas. For, though I should grant sound may mechanically cause a certain motion of the animal spirits in the brains of those birds, whilst the tune is actually playing; and that motion may be continued on to the muscles of the wings, and so the bird mechanically be driven away by certain noises, because this may tend to the bird's preservation; yet that can never be supposed a reason why it should cause mechanically—either whilst the tune is playing, much

---

[1] This about Pascal must be taken with allowance. That he never forgot anything 'which he *tried* to retain' is what Madame Perier records of him.

[2] Instead of 'existing' as they mostly do in the state of being only *revivable*, and that bit by bit, not all simultaneously; and with large portions incapable of resuscitation in this life, under normal conditions at least.

less after it has ceased—such a motion of the organs in the bird's voice as should conform it to the notes of a foreign sound, which imitation can be of no use to the bird's preservation. But, which is more, it cannot with any appearance of reason be supposed (much less proved) that birds, without sense and memory, can approach their notes nearer and nearer by degrees to a tune played yesterday; which if they have no idea of in their memory, is now nowhere, nor can be a pattern for them to imitate, or which any repeated essays can bring them nearer to. Since there is no reason why the sound of a pipe should leave traces in their brains, which, not at first, but by their after-endeavours, should produce the like sounds; and why the sounds they make themselves, should not make traces which they should follow, as well as those of the pipe, is impossible to conceive[1].

[1] The phenomena and laws of unconscious cerebration were imperfectly known when Locke wrote.

CHAPTER XI.

OF DISCERNING, AND OTHER OPERATIONS OF THE MIND [1].

BOOK II.

CHAP. XI.

No Knowledge without Discernment.

1. ANOTHER faculty we may take notice of in our minds is that of *discerning* and *distinguishing* between the several ideas it has [2]. It is not enough to have a confused perception of something in general. Unless the mind had a distinct perception of different objects and their qualities, it would be capable of very little knowledge, though the bodies that affect us were as busy about us as they are now, and the mind were continually employed in thinking. On this faculty of distinguishing one thing from another depends the evidence and certainty of several, even very general, propositions, which have passed for innate truths;— because men, overlooking the true cause why those propositions find universal assent, impute it wholly to native uniform impressions; whereas it in truth depends upon this clear discerning faculty of the mind, whereby it *perceives* two ideas to be the same, or different. But of this more hereafter.

The Difference of Wit and Judgment.

2. How much the imperfection of accurately discriminating ideas one from another lies, either in the dulness or faults of the organs of sense; or want of acuteness, exercise, or attention in the understanding; or hastiness and precipitancy, natural to some tempers, I will not here examine: it suffices to take notice, that this is one of the operations that the mind may reflect on and observe in itself. It is of that con-

---

[1] It is with the operations of elaborative thought that this chapter is concerned.

[2] Locke's descendants, we are told, have neglected the study of discrimina-
tion or dissociation for that of association of ideas; although 'experience is trained by both association and dissociation.' (See James's *Psychology*, i. p. 487.)

sequence to its other knowledge, that so far as this faculty is
in itself dull, or not rightly made use of, for the distinguishing
one thing from another,—so far our notions are confused, and
our reason and judgment disturbed or misled. If in having
our ideas in the memory ready at hand consists quickness of
parts; in this, of having them unconfused, and being able
nicely to distinguish one thing from another, where there is
but the least difference, consists, in a great measure, the
exactness of judgment, and clearness of reason, which is to be
observed in one man above another. And hence perhaps
may be given some reason of that common observation,—that
men who have a great deal of wit, and prompt memories,
have not always the clearest judgment or deepest reason. For
wit lying most in the assemblage of ideas, and putting those
together with quickness and variety, wherein can be found
any resemblance or congruity, thereby to make up pleasant
pictures and agreeable visions in the fancy[1]; *judgment,* on
the contrary, lies quite on the other side, in separating carefully, one from another, ideas wherein can be found the
least difference, thereby to avoid being misled by similitude,
and by affinity to take one thing for another[2]. This is a
way of proceeding quite contrary to metaphor and allusion;
wherein for the most part lies that entertainment and plea-
santry of wit, which strikes so lively on the fancy, and therefore is so acceptable to all people, because its beauty appears
at first sight, and there is required no labour of thought to
examine what truth or reason there is in it. The mind,

---

[1] Wit, according to Hobbes, is
'quick discernment of similitude in
things otherwise much unlike, or of
dissimilitude in things that otherwise
appear the same.' It is thus more akin
to imagination than to intellect proper.

[2] This is only one way in which the
faculty of comparison, or of elaborative affirmation and denial, is exercised. Locke further modifies the
meaning of 'judgment' in the Fourth
Book, where he distinguishes it from
'knowledge,' and confines it to presumption of probability only. See

Bk. IV. chh. xiv, xv, xvi. The exercise of 'discernment' implies that our
mental experience is originally confused but complex, and that recognition
of ideas in their simplicity is the result
of discriminative analysis. Things,
presented in sense as confused aggregates, reveal their constituent elements
as intelligence evolves. This evolution,
through dissociation of our complex
ideas of individual things, leads to re-
association, under concepts, scientific
or physical, and at last philosophic or
metaphysical.

BOOK II.
Chap. XI.

without looking any further, rests satisfied with the agreeableness of the picture and the gaiety of the fancy. And it is a kind of affront to go about to examine it, by the severe rules of truth and good reason ; whereby it appears that it consists in something that is not perfectly conformable to them.

Clearness alone hinders Confusion.

3. To the well distinguishing our ideas, it chiefly contributes that they be *clear* and *determinate*. And when they are so, it will not breed any confusion or mistake about them, though the senses should (as sometimes they do) convey them from the same object differently on different occasions, and so seem to err. For, though a man in a fever should from sugar have a bitter taste, which at another time would produce a sweet one, yet the idea of bitter in that man's mind would be as clear and distinct from the idea of sweet as if he had tasted only gall. Nor does it make any more confusion between the two ideas of sweet and bitter, that the same sort of body produces at one time one, and at another time another idea by the taste, than it makes a confusion in two ideas of white and sweet, or white and round, that the same piece of sugar produces them both in the mind at the same time. And the ideas of orange-colour and azure, that are produced in the mind by the same parcel of the infusion of *lignum nephriticum*, are no less distinct ideas than those of the same colours taken from two very different bodies.

Comparing.

4. The COMPARING them one with another, in respect of extent, degrees, time, place, or any other circumstances, is another operation of the mind about its ideas, and is that upon which depends all that large tribe of ideas comprehended under *relation* ; which, of how vast an extent it is, I shall have occasion to consider hereafter [1].

Brutes compare but imperfectly.

5. How far brutes partake in this faculty, is not easy to determine. I imagine they have it not in any great degree: for, though they probably have several ideas distinct enough, yet it seems to me to be the prerogative of human under-

[1] See chh. xxv–xxviii.

standing, when it has sufficiently distinguished any ideas, so as to perceive them to be perfectly different, and so consequently two, to cast about and consider in what circumstances they are capable to be compared. And therefore, I think, beasts compare not their ideas further than some sensible circumstances annexed to the objects themselves. The other power of comparing[1], which may be observed in men, belonging to general ideas, and useful only to abstract reasonings, we may probably conjecture beasts have not.

6. The next operation we may observe in the mind about its ideas is COMPOSITION ; whereby it puts together several of those simple ones it has received from sensation and reflection, and combines them into complex ones. Under this of composition may be reckoned also that of *enlarging*[2], wherein, though the composition does not so much appear as in more complex ones, yet it is nevertheless a putting several ideas together, though of the same kind[3]. Thus, by adding several units together, we make the idea of a dozen ; and putting together the repeated ideas of several perches, we frame that of a furlong.

7. In this also, I suppose, brutes come far short of man. For, though they take in, and retain together, several combinations of simple ideas, as possibly the shape, smell, and voice of his master make up the complex idea a dog has of him, or rather are so many distinct marks whereby

BOOK II.
CHAP. XI.

Com-
pounding.

Brutes
compound
but little.

---

[1] The power of elaborating intellectual concepts of things—as distinguished from sensuous representation, determined merely by automatic association.

[2] 'En conversant un jour avec M. Locke, le discours venant à tomber sur les *idées innées*, je lui fis cette objection : Que penser de certains petits oiseaux, du chardonneret, par exemple, qui, éclos dans un nid que le père ou la mère lui ont fait, s'envole enfin dans les champs pour y chercher sa nourriture, sans que le père ou la mère prenne aucune soin de lui, et qui, l'année suivante, sait forte bien trouver et démêler tous les matériaux dont il a besoin pour se bâtir un nid, qui, par son industrie, se trouve fait et agencé avec autant ou plus l'art que celui où il est éclos lui-même ? D'où lui sont venues les idées de ces différents matériaux, et l'art d'en construire ce nid ? M. Locke me répondit brusquement : *Je n'ai pas écrit mon livre pour expliquer les actions des bêtes.*' (Coste.)

[3] In what Locke calls 'simple modes' of our simple ideas. See chh. xiii-xxi.

he knows him; yet I do not think they do of themselves ever compound them, and make complex ideas[1]. And perhaps even where we think they have complex ideas, it is only one simple one that directs them in the knowledge of several things, which possibly they distinguish less by their sight than we imagine. For I have been credibly informed that a bitch will nurse, play with, and be fond of young foxes, as much as, and in place of her puppies, if you can but get them once to suck her so long that her milk may go through them. [[2] And those animals which have a numerous brood of young ones at once, appear not to have any knowledge of their number; for though they are mightily concerned for any of their young that are taken from them whilst they are in sight or hearing, yet if one or two of them be stolen from them in their absence, or without noise, they appear not to miss them, or to have any sense that their number is lessened.]

Naming.

8. When children have, by repeated sensations, got ideas fixed in their memories, they begin by degrees to learn the use of signs. And when they have got the skill to apply the organs of speech to the framing of articulate sounds, they begin to make use of words, to signify their ideas to others. These verbal signs they sometimes borrow from others, and sometimes make themselves, as one may observe among the new and unusual names children often give to things in the first use of language.

Abstraction.

9. The use of words then being to stand as outward marks of our internal ideas, and those ideas being taken from particular things, if every particular idea that we take in should have a distinct name, names must be endless. To prevent this, the mind makes the particular ideas received

---

[1] That is to say, brutes receive their simple ideas in complexity, and thus seem to have complex ideas made for them. But so too often with men. Many of *our* complex ideas, too, are not formed by our will. They are made *for* us, not *by* us; as Locke himself sees. Even in sense we receive from particular substances *aggregates* of simple ideas, and this through various senses; and the ideas of *existence, unity, succession,* and *power* are suggested by all of them (ch. vii. §§ 7–9)—implying that simple ideas are never presented in their simplicity.

[2] Added in second edition.

from particular objects to become general; which is done by
considering them as they are in the mind such appearances,
—separate from all other existences, and the circumstances of
real existence, as time, place, or any other concomitant ideas [1].
This is called ABSTRACTION [2], whereby ideas taken from particular beings become general representatives of all of the
same kind; and their names general names, applicable to
whatever exists conformable to such abstract ideas. Such
precise, naked appearances in the mind, without considering
how, whence, or with what others they came there, the understanding lays up (with names commonly annexed to them)
as the standards to rank real existences into sorts, as they
agree with these patterns, and to denominate them accordingly. Thus the same colour being observed to-day in chalk
or snow, which the mind yesterday received from milk, it
considers that appearance alone, makes it a representative of
all of that kind; and having given it the name *whiteness*, it
by that sound signifies the same quality wheresoever to be
imagined or met with; and thus universals, whether ideas or
terms, are made.

10. If it may be doubted whether beasts compound and
enlarge their ideas that way to any degree; this, I think,
I may be positive in,—that the power of abstracting is not
at all in them; and that the having of general ideas is

---

[1] Our *ideas* are, all of them, '*particular* existences,' according to Locke;
and our knowledge is confined to perception of the agreements or disagreements of particular ideas—*universality*
being only accidental to it, when our
particular ideas of the moment happen
to represent other particular ideas,
with which they are in a way identical. (Bk. IV. ch. xvii. § 8.)

[2] The words in capitals, here and in
§§ 4 and 5, are so printed in the
editions which appeared in Locke's
lifetime. This and the two next sections are the first passages in the
Essay which expressly treat of the
'abstract' ideas, rejected by Berkeley
in the Introduction to his *Principles*

and elsewhere, as 'remote from common sense, though countenanced by
Locke, who seems to think that
having abstract ideas is what puts the
difference in point of understanding
between man and beast.' But if this
be so, 'I fear,' Berkeley adds, 'that a
great many of those that pass for men
must be reckoned into the number of
beasts, who, though they *use general
words*, are incapable of *abstracting their
ideas*.' Berkeley's criticism is due to
misunderstanding. Cf. Bk. III. ch. iii.
§ 6; Bk. IV. ch. vii. § 9 of the *Essay*.
Locke does not, like Berkeley, confine
'idea' to individual percepts of sense,
and images of sensuous imagination,
but includes individualisable concepts.

that which puts a perfect distinction betwixt man and brutes, and is an excellency which the faculties of brutes do by no means attain to. For it is evident we observe no footsteps in them of making use of general signs for universal ideas; from which we have reason to imagine that they have not the faculty of abstracting, or making general ideas, since they have no use of words, or any other general signs.

Brutes abstract not, yet are not bare machines.

11. Nor can it be imputed to their want of fit organs to frame articulate sounds, that they have no use or knowledge of general words; since many of them, we find, can fashion such sounds, and pronounce words distinctly enough, but never with any such application. And, on the other side, men who, through some defect in the organs, want words, yet fail not to express their universal ideas by signs, which serve them instead of general words, a faculty which we see beasts come short in. And, therefore, I think, we may suppose, that it is in this that the species of brutes are discriminated from man : and it is that proper difference wherein they are wholly separated, and which at last widens to so vast a distance. For if they have any ideas at all, and are not bare machines[1], (as some would have them[2],) we cannot deny them to have some reason. It seems as evident to me, that they do [[3] some of them in certain instances] reason, as that they have sense ; but it is only in particular ideas, just as they received them from their senses. They are the best of them tied up within those narrow bounds, and have not (as I think) the faculty to enlarge them by any kind of abstraction [4].

---

[1] 'Machines'—'machins' in the early editions.

[2] The Cartesians, who regarded brutes as sentient machines, or organisms that are unconscious instruments of the Supreme Power. Cf. on the other hand, Butler, *Analogy*, ch. i.—on the 'latent powers' and possible 'natural immortality' of brutes.

[3] Added in *fourth* edition.

[4] Leibniz thus comments, distinguishing intellect proper from sensuous association mechanically determined by natural law :—' Je suis de même sentiment. . . . Les bêtes passent d'une imagination à une autre par la liaison qu'elles y ont sentie autrefois. . . . On pourrait appeler cela *conséquence* et *raisonnement* dans un sens fort étendu. Mais j'aime mieux me conformer à l'usage reçu, en consacrant ces mots à l'homme, et

12. How far idiots are concerned in the want or weakness of any, or all of the foregoing faculties, an exact observation of their several ways of faultering [1] would no doubt discover. For those who either perceive but dully, or retain the ideas that come into their minds but ill, who cannot readily excite or compound them, will have little matter to think on. Those who cannot distinguish, compare, and abstract, would hardly be able to understand and make use of language, or judge or reason to any tolerable degree ; but only a little and imperfectly about things present, and very familiar to their senses. And indeed any of the forementioned faculties, if wanting, or out of order, produce suitable defects in men's understandings and knowledge.

13. In fine, the defect in naturals seems to proceed from want of quickness, activity, and motion in the intellectual faculties, whereby they are deprived of reason ; whereas madmen, on the other side, seem to suffer by the other extreme. For they do not appear to me to have lost the faculty of reasoning, but having joined together some ideas very wrongly, they mistake them for truths ; and they err as men do that argue right from wrong principles. For, by the violence of their imaginations, having taken their fancies for realities, they make right deductions from them. Thus you shall find a distracted man fancying himself a king, with a right inference require suitable attendance, respect, and obedience : others who have thought themselves made of glass, have used the caution necessary to preserve such brittle bodies. Hence it comes to pass that a man who is very sober, and of a right understanding in all other things, may in one particular be as frantic as any in Bedlam ; if either by any sudden very strong impression, or long fixing his fancy upon one sort of thoughts, incoherent ideas have been

---

en les restreignant à la connaissance de quelque *raison* de la liaison des perceptions, *que les sensations seules ne sauraient donner* ; leur effet n'étant que de faire que naturellement on s'attende une autre fois à cette même liaison qu'on a remarquée auparavant, quoique peut-être les raisons ne soient plus les mêmes ; ce qui trompe souvent ceux qui ne se gouvernent que par les sens.' (*Nouveaux Essais*, II. xi.)

[1] 'Faultering,'—failing, or being deficient.

BOOK II.
CHAP. XI.

cemented together so powerfully, as to remain united. But there are degrees of madness, as of folly; the disorderly jumbling ideas together is in some more, and some less. In short, herein seems to lie the difference between idiots and madmen: that madmen put wrong ideas together, and so make wrong propositions, but argue and reason right from them; but idiots make very few or no propositions, and reason scarce at all.

Method followed in this explication of Faculties.

14. These, I think, are the first faculties and operations of the mind, which it makes use of in understanding; and though they are exercised about all its ideas in general, yet the instances I have hitherto given have been chiefly in simple ideas. And I have subjoined the explication of these faculties of the mind to that of simple ideas [1], before I come to what I have to say concerning complex ones, for these following reasons :—

First, Because several of these faculties being exercised at first principally about simple ideas [2], we might, by following nature in its ordinary method, trace and discover them [3], in their rise, progress, and gradual improvements.

Secondly, Because observing the faculties of the mind, how they operate about simple ideas,—which are usually, in most men's minds, much more clear, precise, and distinct than complex ones,—we may the better examine and learn how the mind extracts, denominates, compares, and exercises, in its other operations about those which are complex, wherein we are much more liable to mistake.

[1] 'simple ideas,'—especially of 'sensation,'—treated of in ch. ii–viii.

[2] According to some interpreters of the *Essay* (Cousin, Green, &c.), Locke supposes that men begin to have experience in the form of a consciousness of isolated phenomena, i. e. of simple ideas in their simplicity; and that all their complex ideas are afterwards elaborated by themselves out of these; while the actual history of the human understanding is the reverse—beginning with apprehension of the complex or concrete, advancing, by abstraction, to the simple in their simplicity, gradually rendering original experience more determinate. But, though here and elsewhere occasional expressions may seem to countenance this interpretation, we have already seen that he mentions certain ideas as invariably connected with all other ideas; and in the sequel he makes comparison of ideas in mental propositions the essence of knowledge. (Bk. IV. ch. i. § 2.)

[3] 'them,' i. e. 'ideas and their correlative faculties.'

Thirdly, Because these very operations of the mind about BOOK II.
ideas received from sensations, are themselves, when reflected ⎯⎯⎯
on, another set of ideas, derived from that other source of our CHAP. XI.
knowledge, which I call reflection; and therefore fit to be
considered in this place after the simple ideas of sensation.
Of compounding, comparing, abstracting, &c., I have but
just spoken, having occasion to treat of them more at large
in other places [1].

15. And thus I have given a short, and, I think, true The true
history [2] *of the first beginnings of human knowledge*;—whence Beginning of
the mind has its first objects; and by what steps it makes Human
its progress to the laying in and storing up those ideas, out ledge.
of which is to be framed all the knowledge it is capable of:
wherein I must appeal to experience and observation whether
I am in the right: the best way to come to truth being
to examine things as really they are, and not to conclude
they are, as we fancy of ourselves, or have been taught by
others to imagine.

16. To deal truly, this is the only way that I can discover, Appeal to
whereby the *ideas of things* are brought into the under- Experi-
standing. If other men have either innate ideas or infused ence.
principles, they have reason to enjoy them; and if they
are sure of it, it is impossible for others to deny them the
privilege that they have above their neighbours. I can speak
but of what I find in myself, and is agreeable to those
notions, which, if we will examine the whole course of
men in their several ages, countries, and educations, seem to
depend on those foundations which I have laid, and to correspond with this method in all the parts and degrees thereof.

17. I pretend not to teach, but to inquire; and therefore Dark
cannot but confess here again,—that external and internal Room.
sensation are the only passages I can find of knowledge to
the understanding [3]. These alone, as far as I can discover,

---

[1] Chh. xiii–xxviii, xxxii. § 6-8; Bk.
III. ch. iii., &c.

[2] The 'historical' plain matter of
fact method. (Introd. § 2.)

[3] If the original 'materials'—the
'ideas' or phenomena of the sub-

stances that are presented in sense
for elaboration—are in fact found,
when subjected to analysis, as above,
to consist of the aforesaid sorts of
simple ideas, and of none others—Why
should we rebel against this fact?

BOOK II.
CHAP. XI.
are the windows by which light is let into this *dark room*. For, methinks, the understanding is not much unlike a closet wholly shut from light, with only some little openings left, to let in external visible [1] resemblances, or ideas of things without: [[2] would the pictures coming into such a dark room but stay there], and lie so orderly as to be found upon occasion, it would very much resemble the understanding of a man, in reference to all objects of sight, and the ideas of them [3].

These are my guesses concerning the means whereby the understanding comes to have and retain simple ideas [4], and the modes of them, with some other operations about them.

I proceed now to examine some of these simple ideas and their modes a little more particularly.

'Things are what they are, and are not other things; why therefore should we desire to be deceived?'

[1] Why 'visible,' or of 'sight' only? for Locke does not (like some of his contemporaries) mean by *idea* only what can be *seen*. His *ideas* are phenomena of whatever sort—extended and unthinking, or unextended and thinking; apprehended in complexity, as particular, in the senses and sensuous imagination, or abstracted and in their most general relations.

[2] 'Which, would they but stay there'—in first three editions.

[3] Reid founds, mainly on the figurative language of this section, his interpretation of Locke's account of external perception—as non-presentative, because reached through the medium of the ideas of the percipient. He also assumes that Plato intends by his 'similitude of the cave,' to illustrate the manner in which the images of external things are introduced into the mind of man. 'Plato's subterranean cave, and Mr. Locke's dark closet,' Reid says, 'may be applied with ease to all the systems of perception that have been invented; for they all suppose that we perceive not external objects immediately, and that the immediate objects of perception are only certain shadows of the external objects. These shadows or images, which we immediately perceive, were by the ancients called *species, forms, phantasms*. Since the time of Descartes they have commonly been called *ideas*, and by Hume, *impressions*. But all philosophers, from Plato to Hume, agree in this—that we do not perceive *external* objects immediately; and that the immediate object of perception must be some image present to the mind.' (*Intellectual Powers*, Essay II. ch. vii.) But, according to Locke, ideas are the 'medium' of each man's knowledge of his own mental operations, as well as of the qualities of 'external' objects. He can no more apprehend his inner life without *ideas* of its 'operations' than he can things in surrounding space without *ideas* of their qualities. In both alike there must be phenomena, with an apprehension of them that is dependent on, or relative to, the percipient subject. On the meaning of Plato's comparison of the cave, see Hamilton's *Reid*, p. 262, *note*.

[4] This need not mean, that the simple ideas were *originally* apprehended *in their simplicity*.

CHAPTER XII.

OF COMPLEX IDEAS.

BOOK II.

Chap. XII.
Made by
the Mind
out of
simple
Ones.

1. WE have hitherto considered those ideas, in the reception whereof the mind is only passive[1], which are those simple ones received from sensation and reflection before mentioned, whereof the mind cannot make one to itself, nor have any idea which does not wholly consist of them. [2 But as the mind is wholly passive in the reception of all its simple ideas, so it exerts several acts of its own, whereby out of its simple ideas, as the materials and foundations of the rest, the others are framed[3]. The acts of the mind, wherein it exerts its power over its simple ideas, are chiefly these three: (1) Combining several simple ideas into one compound one; and thus all *complex*[4] *ideas* are made. (2) The second is bringing two ideas, whether simple or complex, together, and setting them by one another, so as to take a view of them at once, without uniting them into one; by which way it gets all its *ideas of relations.* (3) The third is separating them from all other ideas that

---

[1] 'passive,' i. e. they are presented involuntarily,—what is actually presented in the senses, and in the operations of which we are conscious, being independent of the *will* of the conscious subject; who is moreover dependent upon what is so presented for all the ideas of things and of spirits that he is capable of having, being also in this respect 'passive,' for one born blind cannot image colour. But all this may consist with attention and active intelligence in perception.

[2] Added in *fourth* edition.

[3] 'framed'—'by us,' and 'for us,' in the complex constitution of the qualified things.

[4] 'complex.' In ch. ii. Locke divided our ideas into *simple* and *complex*; here he seems to make 'complex ideas' one class only of those which result from 'the acts of mind wherein it exerts its power over its simple ideas.' Cf. Hume, *Treatise*, I. i. § 1,—on ideas as simple and complex.

accompany them in their real existence : this is called abstraction : and thus all its *general ideas* are made. This shows man's power, and its ways of operation, to be much the same in the material and intellectual world. For the materials in both being such as he has no power over, either to make or destroy, all that man can do is either to unite them together, or to set them by one another, or wholly separate them. I shall here begin with the first of these in the consideration of complex ideas, and come to the other two in their due places.] As simple ideas are observed to exist in several combinations united together [1], so the mind has a power to consider several of them united together as one idea; and that not only as they are united in external objects, but as itself has joined them together. Ideas thus made up of several simple ones put together, I call *complex*;—such as are beauty, gratitude, a man, an army, the universe; which, though complicated of various simple ideas, or complex ideas made up of simple ones, yet are, when the mind pleases, considered each by itself, as one entire thing, and signified by one name.

Made voluntarily.

2. In this faculty of repeating and joining together its ideas, the mind has great power in varying and multiplying the objects of its thoughts, infinitely beyond what sensation or reflection furnished it with : but all this still confined to those simple ideas which it received from those two sources, and which are the ultimate materials of all its compositions. For simple ideas are all from things themselves, and of these the mind *can* have no more, nor other than what are suggested to it [2]. It can have no other ideas of sensible qualities than what come from without by the senses ; nor any ideas of other kind of operations of a thinking substance [3], than what it finds in itself. But when

---

[1] When the *combinations* are made for, and not by the individual mind,— as in individual things presented to the senses.

[2] As already remarked, it is in this respect that he means that we are 'passive' in dealing with simple ideas. The born blind *cannot* perceive or image variety in colour, and the human mind can by no effort of will have more or other particular ideas of things and persons, than those presented in experience.

[3] Including God. Cf. Bk. II. ch. xxiii. § 33.

it has once got these simple ideas, it is not confined barely
to observation, and what offers itself from without ; it can,
by its own power, put together those ideas it has, and make
new complex ones, which it never received so united [1].

3. *Complex ideas*, however compounded and decompounded,
though their number be infinite, and the variety endless,
wherewith they fill and entertain the thoughts of men ; yet
I think they may be all reduced under these three heads :—

Complex
ideas are
either of
Modes,
Sub-
stances, or
Relations.

    1. MODES.
    2. SUBSTANCES.
    3. RELATIONS [2].

4. First, *Modes* I call such complex ideas which, however
compounded, contain not in them the supposition of subsisting by themselves, but are considered as dependences
on, or affections of substances ;—such as are the ideas signified by the words triangle, gratitude, murder, &c. And if
in this I use the word mode in somewhat a different sense
from its ordinary signification, I beg pardon ; it being unavoidable in discourses, differing from the ordinary received
notions, either to make new words, or to use old words in
somewhat a new signification ; the later whereof, in our
present case, is perhaps the more tolerable of the two [3].

Ideas of
Modes.

5. Of these *modes*, there are two sorts which deserve distinct
consideration :—

First, there are some which are only variations, or different
combinations of the same simple idea, without the mixture
of any other ;—as a dozen, or score ; which are nothing but
the ideas of so many distinct units added together, and
these I call *simple modes* [4] as being contained within the
bounds of one simple idea [4].

Simple
and mixed
Modes of
simple
ideas.

Secondly, there are others compounded of simple ideas of

---

[1] In its own plastic imaginations,
and arbitrary generalisations.

[2] Here he makes ' ideas of relation '
one species of ' complex idea '; whereas, in § 1, he spoke of ' complex ideas '
and ' ideas of relation ' as coordinate
species of the genus ' ideas made by
the mind,' and elsewhere he acknowledges ' relation ' in all ' complex '
ideas.

[3] Locke's ' modes '—' simple ' and
' mixed '—are names for the ideas we
have of qualities, and collections of
qualities, considered in abstraction from
substances.

[4] Treated in chapters xiii–xxi.

several kinds, put together to make one complex one;—v. g. beauty, consisting of a certain composition of colour and figure, causing delight to the beholder; theft, which being the concealed change of the possession of anything, without the consent of the proprietor, contains, as is visible, a combination of several ideas of several kinds: and these I call *mixed modes* [1].

Ideas of Substances, single or collective.

6. Secondly, the ideas of *substances* are such combinations of simple ideas as are taken to represent distinct *particular* things subsisting by themselves; in which the supposed or confused idea of substance, such as it is, is always the first and chief. Thus if to substance be joined the simple idea of a certain dull whitish colour, with certain degrees of weight, hardness, ductility, and fusibility, we have the idea of lead; and a combination of the ideas of a certain sort of figure, with the powers of motion, thought and reasoning, joined to substance, make the ordinary idea of a man. Now of substances also, there are two sorts of ideas:—one of *single* substances, as they exist separately, as of a man or a sheep; the other of several of those put together, as an army of men, or flock of sheep—which *collective* ideas of several substances thus put together are as much each of them one single idea as that of a man or an unit.

Ideas of Relation.

7. Thirdly, the last sort of complex ideas is that we call *relation*, which consists in the consideration and comparing one idea with another [2].

Of these several kinds we shall treat in their order [3].

The abstrusest Ideas we

8. If we trace the progress of our minds [4], and with attention observe how it repeats, adds together, and unites

---

[1] See ch. xxii.

[2] Properly speaking all the three sorts of complex ideas involve comparison, and therefore 'relation,' as Locke himself acknowledges in other places.

[3] 'Cette division des objets de nos pensées, en *substances, modes,* et *relations,* est assez à mon goût. Je crois que les qualités ne sont que modifications des substances, et l'entendement y ajoute les relations.' (*Nouveaux Essais.*)

[4] According to Locke's 'historical' method, which is bound to seek in *past* ideas or phenomena for its 'explanations.'

its simple ideas received [1] from sensation or reflection, it
will lead us further than at first perhaps we should have
imagined. And, I believe, we shall find, if we warily observe
the originals of our notions, that *even the most abstruse ideas,*
how remote soever they may seem from sense, or from any
operations of our own minds, are yet only such as the understanding frames to itself, by repeating and joining together
ideas that it had either from objects of sense, or from its
own operations about them : so that those even large and
abstract ideas are derived from sensation or reflection, being
no other than what the mind, by the ordinary use of its
own faculties, employed about ideas received from objects
of sense, or from the operations it observes in itself about
them, may, and does, attain unto.

This I shall endeavour to show in the ideas we have of
space, time, and infinity, and some few others that seem the
most remote [2], from those originals.

BOOK II.

CHAP. XII.
can have
are all
from two
Sources.

---

[1] ' received ' — yet originally received in complexity—a complexity
however that can always, by abstraction and analysis, be refunded into
simple ideas of external or internal
sense.

[2] In the following chapters,—to the
end of the twenty-eighth,—the examples of ideas in their *modes,* of
ideas of *substances,* and of ideas of
their *relations,* are what Bacon would
call ' crucial instances,'—in verification
of the hypothesis that even our ' most
abstruse ideas' in science and philosophy all gradually rise out of phenomena of the five senses or of reflection.
But are the ' abstruse ideas' in all
cases results of *empirical* comparison ?
Do they not often issue from *intellectual
necessities,* a point of view not familiar
to Locke, who sometimes seems to
sensualise ' human understanding,' in
an exclusive desire to show its dependence upon ' experience ' ?

CHAPTER XIII.

COMPLEX IDEAS OF SIMPLE MODES:—AND FIRST, OF THE SIMPLE MODES OF IDEA OF SPACE.

BOOK II.

Chap. XIII.

Simple
modes of
simple
ideas.

1. Though in the foregoing part I have often mentioned simple ideas, which are truly the materials of all our knowledge; yet having treated of them there, rather in the way that they come into the mind, than as distinguished from others more compounded[1], it will not be perhaps amiss to take a view of some of them again under this consideration, and examine those different modifications of the *same* idea; which the mind either finds in things existing[2], or is able to make within itself without the help of any extrinsical object, or any foreign suggestion[3].

Those modifications of any *one* simple idea (which, as has been said, I call *simple modes*) are as perfectly different and distinct ideas in the mind as those of the greatest distance or contrariety. For the idea of two is as distinct from that of one, as blueness from heat, or either of them from any number: and yet it is made up only of that simple idea of an unit repeated; and repetitions of this kind joined together make those distinct simple modes, of a dozen, a gross, a million.

---

[1] ' *More* compounded' suggests that, *from the first*, experience implies some degree of complexity in the ideas of which it consists.

[2] The mind accordingly 'finds' complex ideas *made for it* in things existing, which are perceived as qualities united in substances, accompanied always by ideas of 'existence' and 'power'—all obscurely present even in our early sense perceptions.

[3] That is, they are either made *by* or *for* the individual mind.

2. I shall begin with the simple idea of *space*[1]. I have
showed above, chap. 4, that we get[2] the idea of space, both
by our sight and touch[3]; which, I think, is so evident, that it
would be as needless to go to prove that men perceive, by
their sight, a distance between bodies of different colours, or
between the parts of the same body, as that they see colours
themselves[4]: nor is it less obvious, that they can do so in
the dark by feeling and touch.

[1] The idea of the immensity of space, and also our mathematical ideas of space relations, might seem too remote from the simple phenomena of sense to be explained by them. In what follows, Locke tries to meet this objection, and treats our ideas of the modes of space as crucial instances, in verification of his theory of the dependence of all our ideas on experience. If the simple phenomena of extension, presented in the senses, can give rise to the idea of boundless space, *a fortiori* the sublimest ideas of which man is conscious may depend in like manner upon data of sense.

In this and the four following chapters, Locke tries to reconcile our idea of the *Infinite in Quantity*—as in space, duration, and number—with his theory of the necessary dependence of all our ideas upon the exercise of our faculties in experience.

[2] 'get,' i.e. dependently on perceptions of sight or touch, in the order of time, and thus of history; but not therefore in the order of reason, according to which space is necessarily 'suggested' by, and thus 'innate' in, those sense perceptions. 'Getting an idea' is, with Locke, *becoming percipient of an attribute for the first time*; and demands a history of the circumstances in which the consciousness has arisen, and had its natural 'origin'—the history of the rise of an idea superseding in the *Essay* that critical analysis of its ultimate constitution which

may reveal other elements than the merely sensuous phenomena in which it arose.

[3] To regard space moreover as a datum of *touch*, Cousin argues, is to identify space and body. This he alleges that Locke accordingly does, or at least is logically bound to do, and so to make the idea of immensity that of body *indefinitely* enlarged. Locke does not ask whether the perce ptionof space is exclusively tactual and visual, or whether it is not more or less occasioned by, and so implied in, *every* organic sensation; also whether the idea of extension given in seeing is identical with, or different in kind from that given in touch; and whether in 'touch' it is given chiefly in the sense of simple contact (touch proper), or in the muscular sense.

[4] This means that some perception of extension is *necessarily* given in perception of colour—at least a vague superficial extension; for the question about *distance outwards in the line of sight*, afterwards discussed by Berkeley, is hardly raised by Locke. Body, according to him, immediately reveals itself, in its chief primary quality of extension, through both sight and touch. Berkeley, on the other hand, concludes that space proper is not, as Locke held, both seen and felt, but is only felt; and the idea is thus ultimately resolved into the succession of tactual sensations. *Touch* is made the *only* original occasion of the idea of *room*, which is supposed to be gradually attached to

3. This space, considered barely in length between any two beings, without considering anything else between them, is called *distance*: if considered in length, breadth, and thickness, I think it may be called *capacity*. [¹ The term *extension* is usually applied to it in what manner soever considered.]

4. Each different distance is a different modification of space; and each idea of any different distance, or space, is a *simple mode* of this idea. [² Men, for the use and by the custom of measuring, settle in their minds the ideas of certain stated lengths,—such as are an inch, foot, yard, fathom, mile, diameter of the earth, &c., which are so many distinct ideas made up only of space. When any such stated lengths or measures of space are made familiar to men's thoughts, they] can, in their minds, repeat them as often as they will, without mixing or joining to them the idea of body, or anything else; and frame to themselves the ideas of long, square, or cubic feet, yards or fathoms, here amongst the bodies of the universe, or else beyond the utmost bounds of all bodies; and, by adding these still one to another, enlarge their ideas of space as much as they please. The power of repeating or doubling any idea we have of any distance, and adding it to the former as often as we will, without being ever able to come to any stop or

---

the original data of the other senses, as a 'suggestion' of recollected experience;—in antithesis to the opposite extreme view, which finds the idea vaguely involved in *every organic sensation*, as the germ of its objective constitution. Objectivity, however, is not necessarily *spacial*, and must not be confused with the sense or idea of space.

¹ Here the first three editions read thus:—'When considered between the extremities of matter, which fills the capacity of space with something solid, tangible, and moveable, it is properly called *extension*. And so extension is an idea belonging to body only; but space may, as is evident, be con-

sidered without it. At least I think it most intelligible, and the best way to avoid confusion, if we use the word extension for an affection of matter, or the distance of the extremities of particular solid bodies; and space in the more general signification, for distance, with or without solid matter possessing it.'

² The first edition here reads as follows:—'Men having, by accustoming themselves to stated lengths of space, which they use for measuring of other distances—as a foot, a yard, or a fathom, a league, or diameter of the earth—made those ideas familiar to their thoughts, can,' &c.

stint, let us enlarge it as much as we will, is that which gives us the idea of *immensity*[1].

5. There is another modification of this idea, which is nothing but the relation which the parts of the termination of extension, or circumscribed space, have amongst themselves. This the touch discovers in sensible bodies, whose extremities come within our reach; and the eye takes both from bodies and colours, whose boundaries are within its view: where, observing how the extremities terminate,—either in straight lines which meet at discernible angles, or in crooked lines wherein no angles can be perceived; by considering these as they relate to one another, in all parts of the extremities of any body or space, it has that idea we call *figure*, which affords to the mind infinite variety[2]. For, besides the vast number of different figures that do really exist in the coherent masses of matter, the stock that the mind has in its power, by varying the idea of space, and thereby making still new compositions, by repeating its own ideas, and joining them as it pleases, is perfectly inexhaustible. And so it can multiply figures *in infinitum*.

6. For the mind having a power to repeat the idea of any length directly stretched out, and join it to another in the same direction, which is to double the length of that straight line; or else join another with what inclination it thinks fit, and so make what sort of angle it pleases: and being able also to shorten any line it imagines, by taking from it one half, one fourth, or what part it pleases, without being able to come to an end of any such divisions, it can make an angle of any bigness. So also the lines that are its sides, of what length

[1] The idea of *immensity* cannot be a *contingent* datum of sense, if it implies *intellectual obligation to add without limit*. The senses present only what is actually seen or felt, and this is always a finite phenomenon; the obligation to add without limit must come from another source, although without data of sense there can be no perception of the obligation.

[2] 'Immensity' is the term which stands for the mysterious infinite, as suggested by the phenomenon of extension; the ideas of figure and place are finite and positive. Is the mysterious infinite, in its aspect of 'immensity,' properly regarded as only one of the 'modes' of the sensuous idea of space? Particular spaces end, but we cannot think of immensity as ending. Our only positive idea of it is that of *inevitable progress*; but there can be no mental image of the infinity towards which the mind thus tends.

it pleases, which joining again to other lines, of different lengths, and at different angles, till it has wholly enclosed any space, it is evident that it can multiply figures, both in their shape and capacity, *in infinitum* ; all which are but so many different simple modes of space.

The same that it can do with straight lines, it can also do with crooked, or crooked and straight together ; and the same it can do in lines, it can also in superficies ; by which we may be led into farther thoughts of the endless variety of figures that the mind has a power to make, and thereby to multiply the simple modes of space.

Place.

7. Another idea coming under this head, and belonging to this tribe, is that we call *place*[1]. As in simple space, we consider the relation of distance between any two bodies or points ; so in our idea of place, we consider the relation of distance betwixt anything, and any two or more points, which are considered as keeping the same distance one with another, and so considered as at rest. For when we find anything at the same distance now which it was yesterday, from any two or more points, which have not since changed their distance one with another, and with which we then compared it, we say it hath kept the same place : but if it hath sensibly altered its distance with either of those points, we say it hath changed its place : though, vulgarly speaking, in the common notion of place, we do not always exactly observe the distance from these precise points, but from larger portions of sensible objects, to which we consider the thing placed to bear relation, and its distance from which we have some reason to observe[2].

---

[1] The history of the gradual evolution in sense of the idea of locality, and of the localisation of our sensations, is now ascertained with a scientific detail beside which Locke's observations seem meagre and commonplace.

[2] 'No single *quale* of sensation can, by itself, amount to a consciousness of *position*. Suppose no feeling but that of a point ever to be awakened, could that possibly be the feeling of any special *whereness* or *thereness*? Certainly not. *Only when a second point* is felt to arise can the first one acquire a determination up or down, right or left ; and these determinations are all relative to that second point. Each point, so far as it is *placed, is* then only by virtue of what it *is not*, namely, by virtue of another point. This is as much as to say that position has nothing *intrinsic* about it ; and that, although a feeling of *absolute bigness* may, *a feeling of place cannot possibly form an immanent element in any single isolated sensation.*' (James, *Psychology*, vol. ii. p. 154.)

8. Thus, a company of chess-men, standing on the same
squares of the chess-board where we left them, we say they are
all in the *same* place, or unmoved, though perhaps the chess-
board hath been in the mean time carried out of one room into
another ; because we compared them only to the parts of the
chess-board, which keep the same distance one with another.
The chess-board, we also say, is in the same place it was, if it
remain in the same part of the cabin, though perhaps the ship
which it is in sails all the while. And the ship is said to be
in the same place, supposing it kept the same distance with
the parts of the neighbouring land ; though perhaps the earth
hath turned round, and so both chess-men, and board, and
ship, have every one changed place, in respect of remoter
bodies, which have kept the same distance one with another.
But yet the distance from certain parts of the board being
that which determines the place of the chess-men ; and the
distance from the fixed parts of the cabin (with which we
made the comparison) being that which determined the place
of the chess-board ; and the fixed parts of the earth that by
which we determined the place of the ship,—these things
may be said to be in the same place in those respects :
though their distance from some other things, which in
this matter we did not consider, being varied, they have undoubtedly changed place in that respect ; and we ourselves
shall think so, when we have occasion to compare them with
those other.

9. But this modification of distance we call place, being
made by men for their common use, that by it they might
be able to design the particular position of things, where
they had occasion for such designation ; men consider and
determine of this place by reference to those adjacent things
which best served to their present purpose, without considering other things which, to another purpose, would
better determine the place of the same thing. Thus in the
chess-board, the use of the designation of the place of each
chess-man being determined only within that chequered
piece of wood, it would cross that purpose to measure it by
anything else ; but when these very chess-men are put up in
a bag, if any one should ask where the black king is, it

would be proper to determine the place by the part of the room it was in, and not by the chess-board; there being another use of designing the place it is now in, than when in play it was on the chess-board, and so must be determined by other bodies. So if any one should ask, in what place are the verses which report the story of Nisus and Euryalus, it would be very improper to determine this place, by saying, they were in such a part of the earth, or in Bodley's library: but the right designation of the place would be by the parts of Virgil's works; and the proper answer would be, that these verses were about the middle of the ninth book of his Æneids[1], and that they have been always constantly in the same place ever since Virgil was printed: which is true, though the book itself hath moved a thousand times, the use of the idea of place here being, to know in what part of the book that story is, that so, upon occasion, we may know where to find it, and have recourse to it for use.

Place of the universe.

10. That our idea of place is nothing else but such a relative position of anything as I have before mentioned, I think is plain, and will be easily admitted, when we consider that we can have no idea of the place of the universe, though we can of all the parts of it; because beyond that we have not the idea of any fixed, distinct, particular beings, in reference to which we can imagine it to have any relation of distance; but all beyond it is one uniform space or expansion, wherein the mind finds no variety, no marks. For to say that the world is somewhere, means no more than that it does exist; this, though a phrase borrowed from place, signifying only its existence, not location: and when one can find out, and frame in his mind, clearly and distinctly, the place of the universe, he will be able to tell us whether it moves or stands still in the undistinguishable inane of infinite space: though it be true that the word place has sometimes a more confused sense[2], and stands for that space which anybody takes up; and so the universe is in a place.

---

[1] Bk. iv, lines 176–502.

[2] An absolute meaning is then given to a term properly relative; for 'place' with Locke is relation to bodies external to the place itself. But to identify absolutely the *existence of the*

The idea, therefore, of place we have by the same means that we get the idea of space, (whereof this is but a particular limited consideration,) viz. by our sight and touch; by either of which we receive into our minds the ideas of extension or distance [1].

11. There are some that would persuade us, that body and extension are the same thing [2], who either change the signification of words, which I would not suspect them of,—they having so severely condemned the philosophy of others, because it hath been too much placed in the uncertain meaning, or deceitful obscurity of doubtful or insignificant terms. If, therefore, they mean by body and extension the same that other people do, viz. by *body* something that is solid and extended, whose parts are separable and movable different ways; and by *extension,* only the space that lies between the extremities of those solid coherent parts, and which is possessed by them,—they confound very different ideas one with another; for I appeal to every man's own thoughts, whether the idea of space be not as distinct from that of solidity, as it is from the idea of scarlet colour?

universe in place with *its bare existence* would be to identify space and body, which Locke refuses to do.

[1] When thus defining our perceptions of distance, figure, place, and other space relations, Locke fails to investigate in detail the *physical conditions* through which our originally vague idea of space or room is transformed into the spacial universe, in the manifold relations under which adults contemplate the world of the senses—an inquiry which has since led to interesting results in physiological psychology.

[2] The Cartesians (thus referred to) regarded *extension* as the *essence* of matter. Locke insists on the antithesis between our idea of body and our idea of space; but he fails to represent adequately the distinctive characteristics of the idea of space; or to show how, even under his own inadequate account of the idea, it can

be regarded as an empirical datum of sense. It must be remembered, however, that, in his 'historical plain method,' he is looking only to the rise of the idea of space, *as an event in the history of the conscious life of man,* and to the sensuous phenomena in combination with which it arises. These he finds in sight and touch, without using which we could not have our idea of space. That the risen idea includes what was neither seen nor touched, is hardly recognised. His method makes him apt to overlook the spiritual activity of intellect, and direct attention exclusively to the phenomena supplied by experience, with their organic accompaniments under the present constitution of things. Physical coexistences and sequences, not their universal and necessary, i. e. metaphysical, presuppositions, recommend themselves to him in this regard.

It is true, solidity[1] cannot exist without extension, neither can scarlet colour exist without extension[2], but this hinders not, but that they are distinct ideas. Many ideas require others, as necessary to their existence or conception[3], which yet are very distinct ideas. Motion can neither be, nor be conceived, without space; and yet motion is not space, nor space motion; space can exist without it, and they are very distinct ideas; and so, I think, are those of space and solidity. Solidity[4] is so inseparable an idea from body, that upon that depends its filling of space, its contact, impulse, and communication of motion upon impulse. And if it be a reason to prove that spirit is different from body, because thinking includes not the idea of extension in it ; the same reason will be as valid, I suppose, to prove that space is not body, because it includes not the idea of solidity in it ; *space* and *solidity* being as distinct ideas as *thinking* and *extension,* and as wholly separable in the mind one from another. Body then and extension, it is evident, are two distinct ideas. For,

Extension not solidity.

12. First, Extension includes no solidity, nor resistance to the motion of body, as body does.

The parts of space inseparable, both really and mentally.

13. Secondly, The parts of pure space are inseparable one from the other ; so that the continuity cannot be separated, neither really nor mentally. For I demand of any one to remove any part of it from another, with which it is continued, even so much as in thought. To divide and separate actually is, as I think, by removing the parts one from another, to make two superficies, where before there was a continuity : and to divide mentally is, to make in the mind two superficies, where before there was a continuity, and consider them as removed one from the other ; which can only

---

[1] A solid is that which fills or occupies a space that is extended in three dimensions; and that is physically impenetrable, or incapable of being transformed by pressure or otherwise, from an extended into an unextended being.

[2] Does not this imply that extension is *necessarily given* in all sensuous perception of colour ?

[3] This concession might have led Locke to a fuller recognition of metaphysical priority of ideas in reason (*origo*), as distinguished from their merely ' historical ' priority (*exordium*) in the individual consciousness.

[4] Cf. Bk. II. ch. iv.

be done in things considered by the mind as capable of being separated; and by separation, of acquiring new distinct superficies, which they then have not, but are capable of. But neither of these ways of separation, whether real or mental, is, as I think, compatible to pure space [1].

It is true, a man may consider so much of such a space as is answerable or commensurate to a foot, without considering the rest, which is, indeed, a partial consideration, but not so much as mental separation or division; since a man can no more mentally divide, without considering two superficies separate one from the other, than he can actually divide, without making two superficies disjoined one from the other: but a partial consideration is not separating. A man may consider light in the sun without its heat, or mobility in body without its extension, without thinking of their separation. One is only a partial consideration, terminating in one alone; and the other is a consideration of both, as existing separately.

14. Thirdly, The parts of pure space are immovable, which follows from their inseparability; motion being nothing but change of distance between any two things; but this cannot be between parts that are inseparable, which, therefore, must needs be at perpetual rest one amongst another. *The parts of space immovable.*

Thus the determined idea of simple space distinguishes it plainly and sufficiently from body; since its parts are inseparable, immovable, and without resistance to the motion of body [2].

---

[1] 'Infinites are composed of finites in no other sense than as finites are composed of infinitesimals. Parts, in the corporeal sense of the word, are separable, compounded, ununited, independent on, and moveable from each other. But infinite space, though it may by us be *partially* apprehended, i. e. may in our imagination be conceived as composed of *parts*; yet those parts (improperly so called) being essentially indiscerptible, and immoveable from each other, and not partable without an express contradiction in terms.

Space is consequently in itself essentially one, and absolutely indivisible.' (Clarke to Leibniz, *Collection of Papers*, p. 131.) So too Spinoza. Cf. *Ethica*, Schol. Prop. xv. Pars i.

[2] The *necessary* 'continuity' of space implies its necessarily illimitable character—that beyond any occupied space there *must* still be room for more, which room is thus necessarily inexhaustible. We can imagine an end of body, but not of space, i. e. of potential room for more bodies. We can form a sensuous image of a body; space

BOOK II.

CHAP. XIII.

The Definition of Extension explains it not.

15. If any one ask me *what* this space I speak of *is*, I will tell him when he tells me what his extension is[1]. For to say, as is usually done, that extension is to have *partes extra partes*, is to say only, that extension is extension. For what am I the better informed in the nature of extension, when I am told that extension is to have parts that are extended, exterior to parts that are extended, i. e. extension consists of extended parts[2]? As if one, asking what a fibre was, I should answer him,—that it was a thing made up of several fibres. Would he thereby be enabled to understand what a fibre was better than he did before? Or rather, would he not have reason to think that my design was to make sport with him, rather than seriously to instruct him?

Division of Beings into Bodies and Spirits proves not Space and Body the same.

16. Those who contend that space and body are the same, bring this dilemma :—either this space is something or nothing ; if nothing be between two bodies, they must necessarily touch ; if it be allowed to be something, they ask, Whether it be body or spirit ? To which I answer by another question, Who told them that there was, or could be, nothing but *solid beings, which could not think*, and *thinking beings that were not extended* ?—which is all they mean by the terms *body* and *spirit.*

Substance, which we know not, no Proof against Space without Body.

17. If it be demanded (as usually it is) whether this space, void of body, be *substance* or *accident,* I shall readily answer I know not ; nor shall be ashamed to own my ignorance, till they that ask show me a clear distinct idea of substance.

Different meanings

18. I endeavour as much as I can to deliver myself from those fallacies which we are apt to put upon ourselves, by taking words for things[3]. It helps not our ignorance to feign

---

per se is unimaginable. Locke's history of the experience in which the idea rises fails to show how, *when arisen,* it must be *so* constituted.

[1] In §§ 15–20 the ontological question about space arises—whether it is matter, spirit, or neither ; whether it is nothing or something, and if something, a substance or an attribute ; whether it is absolutely independent or dependent upon God. This introduces the idea of 'substance' (§§ 17–

20), already referred to in Bk. I. ch. iii. § 18, of which Locke makes light, regarding it as of little use, while Leibniz believes that it is 'a point in philosophy of the greatest importance.' (*Nouv. Essais.*)

[2] He has already said (§ 3) that by ' extension ' he means ' space in whatever manner considered.'

[3] It must never be forgotten that the deliverance of the human mind from the bondage of empty and ambiguous

a knowledge where we have none, by making a noise with
sounds, without clear and distinct significations. Names
made at pleasure, neither alter the nature of things, nor make
us understand them, but as they are signs of and stand for
determined[1] ideas. And I desire those who lay so much
stress on the sound of these two syllables, *substance*, to consider whether applying it, as they do, to the infinite, incomprehensible God, to finite spirits, and to body, it be in the same
sense ; and whether it stands for the same idea, when each of
those three so different beings are called substances. If so,
whether it will thence follow—that God, spirits, and body,
agreeing in the same common nature of substance, differ not
any otherwise than in a bare different *modification* of that
substance ; as a tree and a pebble, being in the same sense
body, and agreeing in the common nature of body, differ only
in a bare modification of that common matter, which will be
a very harsh doctrine[2]. If they say, that they apply it to God,
finite spirit, and matter, in three different significations and
that it stands for one idea when God is said to be a substance ;
for another when the soul is called substance ; and for a third
when body is called so ;—if the name substance stands for
three several distinct ideas, they would do well to make known
those distinct ideas, or at least to give three distinct names
to them, to prevent in so important a notion the confusion
and errors that will naturally follow from the promiscuous use
of so doubtful a term ; which is so far from being suspected to
have three distinct, that in ordinary use it has scarce one
clear distinct signification. And if they can thus make three

---

metaphysical words was one of Locke's
chief motives to the inquiry in which
he engaged in the *Essay*.

[1] 'clear and distinct'—in first three
editions.

[2] Spinoza, as well as Descartes,
was probably here in Locke's view.
According to the definition of Substance in the *Ethica*, only one substance is possible, and all things
and persons must be conceived as its
modifications. The one substance is
Spinoza's 'God.' 'Praeter Deum nulla

dari neque concipi potest substantia.'
(*Ethica*, Prop. xiv.) Locke's idea of
God, as the human spirit magnified to
infinity—one spirit among many, yet
supreme—leads him here to alter this so
far as to speak of God as a 'modification' of the one substance which underlies them all. Spinoza does not think of
God as Creator or cause of things and
persons, or as working towards ends,
in the way Locke does. The Spino-
zistic *unica substantia* is the intellectual
presupposition of all that exists—the

BOOK II.

CHAP. XIII.

Substance
and acci-
dents of
little use
in Philo-
sophy.

distinct ideas of substance, what hinders why another may not make a fourth [1]?

19. They who first ran into the notion of *accidents,* as a sort of real beings that needed something to inhere in, were forced to find out the word *substance* to support them. Had the poor Indian philosopher (who imagined that the earth also wanted something to bear it up) but thought of this word substance, he needed not to have been at the trouble to find an elephant to support it, and a tortoise to support his elephant : the word substance would have done it effectually. And he that inquired might have taken it for as good an answer from an Indian philosopher,—that substance, without knowing what it is, is that which supports the earth, as we take it for a sufficient answer and good doctrine from our European philosophers, — that substance, without knowing what it is, is that which supports accidents. So that of substance, we have no idea of what it is, but only a confused, obscure one of what it does [2].

20. Whatever a learned man may do here, an intelligent American, who inquired into the nature of things, would scarce take it for a satisfactory account, if, desiring to learn our architecture, he should be told that a pillar is a thing supported by a basis, and a basis something that supported a pillar. Would he not think himself mocked, instead of taught, with such an account as this? And a stranger to them would be very liberally instructed in the nature of books, and the things they contained, if he should be told that all learned books consisted of paper and letters, and that

conception in which all true conceptions of things and persons are logically contained, and from which they may be deduced with mathematical rigour, even as the relations of triangles and circles may be logically found in the space which contains them. For Descartes, cf. *Principles,* Part i. Prop. 51–54, where Locke's question about the meanings of ' substance ' is raised.

[1] So far from regarding *space* as a fourth substance, Locke, in the manuscripts which record his thoughts when he was preparing the *Essay,*

suggests that ' space in itself seems to be nothing but a capacity or possibility for *extended* being to exist, *which we are apt to conceive infinite, because there is in nothing no substance.* That space cannot be perceived apart from body was the argument against a vacuum.

[2] ' Here Locke himself banters the idea of substance in *matter.*' (Berkeley, *C. Pl. B.* p. 473.) But it is substance in mind, as well as in matter, that is here in question and misconceived.

letters were things inhering in paper, and paper a thing that
held forth letters: a notable way of having clear ideas of
letters and paper. But were the Latin words, *inhaerentia*
and *substantio*, put into the plain English ones that answer
them, and were called *sticking on* and *under-propping*, they
would better discover to us the very great clearness there is
in the doctrine of substance and accidents, and show of what
use they are in deciding of questions in philosophy.

21. But to return to our idea of space. If body be not
supposed infinite, (which I think no one will affirm,) I would
ask, whether, if God placed a man at the extremity of corporeal beings[1], he could not stretch his hand beyond his
body? If he could, then he would put his arm where there
was before space without body; and if there he spread his
fingers, there would still be space between them without body.
If he could not stretch out his hand, it must be because of
some external hindrance; (for we suppose him alive, with
such a power of moving the parts of his body that he hath
now, which is not in itself impossible, if God so pleased to
have it; or at least it is not impossible for God so to move
him:) and then I ask,—whether that which hinders his hand
from moving outwards be substance or accident, something or
nothing? And when they have resolved that, they will be
able to resolve themselves,—what that is, which is or may be
between two bodies at a distance, that is not body, and has
no solidity. In the mean time, the argument is at least as
good, that, where nothing hinders, (as beyond the utmost
bounds of all bodies,) a body put in motion may move on, as
where there is nothing between, there two bodies must
necessarily touch. For pure space between is sufficient to
take away the necessity of mutual contact; but bare space in

[1] Although body is not continuous like space,—inasmuch as we find intervals of empty space which make motion possible—have we any right to assume that there is a point in the material universe at which, if a man were placed on it, he would be 'at the extremity even of corporeal beings,' thus separated? Is there need to suppose any 'extremity,' or that the universe of bodies is in this respect finite; or even that they are not ever-lasting, although, through all their metamorphoses, everlastingly subject to divine law, and charged with divine purpose?

the way is not sufficient to stop motion. The truth is, these men must either own that they think body infinite, though they are loth to speak it out, or else affirm that space is not body. For I would fain meet with that thinking man that can in his thoughts set any bounds to space, more than he can to duration ; or by thinking hope to arrive at the end of either. And therefore, if his idea of eternity be infinite, so is his idea of immensity ; they are both finite or infinite alike.

22. Farther, those who assert the impossibility of space existing without matter, must not only make body infinite, but must also deny a power in God to annihilate any part of matter. No one, I suppose, will deny that God can put an end to all motion that is in matter, and fix all the bodies of the universe in a perfect quiet and rest, and continue them so long as he pleases. Whoever then will allow that God can, during such a general rest, *annihilate* either this book or the body of him that reads it, must necessarily admit the possibility of a vacuum. For, it is evident that the space that was filled by the parts of the annihilated body will still remain, and be a space without body. For the circumambient bodies being in perfect rest, are a wall of adamant, and in that state make it a perfect impossibility for any other body to get into that space. And indeed the necessary motion of one particle of matter into the place from whence another particle of matter is removed, is but a consequence from the supposition of plenitude ; which will therefore need some better proof than a supposed matter of fact, which experiment can never make out ;—our own clear and distinct ideas plainly satisfying us, that there is no necessary connexion between space and solidity, since we can conceive the one without the other. And those who dispute for or against a vacuum, do thereby confess they have distinct *ideas* of vacuum and plenum, i. e. that they have an idea of extension void of solidity, though they deny its *existence* ; or else they dispute about nothing at all. For they who so much alter the signification of words, as to call extension body, and consequently make the whole essence of body to be nothing but pure extension without solidity, must talk absurdly whenever they speak of *vacuum* ; since it is impossible for extension to be without extension.

For *vacuum*, whether we affirm or deny its existence, signifies space without body; whose very existence no one can deny to be possible, who will not make matter infinite, and take from God a power to annihilate any particle of it [1].

23. But not to go so far as beyond the utmost bounds of body in the universe, nor appeal to God's omnipotency to find a *vacuum*, the motion of bodies that are in our view and neighbourhood seems to me plainly to evince it. For I desire any one so to divide a solid body, of any dimension he pleases, as to make it possible for the solid parts to move up and down freely every way within the bounds of that superficies, if there be not left in it a void space as big as the least part into which he has divided the said solid body. And if, where the least particle of the body divided is as big as a mustard-seed, a void space equal to the bulk of a mustard-seed be requisite to make room for the free motion of the parts of the divided body within the bounds of its superficies, where the particles of matter are 100,000,000 less than a mustard-seed, there must also be a space void of solid matter as big as 100,000,000 part of a mustard-seed; for if it hold in the one it will hold in the other, and so on *in infinitum*. And let this void space be as little as it will, it destroys the hypothesis of plenitude. For if there can be a space void of body equal to the smallest separate particle of matter now existing in nature, it is still space without body; and makes as great a difference between space and body as if it were μέγα χάσμα, a distance as wide as any in nature. And therefore, if we suppose not the void space necessary to motion equal to the least parcel of the divided solid matter, but to $\frac{1}{10}$ or $\frac{1}{1000}$ of it, the same consequence will always follow of space without matter.

Motion proves a Vacuum.

24. But the question being here,—Whether the idea of space or extension be the same with the idea of body? it is not necessary to prove the real existence of a *vacuum*, but the

The Ideas of Space and Body distinct.

[1] '*Vacuum*, sive *inane*, tribus modis dicitur. 1mo in quo non est conspicuum corpus. . . . 2do in quo non est solidum corpus. . . . 3^{tio} in quo nullum omnino est corpus, ut tenent Epicurei. . . . Cartesiani nec dari actu, neque etiam dari posse vacuum, ex eo probant, quod ubicunque ponitur extensio, necessario concipi debet corpus; quia ratio essentialis corporis in extensione sita est: at in spatio vacuo ponitur extensio, ergo et corpus.' (Chauvini, *Lexicon.*)

idea of it; which it is plain men have when they inquire and dispute whether there be a *vacuum* or no. For if they had not the idea of space without body, they could not make a question about its existence: and if their idea of body did not include in it something more than the bare idea of space, they could have no doubt about the plenitude of the world; and it would be as absurd to demand, whether there were space without body, as whether there were space without space, or body without body, since these were but different names of the same idea.

Extension being inseparable from Body, proves it not the same.
25. It is true, the idea of extension joins itself so inseparably with all visible, and most tangible qualities, that it suffers us to *see* no one, or *feel* very few external objects, without taking in impressions of extension too[1]. This readiness of extension to make itself be taken notice of so constantly with other ideas, has been the occasion, I guess, that some have made the whole essence of body to consist in extension; which is not much to be wondered at, since some have had their minds, by their eyes and touch, (the busiest of all our senses,) so filled with the idea of extension, and, as it were, wholly possessed with it, that they allowed no existence to anything that had not extension. I shall not now argue with those men, who take the measure and possibility of all being only from their narrow and gross imaginations: but having here to do only with those who conclude the essence of body to be extension, because they say they cannot imagine any sensible quality of any body without extension,—I shall desire them to consider, that, had they reflected on their ideas of tastes and smells as much as on those of sight and touch; nay, had they examined their ideas of hunger and thirst, and several other pains, they would have found that *they* included in them no idea of extension at all, which is but an affection of body, as well as the rest, discoverable by our senses, which are scarce acute enough to look into the pure essences of things.

[1] Does Locke mean here to distinguish between the visible and tangible extensions which happen to present themselves in sight and touch, and an idea of space necessarily 'suggested' by what is actually seen and touched, but which is itself neither seen nor touched?

26. If those ideas which are constantly joined to all others [1], BOOK II. must therefore be concluded to be the essence of those things which have constantly those ideas joined to them, and are inseparable from them ; then unity is without doubt the essence of everything. For there is not any object of sensation or reflection which does not carry with it the idea of one : but the weakness of this kind of argument we have already shown sufficiently.

CHAP. XIII.
Essences of things.

27. To conclude: whatever men shall think concerning the existence of a *vacuum,* this is plain to me—that we have as clear an idea of space distinct from solidity, as we have of solidity distinct from motion, or motion from space. We have not any two more distinct ideas ; and we can as easily conceive space without solidity, as we can conceive body or space without motion, though it be never so certain that neither body nor motion can exist without space. But whether any one will take space to be only a *relation* resulting from the existence of other beings at a distance ; or whether they will think the words of the most knowing King Solomon, 'The heaven, and the heaven of heavens, cannot contain thee;' or those more emphatical ones of the inspired philosopher St. Paul, 'In him we live, move, and have our being,' are to be understood in a literal sense, I leave every one to consider : only our idea of space is, I think, such as I have mentioned, and distinct from that of body. For, whether we consider, in matter itself, the distance of its coherent solid parts, and call it, in respect of those solid parts, extension; or whether, considering it as lying between the extremities of any body in its several dimensions, we call it length, breadth, and thickness [2] ; or else, considering it as lying between any two bodies or

Ideas of Space and Solidity distinct.

---

[1] Therefore no phenomenon, as presented in sensation or reflection, can be 'simple' although it may be afterwards abstracted by analysis, from the concrete experience. Our ideas are *necessarily complex,* if there are 'ideas which *must* be constantly joined to all others'; although their 'simple' elements may be considered separately afterwards. The necessary superaddition of elements not presented contingently in sense seems to be implied here, but without sufficient apprehension of its immense philosophical significance.

[2] Trinal space. We can *suppose* a space with more than three dimensions; but we cannot *imagine* space with another dimension than length, breadth, and thickness.

positive beings, without any consideration whether there be any matter or not between, we call it distance;—however named or considered, it is always the same uniform simple idea of space, taken from objects about which our senses have been conversant ; whereof, having settled ideas in our minds, we can revive, repeat, and add them one to another as often as we will, and consider the space or distance so imagined, either as filled with solid parts, so that another body cannot come there without displacing and thrusting out the body that was there before; or else as void of solidity, so that a body of equal dimensions to that empty or pure space may be placed in it, without the removing or expulsion of anything that was there. [[1] But, to avoid confusion in discourses concerning this matter, it were possibly to be wished that the name *extension* were applied only to matter, or the distance of the extremities of particular bodies ; and the term *expansion* to space in general, with or without solid matter possessing it,— so as to say space is expanded and body extended. But in this every one has his liberty : I propose·it only for the more clear and distinct way of speaking.]

Men differ little in clear, simple Ideas.

28. The knowing precisely what our words stand for, would, I imagine, in this as well as a great many other cases, quickly end the dispute. For I am apt to think that men, when they come to examine them, find their simple ideas all generally to agree, though in discourse with one another they perhaps confound one another with different names. I imagine that men who abstract their thoughts, and do well examine the ideas of their own minds, cannot much differ in thinking; however they may perplex themselves with words, according to the way of speaking of the several schools or sects they have been bred up in: though amongst unthinking men, who examine not scrupulously and carefully their own ideas, and strip them not from the marks men use for them, but confound them with words, there must be endless dispute, wrangling, and jargon ; especially if they be learned, bookish men, devoted to some sect, and accustomed to the language of it, and have learned

---

[1] Added in *fourth* edition. Locke does not always keep to these definitions.

to talk after others. But if it should happen that any two thinking men should really have different ideas, I do not see how they could discourse or argue one with another. Here I must not be mistaken, to think that every floating imagination in men's brains is presently of that sort of ideas I speak of. It is not easy for the mind to put off those confused notions and prejudices it has imbibed from custom, inadvertency, and common conversation. It requires pains and assiduity to examine its ideas, till it resolves them into those clear and distinct simple ones, out of which they are compounded ; and to see which, amongst its simple ones, have or have not a *necessary* connexion and dependence one upon another[1]. Till a man doth this in the primary and original notions of things, he builds upon floating and uncertain principles, and will often find himself at a loss[2].

[1] Reaction against the abuse of words, also against *a priori* assumptions and the authority of books, here again finds expression. Locke is sparing of quotations, and refuses to rest conclusions upon an array of authorities. The last sentence again implies that, among our 'simple ideas' some are 'necessarily connected' together, so that they *must* rise in consciousness in complexity. In concrete experience our ideas are so complex that it requires pains to resolve them into those simple ones of which the compound consists.

[2] Locke here expresses, more emphatically than is common with him, the metaphysical craving for a *foundation* of *absolute* certainty in knowledge and in action ; not merely one of the highest attainable probability, in which he is often disposed to leave men to exercise their judgment among the facts which happen to be presented in their experience.

CHAPTER XIV.

IDEA OF DURATION AND ITS SIMPLE MODES.

1. THERE is another sort of distance, or length, the idea whereof we get not from the permanent parts of space, but from the fleeting and perpetually perishing parts of succession. This we call *duration*; the simple modes whereof are any different lengths of it whereof we have distinct ideas, as *hours, days, years,* &c., *time* and *eternity*.

Its Idea
from Re-
flection on
the Train
of our
Ideas.

2. The answer of a great man [1], to one who asked what time was: *Si non rogas intelligo,* (which amounts to this; The more I set myself to think of it, the less I understand it,) might perhaps persuade one that time, which reveals all other things, is itself not to be discovered. Duration, time, and eternity, are, not without reason, thought to have something very abstruse in their nature. But however remote these may seem from our comprehension, yet if we trace them right to their originals, I doubt not but one of those sources of all our knowledge, viz. sensation and reflection, will be able to furnish us with these ideas, as clear and distinct as many others which are thought much less obscure; and we shall find that the idea of eternity itself is derived from the same common original [2] with the rest of our ideas.

---

[1] St. Augustine. Duration is a simple and unique, therefore an undefinable idea. We may ascertain the history of its appearance in consciousness, but we cannot analyse it after it has appeared.

[2] The phenomenal antecedents, not the function in intelligence, and necessary inadequacy in a human understanding, of the idea of eternity, is here in Locke's view. A natural explanation of the supernatural, rather than a supernatural explanation of the natural, is what his method inclines to.

3. To understand *time* and *eternity* aright, we ought with attention to consider what idea it is we have of *duration,* and how we came by it. It is evident to any one who will but observe what passes in his own mind, that there is a train of ideas which constantly succeed one another in his understanding, as long as he is awake. Reflection on these appearances of several ideas one after another in our minds, is that which furnishes us with the idea of *succession*[1]: and the distance between any parts of that succession, or between the appearance of any two ideas in our minds, is that we call *duration*[2]. For whilst we are thinking, or whilst we receive successively several ideas in our minds, we know that we do exist ; and so we call the existence, or the continuation of the existence of ourselves, or anything else, commensurate to the succession of any ideas in our minds, the duration of ourselves, or any such other thing co-existent with our thinking.

4. That we have our notion of succession and duration from this original, viz. from reflection on the train of ideas, which we find to appear one after another in our own minds, seems plain to me, in that we have no perception of duration but by considering the train of ideas that take their turns in our understandings. When that succession of ideas ceases, our perception of duration ceases with it; which every one clearly experiments in himself, whilst he sleeps soundly, whether an hour or a day, a month or a year ; of which duration of things, while he sleeps or thinks not, he has no perception at all, but it is quite lost to him ; and the moment wherein he leaves off to think, till the moment he begins to think again, seems to him to have no distance. And so I doubt not it would be to a waking man, if it were possible for him to keep *only one* idea in his mind, without variation and the succession of others[2]. And we see, that one who fixes

[1] Succession, in which the idea of duration is necessarily contained, is, according to Locke, an idea which accompanies every other idea, as all our ideas are changing. Duration is therefore presupposed, as the condition of our apprehension of phenomena presented in experience. This apprehension of succession or change implies memory.

[2] 'Nothing is more certain than that every elementary part of duration

his thoughts very intently on one thing, so as to take but little notice of the succession of ideas that pass in his mind, whilst he is taken up with that earnest contemplation, lets slip out of his account a good part of that duration, and thinks that time shorter than it is. But if sleep commonly unites the distant parts of duration, it is because during that time we have no succession of ideas in our minds. For if a man, during his sleep, dreams, and variety of ideas make themselves perceptible in his mind one after another, he hath then, during such dreaming, a sense of duration, and of the length of it. By which it is to me very clear, that men derive their ideas of duration from their reflections on the train of the ideas they observe to succeed one another in their own understandings; without which observation they can have no notion of duration, whatever may happen in the world [1].

The Idea of Duration applicable to Things whilst we sleep.

5. Indeed a man having, from reflecting on the succession and number of his own thoughts, got the notion or idea of duration, he can apply that notion to things which exist while he does not think; as he that has got the idea of extension from bodies by his sight or touch, can apply it to distances, where no body is seen or felt. And therefore, though a man has no perception of the length of duration which passed whilst he slept or thought not; yet, having observed the revolution of days and nights, and found the length of their duration to be in appearance regular and

must have duration, as every elementary part of extension must have extension. Now, in these elements of duration, or single intervals of successive ideas, there is no succession of ideas; yet we must conceive *them* to have duration;—whence we may conclude with certainty that there is a conception of duration where there is no succession of ideas in the mind.' (Hamilton's *Reid*, pp. 348-9.) Reid looks, through analytic reflection, to the idea produced: Locke regards the natural history of its production. To suppose that a single idea should have

no duration, and yet that a multiplication of that no duration should have duration, seems, at Reid's point of view, as absurd as that the multiplication of nothing should produce something.

[1] *Pastness* and *futurity* must mean more than change in *my* ideas, as otherwise if I were to become unconscious, there would be no duration till conscious activity revived in *me*. Change of conscious state awakens the perception of duration in me, but the perception thus awakened involves more than the items of the change.

constant, he can, upon the supposition that that revolution
has proceeded after the same manner whilst he was asleep or thought not, as it used to do at other times, he can, I say, imagine and make allowance for the length of duration whilst he slept. But if Adam and Eve, (when they were alone in the world,) instead of their ordinary night's sleep, had passed the whole twenty-four hours in one continued sleep, the duration of that twenty-four hours had been irrecoverably lost to them, and been for ever left out of their account of time.

6. Thus by reflecting [1] on the appearing of various ideas one after another in our understandings, we get the notion of succession; which, if any one should think we did rather get from our observation of motion by our senses, he will perhaps be of my mind when he considers, that even motion The Idea of Succession not from Motion.

---

[1] If 'reflection' means consciousness of a *present* operation of mind, no *succession*, Reid remarks, can be an object either of immediate consciousness or of sense; '*because the operations of both are confined to the present point of time.*' Change could not be observed by the senses alone, without the aid of memory. 'Reflecting upon the train of ideas can be nothing but remembering it. Reflection here includes remembrance, without which there could be no reflection on what is past, and consequently no idea of succession.' (Hamilton's *Reid*, p. 343.) But is consciousness of an indivisible present impossible, wholly divorced from a past and a future? 'Let anyone try to notice or attend to the *present* moment of time. One of the most baffling experiences occurs. *Where is it, this present?* . . . It is in fact an altogether ideal abstraction, not only never realised in sense [external or internal], but probably never even conceived of by those unaccustomed to philosophic meditation. Reflection leads us to the conclusion that it *must* exist, but that it *does* exist can never be a fact of our immediate experience.

. . . The practically cognised present is no knife-edge, but a saddle-back with a certain breadth of its own, from which we look in two directions into time. The unit of composition of our perception of time is a *duration*—with a bow and a stern, as it were, a rear-ward and a forward-looking end. It is only as *parts* of this *duration-block* that the relation of *succession* of one end to the other is perceived. We do not first feel one end, and then feel the other after it, and from the perception of the succession infer an interval of time between, but we seem to feel the interval of time as a whole, with its two ends embedded in it. The experience is from the outset a synthetic datum, not a simple one; and to *sensible perception* its elements are inseparable, although attention, looking back, may easily decompose the experience, and distinguish its beginning from its end.' (James's *Psychology*, vol. i. pp. 608–10.) The present, which we recognise in our concrete experience is never the absolutely indivisible present of philosophical abstraction.

produces in his mind an idea of succession no otherwise than as it produces there a continued train of distinguishable ideas. For a man looking upon a body really moving, perceives yet no motion at all unless that motion produces a constant train of successive ideas: v. g. a man becalmed at sea, out of sight of land, in a fair day, may look on the sun, or sea, or ship, a whole hour together, and perceive no motion at all in either; though it be certain that two, and perhaps all of them, have moved during that time a great way. But as soon as he perceives either of them to have changed distance with some other body, as soon as this motion produces any new idea in him, then he perceives that there has been motion. But wherever a man is, with all things at rest about him, without perceiving any motion at all,—if during this hour of quiet he has been thinking, he will perceive the various ideas of his own thoughts in his own mind, appearing one after another, and thereby observe and find succession where he could observe no motion.

Very slow motions unperceived.

7. And this, I think, is the reason why motions very slow, though they are constant, are not perceived by us; because in their remove from one sensible part towards another, their change of distance is so slow, that it causes no new ideas in us, but a good while one after another. And so not causing a constant train of new ideas to follow one another immediately in our minds, we have no perception of motion; which consisting in a constant succession, we cannot perceive that succession without a constant succession of varying ideas arising from it.

Very swift motions unperceived.

8. On the contrary, things that move so swift as not to affect the senses distinctly with several distinguishable distances of their motion, and so cause not any train of ideas in the mind, are not also perceived. For anything that moves round about in a circle, in less times than our ideas are wont to succeed one another in our minds, is not perceived to move; but seems to be a perfect entire circle of that matter or colour, and not a part of a circle in motion [1].

---

[1] So when a duration is empty, or seems empty, because of the extreme slowness or the extreme swiftness of the changes, we can have no idea of that duration. It is familiar to us that the *apparent* length of a time is de-

9. Hence I leave it to others to judge, whether it be not probable that our ideas do, whilst we are awake, succeed one another in our minds at certain distances; not much unlike the images in the inside of a lantern, turned round by the heat of a candle. This appearance of theirs in train, though perhaps it may be sometimes faster and sometimes slower, yet, I guess [1], varies not very much in a waking man: there seem to be certain bounds to the quickness and slowness of the succession of those ideas one to another in our minds, beyond which they can neither delay nor hasten.

10. The reason I have for this odd conjecture is, from observing that, in the impressions made upon any of our senses, we can but to a certain degree perceive any succession; which, if exceeding quick, the sense of succession is lost, even in cases where it is evident that there is a real succession. Let a cannon-bullet pass through a room, and in its way take with it any limb, or fleshy parts of a man, it is as clear as any demonstration can be, that it must strike successively the two sides of the room: it is also evident, that it must touch one part of the flesh first, and another after, and so in succession: and yet, I believe, nobody who ever felt the pain of such a shot, or heard the blow against the two distant walls, could perceive any succession either in the pain or sound of so swift a stroke. Such a part of duration as this, wherein we perceive no succession, is that which we call an *instant*, and is that which takes up the time of only one idea in our minds, without the succession of another; wherein, therefore, we perceive no succession at all.

11. This also happens where the motion is so slow as not to supply a constant train of fresh ideas to the senses, as fast as the mind is capable of receiving new ones into it; and so other ideas of our own thoughts, having room to come into our minds between those offered to our senses by the moving body, there the sense of motion is lost; and the body, though

termined by the variety and interest of the phenomena which suggest the time, and thus as one grows older each period seems shorter in retrospect.

[1] ' guess '—used by Locke for ' conjecture ' in several places. (See ch. xiii. § 25.)

it really moves, yet, not changing perceivable distance with some other bodies as fast as the ideas of our own minds do naturally follow one another in train, the thing seems to stand still ; as is evident in the hands of clocks, and shadows of sun-dials, and other constant but slow motions, where, though, after certain intervals, we perceive, by the change of distance, that it hath moved, yet the motion itself we perceive not.

ThisTrain, the Measure of other Successions.

12. So that to me it seems, that the constant and regular succession of *ideas* in a waking man, is, as it were, the measure and standard of all other successions[1]. Whereof, if any one either exceeds the pace of our ideas, as where two sounds or pains, &c., take up in their succession the duration of but one idea ; or else where any motion or succession is so slow, as that it keeps not pace with the ideas in our minds, or the quickness in which they take their turns, as when any one or more ideas in their ordinary course come into our mind, between those which are offered to the sight by the different perceptible distances of a body in motion, or between sounds or smells following one another,—there also the sense of a constant continued succession is lost, and we perceive it not, but with certain gaps of rest between.

The Mind cannot fix long on one in-variable Idea.

13. If it be so, that the ideas of our minds, whilst we have any there, do constantly change and shift in a continual succession, it would be impossible, may any one say, for a man to think long of any one thing. By which, if it be meant that a man may have one self-same single idea a long time alone in his mind, without any variation at all, I think, in matter of fact, it is not possible. For which (not knowing how the ideas of our minds are framed, of what materials they are made, whence they have their light, and how they come to make their appearances)[2] I can give no other reason but

---

[1] We conceive duration as a relation that is in itself independent of that succession of our ideas by which it is awakened. The 'measure and stan-dard' of 'succession,' which Locke finds in each man's ideas, is not to be confused with 'motion,' the objective measure of duration, treated of in the sequel, out of which his idea of time (distinguished from duration) issues.

[2] This seems to be only a confession of ignorance of the organic conditions of our mental operations, on which physiology has now thrown more light. 'This,' Mr. Webb remarks, 'is the only passage in the four

experience: and I would have any one try, whether he can BOOK II.
keep one unvaried single idea in his mind, without any other, CHAP. XIV.
for any considerable time together.

14. For trial, let him take any figure, any degree of light Proof.
or whiteness, or what other he pleases, and he will, I suppose,
find it difficult to keep all other ideas out of his mind ; but
that some, either of another kind, or various considerations of
that idea, (each of which considerations is a new idea,) will
constantly succeed one another in his thoughts, let him be as
wary as he can[1].

15. All that is in a man's power in this case, I think, is The extent
only to mind and observe what the ideas are that take their of our power
turns in his understanding ; or else to direct the sort, and over the
call in such as he hath a desire or use of: but hinder the succession of our
constant succession of fresh ones, I think he cannot, though ideas.
he may commonly choose whether he will heedfully observe
and consider them.

16. Whether these several ideas in a man's mind be made Ideas,
by certain motions, I will not here dispute ; but this I am however made,
sure, that they include no idea of motion in their appearance[2]; include no
and if a man had not the idea of motion otherwise, I think Motion.
he would have none at all, which is enough to my present
purpose ; and sufficiently shows that the notice we take of
the ideas of our own minds, appearing there one after another,
is that which gives us the idea of succession and duration,
without which we should have no such ideas at all. It is not
then *motion*, but the constant train of *ideas* in our minds
whilst we are waking, that furnishes us with the idea of
duration ; whereof motion no otherwise gives us any perception than as it causes in our minds a constant succession
of ideas, as I have before showed : and we have as clear an

---

books of the *Essay* which gives the
slightest countenance to the views
of Sir W. Hamilton and Reid,' when
they imply that Locke supposed ideas
to be entities numerically and substantially distinct both from the percipient mind, and from the reality
perceived.

[1] 'No one can possibly attend continuously to an object that does not
change.' (James, *Psychology*, i. 421.)

[2] Here the perception is distinguished from the organic ' motions '
which, under the actual constitution
of things, determine its appearance to
individual men.

idea of succession and duration, by the train of other ideas succeeding one another in our minds, without the idea of any motion, as by the train of ideas caused by the uninterrupted sensible change of distance between two bodies, which we have from motion ; and therefore we should as well have the idea of duration were there no sense of motion at all.

Time is Duration set out by Measures.

17. Having thus got the idea of duration, the next thing natural for the mind to do, is to get some *measure* of this common duration, whereby it might judge of its different lengths, and consider the distinct order wherein several things exist ; without which a great part of our knowledge would be confused, and a great part of history be rendered very useless. This consideration of duration, as set out by certain periods, and marked by certain measures or epochs, is that, I think, which most properly we call *time* [1].

A good Measure of Time must divide its whole Duration into equal Periods.

18. In the measuring of extension, there is nothing more required but the application of the standard or measure we make use of to the thing of whose extension we would be informed. But in the measuring of duration this cannot be done, because no two different parts of succession can be put together to measure one another. And nothing being a measure of duration but duration, as nothing is of extension but extension, we cannot keep by us any standing, unvarying measure of duration, which consists in a constant fleeting succession, as we can of certain lengths of extension, as inches, feet, yards, &c., marked out in permanent parcels of matter. Nothing then could serve well for a convenient measure of time, but what has divided the whole length of its duration into apparently equal portions, by constantly repeated periods. What portions of duration are not distinguished, or considered as distinguished and measured, by

---

[1] Uniform change gives us the idea of *time,* or *objectively measured duration.* Yet if there had been nothing uniform in nature, duration, or room for events would not cease to be the necessary condition of change, even as *space,* or *room for extended beings,* would not cease to be the necessary presupposition of body. Duration and space thus supply eternal truths, which determine alike the actual and the possible—the concrete and the abstract— the occupied and the empty.

such periods, come not so properly under the notion of time ; BOOK II.
as appears by such phrases as these, viz. 'Before all time,'
and 'When time shall be no more[1].' CHAP. XIV.

19. The diurnal and annual revolutions of the sun, as The Revo-
having been, from the beginning of nature, constant, regular, lutions of
and universally observable by all mankind, and supposed and Moon,
equal to one another, have been with reason made use of the pro-
perest
for the measure of duration[2]. But the distinction of days Measures
and years having depended on the motion of the sun, it has for man-
brought this mistake with it, that it has been thought that kind.
motion and duration were the measure one of another. For
men, in the measuring of the length of time, having been
accustomed to the ideas of minutes, hours, days, months,
years, &c., which they found themselves upon any mention
of time or duration presently to think on, all which portions
of time were measured out by the motion of those heavenly
bodies, they were apt to confound time and motion ; or at
least to think that they had a necessary connexion one
with another. Whereas any constant periodical appearance,
or alteration of ideas, in seemingly equidistant spaces of duration, if constant and universally observable, would have as well
distinguished the intervals of time, as those that have been
made use of. For, supposing the sun, which some have taken
to be a fire, had been lighted up at the same distance of time
that it now every day comes about to the same meridian,
and then gone out again about twelve hours after, and that
in the space of an annual revolution it had sensibly increased
in brightness and heat, and so decreased again,—would not
such regular appearances serve to measure out the distances
of duration to all that could observe it, as well without as with
motion ? For if the appearances were constant, universally
observable, in equidistant periods, they would serve mankind
for measure of time as well were the motion away.

[1] Sense presents to us only concrete measures of duration, not the ultimate idea. If with Locke we mean by *time*, duration measured by *regulated* changes, then if all regular order in external nature had a beginning, that which preceded it must have been duration 'before time'; and after the extinction of the physical order, time (not duration) could no more be. Cf. § 24.

[2] Could men have had the idea of time (not duration) without the regular movements of the bodies that make up our solar system ?

BOOK II.
—+—
CHAP. XIV.
But not
by their
Motion, but
periodical
Appear-
ances.

20. For the freezing of water, or the blowing of a plant, returning at equidistant periods in all parts of the earth, would as well serve men to reckon their years by, as the motions of the sun : and in effect we see, that some people in America counted their years by the coming of certain birds amongst them at their certain seasons, and leaving them at others. For a fit of an ague ; the sense of hunger or thirst ; a smell or a taste ; or any other idea returning constantly at equidistant periods, and making itself universally be taken notice of, would not fail to measure out the course of succession, and distinguish the distances of time. Thus we see that men born blind count time well enough by years, whose revolutions yet they cannot distinguish by motions that they perceive not. And I ask whether a blind man, who distinguished his years either by the heat of summer, or cold of winter ; by the smell of any flower of the spring, or taste of any fruit of the autumn, would not have a better measure of time than the Romans had before the reformation of their calendar by Julius Cæsar, or many other people, whose years, notwithstanding the motion of the sun, which they pretended to make use of, are very irregular? And it adds no small difficulty to chronology, that the exact lengths of the years that several nations counted by, are hard to be known, they differing very much one from another, and I think I may say all of them from the precise motion of the sun. And if the sun moved from the creation to the flood constantly in the equator, and so equally dispersed its light and heat to all the habitable parts of the earth, in days all of the same length, without its annual variations to the tropics, as a late ingenious author [1] supposes, I do not think it very easy to imagine, that (notwithstanding the motion of the sun) men should in the antediluvian world, from the beginning, count by years, or measure their time by periods that had no sensible marks very obvious to distinguish them by [2].

[1] Thomas Burnet, in his *Theory of the Earth.*

[2] The various external measures of duration which mankind have adopted in the ancient and modern world (a curious subject) illustrate the difference between the intellectually necessary relations involved in duration itself, and these their contingent symbols which determine our ideas of time.

21. But perhaps it will be said,—without a regular motion,
such as of the sun, or some other, how could it ever be known
that such periods were equal? To which I answer,—the
equality of any other returning appearances might be known
by the same way that that of days was known, or presumed
to be so at first; which was only by judging of them by the
train of ideas which had passed in men's minds in the
intervals; [¹ by which train of ideas discovering inequality in
the natural days, but none in the artificial days, the artificial
days, or νυχθήμερα, were guessed ¹] to be equal, which was
sufficient to make them serve for a measure; though exacter
search has since discovered inequality in the diurnal revolutions of the sun, and we know not whether the annual also be
not unequal. These yet, by their presumed ² and apparent
equality, serve as well to reckon time by (though not to
measure the parts of duration exactly) as if they could be
proved to be exactly equal. We must, therefore, carefully
distinguish betwixt duration itself, and the measures we make
use of to judge of its length. Duration, in itself, is to be considered as going on in one constant, equal, uniform course:
but none of the measures of it which we make use of can be
known to do so ³, nor can we be assured that their assigned
parts or periods are equal in duration one to another; for
two successive lengths of duration, however measured, can
never be demonstrated to be equal. The motion of the sun,
which the world used so long and so confidently for an exact
measure of duration, has, as I said, been found in its several
parts unequal. And though men have, of late, made use of
a pendulum, as a more steady and regular motion than that
of the sun, or, (to speak more truly,) of the earth;—yet if any

CHAP. XIV.

No two
Parts of
Duration
can be
certainly
known to
be equal.

---

¹ 'Whereby they guessed them'—
in the first edition.

² We cannot rise above 'guess,'—
'presumption,'—'hypothesis,'—when
we take for granted the *objective regu-
larity* of the motions of the heavenly
bodies, or of any other adopted measures of duration. According to Locke,
the *idea* of duration is (at first vaguely)
suggested by changes in our own conscious state; duration is *measured*, and

the idea is thus elaborated, by certain
motions in the material world which
are 'presumed' to be regular.

³ No two parts of duration can be
shown certainly to be equal, because
their common measure cannot be placed
in juxtaposition with the parts, as in
the case of measures of space, which
stands still and submits to be measured.

one should be asked how he certainly knows that the two successive swings of a pendulum are equal, it would be very hard to satisfy him that they are infallibly so; since we cannot be sure that the cause of that motion, which is unknown to us, shall always operate equally; and we are sure that the medium in which the pendulum moves is not constantly the same: either of which varying, may alter the equality of such periods, and thereby destroy the certainty and exactness of the measure by motion, as well as any other periods of other appearances; the notion of duration still remaining clear, though our measures of it cannot (any of them) be demonstrated to be exact. Since then no two portions of succession can be brought together, it is impossible ever certainly to know their equality. All that we can do for a measure of time is, to take such as have continual successive appearances at seemingly equidistant periods; of which seeming equality we have no other measure, but such as the train of our own ideas have lodged in our memories, with the concurrence of other *probable* reasons, to persuade us of their equality.

Time not the Measure of Motion. 22. One thing seems strange to me,—that whilst all men manifestly measured time by the motion of the great and visible bodies of the world, time yet should be defined to be the 'measure of motion': whereas it is obvious to every one who reflects ever so little on it, that to measure motion, space is as necessary to be considered as time; and those who look a little farther will find also the bulk of the thing moved necessary to be taken into the computation, by any one who will estimate or measure motion so as to judge right of it. Nor indeed does motion any otherwise conduce to the measuring of duration, than as it constantly brings about the return of certain sensible ideas, in seeming equidistant periods. For if the motion of the sun were as unequal as of a ship driven by unsteady winds, sometimes very slow, and at others irregularly very swift; or if, being constantly equally swift, it yet was not circular, and produced not the same appearances,—it would not at all help us to measure time, any more than the seeming unequal motion of a comet does.

23. Minutes, hours, days, and years are, then, no more

necessary to time or duration, than inches, feet, yards, and
miles, marked out in any matter, are to extension. For,
though we in this part of the universe, by the constant use of
them, as of periods set out by the revolutions of the sun, or as
known parts of such periods, have fixed the ideas of such
lengths of duration in our minds, which we apply to all parts
of time whose lengths we would consider; yet there may be
other parts of the universe, where they no more use these
measures of ours, than in Japan they do our inches, feet, or
miles; but yet something analogous to them there must be.
For without some regular periodical returns, we could not
measure ourselves, or signify to others, the length of any
duration; though at the same time the world were as full of
motion as it is now, but no part of it disposed into regular and
apparently equidistant revolutions. But the different measures
that may be made use of for the account of time, do not at
all alter the notion of duration, which is the thing to be
measured; no more than the different standards of a foot and
a cubit alter the notion of extension to those who make use
of those different measures.

24. The mind having once got such a measure of time as
the annual revolution of the sun, can apply that measure to
duration wherein that measure itself did not exist, and with
which, in the reality of its being, it had nothing to do.
For should one say, that Abraham was born in the two
thousand seven hundred and twelfth year of the Julian
period, it is altogether as intelligible as reckoning from the
beginning of the world, though there were so far back no
motion of the sun, nor any motion at all [1]. For, though the
Julian period be supposed to begin several hundred years
before there were really either days, nights, or years, marked
out by any revolutions of the sun,—yet we reckon as right,
and thereby measure durations as well, as if really at that
time the sun had existed, and kept the same ordinary motion
it doth now. The idea of duration equal to an annual
revolution of the sun, is as easily *applicable* in our thoughts
to duration, where no sun or motion was, as the idea of a
foot or yard, taken from bodies here, can be applied in our

[1] Locke supposes a lately-created solar system.

thoughts to duration, where no sun or motion was, as the idea of a foot or yard, taken from bodies here, can be applied in our thoughts to distances beyond the confines of the world, where are no bodies at all [1].

As we can measure space in our thoughts where there is no body.

25. For supposing it were 5639 miles, or millions of miles, from this place to the remotest body of the universe, (for, being finite, it must be at a certain distance,) as we suppose it to be 5639 years from this time to the first existence of any body in the beginning of the world;—we can, in our thoughts, apply this measure of a year to duration before the creation, or beyond the duration of bodies or motion, as we can this measure of a mile to space beyond the utmost bodies; and by the one measure duration, where there was no motion, as well as by the other measure space in our thoughts, where there is no body.

The assumption that the world is neither boundless nor eternal.

26. If it be objected to me here, that, in this way of explaining of time, I have begged what I should not, viz. that the world is neither eternal nor infinite; I answer, That to my present purpose it is not needful, in this place, to make use of arguments to evince the world to be finite both in duration and extension. But it being at least as conceivable as the contrary, I have certainly the liberty to suppose it, as well as any one hath to suppose the contrary; and I doubt not, but that every one that will go about it, may easily conceive in his mind the beginning of motion, though not of all duration, and so may come to a step and *non ultra* in his consideration of motion. So also, in his thoughts, he may set limits to body, and the extension belonging to it; but not to space, where no body is, the utmost bounds of space and duration being beyond the reach of thought, as well as the utmost bounds of number are beyond the largest comprehension of the mind; and all for the same reason, as we shall see in another place.

Eternity.

27. By the same means, therefore, and from the same original that we come to have the idea of time, we have also that idea which we call Eternity; viz. having got

---

[1] 'Ce *vide*, qu'on peut concevoir dans le temps, marquerait, comme celui de l'espace, que le temps et l'es- pace vont aussi bien aux possibles qu'aux existants.' (Leibniz.)

the idea of succession and duration, by reflecting on the
train of our own ideas, caused in us either by the natural
appearances of those ideas coming constantly of themselves
into our waking thoughts, or else caused by external objects
successively affecting our senses ; and having from the revolutions of the sun got the ideas of certain lengths of duration,
—we can in our thoughts add such lengths of duration to one
another, as often as we please, and apply them, so added, to
durations past or to come. And this we can continue to do
on, without bounds or limits, and proceed *in infinitum*[1], and
apply thus the length of the annual motion of the sun to
duration, supposed before the sun's or any other motion had
its being ; which is no more difficult or absurd, than to
apply the notion I have of the moving of a shadow one hour
to-day upon the sun-dial to the duration of something last
night, v. g. the burning of a candle, which is now absolutely
separate from all actual motion ; and it is as impossible for
the duration of that flame for an hour last night to co-exist
with any motion that now is, or for ever shall be, as for any
part of duration, that was before the beginning of the world,
to co-exist with the motion of the sun now. But yet this
hinders not but that, having the *idea* of the length of the
motion of the shadow on a dial between the marks of two
hours, I can as distinctly measure in my thoughts the duration of that candle-light last night, as I can the duration of
anything that does now exist : and it is no more than to

[1] 'Mais, pour tirer la notion de l'é-
ternité, il faut concevoir de plus que
la même raison subsiste *toujours* pour
aller plus loin. C'est cette considération des raisons qui achève la
notion de l'infini, ou de l'indéfini,
dans les progrès possibles. *Ainsi
les sens ne sauraient suffire à faire
former ces notions.*' (Leibniz.) The
notion of eternity, when it means *the
unbeginning and unending*, implies not
merely that we *may*, but that we *must*,
continue to add to any finite duration,
however great. In it intelligence
expresses dissatisfaction with *every*
merely finite quantity of duration.

This conscious dissatisfaction, as an
object of reflection, gives a positive
idea, and also suggests the negative
idea of duration without beginning
or end, in which the positive idea
disappears in the mystery of Eternity.
Thus from a sense perception of what
is finite, necessities of reason carry us
towards the necessarily incomplete
idea of boundless room for change,—
time merged in the timeless. Is this
timeless Eternity—this mysterious infinite, in which the idea of duration is
lost—rightly called a ' mode ' of our
' simple idea ' of duration ?

think, that, had the sun shone then on the dial, and moved after the same rate it doth now, the shadow on the dial would have passed from one hour-line to another whilst that flame of the candle lasted.

Our measures of Duration dependent on our ideas.

28. The notion of an hour, day, or year, being only the idea I have of the length of certain periodical regular motions, neither of which motions do ever all at once exist, but only in the ideas I have of them in my memory derived from my senses or reflection ; I can with the same ease, and for the same reason, apply it in my thoughts to duration antecedent to all manner of motion, as well as to anything that is but a minute or a day antecedent to the motion that at this very moment the sun is in. All things past are equally and perfectly at rest ; and to this way of consideration of them are all one, whether they were before the beginning of the world, or but yesterday : the measuring of any duration by some motion depending not at all on the *real* co-existence of that thing to that motion, or any other periods of revolution, but the having a clear *idea* of the length of some periodical known motion, or other interval of duration, in my mind, and applying that to the duration of the thing I would measure.

The Duration of anything need not be co-existent with the motion we measure it by.

29. Hence we see that some men imagine the duration of the world, from its first existence to this present year 1689, to have been 5639 years, or equal to 5639 annual revolutions of the sun, and others a great deal more; as the Egyptians of old, who in the time of Alexander counted 23,000 years from the reign of the sun ; and the Chinese now, who account the world 3,269,000 years old, or more ; which longer duration of the world, according to their computation, though I should not believe to be true, yet I can equally imagine it with them, and as truly understand, and say one is longer than the other, as I understand, that Methusalem's life was longer than Enoch's. And if the common reckoning of 5639 should be true, (as it may be as well as any other assigned,) it hinders not at all my imagining what others mean, when they make the world one thousand years older, since every one may with the same facility imagine (I do not say believe) the world to be 50,000 years old, as 5639 ;

and may as well conceive the duration of 50,000 years as
5639. Whereby it appears that, to the measuring the
duration of anything by time, it is not requisite that that
thing should be co-existent to the motion we measure by, or
any other periodical revolution; but it suffices to this purpose,
that we have the idea of the length of *any* regular periodical
appearances, which we can in our minds apply to duration,
with which the motion or appearance never co-existed.

30. For, as in the history of the creation delivered by Infinity in
Moses, I can imagine that light existed three days before Duration.
the sun was, or had any motion, barely by thinking that
the duration of light before the sun was created was so
long as (*if* the sun had moved then as it doth now) would
have been equal to three of his diurnal revolutions; so by
the same way I can have an idea of the chaos, or angels,
being created before there was either light or any continued
motion, a minute, an hour, a day, a year, or one thousand
years. For, if I can but consider duration equal to one
minute, before either the being or motion of any body, I can
add one minute more till I come to sixty; and by the same
way of adding minutes, hours, or years (i. e. such or such
parts of the sun's revolutions, or any other period whereof
I have the idea) proceed *in infinitum*, and suppose a duration exceeding as many such periods as I can reckon, let
me add whilst I will, which I think is the notion we have
of eternity; of whose infinity we have no other notion than
we have of the infinity of number, to which we can add for
ever without end [1].

31. And thus I think it is plain, that from those two Origin of
fountains of all knowledge before mentioned, viz. reflection and our ideas
of Dura-
sensation, we got the ideas of duration, and the measures of it. tion, and
of the
measures
For, First, by observing what passes in our minds, how our of it.
ideas there in train constantly some vanish and others begin
to appear, we come by the idea of *succession*.

---

[1] Can the mysterious idea of the
Innumerable be called a 'mode' of
the positive idea of number? The
ultimate reality is not numerable
not measurable—transcends the category of quantity, and the positive
element, which gives meaning to our
words when we speak of it, is the
feeling of *irresistible progress* in the
idea.

Secondly, by observing a distance in the parts of this succession, we get the idea of *duration*.

Thirdly, by sensation observing certain appearances, at certain regular and seeming equidistant periods, we get the ideas of certain *lengths* or *measures of duration*, as minutes, hours, days, years, &c.

Fourthly, by being able to repeat those measures of time, or ideas of stated length of duration, in our minds, as often as we will, we can come to imagine *duration, where nothing does really endure or exist*; and thus we imagine to-morrow, next year, or seven years hence.

Fifthly, by being able to repeat ideas of any length of time, as of a minute, a year, or an age, as often as we will in our own thoughts, and adding them one to another, without ever coming to the end of such addition, any nearer than we can to the end of number, to which we can always add; we come by the idea of *eternity*, as the future eternal duration of our souls, as well as the eternity of that infinite Being which must necessarily have always existed.

Sixthly, by considering any part of infinite duration, as set out by periodical measures, we come by the idea of what we call *time* in general.

CHAPTER XV.

IDEAS OF DURATION AND EXPANSION, CONSIDERED
TOGETHER.

1. THOUGH we have in the precedent chapters dwelt pretty long on the considerations of space and duration, yet, they being ideas of general concernment, that have something very abstruse and peculiar in their nature, the comparing them one with another may perhaps be of use for their illustration; and we may have the more clear and distinct conception of them by taking a view of them together[1]. Distance or space, in its simple abstract conception, to avoid confusion, I call *expansion*, to distinguish it from extension, which by some is used to express this distance only as it is in the solid parts of matter, and so includes, or at least intimates, the idea of body: whereas the idea of pure distance includes no such thing[2]. I prefer also the word expansion to space, because space is often applied to distance of fleeting successive parts, which never exist together[3], as

---

[1] These ideas, along with number, are modes of Quantity, or that which is conceived to consist of *parts*, as contrasted with other ideas which consist of *degrees* in Quality, and are not lost in *boundless* addition and division of quantitative parts.

[2] '*Space void of body is the property of an incorporeal substance.* . . . Void space is not an attribute without a subject; because by *void* space we never mean space void of everything, but void of body only. In all void space God is certainly present; and possibly many other substances which are not matter, being neither tangible, nor objects of any of *our* senses. . . . Space and duration are not *hors de Dieu*, but are created by, and are immediate and necessary consequences of, his existence. And without them his Eternity and Omnipresence would be taken away.' (Clarke to Leibniz, *Papers,* pp. 127–91.)

[3] e.g. distance or 'space' of duration. Cf. § 8.

BOOK II.
CHAP. XV.

well as to those which are permanent[1]. In both these (viz. expansion and duration) the mind has this common idea of continued lengths, capable of greater or less quantities. For a man has as clear an idea of the difference of the length of an hour and a day, as of an inch and a foot.

Expansion not bounded by Matter.

2. The mind, having got the idea of the length of any part of expansion[2], let it be a span, or a pace, or what length you will, *can*, as has been said, repeat that idea, and so, adding it to the former, enlarge its idea of length, and make it equal to two spans, or two paces; and so, as often as it will, till it equals the distance of any parts of the earth one from another, and increase thus till it amounts to the distance of the sun or remotest star. By such a progression as this, setting out from the place where it is, or any other place, it can proceed and pass beyond all those lengths, and find nothing to stop its going on, either in or without body. It is true, we can easily in our thoughts come to the end of *solid* extension; the extremity and bounds of all body we have no difficulty to arrive at: but when the mind is there, it finds nothing to hinder its progress into this endless expansion; of that it can neither find nor conceive any end. Nor let any one say, that beyond the bounds of body, there is nothing at all; unless he will confine God within the limits of matter. Solomon, whose understanding was filled and enlarged with wisdom, seems to have other thoughts when he says, 'Heaven, and the heaven of heavens, cannot contain thee.' And he, I think, very much magnifies to himself the capacity of his own understanding, who persuades himself that he can extend his

[1] Cf. ch. xiii. § 2. Locke vacillates, nevertheless, as in other instances, in his use of these terms, and occasionally uses extension, and also space, instead of expansion, as here defined.
[2] Originally by sight or touch. Either gives an incomplete idea; but without one or other of those senses it seems to Locke that we must have wanted the idea of 'expansion' altogether; and, as it is, we could not by them have perceived it, in the absence of all perceived bodies. Yet, after the idea has thus arisen, it remains as a necessary relation, under which things must be perceived in sense, and also as a capacity or possibility for the existence of *extended* beings.

thoughts further than God exists, or imagine any expansion
where He is not [1].

3. Just so is it in duration. The mind having got the
idea of any length of duration, *can* double, multiply, and
enlarge it, not only beyond its own, but beyond the existence
of all corporeal beings, and all the measures of time, taken
from the great bodies of all the world and their motions.
But yet every one easily admits, that, though we make
duration boundless, as certainly it is, we cannot yet extend
it beyond all being. God, every one easily allows, fills
eternity ; and it is hard to find a reason why any one should
doubt that he likewise fills immensity. His infinite being
is certainly as boundless one way as another ; and methinks
it ascribes a little too much to matter to say, where there
is no body, there is nothing [2].

4. Hence I think we may learn the reason why every one
familiarly and without the least hesitation speaks of and
supposes Eternity, and sticks not to ascribe *infinity* to *dura-*
tion ; but it is with more doubting and reserve that many
admit or suppose the *infinity* of *space*. The reason whereof
seems to me to be this,—That duration and extension being
used as names of affections belonging to other beings, we easily
conceive in God infinite duration, and we cannot avoid doing
so : but, not attributing to him extension, but only to matter,
which is finite, we are apter to doubt of the existence of

---

[1] Although Locke holds (as after-wards Samuel Clarke) that in some way God occupies and sustains space, this cannot mean that God must be conceived to consist of *partes extra partes*, but only that signs of active Reason and Purpose must appear wherever extended beings are, or can exist,—that the extended universe cannot be supposed, in any part of it, or as a whole, to be purposeless chaos. ' Si Dieu était étendu,' says Leibniz, ' il aurait des parties, mais la durée n'en donne qu'à ses opérations. Cependant, par rapport à l'espace, il faut lui attribuer l'immensité, qui donne aussi des parties, et de l'ordre, aux opérations immédiates du Dieu. Il est la source des possibilités comme des existences, des unes par son essence, des autres par sa volonté. Ainsi l'espace comme le temps n'ont leur réalité que de lui, et il peut remplir le vide quand bon lui semble.' (*Nouv. Essais.*)

[2] Neither space nor duration is limited by the concrete things which are used to measure them by, the one not being bounded by matter, nor the other by its motions. Locke describes the ideas of pure space and duration as ideas of that which is independent of all objects and events,—ready to receive concrete existences—the universe of finite objects, and the universe of finite changes.

expansion without matter; of which alone we commonly suppose it an attribute. And, therefore, when men pursue their thoughts of space, they are apt to stop at the confines of body: as if space were there at an end too, and reached no further. Or if their ideas, upon consideration, carry them further, yet they term what is beyond the limits of the universe, imaginary space: as if *it* were nothing, because there is no body existing in it [1]. Whereas duration, antecedent to all body, and to the motions which it is measured by, they never term imaginary: because it is never supposed void of some other real existence [2]. And if the names of things may at all direct our thoughts towards the original of men's ideas, (as I am apt to think they may very much,) one may have occasion to think by the name *duration*, that the continuation of existence, with a kind of resistance to any destructive force, and the continuation of solidity (which is apt to be confounded with, and if we will look into the minute anatomical parts of matter, is little different from, hardness) were thought to have some analogy, and gave occasion to words so near of

---

[1] Cf. ch. xiii. § 27. Locke wrote, in 1676, that 'space, in itself, seems to be nothing but a *possibility* for *extended* beings to be, or exist'; and that '*in itself it is really nothing but a bare relation . . . not any real thing.*' (*Miscellaneous Papers.*) Against this of *space* being a mere relation (as held by Leibniz), Samuel Clarke argues, that, 'if so, it would follow, that if God should remove in a straight line the whole material world entire, it would still remain in the same place; and that if *time* is only order of succession, it would follow, that if God had created the world millions of ages sooner than he did, yet it would not have been created at all the sooner. Space and time are quantities, which situation and order are not.' (See *Papers*, p. 79.) Leibniz, and Kant in the 'Aesthetic,' refer to the idea of space and time held by the mathematical natural philosophers, as of 'two self-subsisting entities.'

[2] Is not the idea of *duration* a mental necessity in a deeper sense than the idea of *space* is? Might we not conceive an objective universe, without having the idea of *space* in any of its modes; while the absence of the idea of *duration* and its modes seems inconsistent with finite consciousness, which presupposes changing phenomena? We can suppose sentient intelligence, otherwise like ours, without the idea of space and its modes; matter being thus manifested in none of the qualities, primary or secondary, of *our* world, but in qualities of other sorts, unimaginable by man. But can we equally suppose intelligence in the absence of all change, and without an idea of duration? The ideas of space and duration are not on the same level, if the former are essential to finite intelligence, while the other depends on the organisation in which the conscious life of man is at present embodied.

kin as *durare* and *durum esse*. And that *durare* is applied BOOK II.
to the idea of hardness, as well as that of existence, we see in —◆◆—
Horace, Epod. xvi. *ferro duravit secula.* But, be that as it CHAP. XV.
will, this is certain, that whoever pursues his own thoughts,
will find them sometimes launch out beyond the extent of
body, into the infinity of space or expansion; the idea
whereof is distinct and separate from body and all other
things: which may, (to those who please,) be a subject of
further meditation[1].

5. Time in general is to duration as place to expansion. Time to
They are so much of those boundless oceans of eternity and Duration
immensity as is set out and distinguished from the rest, as it to Ex-
were by landmarks; and so are made use of to denote the pansion.
position of *finite* real beings, in respect one to another, in
those uniform infinite oceans of duration and space. These,
rightly considered, are only ideas of determinate distances from
certain known points, fixed in distinguishable sensible things,
and supposed to keep the same distance one from another.
From such points fixed in sensible beings we reckon, and
from them we measure our portions of those infinite quantities; which, so considered, are that which we call *time* and
place. For duration and space being in themselves uniform
and boundless, the order and position of things, without such
known settled points, would be lost in them; and all things
would lie jumbled in an incurable confusion[2].

---

[1] 'Further meditation' would show
that the necessities of reason carry
finite intelligence into ideas that
are at once essentially obscure, because *necessarily* incomplete, and also
incapable of being mentally imaged;
nevertheless *finite* minds cannot dispense with them. It is ultimate
ideas of this sort that are apt to be
inadequately dealt with at Locke's
point of view.

[2] *Time* has been called the *place of
events,* as space is the *place of bodies.*
If we had no perception of change or
'succession,' we could have no idea of
time, and therefore no consciousness
of anything; and if we had no perception of body, we could have no
idea of space. Changes and bodies,
presented in experience, are said to
be the 'explanation' of each, at the
physical point of view; but as neither
bodies nor changes can be conceived,
except as placed and dated, duration and space are presupposed,
and thus cannot be explained, by
data of sense. Change or succession
awakens and measures the idea of
time, and sensuous things awaken and
measure the idea of space; but those
ideas themselves are not to be confused with their physical occasions and
concrete measures.

BOOK II.

CHAP. XV.

Time and Place are taken for so much of either as are set out by the Existence and Motion of Bodies.

6. Time and place, taken thus for determinate distinguishable portions of those infinite abysses of space[1] and duration, set out or supposed to be distinguished from the rest, by marks and known boundaries, have each of them a twofold acceptation.

First, Time in general is commonly taken for so much of infinite duration as is measured by, and co-existent with, the existence and motions of the great bodies of the universe, as far as we know anything of them : and in this sense time begins and ends with the frame of this sensible world, as in these phrases before mentioned, 'Before all time,' or, 'When time shall be no more[2].' Place likewise is taken sometimes for that portion of infinite space which is possessed by and comprehended within the material world ; and is thereby distinguished from the rest of expansion ; though this may be more properly called extension than place. Within these two are confined, and by the observable parts of them are measured and determined, the particular time or duration, and the particular extension and place, of all corporeal beings.

7. *Secondly*, sometimes the word time is used in a larger sense, and is applied to parts of that infinite duration, not that were really distinguished and measured out by this real existence, and periodical motions of bodies, that were appointed from the beginning to be for signs and for seasons and for days and years, and are accordingly our measures of time; but such other portions too of that infinite uniform duration, which we upon any occasion do suppose equal to certain lengths of measured time; and so consider them as bounded and determined. For, if we should suppose the creation, or fall of the angels, was at the beginning of the Julian period, we should speak properly enough, and should be understood if we said, it is a longer time since the creation

---

[1] Expansion.

[2] That is, when we intend by *time* only those motions by which we are accustomed to measure it, of which we *can* suppose a beginning and an ending; in contrast with time (in the wider meaning of this term, or, in Locke's language, duration) undistinguished by change, preceding and following the existence of the motions by which it is measured. A beginning or ending of duration, i. e. of time in its wider sense, would be an express contradiction.

of angels than the creation of the world, by 7640 years : BOOK II.
whereby we would mark out so much of that undistinguished
duration as we suppose equal to, and would have admitted, CHAP. XV.
7640 annual revolutions of the sun, moving at the rate it now
does. And thus likewise we sometimes speak of place, distance, or bulk, in the great *inane*, beyond the confines of the
world, when we consider so much of that space as is equal to,
or capable to receive, a body of any assigned dimensions, as
a cubic foot; or do suppose a point in it, at such a certain
distance from any part of the universe[1].

8. *Where* and *when* are questions belonging to all finite They be-
existences, and are by us always reckoned from some known long to all
parts of this sensible world, and from some certain epochs beings.
marked out to us by the motions observable in it. Without
some such fixed parts or periods, the order of things would be
lost, to our finite understandings, in the boundless invariable
oceans of duration and expansion, which comprehend in
them all finite beings, and in their full extent belong only to
the Deity[2]. And therefore we are not to wonder that we
comprehend them not, and do so often find our thoughts at
a loss, when we would consider them, either abstractly in
themselves, or as any way attributed to the first incomprehensible Being. But when applied to any particular finite
beings, the extension of any body is so much of that infinite
space as the bulk of the body takes up. And place is the
position of any body, when considered at a certain distance
from some other. As the idea of the particular duration of

---

[1] Accordingly, all *measurable* realities are tested by those concrete
measures which constitute *places* and
dates. In this sense, space, duration,
and number are measurable quantities,
—the ideas out of which mathematics
is formed. Measurable or finite spaces
and durations are mathematically intelligible while, the *immeasurable* expansion and eternity in which space and
duration are lost at last (reason itself
thus transcending the finite category
of quantity) are necessarily *mysteries*
to a human understanding measured

by sense.

[2] 'Expansion' is that which makes
it possible for extended things to have
places, and duration is what makes it
possible for changes of any sort to have
dates. Except as relations of things
and their events, into which they introduce order, neither has any positive
meaning for a human mind, although
Locke sometimes pictures them as
receptacles—pre-existing objectively
—capable of receiving the finite universe into their capacious embrace.

anything is, an idea of that portion of infinite duration[1] which passes during the existence of that thing; so the time when the thing existed is, the idea of that space of duration which passed between some known and fixed period of duration, and the being of that thing. One shows the distance of the extremities of the bulk or existence of the same thing, as that it is a foot square, or lasted two years; the other shows the distance of it in place, or existence from other fixed points of space or duration, as that it was in the middle of Lincoln's Inn Fields, or the first degree of Taurus, and in the year of our Lord 1671[2], or the 1000th year of the Julian period. All which distances we measure by preconceived ideas of certain lengths of space and duration,—as inches, feet, miles, and degrees, and in the other, minutes, days, and years, &c.

9. There is one thing more wherein space and duration have a great conformity, and that is, though they are justly reckoned amongst our *simple ideas*[3], yet none of the distinct ideas we have of either is without all manner of composition: it is the very nature of both of them to consist of parts: but their parts being all of the same kind, and without the mixture of any other idea, hinder them not from having a place amongst simple ideas[4]. Could the mind, as in number, come

---

[1] Can we speak consistently of a *portion* of *infinite* duration, thus implying that the 'infinite' is a finite quantity? Is not infinite duration the abstract, inexhaustible, possibility of events happening; and infinite space the abstract, inexhaustible, possibility of bodies, composed of extended parts, existing? This is abstract duration and space; incapable of being realised without a universe of finite things, and without conscious mind. Whether the mysteries of immensity, in which all finite spaces, and of eternity, in which all finite durations are lost, might subsist, though all finite spaces and durations should be annihilated, we cannot tell, but it is the ideas of particular spaces and durations that suggest those mysteries to man.

[2] The year in which Locke undertook the inquiry which issued in the *Essay*.

[3] 'I know of no ideas or notions that have a better claim to be accounted simple and original than those of space and time.' (Reid.)

[4] An objection, that if 'none of the distinct ideas that we have of either extension or duration' is 'without all manner of composition,' neither of these can be classed among 'simple ideas'; and that in ch. ii. of this book, in which Locke introduces the subject of 'simple ideas,' he has failed to give an exact enough definition of their *simplicity*, is thus referred to by M. Coste, in his French version of the *Essay*:—
'C'est M. Barbyrac, professeur en droit à Groningue, qui me communique ces objections, dans une lettre que je

to so small a part of extension or duration as excluded BOOK II.
divisibility[1], *that* would be, as it were, the indivisible unit or CHAP. XV.

fis voir à M. Locke. Et voici la réponse que M. Locke me dicta peu de jours après : Pour commencer par la dernière objection, M. Locke déclare d'abord, qu'il n'a pas traité son sujet dans un ordre parfaitement *scholastique*, n'ayant pas eu beaucoup de familiarité avec ces sortes de livres, lorsqu'il a écrit le sien, ou plutôt ne se souvenant guère plus alors de la méthode qu'on y observe ; et qu'ainsi ses lecteurs ne doivent pas s'attendre à des définitions régulièrement placées à la tête de chaque nouveau sujet. Il est content d'employer les principaux termes dont il se sert de telle sorte que, d'une manière ou d'autre, il fasse comprendre nettement à ses lecteurs ce qu'il entend par ces termes-là. Et en particulier à l'égard du terme d'*idées simples*, il a eu le bonheur de le définir dans l'endroit cité dans l'objection ; et par conséquent il n'aura pas besoin de suppléer à ce défaut. La question se réduit donc à savoir si l'idée d'*extension* peut s'accorder avec cette définition qui lui conviendra, si elle est entendue dans le sens que M. Locke a eu principalement en vue. Or, la composition qu'il a eu proprement dessein d'exclure dans cette définition, c'est une composition de différentes idées dans l'esprit, et non une composition d'idées de même espèce et où l'on ne peut venir à une dernière entièrement exempte de cette composition ; de sorte que si l'idée d'étendu consiste à avoir *partes extra partes,* comme on parle dans les écoles, c'est toujours, au sens de M. Locke, une idée simple ; parce que l'idée d'avoir *partes extra partes* ne peut être résolue en deux autres idées. Du reste, l'objection qu'on fait à M. Locke, à propos de la nature de l'étendue, ne lui avait pas entièrement échappée, comme on peut le voir dans le § 9 de chapitre xv, où il dit que la moindre portion d'espace ou

d'étendue, *dont nous ayons une idée claire et distincte,* est la plus propre à être regardée comme l'idée *simple* de cette espèce, dont les modes complexes d'espace et d'étendue sont composés ; et à son avis, on peut fort l'appeler une *idée simple,* puisque c'est la plus petite idée de l'espace que l'esprit se puisse former à lui-même, et qu'il ne peut par conséquent la diviser en deux plus petites. D'où il ensuit qu'elle est *à l'esprit* une idée simple : ce qui suffit dans cette occasion. *Car, l'affaire de M. Locke n'est pas de discourir, en cet endroit de la réalité des choses, mais des idées de l'esprit.* Et si cela ne suffit pour éclaircir la difficulté, M. Locke n'a plus rien à ajouter, sinon que si l'idée *d'étendue* est si singulaire qu'elle ne puisse s'accorder exactement avec la définition qu'il a donnée des idées simples, de sorte qu'elle diffère en quelque manière de toutes les autres de cette espèce, il croit qu'il vaut mieux la laisser là exposée à cette difficulté, que de faire une nouvelle division en sa faveur. C'est assez pour M. Locke qu'on puisse comprendre sa pensée. Il n'est pas trop ordinaire de voir des discours très-intelligibles, gâtés par trop de délicatesse sur ces pointilleries. Nous devons assortir les choses le mieux que nous pouvons, *doctrinae causa* ; mais, après tout, il se trouvera toujours quantité de choses qui ne pourront pas s'ajuster exactement avec nos conceptions et nos façons de parler.' This explanation throws some light upon Locke's use of language in the *Essay.* Minima sensibilia are thus his simple ideas of sensation ; and division carried beyond what is sensible transcends the sphere of *positive* ideas at one extreme, even as when too large to be mentally imaged, it transcends it at the other.

[1] The idea of number is accordingly called discrete, not continuous, be-

idea; by repetition of which, it would make its more enlarged ideas of extension and duration. But, since the mind is not able to frame an idea of *any* space without parts, instead thereof it makes use of the common measures, which, by familiar use in each country, have imprinted themselves on the memory (as inches and feet; or cubits and parasangs; and so seconds, minutes, hours, days, and years in duration);— the mind makes use, I say, of such ideas as these, as simple ones: and these are the component parts of larger ideas, which the mind upon occasion makes by the addition of such known lengths which it is acquainted with. On the other side, the ordinary smallest measure we have of either is looked on as an unit in number, when the mind by division would reduce them into less fractions. Though on both sides, both in addition and division, either of space or duration, when the idea under consideration becomes very big or very small, its precise bulk becomes very obscure and confused; and it is the *number* of its repeated additions or divisions that alone remains clear and distinct; as will easily appear to any one who will let his thoughts loose in the vast expansion of space, or divisibility of matter. Every part of duration is duration too; and every part of extension is extension, both of them capable of addition or division *in infinitum*. But *the least portions of either of them, whereof we have clear and distinct ideas*, may perhaps be fittest to be considered by us, as the *simple ideas* of that kind out of which our complex[1] modes of space, extension, and duration are made up, and into which they can again be distinctly resolved. Such a small part in duration may be called a *moment*, and is the time of one idea in our minds, in the train of their ordinary succession there. The other, wanting a proper name, I know not whether I may be allowed to

cause of *indivisible* parts or units; whereas the ideas of space and duration are of parts that are necessarily supposed to be *divisible without end*, and thus *at last* transcend the category of Quantity in the form of infinite (or mysterious) divisibility.

[1] Simple ideas of space are thus the *minima sensibilia*, and *moments* are our simple ideas of duration. This need not imply a denial of the continuity of space and time. Locke elsewhere recognises that their parts are inseparable.

call a *sensible point*, meaning thereby the least particle of matter or space we can discern, which is ordinarily about [¹ a minute, and to the sharpest eyes seldom less than thirty seconds of a circle,] whereof the eye is the centre.

10. Expansion and duration have this further agreement, that, though they are both considered by us as having parts ², yet their parts are not separable one from another, no not even in thought : though the parts of bodies from whence we take our *measure* of the one; and the parts of motion, or rather the succession of ideas in our minds, from whence we take the *measure* of the other, may be interrupted and separated ; as the one is often by rest, and the other is by sleep, which we call rest too.

Their Parts inseparable.

11. But there is this manifest difference between them,— That the ideas of length which we have of expansion are turned every way, and so make figure, and breadth, and thickness ³; but duration is but as it were the length of one straight line, extended *in infinitum*, not capable of multiplicity, variation, or figure ; but is one common measure of all existence whatsoever, wherein all things, whilst they exist, equally partake. For this present moment is common to all things that are now in being, and equally comprehends that part of their existence, as much as if they were all but one single being; and we may truly say, they all exist in the *same* moment of time. Whether angels and spirits have any analogy to this, in respect to expansion, is beyond my comprehension : and perhaps for us, who have understandings and comprehensions suited to our own preservation, and the ends of our own being, but not to the reality and extent of all other beings, it is near as hard to conceive

Duration is as a Line, Expansion as a Solid.

---

¹ 'a second of a circle,' in first edition. Molyneux (March 2, 1693) drew Locke's attention to this error, which he promised to correct, as he did.

² Cf. former notes, on the mysteries of Immensity and Eternity, as inconsistent with ideas of ' parts.'

³ The various relations of this trinal extension afford the material of geometry. Figure, trinal extension, and other *finite modes* of space are the objects of the most lucid and certain of the sciences; while the mystery of immensity is an obtrusive manifestation of the ultimate mystery to which, through various avenues, the finite ideas of experience necessarily lead us at last.

BOOK II.
CHAP. XV.

any existence, or to have an idea of any real being, with a perfect negation of all manner of expansion, as it is to have the idea of any real existence with a perfect negation of all manner of duration. And therefore, what spirits[1] have to do with space, or how they communicate in it, we know not. All that we know is, that bodies do each singly possess its proper portion of it, according to the extent of solid parts; and thereby exclude all other bodies from having any share in that particular portion of space, whilst it remains there.

Duration has never two Parts together, Expansion altogether.

12. *Duration,* and *time* which is a part of it, is the idea we have of *perishing* distance, of which no two parts exist together, but follow each other in succession; an *expansion* is the idea of *lasting* distance, all whose parts exist together, and are not capable of succession. And therefore, though we cannot conceive any duration without succession, nor can put it together in our thoughts that any being does *now* exist to-morrow, or possess at once more than the present moment of duration; yet we can conceive the eternal duration of the Almighty far different from that of man, or any other finite being. Because man comprehends not in his knowledge or power all past and future things: his thoughts are but of yesterday, and he knows not what to-morrow will bring forth. What is once past he can never recal; and what is yet to come he cannot make present. What I say of man, I say of all finite beings; who, though they may far exceed man in knowledge and power, yet are no more than the meanest creature, in comparison with God himself. Finite or any magnitude holds not any proportion to infinite[2]. God's infinite duration, being accompanied with infinite knowledge and infinite power, he sees all things, past and to come; and they are no more distant from his knowledge, no further removed from his sight, than the present: they all lie under the same view: and there is nothing which he cannot make exist each moment he pleases. For the existence of all

---

[1] 'Spirits,' i. e. unembodied spirits.

[2] Hence so-called 'infinite quantity,' either in space or in duration, is not properly quantity at all, but *unquantifiable reality*, in which quantity is lost in mystery.

things, depending upon his good pleasure, all things exist BOOK II.
every moment that he thinks fit to have them exist. To CHAP. XV.
conclude: expansion and duration do mutually embrace and
comprehend each other; every part of space being in every
part of duration, and every part of duration in every part of
expansion. Such a combination of two distinct ideas is, I
suppose, scarce to be found in all that great variety we do or
can conceive, and may afford matter to further speculation [1].

[1] Duration is in idea in every place, and space throughout endures. It is impossible to have an idea of the annihilation of either; each is so much allied to *nothing*, that it seems incapable either of annihilation or creation,—the one being the idea of the abstract possibility of something extended, and the other of the abstract possibility of something changing. In nature or the reason of things, they disappear in the *boundless* and in the *infinitely* divisible. Imagination and sensuous understanding cannot represent either the boundlessness or the infinite divisibility, in which they are thus, by a necessity of the reason in things, mysteriously lost. In describing the ideas of space and duration, Locke leaves in the background this *intellectual necessity*—this absolute inability to conceive *body* without ideas of its space-relations, or changes without ideas of a duration in which they must have taken place; and the necessarily illimitable character of each. This *intellectual necessity* cannot be explained as an event, under the merely physical order of its rise in consciousness, in the 'historical plain' method,—any more than the inability of either of these relations, abstracted from their concrete measures, to submit to the grasp of sensuous imagination, can be *so* explained.

CHAPTER XVI.

IDEA OF NUMBER.

BOOK II.
—⫰—
CHAP. XVI.
Number
the
simplest
and most
universal
Idea.

1. AMONGST all the ideas we have, as there is none suggested to the mind by more ways, so there is none more simple, than that of *unity*, or one : it has no shadow of variety or composition in it : every object our senses are employed about ; every idea in our understandings ; every thought of our minds, brings this idea along with it. And therefore it is the most intimate to our thoughts, as well as it is, in its agreement to all other things, *the most universal idea we have.* For number applies itself to men, angels, actions, thoughts ; everything that either doth exist, or can be imagined [1].

2. By repeating this idea in our minds, and adding the repetitions together, we come by the *complex* ideas of the *modes* of it. Thus, by adding one to one, we have the complex idea of a couple ; by putting twelve units together, we have the complex idea of a dozen ; and so of a score, or a million, or any other number [2].

3. The *simple modes* of *number* are of all other the most distinct ; every the least variation, which is an unit, making each combination as clearly different from that which approacheth nearest to it, as the most remote ; two being as distinct from one, as two hundred ; and the idea of

---

[1] Cf. ch. vii. § 7. This necessary co-existence of the 'suggested' idea of unity with all our other ideas, in concrete experience, hinders any of them from being therein simple. As thus inevitably blended with them all, number has been referred to the essential constitution of reason, instead of to the contingent phenomena of sense, which presuppose and exemplify number.

[2] The idea of number is specially important with Locke, as he makes it the means through which we get our clearest idea of infinity. Cf. § 8; ch. xvii. § 9. It has attracted metaphysical speculation since Pythagoras.

two as distinct from the idea of three, as the magnitude of the whole earth is from that of a mite[1]. This is not so in other simple modes, in which it is not so easy, nor perhaps possible for us to distinguish betwixt two approaching ideas, which yet are really different. For who will undertake to find a difference between the white of this paper and that of the next degree to it : or can form distinct ideas of every the least excess in extension ?

4. The clearness and distinctness of each mode of number Therefore Demon- strations in Numbers the most precise. from all others, even those that approach nearest, makes me apt to think that demonstrations in numbers, if they are not more evident and exact than in extension, yet they are more general in their use, and more determinate in their appli- cation. Because the ideas of numbers are more precise and distinguishable than in extension ; where every equality and excess are not so easy to be observed or measured ; because our thoughts cannot in space arrive at any determined small- ness beyond which it cannot go, as an unit ; and therefore the quantity or proportion of any the least excess cannot be discovered ; which is clear otherwise in number, where, as has been said, 91 is as distinguishable from 90 as from 9000, though 91 be the next immediate excess to 90. But it is not so in extension, where, whatsoever is more than just a foot or an inch, is not distinguishable from the standard of a foot or an inch ; and in lines which appear of an equal length, one may be longer than the other by innumerable parts : nor can any one assign an angle, which shall be the next biggest to a right one[2].

5. By the repeating, as has been said, the idea of an unit, and joining it to another unit, we make thereof one collective

---

[1] ' Numerical difference,' accord- ingly, with its *unit*, is the most distinct and measurable standard of Quantity, each variation in its mode be- ing as distinguishable from that which comes nearest to it as from the most remote number that can be conceived.

[2] ' Cela se doit entendre du nombre *entier* ; car autrement le nombre, dans sa latitude, comprenant le sourd, le rompu et le transcendant, et tout ce qui peut se prendre entre deux nombres entiers, est proportionnel à la ligne, et il y a là aussi peu de *minimum* que dans le contenu. Ainsi cette définition que le nombre est une multitude d'unités, n'a lieu que pour les entiers.' (Leibniz, *Nouveaux Essais.*) Locke seems to exclude *fractions* from his idea of number.

BOOK II.

CHAP. XVI.

Names
necessary
to Num-
bers.

idea, marked by the name two. And whosoever can do this, and proceed on, still adding one more to the last collective idea which he had of any number, and gave a name to it, may count, or have ideas, for several collections of units, distinguished one from another, as far as he hath a series of names for following numbers, and a memory to retain that series, with their several names: all numeration being but still the adding of one unit more, and giving to the whole together, as comprehended in one idea, a new or distinct name or sign, whereby to know it from those before and after, and distinguish it from every smaller or greater multitude of units. So that he that can add one to one, and so to two, and so go on with his tale, taking still with him the distinct names belonging to every progression; and so again, by subtracting an unit from each collection, retreat and lessen them, is capable of all the ideas of numbers within the compass of his language, or for which he hath names, though not perhaps of more. For, the several simple modes of numbers being in our minds but so many combinations of units, which have no variety, nor are capable of any other difference but more or less, names or marks for each distinct combination seem more necessary than in any other sort of ideas. For, without such names or marks, we can hardly well make use of numbers in reckoning, especially where the combination is made up of any great multitude of units; which put together, without a name or mark to distinguish that precise collection, will hardly be kept from being a heap in confusion.

Another
reason
for the
necessity
of names
to num-
bers.

6. This I think to be the reason why some Americans[1] I have spoken with, (who were otherwise of quick and rational parts enough,) could not, as we do, by any means count to 1000; nor had any distinct idea of that number, though they could reckon very well to 20. Because their language being scanty, and accommodated only to the few necessaries of a needy, simple life, unacquainted either with trade or mathematics, had no words in it to stand for 1000; so that when they were discoursed with of those greater numbers, they would show the hairs of their head, to express a great mul-

---

[1] American Indians.

titude, which they could not number; which inability, I suppose, proceeded from their want of names. The *Tououpinambos* had no names for numbers above 5; any number beyond that they made out by showing their fingers, and the fingers of others who were present[1]. And I doubt not but we ourselves might distinctly number in words a great deal further than we usually do, would we find out but some fit denominations to signify them by; whereas, in the way we take now to name them, by millions of millions of millions, &c., it is hard to go beyond eighteen, or at most, four and twenty, decimal progressions, without confusion. But to show how much distinct names conduce to our well reckoning, or having useful ideas of numbers, let us see all these following figures in one continued line, as the marks of one number: v. g.

Nonillions.	Octillions.	Septillions.	Sextillions.	Quintrillions.	Quartrillions.	Trillions.	Billions.	Millions.	Units.
857324	162486	345896	437918	423147	248106	235421	261734	368149	623137

The ordinary way of naming this number in English, will be the often repeating of millions, of millions, of millions, of millions, of millions, of millions, of millions, of millions, (which is the denomination of the second six figures[2]. In which way, it will be very hard to have any distinguishing notions of this number. But whether, by giving every six figures a new and orderly denomination, these, and perhaps a great many more figures in progression, might not easily be counted distinctly, and ideas of them both got more easily to ourselves, and more plainly signified to others, I leave it to be considered. This I mention only to show how necessary distinct names are to numbering, without pretending to introduce new ones of my invention.

7. Thus children, either for want of names to mark the several progressions of numbers, or not having yet the faculty to collect scattered ideas into complex ones, and range them in a regular order, and so retain them in their memories, as is

Why Children number not earlier.

---

[1] *Histoire d'un Voyage, fait en la Terre du Brésil,* par Jean de Lery, chap. xx. pp. 307-382.

[2] Any number, however great, is finite, and measures a space or a duration without being fit to measure Immensity or Eternity, which transcend the idea or category of number, and are lost in the not-numerable.

necessary to reckoning, do not begin to number very early, nor proceed in it very far or steadily, till a good while after they are well furnished with good store of other ideas: and one may often observe them discourse and reason pretty well, and have very clear conceptions of several other things, before they can tell twenty. And some, through the default of their memories, who cannot retain the several combinations of numbers, with their names, annexed in their distinct orders, and the dependence of so long a train of numeral progressions, and their relation one to another, are not able all their lifetime to reckon, or regularly go over any moderate series of numbers. For he that will count twenty, or have any idea of that number, must know that nineteen went before, with the distinct name or sign of every one of them, as they stand marked in their order; for wherever this fails, a gap is made, the chain breaks, and the progress in numbering can go no further. So that to reckon right, it is required, (1) That the mind distinguish carefully two ideas, which are different one from another only by the addition or subtraction of *one* unit: (2) That it retain in memory the names or marks of the several combinations, from an unit to that number; and that not confusedly, and at random, but in that exact order that the numbers follow one another. In either of which, if it trips, the whole business of numbering will be disturbed, and there will remain only the confused idea of multitude, but the ideas necessary to distinct numeration will not be attained to.

Number measures all Measurables

8. This further is observable in number, that it is that which the mind makes use of in measuring all things that by us are measurable, which principally are *expansion* and *duration*; and our idea of infinity, even when applied to those, seems to be nothing but the infinity of number. For what else are our ideas of Eternity and Immensity, but the repeated additions of certain ideas of imagined parts of duration and expansion, with the infinity of number; in which we can come to no end of addition? For such an inexhaustible stock, number (of all other our ideas) most clearly furnishes us with, as is obvious to every one. For let a man collect into one sum as great a number as he pleases, this multitude, how great soever, lessens not one jot the power of adding to

it, or brings him any nearer the end of the inexhaustible stock of number; where still there remains as much to be added, as if none were taken out. And this *endless addition* or *addibility* (if any one like the word better) of numbers, so apparent to the mind, is that, I think, which gives us the clearest and most distinct idea of infinity: of which more in the following chapter.

CHAPTER XVII.

OF INFINITY.

BOOK II.

—→•←—

CHAP.
XVII.

Infinity,
in its
original
Intention,
attributed
to Space,
Duration,
and Num·
ber.

1. HE that would know what kind of idea it is to which we give the name of *infinity*, cannot do it better than by considering to what infinity is by the mind more immediately attributed ; and then how the mind comes to frame it.

Finite and *infinite* seem to me to be looked upon by the mind as the *modes of quantity*, and to be attributed primarily in their first designation only to those things which have parts, and are capable of increase or diminution by the addition or subtraction of any the least part : and such are the ideas of space, duration, and number, which we have considered in the foregoing chapters [1]. It is true, that we cannot but be assured, that the great God, of whom and from whom are all things, is incomprehensibly infinite : but yet, when we apply to that first and supreme Being our idea of infinite, in our weak and narrow thoughts, we do it primarily in respect to his duration and ubiquity ; and, I think, more figuratively to his power, wisdom, and goodness, and other attributes, which are properly inexhaustible and incomprehensible, &c.[2]

---

[1] In which it is argued that we can have no positive idea, or mental image of an infinite quantity of anything ; while it seems to be implied that we have a positive idea of the *felt irresistible necessity to advance*, which makes infinity an idea of reflection, so far as it is positive, and suggested by space or time.

[2] Locke's idea of Infinity, as illustrated in the four preceding chapters, is a quantitative infinity, in abstract space and duration ; composed of finite parts, inexhaustible in number and relations. The concrete, qualitative Infinite is found in God ; perfect Reason and Purpose personified, yet immanent and Supreme in nature and spirit, mysteriously independent of our ideas of space and duration.

For, when we call *them* infinite, we have no other idea of this
infinity but what carries with it some reflection on, and
imitation of, that number or extent of the acts or objects of
God's power, wisdom, and goodness, which can never be
supposed so great, or so many, which these attributes will not
always surmount and exceed, let us multiply them in our
thoughts as far as we can, with all the infinity of endless
number. I do not pretend to say how these attributes are in
God, who is infinitely beyond the reach of our narrow capacities : they do, without doubt, contain in them all possible
perfection : but this, I say, is our way of conceiving them,
and these our ideas of their infinity.

2. Finite then, and infinite, being by the mind looked on The Idea
of Finite
easily got.
as *modifications* of expansion and duration, the next thing to
be considered, is,—*How the mind comes by them.* As for the
idea of finite, there is no great difficulty. The obvious portions of extension that affect our senses, carry with them into
the mind the idea of finite : and the ordinary periods of succession, whereby we measure time and duration, as hours,
days, and years, are bounded lengths. The difficulty is, how
we come by those *boundless ideas* of eternity and immensity ;
since the objects we converse with come so much short of
any approach or proportion to that largeness[1].

3. Every one that has any idea of any stated lengths of How we
come by
the Idea of
Infinity.
space, as a foot, finds that he can repeat that idea ; and
joining it to the former, make the idea of two feet ; and by
the addition of a third, three feet ; and so on, without ever
coming to an end of his additions, whether of the same idea
of a foot, or, if he pleases, of doubling it, or any other idea he
has of any length, as a mile, or diameter of the earth, or of
the *orbis magnus* : for whichever of these he takes, and how
often soever he doubles, or any otherwise multiplies it, he finds,
that, after he has continued his doubling in his thoughts, and
enlarged his idea as much as he pleases, he has no more

---

[1] We have never perceived, and
could not perceive an object that is
boundless, either in extent or duration,
and yet we are necessarily impelled
towards an obscure idea of boundlessness. This fact Locke tries to reconcile
with his fundamental hypothesis of
the dependence of all our ideas upon
corresponding simple ideas, or primary
impressions.

BOOK II.

—◆—

CHAP.
XVII.

Our Idea
of Space
boundless.

reason to stop, nor is one jot nearer the end of such addition, than he was at first setting out: the power of enlarging his idea of space by further additions remaining still the same, he hence takes the idea of infinite space.

4. This, I think, is the way whereby the mind gets the *idea* of infinite space[1]. It is a quite different consideration, to examine whether the mind has the idea of such a boundless space *actually existing*; since our ideas are not always proofs of the existence of things: but yet, since this comes here in our way, I suppose I may say, that we are *apt to think* that space in itself is actually boundless, to which imagination the idea of space or expansion of itself naturally leads us. For, it being considered by us, either as the extension of body, or as existing by itself, without any solid matter taking it up, (for of such a void space we have not only the idea, but I have proved, as I think, from the motion of body, its necessary existence,) it is impossible the mind should be ever able to find or suppose any end of it, or be stopped anywhere in its progress in this space, how far soever it extends its thoughts. Any bounds made with body, even adamantine walls, are so far from putting a stop to the mind in its further progress in space and extension that it rather facilitates and enlarges it. For so far as that body reaches, so far no one can doubt of extension; and when we are come to the utmost extremity of body, what is there that can there put a stop, and satisfy the mind that it is at the end of space, when it perceives that it is not; nay, when it is satisfied that body itself can move into it? For, if it be necessary for the motion of body, that there should be an empty space, though ever so little, here amongst bodies; and if it be possible for body to move in or through that empty space;—nay, it is impossible for any particle of matter to move but into an empty space; the same possibility of a body's moving into a void space, beyond the utmost

---

[1] A merely empirical 'repetition' of phenomena does not explain the *intellectual need* for *continuing without end* the process of repetition, which, as Locke himself seems to allow, is implied in the idea of space. Is not this necessity due to something in mind, and in the rational nature of things, not to the merely sensuous presentations, which *per se* cannot transcend their own finitude and transitoriness?

bounds of body, as well as into a void space interspersed amongst bodies, will always remain clear and evident: the idea of empty pure space, whether within or beyond the confines of all bodies, being exactly the same, differing not in nature, though in bulk; and there being nothing to hinder body from moving into it. So that wherever the mind places itself by any thought, either amongst, or remote from all bodies, it can, in this uniform idea of space, nowhere find any bounds, any end; and so must necessarily conclude it, by the very nature and idea of each part of it, to be actually infinite[1].

5. As, by the power we find in ourselves of repeating, as often as we will, any idea of space, we get the idea of *immensity*; so, by being able to repeat the idea of any length of duration we have in our minds, with all the endless addition of number, we come by the idea of *eternity*. For we find in ourselves[2], we can no more come to an end of such repeated ideas than we can come to the end of number; which every one perceives he cannot. But here again it is another question, quite different from our having an *idea* of eternity, to know whether there were *any real being*, whose duration has been eternal. And as to this, I say, he that considers something now existing, must necessarily come to Something eternal. But having spoke of this in another place[3], I shall say here no more of it, but proceed on to some other considerations of our idea of infinity.

And so of Duration.

6. If it be so, that our idea of infinity be got from the power[4] we observe in ourselves of repeating, without end, our own ideas, it may be demanded,—Why we do not attribute infinity

Why other Ideas are not capable of Infinity.

---

[1] 'Pure space,' Locke asserts elsewhere, is purely nothing, but merely infinite possibility that something extended might there exist. 'Having been all our lifetime accustomed to phrases, that import it to be a real thing, we come at last to be possessed with this prejudice, that it *is* a real thing and not *a bare relation.*' (*Miscellaneous Papers.*)

[2] We 'find in ourselves,' i.e. not in the presented phenomena, but 'in ourselves,' we find something that forbids

us to rest absolutely in any limited duration.

[3] Cf. Bk. IV. ch. x. § 3. The reference might imply that the chapter in the Fourth Book, here referred to, was written before this on 'Infinity.' He finds it impossible to suppose that *duration* could be empty; but the distinction of space from body, so that there is room for motion, means that portions of *space* are empty.

[4] Rather, in the ideas of space and duration, the *mental obligation.*

to other ideas, as well as those of space and duration; since they may be as easily, and as often, repeated in our minds as the other: and yet nobody ever thinks of infinite sweetness, or infinite whiteness, though he can repeat the idea of sweet or white, as frequently as those of a yard or a day? To which I answer,—All the ideas that are considered as having parts, and are capable of increase by the addition of any equal or less parts, afford us, by their repetition, the idea of infinity; because, with this endless repetition, there is continued an enlargement of which there *can* be no end. But in other ideas it is not so. For to the largest idea of extension or duration that I at present have, the addition of any the least part makes an increase; but to the perfectest idea I have of the whitest whiteness, if I add another of a less or equal whiteness, (and of a whiter than I have, I cannot add the idea,) it makes no increase, and enlarges not my idea at all; and therefore the different ideas of whiteness, &c. are called degrees. For those ideas that consist of parts[1] are capable of being augmented by every addition of the least part; but if you take the idea of white, which one parcel of snow yielded yesterday to our sight, and another idea of white from another parcel of snow you see to-day, and put them together in your mind, they embody, as it were, and run into one, and the idea of whiteness is not at all increased; and if we add a less degree of whiteness to a greater, we are so far from increasing, that we diminish it. Those ideas that consist not of parts cannot be augmented to what proportion men please, or be stretched beyond what they have received by their senses[1]; but space, duration, and number, being capable of increase by repetition, leave in the mind an idea

---

[1] Locke's quantitative Infinite consists of *innumerable* parts, and this cannot be conceived as an absolute whole or completed idea. Endless repetition cannot end in a positive idea of infinite quantity. A completed or comprehensible infinite quantity (great or small) in space, time, or number, would be incapable of further increase. This sort of infinite is repelled by the category of quantity, as self-contradictory, a *finite* infinite. The *obligation* to continue expanding these ideas of space and duration leaves us, at our furthest stage, with that sense of incompleteness and mystery, which seems to be our only relation to the Infinite through this avenue.

of endless room for more ; nor can we conceive anywhere a stop to a further addition or progression : and so those ideas *alone* lead our minds towards the thought of infinity.

7. Though our idea of infinity arise from the contemplation of quantity, and the endless increase the mind is able to make in quantity, by the repeated additions of what portions thereof it pleases ; yet I guess we cause great confusion in our thoughts, when we join infinity to any supposed idea of quantity the mind can be thought to have, and so discourse or reason about an infinite quantity, as an infinite space, or an infinite duration. For, as our idea of infinity being, as I think, *an endless growing idea*, but the idea of any quantity the mind has, being at that time *terminated* in that idea, (for be it as great as it will, it can be no greater than it is,)—to join infinity to it, is to adjust a standing measure to a growing bulk ; and therefore I think it is not an insignificant subtilty, if I say, that we are carefully to distinguish between the idea of the infinity of space, and the idea of a space infinite. The first is nothing but a supposed endless progression of the mind, over what repeated ideas of space it pleases ; but to have actually in the mind the idea[1] of a space infinite, is to suppose the mind already passed over, and actually to have a view of *all* those repeated ideas of space which an *endless* repetition can never totally represent to it ; which carries in it a plain contradiction[2].

8. This, perhaps, will be a little plainer, if we consider it in numbers. The infinity of numbers, to the end of whose addition every one perceives there is no approach, easily appears to any one that reflects on it. But, how clear soever this idea of the infinity of number be, there is nothing yet more evident than the absurdity of the actual idea[3] of an infinite number. Whatsoever *positive* ideas we have in our minds of any space, duration, or number, let them be ever so

---

[1] Idea, i. e. completed or finite image in the mind.

[2] This suggests that the ideas of Quantity (in space, duration, or number) and Infinity are incompatible, and that the true infinite is *unquantifiable.* Accordingly space and duration at last disappear in the *mysteries* of Immensity and Eternity. This section may be compared with Kant's solution of his first antinomy. See also Prof. Caird's *Philosophy of Kant,* Pt. II. ch. xvii.

[3] That is, completed sensuous image.

great, they are still finite; but when we suppose an inexhaustible remainder, from which we remove all bounds, and wherein we allow the mind an endless progression of thought, without ever completing the idea, there we have our idea of infinity : which, though it seems to be pretty clear when we consider nothing else in it but the negation of an end, yet, when we would frame in our minds the idea[1] of an infinite space or duration, that idea is very obscure and confused, because it is made up of two parts, very different, if not inconsistent. For, let a man frame in his mind an idea of any space or number, as great as he will; it is plain the mind *rests and terminates* in that idea, which is contrary to the idea of infinity, which *consists in a supposed endless progression*[1]. And therefore I think it is that we are so easily confounded, when we come to argue and reason about infinite space or duration, &c.[2] Because the parts of such an idea not being perceived to be, as they are, inconsistent[3], the one side or other always perplexes, whatever consequences we draw from the other ; as an idea of motion not passing on would perplex any one who should argue from such an idea, which is not better than an idea of motion at rest. And such another seems to me to be the idea of a space, or (which is the same thing) a number infinite, i. e. of a space or number which the mind actually has, and so views and terminates in ; and of a space or number, which, in a constant and endless enlarging and progression, it can in thought never attain to. For, how

---

[1] Not in a *mental image* of *endless* progression, which is not merely unimaginable by man, but is in its nature unimaginable. The imagination of 'progress' is positive and possible ; but there can be no image of '*endless* progression,' which involves what is necessarily incomplete and mysterious.

[2] The puzzles of the infinitely little, and the infinite divisibility of space and duration were raised by Berkeley, in his controversies with the mathematicians. They are discussed in Hume's *Treatise*, Bk. I. pt. ii., and *Inquiry*, sect. xii., in their sceptical aspects. But all necessarily imperfect truths involve contradiction, when forced under the categories of an understanding that judges according to the measure of the sensuous imagination. Locke, in his own way, accepted them in their obscurity, and insists, in his letters to Stillingfleet, that he never intended to say that *all* our legitimate ideas must be clear and distinct.

[3] 'Inconsistent,' i.e. if we insist on arguing from the necessarily inadequate idea, on the assumption that it is adequate and imaginable.

large soever an idea of space I have in my mind, it is no
larger than it is that instant that I have it, though I be
capable the next instant to double it, and so on *in infinitum*;
for that alone is infinite which has no bounds; and that the
idea of infinity, in which our thoughts can find none[1].

9. But of all other ideas, it is number, as I have said, which
I think furnishes us with the clearest and most distinct idea
of infinity we are capable of[2]. For, even in space and duration, when the mind pursues the idea of infinity, it there makes
use of the ideas and repetitions of numbers, as of millions and
millions of miles, or years, which are so many distinct ideas,—
kept best by number from running into a confused heap,
wherein the mind loses itself; and when it has added together
as many millions, &c., as it pleases, of known lengths of space
or duration, the clearest idea it can get of infinity, is the
confused incomprehensible remainder of endless addible
numbers, which affords no prospect of stop or boundary[3].

10. It will, perhaps, give us a little further light into the
idea we have of infinity, and discover to us, that it is *nothing
but the infinity of number applied to determinate parts, of
which we have in our minds the distinct ideas*, if we consider
that number is not generally thought by us infinite, whereas
duration and extension are apt to be so; which arises from
hence,—that in number we are at one end, as it were: for
there being in number nothing *less* than an unit[4], we there
stop, and are at an end; but in addition, or increase of number,
we can set no bounds: and so it is like a line, whereof one
end terminating with us, the other is extended still forwards,
beyond all that we can conceive. But in space and duration
it is otherwise. For in duration we consider it as if this line
of number were extended *both* ways—to an unconceivable,

BOOK II.

CHAP.
XVII.

Number
affords us
the clear-
est Idea of
Infinity.

Our differ-
ent Con-
ceptions
of the
Infinity of
Number
contrasted
with those
of Dura-
tion and
Expan-
sion.

---

[1] As already noted, we can imagine
progression, but not *endless* progress.

[2] That is to say, the unimaginable
idea of infinity is suggested by all
finite, or imaginable, things, which
may be numbered; for number is
finite, till it is lost in the mystery of
the *numberless*. ' Le vrai infini,' says
Leibniz, ' à la rigueur n'est que dans

l'absolu, qui est *antérieur à toute composition, et n'est point formé par l'addition des parties*.'

[3] If ' endless,' it not only ' affords
no prospect ' of a stop : a stop is impossible, on pain of express contradiction. Thus endlessness transcends the
category of quantity.

[4] What of fractions ?

undeterminate, and infinite length[1]; which is evident to any one that will but reflect on what consideration he hath of Eternity; which, I suppose, will find to be nothing else but the turning this infinity of number both ways, *à parte ante*, and *à parte post*, as they speak. For, when we would consider eternity, *à parte ante*, what do we but, beginning from ourselves and the present time we are in, repeat in our minds the ideas of years, or ages, or any other assignable portion of duration past, with a prospect of proceeding in such addition with all the infinity of number[2]: and when we would consider eternity, *à parte post*, we just after the same rate begin from ourselves, and reckon by multiplied periods yet to come, still extending that line of number as before. And these two being put together, are that infinite duration we call *Eternity*: which, as we turn our view either way, forwards or backwards, appears infinite, because we still turn that way the infinite end of number, i. e. the power[3] still of adding more.

How we conceive the Infinity of Space.

11. The same happens also in space, wherein, conceiving ourselves to be, as it were, in the centre, we do on all sides pursue those indeterminable lines of number; and reckoning any way from ourselves, a yard, mile, diameter of the earth, or *orbis magnus*,—by the infinity of number, we add others to them, as often as we will. And having no more reason[4] to set bounds to those repeated ideas than we have to set bounds to number, we have that indeterminable idea of immensity.

Infinite Divisibility.

12. And since in any bulk of matter[5] our thoughts can never arrive at the utmost divisibility, therefore there is an

---

[1] Of which we can have no mental image; although we may of the (*necessarily ineffectual*) *mental struggle to reach it*.

[2] If the *à parte ante* and *à parte post* is infinite, can it be spoken of as 'parts,' or as 'two'—number being finite or quantitative? 'De spatio et tempore interminabili,' says Hobbes, 'dici non potest quod sit *totum* aut *unum*; non *totum*, quia ex nullis partibus componi potest; partes enim quotcunque, cum singulae sint finitae, etiam simul sumptae facient totum finitum. Non *unum*, quia unum non dicitur nisi ut comparatum ad aliud; duo autem infinita spatia, vel duo tempora infinita esse, intelligi non potest. Denique cum quaeritur an mundus finitus an infinitus, nihil in animo est sub voce *mundus*; quicquid enim *imaginamur*, eo ipso finitum est.' (*Philosophia Prima*, cap. vii. 12.) This assumes sensuous imagination to be the measure of intelligence.

[3] Rather, are subject to a constant mental necessity of ' adding more.'

[4] Rather, having reason *not* to do so.

[5] Or, as it has been put—'non *datur* quantitatis minimum divisibile,' and 'quavis quantitate data, sumi posse minorem.'

apparent infinity to us also in that, which has the infinity also
of number ; but with this difference,—that, in the former considerations of the infinity of space and duration, we only use
addition of numbers ; whereas this is like the division of an
unit into its fractions, wherein the mind also can proceed *in
infinitum*, as well as in the former additions ; it being indeed
but the addition still of new numbers : though in the addition
of the one, we can have no more the *positive* idea of a space infinitely great, than, in the division of the other, we can have
the [positive] idea of a body infinitely little ;—our idea of infinity being, as I may say, a growing or fugitive idea, still in
a boundless progression, that can stop nowhere[1].

13. Though it be hard, I think, to find anyone so absurd as
to say he has the *positive* idea of an actual infinite number[2] ;—
the infinity whereof lies only in a power still of adding any
combination of units to any former number, and that as long
and as much as one will ; the like also being in the infinity of
space and duration, which power leaves always to the mind
room for endless additions ;—yet there be those who imagine
they have *positive* ideas of infinite duration and space[3]. It
would, I think, be enough to destroy any such positive idea of
infinite, to ask him that has it,—whether he could add to it or
no ; which would easily show the mistake of such a positive
idea. We can, I think, have no positive idea of any space
or duration which is not made up of, and commensurate to, repeated numbers of feet or yards, or days and years ; which are
the common measures, whereof we have the ideas in our minds,
and whereby we judge of the greatness of this sort of quantities.

BOOK II.

CHAP.
XVII.

No posi-
tive Idea
of Infinity.

---

[1] Hence it is inadequate, when regarded, as here by Locke, from the
point of view of the sensuous imagination, and therefore of quantity, in
space, duration, and number ; and misleading when the inadequate idea,
which alone. is possible at the human
point of view, is treated in our reasonings as if it were the whole.

[2] Infinite in number, that is to say,
cannot be phenomenalised—individualised—although the mental tendency
towards it can, regarded as a state of
the finite mind ; including, as it does,
the (negative) idea, that we can have
no quantified image of that towards
which we are, nevertheless, obliged to
tend.

[3] God, and finite persons too are
found transcending human understanding, measured by the phenomena of
external and internal sense, whenever
man tries to represent either as *without
beginning* or *without end*, i. e. as self-
conscious persons somehow transcending time and quantity.

And therefore, since an infinite idea of space or duration must needs be made up of infinite parts, it can have no other infinity than that of number *capable* still of further addition ; but not an actual positive idea of a number infinite. For, I think it is evident, that the addition of finite things together (as are all lengths whereof we have the positive ideas) can never otherwise produce the idea of infinite than as number does ; which, consisting of additions of finite units one to another, suggests [1] the idea of infinite, only by a power we find we have of still increasing the sum, and adding more of the same kind ; without coming one jot nearer the end of such progression.

How we cannot have a positive idea of infinity in Quantity.

14. They who would prove their idea of infinite to be positive, seem to me to do it by a pleasant argument, taken from the negation of an end; which being negative, the negation of it is positive. He that considers that the end is, in body [2], but the extremity or superficies of that body, will not perhaps be forward to grant that the end is a bare negative : and he that perceives the end of his pen is black or white, will be apt to think that the end is something more than a pure negation. Nor is it, when applied to duration, the bare negation of existence, but more properly the last moment of it. But if they will have the end to be nothing but the bare negation of existence, I am sure they cannot deny but the beginning is the first instant of being, and is not by any body conceived to be a bare negation ; and therefore, by their own argument, the idea of eternal, *à parte ante*, or of a duration without a beginning, is but a negative idea.

What is positive, what negative, in our Idea of infinite.

15. The idea of infinite has, I confess, something of positive in all those things we apply to it. When we would think of infinite space or duration, we at first step usually make some very large idea, as perhaps of millions of ages, or miles, which possibly we double and multiply several times. All that we

---

[1] This makes the idea of the infinite that arises in quantity, a mysterious 'suggestion' of *intelligence*, not a datum of *sense*, elaborated by an understanding that judges under sensuous imagination. Locke's infinite is only the ideally incomplete outcome of the finite; which would involve contradiction, if the infinite, struggled after, and which baffles the imagination, were *itself* supposed to be a quantity. Cf. *Novum Organum*, Lib. i. 48, and Dr. Fowler's notes.

[2] 'body,' i.e. in a finite body—a finite object.

thus amass together in our thoughts is positive, and the assemblage of a great number of positive ideas of space or duration. But what still remains beyond this we have no more a positive distinct notion of than a mariner has of the depth of the sea; where, having let down a large portion of his sounding-line, he reaches no bottom. Whereby he knows the depth to be so many fathoms, and more ; but how much the more is [1], he hath no distinct notion at all: and could he always supply new line, and find the plummet always sink, without ever stopping, he would be something in the posture of the mind reaching after a complete and positive idea of infinity [2]. In which case, let this line be ten, or ten thousand fathoms long, it equally discovers what is beyond it, and gives only this confused and comparative idea, that this is not all, but one may yet go farther. So much as the mind comprehends of any space, it has a positive idea of : but in endeavouring to make it infinite,—it being always enlarging, always advancing,—the idea is still imperfect and incomplete. So much space as the mind takes a view of in its comtemplation of greatness, is a clear picture, and positive in the understanding : but infinite is still greater. 1. Then the idea of *so much* is positive and clear. 2. The idea of *greater* is also clear; but it is but a comparative idea, the idea of *so much greater as cannot be comprehended.* 3. And this is plainly negative : not positive. For he has no positive clear idea of the largeness of any extension, (which is that sought for in the idea of infinite), that has not a comprehensive idea of the dimensions of it : and such, nobody, I think, pretends to in what is infinite. For to

---

[1] This is still to compare a lesser finite with a (by us) unimaginable greater *finite*, but not to compare it with the infinite, to which ' how much' is inapplicable, without assuming the supposed infinite to be a measurable quantity. ' How much ' and ' the more ' are expressions which keep us still within the conception of a quantity.

[2] This ' posture of the mind ' we *may* have a positive idea of,—as a phenomenon that can be individualised ; but this cannot be said of the idea of the infinity, to which the ' posture' relates ; for the idea, if completed, or comprehended in imagination, would give evidence on its face that it was not the infinity the mind was ' reaching after.' *The feeling of a mental necessity which urges us beyond the idea of what is finite or completed,* but not *the incomplete or incomprehensible itself, towards which we are thus urged,* is within the compass of an understanding confined to what is imaginable.

BOOK II.

CHAP. XVII.

say a man has a positive clear idea of any quantity, without knowing how great it is, is as reasonable as to say, he has the positive clear idea of the number of the sands on the sea-shore, who knows not how many there be, but only that they are more than twenty. For just such a perfect and positive idea has he of an infinite space or duration, who says it is *larger than* the extent or duration of ten, one hundred, one thousand, or any other number of miles, or years, whereof he has or can have a positive idea; which is all the idea, I think, we have of infinite[1]. So that what lies beyond our positive idea *towards* infinity, lies in obscurity, and has the indeterminate confusion of a negative idea, wherein I know I neither do nor can comprehend all I would, it being too large[1] for a finite and narrow capacity. And that cannot but be very far from a positive complete idea, wherein the greatest part of what I would comprehend is left out, under the undeterminate intimation of being still greater. For to say, that, having in any quantity measured so much, or gone so far, you are not yet at the end, is only to say that that quantity is greater. So that the negation of an end in any quantity is, in other words, only to say that it is bigger; and a total negation of an end is but carrying this bigger still with you, in all the progressions your thoughts shall make in quantity; and adding this *idea of still greater* to *all* the ideas you have, or can be supposed to have, of quantity[2]. Now, whether such an idea as that be positive, I leave any one to consider.

We have no positive Idea of an infinite Duration.

16. I ask those who say they have a positive idea of eternity, whether their idea of duration includes in it succession[3], or not? If it does not, they ought to show the difference of their notion of duration, when applied to an eternal Being, and to a finite; since, perhaps, there may be others as well as I, who will own to them their weakness of understanding in this point, and

---

[1] Can we properly speak of the infinite which quantity suggests as 'larger' in quantity than any finite quantity? This would make the infinite differ only in degree from the finite.

[2] Is largeness of quantity, to whatever extent, or 'part,' however large, applicable to infinity at all, or consistent with its unimaginableness?

[3] 'Succession,' or change (as conceived by man) consists of parts, and is thus quantitative and finite in its constitution.

acknowledge that the notion they have of duration forces them
to conceive, that whatever has duration, is of a longer continuance to-day than it was yesterday. If, to avoid succession
in external existence, they return to the *punctum stans* of the
schools, I suppose they will thereby very little mend the
matter, or help us to a more clear and positive idea of infinite
duration ; there being nothing more inconceivable to me than
duration without succession. Besides, that *punctum stans* [1], if
it signify anything, being not *quantum*, finite or infinite cannot
belong to it. But, if our weak apprehensions cannot separate
succession from any duration whatsoever, our idea of eternity
can be nothing but of *infinite succession of moments of duration
wherein anything does exist;* and whether any one has, or can
have, a positive idea of an actual infinite number, I leave him
to consider, till his infinite number be so great that he himself
can add no more to it ; and as long as he can [2] increase it,
I doubt he himself will think the idea he hath of it a little too
scanty for positive infinity.

17. I think it unavoidable for every considering, rational No com-
creature, that will but examine his own or any other existence, plete Idea of Eternal
to have the notion of an eternal, wise Being, who had no begin- Being.
ning : and such an idea of infinite duration I am sure I have.
But this negation of a beginning, being but the negation of
a positive thing, scarce gives me a positive idea of infinity ;
which, whenever I endeavour to extend my thoughts to, I
confess myself at a loss, and I find I cannot attain any clear
comprehension of it.

18. He that thinks he has a positive idea of infinite space, No posi-
will, when he considers it, find that he can no more have a tive Idea of infinite
positive idea of the greatest, than he has of the least space. Space.
For in this latter, which seems the easier of the two, and more
within our comprehension, we are capable only of a comparative idea of smallness, which will always be less than any one
whereof we have the positive idea. All our *positive* ideas
of any quantity, whether great or little, have always bounds,

---

[1] See Green's 'Introduction' to
Hume, p. 121, on the presence of consciousness to itself as the true *punctum*

stans, and not an event in time.

[2] 'can,' and also *must*, if in virtue of
a mental necessity.

BOOK II.
CHAP.
XVII.

though our *comparative* idea, whereby we can always add to the one, and take from the other, hath no bounds. For that which remains, either great or little, not being comprehended in that positive idea which we have, lies in obscurity; and we have no other idea of it, but of the power of enlarging the one and diminishing the other, *without ceasing*. A pestle and mortar will as soon bring any particle of matter to indivisibility, as the acutest thought of a mathematician; and a surveyor may as soon with his chain measure out infinite space, as a philosopher by the quickest flight of mind reach it, or by thinking comprehend it; which is to have a positive idea of it. He that thinks on a cube of an inch diameter, has a clear and positive idea of it in his mind, and so can frame one of $\frac{1}{2}, \frac{1}{4}, \frac{1}{8}$, and so on, till he has the idea in his thoughts of something very little; but yet reaches not the idea of that incomprehensible littleness which division can produce. What remains of smallness is as far from his thoughts as when he first began; and therefore he never comes at all to have a clear and positive idea of that smallness[1] which is consequent to infinite divisibility.

What is positive, what negative, in our Idea of Infinite.

19. Every one that looks towards infinity does, as I have said, at first glance make some very large idea of that which he applies it to, let it be space or duration; and possibly he wearies his thoughts, by multiplying in his mind that first large idea: but yet by that he comes no nearer[2] to the having a positive clear idea of what remains to make up a positive infinite, than the country fellow had of the water which was yet to come, and pass the channel of the river where he stood:

'Rusticus expectat dum defluat amnis, at ille
Labitur, et labetur in omne volubilis ævum[3].'

Some think they

20. There are some I have met that put so much difference between infinite duration and infinite space, that they persuade

---

[1] 'smallness'—rather no complete idea of *what* the intellectual outcome would be of the divisibility towards which one is intellectually impelled.

[2] 'no nearer'—the two states of intelligence are *incommensurate* in the case of infinity, but not in the other case.

[3] Horat. *Epist.* I. ii. 42.

themselves that they have a positive idea of eternity, but that
they have not, nor can have any idea of infinite space. The
reason of which mistake I suppose to be this—that finding,
by a due contemplation of causes and effects, that it is necessary to admit some Eternal Being, and so to consider the real
existence of that Being as taken up and commensurate to
their idea of eternity; but, on the other side, not finding it
necessary, but, on the contrary, apparently absurd, that body
should be infinite, they forwardly conclude that they can have
no idea of infinite space, because they can have no idea of
infinite matter [1]. Which consequence, I conceive, is very ill
collected, because the existence of matter is no ways necessary
to the existence of space, no more than the existence of
motion, or the sun, is necessary to duration, though duration
uses to be measured by it. And I doubt not but that a man
may have the idea of ten thousand miles square, without any
body so big, as well as the idea of ten thousand years, without
any body so old. It seems as easy to me to have the idea of
space empty of body, as to think of the capacity of a bushel
without corn, or the hollow of a nut-shell without a kernel
in it: it being no more necessary that there should be existing
a solid body, infinitely extended, because we have an idea of
the infinity of space, than it is necessary that the world should
be eternal, because we have an idea of infinite duration. And
why should we think our idea of infinite space requires the
real existence of matter to support it, when we find that we
have as clear an idea of an infinite duration to come, as we
have of infinite duration past? Though I suppose nobody
thinks it conceivable that anything does or has existed in that
future duration. Nor is it possible to join our idea of future
duration with present or past existence, any more than it is
possible to make the ideas of yesterday, to-day, and to-morrow
to be the same; or bring ages past and future together, and
make them contemporary. But if these men are of the mind,
that they have clearer ideas of infinite duration than of infinite
space, because it is past doubt that God has existed from all
eternity, but there is no real matter co-extended with infinite

[1] cf. ch. xv. § 4.

space; yet those philosophers who are of opinion that infinite space is possessed by God's infinite omnipresence [1], as well as infinite duration by his eternal existence, must be allowed to have as clear an idea of infinite space as of infinite duration; though neither of them, I think, has any positive idea of infinity in either case. For whatsoever positive ideas a man has in his mind of any quantity, he can repeat it, and add it to the former, as easy as he can add together the ideas of two days, or two paces, which are positive ideas of lengths he has in his mind, and so on as long as he pleases: whereby, if a man had a positive idea of infinite, either duration or space, he could add two infinites together; nay, make one infinite infinitely bigger than another—absurdities too gross to be confuted.

21. But yet if after all this, there be men who persuade themselves that they have clear positive comprehensive ideas of infinity, it is fit they enjoy their privilege: and I should be very glad (with some others that I know, who acknowledge they have none such) to be better informed by their communication. For I have been hitherto apt to think that the great and inextricable difficulties which perpetually involve all discourses concerning infinity,—whether of space, duration, or divisibility, have been the certain marks of a defect in our ideas of infinity, and the disproportion the nature thereof has to the comprehension of our narrow capacities. For, whilst men talk and dispute of infinite space or duration, as if they had as complete and positive ideas of them as they have of the names they use for them, or as they have of a yard, or an hour, or any other determinate quantity; it is no wonder if the incomprehensible nature of the thing they discourse of, or reason about, leads them into perplexities and contradictions, and their minds be overlaid by an object too large and mighty to be surveyed and managed by them [2].

[1] Not that God is *extended*, as solid and extended things are, but that Divine Reason is *everywhere* manifested and operative. The expression also suggests Samuel Clarke's attempt to demonstrate, that the existence of God is implied in the necessary infinity of space—which is thus regarded as an attribute of the Divine Being.

[2] Are not these 'perplexities and contradictions' evidence of the inadequacy of the supposition that the (unimaginable) Infinite consists of parts, is thus numerable? Leibniz refers to

22. If I have dwelt pretty long on the consideration of BOOK II.
duration, space, and number, and what arises from the contemplation of them,—Infinity, it is possibly no more than the CHAP.
XVII.
matter requires; there being few simple ideas whose *modes* All these
give more exercise to the thoughts of men than those do. I are modes
of Ideas
pretend not to treat of them in their full latitude [1]. It suffices got from
to my design to show how the mind receives them, such as Sensation
and Re-
they are, from sensation and reflection; and how even the flection.
idea we have of infinity, how remote soever it may seem to
be from any object of sense, or operation of our mind, has,
nevertheless, as all our other ideas, its original there [2]. Some
mathematicians perhaps, of advanced speculations, may have
other ways to introduce into their minds ideas of infinity.
But this hinders not but that they themselves, as well as all
other men, got the first ideas which they had of infinity [3]
from sensation and reflection, in the method we have here set
down.

Locke's exposition of them in this chapter, when he writes as follows in 1696:—'Je crois avec M. Locke qu'à proprement parler on peut dire qu'il n'y a point d'espace, de tems, ni de nombre, qui soit infini; mais qu'il est seulement vrai que pour grand que soit un espace, un tems, ou un nombre, il y en a toujours un autre plus grand que lui sans fin; *et qu'ainsi le véritable Infini ne se trouve point dans un tout composé de parties.*' (*Opera*, Erdman, p. 138.) But it is not on that account, he argues, unreal; for we find infinity absolutely in God, *without parts*, so that the true idea is presupposed in the idea of the finite. Thus with Locke the idea of the Infinite is that of endless increase of a finite positively given in sense; with Leibniz it is rationally given reality, mysteriously limited in our experience, under real *relations* of space, duration, and number.

[1] Not 'in their full latitude,' but only so far as they admit of being treated according to the 'historical plain method,' which only discovers the occasions, under natural law, on which they arise, 'such as they are,'—with their implied intellectual necessity and incompleteness, which he 'pretends not to treat of.'

[2] In *minima tangibilia* and *visibilia*, —coexisting and successive modes of quantity—which we can multiply in a constant process, without any *imaginable* final issue. Why those quantitative relations are necessarily presupposed, as conditions of our concrete experience; and why the 'process of multiplying is necessarily supposed to be inexhaustible, are considerations foreign to the 'historical' method of Locke, and to the categories within which his speculations are apt to be confined.

[3] 'First ideas,' i. e. first occasions of our having those indeterminate, inadequate, mysterious ideas that constitute reason—'first ideas,' so to speak, by which the 'candle of the Lord' is lighted in man.

CHAPTER XVIII.

OTHER SIMPLE MODES.

BOOK II.
—◆—
CHAP.
XVIII.
Other
simple
Modes of
simple
Ideas of
sensation.

1. THOUGH I have, in the foregoing chapters, shown how, from simple ideas taken in by sensation, the mind comes to extend itself[1] even to infinity; which, however it may of all others seem most remote from any sensible perception, yet at last hath nothing in it[2] but what is made out of simple ideas: received into the mind by the senses, and afterwards there put together, by the faculty the mind has to repeat its own ideas; —Though, I say, these might be instances enough of simple modes of the simple ideas of sensation, and suffice to show how the mind comes by them, yet I shall, for method's sake, though briefly, give an account of some few more, and then proceed to more complex ideas.

2. To slide, roll, tumble, walk, creep, run, dance, leap, skip, and abundance of others that might be named, are words which are no sooner heard but every one who understands English has presently in his mind distinct ideas, which are all but the different modifications of motion. Modes of motion answer those of extension; swift and slow are two different ideas of motion, the measures whereof are made of the distances

---

[1] 'extend itself,' i.e. in its complex ideas.

[2] i.e. nothing imaginable and immediately useful. Without the data of experience the understanding is empty and dormant; and this is the lesson which the *Essay* throughout emphasises, in teaching that human knowledge rises from the observation and comparison of concrete things. But it is not less true—this truth is indeed the indispensable ultimate support of human life—that the universe of things and persons, with all its natural and moral laws, is rooted in the Active Reason called God, in whom men and their world of sense have their being.

of time and space put together; so they are complex ideas, comprehending time and space with motion.

3. The like variety have we in sounds. Every articulate word is a different modification of sound; by which we see that, from the sense of hearing, by such modifications, the mind may be furnished with distinct ideas, to almost an infinite number. Sounds also, besides the distinct cries of birds and beasts, are modified by diversity of notes of different length put together, which make that complex idea called a tune, which a musician may have in his mind when he hears or makes no sound at all, by reflecting on the ideas of those sounds, so put together silently in his own fancy.

4. Those of colours are also very various: some we take notice of as the different degrees, or as they were termed shades, of the same colour. But since we very seldom make assemblages of colours, either for use or delight, but figure is taken in also, and has its part in it, as in painting, weaving, needleworks, &c.;—those which are taken notice of do most commonly belong to *mixed modes*, as being made up of ideas of divers kinds, viz. figure and colour, such as beauty, rainbow, &c.

5. All compounded tastes and smells are also modes, made up of the simple ideas of those senses. But they, being such as generally we have no names for, are less taken notice of, and cannot be set down in writing; and therefore must be left without enumeration to the thoughts and experience of my reader.

6. In general it may be observed, that those simple modes which are considered but as different *degrees* of the same simple idea, though they are in themselves many of them very distinct ideas, yet have ordinarily no distinct names, nor are much taken notice of, as distinct ideas, where the difference is but very small between them. Whether men have neglected these modes, and given no names to them, as wanting measures nicely to distinguish them; or because, when they were so distinguished, that knowledge would not be of general or necessary use, I leave it to the thoughts of others. It is sufficient to my purpose to show, that all our simple ideas come to our minds only by sensation and reflection; and that

when the mind has them, it can variously repeat and compound them, and so make new complex ideas. But, though white, red, or sweet, &c. have not been modified, or made into complex ideas, by several combinations, so as to be named, and thereby ranked into species; yet some others of the simple ideas, viz. those of unity, duration, and motion, &c., above instanced in, as also power and thinking, have been thus modified to a great variety of complex ideas, with names belonging to them.

7. The reason whereof, I suppose, has been this,—That the great concernment of men being with men one amongst another, the knowledge of men, and their actions, and the signifying of them to one another, was most necessary; and therefore they made ideas of *actions* very nicely modified, and gave those complex ideas names, that they might the more easily record and discourse of those things they were daily conversant in, without long ambages and circumlocutions; and that the things they were continually to give and receive information about might be the easier and quicker understood. That this is so, and that men in framing different complex ideas, and giving them names, have been much governed by the end of speech in general, (which is a very short and expedite way of conveying their thoughts one to another), is evident in the names which in several arts have been found out, and applied to several complex ideas of modified actions, belonging to their several trades, for dispatch sake, in their direction or discourses about them. Which ideas are not generally framed in the minds of men not conversant about these operations. And thence the words that stand for them, by the greatest part of men of the same language, are not understood: v. g. *coltshire, drilling, filtration, cohobation,* are words standing for certain complex ideas, which being seldom in the minds of any but those few whose particular employments do at every turn suggest them to their thoughts, those names of them are not generally understood but by smiths and chymists; who, having framed the complex ideas which these words stand for, and having given names to them, or received them from others, upon hearing of these names in communication, readily conceive those ideas in their

minds ;—as by *cohobation* all the simple ideas of distilling, and the pouring the liquor distilled from anything back upon the remaining matter, and distilling it again. Thus we see that there are great varieties of simple ideas, as of tastes and smells, which have no names; and of modes[1] many more; which either not having been generally enough observed, or else not being of any great use to be taken notice of in the affairs and converse of men, they have not had names given to them, and so pass not for species[2]. This we shall have occasion hereafter to consider more at large, when we come to speak of *words*[3].

---

[1] 'Modes,' i. e. simple modes of simple ideas.

[2] See Bk. III. 'La plupart des *modes* dont l'auteur parle dans ce chapitre, ne sont pas assez simples, et pourraient être comptés parmi les complexes ; par exemple, pour expliquer ce que c'est que *glisser* ou *rouler*, outre le mouvement, il faut considérer la résistance de la surface.' (Leibniz.)

[3] In Bk. III. chh. v, vi.

CHAPTER XIX.

OF THE MODES OF THINKING.

BOOK II.

CHAP.
XIX.

Sensation,
Remembrance,
Contemplation,
&c., modes
of thinking.

1. WHEN the mind turns its view inwards upon itself, and contemplates its own actions, *thinking*[1] is the first that occurs. In it the mind observes a great variety of modifications, and from thence receives distinct ideas. Thus the perception or thought which actually accompanies, and is annexed to, any impression on the body, made by an external[1] object, being distinct from all other modifications of thinking, furnishes the mind with a distinct idea, which we call *sensation*;—which is, as it were, the actual entrance of any idea into the understanding by the senses[2]. The same idea, when it again recurs without the operation of the like object on the external sensory, is *remembrance*: if it be sought after by the mind, and with pain and endeavour found, and brought again in view, it is *recollection*: if it be held there long under attentive consideration, it is *contemplation*: when ideas float in our mind, without any reflection or regard of the understanding, it is that which the French call *rêverie*; our language has scarce a name for it: when the ideas that offer themselves (for, as I have observed in another place, whilst we are awake, there will always be a train of ideas succeeding one another in

---

[1] We must not forget that Locke uses 'thinking,' not in its narrow meaning of elaborative intelligence, but as synonymous with cognition in all its gradations of development, and occasionally, like Descartes, as coextensive with conscious state of whatever sort.

[2] In this definition of *sensation*, 'entrance into the understanding' is the prominent element, but in ch. i. § 23 'sensation' is applied to 'a *motion in some part of the body*.'

our minds) are taken notice of, and, as it were, registered in
the memory, it is *attention*: when the mind with great
earnestness, and of choice, fixes its view on any idea, considers it on all sides, and will not be called off by the ordinary
solicitation of other ideas, it is that we call *intention* or *study*:
sleep, without dreaming, is rest from all these: and *dreaming*
itself is the having of ideas (whilst the outward senses are
stopped, so that they receive not outward objects with their
usual quickness) in the mind, not suggested by any external
objects, or known occasion ; nor under any choice or conduct
of the understanding at all : and whether that which we call
ecstasy be not dreaming with the eyes open, I leave to be
examined.

2. These are some few instances of those various modes of
thinking, which the mind may observe in itself, and so have
as distinct ideas of as it hath of white and red, a square or a
circle. I do not pretend to enumerate them all, nor to treat
at large of this set of ideas, which are got from reflection :
that would be to make a volume. It suffices to my present
purpose to have shown here, by some few examples, of what
sort these ideas are, and how the mind comes by them ; especially since I shall have occasion hereafter [1] to treat more at
large of *reasoning*, *judging*, *volition*, and *knowledge*, which are
some of the most considerable operations of the mind, and
modes of thinking.

3. But perhaps it may not be an unpardonable digression,
nor wholly impertinent to our present design, if we reflect
here upon the different state of the mind in thinking, which
those instances of attention, reverie, and dreaming, &c.,
before mentioned, naturally enough suggest. That there are
ideas, some or other, always present in the mind of a waking
man, every one's experience convinces him ; though the mind
employs itself about them with several degrees of attention.
Sometimes the mind fixes itself with so much earnestness on
the contemplation of some objects, that it turns their ideas on

---

[1] In Bk. IV., which, in treating of
'knowledge,' 'judgment,' and their
correlates, is by implication concerned with the *ideas* which those
terms stand for. The idea of 'volition,'
as a mode of the idea of *power*, is
considered in ch. xxi.

all sides; marks their relations and circumstances; and views every part so nicely and with such intention, that it shuts out all other thoughts, and takes no notice of the ordinary impressions made then on the senses, which at another season would produce very sensible perceptions: at other times it barely observes the train of ideas that succeed in the understanding, without directing and pursuing any of them: and at other times it lets them pass almost quite unregarded, as faint shadows that make no impression.

Hence it is probable that Thinking is the Action, not the Essence of the Soul.

4. This difference of intention, and remission of the mind in thinking, with a great variety of degrees between earnest study and very near minding nothing at all, every one, I think, has experimented in himself. Trace it a little further, and you find the mind in sleep retired as it were from the senses, and out of the reach of those motions made on the organs of sense, which at other times produce very vivid and sensible ideas. I need not, for this, instance in those who sleep out whole stormy nights, without hearing the thunder, or seeing the lightning, or feeling the shaking of the house, which are sensible enough to those who are waking. But in this retirement of the mind from the senses, it often retains a yet more loose and incoherent manner of thinking, which we call dreaming. And, last of all, sound sleep closes the scene quite, and puts an end to all appearances. This, I think almost every one has experience of in himself, and his own observation without difficulty leads him thus far[1]. That which I would further conclude from hence is, that since the mind can sensibly put on, at several times, several degrees of

[1] This implies complete unconsciousness in sleep. That mental activity exists in different degrees of intensity, from deliberate attention down to semi-consciousness, and even latency, which cannot be disturbed, at least in this life, is obvious to reflection. Thus in memory an idea may exist so little out of consciousness, as that it can be recalled by a common act of reminiscence. In profounder latency, it may be impossible to recover it by any ordinary act of voluntary recollection; yet some unexpected association may make it flash into consciousness after a long oblivion. Or it may be obscured in a latency so much more profound than this, that it can be resuscitated only by some morbid affection of the organism. Finally, it may be absolutely lost for the individual consciousness in this life, and destined for reminiscence only in a life to come.

thinking, and be sometimes, even in a waking man, so remiss,
as to have thoughts dim and obscure to that degree that they
are very little removed from none at all ; and at last, in the
dark retirements of sound sleep, loses the sight perfectly of
all ideas whatsoever : since, I say, this is evidently so in
matter of fact and constant experience, I ask whether it be
not probable, that thinking is the action and not the essence
of the soul ? Since the operations of agents will easily admit
of intention and remission : but the essences of things are
not conceived capable of any such variation [1]. But this by
the by.

[1] Cf. ch. i. §§ 10–19. 'Nous ne
sommes jamais sans *perceptions*, mais il
est nécessaire que nous soyons souvent
sans *aperceptions*, savoir, lorsqu'il n'y a
point de perceptions distinguées. J'ai montré que nous avons *toujours* une infinité de petites perceptions sans nous
en apercevoir.' (Leibniz.) For Locke,
on the other hand, to be 'in the mind'
means, to be *consciously* apprehended.

CHAPTER XX.

OF MODES OF PLEASURE AND PAIN.

BOOK II.

CHAP. XX.
Pleasure
and Pain,
simple
Ideas.

1. AMONGST the simple ideas which we receive both from sensation and reflection, *pain* and *pleasure* are two very considerable ones[1]. For as in the body there is sensation barely in itself, or accompanied with pain or pleasure, so the thought or perception of the mind is simply so, or else accompanied also with pleasure or pain, delight or trouble, call it how you please[2]. These, like other simple ideas, cannot be described, nor their names defined; the way of knowing them is, as of the simple ideas of the senses, only by experience. For, to define them by the presence of good or evil, is no otherwise to make them known to us than by making us reflect on what we feel in ourselves, upon the several and various operations of good and evil upon our minds, as they are differently applied to or considered by us.

---

[1] Cf. ch. vii. §§ 1-6, for the origin of the simple phenomena of pleasure and pain. Pleasure and pain, as appears in the sequel, play a supreme part in Locke's ethical system, as *motives* for conforming to moral relations that are themselves acknowledged by him to be immutable and eternal. This appears in chh. xxi. and xxviii. If men were destitute of all capacity for pleasure and pain, human life would be transformed; its springs of action dried up; and our knowledge of the universe, including even that of our bodies and of our minds *as our own*, would be obscured.

[2] That is, there are (*a*) absolutely indifferent sensations, and (*b*) sensations that are accompanied with pain or pleasure; also objects of 'reflection' that are (*a*) indifferent, and others that are (*b*) pleasurable or painful. ' Je crois,' says Leibniz, in relation to this, ' qu'il n'y a point de perceptions qui nous soient tout à fait indifférentes; mais c'est assez que leur effet ne soit point notable, pour qu'on les puisse appeler ainsi.' Whether *nerves of pain* and of *pleasure* are distinguishable from one another, and also from the *nerves* of *sensation* is a relative physiological question still in debate.

2. Things then are good or evil, only in reference to
pleasure or pain[1]. That we call *good*, which is apt to cause
or increase pleasure, or diminish pain in us; or else to
procure or preserve us the possession of any other good or
absence of any evil. And, on the contrary, we name that
evil which is apt to produce or increase any pain, or diminish
any pleasure in us: or else to procure us any evil, or deprive us
of any good[2]. By pleasure and pain, I must be understood to
mean of body or mind, as they are commonly distinguished ;
though in truth they be only different constitutions of the
mind, sometimes occasioned by disorder in the body, sometimes by thoughts of the mind.

3. Pleasure and pain and that which causes them,—good
and evil, are the hinges on which our passions turn. And if
we reflect on ourselves, and observe how these, under various
considerations, operate in us ; what modifications or tempers
of mind, what internal sensations (if I may so call them) they
produce in us we may thence form to ourselves the ideas of
our passions[3].

4. Thus any one reflecting upon the thought he has of the
delight which any present or absent thing is apt to produce
in him, has the idea we call *love*[4]. For when a man declares

---

[1] It is by pleasure and pain that we
are helped to distinguish our individual conscious states *as our own*, and
especially to distinguish our own bodies
from the extra-organic world—called
'external,' because visibly outside-the
small aggregates of matter which men
call their own bodies.

[2] 'Every man calleth that which
pleaseth and is delightful to himself,
good; and that *evil* which displeaseth
him : insomuch that, as every man dif-
fereth from every other in constitution,
they differ also concerning the distinction of good and evil.' (Hobbes,
Human Nature, ch. vii. § 3.)

[3] On which Leibniz remarks 'qu'*ai-
mer* est être porté à prendre du
plaisir dans la perfection, bien, ou

bonheur de l'object aimé'—recognising
the disinterestedness of love more than
Locke does, and limiting the application of the term to persons. It is not
properly love, he says, when we say
that we love a beautiful picture.

[4] Compared with Aristotle, in his
Rhetoric, or even with Hobbes, in his
Human Nature, Locke's account of the
Passions, in what follows, is desultory
and superficial. But it is not intended
as an adequate analysis,—only as illustration of the dependence of our *complex ideas of reflection* on phenomena
presented in internal sense. For it
is only through reflection that we
obtain ideas of our ' passions,' and
are able to put meaning into the
words that represent them. He takes

BOOK II.

CHAP. XX.

in autumn when he is eating them, or in spring when there are none, that he loves grapes, it is no more but that the taste of grapes delights him : let an alteration of health or constitution destroy the delight of their taste, and he then can be said to love grapes no longer.

Hatred.

5. On the contrary, the thought of the pain which anything present or absent is apt to produce in us, is what we call *hatred.* Were it my business here to inquire any further than into the bare ideas of our passions, as they depend on different modifications of pleasure and pain, I should remark, that our love and hatred of inanimate insensible beings is commonly founded on that pleasure and pain which we receive from their use and application any way to our senses, though with their destruction. But hatred or love, to beings capable of happiness or misery, is often the uneasiness or delight which we find in ourselves, arising from [¹ a consideration of] their very being or happiness. Thus the being and welfare of a man's children or friends, producing constant delight in him, he is said constantly to love them. But it suffices to note, that our ideas of love and hatred are but the dispositions of the mind, in respect of pleasure and pain in general, however caused in us.

Desire.

6. The uneasiness a man finds in himself upon the absence of anything whose present enjoyment carries the idea of delight with it, is that we call *desire* ; which is greater or less, as that uneasiness is more or less vehement. [² Where, by the by, it may perhaps be of some use to remark, that the chief, if not only spur to human industry and action is *uneasiness* ³. For whatsoever good is proposed, if its absence

no account of the organic conditions of their manifestation, of which recent psychology makes much. These are irrelevant to Locke's purpose here.

¹ Added in the fourth edition.

² Added in the second edition.

³ ' Cette considération de *l'inquié-tude,*' says Leibniz, ' est un point capital où cet auteur montre particulièrement son esprit pénétrant et profond.' He proceeds to apply his principle of *per-ception without apperception* to desires which operate without *conscious* uneasiness — ' petites douleurs inaperceptibles, afin que nous *jouissions de l'avantage du mal, sans en recevoir l'incommodité.*' Such are confused impulses, in which we have no idea of what we need, but which act like springs when they try to unbend, making us machines.

carries no displeasure or pain with it, if a man be easy and content without it, there is no desire of it, nor endeavour after it ; there is no more but a bare velleity[1], the term used to signify the lowest degree of desire, and that which is next to none at all, when there is so little uneasiness in the absence of anything, that it carries a man no further than some faint wishes for it, without any more effectual or vigorous use of the means to attain it.   Desire also is stopped or abated by the opinion of the impossibility or unattainableness of the good proposed, as far as the uneasiness is cured or allayed by that consideration.   This might carry our thoughts further, were it seasonable in this place.]

7. *Joy* is a delight of the mind, from the consideration of the present or assured approaching possession of a good ; and we are then possessed of any good, when we have it so in our power that we can use it when we please.   Thus a man almost starved has joy at the arrival of relief, even before he has the pleasure of using it : and a father, in whom the very well-being of his children causes delight, is always, as long as his children are in such a state, in the possession of that good; for he needs but to reflect on it, to have that pleasure. Joy.

8. *Sorrow* is uneasiness in the mind, upon the thought of a good lost, which might have been enjoyed longer; or the sense of a present evil. Sorrow.

9. *Hope* is that pleasure in the mind, which every one finds in himself, upon the thought of a probable future enjoyment of a thing which is apt to delight him[2]. Hope.

10. *Fear* is an uneasiness of the mind, upon the thought of future evil likely[3] to befal us. Fear.

11. *Despair* is the thought of the unattainableness of any Despair.

---

[1] '*Velleitas* est quoddam languida remissa et ignava voluntas, aut impotentiam arguit perficiendi quod cuperemus.' (Chauvini Lexicon.) But see its meaning according to Hobbes. (*Human Nature*, ch. ix. § 1.)

[2] 'Hope,' says Hobbes, 'is expectation of good to come, as fear is the expectation of evil.' (Cf. Arist. *Rhet.* i. 11.)

[3] Hope and fear, accordingly, as Hume says, ' are *mixed passions,* being derived from the *probability* of any good or evil—probability arising from an opposition of contrary chances or causes, by which the mind is not allowed to fix on either side, but is incessantly tossed from one to another.' (*Dissertation on the Passions.*)

BOOK II.

CHAP. XX.

Anger.

good, which works differently in men's minds, sometimes producing uneasiness or pain, sometimes rest and indolency.

12. *Anger* is uneasiness or discomposure of the mind, upon the receipt of any injury, with a present purpose of revenge.

Envy.

13. *Envy* is an uneasiness of the mind, caused by the consideration of a good we desire obtained by one we think should not have had it before us.

What Passions all Men have.

14. These two last, *envy* and *anger*, not being caused by pain and pleasure simply in themselves, but having in them some mixed considerations of ourselves and others, are not therefore to be found in all men, because those other parts, of valuing their merits, or intending revenge, is wanting[1] in them. But all the rest, terminating purely in pain and pleasure, are, I think, to be found in all men. For we love, desire, rejoice, and hope, only in respect of pleasure ; we hate, fear, and grieve, only in respect of pain ultimately. In fine, all these passions are moved by things, only as they appear to be the causes of pleasure and pain, or to have pleasure or pain some way or other annexed to them[2]. Thus we extend our hatred usually to the subject (at least, if a sensible or voluntary agent) which has produced pain in us ; because the fear it leaves is a constant pain : but we do not so constantly love what has done us good ; because pleasure operates not so strongly on us as pain, and because we are not so ready to have hope it will do so again. But this by the by.

Pleasure and Pain, what.

15. By pleasure and pain, delight and uneasiness, I must all along be understood (as I have above intimated) to mean not only bodily pain and pleasure, but whatsoever delight or uneasiness is felt by us, whether arising from any grateful or unacceptable sensation or reflection.

Removal or lessening of either.

16. It is further to be considered, that, in reference to the passions, the removal or lessening of a pain is considered, and

---

[1] Undeveloped in the individual, rather than absolutely 'wanting.'

[2] Our original capacities for different kinds of uneasiness and ease, are the *natural* explanation of our various *appetites* and *desires*, as these are distinguished from *will*, self-originated or *supernatural.* In the former, man is subject to, and a part of the mechanism of nature ; in the latter he manifests *himself*, as a first cause, in the exercise of a free, and therefore responsible, personality.

operates, as a pleasure: and the loss or diminishing of a
pleasure, as a pain.

17. The passions too have most of them, in most persons, operations on the body, and cause various changes in it; which not being always sensible, do not make a necessary part of the idea of each passion. For *shame*, which is an uneasiness of the mind upon the thought of having done something which is indecent, or will lessen the valued esteem which others have for us, has not always blushing accompanying it.

18. I would not be mistaken here, as if I meant this as a Discourse of the Passions; they are many more than those I have here named: and those I have taken notice of would each of them require a much larger and more accurate discourse. I have only mentioned these here, as so many instances of modes of pleasure and pain resulting in our minds from various considerations of good and evil. I might perhaps have instanced in other modes of pleasure and pain, more simple than these; as the pain of hunger and thirst, and the pleasure of eating and drinking to remove them: the pain of teeth set on edge; the pleasure of music; pain from captious uninstructive wrangling, and the pleasure of rational conversation with a friend, or of well-directed study in the search and discovery of truth. But the passions being of much more concernment to us, I rather made choice to instance in them, and show how the ideas we have of them are derived from sensation or reflection.

CHAPTER XXI.

OF POWER.

1. THE mind being every day informed, by the senses, of the alteration of those simple ideas it observes in things without; and taking notice how one comes to an end, and ceases to be, and another begins to exist which was not before; reflecting also on what passes within itself, and observing a constant change of its ideas, sometimes by the impression of outward objects on the senses, and sometimes by the determination of its own choice; and concluding from what it has so constantly observed to have been, that the like changes will for the future be made in the same things, by like agents, and by the like ways,—considers in one thing the possibility of having any of its simple ideas changed, and in another the possibility of making that change; and so comes by that idea which we call *power*[1]. Thus we say, Fire has a

---

[1] In ch. vii. § 8 the idea of 'power' is said to be one of the 'simple ideas,' received both from sensation and reflection, being presented to us in every change we observe, obtrusively in the movements we make in our own bodies, and in the movements of bodies among themselves. Here, reasoning as well as sense seems to be called in to account for the idea. He speaks of 'concluding,' and implies that in the idea of power we are carried beyond what is immediately present to the senses or reflection. A similar account is given in the description of the rise of the idea of cause and effect (ch. xxvi. § 1), awk-

wardly separated in the *Essay* from the idea of power. Now, as Hume remarks, 'no reasoning can ever give us a new simple idea.' (*Inquiry*, sect. vi., note; also *Treatise*, pt. iii. sect. 11.) Probably what Locke, in his own too inexact fashion, means to say is, that on observing any change, something in the human mind, and in the very constitution of reason itself, forbids the observer to regard the change as *isolated absolutely*; and obliges him to go in quest of an agent. It is in short a simple or inexplicable fact, that the mind is dissatisfied with change, *as such*, and it is forced to recognise the obscure idea of power

power to melt gold, i. e. to destroy the consistency of its
insensible parts, and consequently its hardness, and make it
fluid; and gold has a power to be melted; that the sun has
a power to blanch wax, and wax a power to be blanched by
the sun, whereby the yellowness is destroyed, and whiteness
made to exist in its room. In which, and the like cases, the
power we consider is in reference to the change of perceivable
ideas. For we cannot observe any alteration to be made in,
or operation upon anything, but by the observable change of
its sensible ideas; nor conceive any alteration to be made,
but by conceiving a change of some of its ideas[1].

2. Power thus considered is two-fold, viz. as able to make, Power,
or able to receive any change. The one may be called *active*, active and
and the other *passive* power[2]. Whether matter be not wholly passive.
destitute of active power[3], as its author, God, is truly above
all passive power; and whether the intermediate state of

---

in the change. What it is that is
thus recognised, and in what 'modes'
this 'simple idea' arises, the present
chapter professes to consider. Why
the ideas of 'power' and 'cause' are
treated in separate chapters, is not
made clear. Perhaps it is on the
principle that the idea of cause is conceived to presuppose the complex idea
of substance (ch. xxii. § 11), the analysis of which is interposed (ch. xxiii),
and so causality is regarded as an idea
of relation between substances, while
power is conceived as a simple idea
occasioned by change.

[1] Observed change evokes the idea
of power, but the idea thus evoked, not
being an observed, nor an observable
object, is hence dismissed by Hume
as an illusion.

[2] This is the Aristotelian distinction
of δύναμις τοῦ ποιεῖν and δύναμις τοῦ
πάσχειν, according to which substances
may be either efficacious in producing
change, or susceptible of change. The
one is the δύναμις ἐνεργητική, and the
other the δύναμις παθητική of the Peripatetics.

[3] The inactivity of matter and the
things of the natural world; the eternal activity of Divine Reason; and
the intermediate position of man,
as a passive sentient organism and
also a moral agent, who participates
at once in the system of nature and
in the active supernatural system, to
which the sequences and coexistences
of nature are subordinated—is a conception of the universe that is not
wholly inconsistent with Locke's principles. It is only the derived and
passive power implied in physical law
that he presupposes, when he explains
the secondary qualities and powers
of bodies by the primary, or the dependence of perceptions of sense on
their organs. For his view of the bases
of our ideas and knowledge of ourselves, of God, and of things external,
regarded as substances and as powers
—the central problem of metaphysical
philosophy, cf. Bk. II. ch. xiii. § 18, chh.
xxiii, xxvii. § 2; Bk. IV. chh. ix, x, xi.
Aristotle distinguishes the unintelligent power of matter from the power
of intelligence—τῶν δυνάμεων αἱ μὲν
ἔσονται ἄλογοι, αἱ δὲ μετὰ λόγου. *Metaph.*
Bk. viii.

BOOK II.
CHAP. XXI.

created spirits be not that alone which is capable of both active and passive power, may be worth consideration. I shall not now enter into that inquiry[1], my present business being not to search into the original of power, but how we come by the *idea* of it[2]. But since active powers make so great a part of our complex ideas of natural substances, (as we shall see hereafter[3],) and I mention them as such, according to common apprehension; yet they being not, perhaps, so truly *active* powers as our hasty thoughts are apt to represent them, I judge it not amiss, by this intimation, to direct our minds to the consideration of God and spirits, for the clearest idea of *active* power[4].

Power includes Relation.

3. I confess power includes in it some kind of *relation*, (a relation to action or change,) as indeed which of our ideas, of what kind soever, when attentively considered, does not? For, our ideas of extension, duration, and number, do they not all contain in them a secret relation of the parts? Figure and motion have something relative in them much more visibly. And sensible qualities[5], as colours and smells, &c., what are they but the powers of different bodies, in relation

---

[1] As Berkeley soon after did, who could see active power only in spirits, created and divine; in the sensible world only a divinely maintained order and uniformity of phenomena, commonly called the uniformity of nature.

[2] His inquiry is neither ontological nor cosmological, but psychological and epistemological. One could wish that he had inquired more into the nature of the idea, as well as 'how we come by it.' Is it an idea of changes that appear in things and persons, or of something in the mind's manner of regarding changes? Can we go further than succession of phenomena in our idea of power, and yet preserve meaning in what we say? If he defines power by saying it is something 'productive' of something, what does this imply? In saying this, Hume tells us, he can mean nothing. 'For what does he mean by *production*?

Can he give any definition of it that will not be the same with that of causation [power]? If he can; I desire it may be produced. If he cannot; he here runs in a circle, and gives a synonymous term, instead of a definition.' (*Treatise*, Bk. I. pt. iii. sect. 2.)

[3] Bk. II. ch. xxiii. §§ 7-11; also ch. viii. §§ 23-26.

[4] *Power* and *substance* he regards as correlative ideas — powers presupposing substance, whose powers they are. The ideas of God and of intelligent agents imply the idea of *active* power. Religion is the state of mind that is due to faith in power that determines the destiny of man, and the universe, in accordance with a complete idea of the good that is of necessity imperfectly apprehended by a human mind.

[5] 'sensible qualities,' i. e. the secondary or imputed qualities of matter.

to our perception, &c.? And, if considered in the things themselves, do they not depend on the bulk, figure, texture, and motion of the parts[1]? All which include some kind of relation in them. Our idea therefore of power, I think, may well have a place amongst other *simple ideas*[2], and be considered as one of them ; being one of those that make a principal ingredient in our complex ideas of substances, as we shall hereafter have occasion to observe[3].

4. [[4]We are abundantly furnished with the idea of *passive* power by almost all sorts of sensible things. In most of them we cannot avoid observing their sensible qualities, nay, their very substances[5], to be in a continual flux.] And therefore with reason we look on them as liable still to the same change. Nor have we of *active* power (which is the more proper signification of the word power[6]) fewer instances. Since whatever change is observed, the mind must collect a power somewhere able to make that change[7], as well as a possibility in the thing itself to receive it. But yet, if we will consider it attentively, bodies, by our senses, do not afford us so clear and distinct an idea of active power, as we have from reflection on the operations of our minds[8]. For all power relating to action, and there being but two sorts of

---

[1] Ch. viii. §§ 10, 13, 14.

[2] Yet the preceding sentences rather imply that the idea of power is an idea of relation, and not a simple idea. Locke calls it *simple*, because 'power,' while involving the idea of relation to its effects, is in itself incapable of being defined. While the word is not meaningless, its meaning cannot be conveyed by words to those not prepared by the experience in which it is involved.

[3] Ch. xxiii. § 8.

[4] The first three editions here read thus :—'Of passive power all sensible things abundantly furnish us with sensible ideas; whose sensible qualities and beings we find to be in a continual flux.'

[5] 'their very substances,' i. e. their substances as manifested in their

primary or real qualities ; it being only in and through the appearances which they make of themselves that we can have positive ideas of particular substances.

[6] Cf. Hobbes on 'active power.' (*First Grounds of Philosophy*, Pt. II. ch. x.)

[7] This *necessity* to 'collect' implies that *something in the mind obliges us* to form the idea (notion) of power, whenever ' change is observed '; so that the idea is an intellectual suggestion, not a mere visible or tangible phenomenon.

[8] The feeling of exertion in our mental operations is in itself only a psychical phenomenon, preceding other phenomena, and cannot give what is added to mere phenomenal succession, in the idea of power.

BOOK II.
CHAP. XXI.
action whereof we have an idea, viz. thinking and motion, let us consider whence we have the clearest ideas of the powers which produce these actions. (1) Of thinking, body affords us no idea at all ; it is only from reflection that we have that. (2) Neither have we from body any idea of the beginning of motion [1]. A body at rest affords us no idea of any active power to move; and when it is set in motion itself, that motion is rather a passion than an action in it. For, when the ball obeys the motion of a billiard-stick, it is not any action of the ball, but bare passion. Also when by impulse it sets another ball in motion that lay in its way, it only communicates the motion it had received from another, and loses in itself so much as the other received : which gives us but a very obscure idea of an *active* power of moving in body, whilst we observe it only to *transfer*, but not *produce* any motion. For it is but a very obscure idea of power which reaches not the production of the action, but the continuation of the passion [2]. For so is motion in a body impelled by another; the continuation of the alteration made in it from rest to motion being little more an action, than the continuation of the alteration of its figure by the same blow is an action.

---

[1] To refund imaginable physical phenomena into preceding imaginable physical phenomena is not to explain them, if explanation means referring change to unimaginable active power, on which the transformation somehow depends. It gives the physical occasion, but not the efficient and ultimate cause of the change. It is inadequate, rather than absolutely erroneous; if power or causality, in the full meaning of the word, is more than what is continuously imaginable—change of phenomena into equivalent phenomena. But by what right is conservation of energy, or any other physical law, assumed to be ultimate and supreme, instead of harmoniously subordinate to higher laws of spiritual agency and moral order ?

[2] Yet this 'very obscure idea' is all that enters into the mechanical caus-ality of physical science, which is satisfied with refunding motion continuously into preceding motion, of which it is the imaginable transformation—subject to the natural law of conservation, which forbids absolute loss of motion. Physical science traces body in one form into body in another form, out of which it has issued. But this, as Locke sees, is not 'production'; it is only 'transference'—'continuation of the passion,' of which the body is the passive subject—the effect being connected with its so-called physical cause, by a quantitative relation, in which motion received is *equivalent* to motion lost. A physical effect is thus its merely physical cause in a new form—in an imaginable sequence, or metamorphosis, but emptied of originative power.

The idea of the *beginning* of motion we have only from BOOK II.
reflection on what passes in ourselves ; where we find by
experience, that, barely by willing it, barely by a thought of CHAP. XXI
the mind, we can move the parts of our bodies, which were before
at rest.   So that it seems to me, we have, from the observation
of the operation of bodies by our senses, but a very imperfect
obscure idea of *active* power ; since they afford us not any
idea in themselves of the power to begin any action, either
motion or thought.   But if, from the impulse bodies are
observed to make one upon another, any one thinks he has
a clear idea of power, it serves as well to my purpose [1] ;
sensation being one of those ways whereby the mind comes
by its ideas : only I thought it worth while to consider here,
by the way, whether the mind doth not receive its idea of
active power clearer from reflection on its own operations,
than it doth from any external sensation [2].

5. This, at least, I think evident,—That we find in ourselves Will and
a power to begin or forbear, continue or end several [[3] actions] Under-
of our minds, and motions of our bodies, barely by [[4] a thought] standing two
or preference of the mind [[5] ordering, or as it were commanding, Powers in
the doing or not doing such or such a particular action.]   This Mind or
power which the mind has [[6] thus to order] the consideration Spirit.
of any idea, or the forbearing to consider it ; or to prefer the
motion of any part of the body to its rest, [[7] and *vice versâ*, in
any particular instance,] is that which we call the *Will*.   The
actual [[8] exercise of that power, by directing any particular
action, or its forbearance,] is that which we call *volition* or

---

[1] That ' purpose ' being to show that
elaborative activity, *per se*, cannot be
productive of real discoveries, independently of data of experience, supplied
in ideas of the senses, and of our mental
operations.

[2] Are we not led, by the analogy of
the ' operations ' to which we attribute
personal responsibility, to refer all
motion in the universe ultimately to
Divine Reason,—continuity of motion
and the ' conservation of energy' being
methods according to which the immanent Reason determines motion or

change in bodies ?

[3] ' thoughts,' in first edition.

[4] ' the choice,' in first edition.

[5] Added in second edition.

[6] ' thus to order ': ' to prefer,' in
first edition.

[7] Added in second edition.

[8] ' preferring one to another,' in first
edition. A man may be free to *will*,
even when he is not free in the sense
of being able, by willing, to regulate
the course of his ideas, or motions of
his body, and motions in extra-organic
bodies, which he seeks to cause.

BOOK II.
CHAP. XXI.

willing. [¹ The forbearance of that action, consequent to such order or command of the mind, is called *voluntary*. And whatsoever action is performed without such a thought of the mind, is called *involuntary*.] The power of perception is that which we call the *Understanding*. Perception, which we make the act of the understanding, is of three sorts :—1. The perception of ideas in our minds. 2. The perception of the signification of signs. 3. The perception of the [² connexion or repugnancy,] agreement or disagreement, [³ that there is between any of our] ideas. All these are attributed to the understanding, or perceptive power, though it be [⁴ the two latter only that use allows us to say we understand ⁵.]

Faculties, not real beings.

6. These powers of the mind, viz. of perceiving, and of preferring, are usually called by another name. And the ordinary way of speaking is, that the understanding and will are two *faculties* of the mind ; a word proper enough, if it be used, as all words should be, so as not to breed any confusion in men's thoughts, by being supposed (as I suspect it has been) to stand for some real beings in the soul that performed those actions of understanding and volition. For when we say the *will* is the commanding and superior faculty of the soul ; that it is or is not free ; that it determines the inferior faculties ; that it follows the dictates of the understanding, &c.,—though these and the like expressions, by those that carefully attend to their own ideas, and conduct their thoughts more by the evidence of things than the sound of words, may be understood in a clear and distinct sense—yet I suspect, I say, that this way of speaking of *faculties* has misled many into a con-

¹ Added in second edition.

² Added in second edition.

³ ' of any distinct,' in first edition.

⁴ ' to the two latter that, in strictness of speech, the act of understanding is usually applied,' in first edition.

⁵ Here, and in ch. vi. § 2, Locke presents the operations of ' understanding,' ' thinking,' or ' perception,' and those of ' will,' as ' the two great and principal actions of the mind.' In ch. xx. he distinguishes also the sus-

ceptibilities of pleasure and pain, which play an important part in relation to the determinations of the will in this chapter. ' Perception,' he here explains, signifies in the *Essay,* either (*a*) ' simple idea '; (*b*) comprehension of the meanings of words ; (*c*) discernment of the relations which make knowledge or certainty. It appears in the first of these meanings chiefly in the second, and in the third meaning in the fourth Book.

fused notion of so many distinct agents in us [1], which had
their several provinces and authorities, and did command,
obey, and perform several actions, as so many distinct
beings ; which has been no small occasion of wrangling,
obscurity, and uncertainty, in questions relating to them.

7. Every one, I think, finds in *himself* a power to begin or Whence
the Ideas
of Liberty
and Ne-
cessity.
forbear, continue or put an end to several actions in himself.
[[2] From the consideration of the extent of this power of the
mind over the actions [3] of the man, which everyone finds in
himself, arise the *ideas* of *liberty* and *necessity*.]

8. All the actions that we have any idea of reducing them- Liberty,
what.
selves, as has been said, to these two, viz. thinking and
motion [3] ; so far as a man has power to think or not to think,
to move or not to move, according to the preference or direction of his own mind, so far is a man *free* [4]. Wherever any
performance or forbearance are not equally in a man's power ;
wherever doing or not doing will not equally *follow* upon the
preference of his mind directing it, there he is not free, though

---

[1] Instead of meaning by 'faculties,' as Locke does, *the human agents*, regarded as manifesting passive and active powers, in states of intelligence of different degrees, and exertions of will, under various motives, Locke characteristically wants to keep concrete meaning in 'mind,' its 'powers,' 'faculties,' 'capacities,' and cognate words. In a more exact usage, 'faculty' is applied to the self-originated energies, and 'capacity' to the passive susceptibilities of self-conscious life, confused together by Locke as 'operations.'

[2] The first edition has it thus :— 'The power the mind has at any time to prefer any particular one of these actions to its forbearance, or *vice versa*, is that faculty which, as I have said, we call the *Will*; the actual exercise of that power we call *volition*; and the forbearance or performance of that

action, consequent to such a preference of the mind, is called *voluntary*. Hence we have the ideas of *liberty* and *necessity*, which arise from the consideration of the extent of this power of the mind over the actions, not only of the mind, but the whole agent, the whole man.'

[3] The production of motion is the immediate palpable effect of willing. But the mechanism of visible movements, and the idea of 'power' got from this, must not be confounded with what is implied in that primary causality of will for which alone we are accountable.

[4] But the 'freedom' of a moral agent refers to the hyper-physical *origin* of the 'preference or direction' —the voluntary determination itself— for which alone, and not for its consequences, the agent is accountable, as properly his own.

perhaps the action may be voluntary [1]. So that the idea of *liberty* is, the idea of a power in any agent to do or forbear any particular action, according to the determination or thought of the mind, whereby either of them is preferred to the other : where either of them is not in the power of the agent to be produced by him according to his volition, there he is not at liberty ; that agent is under *necessity*. So that liberty cannot be where there is no thought, no volition, no will ; but there may be thought, there may be will, there may be volition, where there is no liberty [2]. A little consideration of an obvious instance or two may make this clear.

Supposes Under-standing and Will.

9. A tennis-ball, whether in motion by the stroke of a racket, or lying still at rest, is not by any one taken to be a free agent. If we inquire into the reason, we shall find it is because we conceive not a tennis-ball to think, and consequently not to have any volition, or *preference* of motion to rest, or *vice versâ* ; and therefore has not liberty, is not a free agent ; but all its both motion and rest come under our idea

---

[1] He may ineffectually will to do it, erroneously supposing that the expected consequence will follow, and he is still accountable for the *ineffectual* voluntary determination ; but not for the failure, which depends upon natural law.

[2] The idea of ' power,' as suggested by voluntary activity, is the subject of the remaining sections of this chapter, with which Locke himself was still dissatisfied, even after the many changes which they underwent in successive editions. This appears in his correspondence with Molyneux. The difficulty of reconciling free power to will, in a finite agent, with the supremacy of Divine power and perfection of Divine knowledge, was obvious to him :— ' If you will argue,' he writes to Molyneux (Jan. 20, 1693), ' for or against liberty from consequences, I will not undertake to answer you ; for I own freely to you the weakness of my understanding—that though it be unquestionable that there is omni-potence and omniscience in God our Maker, yet I cannot make freedom in man consistent with omnipotence or omniscience in God ;—though I am as fully persuaded of *both* as of any truths I most freely assent to. And therefore I have long left off the consideration of that question, resolving all into this short conclusion—that if it be possible for God to make a free agent, then man is free, though I see not the way of it.' (Letter to Molyneux, Jan. 20, 1693.) The reasoning in this chapter presupposes that volitions follow motives in a natural sequence, not recognising that their supernatural character of a volition is implied in the accountability of the agent. The ultimate relation of the mechanism of nature itself, by which they are thus supposed to be determined, to the ' omnipotence and omniscience of God ' is not contemplated ; nor is the answer to the question raised about the will seen to be the turning point between philosophical materialism and a spiritual philosophy.

of necessary, and are so called. Likewise a man falling into the water, (a bridge breaking under him,) has not herein liberty, is not a free agent. For though he has volition, though he prefers his not falling to falling; yet the forbearance of that motion not being in his power, the stop or cessation of that motion follows not [1] upon his volition ; and therefore therein he is not free. So a man striking himself, or his friend, by a convulsive motion of his arm, which it is not in his power, by volition or the direction of his mind, to stop or forbear, nobody thinks he has in this liberty ; every one pities him, as acting by necessity and constraint [2].

10. Again : suppose a man be carried, whilst fast asleep, into a room where is a person he longs to see and speak with ; and be there locked fast in, beyond his power to get out : he awakes, and is glad to find himself in so desirable company, which he stays willingly in, i. e. prefers his stay to going away. I ask, is not this stay voluntary ? I think nobody will doubt it : and yet, being locked fast in, it is evident he is not at liberty not to stay, he has not freedom to be gone. So that liberty is not an idea belonging to volition, or preferring ; but to the person having the power of doing, or forbearing to do, according as the mind shall choose or direct [3]. Our idea of liberty reaches as far as that power, and no farther [4]. For wherever restraint comes to check that power, or compulsion takes away that indifferency of ability to act, or to for-

Belongs not to Volition.

---

[1] Here again it is to *what follows volition*, not to the *origin* of the volition, that Locke looks. Are acts of will, for which the subject is responsible, free from natural necessity to will them ?

[2] Because *he* is not the moral agent in an act for which he is not responsible, as it has not ultimately originated in him, but must be referred to the mechanism of nature ; whether or not that mechanism is ultimately determined by supreme Reason and Purpose that is immanent in nature. 'Aristotle a déjà bien remarqué que, pour appeler les actions libres, nous demandons qu'elles soient non seulement *spontanées*, mais encore *délibérées*.' (Leibniz.)

[3] But how does this ' choice of the mind' originate ?—in the mechanism of nature ; or in something above nature (in its ordinary meaning), in the agents himself, in virtue of which he rises into a moral person ?

[4] Since 'liberty' of willing is the measure of man's responsibility, it is surely important to him, as an accountable agent, to know *what* actions are, in this regard, *his own* actions, for which he deserves praise or blame ; and *why* they have this character.

BOOK II.
━━
CHAP. XXI.
Voluntary
opposed to
involun-
tary, not to
necessary.

bear acting, there liberty, and our notion of it, presently ceases.

11. We have instances enough, and often more than enough, in our own bodies. A man's heart beats, and the blood circulates, which it is not in his power by any thought or volition to stop ; and therefore in respect of these motions, where rest depends not on his choice, nor would follow the determination of his mind, if it should prefer it, he is not a free agent. Convulsive motions agitate his legs, so that though he wills it ever so much, he cannot by any power of his mind stop their motion, (as in that odd disease called *chorea sancti viti*), but he is perpetually dancing ; he is not at liberty in this action, but under as much necessity of moving, as a stone that falls, or a tennis-ball struck with a racket. On the other side, a palsy or the stocks hinder his legs from obeying the determination of his mind, if it would thereby transfer his body to another place. In all these there is want of freedom ; though the sitting still, even of a paralytic, whilst he prefers it to a removal, is truly voluntary. Voluntary, then, is not opposed to necessary, but to involuntary. For a man may prefer what he can do, to what he cannot do ; the state he is in, to its absence or change ; though necessity has made it in itself unalterable[1].

12. As it is in the motions of the body, so it is in the thoughts of our minds : where any one is such, that we have power to take it up, or lay it by, according to the preference of the mind, there we are at liberty[2]. A waking man, being under the necessity of having some ideas constantly in his mind, is not at liberty to think or not to think ; no more than he is at liberty, whether his body shall touch any other or no : but whether he will remove his contemplation from one idea to another is many times in his choice ; and then he is, in respect of his ideas, as much at liberty as he is in respect of

---

[1] Here again it is in the efficacy or the impotence of the voluntary act, not in the origin of the act itself, that Locke finds his idea of power.

[2] He is not morally responsible for 'motions' and 'thoughts' that are not causally connected with his antece-dent volition ; but he is nevertheless responsible for the volition itself. 'Ceux qui opposent la *liberté* à la *nécessité* entendent parler, non pas des actions exterieures, mais de l'acte même de vouloir.' (Leibniz, *Nouveaux Essais.*)

bodies he rests on ; he can at pleasure remove himself from one
to another. But yet some ideas to the mind, like some motions
to the body, are such as in certain circumstances it cannot
avoid, nor obtain their absence by the utmost effort it can use.
A man on the rack is not at liberty to lay by the idea of pain,
and divert himself with other contemplations : and sometimes
a boisterous passion hurries our thoughts, as a hurricane does
our bodies, without leaving us the liberty of thinking on other
things, which we would rather choose [1]. But as soon as the
mind regains the power to stop or continue, begin or forbear,
any of these motions of the body without, or thoughts within,
according as it thinks fit to prefer either to the other, we then
consider the man as a *free agent* again.

13. Wherever thought is wholly wanting, or the power to Necessity,
act or forbear according to the direction of thought, there what.
necessity takes place. This, in an agent capable of volition,
when the beginning or continuation of any action is contrary
to that preference of his mind, is called compulsion ; when the
hindering or stopping any action is contrary to his volition, it
is called restraint. Agents that have no thought, no volition
at all, are in everything *necessary agents* [2].

14. If this be so, (as I imagine it is,) I leave it to be con- Liberty
sidered, whether it may not help to put an end to that long belongs
agitated, and, I think, unreasonable, because unintelligible Will.
question, viz. *Whether man's will be free or no?* For if I
mistake not, it follows from what I have said, that the
question itself is altogether improper ; and it is as insignificant to ask whether man's *will* be free, as to ask whether his
sleep be swift, or his virtue square : liberty being as little
applicable to the will, as swiftness of motion is to sleep, or
squareness to virtue. Every one would laugh at the absurdity

---

[1] His responsibility, and the implied
personal freedom, must be tested by
the man's power to prevent the pain
and passion—to will their absence,
being self-originated, and not determined for him as a physical sequence.

[2] An agent whose volitions could,
according to the laws of nature, in no

case be followed by the motions or
thoughts which he intended, would
still be responsible *for the volitions
themselves* ; but not for physically impossible consequences, these being
in that case determined according to
the mechanism of nature, not by his
own power.

BOOK II.

CHAP. XXI.

of such a question as either of these : because it is obvious that the modifications of motion belong not to sleep, nor the difference of figure to virtue ; and when any one well considers it, I think he will as plainly perceive that liberty, which is but a power, belongs only to *agents*, and cannot be an attribute or modification of the will, which is also but a power.

Volition.

15. [¹ Such is the difficulty of explaining and giving clear notions of internal actions by sounds, that I must here warn my reader, that *ordering*, *directing*, *choosing*, *preferring*, &c., which I have made use of, will not distinctly enough express volition, unless he will reflect on what he himself does when he wills. For example, preferring, which seems perhaps best to express the act of volition, does it not precisely. For though a man would prefer flying to walking, yet who can say he ever wills it ? Volition, it is plain, is an act of the mind knowingly exerting² that dominion it takes itself to have over any part of the man, by employing it in, or withholding it from, any particular action.] And what is the will, but the faculty to do this ? And is that faculty anything more in effect than a power ; the power of [³ the mind to determine its thought, to the producing, continuing, or stopping any action⁴, as far as it depends on us ?] For can it be denied that whatever agent has a power to think on its own actions, and to prefer their doing or omission either to other, has that faculty called will ? *Will*, then, is nothing but such a power. *Liberty*, on the other side, is the power a *man* has to do or forbear doing any particular action ⁴ according as its doing or forbearance has the actual preference in the mind ; which is the same thing as to say, according as he himself wills it.

Powers.

16. It is plain then that the will is nothing but one power

---

¹ In first edition :—'Volition, 'tis plain, is nothing but the *actual* choosing or preferring forbearance to the doing, or doing to the forbearance, of any particular action in our power that we think on.'

² 'exerting'— freedom lies essentially in the power to originate exertion, not in the necessary intellectual conditions, nor in the natural effects of the exertion.

³ In first edition :—'preferring any action to its forbearance, or *vice versa*, as far as it appears to depend on us.'

⁴ 'action,' i. e. event intended to follow the volition, as distinguished from the volition itself. But are volitions themselves acts done in and for us, under natural law, or are they done by us so that we are accountable for them ?

or ability, and *freedom* another power or ability [1] so that, to

ask, whether the will has freedom, is to ask whether one power has another power, one ability another ability; a question at first sight too grossly absurd to make a dispute, or need an answer. For, who is it that sees not that powers belong only to agents, and are attributes only of substances, and not of powers themselves? So that this way of putting the question (viz. whether the will be free) is in effect to ask, whether the will be a substance, an agent, or at least to suppose it, since freedom can properly be attributed to nothing else. If freedom can with any propriety of speech be applied to power, it may be attributed to the power that is in a man to produce, or forbear producing, motion in parts of his body, by choice or preference; which is that which denominates him free, and is freedom itself [2]. But if any one should ask, whether freedom were free, he would be suspected not to understand well what he said; and he would be thought to deserve Midas's ears [3], who, knowing that rich was a denomination for the possession of riches, should demand whether riches themselves were rich.

17. However, the name *faculty*, which men have given to
this power called the will, and whereby they have been led into a way of talking of the will as acting, may, by an appropriation that disguises its true sense, serve a little to palliate the absurdity; yet the will, in truth, signifies nothing but a power or ability to prefer or choose: and when the will, under the name of a faculty, is considered as it is, barely as an ability to do something, the absurdity in saying it is free, or not free, will easily discover itself. For, if it be reasonable to suppose and talk of faculties as distinct beings that can act, (as we do, when we say the will orders, and the will is free,) it is fit that we should make a speaking faculty, and a

---

[1] For, according to Locke's argument, an agent may will when he has no 'freedom' to execute what he wills —the only freedom here contemplated. But does not moral freedom mean the power of the voluntary agent to *originate* his own moral or immoral volitions, so that he is their absolutely ultimate cause?

[2] Here again he finds the idea of power in what *follows* 'choice or preference.' So too in his letters to Limborch.

[3] The ears of Midas were changed into those of an ass.

BOOK II.
—✦—
CHAP. XXI.

walking faculty, and a dancing faculty, by which these actions are produced, which are but several modes of motion; as well as we make the will and understanding to be faculties, by which the actions of choosing and perceiving are produced, which are but several modes of thinking[1]. And we may as properly say that it is the singing faculty sings, and the dancing faculty dances, as that the will chooses, or that the understanding conceives; or, as is usual, that the will directs the understanding, or the understanding obeys or obeys not the will: it being altogether as proper and intelligible to say that the power of speaking directs the power of singing, or the power of singing obeys or disobeys the power of speaking[2].

This way of talking causes confusion of thought.

18. This way of talking, nevertheless, has prevailed, and, as I guess, produced great confusion. For these being all different powers in the mind, or in the man, to do several actions, he exerts them as he thinks fit: but the power to do one action is not operated on by the power of doing another action. For the power of thinking operates not on the power of choosing, nor the power of choosing on the power of thinking; no more than the power of dancing operates on the power of singing, or the power of singing on the power of dancing, as any one who reflects on it will easily perceive. And yet this is it which we say when we thus speak, that the will operates on the understanding, or the understanding on the will.

Powers are relations, not agents.

19. I grant, that this or that actual thought may be the occasion of volition, or exercising the power a man has to choose; or the actual choice of the mind, the cause of actual thinking on this or that thing: as the actual singing of such a tune may be the cause of dancing such a dance, and the actual dancing of such a dance the occasion of singing such a tune. But in all these it is not one *power* that operates on

---

[1] Here 'thinking' is applied to any sort of conscious act or state.

[2] The real question is, whether in willing freely the man is conceived as the power to which his own volitions are ultimately and absolutely referable, so far as he is morally accountable for them; or whether, in this as otherwise, he is only a link in the succession of natural causes that are themselves natural effects. Does 'I ought' mean that *I* can, or only that *nature* can?

another : but it is the mind that operates, and exerts these

powers ; it is the man that does the action ; it is the agent that has power, or is able to do. For powers are relations, not agents : and that which has the power or not the power to operate, is that alone which is or is not free, and not the power itself[1]. For freedom, or not freedom, can belong to nothing but what has or has not a power to act[2].

20. The attributing to faculties that which belonged not to them, has given occasion to this way of talking : but the introducing into discourses concerning the mind, with the name of faculties, a notion of *their* operating, has, I suppose, as little advanced our knowledge in that part of ourselves, as the great use and mention of the like invention of faculties, in the operations of the body, has helped us in the knowledge of physic. Not that I deny there are faculties, both in the body and mind : they both of them have their powers of operating, else neither the one nor the other could operate. For nothing can operate that is not able to operate ; and that is not able to operate that has no power to operate[3]. Nor do I deny that those words, and the like, are to have their place in the common use of languages that have made them current. It looks like too much affectation wholly to lay them by : and philosophy itself, though it likes not a gaudy dress, yet, when it appears in public, must have so much complacency as to be clothed in the ordinary fashion and

---

[1] Power *per se* is of course an abstraction, and the idea of free active power is suggested by an agent to whom the effects are ultimately referred as their origin.

[2] That, in the case of a moral agent, is to *originate*, or be the *first cause* of a volition, and of all that the volition naturally carries with it, as an agent in nature. If all activity is spiritual, then every physical event exhibits immanent Spirit, or Active Reason, determining motions in bodies ; so that physical events or effects are all *transformations* of, but are not *produced by*, preceding physical phenomena. Voluntary activity is, accordingly,

inexplicable by natural science, or as conditioned by mechanical causality. Reason and Will interpose, nevertheless, in the physical system, unless the overt acts attributed to Alexander the Great or to Caesar, or the works of Plato or Milton, are explicable as the issue of undirected changes in solid and extended bodies, apart from consciousness.

[3] But is our idea of the 'power' that is exercised in willing an idea of mechanical and dependent power, or of a power that is supernatural, in the sense of being somehow superior to passive natural economy, and under the higher law of moral government ?

language of the country, so far as it can consist with truth and perspicuity.   But the fault has been, that faculties have been spoken of and represented as so many distinct agents. For, it being asked, what it was that digested the meat in our stomachs? it was a ready and very satisfactory answer to say, that it was the *digestive faculty.*   What was it that made anything come out of the body? the *expulsive faculty.*   What moved? the *motive faculty.*   And so in the mind, the *intellectual faculty,* or the understanding, understood; and the *elective faculty,* or the will, willed or commanded.   This is, in short, to say, that the ability to digest, digested; and the ability to move, moved; and the ability to understand, understood.   For faculty, ability, and power, I think, are but different names of the same things: which ways of speaking, when put into more intelligible words, will, I think, amount to thus much;—That digestion is performed by something that is able to digest, motion by something able to move, and understanding by something able to understand.   And, in truth, it would be very strange if it should be otherwise; as strange as it would be for a man to be free without being able to be free [1].

But to
the Agent,
or Man.
21. To return, then, to the inquiry about liberty, I think the question is not proper, *whether the will be free,* but *whether a man be free.*   Thus, I think,

First, That so far as any one can, by [[2] the direction or choice of his mind, preferring] the existence of any action to the non-existence of that action, and *vice versâ,* make *it* to exist or not exist, so far *he* is free.   For if I can, by [[3] a thought directing] the motion of my finger [4], make it move

---

[1] Freedom of moral acts from merely natural uniformity, the postulate of morality, transcends a physical science of man, or the science which is concerned only with the succession of causal uniformities, and ignores the supernatural in man.   'Psychology will be psychology, and science science, as much as ever (as much and no more) whether free will be true or not.   Science however must be constantly reminded that her pur-

poses are not the only purposes, and that the order of uniform causation which she has use for, and is therefore right in postulating, *may be enveloped in a wider order on which she has no claims at all.*'   (James's *Psychology,* vol. ii. p. 570.)

[2] 'choice or preference of'—in first edition.

[3] 'the preference of'—in first edition.

[4] 'to its rest'—added in first edition.

when it was at rest, or *vice versâ*, it is evident, that in respect of that I am free: and if I can, by a like thought of my mind, preferring one to the other, produce either words or silence, I am at liberty to speak or hold my peace: and as far as this power reaches, of acting or not acting, by the determination of his own thought preferring either, so far is a man free. For how can we think any one freer, than to have the power to do what he will? And so far as any one can, by preferring any action to its not being, or rest to any action, produce that action or rest, so far can he do what he will. For such a preferring of action to its absence, is the willing of it: and we can scarce tell how to imagine any being freer, than to be able to do what he wills[1]. So that in respect of actions within the reach of such a power in him, a man seems as free as it is possible for freedom to make him.

22. But the inquisitive mind of man, willing to shift off from himself, as far as he can, all thoughts of guilt, though it be by putting himself into a worse state than that of fatal necessity, is not content with this: freedom, unless it reaches further than this, will not serve the turn: and it passes for a good plea, that a man is not free at all, if he be not as *free to will* as he is to *act what he wills*. Concerning a man's liberty, there yet, therefore, is raised this further question, *Whether a man be free to will?* which I think is what is meant, when it is disputed whether the will be free. And as to that I imagine. *In respect of willing, a Man is not free.*

23. Secondly, That willing, or volition, being an action, and freedom consisting in a power of acting or not acting, a man in respect of willing [2 or the act of volition], when any action in his power is once proposed to his thoughts, [3 as presently to be done,] cannot be free. The reason whereof is very manifest. For, it being unavoidable that the action depending on his will should exist or not exist, and its *How a man cannot be free to will.*

---

[1] He *is* 'freer' if, in virtue of his moral accountability for his own voluntary determinations, he is, as a voluntary agent, so far extricated from the mechanism of natural causation, and included in the moral and spiritual economy to which the natural mechanism is in harmonious subordination.

[2] Added in posthumous edition.

[3] Added in posthumous edition.

existence or not existence following perfectly the determination and preference of his will, he cannot avoid willing the existence or non-existence of that action ; it is absolutely necessary that he will the one or the other ; i. e. prefer the one to the other : since one of them must necessarily follow ; and that which does follow follows by the choice and determination of his mind ; that is, by his willing it : for if he did not will it, it would not be. So that, in respect of the act of willing, a man [¹in such a case] is not free : liberty consisting in a power to act or not to act ; which, in regard of volition, a man, [² upon such a proposal] has not. [³ For it is unavoidably necessary to prefer the doing or forbearance of an action in a man's power, which is once so proposed to his thoughts ; a man must necessarily will the one or the other of them ; upon which preference or volition, the action or its forbearance certainly follows, and is truly voluntary. But the act of volition, or preferring one of the two, being that which he cannot avoid, a man, in respect of that act of willing, is under a necessity, and so cannot be free ; unless necessity and freedom can consist together, and a man can be free and bound at once ⁴.] [⁵ Besides to make a man free after this manner, by making the action of willing to depend on his will, there must be another antecedent will, to determine the acts of this will, and another to determine that, and so *in infinitum* : for wherever one stops, the actions of the last will cannot be free. Nor is any being, as far I can comprehend beings

¹ Added in posthumous edition.
² Added in posthumous edition.
³ Added in fourth edition.
⁴ Here at last Locke comes to the idea of a free power to act for which the agent is accountable ; but without an adequate estimate of it, as the turning point between materialism or naturalism, and a spiritual philosophy of the universe. He concludes, under this inadequate conception, that, in his volitions, man is *under causal necessity to avoid uneasiness*, so that he cannot be under higher law than mechanism of nature, even in his voluntary determinations.

⁵ The sentences within brackets do not appear in the French version, or in the posthumous editions of the *Essay*, while they are found in the four English editions published in Locke's lifetime, and in the Latin version. The argument supposes that 'freedom of will' means determination of volitions *by previous volitions*, as part of the mechanism of nature, instead of independence of that mechanism altogether ; and this on the ground that no events, volitions included, can come to pass, without a previous *physical* or *caused* cause of their occurrence.

above me, capable of such a freedom of will, that it can forbear to will, i. e. to prefer the being or not being of anything
in its power, which it has once considered as such.]

24. This, then, is evident, That *a man is not at liberty to will,
or not to will, anything in his power that he once considers of* :
liberty consisting in a power to act or to forbear acting, and
in that only. For a man that sits still is said yet to be at
liberty; because he can walk if he wills it. A man that
walks is at liberty also, not because he walks or moves ; but
because he can stand still if he wills it. But if a man sitting
still has not a power to remove himself, he is not at liberty ;
so likewise a man falling down a precipice, though in motion,
is not at liberty, because he cannot stop that motion if he
would. This being so, it is plain that a man that is
walking, to whom it is proposed to give off walking, is
not at liberty, whether he will determine himself[1] to walk, or
give off walking or not : he must necessarily prefer one
or the other of them ; walking or not walking. And so it
is in regard of all other actions in our power [[2] so proposed,
which are the far greater number. For, considering the vast
number of voluntary actions that succeed one another every
moment that we are awake in the course of our lives, there
are but few of them that are thought on or proposed to the
will, till the time they are to be done ; and in all such actions,
as I have shown, the mind, in respect of willing,] has not a
power to act or not to act, wherein consists liberty. The
mind, in that case, has not a power to forbear *willing* ; it
cannot avoid some determination concerning them, let the
consideration be as short, the thought as quick as it will, it
either leaves the man in the state he was before thinking, or
changes it ; continues the action, or puts an end to it.
Whereby it is manifest, that *it* orders and directs one, in

---

[1] In the French version, ' n'est plus
en liberté de *vouloir vouloir* (permittez
moi cette expression).' On which
Leibniz comments thus :—' Il est vrai
qu'on parle peu juste, lorsqu'on
parle comme si nous *voulions vouloir.*
Nous ne voulons point *vouloir,* mais
nous voulons *faire* ; et si nous voulions
vouloir, nous voudrions vouloir vouloir,
et cela irait à l'infini.'

[2] Instead of the words within brackets, introduced in the French version,
the first four editions read :—' they
being once proposed, the mind.'

BOOK II.
Chap. XXI.

The Will determined by something without it.

preference to, or with neglect of the other, and thereby either the continuation or change becomes *unavoidably* voluntary[1].

25. Since then it is plain that, in most cases, a man is not at liberty, whether he will or no, (for, when an action in his power is proposed to his thoughts, he *cannot* forbear volition; he *must* determine one way or the other;) the next thing demanded is,— *Whether a man be at liberty to will which of the two he pleases, motion or rest?* This question carries the absurdity of it so manifestly in itself, that one might thereby sufficiently be convinced that liberty concerns not the will. For, to ask whether a man be at liberty to will either motion or rest, speaking or silence, which he pleases, is to ask whether a man can will what he wills, or be pleased with what he is pleased with? A question which, I think, needs no answer: and they who can make a question of it must suppose one will to determine the acts of another, and another to determine that, and so on *in infinitum*[2].

The ideas of *liberty* and *volition* must be defined.

26. To avoid these and the like absurdities[3], nothing can be of greater use than to establish in our minds determined ideas of the things under consideration. If the ideas of liberty and volition were well fixed in our understandings, and

---

[1] On the principle of an excluded middle between contradictories, he *must* either act or not act.

[2] The words, 'an absurdity before taken notice of,' which follow in the fourth edition, afterwards omitted. Cf. sentences in brackets in § 23.

[3] That volition cannot be free, in the sense of being self-determined in all cases by *a preceding volition*, in the order of natural sequence, is thus argued by Jonathan Edwards:—' If the will determines all its own acts, then every free act of choice is determined by a preceding act of choice, choosing that act. And if that preceding act of the will be also a free act, then, by these principles, in this act too the will is self-determined, or is an act determined still by a preceding act of the will choosing that. And the like may again be observed of the last-

mentioned act, which brings us directly to a contradiction; for it supposes an act of the will preceding the first act in the whole train, directing the rest; —or a free act of the will before the first free act of the will. Or else we must come at last to an act of the will determining the consequent acts, wherein the will is not self-determined [i. e. by a preceding volition], and so is not free, in this notion of freedom. But if the first act in the train determining and fixing the next, be not free, none of them all can be free.' (*Inquiry respecting that Freedom of Will which is supposed to be essential to Moral Agency*, pt. ii. § 1.) This argument proceeds on the unwarranted assumption, that 'free will' is volition naturally caused by preceding volition, instead of being itself a first cause.

carried along with us in our minds, as they ought, through BOOK II.
all the questions that are raised about them, I suppose a
great part of the difficulties that perplex men's thoughts, CHAP. XXI.
and entangle their understandings, would be much easier
resolved; and we should perceive where the confused signification of terms, or where the nature of the thing caused
the obscurity.

27. First, then, it is carefully to be remembered, That free- Freedom.
dom consists in the dependence of the existence, or not
existence of any *action*, upon our *volition* of it; and not in
the dependence of any action, or its contrary, on our *preference*. A man standing on a cliff, is at liberty to leap
twenty yards downwards into the sea, not because he has a
power to do the contrary action, which is to leap twenty yards
upwards, for that he cannot do; but he is therefore free, because he has a power to leap or not to leap. But if a greater
force than his, either holds him fast, or tumbles him down, he
is no longer free in that case; because the doing or forbearance of that particular action is no longer in his power. He
that is a close prisoner in a room twenty feet square, being at
the north side of his chamber, is at liberty to walk twenty feet
southward, because he can walk or not walk it; but is not, at
the same time, at liberty to do the contrary, i.e. to walk
twenty feet northward.

In this, then, consists *freedom*, viz. in our being able to act
or not to act, according as we shall choose or will[1].

[28. [2] Secondly, we must remember, that *volition* or *willing* What
Volition

---

[1] This is the necessitarian idea of
a free agent, as in Hobbes's *Treatise
of Liberty and Necessity*, for instance.
Locke's idea is only that of freedom
from obstruction in executing what
we have willed. The prisoner, moreover, might originate an (ineffectual)
voluntary determination to escape;
although, in his circumstances, this
volition must be inefficacious, under
the established laws of nature, and
would therefore be an *irrational* exercise of his moral freedom. 'Quand on

raisonne sur la liberté de la volonté, on
ne demande pas si l'homme peut faire
ce qu'il veut, *mais s'il y a assez d'inde-
pendance dans sa volonté même*; on ne
demande pas s'il a les jambes libres
ou les coudées franches, *mais s'il a
l'esprit libre, et en quoi cela consiste.*'
(Leibniz.)

[2] This section and those which follow to the end of § 62 (some parts of
which correspond to the original text)
were substituted, in the second and
subsequent editions, for §§ 28–38 in

BOOK II.

CHAP. XXI.

and action mean.

is an act of the mind directing its thought to the production of any action, and thereby exerting its power to produce it. To avoid multiplying of words, I would crave leave here, under the word *action*, to comprehend the forbearance too of any action proposed : sitting still, or holding one's peace, when walking or speaking are proposed, though mere forbearances, requiring as much the determination of the will, and being as often weighty in their consequences, as the contrary actions, may, on that consideration, well enough pass for actions too : but this I say, that I may not be mistaken, if (for brevity's sake) I speak thus [1].

What determines the Will.

29. Thirdly, the will being nothing but a power in the mind to direct the operative faculties of a man to motion or rest, as far as they depend on such direction ; to the question, What is it determines the will? the true and proper answer is, The mind. For that which determines the general power of directing, to this or that particular direction, is nothing but the agent itself exercising the power it has that particular way. If this answer satisfies not, it is plain the meaning of the question, What determines the will? is this,—What moves the mind, in every particular instance, to determine its general power of directing, to this or that particular motion or rest ?

the first edition. The eleven omitted sections are, in this edition, printed at the end of this chapter, for collation with the present text. The alteration was due to Locke's change of his original opinion,—that our volitions are ultimately determined by our judgment of the *greater good*,—in favour of the view that *felt uneasiness* is the natural cause of willing. The thirty-five sections that take their place only present Locke's ' second thoughts ' of liberty, as consisting in power to 'suspend' volition, pending judgment. The letters which passed between Locke and Molyneux, in 1693, when the second edition of the *Essay* was in preparation, and letters to Limborch, show the grounds of this change, and also Locke's perplexities throughout the reasonings of this chapter.

[1] Locke means by ' action ' only the effect of willing. His contemporary, Samuel Clarke, carefully distinguishes action proper, in the following, among many similar passages :—' To be an *agent* signifies to have a power of beginning motion (or change); and motion cannot begin necessarily, because *necessity* of motion supposes an efficiency superior to, and irresistible by, the thing moved ; and consequently the beginning of motion cannot be in that which is moved necessarily, but in the superior cause, and then in the efficiency of some other cause, still superior to that.' (*Remarks upon ' Inquiry concerning Liberty*,' p. 6.) A *necessary agent* would thus be a contradiction in terms, and there could be no *active* power in a mechanical or caused cause.

And to this I answer,—The motive for continuing in the same
state or action, is only the present satisfaction in it ; the motive
to change is always some uneasiness : nothing setting us upon
the change of state, or upon any new action, but some uneasiness [1]. This is the great motive that works on the mind
to put it upon action, which for shortness' sake we will call
determining of the will, which I shall more at large explain.

30. But, in the way to it, it will be necessary to premise,
that, though I have above endeavoured to express the act of
volition, by *choosing*, *preferring*, and the like terms, that signify
desire as well as volition, for want of other words to mark that
act of the mind whose proper name is *willing* or *volition* ; yet,
it being a very simple act, whosoever desires to understand
what it is, will better find it by reflecting on his own mind, and
observing what it does when it wills, than by any variety of
articulate sounds whatsoever. This caution of being careful
not to be misled by expressions that do not enough keep up
the difference between the *will* and several acts of the mind
that are quite distinct from it, I think the more necessary, because I find the will often confounded with several of the
affections, especially *desire*, and one put for the other ; and
that by men [2] who would not willingly be thought not to have
had very distinct notions of things, and not to have writ very
clearly about them. This, I imagine, has been no small
occasion of obscurity and mistake in this matter ; and therefore is, as much as may be, to be avoided. For he that shall
turn his thoughts inwards upon what passes in his mind when
he wills, shall see that the will or power of volition is conversant about nothing but our own *actions* ; terminates there ;
and reaches no further ; and that volition is nothing but that
particular determination of the mind, whereby, barely by a
thought, the mind endeavours to give rise, continuation, or
stop, to any action which it takes to be in its power [3]. This,

---

[1] Then the so-called 'agent' is himself, in each particular 'act' of willing,
ultimately the passive subject of a natural necessity consequent upon 'uneasiness ;' he is merged in nature, and is
not the agent of the action that is nomi-
nally his. A motive thus is the physical

cause of a volition. The supposed 'freedom' of man is only the freedom of
external nature: whatever that may be.

[2] He probably alludes to Malebranche.

[3] According to this account will and
desire differ not in their origin, nor in

well considered, plainly shows that the will is perfectly distinguished from desire; which, in the very same action, may
have a quite contrary tendency from that which our will sets
us upon. A man, whom I cannot deny, may oblige me to use
persuasions to another, which, at the same time I am speaking,
I may wish may not prevail on him. In this case, it is plain
the will and desire run counter. I will the action; that
tends one way, whilst my desire tends another, and that the
direct contrary way. A man who, by a violent fit of the gout
in his limbs, finds a doziness in his head, or a want of appetite
in his stomach removed, desires to be eased too of the pain of
his feet or hands, (for wherever there is pain, there is a desire
to be rid of it,) though yet, whilst he apprehends that the removal of the pain may translate the noxious humour to a more
vital part, his will is never determined to any one action that
may serve to remove this pain. Whence it is evident that
desiring and willing are two distinct acts of the mind; and
consequently, that the will, which is but the power of volition,
is much more distinct from desire [1].

*Uneasi-
ness deter-
mines the
Will.*

31. To return, then, to the inquiry, what is it that determines the will in regard to our actions? And that, upon
second thoughts, I am apt to imagine is not, as is generally
supposed, the greater good in view; but some (and for the
most part the most pressing) *uneasiness* a man is at present
under [2]. This is that which successively determines the will,

their relation to the system of physical
causes, but only in their consequences.
Volitions and desires are equally a
part of nature, but a volition issues in
overt action, while it is itself the natural effect of the *dominant* uneasiness
or desire of the moment. Volition is
victorious desire.

[1] The mechanism and production of
voluntary movements—a complex problem in natural science—instead of the
idea of power suggested by the voluntary act, is what Locke still keeps to.
Ineffectual volition, however deliberate, is regarded as *wish* or *desire*
only.

[2] The 'second thoughts,' which led

Locke to place the motive or cause,
by which voluntary determination
is naturally determined, in a felt
'uneasiness,' rather than in an ideal
'good' (by which he means pleasure,
cf. ch. xx. § 2), equally with his
first thoughts, make volition an issue
of the physical system, and man,
even in the deepest root of his being,
a part of nature. Yet, in writing to
Molyneux (15 July, 1693), he congratu-
lates himself as having 'got into a
new view of things, which, if I mistake not, will satisfy you, and give a
clearer account of human freedom
than hitherto I have done.' He makes
'uneasiness' practically one with the

and sets us upon those actions we perform.   This uneasiness
we may call, as it is, *desire*; which is an uneasiness of the
mind for want of some absent good.   All pain of the body,
of what sort soever, and disquiet of the mind, is uneasiness :
and with this is always joined desire, equal to the pain or uneasiness felt; and is scarce distinguishable from it.   For desire
being nothing but an uneasiness in the want of an absent good,
in reference to any pain felt, ease is that absent good ; and till
that ease be attained, we may call it desire ; nobody feeling
pain that he wishes not to be eased of, with a desire equal to
that pain, and inseparable from it [1].   Besides this desire of
ease from pain, there is another of absent positive good ; and
here also the desire and uneasiness are equal.   As much as we
desire any absent good, so much are we in pain for it.   But
here all absent good does not, according to the greatness it
has, or is acknowledged to have, cause pain equal to that
greatness ; as all pain causes desire equal to itself : because
the absence of good is not always a pain, as the presence of
pain is.   And therefore absent good may be looked on and
considered without desire.   But so much as there is anywhere
of desire, so much there is of uneasiness [2].

32. That desire is a state of uneasiness, every one who
reflects on himself will quickly find.   Who is there that has
not felt in desire what the wise man [3] says of hope, (which is
not much different from it,) that it being ' deferred makes the

Desire
is Uneasi-
ness.

desire, which necessarily goes with it ;
and *will* to differ from *desire* only in
being followed by the event intended.
But ' every good, nay every greater
good' (so he argues in favour of his
' second thoughts') does not *constantly*
move desire ; because it may not make,
or may not be taken to make, any necessary part of our happiness ; for ' all
that we desire is only to be happy.'
The absence of good is not always a
pain, but the presence of pain must of
course always be painful.

[1] So Montaigne in his *Essais* :—
' Notre bien-être, ce n'est que la privation d'être mal' (Liv. II. ch. xii.), and
in sundry other passages.

[2] And so ' the greater good' is not,
as maintained in the first edition, ' that
which always determines the will.'
' Freedom ' in willing would thus consist in a man being naturally determined to will by *his desire or feeling
of uneasiness, guided by judgment*, and
volition is based upon capacity for
being made uneasy.   He afterwards
qualifies this (§§ 48–53) by inconsistently claiming for ' free agents '
power to '*suspend*' volition, pending
deliberation, thus mixing the natural
passivity with a semblance of moral
superiority to this.

[3] Proverbs xiii. 12.

BOOK II.
——◆——
CHAP. XXI.

heart sick'; and that still proportionable to the greatness of the desire, which sometimes raises the uneasiness to that pitch, that it makes people cry out, 'Give me children,' give me the thing desired, 'or I die[1].' Life itself, and all its enjoyments, is a burden cannot be borne under the lasting and unremoved pressure of such an uneasiness.

The Uneasiness of Desire determines the Will.

33. Good and evil, present and absent, it is true, work upon the mind. But that which *immediately* determines the will, from time to time, to every voluntary action, is the *uneasiness of desire*, fixed on some absent good : either negative, as indolence to one in pain ; or positive, as enjoyment of pleasure. That it is this uneasiness that determines the will to the successive voluntary actions, whereof the greatest part of our lives is made up, and by which we are conducted through different courses to different ends, I shall endeavour to show, both from experience[2], and the reason of the thing[3].

This is the Spring of Action.

34. When a man is perfectly content with the state he is in—which is when he is perfectly without any uneasiness—what industry, what action, what will is there left, but to continue in it ? Of this every man's observation will satisfy him. And thus we see our all-wise Maker, suitably to our constitution and frame, and knowing what it is that determines the will, has put into man the uneasiness of hunger and thirst, and other natural desires, that return at their seasons, to move and determine their wills[4], for the preservation of themselves, and the continuation of their species. For I think we may conclude, that, if the *bare contemplation* of these good ends to which we are carried by these several uneasinesses had been sufficient to determine the will, and set us on work, we should have had none of these natural pains, and perhaps in this world little or no pain at all. 'It is better to marry than to burn,' says St. Paul[5], where we may see what it is that chiefly drives men into the enjoyments of a conjugal life. A little burning felt pushes us more powerfully than greater pleasures in prospect draw or allure.

---

[1] Genesis xxx. 1.

[2] §§ 34–35.

[3] §§ 36, &c.

[4] As 'motives' which necessitate their volitions ?

[5] 1 Corinth. vii. 9.

35. It seems so established and settled a maxim, by the
general consent of all mankind, that good, the greater good,
determines the will, that I do not at all wonder that, when
I first published my thoughts on this subject[1] I took it for
granted ; and I imagine that, by a great many, I shall be
thought more excusable for having then done so, than that
now I have ventured to recede from so received an opinion.
But yet, upon a stricter inquiry, I am forced to conclude that
good, the *greater good*, though apprehended and acknowledged to be so, does not determine the will, until our desire,
raised proportionably to it, makes us uneasy in the want of
it. Convince a man never so much, that plenty has its advantages over poverty; make him see and own, that the handsome conveniences of life are better than nasty penury : yet,
as long as he is content with the latter, and finds no uneasiness in it, he moves not; his will never is determined to any
action that shall bring him out of it. Let a man be ever so
well persuaded of the advantages of virtue, that it is as
necessary to a man who has any great aims in this world, or
hopes in the next, as food to life : yet, till he hungers or
thirsts after righteousness, till he *feels an uneasiness* in the
want of it, his *will* will not be determined to any action in
pursuit of this confessed greater good ; but any other
uneasiness he feels in himself shall take place, and carry his
will to other actions. On the other side, let a drunkard see
that his health decays, his estate wastes; discredit and
diseases, and the want of all things, even of his beloved
drink, attends him in the course he follows : yet the returns
of uneasiness to miss his companions, the habitual thirst after
his cups at the usual time, drives him to the tavern, though
he has in his view the loss of health and plenty, and perhaps
of the joys of another life : the least of which is no inconsiderable good, but such as he confesses is far greater than
the tickling of his palate with a glass of wine, or the idle
chat of a soaking club. It is not want of viewing the
greater good : for he sees and acknowledges it, and, in the
intervals of his drinking hours, will take resolutions to

---

[1] In 1690, in the first edition of the *Essay*.

pursue the greater good ; but when the uneasiness to miss his accustomed delight returns, the greater acknowledged good loses its hold, and the present uneasiness determines the will to the accustomed action ; which thereby gets stronger footing to prevail against the next occasion, though he at the same time makes secret promises to himself that he will do so no more ; this is the last time he will act against the attainment of those greater goods. And thus he is, from time to time, in the state of that unhappy complainer[1], *Video meliora, proboque, deteriora sequor*: which sentence, allowed for true, and made good by constant experience, may in this, and possibly no other way, be easily made intelligible.

Because the Removal of Uneasiness is the first Step to Happiness.

36. If we inquire into the reason of what experience makes so evident in fact, and examine, why it is uneasiness alone operates on the will, and determines it in its choice, we shall find that, we being capable but of one determination of the will to one action at once, the present uneasiness that we are under does *naturally* determine the will, in order to that happiness which we all aim at in all our actions. For, as much as whilst we are under any uneasiness, we cannot apprehend ourselves happy, or in the way to it ; pain and uneasiness being, by every one, concluded and felt to be inconsistent with happiness, spoiling the relish even of those good things which we have : a little pain serving to mar all the pleasure we rejoiced in. And, therefore, that which of course determines the choice of our will to the next action will always be—the removing of pain, as long as we have any left, as the first and necessary step towards happiness.

Because Uneasiness alone is present.

37. Another reason why it is uneasiness alone determines the will, is this : because that alone is present and, it is against the nature of things, that what is absent should operate where it is not. It may be said that absent good may, by contemplation, be brought home to the mind and made present. The idea of it indeed may be in the mind, and viewed as present there ; but nothing will be in the mind as a present good, able to counterbalance the removal of any

---

[1] Ovid, *Metamorph*. lib. vii., vv. 20, 21.

uneasiness which we are under, till it raises our desire; and
the uneasiness of that has the prevalency in determining the
will. Till then, the idea in the mind of whatever is good is
there only, like other ideas, the object of bare unactive
speculation; but operates not on the will, nor sets us on work;
the reason whereof I shall show by and by. How many are
to be found that have had lively representations set before
their minds of the unspeakable joys of heaven, which they
acknowledge both possible and probable too, who yet would
be content to take up with their happiness here? And so the
prevailing uneasiness of their desires, let loose after the enjoyments of this life, take their turns in the determining their
wills; and all that while they take not one step, are not one
jot moved, towards the good things of another life, considered
as ever so great.

38. Were the will determined by the views of good, as
it appears in contemplation greater or less to the understanding, which is the state of all absent good, and that
which, in the received opinion, the will is supposed to move
to, and to be moved by,—I do not see how it could ever get
loose from the infinite eternal joys of heaven, once proposed
and considered as possible. For, all absent good, by which
alone, barely proposed, and coming in view, the will is
thought to be determined, and so to set us on action, being
only possible, but not infallibly certain, it is unavoidable
that the infinitely greater possible good should regularly and
constantly determine the will in all the successive actions it
directs; and then we should keep constantly and steadily in
our course towards heaven, without ever standing still, or
directing our actions to any other end: the eternal condition
of a future state infinitely outweighing the expectation of
riches, or honour, or any other worldly pleasure which we
can propose to ourselves, though we should grant these the
more probable to be obtained: for nothing future is yet in
possession, and so the expectation even of these may deceive
us. If it were so that the greater good in view determines
the will, so great a good, once proposed, could not but seize
the will, and hold it fast to the pursuit of this infinitely
greatest good, without ever letting it go again: for the will

having a power over, and directing the thoughts, as well as other actions, would, if it were so, hold the contemplation of the mind fixed to that good.

But any great Uneasiness is never neglected.

39. This would be the state of the mind, and regular tendency of the will in all its determinations, were it determined by that which is considered and in view the greater good. But that it is not so, is visible in experience; the infinitely greatest confessed good being often neglected, to satisfy the successive uneasiness of our desires pursuing trifles. But, though the greatest allowed, even everlasting unspeakable, good, which has sometimes moved and affected the mind, does not stedfastly hold the will, yet we see any very great and prevailing uneasiness having once laid hold on the will, let it not go; by which we may be convinced, what it is that determines the will. Thus any vehement pain of the body; the ungovernable passion of a man violently in love; or the impatient desire of revenge, keeps the will steady and intent; and the will, thus determined, never lets the understanding lay by the object, but all the thoughts of the mind and powers of the body are uninterruptedly employed that way, by the determination of the will, influenced by that topping uneasiness, as long as it lasts; whereby it seems to me evident, that the will, or power of setting us upon one action in preference to all others, is determined in us by uneasiness: and whether this be not so, I desire every one to observe in himself.

Desire accompanies all Uneasiness.

40. I have hitherto chiefly instanced in the *uneasiness* of desire, as that which determines the will: because that is the chief and most sensible; and the will seldom[1] orders any action, nor is there any voluntary action performed, without some desire accompanying it; which I think is the reason why the will and desire are so often confounded. But yet we are not to look upon the uneasiness which makes up, or at least accompanies, most of the other passions, as wholly excluded in the case. Aversion, fear, anger, envy, shame, &c. have each their uneasinesses too, and thereby influence the

---

[1] 'seldom'—*never*, if 'wherever there is uneasiness there *must* be desire' for relief, and if 'the will *must* in all cases be *naturally* determined by present uneasiness only.'

will. These passions are scarce any of them, in life and practice, simple and alone, and wholly unmixed with others ; though usually, in discourse and contemplation, that carries the name which operates strongest, and appears most in the present state of the mind. Nay, there is, I think, scarce any of the passions to be found without desire joined with it. I am sure wherever there is uneasiness, there is desire. For we constantly desire happiness ; and whatever we feel of uneasiness, so much it is certain we want of happiness ; even in our own opinion, let our state and condition otherwise be what it will. Besides, the present moment not being our eternity, whatever our enjoyment be, we look beyond the present, and desire goes with our foresight, and that still carries the will with it. So that even in joy itself, that which keeps up the action whereon the enjoyment depends, is the desire to continue it, and fear to lose it : and whenever a greater uneasiness than that takes place in the mind, the will presently is by that determined to some new action, and the present delight neglected.

41. But we being in this world beset with sundry uneasinesses, distracted with different desires, the next inquiry naturally will be,—Which of them has the precedency in determining the will to the next action? and to that the answer is,—That ordinarily which is the most pressing of those that are judged capable of being then removed. For, the will being the power of directing our operative faculties to some action, for some end, cannot at any time be moved towards what is judged at that time unattainable : that would be to suppose an intelligent being designedly to act for an end, only to lose its labour ; for so it is to act for what is judged not attainable ; and therefore very great uneasinesses move not the will, when they are judged not capable of a cure : they in that case put us not upon endeavours [1]. But, these set apart, the most important and urgent uneasiness we at that time feel, is that which ordinarily determines the will, successively, in that train of voluntary actions which makes up our

---

[1] The spontaneous feeling of uneasiness, and relative desire for relief, lose their natural influence, when relief is believed to be unattainable,—volition being thus naturally conditioned by the judgment of the understanding.

lives. The greatest present uneasiness is the spur to action, that is constantly most felt, and for the most part determines the will in its choice of the next action. For this we must carry along with us, that the proper and only object of the will is some action of ours, and nothing else. For we producing nothing by our willing it, but some action in our power[1], it is there the will terminates, and reaches no further.

All desire Happiness.

42. If it be further asked,—What it is moves desire? I answer,—happiness, and that alone. Happiness and misery are the names of two extremes, the utmost bounds whereof we know not; it is what 'eye hath not seen, ear hath not heard, nor hath it entered into the heart of man to conceive.' But of some degrees of both we have very lively impressions; made by several instances of delight and joy on the one side, and torment and sorrow on the other; which, for shortness' sake, I shall comprehend under the names of pleasure and pain; there being pleasure and pain of the mind as well as the body,—'With him is fulness of joy, and pleasure for evermore.' Or, to speak truly, they are all of the mind; though some have their rise in the mind from thought, others in the body from certain modifications of motion[2].

Happiness and misery, good and evil, what they are.

43. *Happiness*, then, in its full extent, is the utmost pleasure we are capable of, and *misery* the utmost pain; and the lowest degree of what can be called happiness is so much ease from all pain, and so much present pleasure, as without which any one cannot be content. Now, because pleasure and pain are produced in us by the operation of certain objects, either on our minds or our bodies, and in different degrees; therefore, what has an aptness to produce pleasure in us is that we call *good*, and what is apt to produce pain in us we call *evil*; for no other reason but for its aptness to produce pleasure and pain in us, wherein consists our happiness and misery. Further, though what is apt to produce any degree of pleasure

[1] That the overt action should be the unimpeded natural consequence of volition, without regard to the origin of the voluntary determination itself, is still the freedom contemplated by Locke.

[2] The only real qualities in bodies being their primary qualities, and all their other so-called qualities and powers being correlative mental sensibilities, of which the former are the occasions, under the established laws of nature.

be in itself good ; and what is apt to produce any degree of pain be evil ; yet it often happens that we do not call it so when it comes in competition with a greater of its sort ; because, when they come in competition, the degrees also of pleasure and pain have justly a preference. So that if we will rightly estimate what we call good and evil, we shall find it lies much in comparison : for the cause of every less degree of pain, as well as every greater degree of pleasure, has the nature of good, and *vice versâ* [1].

44. Though this be that which is called good and evil, and all good be the proper object of desire in general ; yet all good, even seen and confessed to be so, does not necessarily move every particular man's desire ; but only that part, or so much of it as is considered and taken to make a necessary part of *his* happiness. All other good, however great in reality or appearance, excites not a man's desires who looks not on it to make a part of that happiness wherewith he, in his present thoughts, can satisfy himself. Happiness, under this view, every one constantly pursues, and desires what makes any part of it : other things, acknowledged to be good, he can look upon without desire, pass by, and be content without. There is nobody, I think, so senseless as to deny that there is pleasure in knowledge : and for the pleasures of sense, they have too many followers to let it be questioned whether men are taken with them or no. Now, let one man place his satisfaction in sensual pleasures, another in the delight of knowledge : though each of them cannot but confess, there is great pleasure in what the other pursues ; yet, neither of them making the other's delight a part of *his* happiness, their desires are not moved, but each is satisfied without what the other enjoys ; and so his will is not determined to the pursuit of it. But yet, as soon as the studious man's hunger and thirst make him uneasy, he, whose will was

---

[1] Pleasure thus becomes Locke's ideal of 'good'; his *summum bonum* is logically 'infinite quantity,' not perfect quality, of pleasure. 'Je ne sais,' says Leibniz, 'si le plus grand plaisir est possible. Je croirais plutôt qu'il peut croître à l'infini ; car nous ne savons pas jusqu'où nos connaissances et nos organes peuvent être portés dans toute cette éternité qui nous attend. Je croirais donc que le *bonheur* est un plaisir durable, ce qui ne saurait avoir lieu sans une progression continuelle à de nouveaux plaisirs.'

never determined to any pursuit of good cheer, poignant sauces, delicious wine, by the pleasant taste he has found in them, is, by the uneasiness of hunger and thirst, presently determined to eating and drinking, though possibly with great indifferency, what wholesome food comes in his way. And, on the other side, the epicure buckles to study, when shame, or the desire to recommend himself to his mistress, shall make him uneasy in the want of any sort of knowledge. Thus, how much soever men are in earnest and constant in pursuit of happiness, yet they may have a clear view of good, great and confessed good, without being concerned for it, or moved by it, if they think they can make up their happiness without it. Though as to pain, *that* they are always concerned for; they can feel no uneasiness without being moved. And therefore, being uneasy in the want of whatever is judged necessary to their happiness, as soon as any good appears to make a part of their portion of happiness, they begin to desire it [1].

Why the greatest Good is not always desired.

45. This, I think, any one may observe in himself and others,—That the greater visible good does not always raise men's desires in proportion to the greatness it appears, and is acknowledged, to have: though every little trouble moves us, and sets us on work to get rid of it. The reason whereof is evident from the nature of our happiness and misery itself. All present pain, whatever it be, makes a part of our present misery: but all absent good does not at any time make a necessary part of our present happiness, nor the absence of it make a part of our misery. If it did, we should be constantly and infinitely miserable; there being infinite degrees of happiness which are not in our possession. All uneasiness therefore being removed, a moderate portion of good serves at present to content men; and a few degrees of pleasure, in a succession of ordinary enjoyments, make up a happiness wherein they can be satisfied. If this were not so, there could be no room for those indifferent and visibly trifling actions, to which our wills are so often determined, and wherein we volun-

---

[1] There could thus be no absolute standard of good and evil for man, each man being naturally determined to conceive of good or evil according to the felt strength and variety of his own feelings of uneasiness.

tarily waste so much of our lives ; which remissness could by
no means consist with a constant determination of will or
desire to the greatest apparent good. That this is so, I think
few people need go far from home to be convinced. And
indeed in this life there are not many whose happiness reaches
so far as to afford them a constant train of moderate mean
pleasures, without any mixture of uneasiness ; and yet they
could be content to stay here for ever : though they cannot
deny, but that it is possible there may be a state of eternal
durable joys after this life, far surpassing all the good that is
to be found here. Nay, they cannot but see that it is more
possible than the attainment and continuation of that pittance
of honour, riches, or pleasure which they pursue, and for which
they neglect that eternal state. But yet, in full view of this
difference, satisfied of the possibility of a perfect, secure, and
lasting happiness in a future state, and under a clear conviction that it is not to be had here,—whilst they bound their
happiness within some little enjoyment or aim of this life, and
exclude the joys of heaven from making any necessary part of
it,—their desires are not moved by this greater apparent good,
nor their wills determined to any action, or endeavour for its
attainment.

46. The ordinary necessities of our lives fill a great part of Why not
being
desired,
them with the uneasinesses of hunger, thirst, heat, cold, weari-
ness, with labour, and sleepiness, in their constant returns, &c. it moves
not the
Will.
To which, if, besides accidental harms, we add the fantastical
uneasiness (as itch after honour, power, or riches, &c.) which
acquired habits, by fashion, example, and education, have
settled in us, and a thousand other irregular desires, which
custom has made natural to us, we shall find that a very little
part of our life is so vacant from *these* uneasinesses, as to leave
us free to the attraction of remoter absent good. We are
seldom at ease, and free enough from the solicitation of our
natural or adopted desires, but a constant succession of uneasinesses out of that stock which natural wants or acquired
habits have heaped up, take the will in their turns ; and no
sooner is one action dispatched, which by such a determination
of the will we are set upon, but another uneasiness is ready to
set us on work. For, the removing of the pains we feel, and

are at present pressed with, being the getting out of misery, and consequently the first thing to be done in order to happiness,—absent good, though thought on, confessed, and appearing to be good, not making any part of this unhappiness in its absence, is justled out, to make way for the removal of those uneasinesses we feel; till due and repeated contemplation has brought it nearer to our mind, given some relish of it, and raised in us some desire: which then beginning to make a part of our present uneasiness, stands upon fair terms with the rest to be satisfied, and so, according to its greatness and pressure, comes in its turn to determine the will.

Due Consideration raises Desire.

47. And thus, by a due consideration, and examining any good proposed, it is in our power to raise our desires in a due proportion to the value of that good [1], whereby in its turn and place it may come to work upon the will, and be pursued. For good, though appearing and allowed ever so great, yet till it has raised desires in our minds, and thereby made us uneasy in its want, it reaches not our wills; we are not within the sphere of its activity, our wills being under the determination only of those uneasinesses which are present to us, which (whilst we have any) are always soliciting, and ready at hand to give the will its next determination. The balancing, when there is any in the mind, being only, which desire shall be next satisfied, which uneasiness first removed. Whereby it comes to pass that, as long as any uneasiness, any desire, remains in our mind, there is no room for good, barely as such, to come at the will, or at all to determine it. Because, as has been said, the *first* step in our endeavours after happiness being to get wholly out of the confines of misery, and to feel no part of it, the will can be at leisure for nothing else, till every uneasiness we feel be perfectly removed: which, in the multitude of wants and desires we are beset with in this imperfect state, we are not like to be ever freed from in this world.

The Power to suspend the Prosecution of any Desire

48. There being in us a great many uneasinesses, always soliciting and ready to determine the will, it is natural, as I have said, that the greatest and most pressing should determine the will to the next action; and so it does for the most

---

[1] What is the criterion of its 'value'?

part, but not always. For, the mind having in most cases, as
is evident in experience, a power to *suspend* the execution and
satisfaction of any of its desires; and so all, one after another ; makes way
is at liberty to consider the objects of them, examine them on for Con-
all sides, and weigh them with others.   In this lies the liberty sideration.
man has[1]; and from the not using of it right comes all that
variety of mistakes, errors, and faults which we run into in the
conduct of our lives, and our endeavours after happiness ;
whilst we precipitate the determination of our wills, and
engage too soon, before due examination. To prevent this,
we have a power to suspend the prosecution of this or that
desire ; as every one daily may experiment in himself.   This
seems to me the source of all liberty ; in this seems to consist
that which is (as I think improperly) called *free-will*[2]. For,
during this suspension of any desire, before the will be determined to action, and the action (which follows that determination) done, we have opportunity to examine, view, and judge
of the good or evil of what we are going to do ; and when,
upon due examination, we have judged, we have done our
duty, all that we can, or ought to do, in pursuit of our happiness ; and it is not a fault, but a perfection of our nature, to
desire, will, and act according to the last result of a fair
examination.

49. This is so far from being a restraint or diminution of To be
freedom, that it is the very improvement and benefit of it ; it deter-
is not an abridgment, it is the end and use of our liberty ; and mined by
the further we are removed from such a determination, the our own
Judgment,
nearer we are to misery and slavery[3]. A perfect indifference is no
Restraint
to Liberty.

---

[1] Free agency with Locke thus consists at last in 'power to suspend'
volition. But unless in this man rises
above a merely natural causation of
motives, he is no more ethically free
in suspending the voluntary execution
of a desire than in any other exercise
of will. A power to suspend volition,
necessarily thus dependent, leaves man
still a part of the mechanism of nature.

[2] This recognition of power in the
agent to 'suspend' conversion of

desire into will is the nearest approach
Locke makes to recognition of the
spiritual freedom that is supernatural.
But after all, on his premises, the suspension must be the natural issue of
uneasiness.

[3] He that wills must *conceive* what
he wills, and must have some *motive*
for acting. Intelligence, so far from
being inconsistent with a moral or
supernatural liberty to act, is essential
to it ; although free acts are not in

in the mind, not determinable by its last judgment of the good or evil that is thought to attend its choice, would be so far from being an advantage and excellency of any intellectual nature, that it would be as great an imperfection, as the want of indifferency to act, or not to act, till determined by the will, would be an imperfection on the other side. A man is at liberty to lift up his hand to his head, or let it rest quiet : he is perfectly indifferent in either ; and it would be an imperfection in him, if he wanted that power, if he were deprived of that indifferency. But it would be as great an imperfection, if he had the same indifferency, whether he would prefer the lifting up his hand, or its remaining in rest, when it would save his head or eyes from a blow he sees coming : it is as much a perfection, that desire, or the power of preferring, should be determined by good, as that the power of acting[1] should be determined by the will ; and the certainer such determination is, the greater is the perfection. Nay, were we determined by anything but the last result of our own minds, judging of the good or evil of any action, we were not free ; [2 the very end of our freedom being, that we may attain the good we choose. And therefore, every man is put under a necessity, by his constitution as an intelligent being, to be determined in willing by his own thought and judgment what is best for him to do : else he would be under the determination of some other than himself, which is want of liberty. And to deny that a man's will, in every determination, follows his own judgment, is to say, that a man wills and acts for an end that he would not have, at the time that he wills and acts for it. For if he prefers it in his present thoughts before any other, it is plain he then thinks better of it, and would have it before any other ; unless he can have and not have it, will and not will it, at the same time ; a contradiction too manifest to be admitted [3].]

harmony with reason, when the fallible, finite agent abuses the freedom for which he is responsible.

[1] Desire and will are here distinguished, as ' power of preferring,' and ' power of carrying' preference into overt action.

[2] Added in Coste's French version.

[3] If men are determined, in willing, to follow their judgment of what is best, under a physical necessity, how is it possible for them to will *immorally*, be their judgments ever so erroneous in estimating pleasures and pains? If

50. If we look upon those superior beings above us, who enjoy perfect happiness, we shall have reason to judge that they are more steadily determined in their choice of good than we; and yet we have no reason to think they are less happy, or less free, than we are. And if it were fit for such poor finite creatures as we are to pronounce what infinite wisdom and goodness could do, I think we might say, that God himself *cannot* choose what is not good; the freedom of the Almighty hinders not his being determined by what is best.

51. But to give a right view of this mistaken part of liberty let me ask,—Would any one be a changeling, because he is less determined by wise considerations than a wise man? Is it worth the name of freedom to be at liberty to play the fool, and draw shame and misery upon a man's self? If to break loose from the conduct of reason, and to want that restraint of examination and judgment which keeps us from choosing or doing the worse, be liberty, true liberty, madmen and fools are the only freemen: but yet, I think, nobody would choose to be mad for the sake of such liberty, but he that is mad already. The constant desire of happiness, and the constraint it puts upon us to act for it, nobody, I think, accounts an abridgment of liberty, or at least an abridgment of liberty to be complained of. God Almighty himself is under the necessity of being happy; and the more any intelligent being is so, the nearer is its approach to infinite perfection and happiness. That, in this state of ignorance, we short-sighted creatures might not mistake true felicity, we are endowed with a power to suspend any particular desire, and keep it from determining the will[1], and engaging us in action. This is standing still, where we are not sufficiently assured of the way: examination

---

the man, by a law of external nature, cannot resist his erroneous judgment, and could not have judged differently, how can he be blamed for the resulting volition? Locke only shows that intelligence is one of the conditions of moral freedom—not that volition is the necessary outcome of judgment. A so-called volition that is intel-lectually blind cannot of course be a morally free or really voluntary determination.

[1] Are our determinations to *suspend* our desires naturally necessitated by uneasiness, or is this 'suspending' not a voluntary determination at all; and if not an act of will, what is it?

is consulting a guide. The determination of the will upon inquiry, is following the direction of that guide: and he that has a power to act or not to act, according as *such* determination directs, is a free agent: such determination abridges not that power wherein liberty consists. He that has his chains knocked off, and the prison doors set open to him, is perfectly at liberty, because he may either go or stay, as he best likes; though his preference be determined to stay, by the darkness of the night, or illness of the weather, or want of other lodging. He ceases not to be free; though the desire of some convenience to be had there absolutely determines his preference, and makes him stay in his prison.

The Necessity of pursuing true Happiness the Foundation of Liberty.

52. As therefore the highest perfection of intellectual nature lies in a careful and constant pursuit of true and solid happiness; so the care of ourselves, that we mistake not imaginary for real happiness, is the necessary foundation of our liberty. The stronger ties we have to an unalterable pursuit of happiness in general, which is our greatest good, and which, as such, our desires always follow, the more are we free from any necessary determination of our will to any particular action, and from a necessary compliance with our desire, set upon any particular, and then appearing preferable good, till we have duly examined whether it has a tendency to, or be inconsistent with, our real happiness: and therefore, till we are as much informed upon this inquiry as the weight of the matter, and the nature of the case demands, we are, by the necessity of preferring and pursuing true happiness as our greatest good, obliged to suspend the satisfaction of our desires in particular cases [1].

Power to Suspend.

53. This is the hinge on which turns the *liberty* of intellectual beings, in their constant endeavours after, and a steady prosecution of true felicity,—That they *can suspend* this prose-

---

[1] This is only saying that moral freedom is not blind unintelligent caprice, and that it is rightly used only when we will in accordance with reason. 'À moins que l'appétit ne soit guidé par la raison, il tend au *plaisir present*, et non pas au *bonheur*, *c'est-à-dire au plaisir durable.*' (Leibniz.) Human freedom means original power to act immorally and unreasonably, as well as in accordance with right reason or moral obligation. This is well put in an essay on *Freedom as an Ethical Postulate*, by Prof. James Seth.

cution in particular cases, till they have looked before them, and informed themselves whether that particular thing which is then proposed or desired lie in the way to their main end, and make a real part of that which is their greatest good. For, the inclination and tendency of their nature to happiness is an obligation and motive to them, to take care not to mistake or miss it ; and so necessarily puts them upon caution, deliberation, and wariness, in the direction of their particular actions, which are the means to obtain it. Whatever necessity determines to the pursuit of real bliss, the same necessity, with the same force, establishes suspense, deliberation, and scrutiny of each successive desire, whether the satisfaction of it does not interfere with our true happiness, and mislead us from it. This, as seems to me, is the great privilege of finite [1] intellectual beings ; and I desire it may be well considered, whether the great inlet and exercise of all the liberty men have, are capable of, or can be useful to them, and that whereon depends the turn of their actions, does not lie in this, —That they can suspend their desires, and stop them from determining their wills to any action, till they have duly and fairly examined the good and evil of it, as far forth as the weight of the thing requires. This we are able to do ; and when we have done it, we have done our duty, and all that is in our power ; and indeed all that needs. For, since the will supposes knowledge to guide its choice, all that we can do is to hold our wills undetermined, till we have examined the good and evil of what we desire. What follows after that, follows in a chain of consequences, linked one to another, all depending on the last determination of the judgment [2], which, whether it shall be upon a hasty and precipitate view, or upon a due and mature examination, is in our power ; experience showing us, that in most cases, we are able to suspend the present satisfaction of any desire.

[1] Will always coincides with perfect reason only in the infinite or perfect Being. The moral education of finite agents presupposes the possibility of their willing either irrationally, i.e. immorally, or the reverse.

[2] Does this mean that *in the voluntary act of 'suspending' desires, with a view to test their rationality,* the so-called agent is somehow independent of 'the chain of consequences,' and is not the passive subject of 'uneasiness,' and of those natural consequences of uneasiness which are abusively called *his own* acts?

54. But if any extreme disturbance (as sometimes it happens) possesses our whole mind, as when the pain of the rack, an impetuous uneasiness, as of love, anger, or any other violent passion, running away with us, allows us not the liberty of thought, and we are not masters enough of our own minds to consider thoroughly and examine fairly ;—God, who knows our frailty, pities our weakness, and requires of us no more than we are able to do, and sees what was and what was not in our power, will judge as a kind and merciful Father. But the forbearance of a too hasty compliance with our desires, the moderation and restraint of our passions, so that our understandings may be free to examine, and reason unbiassed give its judgment, being that whereon a right direction of our conduct to true happiness depends ; it is in this we should employ our chief care and endeavours.   In this we should take pains to suit the relish of our minds to the true intrinsic good or ill that is in things ; and not permit an allowed or supposed possible great and weighty good to slip out of our thoughts, without leaving any relish, any desire of itself there, till, by a due consideration of its true worth, we have formed appetites in our minds suitable to it, and made ourselves uneasy in the want of it, or in the fear of losing it.   And how much this is in every one's power, by making resolutions to himself, such as he may keep, is easy for every one to try. Nor let any one say, he cannot govern his passions, nor hinder them from breaking out, and carrying him into action ; for what he can do before a prince or a great man, he can do alone, or in the presence of God, if he will [1].

55. From what has been said, it is easy to give an account how it comes to pass, that, though all men desire happiness, yet their wills carry them so contrarily ; and consequently some of them to what is evil.   And to this I say, that the various and contrary choices that men make in the world do not argue that they do not all pursue good ; but that the same thing is not good to every man alike.   This variety of pursuits shows, that every one does not place his happiness in the same

---

[1] 'Cette remarque est très-bonne, et digne qu'on y réfléchisse souvent.' (Leibniz.)   See Note at the end of this Chapter.

thing, or choose the same way to it. Were all the concerns BOOK II.
of man terminated in this life, why one followed study and
knowledge, and another hawking and hunting : why one chose CHAP. XXI.
luxury and debauchery, and another sobriety and riches,
would not be because every one of these did *not* aim at his
own happiness ; but because their happiness was placed in
different things. And therefore it was a right answer of
the physician to his patient that had sore eyes :—If you
have more pleasure in the taste of wine than in the use
of your sight, wine is good for you ; but if the pleasure of
seeing be greater to you than that of drinking, wine is
naught.

56. The mind has a different relish, as well as the palate ; All men
and you will as fruitlessly endeavour to delight all men with happiness,
riches or glory (which yet some men place their happiness but not of
in) as you would to satisfy all men's hunger with cheese or sort.
lobsters ; which, though very agreeable and delicious fare to
some, are to others extremely nauseous and offensive : and
many persons would with reason prefer the griping of an
hungry belly to those dishes which are a feast to others.
Hence it was, I think, that the philosophers of old did in
vain inquire, whether *summum bonum* consisted in riches, or
bodily delights, or virtue, or contemplation : and they might
have as reasonably disputed, whether the best relish were to
be found in apples, plums, or nuts, and have divided themselves into sects upon it. For, as pleasant tastes depend not
on the things themselves, but on their agreeableness to this or
that particular palate, wherein there is great variety ; so the
greatest happiness consists ·in the having those things which
produce the greatest pleasure, and in the absence of those
which cause any disturbance, any pain. Now these, to different men, are very different things. If, therefore, men in this
life only have hope ; if in this life only they can enjoy, it is
not strange nor unreasonable, that they should seek their
happiness by avoiding all things that disease them here, and
by pursuing all that delight them ; wherein it will be no
wonder to find variety and difference. For if there be no
prospect beyond the grave, the inference is certainly right—
'Let us eat and drink,' let us enjoy what we delight in, 'for

BOOK II.
CHAP. XXI.

to-morrow we shall die[1].' This, I think, may serve to show us the reason, why, though all men's desires tend to happiness, yet they are not moved by the same object. Men may choose different things, and yet all choose right; supposing them only like a company of poor insects; whereof some are bees, delighted with flowers and their sweetness; others beetles, delighted with other kinds of viands, which having enjoyed for a season, they would cease to be, and exist no more for ever[2].

Power to suspend volition explains responsibility for ill choice.

57. [[3] These things, duly weighed, will give us, as I think, a clear view into the state of human liberty. Liberty, it is plain, consists in a power to do, or not to do; to do, or forbear doing, *as we will*. This cannot be denied[4]. But this seeming to comprehend only the actions of a man consecutive to volition, it is further inquired,—Whether he be at liberty to will or no? And to this it has been answered, that, in most cases, a man is not at liberty to forbear the act of volition: he must exert an act of his will, whereby the action proposed is made to exist or not to exist. But yet there is a case wherein a man is at liberty in respect of willing; and that is the choosing of a *remote* good as an end to be pursued[5]. Here a man may *suspend* the act of his choice from being determined

---

[1] 'C'est la seule considération de Dieu et de l'immortalité, qui rend les obligations de la vertu et de la justice absolument indispensables.' (Leibniz.)

[2] This scepticism about the *summum bonum* illustrates Locke's indifference to ideals, and implies that ends cannot be chosen because they are in themselves, or absolutely, good, but only that they are 'good' because the individual finds them by experience to be pleasurable.

[3] The passage within brackets was introduced in Coste's French version. It is not found in any of the English editions which appeared before Locke's death.

[4] That is to say, it 'consists' in the effects of the volition, which is irrelevant to the question, in the view of those who hold that reason requires

us to recognise, in moral and properly personal agency, something to which the 'human understanding' measured by Locke is inadequate.

[5] But may it not be argued, at Locke's point of view, that the previous *uncertainty* as to his choice involves in it an 'uneasiness' which *naturally* makes him will to restrain desire? This voluntary act of restraint or suspension is only a particular instance of volition. Yet, in order to save the fact of responsibility, he treats it as if it were different in kind from other volitions; but he does not show how the *will to suspend* can be supernaturally free, in the face of the evidence which made him conclude that all volitions are naturally determined for the so-called 'agent' by uneasiness.

for or against the thing proposed, till he has examined whether
it be really of a nature, in itself and consequences, to make
him happy or not. For, when he has once chosen it, and
thereby it is become a part of his happiness, it raises desire,
and that proportionably gives him uneasiness ; which determines his will, and sets him at work in pursuit of his choice on
all occasions that offer. And here we may see how it comes
to pass that a man may justly incur punishment, though it be
certain that, in all the particular actions that he wills, he does,
and necessarily does, will that which he then judges to be
good. For, though his will be always determined by that
which is judged good by his understanding, yet it excuses him
not ; because, by a too hasty choice of his own making, he has
imposed on himself wrong measures of good and evil ; which,
however false and fallacious, have the same influence on all
his future conduct, as if they were true and right. He has
vitiated his own palate, and must be answerable to himself
for the sickness and death that follows from it. The eternal
law and nature of things [1] must not be altered to comply with
his ill-ordered choice. If the neglect or abuse of the liberty
he had, to examine what would really and truly make for his
happiness, misleads him, the miscarriages that follow on it
must be imputed to his own election. *He had a power to
suspend his determination* [2] ; it was given him, that he might
examine, and take care of his own happiness, and look that he
were not deceived. And he could never judge, that it was
better to be deceived than not, in a matter of so great and
near concernment.]

58. What has been said may also discover to us the reason
why men in this world prefer different things, and pursue
happiness by contrary courses. But yet, since men are
always constant and in earnest in matters of happiness and
misery, the question still remains, How men come often to

---

[1] With whatever seeming inconsistency, Locke always acknowledges
what he calls ' the *eternal* and *unalterable* nature of right and wrong.' He
elsewhere reminds us that in the *Essay*
he is chiefly treating of the ideas which
finite and *fallible* men are apt to have
of ' the eternal law,' and not of the
immutability of moral distinctions in
themselves.

[2] This ' power' is the essence of
moral freedom, according to the *Essay*.

BOOK II.
CHAP. XXI.

The causes of this.

From bodily Pain.

From wrong Desires arising from wrong Judgments.

Our judgment of present Good or Evil always right.

prefer the worse to the better; and to choose that, which, by their own confession, has made them miserable?

59. To account for the various and contrary ways men take, though all aim at being happy, we must consider whence the *various uneasinesses* that determine the will, in the preference of each voluntary action, have their rise :—

1. Some of them come from causes not in our power ; such as are often the pains of the body from want, disease, or outward injuries, as the rack, &c. ; which, when present and violent, operate for the most part forcibly on the will, and turn the courses of men's lives from virtue, piety, and religion, and what before they judged to lead to happiness ; every one not endeavouring, or, [¹ through disuse], not being able, by the contemplation of remote and future good, to raise in himself desires of them strong enough to counterbalance the uneasiness he feels in those bodily torments, and to keep his will steady in the choice of those actions which lead to future happiness. A neighbouring country² has been of late a tragical theatre from which we might fetch instances, if there needed any, and the world did not in all countries and ages furnish examples enough to confirm that received observation, *Necessitas cogit ad turpia ;* and therefore there is great reason for us to pray, 'Lead us not into temptation.'

2. Other uneasinesses arise from our desires of absent good; which desires always bear proportion to, and depend on, the judgment we make, and the relish we have of any absent good ; in both which we are apt to be variously misled, and that by our own fault.

60. In the first place, I shall consider the wrong judgments men make of *future* good and evil, whereby their desires are misled. For, as to *present* happiness and misery, when that alone comes into consideration, and the consequences are quite removed, a man never chooses amiss : he knows what best pleases him, and that he actually prefers. Things in their present enjoyment are what they seem : the apparent and real good are, in this case, always the same. For, the

---

¹ Added in French version.
² France. He refers to the persecutions on account of religion.

pain or pleasure being just so great and no greater than it is felt, the present good or evil is really so much as it appears. And therefore were every action of ours concluded within itself, and drew no consequences after it, we should undoubtedly never err in our choice of good: we should always infallibly prefer the best. Were the pains of honest industry, and of starving with hunger and cold set together before us, nobody would be in doubt which to choose: were the satisfaction of a lust and the joys of heaven offered at once to any one's present possession, he would not balance, or err in the determination of his choice.

61. But since our voluntary actions carry not all the happiness and misery that depend on them along with them in their present performance, but are the precedent causes of good and evil, which they draw after them, and bring upon us, when they themselves are past and cease to be; our desires look beyond our present enjoyments, and carry the mind out to *absent good*, according to the necessity which we think there is of it, to the making or increase of our happiness. It is our opinion of such a necessity that gives it its attraction: without that, we are not moved by absent good. For, in this narrow scantling of capacity which we are accustomed to and sensible of here, wherein we enjoy but one pleasure at once, which, when all uneasiness is away, is, whilst it lasts, sufficient to make us think ourselves happy, it is not all remote and even apparent good that affects us. Because the indolency and enjoyment we have, sufficing for our present happiness, we desire not to venture the change; since we judge that we are happy already, being content, and that is enough. For who is content is happy. But as soon as any new uneasiness comes in, this happiness is disturbed, and we are set afresh on work in the pursuit of happiness.

62. Their aptness therefore to conclude that they can be happy without it, is one great occasion that men often are not raised to the desire of the greatest *absent* good. For, whilst such thoughts possess them, the joys of a future state move them not; they have little concern or uneasiness about them; and the will, free from the determination of such desires, is left to the pursuit of nearer satisfactions, and to the removal

of those uneasinesses which it then feels, in its want of and longings after them. Change but a man's view of these things; let him see that virtue and religion are necessary to his happiness; let him look into the future state of bliss or misery, and see there God, the righteous Judge, ready to 'render to every man according to his deeds; to them who by patient continuance in well-doing seek for glory, and honour, and immortality, eternal life; but unto every soul that doth evil, indignation and wrath, tribulation and anguish.' To him, I say, who hath a prospect of the different state of perfect happiness or misery that attends all men after this life, depending on their behaviour here, the measures of good and evil that govern his choice are mightily changed. For, since nothing of pleasure and pain in this life can bear any proportion to the endless happiness or exquisite misery of an immortal soul hereafter, actions in his power will have their preference, not according to the transient pleasure or pain that accompanies or follows them here, but as they serve to secure that perfect durable happiness hereafter[1].]

A more particular Account of wrong Judgments.
63. But, to account more particularly for the misery that men often bring on themselves, notwithstanding that they do all in earnest pursue happiness[2], we must consider how things come to be represented to our desires under deceitful appearances: and that is by the judgment pronouncing wrongly concerning them. To see how far this reaches, and what are the causes of wrong judgment, we must remember that things are judged good or bad in a double sense:—

First, *That which is properly good or bad, is nothing but barely pleasure or pain.*

Secondly, But because not only present pleasure and pain, but that also which is apt by its efficacy or consequences to bring it upon us at a distance, is a proper object of our desires, and apt to move a creature that has foresight; therefore *things also that draw after them pleasure and pain, are considered as good and evil.*

---

[1] See p. 329, note 2.
[2] The words 'and always pursue the greatest apparent good'—here follow in first edition, but are omitted in the later ones.

64. The wrong judgment that misleads us, and makes the will often fasten on the worse side, lies in misreporting upon the various comparisons of these. The wrong judgment I am here speaking of is not what one man may think of the determination of another, but what every man himself must confess to be wrong. For, since I lay it for a certain ground, that every intelligent being really seeks happiness, [1 which consists in the enjoyment of pleasure, without any considerable mixture of uneasiness]; it is impossible any one should willingly put into his own draught any bitter ingredient, or leave out anything in his power [2 that would tend to his satisfaction, and the completing of his happiness,] but only by a *wrong judgment.* I shall not here speak of that mistake which is the consequence of *invincible* error[3], which scarce deserves the name of wrong judgment; but of that wrong judgment which every man himself must confess to be so.

65. (I) Therefore, as to present pleasure and pain, the mind, as has been said, never mistakes that which is really good or evil; that which is the greater pleasure, or the greater pain, is really just as it appears. But, though present pleasure and pain show their difference and degrees so plainly as not to leave room to mistake; yet, *when we compare present pleasure or pain with future,* (which is usually the case in most important determinations of the will,) we often make wrong judgments of them; taking our measures of them in different positions of distance. Objects near our view are apt to be thought greater than those of a larger size that are more remote. And so it is with pleasures and pains : the present is apt to carry it ; and those at a distance have the disadvantage in the comparison. Thus most men, like spendthrift heirs, are apt to judge a little in hand better than a great deal to come ; and so, for small matters in possession,

---

[1] In first edition—'and would enjoy all the pleasures he could, and suffer no pain.'

[2] In first edition—'That could add to its sweetness.'

[3] For 'invincible error' a man cannot be accountable, as there cannot be moral obligation to what is impossible. The causes of erroneous judgment are considered in Bk. IV. ch. xx. With Hobbes volition is a necessary consequence of the last judgment of the understanding, which is itself necessarily determined.

part with greater ones in reversion. But that this is a wrong judgment every one must allow, let his pleasure consist in whatever it will : since that which is future will certainly come to be present ; and then, having the same advantage of nearness, will show itself in its full dimensions, and discover his wilful mistake who judged of it by unequal measures. Were the pleasure of drinking accompanied, the very moment a man takes off his glass, with that sick stomach and aching head which, in some men, are sure to follow not many hours after, I think nobody, whatever pleasure he had in his cups, would, on these conditions, ever let wine touch his lips[1]; which yet he daily swallows, and the evil side comes to be chosen only by the fallacy of a little difference in time. But, if pleasure or pain can be so lessened only by a few hours' removal, how much more will it be so by a further distance, to a man that will not, by a right judgment, do what time will, i. e. bring it home upon himself, and consider it as present, and there take its true dimensions? This is the way we usually impose on ourselves, in respect of bare pleasure and pain, or the true degrees of happiness or misery : the future loses its just proportion, and what is present obtains the preference as the greater. I mention not here the wrong judgment, whereby the absent are not only lessened, but reduced to perfect nothing ; when men enjoy what they can in present, and make sure of that, concluding amiss that no evil will thence follow. For that lies not in comparing the greatness of future good and evil, which is that we are here speaking of ; but in another sort of wrong judgment, which is concerning good or evil, as it is considered to be the cause and procurement of pleasure or pain that will follow from it.

Causes of our judging amiss when we compare present pleasure and pain with future.

66. The cause of our judging amiss, when we compare our present pleasure or pain with future, seems to me to be *the weak and narrow constitution of our minds*. We cannot well enjoy two pleasures at once ; much less any pleasure almost, whilst pain possesses us. The present pleasure, if it be not very languid, and almost none at all, fills our narrow souls,

---

[1] So Montaigne :—'Si la douleur de teste nous venait avant l'ivresse, nous nous garderions de trop boire ; mais la volupté, pour nous tromper, marche devant et nous cache sa suite.' (*Essais.*)

and so takes up the whole mind that it scarce leaves any
thought of things absent : or if among our pleasures there are
some which are not strong enough to exclude the consideration of things at a distance, yet we have so great an abhorrence of pain, that a little of it extinguishes all our pleasures.
A little bitter mingled in our cup, leaves no relish of the
sweet. Hence it comes that, at any rate, we desire to be rid
of the present evil, which we are apt to think nothing absent
can equal ; because, under the present pain, we find not ourselves capable of any the least degree of happiness. Men's
daily complaints are a loud proof of this : the pain that any
one actually feels is still of all other the worst ; and it is with
anguish they cry out,—'Any rather than this : nothing can
be so intolerable as what I now suffer.' And therefore our
whole endeavours and thoughts are intent to get rid of the
present evil, before all things, as the first necessary condition
to our happiness ; let what will follow. Nothing, as we
passionately think, can exceed, or almost equal, the uneasiness
that sits so heavy upon us. And because the abstinence from
a present pleasure that offers itself is a pain, nay, oftentimes
a very great one, the desire being inflamed by a near and
tempting object, it is no wonder that that operates after the
same manner pain does, and lessens in our thoughts what is
future ; and so forces us, as it were blindfold, into its
embraces.

67. [[1]Add to this, that absent good, or, which is the same Absent good unable to counterbalance present uneasiness.
thing, future pleasure,—especially if of a sort we are unac-
quainted with,—seldom is able to counterbalance any uneasiness, either of pain or desire, which is present. For, its
greatness being no more than what shall be really tasted when
enjoyed, men are apt enough to lessen that ; to make it give
place to any present desire ; and conclude with themselves
that, when it comes to trial, it may possibly not answer the
report or opinion that generally passes of it : they having often
found that, not only what others have magnified, but even
what they themselves have enjoyed with great pleasure and
delight at one time, has proved insipid or nauseous at another ;

---

[1] Added in second edition.

BOOK II.
CHAP. XXI.

and therefore they see nothing in it for which they should forego a present enjoyment. But that this is a false way of judging, when applied to the happiness of another life, they must confess; unless they will say, God cannot make those happy he designs to be so. For that being intended for a state of happiness, it must certainly be agreeable to every one's wish and desire: could we suppose their relishes as different there as they are here, yet the manna in heaven will suit every one's palate.] Thus much of the wrong judgment we make of present and future pleasure and pain, when they are compared together, and so the absent considered as future.

Wrong judgment in considering Consequences of Actions.

68. (II). As to *things good or bad in their consequences*, and by the aptness that is in them to procure us good or evil in the future, we judge amiss several ways.

1. When we judge that so much evil does not really depend on them as in truth there does.

2. When we judge that, though the consequence be of that moment, yet it is not of that certainty, but that it may otherwise fall out, or else by some means be avoided; as by industry, address, change, repentance, &c.

That these are wrong ways of judging, were easy to show in every particular, if I would examine them at large singly: but I shall only mention this in general, viz. that it is a very wrong and irrational way of proceeding, to venture a greater good for a less, upon uncertain guesses; and before a due examination be made, proportionable to the weightiness of the matter, and the concernment it is to us not to mistake. This I think every one must confess, especially if he considers the usual cause of this wrong judgment, whereof these following are some:—

Causes of this.

69. (i) *Ignorance*: He that judges without informing himself to the utmost that he is capable, cannot acquit himself of judging amiss.

(ii) *Inadvertency*: When a man overlooks even that which he does know. This is an affected and present ignorance, which misleads our judgments as much as the other. Judging is, as it were, balancing an account, and determining on which side the odds lie. If therefore either side be huddled up in haste, and several of the sums that should have gone into the reckoning be overlooked and left out, this precipitancy causes as wrong a judgment as if it were a perfect ignorance. That which most commonly causes this is, the prevalency of some present pleasure or pain, heightened by our feeble passionate nature, most strongly wrought on by what is present. To check this precipitancy, our understanding and reason were given us, if we will make a right use of them, to search and see, and then judge thereupon. [¹Without liberty, the understanding would be to no purpose : and without understanding, liberty (if it could be) would signify nothing. If a man sees what would do him good or harm, what would make him happy or miserable, without being able to move himself one step towards or from it, what is he the better for seeing? And he that is at liberty to ramble in perfect darkness, what is his liberty better than if he were driven up and down as a bubble by the force of the wind? The being acted by a blind impulse from without, or from within, is little odds. The first, therefore, and great use of liberty is to hinder blind precipitancy; the principal exercise of freedom is to stand still, open the eyes, look about, and take a view of the consequence of what we are going to do, as much as the weight of the matter requires.] How much sloth and negligence, heat and passion, the prevalency of fashion or acquired indispositions do severally contribute, on occasion, to these wrong judgments, I shall not here further inquire. [²I shall only add one other false judgment, which I think necessary to mention, because perhaps it is little taken notice of, though of great influence.

70. All men desire happiness, that is past doubt : but, as has been already observed, when they are rid of pain, they are apt to take up with any pleasure at hand, or that custom

Wrong Judgment of what is necessary

---

¹ Added in fourth edition.

² The passage within brackets, ending in § 72, was added in the second edition. The first contains instead the following sentence :—' This, I think, is certain, that the choice of the will is everywhere determined by the greater apparent good, however it may be wrong represented by the understanding ; and it would be impossible men should pursue so different courses as they do in the world, had they not different measures of good and evil. But yet morality established on its true foundations,' &c.

has endeared to them; to rest satisfied in that; and so being happy, till some new desire, by making them uneasy, disturbs that happiness, and shows them that they are not so, they look no further; nor is the will determined to any action in pursuit of any other known or apparent good. For since we find that we cannot enjoy all sorts of good, but one excludes another; we do not fix our desires on every apparent greater good, unless it be judged to be necessary to our happiness: if we think we can be happy without it, it moves us not. This is another occasion to men of judging wrong; when they take not that to be necessary to their happiness which really is so. This mistake misleads us, both in the choice of the good we aim at, and very often in the means to it, when it is a remote good. But, which way ever it be, either by placing it where really it is not, or by neglecting the means as not necessary to it;—when a man misses his great end, happiness, he will acknowledge he judged not right. That which contributes to this mistake is the real or supposed unpleasantness of the actions which are the way to this end; it seeming so preposterous a thing to men, to make themselves unhappy in order to happiness, that they do not easily bring themselves to it.

We can
change
the Agree-
ableness
or Dis-
agreeable-
ness in
Things.
71. The last inquiry, therefore, concerning this matter is, —Whether it be in a man's power to change the pleasantness and unpleasantness that accompanies any sort of action? And as to that, it is plain, in many cases he can. Men may and should correct their palates, and give relish to what either has, or they suppose has none. The relish of the mind is as various as that of the body, and like that too may be altered; and it is a mistake to think that men cannot change the displeasingness or indifferency that is in actions into pleasure and desire, if they will do but what is in their power. A due consideration will do it in some cases; and practice, application, and custom in most. Bread or tobacco may be neglected where they are shown to be useful to health, because of an indifferency or disrelish to them; reason and consideration at first recommends, and begins their trial, and use finds, or custom makes them pleasant. That

this is so in virtue too, is very certain. Actions are pleasing or displeasing, either in themselves, or considered as a means to a greater and more desirable end. The eating of a well-seasoned dish, suited to a man's palate, may move the mind by the delight itself that accompanies the eating, without reference to any other end; to which the consideration of the pleasure there is in health and strength (to which that meat is subservient) may add a new *gusto*, able to make us swallow an ill-relished potion. In the latter of these, any action is rendered more or less pleasing, only by the contemplation of the end, and the being more or less persuaded of its tendency to it, or necessary connexion with it: but the pleasure of the action itself is best acquired or increased by use and practice. Trials often reconcile us to that, which at a distance we looked on with aversion; and by repetitions wear us into a liking of what possibly, in the first essay, displeased us. Habits have powerful charms, and put so strong attractions of easiness and pleasure into what we accustom ourselves to, that we cannot forbear to do, or at least be easy in the omission of, actions, which habitual practice has suited, and thereby recommends to us. Though this be very visible, and every one's experience shows him he can do so; yet it is a part in the conduct of men towards their happiness, neglected to a degree, that it will be possibly entertained as a paradox, if it be said, that men can *make* things or actions more or less pleasing to themselves; and thereby remedy that, to which one may justly impute a great deal of their wandering. Fashion and the common opinion having settled wrong notions, and education and custom ill habits, the just values of things are misplaced, and the palates of men corrupted. Pains should be taken to rectify these; and contrary habits change our pleasures, and give a relish to that which is necessary or conducive to our happiness. This every one must confess he can do; and when happiness is lost, and misery overtakes him, he will confess he did amiss in neglecting it, and condemn himself for it; and I ask every one, whether he has not often done so [1]?

---

[1] All this concerns the *effects* not the *origin* of our voluntary determinations, or whether motives (e. g. the uneasinesses of which men are conscious),

BOOK II.
CHAP. XXI.
Prefer-
ence of
Vice to
Virtue a
manifest
wrong
Judgment.

72. I shall not now enlarge any further on the wrong judgments and neglect of what is in their power, whereby men mislead themselves. This would make a volume, and is not my business. But whatever false notions, or shameful neglect of what is in their power, may put men out of their way to happiness, and distract them, as we see, into so different courses of life, this yet is certain, that] [1] morality, established upon its true foundations [2], cannot but determine the choice in any one that will but consider: and he that will not be so far a rational creature as to reflect seriously upon *infinite* happiness and misery, must needs condemn himself as not making that use of his understanding he should [3]. The rewards and punishments of another life [4], which the Almighty has established, as the enforcements of his law, are of weight enough to determine the choice, against whatever pleasure or pain this life can show, when the eternal state is considered but in its bare possibility, which nobody can make any doubt of [5]. He that will allow

necessitate voluntary determinations, as natural sequences, in which the voluntary determinations form a link. That the reasonable will can, by determining habits, indirectly alter and elevate our natural tastes and desires, is presupposed in the duty of educating taste and desire.

[1] What follows, forming sect. 45 of the first edition, is what moved the enthusiasm of Molyneux in his letter (Dec. 22, 1692).

[2] The government of God, by rewards and punishments, fully developed in a future life, is, according to Locke, the 'foundation' of practical morality.

[3] The ethical consideration implied in this self-condemnation presupposes that the man was able to make right use of his understanding; and that voluntary determination, which he failed to exert, is not a merely passive capacity for being pleased with some things more than others.

[4] The unending duration of *suffering*, in the Divine Order of the universe, rather than of self-created *sin*, is with Locke, as with many others, the prominent idea, in treating of the mystery of moral government. He also makes the motive to conduct arise out of prudent calculation of the probable consequences of actions which are in our power—according to his conception of human liberty to act, as physically determined by felt or prospective pain.

[5] 'A man,' says Bishop Butler, 'is as really bound in prudence to do what, upon the whole, appears, according to the best of his judgment, to be for his happiness, as what he certainly knows to be so. Nay further, in questions of great consequence, a reasonable man will think it concerns him to remark lower probabilities and presumptions than these; such as amount to no more than showing one side of a question to be as supposable and credible as the other; nay, such as but amount to much less even than this.' (*Analogy*, Introduction.) So Butler argues throughout the *Analogy*, as to

exquisite and endless happiness to be but the possible consequence of a good life here, and the contrary state the
possible reward of a bad one, must own himself to judge
very much amiss if he does not conclude,—That a virtuous
life, with the certain expectation of everlasting bliss, which
may come, is to be preferred to a vicious one, with the fear of
that dreadful state of misery, which it is very possible may
overtake the guilty; or, at best, the terrible uncertain hope
of annihilation. This is evidently so, though the virtuous
life here had nothing but pain, and the vicious continual
pleasure: which yet is, for the most part, quite otherwise,
and wicked men have not much the odds to brag of, even in
their present possession; nay, all things rightly considered,
have, I think, even the worse part here. But when infinite
happiness is put into one scale, against infinite misery in the
other; if the worst that comes to the pious man, if he
mistakes, be the best that the wicked can attain to, if he be
in the right, who can without madness run the venture?
Who in his wits would choose to come within a possibility of
infinite misery; which if he miss, there is yet nothing to be
got by that hazard [1]? Whereas, on the other side, the sober
man ventures nothing against infinite happiness to be got,
if his expectation comes not to pass. If the good man be
in the right, he is eternally happy; if he mistakes, he is not
miserable, he feels nothing. On the other side, if the wicked
man be in the right, he is not happy; if he mistakes, he is
infinitely miserable. Must it not be a most manifest wrong
judgment that does not presently see to which side, in this
case, the preference is to be given? I have forborne to
mention anything of the certainty or probability of a future
state, designing here to show the wrong judgment that any

our duty in calculating the consequences
of actions which it is in our power to
do or to forbear—'in questions of
difficulty, or that might be thought so,'
where more satisfactory evidence than
probability, or even possibility, cannot
be had.

[1] This is to show that the will is not
determined, as he had at first supposed,
by 'the greater good in view.' The
joys of heaven are often disregarded.
The absent good is not desired, because not necessary to the man's
happiness, as the removal of present
pain always is; though even this does
not always determine the will, if we
rise above mechanism of nature, when
we 'suspend' the execution of desire.

BOOK II.
CHAP. XXI.

one must allow he makes, upon his own principles, laid how he pleases, who prefers the short pleasures of a vicious life upon any consideration, whilst he knows, and cannot but be certain, that a future life is at least possible.

Recapitulation—
Liberty
of indifferency.

73. [¹ To conclude this inquiry into *human liberty*, which, as it stood before, I myself from the beginning fearing, and a very judicious friend of mine, since the publication, suspecting to have some mistake in it, though he could not particularly show it me, I was put upon a stricter review of this chapter. Wherein lighting upon a very easy and scarce observable slip I had made, in putting one seemingly indifferent word for another² that discovery opened to me this present view, which here, in this second edition, I submit

---

¹ The following section, 46 in the *first* edition, there follows what is now § 72, and was in the first edition § 45: it was afterwards omitted, and part of § 73, with § 74, were introduced instead :—' Under this *simple idea of Power*, I have taken occasion to explain our ideas of *Will*, *Volition*, *Liberty*, and *Necessity*;—which having a greater mixture in them than belongs barely to simple modes, might perhaps be better placed amongst the more complex. For *Will*, for example, contains in it the idea of a power to prefer the doing to the not doing of any particular action (and *vice versa*) which it has thought on ; which preference is truly a mode of thinking : and so the idea which the word *will* stands for is a complex and mixed one, made up of the simple ideas of power, and a certain mode of thinking ; and the idea of *liberty* is yet more complex, being made up of the idea of a power to act, or not to act, in conformity to volition. But I hoped this transgression, against the method I have proposed to myself will be forgiven me, if I have quitted it a little, to explain some ideas of great importance; such as are those of the *will*, *liberty*, and *necessity*, in this place, where they as it were offered themselves, and sprang

up from their proper roots. Besides, having before largely enough instanced in several *simple modes*, to show what I meant by them, and how the mind got them (for I intend not to enumerate all the particular ideas of each sort), these of *will*, *liberty*, and *necessity* may serve as instances of *mixed modes*, which are that sort of *ideas* I propose next to treat of.'

² 'I had not been so long before I acknowledged your last, had I not a design to give you an account of some alterations I intended to make in the chapter on Power, wherein I should have been very glad you had showed me any mistake. I myself being not very well satisfied by the conclusion I was led to that my reasonings were perfectly right, reviewed that chapter again with great care, and by observing only the mistake of one word (viz. having put *things* for *actions*), which was very easy to be done in the place where it is (§ 28, of first edition), I got into a new view of things, which, if I mistake not, will satisfy you, and give a clearer account of *human freedom* than hitherto I have done.' (Locke to Molyneux, 15th July, 1693. See also Molyneux to Locke, August 12, and Locke's reply, August 23.)

to the learned world, and which, in short, is this : *Liberty* is BOOK II.
a power to act or not to act, according as the mind directs. ——
A power to direct the operative faculties to motion or rest CHAP. XXI.
in particular instances is that which we call the *will*. That
which in the train of our voluntary actions determines the
will to any change of operation is *some present uneasiness*,
which is, or at least is always accompanied with that of *desire*.
Desire is always moved by evil, to fly it : because a total
freedom from pain always makes a necessary part of our
happiness : but every good, nay, every greater good, does not
constantly move desire, because it may not make, or may not
be taken to make, any necessary part of our happiness. For
all that we desire, is only to be happy. But, though this
general desire of happiness operates constantly and invariably,
yet the satisfaction of any particular desire *can be suspended*[1]
from determining the will to any subservient action, till we
have maturely examined whether the particular apparent
good which we then desire makes a part of our real happiness,
or be consistent or inconsistent with it. The result of our
judgment upon that examination is what ultimately determines the man ; who could not be *free* if his will were
determined by anything but his own desire, guided by his
own judgment.] [[2] I know that liberty, by some, is placed in
an indifferency of the man ; antecedent to the determination
of his will. I wish they who lay so much stress on such an
antecedent indifferency, as they call it, had told us plainly,
whether this supposed indifferency be antecedent to the

---

[1] If the connection between the
'general desire of happiness,' as a
motive, and a voluntary determination
to act, be as constant or 'uniform' as
in a mechanical sequence, how can
he find the volition, its effect, 'suspended,' even for a time ; unless man,
in virtue of his accountability for his
volitions, is mysteriously able to arrest
them, by an act which originates in
himself, supernaturally, i. e. independently of the mechanism of physical
causality, with *its* not less mysterious
outcome of an 'infinite' succession of

dependent, or caused causes ?

[2] What follows, in objection to the
'liberty' of 'indifferency,' was introduced in Coste's French version of the
Essay. This appears in Locke's letter
to Limborch, 12th August, 1701. Free
agency, suggested by the chapter on
'Power,' was a subject of correspondence between Locke and Limborch in
the course of that year. This and
other arguments of Locke's in this
chapter are criticised in Law's notes
to his translation of Archbishop King's
Essay on the Origin of Evil.

thought and judgment of the understanding, as well as to the decree of the will. For it is pretty hard to state it between them[1], i. e. immediately *after* the judgment of the understanding, and *before* the determination of the will: because the determination of the will immediately follows the judgment of the understanding: and to place liberty in an indifferency, antecedent to the thought and judgment of the understanding, seems to me to place liberty in a state of darkness, wherein we can neither see nor say anything of it; at least it places it in a subject incapable of it, no agent being allowed capable of liberty, but in consequence of thought and judgment[2]. I am not nice about phrases, and therefore consent to say with those that love to speak so, that liberty is placed in indifferency; but it is an indifferency which remains after the judgment of the understanding, yea, even after the determination of the will: and that is an indifferency not of the *man*, (for after he has once judged which is best, viz. to do or forbear, he is no longer indifferent,) but an indifferency of *the operative powers of the man*, which remaining equally able to operate or to forbear operating after as before the decree of the will, are in a state, which, if one pleases, may be called indifferency; and as far as this indifferency reaches, a man is free, and no further: v. g. I have the ability to move my hand, or to let it rest; that operative power[3] is

[1] 'Hard' or not 'to state,' is it not here that the voluntary determination enters for which the man is accountable? Is it not *intermediate* between the *antecedent* motive constituted by the stimulus of desire, interpreted by the 'judgment of the understanding,' and the overt action which *follows* the interposed volition? The true 'indifference,' or independence of caused causality, in which moral freedom consists, belongs, not to the antecedent motive, nor to the consequent overt act, but to the act of will, supplied with sufficient intellectual light.

[2] It is thus that Locke effectually argues against the absurd supposition, that in order to be morally free to choose good or evil, a man must be able to exert his will, without regard either to motives, or to determinations of the understanding, in an irrational 'indifference' to all considerations. Reason is surely an essential element in accountability; although a finite moral agent *may* determine to act irrationally—immorally; and cannot act without a motive. Yet it does not follow that his volitions are only links in the sequences of nature, or that they may not be ultimate facts in a spiritual economy, or moral order, to which the mechanical sequences of nature are somehow in harmonious subordination.

[3] Latent in the agent, under law

indifferent to move or not to move my hand.   I am then, in
that respect perfectly free; my will determines that operative power to rest: I am yet free, because the indifferency of
that my operative power to act, or not to act, still remains;
the power of moving my hand is not at all impaired by the
determination of my will, which at present orders rest; the
indifferency of that power to act, or not to act, is just as it
was before, as will appear, if the will puts it to the trial, by
ordering the contrary.   But if, during the rest of my hand,
it be seized with a sudden palsy, the indifferency of that
operative power is gone, and with it my liberty; I have no
longer freedom in that respect, but am under a necessity of
letting my hand rest [1].   On the other side, if my hand be put
into motion by a convulsion, the indifferency of that operative faculty is taken away by that motion; and my liberty in
that case is lost, for I am under a necessity of having my
hand move [2].   I have added this, to show in what sort of
indifferency liberty seems to me to consist, and not in any
other, real or imaginary.]

74. [[3] True notions concerning the nature and extent of Active and
liberty are of so great importance, that I hope I shall be passive
pardoned this digression, which my attempt to explain it has power, in
led me into [4].   The ideas of will, volition, liberty, and necessity, motions
and in
thinking.

which determines his natural power to
‘ operate ’ with his hand, *if he has the
will to exert it.*

[1] But a man would still be accountable *for his voluntary determination*, say
to murder, or to steal, if he could, and
did deliberately *will* to make his hand
the instrument of murder or theft; even
although, in virtue of its relation to
the system of nature, as in palsy, his
volition could no longer carry, as its
natural consequence, the needed movement of his hand.

[2] But I am not then accountable
for the consequences of its movement;
although, if voluntary determination
goes along with the movement which
I am myself unable to execute by my
volition, I am then responsible for the
volition.

[3] Sect. 74 was introduced in the
second edition.

[4] ‘ I do not wonder,’ writes Locke
to Molyneux (Jan. 20, 1693), ‘ you
think my discourse about liberty a little
too fine spun.   I had so much that
thought of it myself, that I said the
same thing of it myself to some of my
friends, before it was printed, and told
them that upon that account, I judged
it best to leave it out; but they persuaded me to the contrary.   When
the connection of the parts of my subject brought me to the consideration
of *power*, I had no desire to meddle
with the question of *liberty*, but barely
pursued my thoughts in the contemplation of that power in man of choosing
or preferring which we call the *will*, as
far as they would lead me, without any

in this Chapter of Power, came naturally in my way. In a former edition of this Treatise I gave an account of my thoughts concerning them, according to the light I then had. And now, as a lover of truth, and not a worshipper of my own doctrines, I own some change of my opinion; which I think I have discovered ground for. In what I first writ, I with an unbiassed indifferency followed truth, whither I thought she led me. But neither being so vain as to fancy infallibility, nor so disingenuous as to dissemble my mistakes for fear of blemishing my reputation, I have, with the same sincere design for truth only, not been ashamed to publish what a severer inquiry has suggested. It is not impossible but that some may think my former notions right; and some (as I have already found) these latter; and some neither. I shall not at all wonder at this variety in men's opinions: impartial deductions of reason in controverted points being so rare, and exact ones in abstract notions not so very easy, especially if of any length. And, therefore, I should think myself not a little beholden to any one, who would, upon these or any other grounds, fairly clear this subject of *liberty* from any difficulties that may yet remain[1].]

[[2]Before I close this chapter, it may perhaps be to our purpose, and help to give us clearer conceptions about *power*, if

the least bias to one side or the other; or if there was any leaning in my mind, it was rather to the contrary side of that where I found myself at the end of my pursuit. But doubting that it bore a little too hard on man's liberty, I showed it to a very ingenious but professed Arminian, and desired him, after he had considered it, to tell me his objections, if he had any; who frankly confessed he could carry it no further.' (*Familiar Letters.*) In this chapter Locke disposes of the pretended freedom of ' self-determination,' by a *reductio ad absurdum* ; and of the supposed freedom of ' indifference' to motives and to reason. While still claiming for man a freedom of ' suspension,' he is logically obliged to deny it, by the arguments which show the impossibility of either liberty of self-determination, or liberty of indifference. He never rises, through the fundamental postulate of moral government, to the conception of the mechanism of nature being merged in a higher system, which leaves room for determining choice between good and evil, in freedom from nature in the lower meaning of the term nature.

[1] This and the preceding sentence suggested a tract entitled:—*A Vindication of Mankind, or Free Will, asserted in answer to a Philosophical Inquiry concerning Human Liberty. To which is added an examination of Mr. Locke's Scheme of Freedom* (1717).

[2] What follows to the end of the section was added in the fourth edition.

we make our thoughts take a little more exact survey of *action*. I have said above, that we have ideas but of two sorts of action, viz. motion and thinking. These, in truth, though called and counted actions, yet, if nearly considered, will not be found to be always perfectly so. For, if I mistake not, there are instances of both kinds, which, upon due consideration, will be found rather passions than actions ; and consequently so far the effects barely of *passive powers* in those subjects, which yet on their accounts are thought agents. For, in these instances, the substance that hath motion or thought receives the impression, whereby it is put into that action, purely from without, and so acts merely by the capacity it has to receive such an impression from some external agent ; and such a power is not properly an active power, but a mere passive capacity in the subject. Sometimes the substance or agent puts itself into action by its own power, and this is properly *active power*. Whatsoever modification a substance has, whereby it produces any effect, that is called action : v. g. a solid substance, by motion, operates on or alters the sensible ideas of another substance, and therefore this modification of motion we call action. But yet this motion in that solid substance is, when rightly considered, but a passion, if it received it only from some external agent. So that the active power of motion is in no substance which cannot begin motion in itself or in another substance when at rest. So likewise in thinking, a power to receive ideas or thoughts from the operation of any external substance is called a power of thinking : but this is but a passive power, or capacity. But to be able to bring into view ideas out of sight at one's own choice, and to compare which of them one thinks fit, this is an active power. This reflection may be of some use to preserve us from mistakes about powers and actions, which grammar, and the common frame of languages, may be apt to lead us into. Since what is signified by verbs that grammarians call active, does not always signify action : v. g. this proposition : I *see* the moon, or a star, or I *feel* the heat of the sun, though expressed by a verb active, does not signify any action in me, whereby I operate on those substances, but only the reception of the ideas of light, roundness,

BOOK II.
CHAP. XXI.
and heat; wherein I am not active, but barely passive, and cannot, in that position of my eyes or body, avoid receiving them. But when I turn my eyes another way, or remove my body out of the sunbeams, I am properly active; because of my own choice, by a power within myself, I put myself into that motion. Such an action is the product of active power [1].]

[1] Locke's idea of 'power,' as implied in *human will*, explained with circumlocution and digression, and with many modifications, in successive editions of the *Essay*, was worked out, more consistently with its implied principle, in controversies of which this chapter was the occasion, during the half century that followed its publication. Naturalism, or the universal applicability of physical causation, as an adequate account of the voluntary determinations of spiritual agents, equally with events in the material world, notwithstanding his vacillations, is Locke's *implied* principle. Yet the infinite succession of antecedents, to which all natural explanations conduct, is ultimately as mysterious as the mystery of origination or creation of his own volitions by a moral agent. The *caused* causes of science, and the power superior to but in harmony with them, presupposed in a moral agent, are both mysteries. With our necessarily inadequate ideas of each, neither conception of the universe can be used to destroy the other; while, under these conditions, room is left for the absolute supremacy of the conception of the universe as a *moral* government, with nature and natural government subordinate, yet harmonious; all involving as a presupposition dependence on God, who is immanent Reason personified and supreme. The idea of human liberty which makes mechanical necessity the *complete* intellectual system of the universe, implied on the whole in Locke's reasoning, was carried more luminously to its conclusion by his friend Anthony Collins, in his *Philosophical Inquiry concerning Human Liberty*, which appeared in 1717, to which Dr. Samuel Clarke replied in the same year. A rejoinder by Collins, published in 1729 (the year in which they both died), now rarely met with, is entitled:—*A Dissertation on Liberty and Necessity; wherein the process of ideas, from their first entrance into the soul until their production of action, is delineated.* Besides Collins and Clarke, Jackson and a host of other polemics joined in the argumentative fray—so that the literature of 'free will,' in last century in England, might form a small library. The necessitated volition of Collins is argued for with extraordinary acuteness by Jonathan Edwards, in his *Inquiry into the Modern prevailing notions respecting Freedom of Will* (1759). Hume, taking the fact that we can predict with probability human actions and their consequences, as we predict events in external nature, maintains that (whether we call this *necessity* or not) acts of will must be determined by a cause out of the will, under the same law or custom of physical causation that is illustrated in all other changes, and concludes that 'the whole dispute has been merely verbal.' But the antithesis between the *natural* and the *spiritual* interpretation of the universe, which moral accountability supposes, is not got rid of by thus reducing spirit to nature, but by allowing scientific uniformity in nature, along with supernaturality in persons, in their voluntary determinations.

75. And thus I have, in a short draught, given a view of BOOK II.
our original ideas, from whence all the rest are derived, and
of which they are made up ; which, if I would consider as a CHAP. XXI.
philosopher, and examine on what causes they depend, and Summary
of what they are made, I believe they all might be reduced of our Original ideas.
to these very few primary and original ones, viz.

> *Extension,*
> *Solidity,*
> *Mobility,* or the power of being moved ;

which by our senses we receive from body :

> *Perceptivity,* or the power of perception, or thinking ;
> *Motivity,* or the power of moving :

which by reflection we receive from *our minds.*

I crave leave to make use of these two new words, to avoid
the danger of being mistaken in the use of those which are
equivocal.

To which if we add

> *Existence,*
> *Duration,*
> *Number,*

which belong both to the one and the other, we have, perhaps,
all the original ideas on which the rest depend.   For by these,
I imagine, might be *explained* the nature of colours, sounds,
tastes, smells, and *all other ideas we have,* if we had but
faculties acute enough to perceive the severally modified
extensions and motions of these minute bodies, which produce those several sensations in us.   But my present purpose
being only to inquire into the knowledge the mind has of
things, by those ideas and appearances which God has fitted
it to receive from them, and how the mind comes by that
knowledge [1]; rather than into their causes or manner of

---

[1] 'À dire la vérité, je crois que ces idées, qu'on appelle ici originales et primitives, ne le sont pas entièrement pour la plupart, étant susceptibles, à mon avis, d'une résolution ultérieure. Cependant, je ne blâme point l'auteur de s'y être borné, et de n'avoir pas poussé l'analyse plus loin.   D'ailleurs, s'il est vrai que le nombre en pourrait être diminué par ce moyen, je crois qu'il pourrait être augmenté, en y ajoutant d'autres idées plus originales, ou autant.   Pour ce qui est de leur arrangement, je croirais, suivant l'ordre de l'analyse, *l'existence* antérieure aux autres, le *nombre* à *l'étendue,* la *durée* à la *motivité* ; quoi que cet ordre analytique ne soit pas ordinairement celui des

production, I shall not, contrary to the design of this *Essay*, set myself to inquire philosophically into the peculiar constitution of *bodies*, and the configuration of parts, whereby *they* have the power to produce in us the ideas of their sensible qualities. I shall not enter any further into that disquisition ; it sufficing to my purpose to observe, that gold or saffron has a power to produce in us the idea of yellow, and snow or milk, the idea of white, which we can only have by our sight ; without examining the texture of the parts of those bodies, or the particular figures or motion of the particles which rebound from them, to cause in us that particular sensation : though, when we go beyond the bare ideas in our minds, and would inquire into their causes, we cannot conceive anything else to be in any sensible object, whereby it produces different ideas in us, but the different bulk, figure, number, texture, and motion of its insensible parts [1].

occasions qui nous y font penser. *Les sens* nous fournissent la matière aux réflexions, et nous ne penserions pas même à la pensée, *si nous ne pensions à quelque autre chose, c'est-à-dire aux particularités que les sens fournissent.*' (Leibniz.)

[1] As this chapter completes Locke's account of the ' simple modes ' of those ' simple ideas ' to which he refers all the thoughts that can be entertained by a human understanding, he ends it with the summary, contained in this section, of ' the original ideas on which the rest depend.' Some of its expressions might imply, that, if he had been enquiring as a natural philosopher into the natural causes of those ideas, he was inclined to maintain, that not only our ideas of the secondary qualities and powers of bodies, but ' all other ideas we have,' might be explained by ' the severally modified extensions and motions ' of the atoms of which bodies consist. This would not be inconsistent with his repeated suggestion (Bk. IV. ch. iii. § 6, and in other parts of the *Essay*), that ' God can, if he pleases, superadd to matter a faculty of thinking.' But his illustration being taken from the dependence of sensations of the imputed qualities of matter on the motions of its particles, it is probable that this only, or chiefly, was before him here, and not the hypothesis of modified materialism elsewhere suggested.

NOTE TO CHAPTER XXI.

THE following are the sections in the First Edition, immediately after Section 27, which were in great part omitted in
the Second Edition, and in place of them thirty-five others
(§§ 28–60) were introduced :—

28. *Secondly,* In the next place we must remember that *volition* or
willing, regarding only what is in our power, is nothing but the
preferring the doing of anything to the not doing of it ; action to rest,
and *contra.* Well, but what is this *preferring*? It is nothing but
the *being pleased more with the one than the other.* Is then a man
indifferent to be pleased, or not pleased, more with one thing than
another? Is it in his choice, whether he will or will not be better
pleased with one thing than another? And to this I think every
one's experience is ready to make answer, No. From whence it
follows,

29. *Thirdly,* That the will or preference is determined by *something
without itself.* Let us see then what it is determined by. If willing
be but the being better pleased, as has been shown, it is easie to
know what 'tis determines the will, what 'tis pleases best : everyone
knows 'tis happiness, or that which makes any part of happiness, or
contributes to it ; and that is it we call *Good.* Happiness and Misery
are names of two extremes, the utmost bounds whereof we know
not : 'tis what *eye hath not seen, ear hath not heard, nor hath entered into
the heart of man to conceive.* But of some degrees of both we have
very lively impressions, made by several instances of delight and joy
on the one side, and torment and sorrow on the other : which, for
shortness sake, I shall comprehend under the names of pleasure and
pain, there being pleasure and pain of the mind as well as the body :
With him is fulness of joy and pleasures for evermore : Or to speak truly
they are all of the mind, though some have their rise in the mind
from thought, others in the body from motion. Happiness then is
the utmost pleasure we are capable of, and misery the utmost pain.
Now, because pleasure and pain are produced in us, by the operation
of certain objects, either on our minds or our bodies ; and in different
degrees : therefore what has an aptness to produce pleasure in us is
that we labour for, and is that we call *Good* ; and what is apt to
produce pain in us, we avoid and call *Evil* ; for no other reason but
its aptness to produce pleasure and pain in us, wherein consists

BOOK II.

CHAP. XXI.

our happiness or misery. Further, because the degrees of pleasure and pain have also justly a preference; though what is apt to produce any degree of pleasure be in itself good; and what is apt to produce any degree of pain be evil; yet it often happens that we do not call it so, when it comes in competition with a greater of its sort. So that if we will rightly estimate what we call *good* and *evil* we shall find it lies much in comparison: For the cause of every less degree of pain, as well as every greater degree of pleasure, has the nature of good, and *vice versa*, and is that which determines our choice and challenges our preference. *Good*, then, *the greater good, is that which determines the will.*

30. This is not an imperfection in man; it is the highest perfection of intellectual natures: it is so far from being a restraint or diminution of *freedom*, that it is the very improvement and benefit of it: 'tis not an abridgement, 'tis the end and use of our liberty: and the further we are removed from such a determination to good, the nearer we are to misery and slavery [1]. A perfect indifferency in the will, or power of preferring, not determinable by the good or evil that is thought to attend its choice, would be so far from being an advantage and excellency of any intellectual nature, that it would be as great an imperfection as the want of indifferency to act and not to act, till determined by the will, would be an imperfection on the other side. A man is at liberty to lift up his hand to his head, or let it rest quiet: he is perfectly indifferent to either; and it would be an imperfection in him, if he wanted that power, if he be deprived of that indifferency. But it would be as great an imperfection, if he had the same indifferency, whether he would prefer the lifting up his hand, or its remaining in rest, when it would save his head or eyes from a blow he sees coming: 'tis as much a *perfection*, that the power of preferring should be *determined by good*, as that the power of *acting* should be *determined by the will*; and the certainer such determination is, the greater is the perfection.

31. If we look upon those superiour beings above us, who enjoy perfect happiness, we shall have reason to judge they are more steadily determined in their choice of good than we: and yet we have no reason to think they are less happy, or less free, than we are. And if it were fit for such poor finite creatures as we are, to pronounce what infinite wisdom and goodness could do, I think we might say that God himself *cannot choose* what is not good: the freedom of the Almighty hinders not his being determined by what is best.

32. But to consider this mistaken part of liberty right, Would any one be a changeling, because he is less determined by wise considerations than a wise man? Is it worth the name of freedom to be at

---

[1] The loss of power to will what is *good* is the 'slavery' in which, by abuse of moral liberty in a finite person, reason and will have become subject to sense and passion. The subjection of the individual to the universal will is the right use of freedom, but is not human freedom itself.

liberty to play the fool, and draw shame and misery upon a man's self? If want of restraint to chuse, or to do the worse, be liberty, true liberty, madmen and fools are the only free men: but yet I think nobody would choose to be mad for the sake of such liberty, but he that is mad already.

33. But though the preference of the mind be *always* determined by the appearance of good, greater good ; yet the person who has the power, in which alone consists liberty to act, or not to act, according to such preference, is nevertheless free ; such determination abridges not that power. He that has his chains knocked off, and the prison-doors set open to him, is perfectly at liberty, because he may either go or stay *as he best likes* ; though his preference be determined to stay by the darkness of the night, or illness of the weather, or want of other lodging. He ceases not to be free ; though that which at that time appears to him greatest good absolutely determines his preference, and *makes* him stay in his prison. I have rather made use of the word *preference* than *choice*, to express the act of volition, because choice is of a more doubtful signification, and bordering more upon desire, and so is referred to things remote ; whereas volition, or the act of willing, signifies nothing properly, but the actual producing of something that is voluntary.

34. The next thing to be considered is, If our minds be determined by good,—*How it comes to pass that men's wills carry them so contrarily,* and consequently some of them to what is evil? And to this I say, that the various and contrary choices that men make in the world, doe not argue that they do not all chuse good ; but that *the same thing is not good to every man.* Were all the concerns of man terminated in this life ; why one pursued study and knowledge, and another hawking and hunting ; why one chose luxury and debauchery, and another sobriety and riches, would not be, because every one of these did not pursue his own happiness, but because their happiness lay in different things : And therefore 'twas a right answer of the physician to his patient that had sore eyes: If you have more pleasure in the taste of wine than in the use of your sight, wine is good for you : but if the pleasure of seeing be greater to you than that of drinking, wine is naught.

35. The mind has a different relish as well as the palate ; and you will as fruitlessly endeavour to delight all men with riches and glory (which yet some men place their happiness in) as you would to satisfie all men's hunger with cheese or lobsters ; which though very agreeable and delicious fare to some, are to others extremely nauseous and offensive : and many people would with reason prefer the griping of an hungry belly to those dishes which are a feast to others. Hence it was I think that philosophers of old did in vain inquire, whether *Summum Bonum* consisted in riches, or bodily delights, or virtue, or contemplation : and they might have as reasonably disputed, whether the best relish were to be found in apples, plums, or nuts ; and divided into sects upon it. For, as pleasant tastes depend not on

the things themselves, but their agreeableness to this and that particular palate, wherein there is great variety: so the greatest happiness consists, in the having those things which produce the greatest pleasure, and the absence of those which cause any disturbance, any pain; which to different men are very different things. If therefore men in this life only have hope; if in this life only they can enjoy; 'tis not strange nor unreasonable, that they should seek their happiness by avoiding all things that disease them here, and by preferring all things that delight them; wherein it will be no wonder to find variety and difference. For if there be no prospect beyond the grave, the inference is certainly right—*Let us eat and drink*, let us enjoy what we delight in, *for to-morrow we shall die*. This I think may serve to show us the reason why, though all men's wills are determined by good, yet they are not determined by the same object. Men may chuse different things, and yet all chuse right, supposing them only like a company of poor insects, whereof some are bees, delighted with flowers, and their sweetness; others scarabes, delighted with other kind of viands; which, having enjoyed for a season, they should cease to be, and exist no more for ever.

36. This sufficiently discovers to us, why men in this world prefer different things, and pursue happiness by contrary courses: But yet since men are always determined by Good, the greater Good, and are constant and in earnest in matter of happiness and misery, the question still remains, *How men often come to prefer the worse to the better; and to chuse that which, by their own confession, has made them miserable?*

37. To this I answer, That as to *present* happiness or misery, *present* pleasure or pain, when that *alone* comes in consideration, a man never chuses amiss: he knows what best pleases him, and that he actually prefers. Things in their present enjoyment are what they seem: the apparent and real good are, in this case, always the same. For the pain or pleasure being just so great, and no greater than is felt, the present good or evil is really as much as it appears. And therefore, were every action of ours concluded within itself, and drew no consequences after it, we should undoubtedly always will nothing but Good; always infallibly prefer the best. Were the pains of honest industry, and of starving with hunger and cold set together before us, nobody would be in doubt which to chuse: were the satisfaction of a lust, and the joys of heaven offered at once to any one's present possession, he would not balance, or err in the choice and determination of his will. But since our voluntary actions carry not all the happiness and misery that depend on them, along with them in their present performance; but are the precedent causes of good and evil, which they draw after them, and bring upon us, when they themselves are passed, and cease to be; that which has the preference, and makes us will the doing or omitting any action in our power, is the greater good, appearing to result from that choice, in all its consequences, as far as at present they are represented to our view.

38. So that that which determines the choice of the will, and obtains the preference, is still good, the greater good: but it is also only good *that appears*; that which carries with it the expectation of addition to our happiness, by the increase of our pleasures, either in degrees, sorts, or duration; or by preventing, shortening, or lessening of pain. Thus the temptation of a pleasant taste brings a surfeit, a disease, and perhaps death too, on one who looks no further than that apparent good, than the present pleasure; who sees not the remote and concealed evil: and the hopes of easing or preventing some greater pain sweetens another man's draught, and makes that willingly be swallowed, which in itself is nauseous and unpleasant. Both these men were moved to what they did by the appearance of good; though the one found ease and health, and the other a disease and destruction: and therefore to him that looks beyond this world, and is fully persuaded that God, the righteous judge, will render to every man according to his deeds: to them who by patient continuance in well doing, seek for glory, and honour, and immortality, eternal life; but unto every soul that doeth evil, indignation and wrath, tribulation and anguish: To him I say who hath a prospect of the different state of happiness, or misery that attends all men after this life, depending on their behaviour here, the *measures* of good and evil that govern his choice are mightily changed. For, since nothing of pleasure and pain in this life can bear any proportion to endless happiness, or exquisite misery of an immortal soul hereafter, actions in his power will have their preference, not according to the transient pleasure or pain that accompanies or follows them here, but as they serve to secure that perfect, durable happiness hereafter.

———

In the first edition chapter xxi consists of 47 sections only. Those reproduced above were omitted in the second and succeeding editions, partly on account of Locke's change of opinion as to the motive by which the will is ultimately determined. Also in the sections substituted in the second edition, Locke, for the first time, claims for man power to *suspend* the execution of any of his desires, in order to examine them with deliberation in the light of intelligence; seeking thus to recognise that we are able to act 'freely,' in accepting or rejecting different kinds of apparent good, in governing our passions, and in educating our tastes. In this power to deliberate he thinks he has discovered 'the source of all liberty,' in which consists 'that which is (as I think improperly) called *free-will*' (§ 48). The omissions and large additions of the second edition, and the passages inserted in subsequent editions, form a mixture in which his original conception of 'freedom,' as 'power to act according to our will,' and this later conception of freedom, as 'power to suspend volition,' and so to determine it by a deliberate judgment of the understanding, are left in inharmonious conjunction, in a chapter which, notwithstanding all Locke's painful labour, is perhaps the least satisfactory in the *Essay*.

Among the MSS. printed by Lord King are four additional sections, which Locke at one time meant to introduce immediately after § 54. In them he tries to explain how it comes to pass, if men '*can* suspend their desires, stop their actions, and take time to consider and deliberate upon what they are going to do,' that they nevertheless so often 'abandon themselves to the most brutish, vile, irrational actions, during the whole current of a wild or dissolute life ; without any check, or the least appearance of any reflection.' Several causes of this are then mentioned—in particular the loss of power to reflect which is the issue of neglected education and bad habits ; and rejection of 'the thoughts and belief of another world, as a fiction of politicians and divines,' notwithstanding that 'when in this age of the world the belief of another life leaves a man of parts who has been bred up under the sound and opinion of heaven and hell, virtue seldom stays with him.' In the end Locke judged that 'this addition to the chapter might be spared.' (King's *Life of Locke*, vol. ii. pp. 219–222.)

CHAPTER XXII.

OF MIXED MODES.

BOOK II.

CHAP.
XXII.

Mixed
Modes,
what.

1. HAVING treated of *simple modes* in the foregoing chapters, and given several instances of some of the most considerable of them, to show what they are, and how we come by them; we are now in the next place to consider those we call *mixed modes*; such are the complex ideas we mark by the names *obligation, drunkenness,* a *lie,* &c.; which consisting of several combinations of simple ideas of *different* kinds, I have called mixed modes[1], to distinguish them from the more simple modes, which consist only of simple ideas of the *same* kind. These mixed modes, being also such combinations of simple ideas as are not looked upon to be characteristical marks of any real beings that have a steady existence, but scattered and independent ideas put together by the mind, are thereby distinguished from the complex ideas of substances[2].

2. That the mind, in respect of its simple ideas, is wholly passive, and receives them all from the existence and operations of things, such as sensation or reflection offers them, without being able to *make* any one idea, experience shows us[3]. But if we attentively consider these ideas I call mixed

---

[1] The ideas for which Locke devised this (now obsolete) name are described by Reid as '*general conceptions* formed by combination' of simple ideas or attributes 'into one parcel.' (*Intellectual Powers,* v. ch. 4.)

[2] Mixed modes are not ideas of substances, and so supposed to be formed according to the intelligible system of things. They are formed to suit the convenience of men, are their own archetypes, and cease to exist, even in the thoughts of those by whom they

were elaborated, when their names are lost. As they are formed chiefly for their utility in social intercourse, which depends upon ever-varying circumstances, the 'mixed modes' of our simple ideas that are current in one age or country may remain unconceived in other nations and periods.

[3] That is to say, the mind shows *passive* power only, in its acquisition of the phenomena of existence that are presented in sense and reflection; for they cannot be made other than

BOOK II.
CHAP.
XXII.

modes, we are now speaking of, we shall find their original quite different. The mind often exercises an *active* power in making these several combinations. For, it being once furnished with simple ideas, it can put them together in several compositions, and so make variety of complex ideas, without examining whether they exist so together in nature. And hence I think it is that these ideas are called *notions*[1]: as if they had their original, and constant existence, more in the thoughts of men, than in the reality of things; and to form such ideas, it sufficed that the mind put the parts of them together, and that they were consistent in the understanding, without considering whether they had any real being: though I do not deny but several of them might be taken from observation, and the existence of several simple ideas so combined[2], as they are put together in the understanding. For the man who first framed the idea of *hypocrisy*, might have either taken it at first from the observation of one who made show of good qualities which he had not; or else have framed that idea in his mind without having any such pattern to fashion it by. For it is evident that, in the beginning of languages and societies of men, several of those complex ideas, which were consequent to the constitutions established amongst them, must needs have been in the minds of men, before they existed anywhere else; and that many names that stood for such complex ideas were in use, and so those ideas framed, before the combinations they stood for ever existed[3].

Sometimes got by the Explication of their Names.

3. Indeed, now that languages are made, and abound with words standing for such combinations, an usual way of *getting* these complex ideas is, by the explication of those terms that stand for them[4]. For, consisting of a company of simple

they appear, by any voluntary determination of ours.

[1] 'notions,' i.e. attributes which men *specially note* in things. Berkeley afterwards applied this term to those of those 'ideas' of Locke which cannot appear in external sense, or in sensuous imagination, e. g. 'ideas' of the soul in its intellectual and voluntary operations; of personality; of relation;

and of God or the supreme Rational Will.

[2] 'so combined,' i.e. in an objectively real combination.

[3] Cf. Bk. III. ch. v. §§ 5, 6, where Locke gives examples of his meaning.

[4] This 'explication' is done exhaustively in *definition*, which is applicable to 'mixed modes,' but not to 'simple ideas.'

ideas combined, they may, by words standing for those simple
ideas, be represented to the mind of one who understands
those words, though that complex combination of simple
ideas were never 'offered to his mind by the real existence
of things. Thus a man may come to have the idea of *sacrilege*
or *murder*, by enumerating to him the simple ideas which
these words stand for ; without ever seeing either of them
committed.

4. Every mixed mode consisting of many distinct simple
ideas, it seems reasonable to inquire, Whence it has its unity ;
and how such a precise multitude comes to make but one
idea ; since that combination does not always exist together
in nature? To which I answer, it is plain it has its unity
from an act of the mind, combining those several simple
ideas together, and considering them as one complex one,
consisting of those parts ; and the mark of this union, or that
which is looked on generally to complete it, is one *name*
given to that combination. For it is by their names that
men commonly regulate their account of their distinct species
of mixed modes, seldom allowing or considering any number
of simple ideas to make one complex one, but such collections
as there be names for. Thus, though the killing of an old
man be as fit in nature to be united into one complex idea,
as the killing a man's father ; yet, there being no name
standing precisely for the one, as there is the name of *parricide*
to mark the other, it is not taken for a particular complex
idea, nor a distinct species of actions from that of killing
a young man, or any other man.

5. If we should inquire a little further, to see what it is that
occasions men to make several combinations of simple ideas
into distinct, and, as it were, settled modes, and neglect others,
which in the nature of things themselves, have as much an
aptness to be combined and make distinct ideas, we shall find
the reason of it to be the end of language ; which being to
mark, or communicate men's thoughts to one another with
all the dispatch that may be, they usually make *such* collections of ideas into complex modes, and affix names to them,
as they have frequent use of in their way of living and
conversation, leaving others, which they have but seldom an

The Name
ties the
Parts of
mixed
Modes
into one
Idea.

The Cause
of making
mixed
Modes.

BOOK II.
CHAP.
XXII.

occasion to mention, loose and without names that tie them together: they rather choosing to enumerate (when they have need) such ideas as make them up, by the particular names that stand for them, than to trouble their memories by multiplying of complex ideas with names to them, which they seldom or never have any occasion to make use of.

Why Words in one Language have none answering in another.

6. This shows us how it comes to pass that there are in every language many particular words which cannot be rendered by any one single word of another. For the several fashions, customs, and manners of one nation, making several combinations of ideas familiar and necessary in one, which another people have had never an occasion to make, or perhaps so much as take notice of, names come of course to be annexed to them, to avoid long periphrases in things of daily conversation; and so they become so many distinct complex ideas in *their* minds. Thus ὀστρακισμὸς amongst the Greeks, and *proscriptio* amongst the Romans, were words which other languages had no names that exactly answered; because they stood for complex ideas which were not in the minds of the men of other nations. Where there was no such custom, there was no notion of any such actions; no use of such combinations of ideas as were united, and, as it were, tied together, by those terms: and therefore in other countries there were no names for them.

And Languages change.

7. Hence also we may see the reason, why languages constantly change, take up new and lay by old terms. Because change of customs and opinions bringing with it new combinations of ideas, which it is necessary frequently to think on and talk about, new names, to avoid long descriptions, are annexed to them; and so they become new species of complex modes[1]. What a number of different ideas are by this means wrapped up in one short sound, and how much of our time and breath is thereby saved, any one will see, who will but take the pains to enumerate all the ideas that either *reprieve* or *appeal* stand for; and instead of either of those names, use a periphrasis, to make any one understand their meaning.

Mixed Modes

8. Though I shall have occasion to consider this more at

---

[1] 'complex modes,' i. e. *mixed* modes.

large when I come to treat of Words and their use[1], yet
I could not avoid to take thus much notice here of the *names*
of mixed modes;. which being fleeting and transient combinations of simple ideas, which have but a short existence
anywhere but in the minds of men, and there too have no
longer any existence than whilst they are thought on, have
not so much anywhere the appearance of a constant and
lasting existence as in their names : which are therefore, in
this sort of ideas, very apt to be taken for the ideas themselves.
For, if we should inquire where the idea of a *triumph* or
apotheosis exists, it is evident they could neither of them
exist altogether anywhere in the things themselves, being
actions that required time to their performance, and so could
never all exist together; and as to the minds of men, where
the ideas of these actions are supposed to be lodged, they
have there too a very uncertain existence : and therefore we
are apt to annex them to the names that excite them in us.

9. There are therefore three ways whereby we get these
complex ideas of mixed modes :—(1) By experience and
observation of things themselves : thus, by seeing two men
wrestle or fence, we get the idea of wrestling or fencing.
(2) By *invention*, or voluntary putting together of several
simple ideas in our own minds : so he that first invented
printing or etching, had an idea of it in his mind before it
ever existed. (3) Which is the most usual way, by *explaining
the names* of actions we never saw, or motions we cannot
see ; and by enumerating, and thereby, as it were, setting
before our imaginations all those ideas which go to the
making them up, and are the constituent parts of them. For,
having by sensation and reflection stored our minds with
simple ideas, and by use got the names that stand for them,
we can by those means represent to another any complex
idea we would have him conceive ; so that it has in it no
simple ideas but what he knows[2], and has with us the
same name for. For all our complex ideas are ultimately
resolvable into simple ideas, of which they are compounded

---

[1] In Book III.

[2] We could not introduce a ' mixed
mode' which included a positive idea of colour into the imagination of one
born blind.

BOOK II.
CHAP.
XXII.

and originally made up, though perhaps their immediate ingredients, as I may so say, are also complex ideas. Thus, the mixed mode which the word *lie* stands for is made of these simple ideas :—(1) Articulate sounds. (2) Certain ideas in the mind of the speaker. (3) Those words the signs of those ideas. (4) Those signs put together, by affirmation or negation, otherwise than the ideas they stand for are in the mind of the speaker. I think I need not go any further in the analysis of that complex idea we call a lie: what I have said is enough to show that it is made up of simple ideas. And it could not be but an offensive tediousness to my reader, to trouble him with a more minute enumeration of every particular simple idea that goes to this complex one; which, from what has been said, he cannot but be able to make out to himself. The same may be done in all our complex ideas whatsoever; which, however compounded and decompounded, may at last be resolved into simple ideas, which are all the materials[1] of knowledge or thought we have, or can have. Nor shall we have reason to fear that the mind is hereby stinted to too scanty a number of ideas, if we consider what an inexhaustible stock of simple modes number and figure alone afford us[2]. How far then mixed modes, which admit of the various combinations of different simple ideas, and their infinite modes[3], are from being few and scanty, we may easily imagine. So that, before we have done, we shall see that nobody need be afraid he shall not have scope and compass enough for his thoughts to range in, though they be, as I pretend, confined only to simple ideas, received from sensation or reflection, and their several combinations.

---

[1] All the 'materials,' that is to say, that men have, for knowing, or even conjecturing, the actual attributes and behaviour, past, present, and future, of finite beings and the Supreme Being, as to all which we are ignorant at birth,—a *tabula rasa*.

[2] Cf. Bk. II. ch. vii. § 10.

[3] Cf. Bk. II. ch. vii. § 14. The mixed modes of their simple ideas,—i. e. of the original revelations of existence made to them in sense—which men can form, by dint of elaborative activity, are endless. They comprehend, he elsewhere says, 'almost the whole subject about which Divinity, Morality, Law, Politics, and several other sciences, are employed';—and so, after all, some mixed modes are not arbitrary, but have their roots in the intelligible order of things.

10. It is worth our observing, which of all our simple ideas have been *most* modified, and had most mixed ideas made out of them, with names given to them. And those have been these three:—*thinking* and *motion* (which are the two ideas which comprehend in them all action,) and *power*, from whence these actions are conceived to flow. These simple ideas, I say, of thinking, motion, and power, have been those which have been most modified ; and out of whose modifications have been made most complex modes, with names to them. For *action* being the great business of mankind, and the whole matter about which all laws are conversant, it is no wonder that the several modes of thinking and motion should be taken notice of, the ideas of them observed, and laid up in the memory, and have names assigned to them; without which laws could be but ill made, or vice and disorders repressed. Nor could any communication be well had amongst men without such complex ideas, with names to them : and therefore men have settled names, and supposed settled ideas in their minds, of modes of actions, distinguished by their causes, means, objects, ends, instruments, time, place, and other circumstances ; and also of their powers fitted for those actions: v. g. *boldness* is the power to speak or do what we intend, before others, without fear or disorder ; and the Greeks call the confidence of speaking by a peculiar name, παρρησία : which power or ability in man of doing anything, when it has been acquired by frequent doing the same thing, is that idea we name *habit*; when it is forward, and ready upon every occasion to break into action, we call it *disposition*. Thus, *testiness* is a disposition or aptness to be angry.

Motion.
Thinking,
and
Power
have been
most
modified.

To conclude : Let us examine any modes of action, v. g. *consideration* and *assent*, which are actions of the mind; *running* and *speaking*, which are actions of the body ; *revenge* and *murder*, which are actions of both together, and we shall find them but so many collections of simple ideas, which, together, make up the complex ones signified by those names.

11. *Power* being the source from whence all action proceeds, the substances wherein these powers are, when they

BOOK II.

CHAP.
XXII.

signify
Action,
signify but
the Effect.

exert this power into act, are called *causes*[1], and the substances which thereupon are produced, or the simple ideas which are introduced into any subject by the exerting of that power, are called *effects*[2]. The *efficacy* whereby the new substance or idea is produced is called, in the subject exerting that power, *action*[3]; but in the subject wherein any simple idea is changed or produced, it is called *passion*[3]: which efficacy, however various, and the effects almost infinite, yet we can, I think, conceive it, in intellectual agents, to be nothing else but modes of thinking and willing[4]; in corporeal agents, nothing else but modifications of motion[5]. I say, I think we cannot conceive it to be any other but these two. For whatever sort of action besides these produces any effects, I confess myself to have no notion nor idea of; and so it is quite remote from my thoughts, apprehensions, and knowledge; and as much in the dark to me as five other senses, or as the ideas of colours to a blind man. And therefore many words which seem to express some action, signify

---

[1] Power thus presupposes a substance, as the cause in which it resides. Apart from the complex idea of a particular substance, in or by which the power is (passively or actively) manifested, and to which it is referred, the idea of power in its various modes, simple and mixed, is an abstraction. The effects, in their antecedent equivalents, along with active power to evolve the effects, are all latent in the cause; which is thus accountable, physically, if not morally, for its effects. But a free agent, recognised as such by the ethical test, is our one experienced example of a cause, in the highest meaning of the word.

[2] When a tree is evolved from the elements into which it may be refunded, we have an example of what he means by the 'production' of a *substance*; when its leaves change colour, appear, or disappear, *simple ideas* are introduced and withdrawn. Cf. ch. viii. § 23.

[3] Cf. ch. xxi. § 2.

[4] 'Thinking and willing' would thus be the primary qualities of spiritual agents; their modes of extension and motion, those of bodies, on which all their other qualities and powers are said to depend.

[5] This assumes that bodies are themselves 'agents,' and not merely 'modes' in which active reason manifests itself. Are the *modifications of motion* which bodies undergo in their progressive evolution, and in which the changes of the material world consist, *per se* 'efficacious'? Is not motion originated and sustained, in its intelligible order, or *modus operandi*, by an 'efficacy' that is external to the motions themselves, and responsible for them, being that to which, as evolved effects, they are to be referred? Does not the *evolution* of physical effects, from their equivalent physical causes, in which they were potentially contained, presuppose the originative and constant hyper-phenomenal efficacy of an *evolver*, so that evolution itself is ultimately and throughout supernatural?

nothing of the action or *modus operandi* at all, but barely the effect, with some circumstances of the subject wrought on, or cause operating: v. g. *creation, annihilation*[1], contain in them no idea of the action or manner whereby they are produced, but barely of the cause, and the thing done. And when a countryman says the cold freezes water, though the word *freezing* seems to import some action, yet truly it signifies nothing but the effect, viz. that water that was before fluid is become hard and consistent, without containing any idea of the action whereby it is done[2].

12. I think I shall not need to remark here that, though power and action make the greatest part of mixed modes, marked by names, and familiar in the minds and mouths of men, yet other simple ideas, and their several combinations, are not excluded: much less, I think, will it be necessary for me to enumerate all the mixed modes which have been settled, with names to them. That would be to make a dictionary of the greatest part of the words made use of in divinity, ethics, law, and politics, and several other sciences. All that is requisite to my present design, is to show what sort of ideas those are which I call mixed modes; how the mind comes by them; and that they are compositions made up of simple ideas got from sensation and reflection; which I suppose I have done.

---

[1] Words which refer to a 'power' actively operating, according to a *modus operandi*, stand for meanings which cannot, like the *modus operandi* itself, be represented in sensuous imagination. A *modus operandi* can be followed in imagination: originative power is not thus conceivable. It is as inconceivable as the 'infinite' in which the imaginable succession of natural causation is lost at last. The *modus operandi* is not action proper: it is succession of phenomena; their imaginable transformations in the kaleidoscope of nature.

[2] And these physical effects can be the *measurable equivalents* of their natural causes, so that the one can be *shown* to follow the other in an intelligible order.

CHAPTER XXIII.

OF OUR COMPLEX IDEAS OF SUBSTANCES.

BOOK II.

CHAP.
XXIII.

Ideas of
particular
Sub-
stances,
how made.

1. [1] THE mind being, as I have declared, furnished with a great number of the simple ideas, conveyed in by the senses as they are found in exterior things [2], or by reflection on its own operations, takes notice also that a certain number of these simple ideas go constantly together; which being presumed to belong to one thing, and words being suited to common apprehensions, and made use of for quick dispatch, are called, so united in one subject, by one name; which, by inadvertency, we are apt afterward to talk of and consider as one simple idea, which indeed is a complication of many ideas together: because, as I have said, not imagining [3] how these simple ideas *can* subsist by themselves, we accustom ourselves to suppose [3] some *substratum* wherein they do

---

[1] This section is meant to show that the complex idea of an *individual substance* is *occasioned* by phenomena of sense and reflection being found to coexist in aggregates in our experience. It has been mistaken for an account of the *general idea of substance*, which is formed, not by 'complication of many simple ideas together,' but by the opposite process of abstraction; and is at the root of all our complex ideas of particular substances, because of our intellectual inability to conceive phenomena really existing *unsubstantiated*, i. e. existing in abstraction, and not in the concrete.

[2] 'C'est plutôt le *concrétion*—comme savant, chaud, luisant—qui nous vient dans l'esprit, que les *abstractions* ou qualités—comme savoir, chaleur, lumière—qui sont bien plus difficiles à comprendre.' (Leibniz.)

[3] 'not imagining how'—'we accustom ourselves to suppose.' These expressions seem to refer our idea of substance to 'imagination' and 'custom,' instead of finding it implied in the very intelligibility of experience; for although 'custom' may explain our reference of such and such 'simple ideas' or qualities to such and such particular substances, it does not show the need in reason for substantiating them, in order to conceive that they are concrete realities. Locke thus vindicates his language in his third Letter to Stillingfleet (p. 375) :—

subsist, and from which they do result, which therefore we BOOK II.
call *substance.*

2. So that if any one will examine himself concerning his
notion of pure substance in general, he will find he has no
other idea of it at all, but only a supposition of he knows not
what *support*[1] of such qualities which are capable of producing simple ideas in us ; which qualities are commonly
called accidents. If any one should be asked, what is the
subject wherein colour or weight inheres[2], he would have
nothing to say, but the solid extended parts ; and if he were
demanded, what is it that solidity and extension adhere in[2],

CHAP.
XXIII.
Our ob-
scure Idea
of Sub-
stance in
general.

'Your lordship goes on to insist upon
"*supposing*" only, as that which gives
rise to, and is included in, our idea of
substance, thus resting it on mere supposition ; and you yourself, if I understand your reasoning, conclude that
there is substance, because it is *a repugnancy to our conceptions of things*
that modes should subsist by themselves ; and *I conclude the same thing*,
because we *cannot conceive* how qualities should subsist by themselves.' In
other places too he insists that it is
necessary in reason to the reality of
'simple ideas,' that they should be
substantiated.

[1] To substitute for the abstract category of substance this metaphor of a
'support' is apt to mislead, and to
suggest a something—stripped of *all*
perceived qualities—hid from our view
by the very phenomena in and through
which it is really (in part) revealed.
To try to *phenomenalise* substance *per
se*, after *all* the phenomena presented
by particular substances have been
abstracted, is to involve ourselves in
an insurmountable difficulty of our own
making. It is in and through 'simple
ideas' that we have our 'general idea'
of particular substances, which is as
inseparable from them all as they are
from otherwise abstract and unimaginable substance *per se*. Space without body ; duration without events ;
power unrevealed in effects ; and sub-

stance not even in part manifested in
phenomena, all illustrate the necessarily incomplete ideas of finite experience and imagination, thus at last
lost in the infinite. Locke implies that
the idea of 'substance in thought,' i.e.
the 'general' idea, is gradually formed
or suggested *in the individual mind*
by our becoming 'accustomed' to particular substances. 'The ideas of the
modes and actions of substances are
usually in our minds before the [gene-
ral] idea of substance itself.' (Letter
to S. Bold, 16 May, 1699.)

[2] 'inheres'—'adhere in.' Rather
—if asked what that is which is manifested to us as ' coloured and weighty,'
also as 'solid and extended'—should
not our answer be, that (whatever
more may be affirmed of it) it is at
least a substance that is coloured,
heavy, solid, and extended? A perfect
or infinite idea of the substance would
be an idea of *all* the phenomena and
effects which it could present to any intelligence, in all their possible relations.
The contingent, and ' in part ' revelation, which individual substances, corporeal and spiritual, make of themselves, in a *human* experience, surely
differs in degree rather than in kind
from the perfect idea which man would
require infinite time to form. But
Locke and others seem to leave *substances* for ever wholly hid behind *their
manifestations.*

BOOK II.
—◆◆—
CHAP.
XXIII.

he would not be in a much better case than the Indian before mentioned [1] who, saying that the world was supported by a great elephant, was asked what the elephant rested on ; to which his answer was—a great tortoise : but being again pressed to know what gave support to the broad-backed tortoise, replied—*something, he knew not what.* And thus here, as in all other cases where we use words without having clear and distinct ideas, we talk like children : who, being questioned what such a thing is, which they know not, readily give this satisfactory answer, that it is *something* : which in truth signifies no more, when so used, either by children or men, but that they know not what ; and that the thing they pretend to know, and talk of, is what they have no distinct idea of at all, and so are perfectly ignorant of it, and in the dark [2]. The idea then we have, to which we give the *general* name substance, being nothing but the supposed, but unknown, support of those qualities we find existing, which we imagine cannot subsist *sine re substante*, without something to support them, we call that support *substantia*; which, according to the true import of the word, is, in plain English, standing under or upholding [3].

Of the Sorts of Substances.

3. An obscure and relative idea of *substance in general* being thus made we come to have the ideas of *particular sorts of substances* [4], by collecting *such* combinations of simple

---

[1] See Bk. II. ch. xiii. § 19, where the abstract or general idea of substance is in like manner compared to the Indian philosopher's *he-knew-not-what,* which 'supported' the tortoise.

[2] These difficulties, as Leibniz says, would disappear with the resolution to think and speak of substances as in *concretes,* so far revealed in the complex ideas we have of them.

[3] Even in these misleading metaphors Locke recognises, in the constitution of our complex ideas of individual substances, a notion or universal, which he can neither phenomenalise nor eliminate, but which, while hard to harmonise with his principle, that

thought is confined to phenomena presented in our experience, he is too faithful to the facts wholly to reject. He rightly emphasises its ' obscurity,' tested by sensuous imagination — a character which belongs to it in common with other ultimate ideas involved in reason; and he half consciously sees that to treat it as ' fiction' would resolve reality with the sceptics into mere succession of impressions, as Hume afterwards showed.

[4] Locke seems glad to pass from the notion of substance in general—that ' supposed or confused idea,' which nevertheless (as more than a *mere* generalisation) it is ' repugnant to our

ideas as are, by experience and observation of men's senses, taken notice of to exist together ; and are therefore supposed to flow from the particular internal constitution, or unknown essence[1] of that substance. Thus we come to have the ideas of a man, horse, gold, water, &c.; of which substances, whether any one has any other *clear* idea, further than of certain simple ideas co-existent together[2], I appeal to every one's own experience. It is the ordinary qualities observable in iron, or a diamond, put together, that make the true complex idea of those substances, which a smith or a jeweller commonly knows better than a philosopher ; who, whatever *substantial forms*[3] he may talk of, has no other idea of those substances, than what is framed by a collection of those simple ideas which are to be found in them : only we must take notice, that our complex ideas of substances, besides all those simple ideas they are made up of, have always the confused idea of something to which they belong, and in which they subsist[4] : and therefore when we speak of any

conceptions of things' to explain away. He hastens to 'particular sorts of substances,' into all which data of sense or reflection necessarily enter; embodying the abstract, and *per se* unimaginable, notion in ideas of the concrete substances — material and spiritual — which the 'pure notion' constitutes. This chapter is professedly on 'our complex ideas of substances,' not on 'the idea of substance in general' which is the subject of sect. 2, and is repeatedly referred to in the sequel, as the 'support' of our complex ideas of particular substances. That *our experience in sense and reflection*—however it comes about, and whatever it means—*must* be an experience of *substances* manifested (in part), is the lesson suggested by, if not expressed in, this chapter. But an analysis of this intellectual need for substantiating phenomena, lies outside Locke's point of view.

[1] 'Essence.' The essence of a substance is, that in it which makes it be

the *sort* of substance that it is. Cf. Bk. III. ch. iii. § 15.

[2] This coexistence of phenomena, maintained by God in the sensuous presentations of finite spirits, constitutes so-called material substances, according to Berkeley. He thus finds their substance in self-conscious spirit, of which he says we have a 'notion' that cannot be represented in sensuous imagination.

[3] The 'substantial form' of the schoolmen is the *supposed* real and immaterial principle in substances that gives them the character by which they are definable.

[4] The 'confused' or 'obscure' idea of substance *per se*, in which concrete reality consists. Locke is apt to express himself as if this were the idea of something absolutely distinct from the phenomena, or simple ideas, in which it is so really revealed that we can predicate *them* of *it*, and have (thus far) in them a conception of it. What he said about the 'obscurity' of the idea,

sort of substance, we say it is a thing having such or such qualities; as body is a thing that is extended, figured, and capable of motion; spirit, a thing capable of thinking; and so hardness, friability, and power to draw iron, we say, are qualities to be found in a loadstone. These, and the like fashions of speaking, intimate that the substance is supposed always *something besides* the extension, figure, solidity, motion, thinking, or other observable ideas, though we know not what it is [1].

and its origin in the custom of experience, as well as the impossibility of reconciling an idea of the sort with a purely sensuous source of ideas, raised against him a charge of scepticism, against which he thus defends himself, in one of his letters to Stillingfleet :—' It is laid to my charge that I look at the *being* of substance to be doubtful ; and rendered it so by the imperfect and ill-grounded idea I have of it. To which I beg leave to say, that I ground not the *being* but the *idea* of substance, on our accustoming ourselves to suppose some *substratum*: for it is of the *idea* alone that I speak there, and not of the *being* of substance. And having everywhere affirmed and built upon it, that *man* is a substance, I cannot be supposed to question or doubt of the being of substance. Further, I say that sensation convinces us that there *are solid and extended substances*, and reflection that there *are thinking substances*. So that I think the being of substance is not shaken by what I have said ; and if the idea of it should be, yet (the being of things not depending on our ideas) the being of substance would not be shaken by my saying we had but an obscure imperfect idea of it ; and that the idea came from our accustoming ourselves to suppose some *substratum*: or indeed if I should say that *we* had no idea of substance at all. *For a great many things are granted to be of which we have no ideas.*' (First *Letter*, pp. 32, 33.) This, notwithstanding confusion of ex-

pression, may be understood to mean, that although we cannot *represent in sensuous imagination*, and have *in this way* an *idea* of that in which the substantiality or concreteness of things, material and spiritual, consists, we are not therefore bound to deny substantial reality; and also, that although our ' obscure idea' is *occasioned* by the custom of experience, it is ' obscure,' and dependent on that ' custom,' in the way that all ultimate notions must be. We could not have them without experience, or experience without them; but they are necessarily obscure and incomplete, in virtue of the finitude of human understanding and experience.

[1] It is this 'something' in the complex ingredient, the inevitable presence of which Locke is bound to reconcile with the hypothesis, that all our ideas of reality must consist of phenomena presented in the senses and in reflection. We *must* have the idea that they are the phenomena or manifestations of *something on which they depend*. Hence 'substances' neither are in, nor can be affirmed of a subject, and are thus independent; but genera and species (the *second substances* of Aristotle) are affirmable of their subject. So too we cannot understand the name of a substantive noun till we can predicate an adjective of it, while adjectives are unintelligible without substantives understood, on which they depend.

4. Hence, when we talk or think of any particular sort of corporeal substances, as horse, stone, &c., though the idea we have of either of them be but the complication or collection of those several simple ideas of sensible qualities, which we used to find united in the thing called horse or stone ; yet, *because we cannot conceive* [1] *how they should subsist alone, nor one in another*, we suppose them existing in and supported by some common subject; which support we denote by the name substance, though it be certain we have no clear or distinct idea of that thing we suppose a support.

5. The same thing happens concerning the operations of the mind, viz. thinking, reasoning, fearing, &c., which we concluding not to subsist of themselves, nor apprehending how they can belong to body, or be produced by it, we are apt to think these the actions of some other *substance*, which we call *spirit*; whereby yet it is evident that, having no other idea or notion of matter, but something wherein those many sensible qualities which affect our senses do subsist ; by supposing a substance wherein thinking, knowing, doubting, and a power of moving, &c., do subsist, we have as clear a notion of the substance of spirit, as we have of body; the one being supposed to be (without knowing what it is [2]) the *substratum* to those simple ideas we have from without; and the other supposed (with a like ignorance of what it is [3]) to be the *substratum* to those operations we experiment in ourselves within. It is plain then, that the idea of *corporeal substance* in matter is as remote from our conceptions and appre-

---

[1] 'cannot conceive,' i.e. it is repugnant to conception—contrary to reason.

[2] We can have no sensuous idea of it at all till it is manifested—*phenomenalised*—in its qualities ; but these, as manifested, necessarily presuppose what he metaphorically calls a ' support '—something independent, and that persists through the phenomenal changes which reveal it; while by means of the supersensible idea, thus awakened, presented phenomena are conceived in the concrete. But the substance is not one 'thing,' and its phenomena or qualities another 'thing.' The qualities are that in which the substance reveals *itself*, so far as they go.

[3] ' Pour moi,' says Leibniz, ' je crois que cette opinion de notre ignorance vient de ce qu'on demande une manière de connaissance que l'objet ne souffre point.' We do ' know what it is,' so far as it is revealed to us, in such and such modes, and in such and such effects ; and we are obliged to think that ' modes ' and ' effects ' mean *something modified* and *efficient*.

hensions, as that of *spiritual substance,* or spirit : and there-fore, from our not having any notion of the substance of spirit, we can no more conclude its non-existence, than we can, for the same reason, deny the existence of body ; it being as rational to affirm there is no body, because we have no clear and distinct idea of the substance of matter, as to say there is no spirit, because we have no clear and distinct idea of the substance of a spirit[1].

Our ideas of particular Sorts of Sub-stances.

6. Whatever therefore be the secret abstract nature of substance in general[2], all the ideas we have of particular distinct sorts of substances are nothing but several combina-tions of simple ideas, co-existing in such, though unknown, cause of their union[3], as makes the whole subsist of itself. It is by such combinations of simple ideas, and nothing else, that we represent particular sorts of substances to ourselves ; such are the ideas we have of their several species in our minds ; and such only do we, by their specific names, signify to others, v. g. man, horse, sun, water, iron : upon hearing which words, every one who understands the language, frames in his mind a combination of those several simple ideas which he has usually observed, or fancied to exist together under that denomination ; all which he supposes to rest in and be, as it were, adherent to that unknown common subject, which inheres not in anything else[4]. Though, in the meantime, it be manifest, and every one, upon inquiry into his own

---

[1] It is well said by Locke, Leibniz remarks, that spirit is at least as dis-tinctly manifested to us in our experi-ence as body is. 'Et il est très-vrai,' he further adds, 'que l'existence de l'esprit est *plus certaine* que celle des objets sensibles.'

[2] Locke speaks as if this substance were a secret *thing,* something *nume-rically different* from its own modifica-tions, or from substance in the concrete and particular. Yet he is too faithful to the implicates of experience to be satisfied with hollow, unsubstantiated phenomena, as Hume afterwards pro-fessed to be.

[3] 'unknown cause of their union'

—*imperfectly* known, in and through the phenomena in which it 'in part' reveals itself ; and in those inadequate interpretations, scientific and philo-sophic, of its phenomena or effects, which men, with their finite experi-ence, can attain to.

[4] 'inheres not in anything else,' i. e. cannot be predicated *as a mode or quality of anything else,* and so is *thus far* independent. This consists with finite individual substances being causally dependent, as elements in the universal system, in which each needs other substances in order to reveal itself, and God to sustain the whole.

thoughts, will find, that he has no other idea of any substance, v. g. let it be gold, horse, iron, man, vitriol, bread, but what he has barely of those sensible qualities, which he supposes to inhere; with a supposition of such a *substratum* as gives, as it were, a support to those qualities or simple ideas, which he has observed to exist united together. Thus, the idea of the sun,—what is it but an aggregate of those several simple ideas, bright, hot, roundish, having a constant regular motion, at a certain distance from us, and perhaps some other: as he who thinks and discourses of the sun has been more or less accurate in observing those sensible qualities, ideas, or properties, which are in that thing which he calls the sun[1].

7. For he has the perfectest idea of any of the particular sorts of substances, who has gathered, and put together, most of those simple ideas which do exist in it; among which are to be reckoned its active powers, and passive capacities[2], which, though not simple ideas, yet in this respect, for brevity's sake, may conveniently enough be reckoned amongst them[3]. Thus, the power of drawing iron is one of the ideas of the complex one of that substance we call a loadstone; and a power to be so drawn is a part of the complex one we call iron: which powers pass for inherent qualities in those subjects. Because every substance, being as apt, by the

Their active and passive Powers a great part of our complex Ideas of Substances.

---

[1] Locke holds that the ideas of the modes and actions of substances are usually in our minds *before* the general idea of substance itself. The idea (notion) is suggested by the manifestations which substances make of themselves in simple ideas, i. e. in the phenomena presented in sensation or reflection.

[2] In a 'perfect,' or exhaustive, idea of the 'particular substances' that exist, should we not be able to picture them in all their possible manifestations and relations, in the supreme or spiritual, and also in the subordinate or natural, system? The drift of this chapter is to show how far short of this ideal any *human* conception of each substance in the universe must be.

[3] According to Leibniz, every substance, or *monad*, is necessarily active, and revealed only in its unconscious and conscious activities. Locke sees the 'powers' of *material* substances in all their secondary or imported qualities, as well as in the changes in other things, of which they are the occasion; and in *spiritual* substances, in their passive sensibilities and voluntary determinations. On the other hand, in the solidity of bodies, and the conscious personality of spirits, Locke appears to regard material and spiritual substances as revealing *themselves*, rather than revealing *their powers to produce effects in other substances.*

powers we observe in it, to change some sensible qualities in other subjects, as it is to produce in us those simple ideas which we receive immediately from it, does, by those new sensible qualities introduced into other subjects, discover to us those powers which do thereby mediately affect our senses, as regularly as its sensible qualities do it immediately: v. g. we immediately by our senses perceive in fire its heat and colour; which are, if rightly considered, nothing but powers in it to produce those ideas in *us*: we also by our senses perceive the colour and brittleness of charcoal, whereby we come by the knowledge of another power in fire, which it has to change the colour and consistency of *wood.* By the former, fire immediately, by the latter, it mediately discovers to us these several powers; which therefore we look upon to be a part of the qualities of fire, and so make them a part of the complex idea of it. For all those powers that we take cognizance of, terminating only in the alteration of some sensible qualities in those subjects on which they operate, and so making them exhibit to us new sensible ideas [1], therefore it is that I have reckoned these powers amongst the simple ideas which make the complex ones of the sorts of substances [2]; though these powers considered in themselves, are truly complex ideas. And in this looser sense I crave leave to be understood, when I name any of these *potentialities* among the simple ideas which we recollect in our minds when we think of *particular substances.* For the powers that are severally in them are necessary to be considered, if we will have true distinct notions of the several sorts of substances.

And why. 8. Nor are we to wonder that powers make a great part of our complex ideas of substances [3]; since their secondary qualities are those which in most of them serve principally to distinguish substances [4] one from another, and commonly make a considerable part of the complex idea of the several sorts of them. For, our senses failing us in the discovery of

---

[1] 'new sensible ideas,' i. e. new simple ideas, in which ideas powers are manifested.

[2] The idea of power is thus virtually an idea of a quality presented in sense.

[3] 'substances'; *material* substances, not *spiritual*, are what he has in view in §§ 7-14.

[4] Cf. Bk. II. ch. viii. §§ 10, 13, 14, 23-26.

the bulk, texture, and figure of the minute parts of bodies, on which their real constitutions and differences depend[1], we are fain to make use of their secondary qualities as the characteristical notes and marks whereby to frame ideas of them in our minds, and distinguish them one from another: all which secondary qualities, as has been shown, are nothing but bare powers. For the colour and taste of opium are, as well as its soporific or anodyne virtues, mere powers, depending on its primary qualities[2], whereby it is fitted to produce different operations on different parts of our bodies.

9. The ideas that make our complex ones of corporeal substances, are of these three sorts[3]. First, the ideas of the primary qualities of things, which are discovered by our senses, and are in them even when we perceive them not; such are the bulk, figure, number, situation, and motion of the parts of bodies; which are really in them, whether we take notice of them or not[4]. Secondly, the sensible secondary qualities, which, depending on these, are nothing but the powers those substances have to produce several ideas in us by our senses; which ideas are not in the things themselves, otherwise than as anything is in its cause[5]. Thirdly,

Three sorts of Ideas make our complex ones of Corporeal Substances.

---

[1] Cf. Bk. II. ch. viii. §§ 10, 13, 14, 23-26.

[2] The dependence of the secondary qualities, which are those that make material substances interesting, upon the primary, is stated less dogmatically elsewhere, e. g. Bk. IV. ch. iii. § 11.

[3] What follows, in this and next section, is nearly a restatement of what was said in ch. viii, regarding the 'qualities and powers of bodies.'

[4] The chief argument of Berkeley, in his reasonings against the *independent* actual existence of bodies, is directed against this assumption—that all the primary qualities in which they are revealed to us, are in them even when they are unperceived by any one. Extension and solidity, he argues, are words that can have no applicability or meaning, in the absence of all percipient activity, any

more than tastes or smells, in the absence of all sentients. All alike are substantiated only in and through the living experience, and active power of percipient spirit—*actually manifested* in the sense experiences of finite spirits, and all *ultimately determined* by the Supreme Spirit. Solids are thus necessarily dependent for their solidity, as much as for their taste, upon percipients; while percipient personality is not in like manner dependent upon them. A percipient person is therefore a *substance* in a way that a solid object cannot be.

[5] With Leibniz the idea of substances is that of an inconceivable number of self-active powers or monads, so that substance is identified with power; and this monadology is then opposed to Spinoza's central conception of *unica substantia*, which issues in a

the aptness we consider in any substance, to give or receive such alterations of primary qualities, as that the substance so altered should produce in us different ideas from what it did before; these are called active and passive powers: all which powers, as far as we have any notice or notion of them, terminate only in sensible simple ideas. For whatever alteration a loadstone has the power to make in the minute particles of iron, we should have no notion of any power it had at all to operate on iron, did not its sensible motion discover it: and I doubt not, but there are a thousand changes, that bodies we daily handle have a power to cause in one another, which we never suspect, because they never appear in sensible effects.

Powers thus make a great Part of our complex Ideas of particular Substances.

10. *Powers* therefore justly make a great part of our complex ideas of substances[1]. He that will examine his complex idea of gold, will find several of its ideas that make it up to be only powers; as the power of being melted, but of not spending itself in the fire; of being dissolved in *aqua regia*, are ideas as necessary to make up our complex idea of gold, as its colour and weight: which, if duly considered, are also nothing but different powers. For, to speak truly, yellowness is not actually in gold, but is a power in gold to produce that idea in us by our eyes, when placed in a due light: and the heat, which we cannot leave out of our ideas of the sun, is no more really in the sun, than the white colour it introduces into wax. These are both equally powers in the sun, operating, by the motion and figure of its sensible parts, so on a man, as to make him have the idea of heat; and

---

universe of logical consequences emptied of causal efficiency. Locke does not explain what he means by 'powers existing in substances'— things 'existing in their causes'; but he distinguishes between the *direct* manifestation of a material substance, in its primary qualities (more or less,) and its indirect manifestation of itself, in its 'effects' on other substances. Is a cause, i.e. a substance (material or spiritual), when it

is regarded as 'containing active and passive powers,' rightly conceived to be *identical* with the sum of its effects, the effects balancing what is subtracted from the cause by its activity?

[1] That is to say, a thing *is* substantially, *in a great measure*, what it *does*. Leibniz would say that it is simply what it does, or is able to do,—its substance consisting of its doing. He finds the *what* of things exclusively in their activities or behaviour.

so on wax, as to make it capable to produce in a man the BOOK II.
idea of white[1].

CHAP.
XXIII.

11. Had we senses acute enough to discern the minute
particles of bodies, and the real constitution on which their
sensible qualities depend, I doubt not but they would produce quite different ideas in us: and that which is now the
yellow colour of gold, would then disappear, and instead of
it we should see an admirable texture of parts, of a certain
size and figure. This microscopes plainly discover to us;
for what to our naked eyes produces a certain colour, is, by
thus augmenting the acuteness of our senses, discovered to be
quite a different thing; and the thus altering, as it were,
the proportion of the bulk of the minute parts of a coloured
object to our usual sight, produces different ideas from what
it did before. Thus, sand or pounded glass, which is opaque,
and white to the naked eye, is pellucid in a microscope; and
a hair seen in this way, loses its former colour, and is, in a
great measure, pellucid, with a mixture of some bright spark-
ling colours, such as appear from the refraction of diamonds,
and other pellucid bodies. Blood, to the naked eye, appears
all red; but by a good microscope, wherein its lesser parts
appear, shows only some few globules of red, swimming in
a pellucid liquor, and how these red globules would appear,
if glasses could be found that could yet magnify them a
thousand or ten thousand times more, is uncertain[2].

The now
secondary
Qualities
of Bodies
would dis-
appear, if
we could
discover
the pri-
mary ones
of their
minute
Parts.

---

[1] To the practical mind of Locke,
the inquiry, *how substances behave*, i. e.
what their powers are, is more interesting than speculation about the
' obscure' idea of ' substance in
general.' The opposite points of view
at which philosophy is regarded by
the utilitarian Locke, and the purely
speculative Spinoza, appear in their
treatment of substance. Locke dwells
on the inevitable inadequacy of *our*
ideas of individual substances—material
and spiritual; avoiding the ultimate
intellectual necessity to substantiate
phenomena, of which, nevertheless,
he cannot get rid. To the *acosmic*
Spinoza, the individual things and

persons that are all in all with Locke
disappear in the barren notion of One
Substance, the only real existence, in
which all that appears is logically
contained; while the *res particulares*
of Locke are referred to the inadequate ideas of imagination and experience, in a merely individual and
temporal knowledge, wherein nothing
is seen from the philosophic point of
view of the One Substance, or *sub
specie æternitatis*.

[2] That is to say, the sensible or
secondary qualities of bodies would
appear other than they now do, if our
senses were acute enough to perceive
the texture and motions of the atoms

BOOK II.

—✛—

CHAP.
XXIII.

Our
Faculties
for Dis-
covery
of the
Qualities
and
powers
of Sub-
stances
suited to
our State.

12. The infinite wise Contriver of us, and all things about us, hath fitted our senses, faculties, and organs, to the conveniences of life, and the business we have to do here. We are able, by our senses, to know and distinguish things : and to examine them so far as to apply them to our uses, and several ways to accommodate the exigences of this life. We have insight enough into their admirable contrivances and wonderful effects, to admire and magnify the wisdom, power, and goodness of their Author. Such a knowledge as this, which is suited to our present condition, we want not faculties to attain. But it appears not that God intended we should have a perfect, clear, and adequate knowledge of them : that perhaps is not in the comprehension of any finite being. We are furnished with faculties (dull and weak as they are) to discover enough in the creatures to lead us to the knowledge of the Creator, and the knowledge of our duty ; and we are fitted well enough with abilities to provide for the conveniences of living : these are our business in this world[1]. But were our senses altered, and made much quicker and acuter, the appearance and outward scheme of things would have quite another face to us ; and, I am apt to think, would be inconsistent with our being, or at least wellbeing, in this part of the universe which we inhabit. He that considers how little our constitution is able to bear a remove into parts of this air, not much higher than that we commonly breath in, will have reason to be satisfied, that in this globe of earth

---

of which they consist ; which are, he assumes, the physical causes of the sensations that we refer to the so-called ' secondary' qualities. The superficial appearances which substances make to our senses are (so far) real ; but more acute senses, or greater ability on our part to interpret the appearances presented to us, would discover deeper and truer relations, and these in turn deeper and truer still ; our complex ideas of the substance thus undergoing a gradual correction and development, as we advance from our first crude interpretations of what is presented in sense.

[1] Cf. Introduction, § 5. Material substances, by their respective natures, produce effects, or are manifested in sense, in ways practically related to us and our functions in the universe. Deeper and truer ideas of them than those man can attain to, being inconsistent with *his* purpose in the universe, are withheld from his finite intelligence. The *ultimate* construction of sensible things is accordingly a mystery to the ' human understanding' and we can only go a little way towards substituting their ultimate meaning for those ' first appearances' in sense which are apt to delude.

allotted for our mansion, the all-wise Architect has suited our organs, and the bodies that are to affect them, one to another. If our sense of hearing were but a thousand times quicker than it is, how would a perpetual noise distract us. And we should in the quietest retirement be less able to sleep or meditate than in the middle of a sea-fight[1]. Nay, if that most instructive of our senses, seeing, were in any man a thousand or a hundred thousand times more acute than it is by the best microscope, things several millions of times less than the smallest object of his sight now would then be visible to his naked eyes, and so he would come nearer to the discovery of the texture and motion of the minute parts of corporeal things; and in many of them, probably get ideas of their internal constitutions: but then he would be in a quite different world from other people: nothing would appear the same to him and others: the visible ideas of everything would be different. So that I doubt, whether he and the rest of men could discourse concerning the objects of sight, or have any communication about colours, their appearances being so wholly different. And perhaps such a quickness and tenderness of sight could not endure bright sunshine, or so much as open daylight; nor take in but a very small part of any object at once, and that too only at a very near distance. And if by the help of such *microscopical eyes*[2] (if I may so call them) a man could penetrate further than ordinary into the secret composition and radical texture of bodies, he would not make any great advantage by the change, if such an acute sight would not serve to conduct him to the market and exchange; if he could not see things he was to avoid, at a convenient distance; nor distinguish things he had to do with by those sensible qualities others do. He that was sharp-sighted enough to see the configuration of the

---

[1] Thus paraphrased by Pope in the *Essay on Man* :—

'If nature thundered in his opening
    ears,
And stunned him with the music of
    the spheres,
How would he wish that Heaven
    had left him still,

The whispering zephyr and the
    purling rill!'

[2] So Pope again :—

'Why has not man a microscopic
    eye?
For this plain reason—man is not
    a fly.'

BOOK II.
CHAP.
XXIII.

minute particles of the spring of a clock, and observe upon what peculiar structure and impulse its elastic motion depends, would no doubt discover something very admirable: but if eyes so framed could not view at once the hand, and the characters of the hour-plate, and thereby at a distance see what o'clock it was, their owner could not be much benefited by that acuteness; which, whilst it discovered the secret contrivance of the parts of the machine, made him lose its use.

Conjecture about the corporeal organs of some Spirits.

13. And here give me leave to propose an extravagant conjecture of mine, viz. That since we have some reason (if there be any credit to be given to the report of things that our philosophy cannot account for) to imagine, that Spirits can assume to themselves bodies of different bulk, figure, and conformation of parts—whether one great advantage some of them have over us may not lie in this, that they can so frame and shape to themselves organs of sensation or perception, as to suit them to their present design, and the circumstances of the object they would consider. For how much would that man exceed all others in knowledge, who had but the faculty so to alter the structure of his eyes, that one sense, as to make it capable of all the several degrees of vision which the assistance of glasses (casually at first lighted on) has taught us to conceive? What wonders would he discover, who could so fit his eyes to all sorts of objects, as to see when he pleased the figure and motion of the minute particles in the blood, and other juices of animals, as distinctly as he does, at other times, the shape and motion of the animals themselves? But to us, in our present state, unalterable organs, so contrived as to discover the figure and motion of the minute parts of bodies, whereon depend those sensible qualities we now observe in them, would perhaps be of no advantage. God has no doubt made them so as is best for us in our present condition. He hath fitted us for the neighbourhood of the bodies that surround us, and we have to do with; and though we cannot, by the faculties we have, attain to a perfect knowledge of things, yet they will serve us well enough for those ends above-mentioned, which are our great concernment. I beg my reader's pardon for laying before him so wild a fancy con-

cerning the ways of perception of beings above us; but how extravagant soever it be, I doubt whether we can imagine anything about the knowledge of angels but after this manner, some way or other in proportion to what we find and observe in ourselves. And though we cannot but allow that the infinite power and wisdom of God may frame creatures with a thousand other faculties and ways of perceiving things without them than what we have, yet our thoughts can go no further than our own: so impossible it is for us to enlarge our very guesses beyond the ideas received from our own sensation and reflection[1]. The supposition, at least, that angels do sometimes assume bodies, needs not startle us; since some of the most ancient and most learned Fathers of the church seemed to believe that they had bodies: and this is certain, that their state and way of existence is unknown to us.

14. But to return to the matter in hand,—the ideas we have of substances, and the ways we come by them. I say, our *specific* ideas of substances are nothing else but *a collection of a certain number of simple ideas, considered as united in one thing.* These ideas of substances, though they are commonly simple apprehensions, and the names of them simple terms, yet in effect are complex and compounded. Thus the idea which an Englishman signifies by the name swan, is white colour[2], long neck, red beak, black legs, and whole feet, and all these of a certain size, with a power of swimming in the water, and making a certain kind of noise, and perhaps, to a man who has long observed this kind of birds, some other properties: which all terminate in sensible simple ideas, all united in one common subject[3].

---

[1] So with the Sirian traveller in the *Micromegas* of Voltaire. Isaac Taylor's *Physical Theory of another Life* contains some ingenious speculations in analogy with the text.

[2] Black swans have since been found.

[3] Here again Locke emphasises the empirical side of 'substance,' gradually determined by the contingent presentations of sense, leaving in the background the ultimate rational constitution of the 'general idea.' He is habitually averse to the *intellectus sibi permissus*, as apt to intrude when men speculate upon 'abstract necessities of reason,' but without adding to a practical knowledge of the behaviour of particular substances.

BOOK II.
—♦—
CHAP.
XXIII.
Our
Ideas of
spiritual
Sub-
stances,
as clear as
of bodily
Sub-
stances.

15. Besides the complex ideas we have of material sensible substances, of which I have last spoken,—by the simple ideas we have taken from those operations of our own minds [1], which we experiment daily in ourselves, as thinking, understanding, willing, knowing, and power of beginning motion, &c., co-existing in some substance, we are able to frame the *complex idea of an immaterial spirit* [2]. And thus, by putting together the ideas of thinking, perceiving, liberty, and power of moving themselves and other things, we have as clear a perception and notion of immaterial substances as we have of material. For putting together the ideas of thinking and willing, or the power of moving or quieting corporeal motion, joined to substance [3], of which we have no distinct idea, we have the idea of an immaterial spirit; and by putting together the ideas of coherent solid parts, and a power of being moved, joined with substance [3], of which likewise we have no positive idea [4], we have the idea of matter. The one is as clear and distinct an idea as the other: the idea of thinking, and moving a body, being as clear and distinct ideas as the ideas of extension, solidity, and being moved. For our idea of substance is equally obscure, or none at all, in both: it is but a supposed I know not what, to support those ideas we call accidents. [[5] It is for want of reflection that we are apt to think that our senses show us nothing but material things. Every act of sensation [6], when duly considered, gives us an equal view of both parts of nature, the corporeal and spiritual. For whilst I know, by seeing or hearing, &c., that there is some corporeal being without me, the object of that

---

[1] Thus Locke throughout makes perception of 'the operations of our own minds' depend on our ideas of them, in the same way as perception of the qualities of external things.

[2] What follows, to the end of § 28, refers to the complex ideas of *spiritual* substances.

[3] 'substance,' i.e. substance 'in general,' abstracted from all the modes in which it is manifested in particular substances.

[4] 'no positive idea.' The abstract

idea of substance could not without self-contradiction be *phenomenalised*, or represented positively in sensuous imagination.

[5] Added in second edition.

[6] Here, and often elsewhere, Locke means by 'sensation' sensuous perception. A more refined analysis distinguishes this perception, alike from the *organic motion*, and from the *sensuous feeling*, with which the affection in the organism is charged.

sensation, I do more certainly know, that there is some spiritual being within me that sees and hears[1]. This, I must be convinced, cannot be the action of bare insensible matter; nor ever could be, without an immaterial thinking being[2].]

16. By the complex idea of extended, figured, coloured, and all other sensible qualities, which is all that we know of it, we are as far from the idea of the substance of body, as if we knew nothing at all[3]: nor after all the acquaintance and familiarity which we imagine we have with matter, and the many qualities men assure themselves they perceive and know in bodies, will it perhaps upon examination be found, that they have any more or clearer primary ideas belonging to body, than they have belonging to immaterial spirit[4].

No Idea of abstract Substance either in Body or Spirit.

17. The primary ideas we have *peculiar to body*, as contra-distinguished to spirit, are the *cohesion of solid, and consequently separable, parts*, and a *power of communicating motion by impulse*. These, I think, are the original ideas proper and peculiar to body; for figure is but the consequence of finite extension[5].

Cohesion of solid parts and Impulse, the primary ideas peculiar to Body.

18. The ideas we have belonging and *peculiar to spirit*, are *thinking*, and *will*, or *a power of putting body into motion by*

Thinking and Motivity

---

[1] This recognises that internal perception or self-consciousness is implied in all external perception or sense-consciousness: and that, not merely in an equipoise; for he says here and elsewhere (e.g. Bk. IV. chh. ix. and xi.) that our 'certainty' of the existence of the spirit that perceives is *greater* than our certainty of the body that is perceived. Berkeley finds absurdity in the *idea* of independent *material* substance, while he acknowledges a *notion* of *spiritual* substance, as implied in the fact that the personal pronoun 'I' is not a meaningless word.

[2] Locke elsewhere suggests that *God* may have *made* material organisms of a certain sort able to think (e.g. Bk. IV. ch. iii. § 6). What he here says is that 'bare matter' is incapable of superseding Supreme Intelligence, as the blind *ultimate* principle of all that is.

[3] But do we not know this much at least of its substance—that it *is* 'extended and figured'? Sometimes Locke seems to accept a merely physical conception of substance, making it consist in the nature, arrangement, and motion of elementary atoms, which might be brought within the range of senses more acute than ours. Here he inclines more to the Aristotelian *substantial form*, which hyperphysically transcends possible modifications of atoms.

[4] This is directed against those who refuse to believe in anything that is supersensible.

[5] Cf. ch. xxi. § 75, and the enumeration of the real or primary qualities of matter in ch. viii. § 9.

BOOK II.

CHAP.
XXIII.

the
primary
Ideas
peculiar to
Spirit.

Spirits
capable of
Motion.

thought, and, which is consequent to it, liberty[1]. For, as body cannot but communicate its motion by impulse to another body, which it meets with at rest, so the mind can put bodies into motion, or forbear to do so, as it pleases[2]. The ideas of *existence, duration,* and *mobility*, are common to them both[3].

19. There is no reason why it should be thought strange, that I make mobility belong to spirit; for having no other idea of motion, but change of distance with other beings that are considered as at rest; and finding that spirits, as well as bodies, cannot operate but where they are; and that spirits do operate at several times in several places, I cannot but attribute change of place to all finite spirits: (for of the Infinite Spirit I speak not here). For my soul, being a real being as well as my body, is certainly as capable of changing distance with any other body, or being, as body itself; and so is capable of motion[3]. And if a mathematician can consider a certain distance, or a change of that distance between two points, one may certainly conceive a distance, and a change of distance, between two spirits; and so conceive their motion, their approach or removal, one from another.

20. Every one finds in himself that his soul can think, will, and operate on his body in the place where that is, but cannot operate on a body, or in a place, an hundred miles distant from it. Nobody can imagine that his soul can think or move a body at Oxford, whilst he is at London; and cannot but know, that, being united to his body, it constantly changes place all the whole journey between Oxford and London, as the coach or horse does that carries him, and I think may be said to be truly all that while in motion: or if that will not be allowed to afford us a clear idea enough

---

[1] This is Locke's explanation of the ambiguous term, 'liberty,' when applied to voluntary activity (cf. ch. xxi). But it may signify, not only (*a*) power to execute what one wills (as with Locke), but (*b*) power to originate volition; and also (*c*) power to conform to reason or duty, instead of the slavery of passion—supremacy of spirit over sense.

[2] Cf. ch. xxi. § 75. Thinking, or 'having ideas,' and will or 'power to produce motion,' are thus the 'primary qualities' of spirit.

[3] Why is 'mobility' thus made a test of the 'reality' of the 'soul'? Cf. ch. xxi. § 75; also ch. xv. § 2, on the place of spirits, and their relations to space.

of its motion, its being separated from the body in death,
I think, will; for to consider it as going out of the body, or
leaving it, and yet to have no idea of its motion, seems to me
impossible.

21. If it be said by any one that it cannot change place,
because it hath none, for the spirits are not *in loco*, but *ubi*;
I suppose that way of talking will not now be of much weight
to many, in an age that is not much disposed to admire, or
suffer themselves to be deceived by such unintelligible ways
of speaking. But if any one thinks there is any sense in that
distinction, and that it is applicable to our present purpose,
I desire him to put it into intelligible English; and then from
thence draw a reason to show that immaterial spirits are not
capable of motion[1]. Indeed motion cannot be attributed to
God; not because he is an immaterial, but because he is an
infinite spirit[2].

22. Let us compare, then, our complex idea of an immaterial spirit with our complex idea of body, and see
whether there be any more obscurity in one than in the
other, and in which most. Our idea of *body*, as I think,
is *an extended solid substance, capable of communicating motion
by impulse*: and our idea of *soul, as an immaterial spirit*, is of
*a substance that thinks, and has a power of exciting motion in
body, by willing, or thought.* These, I think, are our complex
ideas of soul and body, as contradistinguished; and now let
us examine which has most obscurity in it, and difficulty to
be apprehended. I know that people whose thoughts are
immersed in matter, and have so subjected their minds to
their senses that they seldom reflect on anything beyond
them, are apt to say, they cannot comprehend a *thinking* thing,

---

[1] There is a curious 'tang of the cask' in much of this. This is surely an undue inference from the fact, that a *human* spirit cannot exert powers over extra-organic things that are not in contact with its organism. The 'motion' of human spirits means, that the changes which men can produce in the sensible world are, in this life of sense, conditioned by, or limited to, the places which their bodies occupy, and that they cannot operate effectually where their bodies are not. This need not imply that spirit, as revealed in its operations when we reflect, occupies space, can be measured, or is capable of motion. We cannot attribute size or situation to a feeling, a cognition, or a volition.

[2] And so is supposed to fill immensity, and thus constitute a *plenum*; as well as to fill everlasting duration.

BOOK II.

—++—

CHAP.
XXIII.

Cohesion
of solid
Parts in
Body as
hard to be
conceived
as think-
ing in a
Soul.

which perhaps is true: but I affirm, when they consider it well, they can no more comprehend an *extended* thing.

23. If any one says he knows not what it is thinks in him, he means he knows not what the substance is of that thinking thing: No more, say I, knows he what the substance is of that solid thing. Further, if he says he knows not how he thinks, I answer, Neither knows he how he is extended, how the solid parts of body are united, or cohere together to make extension. For though the pressure of the particles of air may account for the cohesion of several parts of matter that are grosser than the particles of air, and have pores less than the corpuscles of air, yet the weight or pressure of the air will not explain, nor can be a cause of the coherence of the particles of air themselves. And if the pressure of the æther [1], or any subtiler matter than the air, may unite, and hold fast together, the parts of a particle of air, as well as other bodies, yet it cannot make bonds for *itself*, and hold together the parts that make up every the least corpuscle of that *materia subtilis*. So that that hypothesis, how ingeniously soever explained, by showing that the parts of sensible bodies are held together by the pressure of other external insensible bodies, reaches not the parts of the æther itself; and by how much the more evident it proves, that the parts of other bodies are held together by the external pressure of the æther, and can have no other conceivable cause of their cohesion and union, by so much the more it leaves us in the dark concerning the cohesion of the parts of the corpuscles of the æther itself: which we can neither conceive without parts, they being bodies, and divisible, nor yet how their parts cohere, they wanting that cause of cohesion which is given of the cohesion of the parts of all other bodies.

24. But, in truth, the pressure of any ambient fluid, how great soever, can be no intelligible cause of the cohesion of the solid parts of matter. For, though such a pressure may

---

[1] He refers to James Bernoulli, who tried to explain the coherence of the parts of bodies, and their consequent extension, by the pressure of ether, hypothetically assumed—in his essay *De Gravitate Etheris* (1680). The Bernoullis, like the Gregories, were for generations illustrious in natural philosophy.

hinder the avulsion of two polished superficies, one from another, in a line perpendicular to them, as in the experiment of two polished marbles ; yet it can never in the least hinder the separation by a motion, in a line parallel to those surfaces. Because the ambient fluid, having a full liberty to succeed in each point of space, deserted by a lateral motion, resists such a motion of bodies, so joined, no more than it would resist the motion of that body were it on all sides environed by that fluid, and touched no other body ; and therefore, if there were no other cause of cohesion, all parts of bodies must be easily separable by such a lateral sliding motion. For if the pressure of the æther be the adequate cause of cohesion, wherever that cause operates not, there can be no cohesion. And since it cannot operate against a lateral separation, (as has been shown,) therefore in every imaginary plane, intersecting any mass of matter, there could be no more cohesion than of two polished surfaces, which will always, notwithstanding any imaginable pressure of a fluid, easily slide one from another. So that perhaps, how clear an idea soever we think we have of the extension of body, which is nothing but the cohesion of solid parts, he that shall well consider it in his mind, may have reason to conclude, That it is as easy for him to have a clear idea how the soul thinks as how body is extended. For, since body is no further, nor otherwise, extended, than by the union and cohesion of its solid parts, we shall very ill comprehend the extension of body, without understanding wherein consists the union and cohesion of its parts ; which seems to me as incomprehensible as the manner of thinking, and how it is performed.

25. I allow it is usual for most people to wonder how any one should find a difficulty in what they think they every day observe. Do we not see (will they be ready to say) the parts of bodies stick firmly together ? Is there anything more common ? And what doubt can there be made of it ? And the like, I say, concerning thinking and voluntary motion. Do we not every moment experiment it in ourselves, and therefore can it be doubted ? The matter of fact is clear, I confess ; but when we would a little nearer look into it, and consider how it is done, there I think we are at a loss,

We can as little understand how the parts cohere in extension, as how our spirits perceive or move.

both in the one and the other; and can as little understand how the parts of body cohere, as how we ourselves perceive or move. I would have any one intelligibly explain to me, how the parts of gold, or brass, (that but now in fusion were as loose from one another as the particles of water, or the sands of an hour-glass,) come in a few moments to be so united, and adhere so strongly one to another, that the utmost force of men's arms cannot separate them? A considering man will, I suppose, be here at a loss to satisfy his own, or another man's understanding.

The cause of coherence of atoms in extended substances incomprehensible.

26. The little bodies that compose that fluid we call water, are so extremely small, that I have never heard of any one, who, by a microscope, (and yet I have heard of some that have magnified to ten thousand; nay, to much above a hundred thousand times,) pretended to perceive their distinct bulk, figure, or motion; and the particles of water are also so perfectly loose one from another, that the least force sensibly separates them. Nay, if we consider their perpetual motion, we must allow them to have no cohesion one with another; and yet let but a sharp cold come, and they unite, they consolidate; these little atoms cohere, and are not, without great force, separable. He that could find the bonds that tie these heaps of loose little bodies together so firmly; he that could make known the cement that makes them stick so fast one to another, would discover a great and yet unknown secret: and yet when that was done, would he be far enough from making the extension of body (which is the cohesion of its solid parts) intelligible, till he could show wherein consisted the union, or consolidation of the parts of those bonds, or of that cement, or of the least particle of matter that exists. Whereby it appears that this primary and supposed obvious quality of body will be found, when examined, to be as incomprehensible as anything belonging to our minds, and a solid extended substance as hard to be conceived as a thinking immaterial one, whatever difficulties some would raise against it.

The supposed pressure brought to

27. For, to extend our thoughts a little further, that pressure which is brought to explain the cohesion of bodies is as unintelligible as the cohesion itself. For if matter be

considered, as no doubt it is, finite, let any one send his
contemplation to the extremities of the universe, and there
see what conceivable hoops, what bond he can imagine to
hold this mass of matter in so close a pressure together;
from whence steel has its firmness, and the parts of a diamond
their hardness and indissolubility. If matter be finite, it must
have its extremes; and there must be something to hinder it
from scattering asunder. If, to avoid this difficulty, any one
will throw himself into the supposition and abyss of infinite
matter, let him consider what light he thereby brings to the
cohesion of body, and whether he be ever the nearer making
it intelligible, by resolving it into a supposition the most
absurd and most incomprehensible of all other: so far is our
extension of body (which is nothing but the cohesion of solid
parts) from being clearer, or more distinct, when we would
inquire into the nature, cause, or manner of it, than the idea
of thinking.

28. Another idea we have of body is, *the power of communication of motion by impulse*; and of our souls, *the power of
exciting motion by thought.* These ideas, the one of body, the
other of our minds, every day's experience clearly furnishes
us with: but if here again we inquire how this is done, we are
equally in the dark. For, in the communication of motion by
impulse, wherein as much motion is lost to one body as is got
to the other, which is the ordinariest case, we can have no
other conception, but of the passing of motion out of one body
into another; which, I think, is as obscure and inconceivable
as how our minds move or stop our bodies by thought, which
we every moment find they do. The increase of motion by
impulse, which is observed or believed sometimes to happen,
is yet harder to be understood. We have by daily experience
clear evidence of motion produced both by impulse and by
thought; but the manner how, hardly comes within our comprehension: we are equally at a loss in both. So that, however we consider motion, and its communication, either from
body or spirit, the idea which belongs to spirit is at least as
clear as that which belongs to body. And if we consider the
active power of moving, or, as I may call it, motivity, it is
much clearer in spirit than body; since two bodies, placed by

one another at rest, will never afford us the idea of a power in the one to move the other, but by a borrowed motion: whereas the mind every day affords us ideas of an active power of moving of bodies; and therefore it is worth our consideration, whether active power be not the proper attribute of spirits, and passive power of matter. Hence may be conjectured that created spirits are not totally separate from matter, because they are both active and passive. Pure spirit, viz. God, is only active; pure matter is only passive; those beings that are both active and passive, we may judge to partake of both. But be that as it will, I think, we have as many and as clear ideas belonging to spirit as we have belonging to body, the substance of each being equally unknown to us; and the idea of thinking in spirit, as clear as of extension in body; and the communication of motion by thought, which we attribute to spirit, is as evident as that by impulse, which we ascribe to body. Constant experience makes us sensible of both these, though our narrow understandings can comprehend neither. For, when the mind would look beyond those original ideas we have from sensation or reflection, and penetrate into their causes, and manner of production, we find still it discovers nothing but its own short-sightedness [1].

Summary. 29. To conclude. Sensation convinces us that there are solid extended substances; and reflection, that there are thinking ones: experience assures us of the existence of such beings, and that the one hath a power to move body by impulse, the other by thought; this we cannot doubt of. Experience, I say, every moment furnishes us with the clear ideas both of the one and the other. But beyond these ideas, as received from their proper sources, our faculties will not reach. If we would inquire further into their nature, causes, and manner, we perceive not the nature of extension clearer than we do of thinking. If we would explain them any further, one is as easy as the other; and there is no more

---

[1] 'The ultimate cause of the *impressions* which arise from the senses is perfectly inexplicable by human reason.' (Hume, *Treatise*, pt. i. sect. 5.)

difficulty to conceive how *a substance we know not* should,
by thought, set body into motion, than how *a substance we*
know not should, by impulse, set body into motion. So that
we are no more able to discover wherein the ideas belonging
to body consist, than those belonging to spirit. From whence
it seems probable [1] to me, that the simple ideas we receive
from sensation and reflection are the boundaries of our
thoughts; beyond which the mind, whatever efforts it would
make, is not able to advance one jot; nor can it make any
discoveries, when it would pry into the nature and hidden
causes of those ideas.

30. So that, in short, the idea we have of spirit, compared
with the idea we have of body, stands thus : the substance of
spirits is unknown to us; and so is the substance of body
equally unknown to us [2]. Two primary qualities or properties

[1] He here rests the main thesis of the *Essay* on the ground of probability. The particular substances that exist can be known by us only in the manifestations which they make of themselves, and the perceived changes which they cause; though if we had other senses, or additional faculties of reflection, we might discover much in material and in spiritual substances that we are now ignorant of. But to know them perfectly we should need to know all the relations of each substance to every other substance, which presupposes omniscience. Locke however seems to imply that even such knowledge must remain ignorant of ' substance.'

[2] The independent or substantive existence of solid, extended, and moveable things is what Berkeley afterwards argued against as an illusion, when he raised the question, What is to be understood by *matter*? The notion of corporeal substance is in his view not merely difficult but self-contradictory, when matter is put in antithesis to thought; while the substantive, i.e. independent, existence of our own thinking being is manifested by our consciousness of it. We are thus

conscious of a spiritual substance, but we have no perception, nor consciousness in any way, of material substance, all even of the so-called primary qualities of matter revealing their necessary dependence upon a percipient, when we examine them carefully. Thus when Hylas objects that, according to this reasoning, it should follow, that what is called a spiritual substance is only ' a system of floating ideas,' Philopous replies,—' I know or am conscious of my own ideas ; and that *I myself* am not my ideas, but somewhat else, a thinking active *principle*, that perceives, knows, wills, and operates about ideas. But I am not in like manner conscious either of the existence or essence of *matter*. On the contrary, I know that nothing inconsistent can exist, and that the existence of matter implies an inconsistency. Further, I know what I mean when I affirm that there is a spiritual substance, or support of ideas, that is, that a spirit knows and perceives ideas. But I do not know what is meant when it is said, that an *unperceiving* substance hath inherent in it and supports either ideas or the archetypes of ideas. There is therefore upon the whole no parity of case between

BOOK II.
CHAP.
XXIII.

of body, viz. solid coherent parts and impulse, we have distinct clear ideas of: so likewise we know, and have distinct clear ideas, of two primary qualities or properties of spirit, viz. thinking, and a power of action ; i. e. a power of beginning or stopping several thoughts or motions. We have also the

spirit and matter.' (*Third Dialogue.*) That spirit as well as matter is only an aggregate of *abstract manifestations*, without a *concrete substance* manifested, so that all substance is impossible, was the essence of Hume's scepticism. 'For my part,' he argues, 'when I enter most intimately into what I call *myself* I always stumble on some *particular perception or other.* I can never catch myself at any time without a perception. We only ' feign the continued existence of the perceptions of our senses, and run into the notion of a soul, self, or substance.' (*Treatise,* pt. iv. sect. 6.) Language breaks down under the stress of this analysis, and Hume has to contradict himself in order to state it. The substantiality of spirit is thus explained by Lotze :— ' We have found it impossible to conceive the world as built up out of a disconnected multiplicity of real elements of matter ; just as little, on the other hand, have we considered individual souls to be indestructible existences : to us they and these occasions mean simply actions of the one genuine Being or Existence ; only that they are gifted with the strange capacity, which no knowledge can further explain, of feeling and knowing *themselves* as active centres of a life which goes out from them. Only because they do this, and so far as they do this, do we give them the name of *existences* or *substances.* Still we have so named them ; and now the question arises, whether it would not—but for the exigences of imagination—be better to avoid even that name, and the inferences into which it will never cease to seduce men. . . . If the soul in a perfectly dreamless sleep feels and

wills nothing, *is* the soul then at all, and *what* is it ? How often has the answer been given that *if* this could ever happen, the soul *would* have no being. Why have we not had the courage to say that, *as often* as this happens, the soul *is not.* Doubtless if the [human] soul were alone in the world, it would be impossible to understand an alternation of existence and non-existence ; but why should not *its* life be a melody with pauses, while the prime eternal source still acts, of which the existence and activity of the [human] soul is a single deed, and from which that existence and activity arise. From it again the soul would once more arise, and its new existence would be the *consistent* continuation of the old, so soon as those pauses are gone by, during which the conditions of its reappearance were being reproduced by other deeds of the same Primal Being.' (*Metaphysics,* § 307.) This is to apply to the finite spirit the theory by which Berkeley explains the real and continued existence of sensible things, according to which their interrupted existence in finite percipients is sustained by God. But when Lotze and others translate the continuity of the finite spirit into a ' stream ' of consciousness, is not this substituting a metaphor for a unique, indefinable fact ? If the primal or eternal Substance is the only real substance, and if finite spirits are alternately existent and non-existent, or exist as a stream exists, this must be in a sense that is reconcileable with the retrospect of memory in each person, and with the moral responsibility of the ' new existence ' for the acts of the old existence.

ideas of several qualities inherent in bodies, and have the clear
distinct ideas of them; which qualities are but the various
modifications of the extension of cohering solid parts, and
their motion. We have likewise the ideas of the several modes
of thinking viz. believing, doubting, intending, fearing, hoping;
all which are but the several modes of thinking. We have
also the ideas of willing, and moving the body consequent to
it, and with the body itself too; for, as has been shown, spirit
is capable of motion.

31. Lastly, if this notion of immaterial spirit may have, The
perhaps, some difficulties in it not easily to be explained, we Notion of Spirit
have therefore no more reason to deny or doubt the existence involves
of such spirits, than we have to deny or doubt the existence no more Difficulty
of body; because the notion of body is cumbered with some in it than that of
difficulties very hard, and perhaps impossible to be explained Body.
or understood by us. For I would fain have instanced anything in our notion of spirit more perplexed, or nearer a
contradiction, than the very notion of body includes in it;
the divisibility *in infinitum* of any finite extension involving
us, whether we grant or deny it, in consequences impossible
to be explicated or made in our apprehensions consistent;
consequences that carry greater difficulty, and more apparent
absurdity, than anything can follow from the notion of an
immaterial knowing substance [1].

32. Which we are not at all to wonder at, since we having We know
but some few superficial ideas of things, discovered to us only nothing of things
by the senses from without, or by the mind, reflecting on what beyond
it experiments in itself within, have no knowledge beyond that, our simple Ideas of
much less of the internal constitution, and true nature of things, them.
being destitute of faculties to attain it. And therefore ex-
perimenting and discovering in ourselves knowledge, and the
power of voluntary motion, as certainly as we experiment, or
discover in things without us, the cohesion and separation of
solid parts, which is the extension and motion of bodies; we
have as much reason to be satisfied with our notion of immaterial spirit, as with our notion of body, and the existence of
the one as well as the other. For it being no more a con-

---

[1] Cf. with note on last page.

tradition that thinking should exist separate and independent from solidity, than it is a contradiction that solidity
should exist separate and independent from thinking, they
being both but simple ideas, independent one from another :
and having as clear and distinct ideas in us of thinking,
as of solidity, I know not why we may not as well allow
a thinking thing without solidity, i. e. immaterial, to exist, as
a solid thing without thinking, i. e. matter, to exist ; especially since it is not harder to conceive how thinking should
exist without matter, than how matter should think. For
whensoever we would proceed beyond these simple ideas
we have from sensation and reflection, and dive further into
the nature of things, we fall presently into darkness and
obscurity, perplexedness and difficulties, and can discover
nothing further but our own blindness and ignorance. But
whichever of these complex ideas be clearest, that of body, or
immaterial spirit, this is evident, that the simple ideas that
make them up are no other than what we have received from
sensation or reflection : and so is it of all our other ideas of
substances, even of God himself.

Our com-
plex idea
of God.

33. For if we examine the idea we have of the incomprehensible Supreme Being [1], we shall find that we come by it the
same way ; and that the complex ideas we have both of God,
and separate spirits, are made of the simple ideas we receive
from reflection : v. g. having, from what we experiment in ourselves, got the ideas of existence and duration ; of knowledge
and power ; of pleasure and happiness ; and of several other
qualities and powers, which it is better to have than to be
without ; when we would frame an idea the most suitable we
can to the Supreme Being, we enlarge every one of these with
our idea of infinity ; and so putting them together, make our
complex idea of God [2]. For that the mind has such a power

---

[1] This is again the old refrain. We
are born in ignorance of everything,
and all that we can conceive of things
must consist of their ideas or phenomena, gradually presented either in our
senses, or in the successive operations
of our self-conscious spirits.

[2] In what follows, to the end of
sect. 36, he considers the ideas we can
have of the Divine Substance. He
argues that men can attribute to God
only what is in analogy with the
operations of their own spirits ; as
otherwise the words they apply to God

of enlarging some of its ideas, received from sensation and reflection, has been already shown[1].

would be to them meaningless. This inadequacy of our theological conceptions Locke acknowledges to Anthony Collins (June 29, 1704):—'I am content with my own mediocrity. And though I call the thinking faculty in me, *mind*; yet I cannot, because of that name, equal it in anything to that infinite and incomprehensible Being, which, for want of right and distinct conceptions, is called *mind* also, or *the Eternal Mind*.' What might seem to be an inconsistency between the account of our ideas of God given in this chapter, and that in the fourth Book, is thus referred to by Molyneux (March 2, 1693):—'In Bk. IV. ch. xvii. § 2, you say the existence of all things without us (except only of God) is had by our senses. And in Bk. II. ch. xxiii. §§ 33–36, you show how the idea we have of God is made up of the ideas we have gotten by our senses [i. e. by reflection on ' what we experience in ourselves, or in external sense']. Now this, though no repugnancy, yet to unwary readers may seem one. To me it is plain that in Bk. IV. ch. xvii, you speak barely of the *existence* of God; and in Bk. II. ch. xxiii, you speak of the ideas that are ingredient in the complex idea of God; i. e. you say that " all the ideas ingredient in the idea of God are had from sense," and in Bk. IV you only assert that the *existence* of this God, or that really there *are* united in one Being all these ideas, is had, not from sense, but demonstration.' To which Locke replies (March 28):—'The seeming contradiction is just as you take it, and I hope so clearly expressed that it cannot be mistaken, but by a very unwary reader, who cannot distinguish between an idea in the mind, and the real existence of something out of the mind answering that idea.' Locke explicitly recognises, after Descartes, that we have ideas of 'three

sorts of substances' (cf. ch. xiii. § 18; ch. xxvii. § 2; Bk. IV. chh. ix, x, xi); God alone existing in absolute independence, or *per se*; bodies and finite spirits existing partly *in alio*; because dependent on God for continued existence and all their so-called powers, so that Spinoza conceived them as only modifications of God, and God as the one possible substance.

[1] Cf. ch. xvii. §§ 8–10, 13–20. The self-contradiction implied in an imagination of an infinite quantity, and the demonstrable impossibility of an idea of the infinite *in this sense*, is consistent with a conception (inadequate) of Divine Substance, as revealed to us in and through the presented phenomena of body and spirit. Ability to conceive and know God, ' in part,' according to the imperfect revelation given in our experience of the universe; and also as the necessary rational and moral implicate of this experience, must not be confounded with inability to know or conceive infinitely great or infinitely little quantity, in abstract space or duration; or to know and conceive substance and cause, unrevealed in any phenomena, or in any effects. A conception and knowledge of the universe (τὸ πᾶν), real so far as it goes, is consistent with the inadequacy of that conception and knowledge; and also with the inextricable contradictions in which we become involved when we treat this conception as if it were adequate, and as if limited and one-sided experience could be identified with Omniscience. Hence the 'antinomies' of Kant's 'Dialektik'; and cross-purpose in recent controversy about infinity, and a possible knowledge of it, under the limitations of human thought, with which the names of Cousin, Hamilton, Mansel, and Professor Calderwood are connected.

BOOK II.

CHAP. XXIII.

Our complex idea of God as infinite.

34. If I find that I know some few things, and some of them, or all, perhaps imperfectly, I can frame an idea of knowing twice as many; which I can double again, as often as I can add to number; and thus enlarge my idea of knowledge, by extending its comprehension to all things existing, or possible. The same also I can do of knowing them more perfectly; i.e. all their qualities, powers, causes, consequences, and relations, &c., till all be perfectly known that is in them, or can any way relate to them: and thus frame the idea of infinite or boundless knowledge. The same may also be done of power, till we come to that we call infinite; and also of the duration of existence, without beginning or end, and so frame the idea of an eternal being. The degrees or extent wherein we ascribe existence, power, wisdom, and all other perfections (which we can have any ideas of) to that sovereign Being, which we call God, being all boundless and infinite, we frame the best idea of him our minds are capable of: all which is done, I say, by enlarging those simple ideas we have taken from the operations of our own minds, by reflection; or by our senses, from exterior things, to that vastness to which infinity can extend them [1].

God in his own essence incognisable.

35. For it is infinity, which, joined to our ideas of existence, power, knowledge, &c., makes that complex idea, whereby we represent to ourselves, the best we can, the Supreme Being. For, though in his own essence (which certainly we do not know, not knowing the real essence of a pebble, or a fly, or of our own selves [2]) God be simple and uncompounded; yet I think I may say we have no other idea of him, but a complex one of existence, knowledge, power, happiness, &c., infinite and eternal: which are all distinct ideas, and some of them,

[1] Cf. Descartes, *Méditation Troisième* —'De Dieu; Qu'il existe'; also S. Augustine, *Confess.* lib. x. c. 6; lib. xii. c. 31. See also Berkeley's account in *Alciphron*, Dial. iv, of the manner in which existence and character of God are revealed to man in His language of vision; so that a man may be said to see God in the same way as he sees his fellow men, but with an even fuller and more constant evidence of His existence, in the intelligible order of the world of sense.

[2] Cf. Berkeley, *Principles*, § 101, on the 'exaggeration' of 'our blindness as to the true and real nature of things.' Locke shrinks from the ultimate questions. He does not here consider the relation between matter and finite spirits; or between both and substance in its highest meaning, in God. Cf. Bk. IV. chh. ix, x, xi.

being relative, are again compounded of others: all which being, as has been shown, originally got from sensation and reflection, go to make up the idea or notion we have of God [1].

36. This further is to be observed, that there is no idea we attribute to God, bating infinity, which is not also a part of our complex idea of other spirits. Because, being capable of no other simple ideas, belonging to anything but body, but those which by reflection we receive from the operation of our own minds, we can attribute to spirits no other but what we receive from thence [2]: and all the difference we can put between them, in our contemplation of spirits, is only in the several extents and degrees of their knowledge, power, duration, happiness, &c. For that in our ideas, as well of spirits as of other things, we are restrained to *those we receive from sensation and reflection*, is evident from hence,—That, in our ideas of spirits [3], how much soever advanced in perfection beyond those of bodies, even to that of infinite, we cannot yet have any idea of the manner wherein they discover their thoughts one to another: though we must necessarily conclude that separate spirits, which are beings that have perfecter knowledge and greater happiness than we, must needs have also a perfecter way of communicating their thoughts than we have, who are fain to make use of corporeal signs, and particular sounds; which are therefore of most general use, as being the best and quickest we are capable of. But of immediate communication [4] having

---

[1] That is, we can only conceive God according to our experience of what is highest in ourselves. Our own self-consciousness enables us to presuppose intelligently the Supreme Universal Consciousness; but without the former, the words expressive of the latter could for us have no meaning. Locke always leans to the Deistic conception of God, as an individual spirit among other spirits, rather than as Active Reason, immanent in nature and spirit, the necessary presupposition of all that is actual.

[2] 'from thence,' i. e. from reflection upon the operations from our own minds. 'We cannot ascribe anything to God of which we have not some conception ourselves. Did we not perceive some degrees of wisdom we could not call Him All-wise; did we not feel power and understand what it is we could not ascribe Omnipotence to God. For *our* idea of God is only formed by adding *infinite* to every perfection that we have any knowledge of.' (*Remarks upon the Fable of the Bees*, p. 30, by William Law.) That perfect wisdom and goodness are attributable to God is, according to Locke, an induction from experience, rather than self-evident.

[3] Of 'separate' or unembodied spirits, that is to say.

[4] 'immediate,' i. e. independently of sense organs.

BOOK II.
CHAP.
XXIII.

no experiment in ourselves, and consequently no notion of it at all, we have no idea how spirits, which use not words, can with quickness [1]; or much less how spirits that have no bodies can be masters of their own thoughts, and communicate or conceal them at pleasure, though we cannot but necessarily suppose they have such a power [2].

Recapitulation.

37. And thus we have seen what kind of ideas we have of *substances of all kinds*, wherein they consist, and how we came by them. From whence, I think, it is very evident,

First, That all our ideas of the several *sorts* of substances are nothing but collections of simple ideas : with a supposition of *something* to which they belong, and in which they subsist : though of this supposed something we have no clear distinct idea at all [3].

Secondly, That all the simple ideas, that thus united in one common *substratum,* make up our complex ideas of several *sorts* of substances, are no other but such as we have received from sensation or reflection [4]. So that even in those which we think we are most intimately acquainted with, and that come nearest the comprehension of our most enlarged conceptions, we cannot go beyond those simple ideas. And even in those which seem most remote from all we have to do with, and do infinitely surpass anything we can perceive in ourselves by reflection ; or discover by sensation in other things, we can attain to nothing but those simple ideas, which we originally received from sensation or reflection; as is evident in the complex ideas we have of angels, and particularly of God himself.

Thirdly, That most of the simple ideas that make up our complex ideas of substances, when truly considered, are only *powers*, however we are apt to take them for positive qualities ;

---

[1] 'Can with quickness,' i. e. can communicate with quickness.

[2] Cf. Bk. I. ch. iii. §§ 8–17; Bk. II. ch. xv. §§ 2, 12; Bk. IV. ch. x ; xvii. § 2, regarding our complex idea and knowledge of God, in its gradual development. Our complex idea of God determines for us ultimately the sort of universe we are living in, and is thus the most humanly interesting of all ideas.

[3] The virtue of this 'something' is that, by assuming it, 'simple ideas' or phenomena are transformed from *abstracted modes* into *concrete things.*

[4] So that we cannot attribute intelligently to things, or to God, what we have experienced nothing analogous to in sense or reflection.

v.g. the greatest part of the ideas that make our complex idea of *gold* are yellowness, great weight, ductility, fusibility, and solubility in *aqua regia*, &c., all united together in an unknown *substratum* : all which ideas are nothing else but so many relations to other substances ; and are not really in the gold, considered barely in itself[1], though they depend on those real and primary qualities of its internal constitution [2], whereby it has a fitness differently to operate, and be operated on by several other substances [3].

[1] As its 'primary qualities are.' They are assumed to be really in the thing itself, as they are perceived, and not merely to be revealed in and through its effects in something else.

[2] Cf. ch. viii. § 13, and the many passages, in this and other chapters, in which dependence of the secondary qualities and powers of bodies upon their primary atoms is taken for granted.

[3] This chapter, upon our complex ideas of substances, material and spiritual, including the idea of 'substance in general,' may be compared with Bk. I. ch. iii. § 18; Bk. II. ch. xiii. §§ 17-20; Bk. III. ch. vi; Bk. IV. chh. iii, ix-xi. The whole has been the occasion of much criticism and controversy. The chief occasion of Stillingfleet's assault was, that Locke had ' almost discarded substance out of the reasonable part of the world,'—in making the general idea of it ' obscure,' ' an idea of something we know not what,' and ' which we neither have nor can have by sensation or reflection '; while in fact it is the foundation of all reasoning about the concrete and real. Locke's first *Letter* (pp. 4-50), and third *Letter* (pp. 370-408), show how difficult it was for him to reconcile a due recognition of the idea of ' substance ' with a strict interpretation of his theory of the origin of our ideas, and of the dependence of knowledge upon ' clear and distinct' ideas. Instead of an idea formed by arbitrary generalisation, it virtually becomes, in the exigencies of controversy, a *simple idea* which we are obliged to form, because the want of it is repugnant in reason to our first conceptions of things ; while its ' obscurity' makes him confess, more explicitly than in the *Essay*, that ideas need not be irrational because they are obscure, and that this and other ideas at the root of knowledge are necessarily inadequate and mysterious. The development of speculation soon discarded *material* substance out of the world; for to Berkeley it ' became evident that there is not any other substance than spirit, or that which perceives'; while Hume, unable to find ' any impression corresponding to the general idea of substance,' in discarding substance altogether, illustrated the intellectual value and significance of an idea that must be presupposed as the alternative to philosophic nihilism. Locke and Hume in this relation are compared in an essay by Edmund Koenig, *Über den Substanzbegriff bei Locke und Hume* (Leipsig, 1881), one of the signs of revived interest in Locke in Germany. Green, among recent English critics, sees scepticism latent in Locke, inasmuch as, while reality implies substance, Locke tells us that it is only ' complex idea,' made arbitrarily by the individual mind, not, like our 'simple ideas,' taken from things themselves—a mere fiction of the mind, which has no existence in the things known—all which Locke himself often and emphatically repudiates in his Letters to Stillingfleet.

CHAPTER XXIV.

OF COLLECTIVE IDEAS OF SUBSTANCES.

BOOK II.
—+—
CHAP.
XXIV.
A collec-
tive idea
is one
Idea.

1. BESIDES these complex ideas of several *single* substances, as of man, horse, gold, violet, apple, &c., the mind hath also complex *collective* ideas of substances ; which I so call, because such ideas are made up of many particular substances considered together, as united into one idea, and which so joined are looked on as one ; v.g. the idea of such a collection of men as make an *army*, though consisting of a great number of distinct substances, is as much one idea as the idea of a man : and the great collective idea of all bodies whatsoever, signified by the name *world*, is as much one idea as the idea of any the least particle of matter in it ; it sufficing to the unity of any idea, that it be considered as one representation or picture, though made up of ever so many particulars.

2. These collective ideas of substances the mind makes, by its power of composition, and uniting severally either simple or complex ideas into one, as it does, by the same faculty, make the complex ideas of particular substances, consisting of an aggregate of divers simple ideas, united in one substance. And as the mind, by putting together the repeated ideas of unity, makes the collective mode, or complex idea, of any number, as a score, or a gross, &c.,—so, by putting together several particular substances, it makes collective ideas of substances, as a troop, an army, a swarm, a city, a fleet ; each of which every one finds that he represents to his own mind by one idea, in one view ; and so under that notion considers those several things as perfectly one, as one ship, or one atom. Nor is it harder to conceive how an army of ten thousand men should make one idea, than how a man should make one idea ;

it being as easy to the mind to unite into one the idea of a
great number of men, and consider it as one, as it is to unite
into one particular all the distinct ideas that make up the
composition of a man, and consider them all together as one.

3. Amongst such kind of collective ideas are to be counted Artificial
most part of artificial things, at least such of them as are things
made up of distinct substances: and, in truth, if we consider made up of
all these collective ideas aright, as *army, constellation, uni-* distinct
verse, as they are united into so many single ideas, they are substances
are our
but the artificial draughts of the mind; bringing things very collective
remote, and independent on one another, into one view, the Ideas.
better to contemplate and discourse of them, united into one
conception, and signified by one name. For there are no
things so remote, nor so contrary, which the mind cannot, by
this art of composition, bring into one idea; as is visible in
that signified by the name *universe* [1].

---

[1] 'Universe' sometimes means the system of sensible things only; again, the system of finite things and finite spirits—'the creation'; again, all that exists, or the worlds of matter and spirit, united in God, i.e. τὸ πᾶν. Locke's ultimate idea of τὸ πᾶν seems to be—an indefinite number of finite *substances*, placed and timed, and the Divine substance;—with their *modes*, which may be considered abstractly, in simple or mixed combinations, and either finite or infinite in quantity; and existing in infinitely numerous *relations* to one another, only a few of which, and these imperfectly, can be formed into the complex ideas of a human understanding.

CHAPTER XXV.

OF RELATION.

1. Besides the ideas, whether simple or complex, that the mind has of things as they are in themselves, there are others it gets from their comparison one with another[1]. The understanding, in the consideration of anything, is not confined to that precise object: it can carry any idea as it were beyond itself, or at least look beyond it, to see how it stands in con-

---

[1] It is the relations, *considered abstractly*, which *particular substances* may have with one another that Locke has in view in what follows, not the relational constitution of knowledge as such. He here enters on our ideas of possible relations of substances to one another, in virtue of their respective qualities and powers. This is in natural sequence to the preceding account,—first of the *simple ideas* in which things around us, and our own mental operations, are manifested, or which are suggested by the manifestations; then of the simple and mixed *modes* of those manifestations, which the mind arbitrarily, or under intellectual necessity, abstracts from the substances in which they appear; next of the idea of *substance* itself, presupposed in the simple ideas, and in the elaboration of their modes,—all leading up to ideas of relation that result from, or are necessarily involved in, comparison of substances with one another, knowledge of substances being knowledge of these relations in concrete. The chapters on 'complex ideas' may

be regarded as Locke's 'historical' account of the order of intellectual advance in the individual mind, as one gradually becomes aware of what is implied in that rational constitution or meaning of things and life, to the first dim consciousness of which we awake in sense. Green complains that, 'in his account of our complex ideas, Locke explains them under modes, substances, and relations, as if each of these three sorts were independent of the rest' and that he also degrades them, as 'unreal things' of the mind. (Introduction to Hume, pp. 20, 21.) On the contrary, consecutive order and objectivity appear in the narration, when read as a history of the gradual awakening of the individual mind to an ever imperfect interpretation of the reality that is first presented in sense. It must also be kept in view that Locke, in this and the three following chapters, is considering 'relations' as *ideas*, simply apprehended by the mind, reserving for the fourth Book questions about the validity and extent of *knowledge*.

formity to any other. When the mind so considers one thing, that it does as it were bring it to, and set it by another, and carries its view from one to the other—this is, as the words import, *relation* and *respect*; and the denominations given to positive things, intimating that respect, and serving as marks to lead the thoughts beyond the subject itself denominated, to something distinct from it, are what we call *relatives*; and the things so brought together, *related*. Thus, when the mind considers Caius as such a positive being, it takes nothing into that idea but what really exists in Caius; v. g. when I consider him as a man, I have nothing in my mind but the complex idea of the species, man. So likewise, when I say Caius is a white man, I have nothing but the bare consideration of a man who hath that white colour. But when I give Caius the name *husband*, I intimate some other person; and when I give him the name *whiter*, I intimate some other thing: in both cases my thought is led to something beyond Caius, and there are two things brought into consideration. And since any idea, whether simple or complex, may be the occasion why the mind thus brings two things together, and as it were takes a view of them at once, though still considered as distinct: therefore any of our ideas may be the foundation of relation. As in the above-mentioned instance, the contract and ceremony of marriage with Sempronia is the occasion of the denomination and relation of husband; and the colour white the occasion why he is said to be whiter than free-stone.

2. These and the like relations, expressed by relative terms that have others answering them, with a reciprocal intimation, as father and son, bigger and less, cause and effect, are very obvious to every one, and everybody at first sight perceives the relation. For father and son, husband and wife, and such other correlative terms, seem so nearly to belong one to another, and, through custom, do so readily chime and answer one another in people's memories, that, upon the naming of either of them, the thoughts are presently carried beyond the thing so named; and nobody overlooks or doubts of a relation, where it is so plainly intimated. But where languages have failed to give correlative names, there the relation is not always so easily taken notice of. *Concubine* is, no doubt, a relative

name, as well as wife: but in languages where this and the like words have not a correlative term, there people are not so apt to take them to be so, as wanting that evident mark of relation which is between correlatives, which seem to explain one another, and not to be able to exist, but together. Hence it is, that many of those names, which, duly considered, do include evident relations, have been called *external denominations*. But all names that are more than empty sounds must signify some idea, which is either in the thing to which the name is applied, and then it is positive, and is looked on as united to and existing in the thing to which the denomination is given; or else it arises from the respect the mind finds in it to something distinct from it, with which it considers it, and then it includes a relation.

Some seemingly absolute Terms contain Relations.

3. Another sort of relative terms there is, which are not looked on to be either relative, or so much as external denominations: which yet, under the form and appearance of signifying something absolute in the subject, do conceal a tacit, though less observable, relation. Such are the seemingly positive terms of *old, great, imperfect,* &c., whereof I shall have occasion to speak more at large in the following chapters.

Relation different from the Things related.

4. This further may be observed, That the ideas of relation may be the same in men who have far different ideas of the things that are related, or that are thus compared: v. g. those who have far different ideas of a man, may yet agree in the notion of a father; which is a notion superinduced to the substance, or man, and refers only to an act of that thing[1] called man whereby he contributed to the generation of one of his own kind, let man be what it will.

Change of Relation may be without any Change in the things related.

5. The nature therefore of relation consists in the referring or comparing two things one to another; from which comparison one or both comes to be denominated. And if either of those things be removed, or cease to be, the relation ceases, and the denomination consequent to it, though the other receive in itself no alteration at all: v. g. Caius, whom I consider to-day as a father, ceases to be so to-morrow, only by the death of his son, without any alteration made in himself.

---

[1] Locke often applies 'thing' to persons.

Nay, barely by the mind's changing the object to which it compares anything, the same thing is capable of having contrary denominations at the same time : v. g. Caius, compared to several persons, may truly be said to be older and younger, stronger and weaker, &c.

6. Whatsoever doth or can exist, or be considered as one thing is positive : and so not only simple ideas and substances, but modes also, are positive beings : though the parts of which they consist are very often relative one to another : but the whole together considered as one thing, and producing in us the complex idea of one thing, which idea is in our minds, as one picture, though an aggregate of divers parts, and under one name, it is a positive or absolute thing, or idea. Thus a triangle, though the parts thereof compared one to another be relative, yet the idea of the whole is a positive absolute idea. The same may be said of a family, a tune, &c. ; for there can be no relation but betwixt two things considered as two things. There must always be in relation two ideas or things, either in themselves really separate, or considered as distinct, and then a ground or occasion for their comparison.

7. Concerning relation in general, these things may be considered :

First, That there is no one thing, whether simple idea, substance, mode, or relation, or name of either of them, which is not capable of almost an infinite number of considerations in reference to other things : and therefore this makes no small part of men's thoughts and words : v. g. one single man may at once be concerned in, and sustain all these following relations, and many more, viz. father, brother, son, grandfather, grandson, father-in-law, son-in-law, husband, friend, enemy, subject, general, judge, patron, client, professor, European, Englishman, islander, servant, master, possessor, captain, superior, inferior, bigger, less, older, younger, contemporary, like, unlike, &c., to an almost infinite number : he being capable of as many relations as there can be occasions of comparing him to other things, in any manner of agreement, disagreement, or respect whatsoever. For, as I said, relation is a way of comparing or considering two things together, and giving one or both of them some appellation

BOOK II.

CHAP.
XXV.

Our
Ideas of
Relations
often
clearer
than of the
Subjects
related.

from that comparison; and sometimes giving even the relation itself a name.

8. Secondly, This further may be considered concerning relation, that though it be not contained in the real existence of things, but something extraneous and superinduced [1], yet the ideas which relative words stand for are often clearer and more distinct than of those substances to which they do belong. The notion we have of a father or brother is a great deal clearer and more distinct than that we have of a man; or, if you will, *paternity* is a thing whereof it is easier to have a clear idea, than of *humanity*; and I can much easier conceive what a friend is, than what God; because the knowledge of one action, or one simple idea, is oftentimes sufficient to give me the notion of a relation; but to the knowing of any substantial being, an accurate collection of sundry ideas is necessary. A man, if he compares two things together, can hardly be supposed not to know what it is wherein he compares them: so that when he compares any things together, he cannot but have a very clear idea of that relation. *The ideas, then, of relations, are capable at least of being more perfect and distinct in our minds than those of substances* [2]. Because it is commonly hard to know all the simple ideas which are really in any substance, but for the most part easy enough to know the simple ideas that make up any relation I think on, or have a name for: v. g. comparing two men in reference to one common parent, it is very easy to frame the ideas of brothers, without having

---

[1] The so-called 'individualism' and 'nominalism' of Locke appear here. The result deduced by Green from this statement is, that 'real existence can belong only to the present momentary act of consciousness, and to that alone' (p. 35); and that 'the really existent is the unmeaning, so that any statement about it must be impossible' (p. 36). He holds Locke's position to be in antithesis to the conception of 'existence,' as consisting in, or constituted by, *relations*; the withdrawal of which leaves only chaotic feelings,

which are transient, while existence must be permanent. But relations are regarded by Locke only as *abstract possibilities* of something actually existing conformable to them; which become real when embodied or exemplified in particular substances.

[2] That is, our complex ideas of the particular substances which enter into a relation—apart from that in them by which the relation is constituted, and of which we have this 'perfect and distinct idea'—may be obscure and inadequate.

yet the perfect idea of a man. For significant relative words, as well as others, standing only for ideas; and those being all either simple, or made up of simple ones, it suffices for the knowing the precise idea the relative term stands for, to have a clear conception of that which is the foundation of the relation; which may be done without having a perfect and clear idea of the thing it is attributed to. Thus, having the notion that one laid the egg out of which the other was hatched, I have a clear idea of the relation of *dam* and *chick* between the two cassiowaries in St. James's Park; though perhaps I have but a very obscure and imperfect idea of those birds themselves.

9. Thirdly, Though there be a great number of considerations wherein things may be compared one with another, and so a multitude of relations, yet they all terminate in, and are concerned about those simple ideas, either of sensation or reflection, which I think to be the whole materials of all our knowledge. To clear this, I shall show it in the most considerable relations that we have any notion of; and in some that seem to be the most remote from sense or reflection : which yet will appear to have their ideas from thence, and leave it past doubt that the notions we have of them are but certain simple ideas, and so originally derived from sense or reflection [1].

Relations all terminate in simple Ideas.

10. Fourthly, That relation being the considering of one thing with another which is extrinsical to it, it is evident that all words that necessarily lead the mind to any other ideas than are supposed really to exist in that thing to which the words are applied are relative words: v.g. a *man, black, merry, thoughtful, thirsty, angry, extended*; these and the like are all absolute, because they neither signify nor intimate anything but what does or is supposed really to exist in the man thus

Terms leading the Mind beyond the Subject denominated, are relative.

---

[1] Relations presuppose correlative substances, in which they are embodied, and which are the occasion of our intellectual apprehension of the relation. Now Locke holds that the only conceivable correlatives must be manifested in simple ideas, either of sensation or reflection. Simple ideas give the indispensable content to the relational concept or category, and also the condition which must be fulfilled in order to an awakening of our apprehension of it; so that all relations, in this respect, 'terminate in, and are concerned with,' simple phenomena presented in the senses or when we reflect.

BOOK II.

CHAP.
XXV.

All relatives made up of simple ideas.

denominated[1]; but *father, brother, king, husband, blacker, merrier*, &c., are words which, together with the thing they denominate, imply also something else separate and exterior to the existence of that thing.

11. Having laid down these premises concerning relation in general, I shall now proceed to show, in some instances, how all the ideas we have of relation are made up, as the others are, only of simple ideas; and that they all, how refined or remote from sense soever they seem, terminate at last in simple ideas[2]. I shall begin with the most comprehensive relation[3], wherein all things that do, or can exist, are concerned, and that is the relation of *cause* and *effect*: the idea whereof, how derived from the two fountains of all our knowledge, sensation and reflection, I shall in the next place consider.

[1] All predicates imply relation.

[2] Unless simple ideas, i.e. qualities of substances, are presented in sense and reflection, none of the relations of the substances can be apprehended by us. Relation presupposes reality, but the relations into which real terms enter may be real as the terms themselves; and as the same term may enter into various relations, it depends upon the purpose or caprice of the elaborating mind whether it is placed under one relation or another.

[3] There is a point of view (and Locke inclines to it) at which the philosophy that regards phenomena *as successive, in a certain order of changes*, i.e. under the relation of physical sequence, is the philosophy of everything that exists.

CHAPTER XXVI.

OF CAUSE AND EFFECT, AND OTHER RELATIONS.

1. In the notice that our senses take of the constant vicissi- tude of things[1], we cannot but observe that several particular, both qualities and substances, begin to exist; and that they receive this their existence from the due application and operation of some other being. From this observation we get our ideas of *cause* and *effect*. *That which produces any simple or complex idea* we denote by the general name, *cause*, and *that which is produced, effect*[2]. Thus, finding that in that substance

BOOK II.

CHAP.
XXVI.

Whence
the Ideas
of cause
and effect
got.

---

[1] 'The centre round which metaphysical inquiries, so far as their essence is concerned, will always move is the fact of *change* . . . Change completely dominates the whole range of reality. Its various forms—becoming and decay, action and suffering, motion and development—are, as a matter of fact, and history, the constant occasion of those inquiries, which, as forming a doctrine of the flux of *things*, in opposition to the permanent being of *ideas*, have from antiquity been united under the name of metaphysic.' (Lotze, *Metaphysics*, § 1.) Notwithstanding the all-comprehending character of the relation of causality, Locke devotes only two sections to our idea of it, except so far as the discussion is anticipated in the chapter on 'Power.' Cf. ch. xx. §§ 1, 4, where he refers the idea of 'power' to external and internal observation and inductive inference. In his first *Letter* to Stillingfleet he grants that it involves a necessary principle of reason. That ' everything that has a beginning must have a cause is a true principle of reason, which we come to know by perceiving that *the idea of beginning to be* is *necessarily connected* with *the idea of some operation*; and the idea of *operation* with *something operating, which we call a cause*' (p. 135).

[2] 'Should any one pretend to define a cause, by saying it is something productive of another, 'tis evident he would say nothing. For what does he mean by *production*? Can he give any definition of it, that will not be the same with that of causation? If he can, I desire it may be produced. If he cannot, he here runs in a circle, and gives a synonymous term instead of a definition.' (Hume, *Treatise*, pt. iii. sect. ii.) 'Conduce,' 'operate,' 'produce,' 'make,' are terms which profess to carry a new idea, implying that causality is a relation that means more than mere phenomenal contiguity and succession.

which we call wax, fluidity, which is a simple idea that was not in it before, is constantly produced by the application of a certain degree of heat we call the simple idea of heat, in relation to fluidity in wax, the cause of it, and fluidity the effect. So also, finding that the substance, wood, which is a certain collection of simple ideas so called, by the application of fire, is turned into another substance, called ashes; i.e., another complex idea, consisting of a collection of simple ideas, quite different from that complex idea which we call wood ; we consider fire, in relation to ashes, as cause, and the ashes, as effect. So that whatever is considered by us to conduce or operate to the producing any particular simple idea, or collection of simple ideas, whether substance or mode, which did not before exist, hath thereby in our minds[1] the relation of a cause, and so is denominated by us.

Creation Generation, making Alteration.

2. Having thus, from what our senses are able to discover in the operations of bodies[2] on one another, got the notion of cause and effect, viz. that a cause is that which makes any other thing, either simple idea, substance, or mode, begin to be ; and an effect is that which had its beginning from some other thing ; the mind finds no great difficulty to distinguish the several originals of things into two sorts :—

First, When the thing is wholly made new, so that no part thereof did ever exist before ; as when a new particle of

---

[1] ' Hath thereby in our minds,' i. e. by a *necessity* of which Locke takes no account here, although, when he concludes the necessity of an eternal mind, as an application of the principle of causality (Bk. IV. ch. x), he implies the necessity and universality in the idea of causation that is recognised in his *Letter* to Stillingfleet (p. 434, note 1). Hume himself thus recognises necessity :— ' Shall we then rest content with these two relations of *contiguity* and *succession*, as affording a complete idea of causation ? By no means. An object may be contiguous and prior to another, without being considered as its cause. There is a NECESSARY CONNECTION to be taken into consideration ; and that relation is of much greater importance than any of the other two above-mentioned.' (*Treatise*, pt. iii. sect. ii.) But then he proceeds to melt down the ' necessity ' into an issue of custom.

[2] ' our senses . . . bodies.' Here he makes the phenomena presented by bodies, the occasion of our having the idea of causality, whereas, in ch. xxi, ' the clearest idea of active power ' is said to be got ' from spirit,' by reflection. Now the senses present phenomena passing into other phenomena, but not what is signified by efficiency and origination : mere sense moreover does not afford an idea that is necessary in reason, and so of universal application, although universal ideas terminate in, and are concerned about those of sense.

matter doth begin to exist, *in rerum natura*, which had before
no being [1], and this we call *creation*.

Secondly, When a thing is made up of particles, which did all of them before exist; but that very thing, so constituted of pre-existing particles, which, considered all together, make up such a collection of simple ideas, had not any existence before, as this man, this egg, rose, or cherry, &c. And this, when referred to a substance, produced in the ordinary course of nature by internal principle, but set on work by, and received from, some external agent, or cause, and working by insensible ways which we perceive not, we call *generation*. When the cause is extrinsical, and the effect produced by a sensible separation, or juxta-position of discernible parts, we call it *making*; and such are all artificial things. When any simple idea is produced, which was not in that subject before, we call it *alteration*. Thus a man is generated, a picture made; and either of them altered, when any new sensible quality or simple idea is produced in either of them, which was not there before: and the things thus made to exist, which were not there before, are effects; and those things which operated to the existence, causes. In which, and all other cases, we may observe, that the notion of cause and effect has its rise from [2] ideas received by sensation or reflection; and that this relation, how comprehensive soever, terminates at last in them [3]. For to have the idea of cause and effect, it suffices to consider any simple idea or substance, as beginning to exist, by the operation of some other, without knowing the manner of that operation [4].

---

[1] Does this mean no actual existence; though it existed potentially in the Supreme Power? The question brings us back to the δύναμις and ἐνέργεια of Aristotle. The two sorts of cause here distinguished correspond to the *uncaused* causation, exemplified in free moral agency, and the *caused* causes of physical science; each of which (as formerly noted) involves what is mysterious—the former an inconceivable beginning, the latter an inconceivable regress into mysterious infinity.

[2] 'has its rise from'—i.e. was occasioned by, and 'concerned with.' 'Reflection' is here conjoined with 'sensation,' each giving occasion to the idea.

[3] Inasmuch as all the causes and effects of which we can have ideas must be conceived by us as either *material* or *spiritual* substances—named causes, because changes are referred to them, or refunded into them.

[4] Locke prefers to deal with the *idea*

3. Time and place are also the foundations of very large relations; and all finite beings at least are concerned in them. But having already shown in another place [1] how we get those ideas, it may suffice here to intimate, that most of the denominations of things received from *time* are only relations. Thus, when any one says that Queen Elizabeth lived sixty-nine, and reigned forty-five years, these words import only the relation of that duration to some other, and mean no more but this, That the duration of her existence was equal to sixty-nine, and the duration of her government to forty-five annual revolutions of the sun; and so are all words, answering, *How long?* Again, William the Conqueror invaded England about the year 1066; which means this, That, taking the duration from our Saviour's time till now for one entire great length of time, it shows at what distance this invasion was from the two extremes; and so do all words of time answering to the question, *When*, which show only the distance of any point of time from the period of a longer duration, from which we measure, and to which we thereby consider it as related [2].

Some
ideas of
Time
supposed
positive
and found
to be
relative.

4. There are yet, besides those, other words of time, that ordinarily are thought to stand for positive ideas, which yet will, when considered, be found to be relative; such as are, young, old, &c., which include and intimate the relation

of causality in the concrete, rather than with the abstract and ultimate idea. His account of what we mean by a cause and an effect refers each particular sequence to data of sense, but fails to show that sense explains the idea of efficiency in the cause; and fails to explain the intellectual inability to conceive change uncaused, or the intellectual obligation to assume that every change has been caused—all which seems to be involved in our complex idea of the relation. Yet, as already noted, he presupposes this universality and necessity when he applies the idea, in his proof of the existence of sensible things, and still more in his 'demonstration' of the existence of God. (Cf. Bk. IV. chh. x, xi.) In order to

be thus applicable, the idea of causality must be more than an empirical generalisation, from either external or internal sense — data which give too narrow a basis for a universal and absolute conclusion. But Locke's account of the idea of causality seems to contain in solution both the empirical and the rational elements, which controversy has since articulately evolved.

[1] Cf. ch. v. § 1; ch. vii. § 9; chh. xiii and xiv.

[2] We have to conceive 'time' relatively to the concrete ideas or 'phenomena,' by which it is measured, and in which it is manifested to the sensuous imagination.

anything has to a certain length of duration, whereof we have
the idea in our minds. Thus, having settled in our thoughts
the idea of the ordinary duration of a man to be seventy
years, when we say a man is *young*, we mean that his age is
yet but a small part of that which usually men attain to ;
and when we denominate him *old*, we mean that his duration
is run out almost to the end of that which men do not usually
exceed. And so it is but comparing the particular age or
duration of this or that man, to the idea of that duration
which we have in our minds, as ordinarily belonging to that
sort of animals : which is plain in the application of these
names to other things ; for a man is called young at twenty
years, and very young at seven years old : but yet a horse
we call old at twenty, and a dog at seven years, because
in each of these we compare their age to different ideas
of duration, which are settled in our minds as belonging to
these several sorts of animals, in the ordinary course of
nature. But the sun and stars, though they have outlasted
several generations of men, we call not old, because we do not
know what period God hath set to that sort of beings. This
term belonging properly to those things which we can observe
in the ordinary course of things, by a natural decay, to come
to an end in a certain period of time ; and so have in our
minds, as it were, a standard to which we can compare the
several parts of their duration ; and, by the relation they bear
thereunto, call them young or old ; which we cannot, therefore, do to a ruby or a diamond, things whose usual periods
we know not.

5. The relation also that things have to one another in Relations
of Place
and Ex-
tension.
their *places* and distances is very obvious to observe ; as
above, below, a mile distant from Charing-cross, in England,
and in London. But as in duration, so in extension and
bulk, there are some ideas that are relative which we signify
by names that are thought positive ; as *great* and *little* are
truly relations. For here also, having, by observation, settled
in our minds the ideas of the bigness of several species of
things from those we have been most accustomed to, we make
them as it were the standards, whereby to denominate the
bulk of others. Thus we call a great apple, such a one as

is bigger than the ordinary sort of those we have been used to ; and a little horse, such a one as comes not up to the size of that idea which we have in our minds to belong ordinarily to horses ; and that will be a great horse to a Welchman, which is but a little one to a Fleming ; they two having, from the different breed of their countries, taken several-sized ideas to which they compare, and in relation to which they denominate their great and their little [1].

Absolute Terms often stand for Relations.

6. So likewise weak and strong are but relative denominations of power, compared to some ideas we have at that time of greater or less power. Thus, when we say a weak man, we mean one that has not so much strength or power to move as usually men have, or usually those of his size have ; which is a comparing his strength to the idea we have of the usual strength of men, or men of such a size. The like when we say the creatures are all weak things ; weak there is but a relative term, signifying the disproportion there is in the power of God and the creatures [2]. And so abundance of words, in ordinary speech, stand only for relations (and perhaps the greatest part) which at first sight seem to have no such signification : v. g. the ship has necessary stores. *Necessary* and *stores* are both relative words ; one having a relation to the accomplishing the voyage intended, and the other to future use. All which relations, how they are confined to, and terminate in ideas derived from sensation or reflection, is too obvious to need any explication [3].

[1] ‘ Ces remarques,’ says Leibniz, ‘ sont très-bonnes.’ ‘ Space,’ like time, is conceived by us relatively to the sensuous objects by which it is measured, and in which it ‘terminates.’ They form the standard of its quantity, in particular instances.

[2] We interpret ‘ power,’ like duration and space, as embodied in the effects of which, in each particular example, it is the correlative.

[3] Terms which signify relations are ‘ explained,’ according to the analogy of the *Essay*, by that in the data of sense which manifests and measures their meaning. But if relation involves more than any of its particular manifestations, Locke’s account is inadequate. Relation is more than the things or persons or modes related ; on the other hand, an idea of relation presupposes related terms. A sensuous philosophy tends to rest in isolated substances, on which relations are contingently superinduced ; extreme idealism tends to reduce actual reality to a network of empty, colourless relations.

CHAPTER XXVII.

[OF IDENTITY AND DIVERSITY [1].]

[I. ANOTHER occasion the mind often takes of comparing, is the very being of things, when, considering *anything as existing at any determined time and place*, we compare it with *itself existing at another time*, and thereon form the ideas of *identity* and *diversity*. When we see anything to be in any place in any instant of time, we are sure (be it what it will) that it is that very thing, and not another which at that same time exists in another place, how like and undistinguishable soever it may be in all other respects : and in this consists *identity*, when the ideas it is attributed to vary not at all from what they were that moment wherein we consider their former existence, and to which we compare the present. For we never finding, nor conceiving it possible, that two things of the same kind should exist in the same place at the same time, we rightly conclude, that, whatever exists anywhere at any time, excludes all of the same kind, and is there itself alone. When therefore we demand whether anything be the *same* or no [2], it refers always to something that existed such

---

[1] This chapter was added in the second edition, on the suggestion of Molyneux. See Locke's letters to Molyneux, Aug. 23, 1693, and March 8, 1695.

[2] Cf. Bk. I. ch. iii. §§ 4, 5 on the origin of the idea of identity. The numerical sameness or identity here in view must be distinguished from generic or specific unity, i. e. *similarity*, or the sameness that consists in a community of quality. When several objects are alike, one description will equally apply to any of them, and hence they are all said to be of the *same* nature or appearance. When we say, ' This table is made of the *same* wood as that other,' we only mean that the material in the one is undistinguishable in quality from that of which the other was constructed. This is the identity of similarity. Numerical sameness, on the contrary, does not necessarily imply outward similarity in the changing phenomena of the same substance.

a time in such a place, which it was certain, at that instant, was the same with itself, and no other. From whence it follows, that one thing cannot have two beginnings of existence, nor two things one beginning; it being impossible for two things of the same kind to be or exist in the same instant, in the very same place; or one and the same thing in different places[1]. That, therefore, that had one beginning, is the same thing; and that which had a different beginning in time and place from that, is not the same, but diverse[2]. That which has made the difficulty about this relation has been the little care and attention used in having precise notions of the things to which it is attributed[3].

Identity of Substances.

2. We have the ideas but of three sorts of substances: 1. *God.* 2. *Finite intelligences.* 3. *Bodies*[4].

First, *God* is without beginning, eternal, unalterable, and everywhere, and therefore concerning his identity there can be no doubt[5].

Secondly, *Finite spirits* having had each its determinate time and place of beginning to exist, the relation to that time and place will always determine to each of them its identity, as long as it exists.

Thirdly, The same will hold of every *particle of matter*, to which no addition or subtraction of matter being made, it is the same. For, though these three sorts of substances, as we term them, do not exclude one another out of the same place, yet we cannot conceive but that they must necessarily each

---

[1] Leibniz refuses to recognise these *external* relations of time and place as adequate to constitute numerical sameness, and argues for an *internal* principle of distinction (*principium individuationis*), in virtue of which things and persons are distinguishable in themselves, independently of their times and places. This is adversely criticised by Kant.

[2] So Hobbes, in *First Grounds of Philosophy*, ch. xi. §§ 1, 2, where he seeks to explain what it is for one thing to differ from another, and in what identity and individuation consist.

[3] Accordingly he proceeds to distin-

guish our idea of the relation of identity, as it is found in substances and modes, organisms, men, and persons.

[4] Cf. ch. xxiii; also Bk. IV. chh. ix, x, xi on the three ultimate substances—the *Ego*, God, and the World: God alone so existing as to need the existence of no other; the other two existing in dependence on God. The ultimate relations of the three give rise to the antinomies of Kant.

[5] It is with regard to *finite* substances—organisms in which body is blended with spirit as in man—that the perplexities in the idea of identity arise which Locke meets in this chapter.

of them exclude any of the same kind out of the same place: or else the notions and names of identity and diversity would be in vain, and there could be no such distinctions of substances, or anything else one from another[1]. For example: could two bodies be in the same place at the same time; then those two parcels of matter must be one and the same, take them great or little; nay, all bodies must be one and the same. For, by the same reason that two particles of matter may be in one place, all bodies may be in one place: which, when it can be supposed, takes away the distinction of identity and diversity of one and more, and renders it ridiculous. But it being a contradiction that two or more should be one, identity and diversity are relations and ways of comparing well founded, and of use to the understanding.

3. All other things being but modes or relations ultimately terminated in substances[2], the identity and diversity of each particular existence of them too will be by the same way determined: only as to things whose existence is in succession, such as are the actions of finite beings, v. g. *motion* and *thought*, both which consist in a continued train of succession, concerning *their* diversity there can be no question: because each perishing the moment it begins, they cannot exist in different times, or in different places, as permanent beings can at different times exist in distant places; and therefore no motion or thought, considered as at different times, can be the same, each part thereof having a different beginning of existence[3]. Identity of modes and relations.

4. From what has been said, it is easy to discover what is so much inquired after, the *principium individuationis*; and that, it is plain, is existence itself; which determines a being of any sort to a particular time and place, incommunicable to Principium Individuationis.

---

[1] Cf. ch. xxiii. §§ 19-21, as to Locke's meaning, where he supposes spirits to be subject to relations of place, and speaks of God as omnipresent.

[2] Locke thus recognises the *supremacy* of the complex idea of substance among our complex ideas. Modes and relations may be abstracted for separate consideration, as in this Book; but they are all ultimately referable to, and terminate in, the substances that are (so far) manifested to us in the simple ideas we have of them.

[3] Substances are thus distinguished from modes, by their independence and persistence. Hume virtually analyses knowledge and existence into Locke's abstract 'modes' and 'relations.'

two beings of the same kind [1]. This, though it seems easier to conceive in simple substances or modes; yet, when reflected on, is not more difficult in compound ones [2], if care be taken to what it is applied: v. g. let us suppose an atom, i.e. a continued body under one immutable superficies, existing in a determined time and place; it is evident, that, considered in any instant of its existence, it is in that instant the same with itself. For, being at that instant what it is, and nothing else, it is the same, and so must continue as long as its existence is continued; for so long it will be the same, and no other. In like manner, if two or more atoms be joined together into the same mass, every one of those atoms will be the same, by the foregoing rule: and whilst they exist united together, the mass, consisting of the same atoms, must be the same mass, or the same body, let the parts be ever so differently jumbled. But if one of these atoms be taken away, or one new one added, it is no longer the same mass or the same body. In the state of living creatures, their identity depends not on a mass of the same particles, but on something else. For in them the variation of great parcels of matter alters not the identity: an oak growing from a plant to a great tree, and then lopped, is still the same oak; and a colt grown up to a horse, sometimes fat, sometimes lean, is all the while the same horse: though, in both these cases, there may be a manifest change of the parts; so that truly they are not either of them the same masses of matter, though they be truly one of them the same oak, and the other the same horse. The reason whereof is, that, in these two cases— a *mass of matter* and a *living body*—identity is not applied to the same thing [3].

---

[1] Molyneux (March 2, 1693) exhorts Locke to 'insist more particularly and at large on the *principium individuationis.* 'Le principe d'individuation revient, dans les individus, au principe de distinction, dont je viens de parler.' (Leibniz.) Individuality must not be confounded with personality.

[2] 'Compound ones,' e. g. *aggregates* of atoms, as distinguished from the separate particles. He has material substances in view.

[3] The idea we have of our *mental* 'individuality' contained in the consciousness of each *ego* being a *unit*, separated from every other *ego*, with a conscious life that is private, or confined to itself alone, belongs to personality, of which afterwards.

5. We must therefore consider wherein an oak differs from a mass of matter, and that seems to me to be in this, that the one is only the cohesion of particles of matter any how united, the other such a disposition of them as constitutes the parts of an oak ; and such an organization of those parts as is fit to receive and distribute nourishment, so as to continue and frame the wood, bark, and leaves, &c., of an oak, in which consists the vegetable life. That being then one plant which has such an organization of parts in one coherent body, partaking of one common life, it continues to be the same plant as long as it partakes of the same life, though that life be communicated to new particles of matter vitally united to the living plant, in a like continued organization conformable to that sort of plants. For this organization, being at any one instant in any one collection of matter, is in that particular concrete distinguished from all other, and *is* that individual life[1], which existing constantly from that moment both forwards and backwards, in the same continuity of insensibly succeeding parts united to the living body of the plant, it has that identity which makes the same plant, and all the parts of it, parts of the same plant, during all the time that they exist united in that continued organization, which is fit to convey that common life to all the parts so united[2].

6. The case is not so much different in *brutes* but that any one may hence see what makes an animal and continues it the

---

[1] It is only in a loose sense that the ' organisation,' which is visible, can be identified with the ' life ' which is invisible.

[2] He finds the identity of a ' mass ' of unorganised matter in the identity of its aggregated atoms, whereas that of a living organism consists in partici_pation of continuous life on the part of the continuously changing atoms that successively compose the organism. In an organism the fleeting parts are maintained in their organic life by their connection with the whole, while in an inorganic mass the whole is formed and constituted by mere aggregation of the parts. Organisms accordingly seem to be one and the same, in virtue of an immanent principle of life, so that when the parts are separated from the whole they lose their life. A branch separated from a tree, or a limb from an animal body, dissolves into its chemically and mechanically determined elements, from which the life has departed; whereas the separation of a stone into fragments leaves the qualities of the separated parts unaffected by the change. In an organism the parts are connected for a reason, and their union expresses a principle, that is inexplicable under merely mechanical law.

BOOK II.
Chap.
XXVII.

same. Something we have like this in machines, and may serve to illustrate it. For example, what is a watch? It is plain it is nothing but a fit organization or construction of parts to a certain end, which, when a sufficient force is added to it, it is capable to attain. If we would suppose this machine one continued body, all whose organized parts were repaired, increased, or diminished by a constant addition or separation of insensible parts, with one common life, we should have something very much like the body of an animal[1]; with this difference, That, in an animal the fitness of the organization, and the motion wherein life consists, begin together, the motion coming from within; but in machines the force coming sensibly from without, is often away when the organ is in order, and well fitted to receive it.

The Identity of Man.

7. This also shows wherein the identity of the same *man* consists; viz. in nothing but a participation of the same continued life, by constantly fleeting particles of matter, in succession vitally united to the same organized body. He that shall place the identity of man in anything else, but, like that of other animals, in one fitly organized body[2], taken in any one instant, and from thence continued, under one organization of life, in several successively fleeting particles of matter united to it, will find it hard to make an embryo, one of years, mad and sober, the *same* man, by any supposition, that will not make it possible for Seth, Ismael, Socrates, Pilate, St. Austin, and Cæsar Borgia, to be the same man. For if the identity of *soul alone* makes the same *man*; and there be nothing in the nature of matter why the same individual spirit may not be united to different bodies, it will be possible that those men, living in distant ages, and of different tempers, may

---

[1] A watch, by superficial analogy, and yet essential contrast, is an apt illustration of the difference between inorganic masses, conditioned only by mechanical and chemical laws, and bodies which are one and the same in virtue of their continuous life.

[2] The identity of a *man*, placed in 'one fitly organized body,' is thus a *physical* identity, and is contrasted with the *moral* or *personal* identity considered in the sequel. The identity of a *man* is manifested to the senses, in his visible and tangible organism; identity of a person is manifested to the person himself, primarily in his self-consciousness, and by inferences founded on his organism.

have been the same man : which way of speaking must be
from a very strange use of the word man, applied to an idea
out of which body and shape are excluded [1]. And that way
of speaking would agree yet worse with the notions of those
philosophers who allow of transmigration, and are of opinion
that the souls of men may, for their miscarriages, be detruded
into the bodies of beasts, as fit habitations, with organs suited
to the satisfaction of their brutal inclinations. But yet I
think nobody, could he be sure that the *soul* of Heliogabalus
were in one of his hogs, would yet say that hog were a *man*
or *Heliogabalus*.

8. It is not therefore unity of substance that comprehends Idea of
all sorts of identity, or will determine it in every case ; but to Identity
suited to
conceive and judge of it aright, we must consider what idea the Idea
the word it is applied to stands for : it being one thing to be it is ap-
plied to.
the same *substance*, another the same *man*, and a third the same
person, if *person*, *man*, and *substance*, are three names standing
for three different ideas ;—for such as is the idea belonging to
that name, such must be the identity ; which, if it had been
a little more carefully attended to, would possibly have prevented a great deal of that confusion which often occurs about
this matter, with no small seeming difficulties, especially concerning *personal* identity, which therefore we shall in the next
place a little consider.

9. An animal is a living organized body ; and consequently Same man.
the same animal, as we have observed, is the same continued
life communicated to different particles of matter, as they
happen successively to be united to that organized living body.
And whatever is talked of other definitions, ingenious observation puts it past doubt, that the idea in our minds, of which
the sound man in our mouths is the sign, is nothing else but
of an animal of such a certain form. Since I think I may be
confident, that, whoever should see a creature of his own shape

---

[1] ' Body and shape,' as well as self-
consciousness, being, he assumes, included in the ordinary connotation of
' man,' it is argued that if the consciousness of any man were transferred
to the organism of a horse or a dog, so
that its body became his body, and
its motions were determined by his
volitions, we could not, in propriety
of speech, apply the name *man* to the
living being thus endowed with a
human consciousness, but in ' body
and shape,' a horse or a dog.

or make, though it had no more reason all its life than a cat or a parrot, would call him still a *man*; or whoever should hear a cat or a parrot discourse, reason, and philosophize, would call or think it nothing but a *cat* or a *parrot*; and say, the one was a dull irrational man, and the other a very intelligent rational parrot. [[1] A relation we have in an author of great note [2], is sufficient to countenance the supposition of a rational parrot. His words are:

A rational
Parrot.

'I had a mind to know, from Prince Maurice's own mouth, the account of a common, but much credited story, that I had heard so often from many others, of an old parrot he had in Brazil, during his government there, that spoke, and asked, and answered common questions, like a reasonable creature: so that those of his train there generally concluded it to be witchery or possession; and one of his chaplains, who lived long afterwards in Holland, would never from that time endure a parrot, but said they all had a devil in them. I had heard many particulars of this story, and assevered by people hard to be discredited, which made me ask Prince Maurice what there was of it. He said, with his usual plainness and dryness in talk, there was something true, but a great deal false of what had been reported. I desired to know of him what there was of the first. He told me short and coldly, that he had heard of such an old parrot when he had been at Brazil; and though he believed nothing of it, and it was a good way off, yet he had so much curiosity as to send for it: that it was a very great and a very old one; and when it came first into the room where the prince was, with a great many Dutchmen about him, it said presently, *What a company of white men are here!* They asked it, what

---

[1] What follows within brackets was added in the fourth edition.

[2] Sir William Temple, in his *Memoirs of what passed in Christendom from 1672 to 1679*, p. 66. See Stewart's *Elements*, vol. iii. note H, for remarks on this story, of which he says that ' it must have left a deep impression on the memory of all who have ever read Locke's Essay,' adding that ' more than one of his professed admirers

seemed to recollect little else which they had learned from that work than the story of this parrot.' The story is omitted in the French version of the *Essay*. If we met with an animal in outward appearance a parrot, but possessed of all intellectual and moral faculties supposed to be characteristic of man, should we name that animal a *parrot* or a *man*? This is a verbal question of arbitrary definition.

it thought that man was, pointing to the prince. It answered, *Some General or other.* When they brought it close to him, he asked it, *D'où venez-vous?* It answered, *De Marinnan.* The Prince, *À qui estes-vous?* The parrot, *À un Portugais.* The Prince, *Que fais-tu là?* Parrot, *Je garde les poulles.* The Prince laughed, and said, *Vous gardez les poulles?* The parrot answered, *Oui, moi; et je sçai bien faire*[1]; and made the chuck four or five times that people use to make to chickens when they call them. I set down the words of this worthy dialogue in French, just as Prince Maurice said them to me. I asked him in what language the parrot spoke, and he said in Brazilian. I asked whether he understood Brazilian; he said No, but he had taken care to have two interpreters by him, the one a Dutchman that spoke Brazilian, and the other a Brazilian that spoke Dutch; that he asked them separately and privately, and both of them agreed in telling him just the same thing that the parrot had said. I could not but tell this odd story, because it is so much out of the way, and from the first hand, and what may pass for a good one; for I dare say this Prince at least believed himself in all he told me, having ever passed for a very honest and pious man : I leave it to naturalists to reason, and to other men to believe, as they please upon it ; however, it is not, perhaps, amiss to relieve or enliven a busy scene sometimes with such digressions. whether to the purpose or no.'

10. I have taken care that the reader should have the story at large in the author's own words, because he seems to me not to have thought it incredible; for it cannot be imagined that so able a man as he, who had sufficiency enough to warrant all the testimonies he gives of himself, should take so much pains, in a place where it had nothing to do, to pin so close, not only a man whom he mentions as his friend, but on a Prince in whom he acknowledges

Same man.

---

[1] The parrot was asked, 'Whence come ye?' It replied, 'From Marinnan.' The Prince asked, 'To whom do you belong?' The parrot replied, 'To a Portuguese.' 'What do you there?' asked the Prince. The parrot answered, 'I look after the chickens.' The Prince laughed, and said, '*You* look after the chickens?' The parrot answered, 'Yes, I; and I know well enough how to do it.'

BOOK II.
—•+•—
CHAP.
XXVII.

very great honesty and piety, a story which, if he himself thought incredible, he could not but also think ridiculous[1]. The Prince, it is plain, who vouches this story, and our author, who relates it from him, both of them call this talker a parrot: and I ask any one else who thinks such a story fit to be told, whether, if this parrot, and all of its kind, had always talked, as we have a prince's word for it this one did,—whether, I say, they would not have passed for a race of *rational animals*; but yet, whether, for all that, they would have been allowed to be men, and not *parrots*?] For I presume it is not the idea of a thinking or rational being alone that makes the *idea of a man* in most people's sense: but of a body, so and so shaped, joined to it; and if that be the idea of a man, the same successive body not shifted all at once, must, as well as the same immaterial spirit, go to the making of the same man.

Personal
Identity.

11. This being premised, to find wherein personal identity consists, we must consider what *person* stands for;—which, I think, is a thinking intelligent being[2], that has reason and reflection, and can consider itself as itself, the same thinking thing, in different times and places; which it does only by that consciousness[3] which is inseparable from thinking, and,

---

[1] 'That Locke did not give this story of the rational parrot much credit,' says Stewart, 'may be presumed from the cautious scepticism with which he expresses himself—a scepticism greater than might have been expected from that credulity in the admission of extraordinary facts, of which he has given so many proofs in the first Book of his *Essay*, and which seems to have been the chief defect in his intellectual character.' Leibniz describes a dog heard by him to converse with his master in articulate language. Stewart suggests that this phenomenon might probably be explained, 'by supposing the master of the dog to have possessed that peculiar species of imitative power which is called *ventriloquism*.' The spectacle

of a rational parrot, or a rational dog, 'would be,' Stewart adds, 'in an extreme degree offensive and painful; and it is so in some degree merely when presented to the imagination.' But why should one look with 'horror' at an animal differing in shape very widely from ourselves, but possessing similar powers of reason and speech?' What is 'offensive' in the idea of the number of rational and responsible agents on this planet being greater than we had supposed?

[2] '*Being* and *substance* in this place stand for the same idea.' (Butler.)

[3] To the French version the following note on 'consciousness' (*conscience*) is appended: 'Le mot Anglais est *consciousness*, qu'on pourroit exprimer en Latin par celui de *conscientia*, si su-

as it seems to me, essential to it: it being impossible for any one to perceive without *perceiving* that he does perceive. When we see, hear, smell, taste, feel, meditate, or will anything, we know that we do so. Thus it is always as to our present sensations and perceptions: and by this every one is to himself that which he calls *self*:—it not being considered, in this case, whether the same self be continued in the same or divers substances. For, since consciousness always accompanies thinking, and it is that which makes every one to be what he calls self[1], and thereby distinguishes himself from all other thinking things, in this alone consists personal identity[2], i.e. the sameness of a rational being: and as far as this consciousness can be extended backwards to any past action or thought, so far reaches the identity of that person[3]; it is the same self now it was then; and it is by the same self with this present one that now reflects on it, that that action was done[4].

matur pro actu illo hominis qui *sibi* est conscius. Et c'est en ce sens que les Latins ont souvent employé ce mot, témoin cet endroit de Cicéron (*Epist.* Lib. vi. Epist. 4). En François nous n'avons à nos avis que les mots de *sentiment* et de *conviction* qui respondent en quelque sorte à cette idée. Mais, en plusieurs endroits de ce chapitre, ils ne peuvent qu'exprimer fort imperfectement la pensée de M. Locke.' The term ' consciousness,' in the sense of apprehension by the *ego* of its operations and other states as its own, came into use in the seventeenth century, among the Cartesians and in Locke, who sometimes confuses direct consciousness with the reflex act in which self is *explicitly* recognised. Although recently in almost as constant use with some psychologists as the term ' idea ' is with Locke, ' consciousness,' so often introduced in this chapter, hardly occurs in any other part of the *Essay*. See, however, ch. i. §§ 10–19.

[1] ' Self consciousness,' says Ferrier, ' *creates* the ego '—' a being *makes itself* I by thinking itself I.' Locke and Ferrier so far regard the *cogito* as the presupposition of the *sum*, instead of the *sum* as presupposed in the *cogito*; but in the *Essay* the presupposition refers to the order of experience, according to which our idea of continued identity of person is formed.

[2] That is, any positive idea we have of what identity of person means is that given in memory.

[3] Here identity of person is limited to what is remembered—potentially as well as actually (?) ' Wherein,' asks Berkeley, ' consists identity of person ? Not in *actual* consciousness; for then I am not the same person I was this day twelvemonth, but only while I think of what I then did. Not in *potential*; for then all persons may be the same, for ought we know.' (*C.P.B. Works*, vol. iv. p. 481.)

[4] ' All attempts to define personal identity would but perplex it. Yet there is no difficulty at all in ascertaining the *idea*. For as upon two triangles being compared together, there arises to the mind the idea of *similitude*; or upon twice two and four

BOOK II.
—••—
CHAP.
XXVII.
Con-
sciousness
makes
personal
Identity.

10. But it is further inquired, whether it be the same identical substance. This few would think they had reason to doubt of, if these perceptions, with their consciousness, always remained present in the mind, whereby the same thinking thing would be always consciously present, and, as would be thought, evidently the same to itself. But that which seems to make the difficulty is this, that this consciousness being interrupted always by forgetfulness, there being no moment of our lives wherein we have the whole train of all our past actions before our eyes in one view, but even the best memories losing the sight of one part whilst they are viewing another[1]; and we sometimes, and that the greatest part of our lives, not reflecting on our past selves, being intent on our present thoughts, and in sound sleep having no thoughts at all, or at least none with that consciousness which remarks our waking thoughts[2],—I say, in all these cases, our consciousness being interrupted, and we losing the sight of our past selves, doubts are raised whether we are the same thinking thing, i.e. the same *substance* or no. Which, however reasonable or unreasonable, concerns not *personal* identity at all. The question being what makes the same person; and not whether it be the same identical substance, which always thinks in the same person, which, in this case, matters not at all: different substances, by the same consciousness (where they do partake in it) being united into one person, as well as different bodies by the same life are united into one animal, whose identity is preserved in that change of substances by the unity of one continued life[3]. For, it being the

the idea of *equality*; so likewise upon comparing the consciousness of one-self in any two moments, there as immediately arises to the mind the idea of *personal identity*. . . . By reflecting on that which is myself now, and that which was myself twenty years ago, I *discern* that they are not two, but one and the same self. (Bp. Butler, *Dissertation on Personal Identity*.) And it is the 'idea,' or 'what makes personal identity to ourselves'

that Locke is concerned with, in this Book, which deals with ideas, not with knowledge.

[1] Cf. ch. x. § 9.

[2] Cf. ch. i. §§ 10–17.

[3] In thus pressing a distinction between identity of *substance* and identity of *person*, he seeks to show that the latter is independent of the former, and that the personality is continuous as far as memory (latent as well as patent?) can go, whatever changes of

same consciousness that makes a man be himself to himself, personal identity depends on that only[1], whether it be annexed solely to one individual substance, or can be continued in a succession of several substances[2]. For as far as any intelligent being *can* repeat the idea of any past action with the same consciousness it had of it at first, and with the same consciousness it has of any present action; so far it is the same personal self. For it is by the consciousness it has of its present thoughts and actions, that it is *self to itself* now, and so will be the same self, as far as the same consciousness can extend to actions past or to come[3]; and would be by distance of time, or change of substance, no more two persons, than a man be two men by wearing other clothes to-day than he did yesterday, with a long or a short sleep between: the same consciousness uniting those distant

---

annexed bodily or spiritual substances may take place; especially if (as he elsewhere suggests) the substance of a man is perhaps 'material'—as it may 'have pleased God to make' consciousness one of the qualities or powers of organised matter. All that is essential to the idea of personal identity is, that memory *can* bridge over the apparent interruptions in self-conscious life, whatever substance may be united with that life.

[1] Here 'depends on,' not 'is constituted by,' as in other passages. It is the *terms* which contribute to the relation of personal identity—i. e. self now, and self in the past—in which this relation 'terminates,' that Locke has in view. As to our conviction of the identity of those terms, Butler remarks, 'But though we are certain that we are the same agents, living beings, or substances, now, which we were as far back as our remembrance reaches; yet it is asked whether we may not be deceived in it? And this question may be asked at the end of any demonstration whatever; because it is a question concerning the truth of

perception by memory. And he who can doubt whether *perception by memory* may in this case be depended upon, may doubt also whether *perception by deduction and reasoning* which also include memory, or indeed whether *intuitive perception* can. Here then we can go no further. For it is ridiculous to attempt to prove the truth of those perceptions, whose truth we can no otherwise prove than by other perceptions of exactly the same kind with them, and which there is just the same ground to suspect.' (*Dissertation on Personal Identity.*)

[2] As in a change from the 'natural body' to a 'spiritual body'—the person, and his accountability for his past conscious experience, remaining unchanged.

[3] Making itself the same by its memory of itself, and thus in memory *creating*, and not merely discovering, itself—if the expressions in the text are strictly interpreted; the thinking substance 'contributing to the production' of the successive acts, which acts memory 'unites' in one person. (Cf. p. 415, note 2.)

BOOK II.
CHAP.
XXVII.
Personal
Identity in
Change of
Sub-
stance.

actions into the same person, whatever substances[1] contributed to their production[2].

11. That this is so, we have some kind of evidence in our very bodies, all whose particles, whilst vitally united to this same thinking conscious self, so that *we feel* when they are touched, and are affected by, and conscious of good or harm that happens to them, are a part of ourselves; i. e. of our thinking conscious self. Thus, the limbs of his body are to every one a part of himself; he sympathizes and is concerned for them. Cut off a hand, and thereby separate it from that consciousness he had of its heat, cold, and other affections, and it is then no longer a part of that which is himself, any more than the remotest part of matter. Thus, we see the *substance* whereof personal self consisted at one time may be varied at another, without the change of personal identity; there being no question about the same person, though the limbs which but now were a part of it, be cut off[3].

Person-
ality in
Change of
Sub-
stance.

12. But the question is, Whether if the same substance which thinks be changed, it can be the same person; or, remaining the same, it can be different persons?

And to this I answer: First, This can be no question at all to those who place thought in a purely material animal constitution, void of an immaterial substance. For, whether

---

[1] 'change of substance,' e. g. by transmigration into another body—'whatever substances'—whatever organised body, or other substance.

[2] Can the *same personality*—accountability—be 'annexed' to *two or more substances*, which all contribute to the production of the memory by which the personality is constituted?

[3] 'Je suis aussi de cette opinion, que la conscience, ou le sentiment du moi, *prouve* une identité morale ou personnelle. Je ne voudrais point dire que *l'identité personnelle* et même le *soi* ne demeurent point en nous, et que je ne suis point le *moi* qui ait été dans le berceau, sous prétexte que je ne me souviens plus de rien de tout ce que j'ai fait alors. Il suffit,

pour trouver l'identité morale par soi-même, qu'il y ait une *moyenne liaison de consciosité* d'un état voisin, ou même un peu éloigné à l'autre, quand quelque saut ou intervalle oublié y serait mêlé.' (Leibniz.) When Locke makes personal, i. e. moral identity depend on memory, this may include *potential* memory, in which our whole past conscious experience is possibly retained; and when he suggests the transmigration of one man's memory into the bodies of other men, or even of brutes, this may be taken as an emphatic illustration of the essential dependence of the idea of our personality upon self-consciousness *only*, but not as affirming that this transmigration actually occurs under the present order of things.

their supposition be true or no, it is plain they conceive
personal identity preserved in something else than identity of
substance; as animal identity is preserved in identity of life,
and not of substance[1]. And therefore those who place
thinking in an immaterial substance only, before they can
come to deal with these men, must show why personal
identity cannot be preserved in the change of immaterial substances, or variety of particular immaterial substances, as well
as animal identity is preserved in the change of material substances, or variety of particular bodies: unless they will say,
it is one immaterial spirit that makes the same life in brutes,
as it is one immaterial spirit that makes the same person in
men; which the Cartesians at least will not admit, for fear of
making brutes thinking things too.

13. But next, as to the first part of the question, Whether, Whether
if the same thinking substance (supposing immaterial sub- in Change
of think-
stances only to think) be changed, it can be the same person? ing Sub-
I answer, that cannot be resolved but by those who know stances
there can
what kind of substances they are that do think[2]; and whether be one
the consciousness of past actions can be transferred from Person.
one thinking substance to another[3]. I grant were the same
consciousness the same individual action it could not: but
it being a present representation of a past action, why it
may not be possible, that that may be represented to the
mind to have been which really never was, will remain to
be shown. And therefore how far the consciousness of past
actions is annexed to any individual agent, so that another

---

[1] The animal organism is continually changing its particles, and this,
according to Locke, is change of the
' material substance.' Consciousness
that he is the same *person*, cannot be
consciousness that he is the same *substance*, to one who makes his body his
substance.

[2] He maintains (ch. xxiii. §§ 5, 15,
&c.) that we have as clear (or as
obscure) an idea of what spiritual substances are as of material substances.

[3] How does Locke thus distinguish
the spiritual substance from the self

that is given in consciousness? Is not
a person a spiritual substance manifested? Here again he uses words which
seem to imply that a substance, material
or spiritual, is one thing, and its manifestations of itself another and different
thing, by which too the substance is
concealed rather than revealed. But is
not our idea of personality rather the
highest form in which substance can
be conceived by us? On this subject
see Lotze's *Metaphysics*, Bk. III. ch. i.
passim, especially the reference to
Kant, § 244.

cannot possibly have it, will be hard for us to determine, till we know what kind of action it is that cannot be done without a reflex act of perception accompanying it, and how performed by thinking substances, who cannot think without being conscious of it. But that which we call the same consciousness, not being the same individual act, why one intellectual substance may not have represented to it, as done by itself, what *it* never did, and was perhaps done by some other agent—why, I say, such a representation may not possibly be without reality of matter of fact, as well as several representations in dreams are, which yet whilst dreaming we take for true—will be difficult to conclude from the nature of things [1]. And that it never is so, will by us, till we have clearer views of the nature of thinking substances, be best resolved into the goodness of God; who, as far as the happiness or misery of any of his sensible creatures is concerned in it, will not, by a fatal error of theirs, transfer from one to another that consciousness which draws reward or punishment with it [2]. How far this may be an argument against those who would place thinking in a system of fleeting animal spirits, I leave to be considered. But yet, to return to the question before us, it must be allowed, that, if the same consciousness (which, as has been shown, is quite a different thing from the same numerical figure or motion in body) can be transferred from one thinking substance to another, it will be possible that two thinking substances may make but one person. For the same consciousness being preserved, whether in the same or different substances, the personal identity is preserved [3].

---

[1] In other words, we cannot be deceived in our presentative, but we may in our representative experience.

[2] Under the natural order of things, which we are obliged to accept in faith, the identity apparent to the person who feels himself the same, with its implied moral responsibility, is intransferable in fact.

[3] 'According to Mr. Locke, we may always be sure that we are the same persons, that is, the same accountable agents or beings, now which we were as far back as our remembrance reaches: or as far as a perfectly just and good God will cause it to reach.' (Perronet's *Vindication of Locke*, p. 21.) The last clause suggests a conscious revival of the latent stores of memory, which may include all the past experience of the person.

14. As to the second part of the question, Whether the same immaterial substance remaining, there may be two distinct persons; which question seems to me to be built on this,—Whether the same immaterial being, being conscious of the action of its past duration, may be wholly stripped of all the consciousness of its past existence, and lose it beyond the power of ever retrieving it again [1]: and so as it were beginning a new account from a new period, have a consciousness that *cannot* reach beyond this new state. All those who hold pre-existence are evidently of this mind; since they allow the soul to have no remaining consciousness of what it did in that pre-existent state, either wholly separate from body, or informing any other body; and if they should not, it is plain experience would be against them [2]. So that personal identity, reaching no further than consciousness [3] reaches, a pre-existent spirit not having continued so many ages in a state of silence, must needs make different persons. Suppose a Christian Platonist or a Pythagorean should, upon God's having ended all his works of creation the seventh day, think his soul hath existed ever since; and should imagine it has revolved in several human bodies; as I once met with one, who was persuaded his had been the *soul* of Socrates (how reasonably I will not dispute; this I know, that in the post he filled, which was no inconsiderable one, he passed for a very rational man, and the press has shown that he wanted not parts or learning;)—would any one say, that he, being not conscious of any of Socrates's actions or thoughts, could be the same *person* with Socrates [4]? Let any one reflect upon himself, and conclude that he has in himself an immaterial spirit, which is that which thinks in him, and, in the constant

BOOK II.
—✦—
CHAP.
XXVII.
Whether,
the same
immaterial
Substance
remaining,
there can
be two
Persons.

---

[1] There being in that case not only no actual, but no potential memory of a past conscious life.

[2] Hardly so, if the Platonic interpretation of the universal ideas of reason, as reminiscence of what we were conscious of, in a pre-existing state, is taken literally, as rendered in Wordsworth's 'Ode on Intimations of Immortality.'

[3] 'Consciousness,' i. e. memory, including its latent possibilities.

[4] But what if the conscious experience of Socrates, is all the while *latent* in him, and capable of being recollected by him, as on the thread of *his* consciousness? When the recollection occurs, Locke would say, he finds himself the same person who then went under that name. Locke, is satirised in Martinus Scriblerus for his paradoxical illustrations of the idea of personal identity.

BOOK II.   change of his body keeps him the same: and is that which he
CHAP.   calls *himself*: let him also suppose it to be the same soul that
XXVII.   was in Nestor or Thersites, at the siege of Troy, (for souls
being, as far as we know anything of them, in their nature
indifferent to any parcel of matter, the supposition has no
apparent absurdity in it,) which it may have been, as well as
it is now the soul of any other man : but he now having no
consciousness of any of the actions either of Nestor or
Thersites, does or can he conceive himself the same person
with either of them ?   Can he be concerned in either of their
actions'? attribute them to himself, or think them his own,
more than the actions of any other men that ever existed?
So that this consciousness, not reaching to any of the actions
of either of those men, he is no more one *self* with either of
them than if the soul or immaterial spirit that now informs
him had been created, and began to exist, when it began to
inform his present body; though it were never so true, that
the same *spirit* that informed Nestor's or Thersites' body
were numerically the same that now informs his[1].   For this
would no more make him the same person with Nestor, than
if some of the particles of matter that were once a part of
Nestor were now a part of this man; the same immaterial
substance, without the same consciousness, no more making
the same person, by being united to any body, than the same
particle of matter, without consciousness, united to any body,
makes the same person.   But let him once find himself conscious of any of the actions of Nestor, he then finds himself
the same person with Nestor.

The body,   15. And thus may we be able, without any difficulty, to
as well as   conceive the same person at the resurrection[2], though in a
the soul,

---

[1] That is, he cannot have the *idea* of himself now, as one and the same with either of them ; being unable, by memory, to connect his present con- sciousness with theirs.   The supposed identity of ' spiritual substance' does not carry with it the idea of personal responsibility for the actions of Nestor, or of Thersites, unless he also finds himself conscious of their actions as having been once his own.   But is memory the only means for testing or discovering one's personal identity?

[2] One of Stillingfleet's charges against the *Essay* was, that its doctrine regarding personality and personal identity was inconsistent with the Christian doctrine of the resurrection of the body.   For sameness of person, in Locke's account of our idea of

body not exactly in make or parts the same which he had here,—the same consciousness going along with the soul that inhabits it. But yet the soul alone, in the change of bodies, would scarce to any one but to him that makes the soul the man, be enough to make the same man. For should the soul of a prince, carrying with it the consciousness of the prince's past life, enter and inform the body of a cobbler, as soon as deserted by his own soul, every one sees he would be the same *person* with the prince, accountable only for the prince's actions: but who would say it was the same *man*? The body too goes to the making the man, and would, I guess, to everybody determine the man in this case, wherein the soul, with all its princely thoughts about it, would not make another man: but he would be the same cobbler to every one besides himself[1]. I know that, in the ordinary way of speaking, the same person, and the same man, stand for one and the same thing. And indeed every one will always have a liberty to speak as he pleases, and to apply what articulate sounds to what ideas he thinks fit, and change them as often as he pleases. But yet, when we will inquire what makes the same *spirit, man,* or *person,* we must fix the ideas of spirit, man, or person in our minds; and having resolved with ourselves what we mean by them, it will not be hard to determine, in either of them, or the like, when it is the same, and when not[2].

---

personal identity, is indifferent to sameness of body. 'My idea of personal identity,' Locke replies, 'makes the same body not to be necessary to making the same person, either here or after death; and even in this life the particles of the bodies of the same persons change every moment, and there is thus no such identity in the *body* as in the *person*.' Moreover, while the resurrection of the dead is revealed in scripture, we find 'no such express words there as that the body shall rise, or the resurrection of the body; and though I do not question that the dead shall be raised with bodies, as matter of revelation, I think

it our duty to keep close to the words of the scripture.' (Cf. Bk. IV. ch. xviii. § 7.) The question of the identity of the risen body, with any or all the ever fluctuating bodies with which the person has been connected in this life, is irrelevant to Christianity.

[1] Because sameness of person is directly revealed only to the person, or spiritual substance, whose identity is in question; but to all others only indirectly, by those visible signs from which we infer the existence and continued identity of other men.

[2] 'No identity (other than perfect likeness) in any individuals besides

BOOK II.
Chap.
XXVII.
Con-
sciousness
alone
unites
actions
into the
same
Person.

16. But though the same immaterial substance or soul does not alone, wherever it be, and in whatsoever state, make the same *man*; yet it is plain, consciousness, as far as ever it can be extended—should it be to ages past—unites existences and actions very remote in time into the same *person*, as well as it does the existences and actions of the immediately preceding moment: so that whatever [1] has the consciousness of present and past actions, is the same person to whom they both belong. Had I the same consciousness that I saw the ark and Noah's flood, as that I saw an overflowing of the Thames last winter, or as that I write now, I could no more doubt that I who write this now, that saw the Thames overflowed last winter, and that viewed the flood at the general deluge, was the same *self*,—place that self in what *substance* you please—than that I who write this am the same *myself* now whilst I write (whether I consist of all the same substance, material or immaterial, or no) that I was yesterday. For as to this point of being the same self, it matters not whether this present self be made up of the same or other substances—I being as much concerned, and as justly accountable [2] for any action that was done a thousand years since, appropriated to me now by this self-consciousness, as I am for what I did the last moment.

17. *Self* is that conscious thinking thing,—whatever sub-

persons,' says Berkeley (*C. P. B.* p. 486); but by 'person' he means spiritual substance, and not merely (as Locke) a consciousness that is (actually or potentially) aware of its own past, and can more or less anticipate its future.

[1] 'whatever.' Does this mean, whatever *being* or *substance*—as that on which the 'consciousness' depends? 'One should really think it self-evident,' says Bishop Butler, 'that consciousness of personal identity presupposes, and therefore cannot constitute, personal identity, any more than knowledge in any other case can constitute the reality which it presupposes.' But the presented facts in

which the presuppositions of reason are primarily embodied are, throughout the *Essay*, always apt to throw in the background the metaphysical presuppositions which they imply. Concrete examples supersede their principles. Locke prefers the practical consideration of particular facts given in consciousness to elaboration of abstract theories about their 'substance.'

[2] 'Accountability' is with Locke a criterion of personality. We are 'persons' only in respect to what is necessary for this. Person is a 'forensic term.' (Cf. § 26.) It does not mean a man, or any other living agent, merely as such, but only an ego that actually (or potentially?) appropriates

stance made up of, (whether spiritual or material, simple or
compounded, it matters not)—which is sensible or conscious
of pleasure and pain, capable of happiness or misery, and so is
concerned for itself, as far as that consciousness extends[1].
Thus every one finds that, whilst comprehended under that
consciousness, the little finger is as much a part of himself
as what is most so. Upon separation of this little finger,
should this consciousness go along with the little finger, and
leave the rest of the body, it is evident the little finger would
be the person, the same person ; and self then would have
nothing to do with the rest of the body. As in this case it
is the consciousness that goes along with the substance, when
one part is separate[2] from another, which makes the same
person, and constitutes this inseparable self: so it is in reference to substances remote in time. That with which the
consciousness of this present thinking thing *can* join itself,
makes the same person, and is one self with it, and with
nothing else ; and so attributes to itself, and owns all the
actions of that thing[3], as its own, as far as that consciousness
reaches, and no further ; as every one who reflects will
perceive[4].

18. In this personal identity is founded all the right and
justice of reward and punishment ; happiness and misery
being that for which every one is concerned for *himself*, and
not mattering what becomes of any *substance*, not joined to,
or affected with that consciousness. For, as it is evident in
the instance I gave but now, if the consciousness went along
with the little finger when it was cut off, that[5] would be the

---

past actions. No being that is not
capable of recognising his own past
answers this description. So that a
madman, though he is living and a
man, is not, in Locke's forensic sense,
a person. For he cannot be justly
punished for what the sane man did.
Therefore more is necessary to the idea
of a person than to the idea of a man ;
and that, Locke argues, is intelligent
recognition of a past as his own past.

[1] What is this but a definition of a
spiritual substance?

[2] 'separate,' i. e. in place.

[3] 'that thing,' i. e. that substance,
whether material or spiritual.

[4] Facts alleged by physiologists in
evidence of inherited memory, through
which, under abnormal conditions, a
person becomes conscious of acts and
thoughts of an ancestor, as his own,
are, so far, in analogy with the suggestion that, in a sense, all men may
constitute one person.

[5] 'that,' i. e. that finger-conscious-
ness. Appropriation of organ is with

same self which was concerned for the whole body yesterday, as making part of itself, whose actions then it cannot but admit as its own now. Though, if the same body should still live, and immediately from the separation of the little finger have its own peculiar consciousness, whereof the little finger knew nothing, it would not at all be concerned for it, as a part of itself, or could own any of its actions, or have any of them imputed to him.

Which shows wherein Personal identity consists. 19. This may show us wherein personal identity consists : not in the identity of substance, but, as I have said, in the identity of consciousness, wherein if Socrates and the present mayor of Queinborough agree, they are the same person : if the same Socrates [1] waking and sleeping do not partake of the same consciousness, Socrates waking and sleeping is not the same person. And to punish Socrates waking for what sleeping Socrates thought, and waking Socrates was never conscious of, would be no more of right [2], than to punish one twin for what his brother-twin did, whereof he knew nothing, because their outsides were so like, that they could not be distinguished ; for such twins have been seen.

Absolute oblivion separates what is thus forgotten from the person, but not from the man. 20. But yet possibly it will still be objected,—Suppose I wholly lose the memory of some parts of my life, beyond a possibility of retrieving them, so that perhaps I shall never be conscious of them again; yet am I not the same person that did those actions, had those thoughts that I once was conscious of, though I have now forgot them ? To which I answer, that we must here take notice what the word *I* is applied to ; which, in this case, is the *man* only. And the same man being presumed to be the same person, I is easily here supposed to stand also for the same person. But if it

---

Locke determined by consciousness. But consciousness, Leibniz remarks, is not the only means of determining the identity of a person. It can be proved, sufficiently for practical purposes, by certain external appearances, which sufficiently signify that the person continues to be the same, as in questions of personal identity in courts of justice.

[1] 'same Socrates,' i. e. the same bodily appearance which signifies the *man* Socrates.

[2] Because, although outwardly Socrates, he is not really Socrates, either man or person, if the apparent Socrates has ceased to partake of the same 'consciousness.' Disease sometimes deprives persons of consciousness of their identity.

be possible for the same man to have distinct incommunicable
consciousness at different times[1], it is past doubt the same
man would at different times make different persons ; which,
we see, is the sense of mankind in the solemnest declaration
of their opinions, human laws not punishing the mad man
for the sober man's actions, nor the sober man for what the
mad man did,—thereby making them two persons : which is
somewhat explained by our way of speaking in English when
we say such an one is 'not himself,' or is ' beside·himself '; in
which phrases it is insinuated, as if those who now, or at
least first used them, thought that self was changed ; the self-
same person was no longer in that man.

21. But yet it is hard to conceive that Socrates, the same
individual man, should be two persons. To help us a little in
this, we must consider what is meant by Socrates, or the same
individual *man*.

First, it must be either the same individual, immaterial,
thinking substance; in short, the same numerical soul, and
nothing else.

Secondly, or the same animal, without any regard to an
immaterial soul.

Thirdly, or the same immaterial spirit united to the same
animal.

Now, take which of these suppositions you please, it is
impossible to make personal identity to consist in anything
but consciousness; or reach any further than that does.

For, by the first of them, it must be allowed possible that
a man born of different women, and in distant times, may be
the same man[2]. A way of speaking which, whoever admits,
must allow it possible for the same man to be two distinct
persons, as any two that have lived in different ages without
the knowledge of one another's thoughts.

By the second and third, Socrates, in this life and after it,
cannot be the same man any way, but by the same consciousness[3]; and so making human identity to consist in the same

[1] For curious cases of double, and
of alternate personality, see James's
Psychology, vol. i. pp. 379–92.
[2] Because the same thinking *sub-*
stance might conceivably be joined to
the different organisms.
[3] Because the animal organism is
changed.

BOOK II.
CHAP.
XXVII.

thing wherein we place personal identity, there will be no difficulty to allow the same man to be the same person. But then they who place human identity in consciousness only, and not in something else, must consider how they will make the infant Socrates the same man with Socrates after the resurrection[1]. But whatsoever to some men makes a man, and consequently the same individual man, wherein perhaps few are agreed, personal identity can by us be placed in nothing but consciousness, (which is that alone which makes what we call *self,*) without involving us in great absurdities[2].

22. But is not a man drunk and sober the same person? why else is he punished for the fact he commits when

[1] This sentence may have suggested the following by Sir James Mackintosh :—' When the mind is purified from gross notions, it is evident that belief in a future state can no longer rest on the merely selfish idea of preserving its own individuality. When we make a further progress, it becomes indifferent whether the *same* individuals who now inhabit the universe, or others who do not yet exist, are to reach that superior degree of virtue and happiness of which human nature seems to be capable. The object of desire is, the quantity of virtue and happiness, not the identical beings who are to act and enjoy. Even those who distinctly believe in the continued existence (after death) of their fellow men are unable to pursue their opinion through its consequences. The dissimilarity between Socrates at his death, and Socrates in a future state, ten thousand years after death, is so very great, that to call these two beings by the same name is rather consequence of the imperfection of language than of exact views in philosophy. There is no practical identity. The Socrates of Elysium can feel no interest in recollecting what befel the Socrates at Athens. He is infinitely more removed from his former state than Newton was in this world from his infancy.' (*Life*, vol. ii. p. 120.) But

is this so, if the thread of self-consciousness is still maintained, and perhaps with the potential memory transformed into an actual consciousness in which all past experience is revived?

[2] According to Locke, our idea of the identity of a *man* includes participation in the same life by constantly changing particles of matter. Our idea of the identity of a *person*, on the other hand, is *independent of particles of matter, organised or unorganised*; and involves only a conception of the self-conscious being or person as the same, *as far back as memory extends*, and without implying that connection with the same material or other substance is also continued. The same person might thus be incarnated in succession in a series of bodies. Locke's curious speculations on identity of person may have suggested to Jonathan Edwards his paradoxical vindication of the responsibility of all men for Adam's sin, on the ground that personality is a consciousness arbitrarily sustained, by divine will, in a constant creation, so that all men, by divine appointment might make one person, all thus, in a revived consciousness, participating in the act by which mankind rebelled against God. (See Edwards on *Original Sin.*) (Cf. p. 415, note 2.)

drunk, though he be never afterwards conscious of it? Just as much the same person as a man that walks, and does other things in his sleep, is the same person, and is answerable for any mischief he shall do in it. Human laws punish both, with a justice suitable to *their* way of knowledge ;—because, in these cases, they cannot distinguish certainly what is real, what counterfeit : and so the ignorance in drunkenness or sleep is not admitted as a plea. [¹For, though punishment be annexed to personality, and personality to consciousness, and the drunkard perhaps be not conscious of what he did, yet human judicatures justly punish him; because the fact is proved against him, but want of consciousness cannot be proved for him².] But in the Great Day, wherein the secrets of all hearts shall be laid open, it may be reasonable

---

¹ Added in fourth edition.

² 'A man may be punished for any crime which he committed when drunk, *whereof he is not conscious.*' Locke allows, in reply to an objection of Molyneux to the statement in the text, that if a man may be justly punished for a crime committed when he was drunk, his theory of personal identity fails. 'You doubt whether my answer be full in the case of the drunkard. To try whether it be or no, we must consider what I am there doing. As I remember (for I have not that chapter here by me) I am there showing that *punishment* is annexed to *personality*, and *personality* to *consciousness* : how then can a drunkard be punished for what he did whereof he is not conscious ? To this I answer : human judicatures justly punish him, because the *fact* is proved against him ; but *want of consciousness* cannot be proved for him. This you think not sufficient, but would have me add the common reason,—that drunkenness being a crime, one crime cannot be alleged in excuse for another. This reason, how good soever, cannot I think be used by me, as not reaching my case ; for what has this to do with consciousness ?

Nay, it is an argument against me; for if a man may be punished for any crime which he committed when drunk, whereof he is allowed not to be conscious, it overturns my hypothesis' (19th Jan. 1694). In reply to this, Molyneux asks (Feb. 17, 1694), 'How it comes to pass that want of consciousness cannot be proved for a drunkard, as well as for a frantic? One methinks is as manifest as the other : if drunkenness may be counterfeit, so may a frenzy. Wherefore to me it seems that the law has made a difference in these two cases, on this account, viz. that drunkenness is commonly incurred voluntarily and premeditately ; whereas a frenzy is commonly without our consent, or impossible to be prevented.' In the end, Locke replies (May 26, 1694) :— 'I agree with you that drunkenness, being a voluntary defect, want of consciousness ought not to be presumed in favour of the drunkard. But frenzy, being involuntary and a misfortune, not a fault, has a right to that excuse, which certainly is a just one, where it is truly a frenzy. And all that lies upon human justice is, to distinguish carefully between what is real, and what counterfeit in the case.'

Con-
sciousness
alone
unites
remote
existences
into one
Person.

to think, no one shall be made to answer for what he knows nothing of; but shall receive his doom, his conscience accusing or excusing him [1].

23. Nothing but consciousness can unite remote existences into the same person: the identity of substance will not do it; for whatever substance there is, however framed, without consciousness there is no person: and a carcass may be a person, as well as any sort of substance be so, without consciousness.

Could we suppose two distinct incommunicable consciousnesses acting the same body, the one constantly by day, the other by night; and, on the other side, the same consciousness, acting by intervals, two distinct bodies: I ask, in the first case, whether the day and the night—man would not be two as distinct persons as Socrates and Plato? And whether, in the second case, there would not be one person in two distinct bodies, as much as one man is the same in two distinct clothings? Nor is it at all material to say, that this same, and this distinct consciousness, in the cases above mentioned, is owing to the same and distinct immaterial substances, bringing it with them to those bodies; which, whether true or no, alters not the case: since it is evident the personal identity would equally be determined by the consciousness, whether that consciousness were annexed to some individual immaterial substance or no. For, granting that the thinking substance in man must be necessarily supposed immaterial, it is evident that immaterial thinking thing may sometimes part with its past consciousness, and be restored to it again: as appears in the forgetfulness men often have of their past actions; and the mind many times recovers the memory of a past consciousness, which it had lost for twenty years together. Make these intervals of memory and forgetfulness to take their turns regularly by day and night, and you have two persons with the same immaterial spirit,

---

[1] His accountability depending upon the possibility of awakening his latent memory of all that he was ever conscious of; which is thus capable of being brought out of latency, so as to become, as suggested by Coleridge, the Book of Judgment, 'in the mysterious hieroglyphics of which every idle word is recorded.'

as much as in the former instance two persons with the same
body. So that self is not determined by identity or diversity
of substance, which it cannot be sure of[1], but only by identity of consciousness.

24. Indeed it may conceive the substance whereof it is Not the
substance
with
now made up to have existed formerly, united in the same
conscious being : but, consciousness removed, that substance which the
conscious-
is no more itself, or makes no more a part of it, than any ness
other substance ; as is evident in the instance we have already may be
united.
given of a limb cut off, of whose heat, or cold, or other affections, having no longer any consciousness, it is no more of
a man's self than any other matter of the universe. In like
manner it will be in reference to any immaterial substance,
which is void of that consciousness whereby I am myself to
myself : [² if there be any part of its existence which] I cannot
upon recollection join with that present consciousness whereby
I am now myself, it is, in that part of its existence, no more
myself than any other immaterial being. For, whatsoever
any substance has thought or done, which I cannot recollect,
and by my consciousness make my own thought and action,
it will no more belong to me, whether a part of me [3] thought
or did it, than if it had been thought or done by any other
immaterial being anywhere existing.

25. I agree, the more probable opinion is, that this con- Conscious-
sciousness is annexed to, and the affection of, one individual ness unites
substances,
immaterial substance [4]. material or

But let men, according to their diverse hypotheses, resolve spiritual,
with the
of that as they please. This every intelligent being, sensible of same per-
happiness or misery, must grant—that there is something that sonality.

---

[1] Locke cannot mean, by this hu-
morous illustration, to suggest the
probability of a double personality in
the same body being ever exemplified
in fact, which would be a 'fatal error'
(§ 13), God thereby putting our reason
to confusion.

[2] 'so that,' in second edition.

[3] I. e. my substance.

[4] Is it only 'probable' that in 'consciousness' the spiritual substance is
manifesting itself to itself? Berkeley,
on the other hand, sees in 'persons' the
only substances—personality and substantiality being identified. 'Nothing
properly but persons, i. e. conscious
things, do exist. All other things are
not so much (independent?) existences
as modes of the existence of persons.'
(*C.P.B.* p. 469.) In this philosophy
personality and its identity is the
ultimate basis of all actual existence.

is *himself*, that he is concerned for, and would have happy; that this self has existed in a continued duration more than one instant, and therefore it is possible may exist, as it has done, months and years to come, without any certain bounds to be set to its duration ; and may be the same self, by the same consciousness continued on for the future. And thus, by this consciousness he finds himself to be the same self which did such and such an action some years since, by which he comes to be happy or miserable now. In all which account of self, the same numerical *substance* is not considered as making the same self ; but the same continued *consciousness*, in which several substances may have been united, and again separated from it, which, whilst they continued in a vital union with that wherein this consciousness then resided, made a part of that same self. Thus any part of our bodies, vitally united to that which is conscious in us, makes a part of ourselves : but upon separation from the vital union by which that consciousness is communicated, that which a moment since was part of ourselves, is now no more so than a part of another man's self is a part of me : and it is not impossible but in a little time may become a real part of another person. And so we have the same numerical substance become a part of two different persons ; and the same person preserved under the change of various substances. Could we suppose any spirit [1] wholly stripped of all its memory or consciousness of past actions [2], as we find our minds always are of a great part of ours, and sometimes of them all [3]; the union or separation of such a spiritual substance would make no variation of personal identity, any more than that of any particle of matter does. Any substance vitally united to the present thinking being is a part of that very same self which now is ; anything united to it by a consciousness of former actions, makes also a part of the same self, which is the same both then and now.

26. *Person*, as I take it, is the name for this self. Wherever a man finds what he calls himself, there, I think, another

---

[1] Spirit, i. e. spiritual substance.

[2] So that its past actions were all *incapable* of being recollected—neither patent nor latent in memory.

[3] For a time, e. g. in sleep.

may say is the same person [1]. It is a forensic term, appropriating actions and their merit; and so belongs only to intelligent agents, capable of a law, and happiness, and misery. This personality extends itself beyond present existence to what is past, only by consciousness,—whereby it becomes concerned and accountable; owns and imputes to itself past actions, just upon the same ground and for the same reason as it does the present [2]. All which is founded in a concern for happiness, the unavoidable concomitant of consciousness; that which is conscious of pleasure and pain, desiring that that self that is conscious should be happy. And therefore whatever past actions it cannot reconcile or *appropriate* to that present self by consciousness, it can be no more concerned in than if they had never been done: and to receive pleasure or pain, i. e. reward or punishment, on the account of any such action, is all one as to be made happy or miserable

---

[1] Throughout this discussion, what Locke means by 'person' must be kept in view. If person means the living agent, or the man, then appropriation of past actions by present consciousness is not necessary to sameness of personality; since they are the same living agents, whether conscious or not of past and present actions. But a 'person' with Locke means an agent who is *accountable for past actions.* Although present 'appropriation' by consciousness of past actions is not implied in a living agent, it is necessary, according to the *Essay*, to our being persons, i.e. the proper objects of reward or punishment on account of them. If a man is not justly responsible for a past act, he is not the *person* by whom it was done, although he is the *man* or *living agent* through whom it was done; as no man can justly be punished for an action that cannot be brought home to his consciousness and conscience, as in a Book of Judgment. We are thus responsible only for voluntary actions which can by consciousness be appro-

priated to ourselves; consciousness uniting the most distant actions in one and the same personality. Consciousness that I am the same *person* cannot, Locke would say, be consciousness that I am the same *substance*, to any one who makes his body his substance. In short, we need not, he implies, for determining personality, embarrass ourselves with subtle questions about 'substances': they are irrelevant to the practical certainty that we are the same accountable agents, as far back as our remembrance of actions *as ours* can be *made* to reach, by a just and good God. Cf. § 11.

[2] The character of the self in former times and places, as it appears in the memory, is thereby appropriated, i. e. *personified*. The name 'person' (*persona*) was given originally to the mask worn by actors, through the mouthplace of which the voice sent forth its sounds (*personuit*); then to the mask itself; to the wearer of it, the actor; to the character acted; and at last to any assumed character.

BOOK II.
CHAP.
XXVII.

in its first being [1], without any demerit at all. For, supposing a *man* punished now for what he had done in another life, whereof he could be made to have no consciousness at all, what difference is there between that punishment and being *created* miserable [2]? And therefore, conformable to this, the apostle tells us, that, at the great day, when every one shall 'receive according to his doings, the secrets of all hearts shall be laid open.' The sentence shall be justified by the consciousness all persons shall have, that *they themselves*, in what bodies soever they appear, or what substances soever that consciousness adheres to, are the *same* that committed those actions, and deserve that punishment for them [3].

Suppositions that look are strange pardonable in our ignorance.

27. I am apt enough to think I have, in treating of this subject, made some suppositions that will look strange to some readers, and possibly they are so in themselves [4]. But yet, I think they are such as are pardonable, in this ignorance we are in of the nature of that thinking thing that is in us, and which we look on as *ourselves* [5]. Did we know what it

---

[1] 'first being,' i. e. inasmuch as he could not *personify*, or appropriate them to himself, as *formerly* his.

[2] The past consciousness having been finally or for ever obliterated. This implies that his own consciousness in memory is the only means by which he could in reason be satisfied that the action was his.

[3] See § 18, in which it is implied that a murderer for example is not accountable for a murder of which his organism was the instrument, if a consciousness of it, as his own past act, *cannot* be awakened in him! It follows (unless conscious experience is ultimately indelible) that any man who has forgotten that he committed a murder, did not *personally* commit it. Who, in that case, was the murderer?

[4] They called forth a host of critics, Sergeant, Stillingfleet, Lee, Clarke in controversy with Collins, Butler, and Reid, with Vincent Perronet and others in defence. The main objection is thus put by Butler:—'One should think it self-evident that consciousness *presupposes*, and cannot *constitute* personal identity.' But Locke, it must be remembered, defines personality from the forensic point of view. He also views its identity as manifested in consciousness, and not in the mystery of its ultimate constitution, the *conscious manifestations* concealing rather than revealing the *substance* on which they depend.

[5] Cf. Bk. IV. ch. ix.—On our certainty of 'our own existence.' We are apt to take for granted that the idea man can form of his own personality, and that of God, is more adequate to the reality than consists with the necessary limitations of our knowledge. That the personality of men *somehow* rests on the personality of God is the language of religion, according to which God is all, and man can do nothing that is *good* without God.

was; or how it was tied to a certain system of fleeting animal spirits; or whether it could or could not perform its operations of thinking and memory out of a body organized as ours is; and whether it has pleased God that no one such spirit shall ever be united to any but one such body, upon the right constitution of whose organs its memory should depend; we might see the absurdity of some of those suppositions I have made. But taking, as we ordinarily now do (in the dark concerning these matters,) the soul of a man for an immaterial substance, independent from matter, and indifferent alike to it all; there can, from the nature of things, be no absurdity at all to suppose that the same *soul* may at different times be united to different *bodies*, and with them make up for that time one *man*: as well as we suppose a part of a sheep's body yesterday should be a part of a man's body to-morrow, and in that union make a vital part of Meliboeus himself, as well as it did of his ram [1].

28. To conclude: Whatever substance begins to exist, it must, during its existence, necessarily be the same: whatever compositions of substances begin to exist, during the union of those substances, the concrete must be the same: whatsoever mode begins to exist, during its existence it is the same: and so if the composition be of distinct substances and different modes [2], the same rule holds. Whereby it will appear, that the difficulty or obscurity that has been about this matter rather rises from the names ill-used, than from any obscurity in things themselves. For whatever makes the specific idea to which the name is applied, if that idea be steadily kept to, the distinction of anything into the same and divers will easily be conceived, and there can arise no doubt about it.

The Difficulty from ill Use of Names.

29. For, supposing a rational spirit be the idea of a *man* [3],

Continuance of

---

[1] In all this the connection between the soul, or the self-conscious person, and the body is assumed to be accidental or contingent; so that the loss of the body by death or otherwise, is irrelevant to the immortality of the soul, or to that continued *appropriation* by consciousness of past experience on which responsibility or personality depends.

[2] As in man, supposed to comprehend spiritual and also material substance—soul and body.

[3] That is, if we exclude the body, as an accident and not of the essence of man, and mean by 'man' only the soul or 'rational spirit.'

BOOK II.

CHAP. XXVII.

that which we have made to be our complex idea of man makes the same man.

it is easy to know what is the same man, viz. the same spirit— whether separate or in a body—will be the *same man.* Supposing a rational spirit vitally united to a body of a certain conformation of parts to make a man [1]; whilst that rational spirit, with that vital conformation of parts, though continued in a fleeting successive body, remains, it will be the *same man.* But if to any one the idea of a man be but the vital union of parts in a certain shape; as long as that vital union and shape remain in a concrete, no otherwise the same but by a continued succession of fleeting particles, it will be the *same man.* For, whatever be the composition whereof the complex idea is made, whenever existence makes it one particular thing under any denomination [2], *the same existence continued* preserves it the *same* individual under the same denomination [3].

---

[1] And this is what Locke means by 'a man.'

[2] The nominalism of Locke, who is apt to make questions of this sort questions about the meaning of words only, appears in all this.

[3] In the foregoing argument, Locke emphatically distinguishes the person from the man, and from the bodily substance. Should we not rather say that it is in his personality and personal agency that *man* finds what is deepest and truest in himself; and, by analogy, in the constitution of the universe? Locke, working from sensation upward, makes his Book of Ideas culminate in the complex idea of our concrete continuous personality, and in the moral relations to which persons ought to conform,—in this and the following chapter. Transcendental philosophy, from Descartes to Hegel, working from thought downward, ends by making abstract self-consciousness the key to the mysteries of existence.

By implication Locke appears to make the idea of our personal existence a simple idea of reflection, which gives its meaning to the personal pronoun 'I,' in the 'perception' that I am. (Cf. Bk. IV. ch. ix.) The idea of our *continuous* personality, or personal identity, is a complex idea of relation between *myself now* and *myself in the past*, which 'terminates,' and is made concrete in actual consciousnesses, past and present. The identity of myself now with myself in the past; and my separateness from all that is not myself, in a private consciousness in which no other finite person can mingle, afford the unique experience of the spirit as distinguished from the mere animal in man. This experience of identical personal life and moral agency is thus the occasion of the most significant ideas in the human mind.

CHAPTER XXVIII.

OF OTHER RELATIONS.

BOOK II.

—٭—

CHAP.
XXVIII.

Ideas of Propor-
tional rela-
tions.

1. BESIDES the before-mentioned occasions of time[1], place, and causality of comparing or referring things one to another, there are, as I have said, infinite others, some whereof I shall mention.

First, The first I shall name is some one simple idea, which, being capable of parts or degrees, affords an occasion of comparing the subjects wherein it is to one another, in respect of that simple idea, v. g. whiter, sweeter, equal, more, &c. These relations depending on the equality and excess of the same simple idea, in several subjects, may be called, if one will, *proportional*; and that these are only conversant about those simple ideas received from sensation or reflection[2] is so evident that nothing need be said to evince it.

2. Secondly, Another occasion of comparing things together, or considering one thing, so as to include in that consideration some other thing[3], is the circumstances of their origin or beginning; which being not afterwards to be altered, make the relations depending thereon as lasting as the subjects to which they belong, v. g. father and son, brothers, cousin-germans, &c., which have their relations by one community of blood, wherein they partake in several degrees : country-men, i. e. those who were born in the same country or tract

---

[1] Our idea of ' personal identity' is with Locke our idea of a relation which arises under difference of time.

[2] That is, the abstract relation can be embodied or made concrete only in phenomena of which we become aware through sensation or reflection.

[3] An 'idea of relation' thus means a complex idea of one thing, regarded as including some idea of another thing ; or of itself at another time or place.

of ground; and these I call *natural relations*: wherein we may observe, that mankind have fitted their notions and words to the use of common life, and not to the truth and extent of things. For it is certain, that, in reality, the relation is the same betwixt the begetter and the begotten, in the several races of other animals as well as men; but yet it is seldom said, this bull is the grandfather of such a calf, or that two pigeons are cousin-germans. It is very convenient that, by distinct names, these relations should be observed and marked out in mankind, there being occasion, both in laws and other communications one with another, to mention and take notice of men under these relations: from whence also arise the obligations of several duties amongst men: whereas, in brutes, men having very little or no cause to mind these relations, they have not thought fit to give them distinct and peculiar names. This, by the way, may give us some light into the different state and growth of languages; which being suited only to the convenience of communication, are proportioned to the notions men have, and the commerce of thoughts familiar amongst them; and not to the reality or extent of things, nor to the various respects might be found among them; nor the different abstract considerations might be framed about them. Where they had no philosophical notions, there they had no terms to express them: and it is no wonder men should have framed no names for those things they found no occasion to discourse of. From whence it is easy to imagine why, as in some countries, they may have not so much as the name for a horse; and in others, where they are more careful of the pedigrees of their horses, than of their own, that there they may have not only names for particular horses, but also of their several relations of kindred one to another.

Ideas of Instituted or Voluntary relations.

3. Thirdly, Sometimes the foundation of considering things, with reference to one another, is some act whereby any one comes by a moral right, power, or obligation to do something. Thus, a general is one that hath power to command an army; and an army under a general is a collection of armed men, obliged to obey one man. A citizen, or a burgher, is one who has a right to certain privileges in this or that place.

All this sort depending upon men's wills, or agreement in society, I call *instituted*, or *voluntary*; and may be distinguished from the natural, in that they are most, if not all of them, some way or other alterable, and separable from the persons to whom they have sometimes belonged, though neither of the substances, so related, be destroyed. Now, though these are all reciprocal, as well as the rest, and contain in them a reference of two things one to the other; yet, because one of the two things often wants a relative name, importing that reference, men usually take no notice of it, and the relation is commonly overlooked: v. g. a patron and client are easily allowed to be relations, but a constable or dictator are not so readily at first hearing considered as such. Because there is no peculiar name for those who are under the command of a dictator or constable, expressing a relation to either of them; though it be certain that either of them hath a certain power over some others, and so is so far related to them, as well as a patron is to his client, or general to his army.

4. Fourthly, There is another sort of relation, which is the conformity or disagreement men's *voluntary actions* have to a *rule* to which they are referred, and by which they are judged of; which, I think, may be called *moral relation*, as being that which denominates our moral actions, and deserves well to be examined; there being no part of knowledge wherein we should be more careful to get determined ideas, and avoid, as much as may be, obscurity and confusion[1]. Human actions, when with their various ends, objects, manners, and circumstances, they are framed into distinct complex ideas, are, as has been shown, so many *mixed modes*, a great part whereof have names annexed to them[2]. Thus, supposing gratitude to be a readiness to acknowledge and return kindness received; polygamy to

---

[1] We have our idea of the relation of moral good or evil when *persons* are compared with a *law* or *rule*, in respect of their *voluntary acts*; moral law or rule being the manifested will of a person able to reward and punish; and moral good or evil, the agreement or disagreement of the voluntary act with that manifested will.

[2] Cf. ch. xxii.

be the having more wives than one at once : when we frame these notions thus in our minds, we have there so many determined ideas of mixed modes. But this is not all that concerns our actions : it is not enough to have determined ideas of them, and to know what names belong to such and such combinations of ideas. We have a further and greater concernment, and that is, to know whether such actions, so made up, are morally good or bad.

Moral
Good and
Evil.

5. Good and evil, as hath been shown, (B. II. chap. xx. § 2, and chap. xxi. § 43,) are nothing but pleasure or pain, or that which occasions or procures pleasure or pain to us. *Moral good and evil*, then, is only *the conformity or disagreement of our voluntary actions to some law, whereby good or evil is drawn on us, from the will and power of the lawmaker* ; which good and evil, pleasure or pain, attending our observance or breach of the law by the decree of the law-maker, is that we call *reward* and *punishment*[1].

Moral
Rules.

6. Of these moral rules or laws, to which men generally refer, and by which they judge of the rectitude or pravity of their actions, there seem to me to be *three sorts*, with their three different enforcements, or rewards and punishments. For, since it would be utterly in vain to suppose a rule set to the free actions of men, without annexing to it some enforcement of good and evil to determine his will, we must, wherever we suppose a law, suppose also some reward or punishment annexed to that law[2]. It would be in vain for one intelligent being to set a rule to the actions of another, if he had it not in his power to reward the compliance with, and punish deviation from his rule, by some good and evil, that is not the natural product and consequence of the action itself. For that, being a natural convenience or inconvenience, would operate of itself, without a law[3]. This,

---

[1] Thus moral law must be enacted by a *person* who has power to annex natural good or evil to obedience or disobedience ; and what is in moral relation with this law must be the voluntary act of a person, who is free either to obey or disobey the law. He proceeds to distinguish the persons with whose laws *men* come into moral relation (§ 7).

[2] Cf. Butler on moral government by rewards and punishments, in Part I. ch. ii. of the *Analogy*.

[3] This might imply that what we call 'natural' law, is not the expression of Supreme Reason and

if I mistake not, is the true nature of all law, properly so BOOK II.
called.

7. The laws that men generally refer their actions to, CHAP.
to judge of their rectitude or obliquity, seem to me to be Laws.
these three :—1. The *divine* law. 2. The *civil* law. 3. [The
law of *opinion* or *reputation*[1], if I may so call it.] By the
relation they bear to the first of these, men judge whether
their actions are sins or duties ; by the second, whether they
be criminal or innocent ; and by the third, whether they be
virtues or vices.

8. First, [[2] the *divine law*, whereby that law which God has Divine
set to the actions of men,—whether promulgated to them by Law the
the light of nature, or the voice of revelation[3].] That God has of Sin and
given a rule whereby men should govern themselves, I think Duty.
there is nobody so brutish as to deny. He has a right to do
it ; we are his creatures : he has goodness and wisdom to
direct our actions to that which is best: and he has power to
enforce it by rewards and punishments of infinite weight and
duration in another life ; for nobody can take us out of his
hands. [[4] This is the only true touchstone of moral rectitude ;
and,] by comparing them to this law, it is that men judge of
the most considerable moral good or evil of their actions ;
that is, whether, as duties or sins, they are like to procure
them happiness or misery from the hands of the ALMIGHTY[5].

Will. But the changes in the universe
are at once natural and supernatural—natural when regarded only
at the point of view of physical
science ; supernatural at the higher
point of view of philosophy or theology. The ultimate immanence of
Divine active reason in all so-called
natural changes, is an idea foreign to
Locke.

[1] In first edition—'The *philosophical*
law.'

[2] Added in second edition.

[3] 'revelation,' i.e. miraculous, which
he distinguishes from revelation
through natural awakening of our
spiritual intuitions. He elsewhere calls
reason 'natural revelation.' (Bk. IV.
ch. xix. § 4.)

[4] Added in second edition.

[5] This implies that the happiness
and the misery annexed by Divine
law to men's actions, form our test
for distinguishing those which it is
our duty to perform from those which
are 'sinful'; and that the desire for
eternal happiness is also the rightful
motive to the performance of dutiful
actions. So Paley afterwards, in his
definition of virtue. But although
Locke lays stress upon the pleasurable
and painful consequences of actions,
as motives to their performance, he
has faith in the inherent obligation of
moral law, as eternal and immutable,
independently of foresight of consequences.

BOOK II.
CHAP.
XXVIII.
Civil
Law the
Measure
of Crimes
and Inno-
cence.

9. Secondly, the *civil law*—the rule set by the common-wealth to the actions of those who belong to it—is another rule to which men refer their actions; to judge whether they be criminal or no. This law nobody overlooks: the rewards and punishments that enforce it being ready at hand, and suitable to the power that makes it: which is the force of the Commonwealth, engaged to protect the lives, liberties, and possessions of those who live according to its laws, and has power to take away life, liberty, or goods, from him who disobeys; which is the punishment of offences committed against his law.

Philo-
sophical
Law the
Measure
of Virtue
and Vice.

10. [¹ Thirdly, the *law of opinion or reputation*. Virtue and vice are names pretended and supposed everywhere to stand for actions in their own nature right and wrong: and as far as they really are so applied, they so far are coincident with the divine law above mentioned. But yet, whatever is pre-tended, this is visible, that these names, virtue and vice, in the particular instances of their application, through the several nations and societies of men in the world, are con-stantly attributed only to such actions as in each country and society are in reputation or discredit. Nor is it to be thought strange, that men everywhere should give the name of virtue to those actions, which amongst them are judged

---

¹ Instead of this section, the first edition has the following:—'The third—which I call the *philosophical* law, not because philosophers make it, but because they have most busied them-selves to inquire after it, and talk about it—is the law of Virtue and Vice; which though it be more talked of possibly than either of the others, yet how it comes to be established with such authority as it has, to dis-tinguish and denominate the actions of men, and what are the true mea-sures of it, perhaps, is not so generally taken notice of. To comprehend this aright, we must consider that men's uniting into political societies, though they have resigned up to the public the disposal of all their force, so that they cannot employ it against any fellow-citizen, any further than the law of their country directs—yet they still retain the power of thinking well or ill, approving or disapproving the actions of those they live amongst and converse with. If, therefore, we ex-amine it right, we shall find, that the measure of what is everywhere called and esteemed 'virtue' and 'vice' is this approbation or dislike, praise or blame, which, by a secret and tacit consent, establishes itself in the several societies, tribes and clubs of men in the world; whereby several act.ons come to find credit or disgrace amongst them, according to the judgment, maxims, or fashions of that place.'

praiseworthy; and call that vice, which they account blamable: since otherwise they would condemn themselves, if they should think anything right, to which they allowed not commendation, anything wrong, which they let pass without blame. Thus the measure of what is everywhere called and esteemed virtue and vice is this approbation or dislike, praise or blame, which, by a secret and tacit consent, establishes itself in the several societies, tribes, and clubs of men in the world: whereby several actions come to find credit or disgrace amongst them, according to the judgment, maxims, or fashion of that place. For, though men uniting into politic societies, have resigned up to the public the disposing of all their force, so that they cannot employ it against any fellow-citizens any further than the law of the country directs: yet they retain still the power of thinking well or ill, approving or disapproving of the actions of those whom they live amongst, and converse with: and by this approbation and dislike they establish amongst themselves what they will call virtue and vice.]

11. That this is the common *measure* of virtue and vice [1], will appear to any one who considers, that, though that passes for vice in one country which is counted a virtue, or at least not vice, in another, yet everywhere virtue and

The Measure that Men commonly apply to determine

---

[1] In vindicating the *Essay* against some of its critics, Locke emphatically rejects the charge, that here or elsewhere he makes public opinion the ultimate nature of right and wrong, and not, as he intends, only the popular test of morality. In a letter to Tyrrell in this reference, he explains that in this passage he is showing what rules men often, in point of fact, take to be the standards of their actions, 'it not being of concernment to my purpose in that chapter, whether they be as much as true or no' (August 4, 1690). As to Lowde's objection, in like manner he remarks:—'If he had been at pains to reflect on what I had said, he would have known what I think of *the eternal and unalterable nature of right and wrong, and what I call virtue and* vice; and if he had observed that, in the place he quotes, *I only report, as matters of fact, what others call virtue and vice*, he would not have found it liable to any great exception.' An insinuation to the contrary by Burnet he repudiates, 'as if I held the distinction of virtue and vice was to be picked up by our eyes, or ears, or nostrils, showing so much ignorance, or so much malice, in the insinuation, that he desires no other answer but pity.' This is well argued in Mr. Curtis's *Outline of Locke's Ethical Philosophy* (Leipsic, 1890). The law of right and wrong is *in itself* eternal and unalterable, according to Locke, but he does not explain the ground on which this moral faith rests.

BOOK II.

CHAP.
XXVIII.

what they
call Virtue
and Vice.

praise, vice and blame, go together. Virtue is everywhere, that which is thought praiseworthy; and nothing else but that which has the allowance of public esteem is called virtue[1]. Virtue and praise are so united, that they are called often by the same name. *Sunt sua præmia laudi*, says Virgil[2]; and so Cicero, *Nihil habet natura præstantius, quam honestatem, quam laudem, quam dignitatem, quam decus*[3], which he tells you are all names for the same thing. This is the language of the heathen philosophers, who well understood wherein their notions of virtue and vice consisted. And though perhaps, by the different temper, education, fashion, maxims, or interest of different sorts of men, it fell out, that what was thought praiseworthy in one place, escaped not censure in another; and so in different societies, virtues and vices were changed: yet, as to the main, they for the most part kept the same everywhere. For, since nothing can be more natural than to encourage with esteem and reputation that wherein every one finds his advantage, and to blame and discountenance the contrary; it is no wonder that esteem and discredit, virtue and vice, should, in a great measure, everywhere correspond with the unchangeable rule of right and wrong, which the law of God hath established; there being nothing that so directly and visibly secures and advances the general good of mankind in this world, as obedience to the laws he has set them, and nothing that breeds such mischiefs and confusion, as the neglect of them. And therefore men, without renouncing all sense and reason, and their own interest, which they are so constantly true to, could not generally mistake, in placing their commendation and blame on that side that really deserved it not. Nay, even those men whose practice was otherwise, failed not to give their approbation right, few being depraved to that degree as not to condemn, at least in others, the faults they themselves were guilty of; whereby, even in the corruption

---

[1] See 'Epistle to the Reader,' prefixed to the second edition of the *Essay* (pp. 19, 20), where he refers to the criticisms of Mr. Lowde.

[2] 'Sunt hic etiam sua præmia laudi;

Sunt lacrimæ rerum, et mentem mortalia tangunt.' (*Æn.* i. 461.)

[3] *Tuscul. Quæst*; lib. ii. 20. See the context.

of manners, the true boundaries of the law of nature, which BOOK II.
ought to be the rule of virtue and vice, were pretty well
preferred. So that even the exhortations of inspired teachers, CHAP XXVIII.
have not feared to appeal to common repute: 'Whatsoever
is lovely, whatsoever is of good report, if there be any virtue,
if there be any praise,' &c. (Phil. iv. 8.)

12. If any one shall imagine that I have forgot my own ItsInforce
notion of a law, when I make the law, whereby men judge of ment is
Commen-
virtue and vice, to be nothing else but the consent of private dation and
men, who have not authority enough to make a law: especially Discredit.
wanting that which is so necessary and essential to a law, a
power to enforce it: I think I may say, that he who imagines
commendation and disgrace not to be strong motives to men
to accommodate themselves to the opinions and rules of those
with whom they converse, seems little skilled in the nature
or history of mankind: the greatest part whereof we shall
find to govern themselves chiefly, if not solely, by this *law
of fashion*; and so they do that which keeps them in reputation with their company, little regard the laws of God, or
the magistrate. The penalties that attend the breach of
God's laws some, nay perhaps most men, seldom seriously
reflect on: and amongst those that do, many, whilst they
break the law, entertain thoughts of future reconciliation,
and making their peace for such breaches. And as to the
punishments due from the laws of the commonwealth, they
frequently flatter themselves with the hopes of impunity.
But no man escapes the punishment of their censure and
dislike, who offends against the fashion and opinion of the
company he keeps, and would recommend himself to. Nor is
there one of ten thousand, who is stiff and insensible enough,
to bear up under the constant dislike and condemnation of
his own club. He must be of a strange and unusual constitution, who can content himself to live in constant disgrace
and disrepute with his own particular society. Solitude
many men have sought, and been reconciled to: but nobody
that has the least thought or sense of a man about him,
can live in society under the constant dislike and ill opinion
of his familiars, and those he converses with. This is
a burden too heavy for human sufferance: and he must be

BOOK II.
CHAP.
XXVIII.

made up of irreconcileable contradictions, who can take pleasure in company, and yet be insensible of contempt and disgrace from his companions.

These three Laws the Rules of moral Good and Evil.

13. These three then, first, the law of God; secondly, the law of politic societies; thirdly, the law of fashion, or private censure, are those to which men variously compare their actions: and it is by their conformity to one of these laws that they take their measures, when they would judge of their moral rectitude, and denominate their actions good or bad[1].

Morality is the Relation of Voluntary Actions to these Rules.

14. Whether the rule to which, as to a touchstone, we bring our voluntary actions, to examine them by, and try their goodness, and accordingly to name them, which is, as it were, the mark of the value we set upon them: whether, I say, we take that rule from the fashion of the country, or the will of a law-maker[2], the mind is easily able to observe the relation any action hath to it, and to judge whether the action agrees or disagrees with the rule; and so hath a notion of moral goodness or evil, which is either conformity or not conformity of any action to that rule: and therefore is often called moral rectitude. This rule being nothing but a collection of several simple ideas, the conformity thereto is but so ordering the action, that the simple ideas belonging to it may correspond to those which the law requires. And thus we see how moral beings and notions are founded on, and terminated in, these simple ideas we have received from sensation or reflection. For example: let us consider the complex idea we signify by the word murder: and when we have taken it asunder, and examined all the particulars, we shall find them to amount to a collection of simple ideas derived from reflection or sensation, viz. First, from *reflection* on the operations of our own minds, we have

[1] Cf. Bk. I. ch. ii. § 5, in which the grounds of obligation recognised by 'a christian, a Hobbist, and one of the old philosophers,' are distinguished.

[2] Again note that it is the nature and origin of the various ideas men form of moral good and evil, not the absolute standard of morality, that he is concerned with, in this second Book, which deals with the ideas men have, and not with the ultimate nature of things. He is illustrating the various ideas of moral law that prevail among men, and the different standards of an abstract morality in itself immutable which they adopt.

the ideas of willing, considering, purposing beforehand, malice, or wishing ill to another; and also of life, or perception, and self-motion. Secondly, from *sensation* we have the collection of those simple sensible ideas which are to be found in a man, and of some action, whereby we put an end to perception and motion in the man; all which simple ideas are comprehended in the word murder. This collection of simple ideas, being found by me to agree or disagree with the esteem of the country I have been bred in, and to be held by most men there worthy praise or blame, I call the action virtuous or vicious: if I have the will of a supreme invisible Lawgiver for my rule, then, as I supposed the action commanded or forbidden by God, I call it good or evil, sin or duty: and if I compare it to the civil law, the rule made by the legislative power of the country, I call it lawful or unlawful, a crime or no crime. So that whencesoever we take the rule of moral actions; or by what standard soever we frame in our minds the ideas of virtues or vices, they consist only, and are made up of collections of simple ideas, which we originally received from sense or reflection: and their rectitude or obliquity consists in the agreement or disagreement with those patterns prescribed by some law[1].

15. To conceive rightly of moral actions, we must take notice of them under this two-fold consideration. First, as they are in themselves, each made up of such a collection of simple ideas. Thus drunkenness, or lying, signify such or such a collection of simple ideas, which I call mixed modes: and in this sense they are as much *positive absolute* ideas, as the drinking of a horse, or speaking of a parrot. Secondly, our actions are considered as good, bad, or indifferent; and in this respect they are *relative*, it being their conformity to, or disagreement with some rule that makes them to be regular or irregular, good or bad; and so, as far as they are compared with a rule, and thereupon denominated, they come under relation[2]. Thus the challenging and fighting with a

Moral actions may be regarded either absolutely, or as ideas of relation.

---

[1] The ideas we have of the concrete actions which we call virtuous or vicious may be so formed, but what is the origin of the eternity and immutability which he says necessarily belong to ideas of morality?

[2] And it is under 'ideas of relation' that they are here considered.

man, as it is a certain positive mode, or particular sort of action, by particular ideas, distinguished from all others, is called *duelling*: which, when considered in relation to the law of God, will deserve the name of sin; to the law of fashion, in some countries, valour and virtue; and to the municipal laws of some governments, a capital crime. In this case, when the positive mode has one name, and another name as it stands in relation to the law, the distinction may as easily be observed as it is in substances, where one name, v. g. *man*, is used to signify the thing; another, v. g. *father*, to signify the relation.

The Denominations of Actions often mislead us.

16. But because very frequently the positive idea of the action, and its moral relation, are comprehended together under one name, and the same word made use of to express both the mode or action, and its moral rectitude or obliquity: therefore the relation itself is less taken notice of; and there is often no distinction made between the positive idea of the action, and the reference it has to a rule. By which confusion of these two distinct considerations under one term, those who yield too easily to the impressions of sounds, and are forward to take names for things, are often misled in their judgment of actions. Thus, the taking from another what is his, without his knowledge or allowance, is properly called *stealing*: but that name, being commonly understood to signify also the moral pravity of the action, and to denote its contrariety to the law, men are apt to condemn whatever they hear called stealing, as an ill action, disagreeing with the rule of right. And yet the private taking away his sword from a madman, to prevent his doing mischief, though it be properly denominated stealing, as the name of such a mixed mode; yet when compared to the law of God, and considered in its relation to that supreme rule, it is no sin or transgression, though the name stealing ordinarily carries such an intimation with it.

Relations innumerable, and only the most considerable here mentioned.

17. And thus much for the relation of human actions to a law, which, therefore, I call *moral relations*.

It would make a volume to go over all sorts of *relations*: it is not, therefore, to be expected that I should here men-

tion them all. It suffices to our present purpose to show
by these, what the ideas are we have of this comprehensive
consideration called *relation*. Which is so various, and the
occasions of it so many, (as many as there can be of comparing things one to another,) that it is not very easy to
reduce it to rules, or under just heads. Those I have mentioned, I think, are some of the most considerable ; and such
as may serve to let us see from whence we get our ideas of
relations, and wherein they are founded. But before I quit
this argument, from what has been said give me leave to
observe :

18. First, That it is evident, that all relation terminates in,
and is ultimately founded on, those simple ideas we have got
from sensation or reflection : so that all we have in our
thoughts ourselves, (if we think of anything, or have any
meaning,) or would signify to others, when we use words
standing for relations, is nothing but some simple ideas, or
collections of simple ideas, compared one with another[1]. This
is so manifest in that sort called proportional, that nothing
can be more. For when a man says 'honey is sweeter than
wax,' it is plain that his thoughts in this relation terminate in
this simple idea, sweetness ; which is equally true of all the
rest : though, where they are compounded, or decompounded,
the simple ideas they are made up of, are, perhaps, seldom
taken notice of : v.g. when the word father is mentioned :
first, there is meant that particular species, or collective idea,
signified by the word man ; secondly, those sensible simple
ideas, signified by the word generation ; and, thirdly, the
effects of it, and all the simple ideas signified by the word
child. So the word friend, being taken for a man who loves
and is ready to do good to another, has all these following
ideas to the making of it up : first, all the simple ideas, com-

Marginal notes: BOOK II. CHAP. XXVIII. All Relations terminate in simple Ideas.

---

[1] But as, according to Locke, the idea of *substance* is presupposed in all our 'simple ideas,' the only ideas which enter into relations, or form subjects and predicates in our judgments, must be those of abstracted *modes* of ma-terial or spiritual substances, or those of concrete (material or spiritual) *substances* themselves. He illustrates this, by analysing the connotation of some terms which enter into propo-sitions. There can be no actual relations unless there are things related, given by experience, which make the rela-tions actual.

prehended in the word man, or intelligent being; secondly, the idea of love; thirdly, the idea of readiness or disposition; fourthly, the idea of action, which is any kind of thought or motion; fifthly, the idea of good, which signifies anything that may advance his happiness, and terminates at last, if examined, in particular simple ideas, of which the word good in general signifies any one; but, if removed from all simple ideas quite, it signifies nothing at all. And thus also all moral words terminate at last, though perhaps more remotely, in a collection of simple ideas: the immediate signification of relative words, being very often other supposed known relations; which, if traced one to another, still end in simple ideas.

We have ordinarily as clear a Notion of the Relation, as of the simple ideas in things on which it is founded. 19. Secondly, That in relations, we have for the most part, if not always, as clear a notion of *the relation* as we have of *those simple ideas wherein it is founded*: agreement or disagreement, whereon relation depends, being things whereof we have commonly as clear ideas as of any other whatsoever; it being but the distinguishing simple ideas, or their degrees one from another, without which we could have no distinct knowledge at all. For, if I have a clear idea of sweetness, light, or extension, I have, too, of equal, or more, or less, of each of these: if I know what it is for one man to be born of a woman, viz. Sempronia, I know what it is for another man to be born of the same woman Sempronia; and so have as clear a notion of brothers as of births, and perhaps clearer. For if I believed that Sempronia digged Titus out of the parsley-bed, (as they used to tell children,) and thereby became his mother; and that afterwards, in the same manner, she digged Caius out of the parsley-bed, I had as clear a notion of the relation of brothers between them, as if I had all the skill of a midwife: the notion that the same woman contributed, as mother, equally to their births, (though I were ignorant or mistaken in the manner of it,) being that on which I grounded the relation; and that they agreed in that circumstance of birth, let it be what it will. The comparing them then in their descent from the same person, without knowing the particular circumstances of that descent, is enough to found my notion of their having, or not having the relation of brothers. But though the ideas of *particular relations* are capable of being as clear and distinct in the minds of those who will duly consider them as those of mixed modes, and more determinate than those of substances: yet the names belonging to relation are often of as doubtful and uncertain signification as those of substances or mixed modes ; and much more than those of simple ideas. Because relative words, being the marks of this comparison, which is made only by men's thoughts, and is an idea only in men's minds, men frequently apply them to different comparisons of things [1], according to their own imaginations; which do not always correspond with those of others using the same name.

20. Thirdly, That in these I call *moral relations,* I have a true notion of relation, by comparing the action with the rule, whether the rule be true or false. For if I measure anything by a yard, I know whether the thing I measure be longer or shorter than that supposed yard, though perhaps the yard I measure by be not exactly the standard: which indeed is another inquiry. For though the rule be erroneous, and I mistaken in it ; yet the agreement or disagreement observable in that which I compare with, makes me perceive the relation. Though, measuring by a wrong rule, I shall thereby be brought to judge amiss of its moral rectitude ; because I have tried it by that which is not the true rule : yet I am not mistaken in the relation which that action bears to that rule I compare it to, which is agreement or disagreement.

[1] The same things, in virtue of different resembling qualities, may be referred to various classes, and so have various names applied to them, according to the classes men find it convenient to think them in.

CHAPTER XXIX.

OF CLEAR AND OBSCURE, DISTINCT AND CONFUSED IDEAS.

BOOK II.

CHAP.
XXIX.

Ideas,
some clear
and dis-
tinct,
others
obscure
and con-
fused.

1. HAVING shown the original of our ideas, and taken a view of their several sorts ; considered the difference between the simple and the complex ; and observed how the complex ones are divided into those of modes, substances, and relations —all which, I think, is necessary to be done by any one who would acquaint himself thoroughly with the progress of the mind, in its apprehension and knowledge of things—it will, perhaps, be thought I have dwelt long enough upon the examination of *ideas*. I must, nevertheless, crave leave to offer some few other considerations concerning them.

The first is, that some are *clear* and others *obscure* ; some *distinct* and others *confused* [1].

2. The perception of the mind being most aptly explained by words relating to the sight, we shall best understand what is meant by *clear* and *obscure* in our ideas, by reflecting on what we call clear and obscure in the objects of sight. Light being that which discovers to us visible objects, we give the name of *obscure* to that which is not placed in a light sufficient to discover minutely to us the figure and colours which are observable in it, and which, in a better light, would be dis-

---

[1] On the qualities of ideas (simple and complex) as *clear* and *obscure*, *distinct* and *confused*, see Leibniz, *Nouveaux Essais*, Liv. II. ch. xxix. and in *Meditationes de Cognitione, Veritate, et Ideis*, first published in 1684, in the *Acta Eruditorum*, five years before the *Essay* appeared, but of which Locke was probably ignorant. Locke's account of those distinctions is more akin to that in the *Port Royal Logic*, Pt. I. ch. ix. Descartes makes much of clearness and distinctness as the ultimate criterion of truth ; but Locke has here to do with ideas and their qualities, abstracted from the consideration of questions about truth and knowledge. On the terms ' clear ' and ' distinct,' cf. ' Epistle to the Reader,' p. 22.

cernible. In like manner, our simple ideas are *clear*, when
they are such as the objects themselves from whence they
were taken did or might, in a well-ordered sensation or perception, present them. Whilst the memory retains them thus,
and can produce them to the mind whenever it has occasion
to consider them, they are clear ideas. So far as they either
want anything of the original exactness, or have lost any of
their first freshness, and are, as it were, faded or tarnished by
time, so far are they obscure. Complex ideas, as they are
made up of simple ones, so they are clear, when the ideas that
go to their composition are clear, and the number and order
of those simple ideas that are the ingredients of any complex
one is determinate and certain.

3. The causes of obscurity, in simple ideas, seem to be
either dull organs ; or very slight and transient impressions
made by the objects ; or else a weakness in the memory, not
able to retain them as received. For to return again to visible
objects, to help us to apprehend this matter. If the organs,
or faculties of perception, like wax over-hardened with cold,
will not receive the impression of the seal, from the usual
impulse wont to imprint it ; or, like wax of a temper too soft,
will not hold it well, when well imprinted ; or else supposing
the wax of a temper fit, but the seal not applied with a
sufficient force to make a clear impression[1] : in any of these
cases, the print left by the seal will be obscure. This, I suppose, needs no application to make it plainer.

Causes of Obscurity.

4. As a clear idea is that whereof the mind has such a full
and evident perception, as it does receive from an outward
object operating duly on a well-disposed organ, so a *distinct*
idea is that wherein the mind perceives a difference from all
other ; and a *confused* idea is such an one as is not sufficiently
distinguishable from another, from which it ought to be
different[2].

Distinct and con-fused, what.

---

[1] There is a passage in the *Theaete-tus* in analogy with this.

[2] According to the usage of Leibniz and others, an idea is *clear* when it is so apprehended as to be distinguished as a whole from other ideas, and it is *obscure* when confused with others ; it is *distinct* when, besides this, its several constituent elements are discriminated from one another, and it is *indistinct*

5. If no idea be confused, but such as is not sufficiently distinguishable from another from which it should be different, it will be hard, may any one say, to find anywhere a *confused* idea. For, let any idea be as it will, it can be no other but such as the mind perceives it to be; and that very perception sufficiently distinguishes it from all other ideas, which cannot be other, i.e. different, without being perceived to be so. No idea, therefore, can be undistinguishable from another from which it ought to be different, unless you would have it different from itself: for from all other it is evidently different.

6. To remove this difficulty, and to help us to conceive aright what it is that makes the confusion ideas are at any time chargeable with, we must consider, that things ranked under distinct names are supposed different enough to be distinguished, that so each sort by its peculiar name may be marked, and discoursed of apart upon any occasion: and there is nothing more evident, than that the greatest part of different names are supposed to stand for different things. Now every idea a man has, being visibly what it is, and distinct from all other ideas but itself; that which makes it confused, is, when it is such that it may as well be called by another name as that which it is expressed by; the difference which keeps the things (to be ranked under those two different names) distinct, and makes some of them belong rather to the one and some of them to the other of those names, being left out; and so the distinction, which was intended to be kept up by those different names, is quite lost.

7. The defaults which usually occasion this confusion, I think, are chiefly these following:

First, when any complex idea (for it is complex ideas that are most liable to confusion) is made up of too small a number of simple ideas, and such only as are common to other things, whereby the differences that make it deserve a different name,

---

when its several parts are not thus discriminated. Thus one's idea of another man may be clear enough to identify him, but not distinct enough to represent the signs of his identity in detail. Locke's method for relieving complex ideas of these defects would be, to recall into the view of consciousness, the simple ideas of which they consist.

are left out. Thus, he that has an idea made up of barely BOOK II.
the simple ones of a beast with spots, has but a confused idea
of a leopard ; it not being thereby sufficiently distinguished CHAP.
XXIX.
from a lynx, and several other sorts of beasts that are spotted. simple
So that such an idea, though it hath the peculiar name leopard, ones.
is not distinguishable from those designed by the names lynx or
panther, and may as well come under the name lynx as leopard.
How much the custom of defining of words by general terms
contributes to make the ideas we would express by them confused and undetermined, I leave others to consider. This is
evident, that confused ideas are such as render the use of words
uncertain, and take away the benefit of distinct names. When
the ideas, for which we use different terms, have not a difference answerable to their distinct names, and so cannot be
distinguished by them, there it is that they are truly confused.

8. Secondly, Another fault which makes our ideas confused Secondly,
is, when, though the particulars that make up any idea are in or their
simple
number enough, yet they are so jumbled together, that it is ones
not easily discernible whether it more belongs to the name jumbled
disorderly
that is given it than to any other. There is nothing properer together.
to make us conceive this confusion than a sort of pictures,
usually shown as surprising pieces of art, wherein the colours,
as they are laid by the pencil on the table itself, mark out
very odd and unusual figures, and have no discernible order
in their position. This draught, thus made up of parts wherein
no symmetry nor order appears, is in itself no more a confused
thing, than the picture of a cloudy sky ; wherein, though there
be as little order of colours or figures to be found, yet nobody
thinks it a confused picture. What is it, then, that makes it
be thought confused, since the want of symmetry does not ?
As it is plain it does not : for another draught made barely in
imitation of this could not be called confused. I answer, That
which makes it be thought confused is, the applying it to
some name to which it does no more discernibly belong than
to some other : v.g. when it is said to be the picture of a man,
or Cæsar, then any one with reason counts it confused ; because it is not discernible in that state to belong more to the
name man, or Cæsar, than to the name baboon, or Pompey :
which are supposed to stand for different ideas from those

BOOK II.
CHAP.
XXIX.

signified by man, or Cæsar. But when a cylindrical mirror, placed right, had reduced those irregular lines on the table into their due order and proportion, then the confusion ceases, and the eye presently sees that it is a man, or Cæsar; i.e. that it belongs to those names; and that it is sufficiently distinguishable from a baboon, or Pompey; i.e. from the ideas signified by those names. Just thus it is with our ideas, which are as it were the pictures of things. No one of these mental draughts, however the parts are put together, can be called confused (for they are plainly discernible as they are) till it be ranked under some ordinary name to which it cannot be discerned to belong, any more than it does to some other name of an allowed different signification.

Thirdly, or their simple ones mutable and undetermined.

9. Thirdly, A third defect that frequently gives the name of confused to our ideas, is, when any one of them is uncertain and undetermined. Thus we may observe men who, not forbearing to use the ordinary words of their language till they have learned their precise signification, change the idea they make this or that term stand for, almost as often as they use it. He that does this out of uncertainty of what he should leave out, or put into his idea of *church*, or *idolatry*, every time he thinks of either, and holds not steady to any one precise combination of ideas that makes it up, is said to have a confused idea of idolatry or the church: though this be still for the same reason as the former, viz. because a mutable idea (if we will allow it to be one idea) cannot belong to one name rather than another, and so loses the distinction that distinct names are designed for [1].

---

[1] Cf. ch. xxii. § 7; also Bk. III. ch. x. §§ 3, 4, on our habit of using words without realising fully what each word means. So too Hume:—'We do not annex distinct and complete ideas to any term we make use of; and in talking of *government, church, negotiations, conquest,* we seldom *spread out in our minds all the simple ideas of which these complex ones are composed.* Notwithstanding this imperfection we may avoid talking nonsense on these subjects, and may be perceive any repugnance among the ideas, as well as if we had a full comprehension of them.' (*Treatise*, Pt. I. sect. 7.) This is further illustrated in Leibniz's distinction between an intuitive and a symbolical apprehension of things. Human imagination cannot represent a very complex idea as a whole, far less each of the simple ideas it contains; in which case the verbal sign serves as an obscure substitute for the idea, in symbolical or blind thought, in contrast to the intuitive thought in

BOOK II.

CHAP.
XXIX.

Confusion
without
Reference
to Names,
hardly
conceiv-
able.

10. By what has been said, we may observe how much *names*, as supposed steady signs of things, and by their difference to stand for, and keep things distinct that in themselves are different, are the occasion of denominating ideas distinct or confused, by a secret and unobserved reference the mind makes of its ideas to such names. This perhaps will be fuller understood, after what I say of Words in the third Book has been read and considered. But without taking notice of such a reference of ideas to distinct names, as the signs of distinct things, it will be hard to say what a confused idea is. And therefore when a man designs, by any name, a sort of things, or any one particular thing, distinct from all others, the complex idea he annexes to that name is the more distinct, the more particular the ideas are, and the greater and more determinate the number and order of them is, whereof it is made up. For, the more it has of these, the more it has still of the perceivable differences, whereby it is kept separate and distinct from all ideas belonging to other names, even those that approach nearest to it, and thereby all confusion with them is avoided.

11. Confusion making it a difficulty to separate two things that should be separated, concerns always two ideas; and those most which most approach one another. Whenever, therefore, we suspect any idea to be confused, we must examine what other it is in danger to be confounded with, or which it cannot easily be separated from; and that will always be found an idea belonging to another name, and so should be a different thing, from which yet it is not sufficiently distinct : being either the same with it, or making a part of it, or at least as properly called by that name as the other it is ranked under; and so keeps not that difference from that other idea which the different names import.

12. This, I think, is the confusion proper to ideas ; which still carries with it a secret reference to names. At least, if

which we are conscious of the ideas themselves. To repeat the common illustration, one can reason about a polygon with 1000 sides, without being able so to image this figure as to distinguish its image from that of one with 999 sides. Its nature and properties are intelligible to us, although the lower faculties of sense and sensuous imagination are not delicate enough for this discrimination.

there be any other confusion of ideas, this is that which most of all disorders men's thoughts and discourses : ideas, as ranked under names, being those that for the most part men reason of within themselves, and always those which they commune about with others. And therefore where there are supposed two different ideas, marked by two different names, which are not as distinguishable as the sounds that stand for them, there never fails to be confusion; and where any ideas are distinct as the ideas of those two sounds they are marked by, there can be between them no confusion. The way to prevent it is to collect and unite into one complex idea, as precisely as is possible, all those ingredients whereby it is differenced from others ; and to them, so united in a determinate number and order, apply steadily the same name. But this neither accommodating men's ease or vanity, nor serving any design but that of naked truth, which is not always the thing aimed at, such exactness is rather to be wished than hoped for. And since the loose application of names, to undetermined, variable, and almost no ideas, serves both to cover our own ignorance, as well as to perplex and confound others, which goes for learning and superiority in knowledge, it is no wonder that most men should use it themselves, whilst they complain of it in others. Though I think no small part of the confusion to be found in the notions of men might, by care and ingenuity, be avoided, yet I am far from concluding it everywhere wilful. Some ideas are so complex, and made up of so many parts, that the memory does not easily retain the very same precise combination of simple ideas under one name : much less are we able constantly to divine for what precise complex idea such a name stands in another man's use of it. From the first of these, follows confusion in a man's own reasonings and opinions within himself; from the latter, frequent confusion in discoursing and arguing with others. But having more at large treated of Words, their defects, and abuses, in the following Book, I shall here say no more of it.

13. Our complex ideas, being made up of collections, and so variety of simple ones, may accordingly be very clear and distinct in one part, and very obscure and confused in another.

In a man who speaks of a *chiliaedron*, or a body of a thousand sides, the ideas of the figure may be very confused, though that of the number be very distinct; so that he being able to discourse and demonstrate concerning that part of his complex idea which depends upon the number of thousand, he is apt to think he has a distinct idea of a *chiliaedron*; though it be plain he has no precise idea of its figure, so as to distinguish it, by that, from one that has but 999 sides : the not observing whereof causes no small error in men's thoughts, and confusion in their discourses.

14. He that thinks he has a distinct idea of the figure of a *chiliaedron*, let him for trial sake take another parcel of the same uniform matter, viz. gold or wax of an equal bulk, and make it into a figure of 999 sides. He will, I doubt not, be able to distinguish these two ideas one from another, by the number of sides ; and reason and argue distinctly about them, whilst he keeps his thoughts and reasoning to that part only of these ideas which is contained in their numbers; as that the sides of the one could be divided into two equal numbers, and of the others not, &c. But when he goes about to distinguish them by their figure, he will there be presently at a loss, and not be able, I think, to frame in his mind two ideas, one of them distinct from the other, by the bare figure of these two pieces of gold ; as he could, if the same parcels of gold were made one into a cube, the other a figure of five sides. In which incomplete ideas, we are very apt to impose on ourselves, and wrangle with others, especially where they have particular and familiar names. For, being satisfied in that part of the idea which we have clear ; and the name which is familiar to us, being applied to the whole, containing that part also which is imperfect and obscure, we are apt to use it for that confused part, and draw deductions from it in the obscure part of its signification, as confidently as we do from the other.

15. Having frequently in our mouths the name Eternity[1], we are apt to think we have a positive comprehensive idea of

(margin notes:) BOOK II. CHAP. XXIX. one Part, and confused in another.

This, if not heeded, causes Confusion in our Arguings.

Instance in Eternity.

---

[1] Locke imperfectly distinguishes *unimaginable concepts of understanding*, which admit of definition, from *sensuous perception and imagination*. We may be said to have a notion of eternity, but we cannot make a mental image of

BOOK II.
CHAP.
XXIX.

it, which is as much as to say, that there is no part of that duration which is not clearly contained in our idea[1]. It is true that he that thinks so may have a clear idea of duration; he may also have a clear idea of a very great length of duration; he may also have a clear idea of the comparison of that great one with still a greater: but it not being possible for him to include in his idea of any duration, let it be as great as it will, *the whole extent together of a duration, where he supposes no end*[1], that part of his idea, which is still beyond the bounds of that large duration he represents to his own thoughts, is very obscure and undetermined. And hence it is that in disputes and reasonings concerning eternity, or any other infinite, we are very apt to blunder, and involve ourselves in manifest absurdities.

Infinite Divisibility of Matter.

16. In matter, we have no clear ideas of the smallness of parts much beyond the smallest that occur to any of our senses: and therefore, when we talk of the divisibility of matter *in infinitum*, though we have clear ideas of division and divisibility, and have also clear ideas of parts made out of a whole by division; yet we have but very obscure and confused ideas of corpuscles, or minute bodies, so to be divided, when, by former divisions, they are reduced to a smallness much exceeding the perception of any of our senses; and so all that we have clear and distinct ideas of is of what division in general or abstractedly is, and the relation of *totum* and *pars*: but of the bulk of the body, to be thus infinitely divided after certain progressions, I think, we have no clear nor distinct idea at all. For I ask any one, whether, taking the smallest atom of dust he ever saw, he has any distinct idea (bating still the number, which concerns not extension) betwixt the 100,000th and the 1,000,000th part of it. Or if he think he can refine his ideas to that degree, without losing sight of them, let him add ten cyphers to each

it; yet errors in our conclusions concerning eternity need not arise from this weakness of our imagination. It must be remembered that the second Book of the *Essay* is properly concerned with ideas, simple or complex, chiefly as particular ideas, in the concrete of sense and imagination; the consideration of their generality, and its relation to words, belonging properly to the third Book.

[1] Here again he makes *eternity* an obscure complex idea composed of moments of time.

of those numbers. Such a degree of smallness is not unreasonable to be supposed; since a division carried on so far brings it no nearer the end of infinite division, than the first division into two halves does. I must confess, for my part, I have no clear distinct ideas of the different bulk or extension of those bodies, having but a very obscure one of either of them. So that, I think, when we talk of division of bodies *in infinitum*, our idea of their distinct bulks, which is the subject and foundation of division, comes, after a little progression, to be confounded, and almost lost in obscurity. For that idea which is to represent only bigness must be very obscure and confused, which we cannot distinguish from one ten times as big, but only by number: so that we have clear distinct ideas, we may say, of ten and one, but no distinct ideas of two such extensions. It is plain from hence, that, when we talk of infinite divisibility of body or extension, our distinct and clear ideas are only of numbers: but the clear distinct ideas of extension, after some progress of division, are quite lost; and of such minute parts we have no distinct ideas at all; but it returns, as all our ideas of infinite do, at last to that of *number always to be added*; but thereby never amounts to any distinct idea of *actual infinite parts*. We have, it is true, a clear idea of division, as often as we think of it; but thereby we have no more a clear idea of infinite parts in matter, than we have a clear idea of an infinite number, by being able still to add new numbers to any assigned numbers we have: endless divisibility giving us no more a clear and distinct idea of actually infinite parts, than endless addibility (if I may so speak) gives us a clear and distinct idea of an actually infinite number: they both being only in a power still of increasing the number, be it already as great as it will. So that of what remains to be added (*wherein consists the infinity*) we have but an obscure, imperfect, and confused idea; from or about which we can argue or reason with no certainty or clearness, no more than we can in arithmetic, about a number of which we have no such distinct idea as we have of 4 or 100; but only this relative obscure one, that, compared to any other, it is still bigger: and we have no more a clear positive idea of it, when we say or conceive it is bigger, or more than 400,000,000, than if we should say it is bigger than 40 or 4 : 400,000,000 having no nearer a proportion to the end of addition or number than 4. For he that adds only 4 to 4, and so proceeds, shall as soon come to the end of all addition, as he that adds 400,000,000 to 400,000,000. And so likewise in eternity ; he that has an idea of but four years, has as much a positive complete idea of eternity, as he that has one of 400,000,000 of years : for what remains of eternity beyond either of these two numbers of years, is as clear to the one as the other ; i.e. neither of them has any clear positive idea of it at all. For he that adds only 4 years to 4, and so on, shall as soon reach eternity as he that adds 400,000,000 of years, and so on ; or, if he please, doubles the increase as often as he will : the remaining abyss being still as far beyond the end of all these progressions as it is from the length of a day or an hour. For nothing finite bears any proportion to infinite ; and therefore our ideas, which are all finite, cannot bear any. Thus it is also in our idea of extension, when we increase it by addition, as well as when we diminish it by division, and would enlarge our thoughts to infinite space. After a few doublings of those ideas of extension, which are the largest we are accustomed to have, we lose the clear distinct idea of that space : it becomes a confusedly great one, with a surplus of still greater ; about which, when we would argue or reason, we shall always find ourselves at a loss ; confused ideas, in our arguings and deductions from that part of them which is confused, always leading us into confusion [1].

---

[1] The complex ideas of infinity in space and time, 'substance in general,' power and causation, personality and its identity—which Locke uses as crucial instances in support of his fundamental principle of the dependence of all our ideas of things upon data of experience—are also illustrations of the inevitable obscurity and indistinctness which a human understanding, measured by sense, finds itself enveloped in, when it tries to think them out, and finds that at last *omnia exeunt in mysteria.*

CHAPTER XXX.

OF REAL AND FANTASTICAL IDEAS.

1. BESIDES what we have already mentioned concerning ideas, other considerations belong to them, in reference to *things from whence they are taken*, or *which they may be supposed to represent*[1]; and thus, I think, they may come under a threefold distinction, and are :—

First, either real or fantastical ;

Secondly, adequate or inadequate ;

Thirdly, true or false.

First, by *real ideas*, I mean such as have a foundation in nature ; such as have a conformity with the real being and existence of things, or with their archetypes. *Fantastical* or *chimerical*, I call such as have no foundation in nature, nor have any conformity with that reality of being to which they are tacitly referred, as to their archetypes[2]. If we examine

---

[1] In this and the two next chapters our ideas are considered in their possible relation to what really exists. Hitherto, for the most part (except in chap. viii.), the inquiry has been confined to ideas *per se*; they have been viewed in abstraction from their reality, adequacy, and truth, and thus from the propositions into which they enter, or which are presupposed in them. Locke here approaches those considerations and so prepares for the questions about *knowledge* that belong to the fourth Book. Cf. Bk. IV. chh. iii, iv, ix, x, xi.

[2] 'Nothing,' says Berkeley, 'seems of more importance towards erecting a firm system of sound and real knowledge than to lay the beginning in a distinct explication of *what is meant* by *thing, reality, existence*; for in vain shall we dispute concerning the real existence of things, or pretend to any knowledge thereof, so long as we have not fixed the meaning of these words.' (*Principles*, § 89.) In the analysis of our ideas, in the second Book, Locke has not included the idea of *reality*. He refers to it here, but without inquiring

BOOK II.
—+•—
CHAP.
XXX.
Simple
Ideas are
all real
appear·
ances of
things.

the several sorts of ideas before mentioned, we shall find that,

2. First, Our *simple ideas* are all real, all agree to the reality of things : not that they are all of them the images or representations of what does exist ; the contrary whereof, in all but the primary qualities of bodies, hath been already shown. But, though whiteness and coldness are no more in snow than pain is ; yet those ideas of whiteness and coldness, pain, &c., being in us the effects of powers in things without us, ordained by our Maker to produce in us such sensations ; they are real ideas in us, whereby we distinguish the qualities that are really in things themselves. For, these several appearances being designed to be the mark whereby we are to know and distinguish things which we have to do with, our ideas do as well serve us to that purpose, and are as real distinguishing characters, whether they be only *constant effects*, or else *exact resemblances* of something in the things themselves : the reality lying in that steady correspondence they have with the distinct constitutions of real beings. But whether they answer to those constitutions, as to causes [1] or patterns [2], it matters not ; it suffices that they are constantly produced by them. And thus our simple ideas are all real and true, because they answer and agree to those powers of things which produce them in our minds ; that being all that is requisite to make them real, and not fictions at pleasure. For in simple ideas (as has been shown) the mind is wholly confined to the operation of things upon it, and can make to itself no simple idea, more than what it has received [3].

whether it implies dependence on conscious mind ; the question which absorbed Berkeley, and which has since influenced the course of philosophy. 'Real and fantastical' here virtually correspond to that difference between *perception* and *imagination*, which Berkeley finds in the intelligible coherence of what is perceived, but which Hume reduces to the degree of *intensity of feeling* which belongs to 'impressions' or perceptions, as compared with ideas of imagination.

That the *ultimate intelligibility* of things is the test of their reality is the conception of the real, opposed to this of Hume, by Hegel.

[1] As the secondary qualities of bodies are supposed to do.

[2] As the primary qualities of bodies are supposed to be.

[3] In the 'simple ideas of sensation and reflection,' *reality*, he implies, manifests itself to us ; either *directly*, as in the primary or real qualities of matter, and in the operations of our

3. Though the mind be wholly passive in respect of its simple ideas; yet, I think, we may say it is not so in respect of its complex ideas. For those being combinations of simple ideas put together, and united under one general name, it is plain that the mind of man uses some kind of liberty in forming those complex ideas: how else comes it to pass that one man's idea of gold, or justice, is different from another's, but because he has put in, or left out of his, some simple idea which the other has not[1]? The question then is, Which of these are real, and which barely imaginary combinations? What collections agree to the reality of things, and what not? And to this I say that,

BOOK II.
CHAP. XXX.
Complex Ideas are voluntary Combinations.

4. Secondly, *Mixed modes* and *relations*, having no other reality but what they have in the minds of men, there is nothing more required to this kind of ideas to make them real, but that they be so framed, that there be a possibility of existing conformable to them. These ideas themselves, being archetypes, cannot differ from their archetypes, and so cannot

Mixed Modes and Relations, made of consistent Ideas, are real.

---

self-conscious spirits, or *indirectly* in the sensations which, as secondary qualities, we 'impute' to bodies. It is, he maintains, in the simple ideas, or appearances which the real thus presents that all our complex ideas 'terminate,' including those of relation. Hence the momentous import of sense-perception with Reid and his followers; as against the extremes of nihilism and pure idealism. 'In its primary application, the real means something apprehended as existing in opposition to that which is not so apprehended, or in opposition to the absence of any appearance whatever. In the earliest conceivable form of perception there is something apprehended—not nothing; and we mean by the real at first, the appearance, percept, impression ['simple idea' of Locke], whatever we come to call it, which is known to consciousness, as opposed to the blank or negation of it; we call the impression *real*; we speak of the absence of impression as the *unreal*. . . . Unless this form of reality is

given to us, we are powerless to think even of its relations to anything whatever, before or after it. So far as this form of reality is concerned, there can hardly be any mistake about it. The sensation I experience can only be the sensation of the moment; the percept I have can only be the percept of the moment. . . It can only be as I affirm it. It exists as in consciousness.' (Prof. Veitch, *Knowing and Being*, pp. 113–4.) This is in analogy with what, in other language Locke intends in assuming the necessary reality of the 'simple ideas,' or qualities of things, which are presented to us, not imagined by us. Various meanings of 'Reality' are discussed in an interesting essay by Mr. Ritchie, in Prof. Schurman's *Philosophical Review* (May, 1892).

[1] Accordingly Locke calls *our* complex ideas of things 'fictitious,' 'made by the mind,'&c., because they are often out of conformity with the modes and relations constituted by actually existing substances, in the intelligible system of things.

be chimerical, unless any one will jumble together in them inconsistent ideas [1]. Indeed, as any of them have the names of a known language assigned to them, by which he that has them in his mind would signify them to others, so bare possibility of existing is not enough; they must have a conformity to the ordinary signification of the name that is given them, that they may not be thought fantastical: as if a man would give the name of justice to that idea which common use calls liberality. But this fantasticalness relates more to propriety of speech, than reality of ideas. For a man to be undisturbed in danger, sedately to consider what is fittest to be done, and to execute it steadily, is a mixed mode, or a complex idea of an action which may exist. But to be undisturbed in danger, without using one's reason or industry, is what is also possible to be; and so is as real an idea as the other. Though the first of these, having the name *courage* given to it, may, in respect of that name, be a right or wrong idea; but the other, whilst it has not a common received name of any known language assigned to it, is not capable of any deformity, being made with no reference to anything but itself.

5. Thirdly, Our complex ideas of *substances*, being made all of them in reference to things existing without us, and intended to be representations of substances as they really are, are no further real than as they are such combinations of simple ideas as are really united, and co-exist in things without us. On the contrary, those are fantastical which are made up of such collections of simple ideas as were

---

[1] Is the 'consistency' which excludes express self-contradiction the only reality that can be attributed to 'mixed modes' and to our 'ideas of relation'; and that on the ground that these ideas are only capricious products of a human understanding? What of the intellectual necessity which determines our ideas of abstract relations like causation, identity, and morality? 'Les *relations*,' says Leibniz, 'ont une réalité dépendante de l'esprit, comme les *vérites*; mais non pas de l'esprit des hommes; puisqu'il y a une Suprême Intelligence qui les détermine toutes en tous temps. Les *modes mixtes* qui sont distincts des relations, peuvent être des accidents réels; mais soit qu'ils dépendent ou ne dépendent point de l'esprit, il suffit pour la réalité de leurs idées, qu'ils soient possibles, ou ce qui est la même chose, intelligibles distinctement.' (*Nouveaux Essais.*)

really never united, never were found together in any substance : v. g. a rational creature, consisting of a horse's
head, joined to a body of human shape, or such as the *cen-*
taurs are described : or, a body yellow, very malleable, fusible,
and fixed, but lighter than common water : or an uniform,
unorganized body, consisting, as to sense, all of similar parts,
with perception and voluntary motion joined to it. Whether
such substances as these can possibly exist or no, it is probable we do not know : but be that as it will, these ideas of
substances, being made conformable to no pattern existing
that we know ; and consisting of such collections of ideas as
no substance ever showed us united together, they ought to
pass with us for barely imaginary : but much more are those
complex ideas so, which contain in them any inconsistency
or contradiction of their parts [1].

---

[1] Men's complex ideas of the particular substances and their relations,
of which real existence consists, are
largely the workmanship of the individual mind; for they are often found
to be at variance with reality, when
tested by the simple ideas of sense,
which 'all agree with the reality of
things.' As Bacon would put it, men,
in these ideas, often *anticipate* instead
of *interpreting* nature, and substitute
idols of the human mind for the Ideas
of the Divine Mind. Our conceptions of particular substances, and
of their concrete relations to one
another — not given in immediate
perception, as are our simple ideas of
sensation and reflection—are 'things
of the [individual] mind,' which
vary with the intellectual power and
experience of the individual, conforming more and more to the real
as science and philosophy advance.
With Locke, our *simple ideas*, in
which the real is actually manifested
in sense, external and internal, and
our ideas of particular substances, are
the only sorts of ideas which can
have other than *subjective* reality ; and
as the reality of our 'simple ideas' is
presupposed (by him), the problem of
reality is concerned exclusively with
the existence, attributes, and powers
of *finite substances* and *God*. But
what of the reality of moral and
mathematical relations, and the applicability of pure mathematics to real
things ?

CHAPTER XXXI.

OF ADEQUATE AND INADEQUATE IDEAS.

BOOK II.
— ♦♦ —
CHAP.
XXXI.
Adequate
Ideas are
such as
perfectly
represent
their
Arche-
types.

Simple
Ideas all
adequate.

1. OF our real ideas, some are adequate, and some are inadequate. Those I call *adequate*, which perfectly represent those archetypes which the mind supposes them taken from : which it intends them to stand for, and to which it refers them. *Inadequate ideas* are such, which are but a partial or incomplete representation of those archetypes to which they are referred [1]. Upon which account it is plain,

2. First, that *all our simple ideas are adequate*. Because, being nothing but the effects of certain powers in things, fitted and ordained by God to produce such sensations in us, they cannot but be correspondent and adequate to those powers : and we are sure they agree to the reality of things. For, if sugar produce in us the ideas which we call whiteness and sweetness, we are sure there is a power in sugar to produce those ideas in our minds, or else they could not have been produced by it. And so each sensation answering the power that operates on any of our senses, the idea so produced is a real idea, (and not a fiction of the mind, which has no power to produce any simple idea); and cannot but be adequate, since it ought only to answer that power :

---

[1] The 'adequacy' of any idea in an individual mind thus involves its relation to a corresponding reality that is independent of the mind whose idea it is. It presupposes a fixed standard external to our transitory idea, and also perfect correspondence with that standard. 'Inadequacy,' Locke goes on to show, is characteristic only of our ideas of *substances* (material and spiritual), which are *all necessarily inadequate*: *simple ideas* are all adequate so far as they go ; as also *modes* and *ideas of relation*.

and so all simple ideas are adequate [1]. It is true, the things producing in us these simple ideas are but few of them denominated by us, as if they were only the *causes* of them; but as if those ideas were real beings *in* them [2]. For, though fire be called painful to the touch, whereby is signified the power of producing in us the idea of pain, yet it is denominated also light and hot; as if light and heat were really something in the fire, more than a power to excite these ideas in us; and therefore are called qualities in or of the fire. But these being nothing, in truth, but powers to excite such ideas in us, I must in that sense be understood, when I speak of secondary qualities as being in things; or of their ideas as being the objects that excite them in us. Such ways of speaking, though accommodated to the vulgar notions, without which one cannot be well understood, yet truly signify nothing but those powers which are in things to excite certain sensations or ideas in us. Since were there no fit organs to receive the impressions fire makes on the sight and touch, nor a mind joined to those organs to receive the ideas of light and heat by those impressions from the fire or sun, there would yet be no more light or heat in the world than there would be pain if there were no sensible creature to feel it, though the sun should continue just as it is now, and Mount Ætna flame higher than ever it did. Solidity and extension, and the termination of it, figure, with motion and rest, whereof we have the ideas, would be really in the world as they are, whether there were any sensible being to perceive them or no: and therefore we have reason to look on those as the real modifications of matter, and such as are the exciting causes of all our various sensations from bodies [3]. But this being an inquiry not belonging to this place, I shall enter no further

---

[1] This founds our faith in the senses, and in self-consciousness upon our faith in God.

[2] Cf. ch. viii. § 23.

[3] The dependence of all *secondary* qualities of things upon a sentient intelligence—their merely relative existence, as perceived—which Locke here insists on, is, so far, just Berkeley's argument for the dependent and relative nature of *all* the qualities in which the material world is manifested; which, he argues, *all equally* presuppose percipient mind, without which they could not become ideas or phenomena.

BOOK II.

—◦—

CHAP.
XXXI.

Modes
are all
adequate.

into it, but proceed to show what complex ideas are adequate, and what not.

3. Secondly, *our complex ideas of modes*, being voluntary collections of simple ideas, which the mind puts together, without reference to any real archetypes, or standing patterns, existing anywhere, are and cannot but be *adequate ideas*[1]. Because they, not being intended for copies of things really existing, but for archetypes made by the mind, to rank and denominate things by, cannot want anything; they having each of them that combination of ideas, and thereby that perfection, which the mind intended they should: so that the mind acquiesces in them, and can find nothing wanting. Thus, by having the idea of a figure with three sides meeting at three angles, I have a complete idea, wherein I require nothing else to make it perfect. That the mind is satisfied with the perfection of this its idea is plain, in that it does not conceive that any understanding hath, or can have, a more complete or perfect idea of that thing it signifies by the word triangle, supposing it to exist, than itself has, in that complex idea of three sides and three angles, in which is contained all that is or can be essential to it, or necessary to complete it, wherever or however it exists. But in our *ideas of substances* it is otherwise. For there, desiring to copy things as they really do exist, and to represent to ourselves that constitution on which all their properties depend, we perceive our ideas attain not that perfection we intend: we find they still want something we should be glad were in them; and so are all inadequate. But *mixed modes* and *relations*, being archetypes without patterns, and so having nothing to represent but themselves, cannot but be adequate, everything being so to itself. He that at first put together the idea of danger perceived, absence of disorder from fear, sedate consideration of what was justly to be done, and executing that without disturbance, or being deterred by the danger of it, had certainly in his mind that complex idea made up of that combination: and intending it to be nothing else but what is, nor to have

---

[1] What of the *simple modes* of our simple ideas, e.g. of space and duration, as in our ideas of Immensity and Eternity? Are *they* 'adequate' to the reality?

in it any other simple ideas but what it hath, it could not also but be an adequate idea: and laying this up in his memory, with the name *courage* annexed to it, to signify to others, and denominate from thence any action he should observe to agree with it, had thereby a standard to measure and denominate actions by, as they agreed to it. This idea, thus made and laid up for a pattern, must necessarily be adequate, being referred to nothing else but itself, nor made by any other original but the good liking and will of him that first made this combination.

4. Indeed another coming after, and in conversation learning from him the word *courage*, may make an idea, to which he gives the name courage, different from what the first author applied it to, and has in his mind when he uses it. And in this case, if he designs that his idea in thinking should be conformable to the other's idea, as the name he uses in speaking is conformable in sound to his from whom he learned it, his idea may be very wrong and inadequate: because in this case, making the other man's idea the pattern of his idea in thinking, as the other man's word or sound is the pattern of his in speaking, his idea is so far defective and inadequate, as it is distant from the archetype and pattern he refers it to, and intends to express and signify by the name he uses for it; which name he would have to be a sign of the other man's idea, (to which, in its proper use, it is primarily annexed,) and of his own, as agreeing to it: to which if his own does not exactly correspond, it is faulty and inadequate.

Modes, in reference to settled Names, may be inadequate.

5. Therefore these complex ideas of *modes*, which they are referred by the mind, and intended to correspond to the ideas in the mind of some other intelligent being, expressed by the names we apply to them, they may be very deficient, wrong, and inadequate; because they agree not to that which the mind designs to be their archetype and pattern: in which respect only any idea of modes can be wrong, imperfect, or inadequate. And on this account our ideas of mixed modes are the most liable to be faulty of any other; but this refers more to proper speaking than knowing right[1].

Because then meant, in propriety of speech, to correspond to the ideas in some other mind.

[1] If our ideas of abstract modes can be called 'inadequate' only when they are viewed in relation to the ideas which other men choose to express

BOOK II.
——
CHAP.
XXXI.
Ideas
of Sub-
stances, as
referred
to real
Essences,
not ade-
quate.

6. Thirdly, what *ideas we have of substances*, I have above shown [1]. Now, those ideas have in the mind a double reference: 1. Sometimes they are referred to a supposed real essence of each species of things. 2. Sometimes they are only designed to be pictures and representations in the mind of things that do exist, by ideas of those qualities that are discoverable in them. In both which ways these copies of those originals and archetypes are imperfect and inadequate.

First, it is usual for men to make the names of substances stand for things as supposed to have certain real essences, whereby they are of this or that species : and names standing for nothing but the ideas that are in men's minds, they must constantly refer their ideas to such real essences, as to their archetypes. That men (especially such as have been bred up in the learning taught in this part of the world) do suppose certain specific essences of substances, which each individual in its several kinds is made conformable to and partakes of, is so far from needing proof that it will be thought strange if any one should do otherwise [2]. And thus they ordinarily apply the specific names they rank particular substances under, to things as distinguished by such specific real essences. Who is there almost, who would not take it amiss if it should be doubted whether he called himself a man, with any other meaning than as having the real essence of a man ? And yet if you demand what those real essences are, it is plain men

by the words which stand for them, it would follow that the convention of language is the only standard for determining their adequacy or inadequacy. Whence then the controversies about mixed modes, such as *religion, courage, justice,* and the virtues and vices generally ? Are all these disputes only about the proper use of words, which can be settled by their customary connotation, or is there not something deeper involved ? What has been called the 'nominalism' of Locke here appears.

[1] Ch. xxiii.

[2] He refers of course to the scho-lastic theory of the *real essences* which individual substances exemplify or participate in. With Locke this means (in the case of material substances) the primary constitution of the *atoms* of which they are composed, and on which all their 'imputed' qualities are supposed to depend. This he contrasts with their *nominal essence,* i.e. the connotation of their class name; in virtue of which the name is applicable to all actual (or imaginary) things, in which the connoted attributes are to be found. But the subject belongs properly to the third Book, especially in ch. vi.

are ignorant, and know them not. From whence it follows, that the ideas they have in their minds, being referred to real essences, as to archetypes which are unknown, must be so far from being adequate that they cannot be supposed to be any representation of them at all. The complex ideas we have of substances are, as it has been shown [1], certain collections of simple ideas that have been observed or supposed constantly to exist together. But such a complex idea cannot be the real essence of any substance; for then the properties we discover in that body would depend on that complex idea, and be deducible from it, and their necessary connexion with it be known; as all properties of a triangle depend on, and, as far as they are discoverable, are deducible from the complex idea of three lines including a space. But it is plain that in our complex ideas of substances are not contained such ideas, on which all the other qualities that are to be found in them do depend. The common idea men have of iron is, a body of a certain colour, weight, and hardness; and a property that they look on as belonging to it, is malleableness. But yet this property has no necessary connexion with that complex idea, or any part of it: and there is no more reason to think that malleableness depends on that colour, weight, and hardness, than that colour or that weight depends on its malleableness. And yet, though we know nothing of these real essences, there is nothing more ordinary than that men should attribute the sorts of things to such essences. The particular parcel of matter which makes the ring I have on my finger is forwardly by most men supposed to have a real essence, whereby it is gold; and from whence those qualities flow which I find in it, viz. its peculiar colour, weight, hardness, fusibility, fixedness, and change of colour upon a slight touch of mercury, &c. This essence, from which all these properties flow, when I inquire into it and search after it, I plainly perceive I cannot discover: the furthest I can go is, only to presume that, it being nothing but body, its real essence or internal constitution, on which these qualities depend, can be nothing but the figure, size, and connexion of its solid parts; of neither of which having any distinct per-

[1] Chap. xxiii.

ception at all can I have any idea of its essence : which is the cause that it has that particular shining yellowness ; a greater weight than anything I know of the same bulk ; and a fitness to have its colour changed by the touch of quicksilver. If any one will say, that the real essence and internal constitution, on which these properties depend, is not the figure, size, and arrangement or connexion of its solid parts, but something else, called its particular *form,* I am further from having any idea of its real essence than I was before. For I have an idea of figure, size, and situation of solid parts in general, though I have none of the particular figure, size, or putting together of parts, whereby the qualities above mentioned are produced ; which qualities I find in that particular parcel of matter that is on my finger, and not in another parcel of matter, with which I cut the pen I write with. But, when I am told that something besides the figure, size, and posture of the solid parts of that body in its essence, something called *substantial form*[1], of that I confess I have no idea at all, but only of the sound form ; which is far enough from an idea of its real essence or constitution. The like ignorance as I have of the real essence of this particular substance, I have also of the real essence of all other natural ones : of which essences I confess I have no distinct ideas at all ; and, I am apt to suppose, others, when they examine their own knowledge, will find in themselves, in this one point, the same sort of ignorance.

Because men know not the real essences of substances.

7. Now, then, when men apply to this particular parcel of matter on my finger a general name already in use, and denominate it *gold,* do they not ordinarily, or are they not understood to give it that name, as belonging to a particular species of bodies, having a real internal essence ; by having

---

[1] The Aristotelian 'substantial form,' with the relative distinction between form (εἶδος) and matter (ὕλη), which plays so important a part in Peripatetic philosophy, is not what Locke means by the 'real essence' of a substance. For Locke's real essence is the (by us) imperceptible constitution and motions of the primary atoms of sensible things, and is thus a *physical* essence in which matter and form are already combined. According to the Peripatetics, the 'substantial form' of anything is, that which makes it be the thing it actually is, giving it the reality and specific nature which it has, and by which it is distinguished from other substances.

of which essence this particular substance comes to be of that species, and to be called by that name? If it be so, as it is plain it is, the name by which things are marked as having that essence must be referred primarily to that essence; and consequently the idea to which that name is given must be referred also to that essence, and be intended to represent it. Which essence, since they who so use the names know not, their ideas of substances must be all inadequate in that respect, as not containing in them that real essence which the mind intends they should.

8. Secondly, those who, neglecting that useless supposition of unknown real essences, whereby they are distinguished, endeavour to copy the substances that exist in the world, by putting together the ideas of those sensible qualities which are found co-existing in them[1], though they come much nearer a likeness of them than those who imagine they know not what real specific essences : yet they arrive not at perfectly adequate ideas of those substances they would thus copy into their minds : nor do those copies exactly and fully contain all that is to be found in their archetypes. Because those qualities and powers of substances, whereof we make their complex ideas, are so many and various, that no man's complex idea contains them all. That our complex ideas of substances do not contain in them *all* the simple ideas that are united in the things themselves is evident, in that men do rarely put into their complex idea of any substance all the simple ideas they do know to exist in it. Because, endeavouring to make the signification of their names as clear and as little cumbersome

---

[1] In 'neglecting,' that is to say, the metaphysical presupposition of a 'substantial form,' and even the presupposition of a physical constitution, determined by primary qualities, on which all the 'powers' of the substance depend; and forming our ideas of substances solely from the phenomena which they actually present to our observation, our ideas of them are still necessarily inadequate. No one can observe *all* the causal relations of *all* substances; and without this one cannot have an exhaustive complex idea of any of them. In a word, we can have no positive idea of the substantial form of a substance; hardly any idea of the concrete constitution of its elementary atoms (assuming that it originally consists of such); and a very inadequate idea of the qualities or powers in which it might manifest itself to observation. This limitation of *our* adequate ideas does not bar the faith that there must *be* an essence in each thing, on which its nature depends.

as they can, they make their specific ideas of the sorts of substance, for the most part, of a few of those simple ideas which are to be found in them: but these having no original precedency, or right to be put in, and make the specific idea, more than others that are left out, it is plain that both these ways our ideas of substances are deficient and inadequate. The simple ideas whereof we make our complex ones of substances are all of them (bating only the figure and bulk of some sorts [1]) powers; which being relations to other substances, we can never be sure that we know *all* the powers that are in any one body, till we have tried what changes it is fitted to give to or receive from other substances in their several ways of application: which being impossible to be tried upon any one body, much less upon all, it is impossible we should have adequate ideas of any substance made up of a collection of all its properties.

Their powers usually make up our complex ideas of substances.

9. Whosoever first lighted on a parcel of that sort of substance we denote by the word *gold*, could not rationally take the bulk and figure he observed in that lump to depend on its real essence, or internal constitution. Therefore those never went into his idea of that species of body; but its peculiar colour, perhaps, and weight, were the first he abstracted from it, to make the complex idea of that species. Which both are but powers; the one to affect our eyes after such a manner, and to produce in us that idea we call yellow; and the other to force upwards any other body of equal bulk, they being put into a pair of equal scales, one against another. Another perhaps added to these the ideas of fusibility and fixedness, two other passive powers, in relation to the operation of fire upon it; another, its ductility and solubility in *aqua regia*, two other powers, relating to the operation of other bodies, in changing its outward figure, or separation of it into insensible parts. These, or parts of these, put together, usually make the complex idea in men's minds of that sort of body we call *gold*.

Substances have innumerable powers not con-

10. But no one who hath considered the properties of bodies in general, or this sort in particular, can doubt that this, called *gold*, has infinite other properties not contained in that complex idea. Some who have examined this species

---

[1] 'some sorts,' i. e. *bodies* only, not spiritual substances.

more accurately could, I believe, enumerate ten times as many properties in gold, all of them as inseparable from its internal constitution, as its colour or weight : and it is probable, if any one knew all the properties that are by divers men known of this metal, there would be an hundred times as many ideas go to the complex idea of gold as any one man yet has in his; and yet perhaps that not be the thousandth part of what is to be discovered in it. The changes that that one body is apt to receive, and make in other bodies, upon a due application, exceeding far not only what we know, but what we are apt to imagine. Which will not appear so much a paradox to any one who will but consider how far men are yet from knowing all the properties of that one, no very compound figure, a triangle ; though it be no small number that are already by mathematicians discovered of it.

11. So that all our complex ideas of substances are imperfect and inadequate. Which would be so also in mathematical figures, if we were to have our complex ideas of them, only by collecting their properties in reference to other figures. How uncertain and imperfect would our ideas be of an ellipsis, if we had no other idea of it, but some few of its properties ? Whereas, having in our plain idea the *whole* essence of that figure, we from thence discover those properties, and demonstratively see how they flow, and are inseparable from it.

12. Thus the mind has three sorts of abstract ideas or nominal essences :

First, *simple* ideas, which are ἔκτυπα or copies ; but yet certainly adequate. Because, being intended to express nothing but the power in things to produce in the mind such a sensation, that sensation, when it is produced, cannot but be the effect of that power. So the paper I write on, having the power in the light (I speak according to the common notion of light) to produce in men the sensation which I call white, it cannot but be the effect of such a power in something without the mind ; since the mind has not the power to produce any such idea in itself : and being meant for nothing else but the effect of such a power, that simple idea is real and adequate ;

the sensation of white, in my mind, being the effect of that power which is in the paper to produce it, is perfectly adequate to that power ; or else that power would produce a different idea.

Ideas of Substances are ἔκτυπα, and inadequate.

13. Secondly, the *complex* ideas of *substances* are ectypes, copies too ; but not perfect ones, not adequate : which is very evident to the mind, in that it plainly perceives, that whatever collection of simple ideas it makes of any substance that exists, it cannot be sure that it exactly answers all that are in that substance. Since, not having tried all the operations of all other substances upon it, and found all the alterations it would receive from, or cause in, other substances, it cannot have an exact adequate collection of all its active and passive capacities ; and so not have an adequate complex idea of the powers of any substance existing, and its relations ; which is that sort of complex idea of substances we have. And, after all, if we would have, and actually had, in our complex idea, an exact collection of all the secondary qualities or powers of any substance, we should not yet thereby have an idea of the *essence* of that thing. For, since the powers or qualities that are observable by us are not the real essence of that substance, but depend on it, and flow from it, any collection whatsoever of these qualities cannot be the real essence of that thing. Whereby it is plain, that our ideas of substances are not adequate ; are not what the mind intends them to be. Besides, a man has no idea of substance in general, nor knows what substance is in itself.

Ideas of Modes and Relations are Archetypes, and cannot but be adequate.

14. Thirdly, *complex* ideas of *modes and relations* are originals, and archetypes ; are not copies, nor made after the pattern of any real existence, to which the mind intends them to be conformable, and exactly to answer. These being such collections of simple ideas that the mind itself puts together, and such collections that each of them contains in it precisely all that the mind intends that it should, they are archetypes and essences of modes that may exist ; and so are designed only for, and belong only to such modes as, when they do exist, have an exact conformity with those complex ideas.

The ideas, therefore, of modes and relations cannot but be adequate [1].

[1] Thus, according to Locke in this and the preceding chapter, our complex ideas of the qualities and powers of *substances*—finite substances, material or spiritual, and God—are the only ideas that need to be brought into conformity with what really exists, or to be made more adequate. Our *simple ideas*, so far as they go, are as real and adequate as they can be, being the appearances presented by bodies in sense-perception, and by our own minds in self-conscious-ness. Our complex ideas of *modes*, and of abstract *relations*, having no other reality than that they *are* ideas in a human mind, there is nothing more required to make *them* real than that they be 'so formed that there is a possibility of substances existing conformable to them.' As complex ideas of which we are actually conscious, they cannot be unreal; unless 'any one will jumble together in them inconsistent ideas,' in which case they cannot even be formed.

CHAPTER XXXII.

OF TRUE AND FALSE IDEAS.

BOOK II.
––••––
Chap.
XXXII.
Truth and
Falsehood
properly
belong to
Proposi-
tions, not
to Ideas.

1. Though truth and falsehood belong, in propriety of speech, only to *propositions*[1] : yet *ideas* are oftentimes termed true or false (as what words are there that are not used with great latitude, and with some deviation from their strict and proper significations?) Though I think that when ideas themselves are termed true or false, there is still some secret or tacit proposition, which is the foundation of that denomination : as we shall see, if we examine the particular occasions wherein they come to be called true or false. In all which we shall find some kind of affirmation or negation, which is the reason of that denomination. For our ideas, being nothing but bare *appearances*, or perceptions in our minds[2], cannot properly and simply in themselves be said to be true or false, no more than a single name of anything can be said to be true or false[3].

2. Indeed both ideas and words may be said to be true, in a metaphysical sense of the word truth; as all other things that any way exist are said to be true, i. e. really to be such as

---

[1] Propositions may be either mental or verbal.

[2] 'in our minds,' i. e. which are mentally apprehended by us.

[3] Until we (expressly or tacitly) affirm or deny something of the ideas we have of things, the idea itself cannot be called either true or false ; for its truth or falsehood consists in the relation to reality of some

judgment into which it enters. As the second Book of the *Essay* professedly treats of *ideas, in abstraction from the judgments into which they enter,* the consideration of their truth and false-hood rightly belongs to the fourth Book, which deals with the relations of simple and complex ideas in propositions and reasonings.

they exist[1]. Though in things called true, even in that sense, there is perhaps a secret reference to our ideas, looked upon as the standards of that truth; which amounts to a mental proposition, though it be usually not taken notice of.

BOOK II.

CHAP. XXXII.

inasmuch as they really are ideas and words.

No Idea, as an Appearance in the Mind, either true or false.

3. But it is not in that metaphysical sense of truth which we inquire here, when we examine, whether our ideas are capable of being true or false, but in the more ordinary acceptation of those words: and so I say that the ideas in our minds, being only so many perceptions or appearances there, none of them are false; the idea of a centaur having no more falsehood in it when it appears in our minds, than the name centaur has falsehood in it, when it is pronounced by our mouths, or written on paper. For truth or falsehood lying always in some affirmation or negation, mental or verbal, our ideas are not capable, any of them, of being false, till the mind passes some judgment on them; that is, affirms or denies something of them.

4. Whenever the mind refers any of its ideas to anything extraneous to them, they are then capable to be called true or false. Because the mind, in such a reference, makes a tacit supposition of their conformity to that thing; which supposition, as it happens to be true or false, so the ideas themselves come to be denominated. The most usual cases wherein this happens, are these following:

5. First, when the mind supposes any idea it has *conformable* to that in *other men's minds*, called by the same common name; v.g. when the mind intends or judges its ideas of justice, temperance, religion, to be the same with what other men give those names to.

Secondly, when the mind supposes any idea it has in itself to be *conformable* to some *real existence*. Thus the two ideas of a man and a centaur, supposed to be the ideas of real substances, are the one true and the other false; the one having a conformity to what has really existed, the other not.

---

[1] In that sense all ideas are equally true. It is as true that *I have the idea* of a centaur, when I am imagining one, as that *I have the idea* of a man, when I am imagining a man. But if I tacitly imply that a centaur actually exists, *independently of this individual and transitory idea,* then this idea (or rather this judgment, latent in the idea) is false.

BOOK II.

CHAP.
XXXII.

Thirdly, when the mind *refers* any of its ideas to that *real* constitution and *essence* of anything, whereon all its properties depend : and thus the greatest part, if not all our ideas of substances, are false.

The cause of such Reference.

6. These suppositions the mind is very apt tacitly to make concerning its own ideas. But yet, if we will examine it, we shall find it is chiefly, if not only, concerning its *abstract* complex ideas[1]. For the natural tendency of the mind being towards knowledge; and finding that, if it should proceed by and dwell upon only particular things, its progress would be very slow, and its work endless; therefore, to shorten its way to knowledge, and make each perception more comprehensive, the first thing it does, as the foundation of the easier enlarging its knowledge, either by contemplation of the things themselves that it would know, or conference with others about them, is to bind them into bundles, and rank them so into sorts, that what knowledge it gets of any of them it may thereby with assurance extend to all of that sort; and so advance by larger steps in that which is its great business, knowledge. This, as I have elsewhere shown[2], is the reason why we collect things under comprehensive ideas, with names annexed to them, into genera and species; i. e. into kinds and sorts.

Names of things supposed to carry in them knowledge of their essences.

7. If therefore we will warily attend to the motions of the mind, and observe what course it usually takes in its way to knowledge, we shall I think find, that the mind having got an idea which it thinks it may have use of either in contemplation or discourse, the first thing it does is to abstract it, and then get a name to it; and so lay it up in its storehouse, the memory, as containing the essence[3] of a sort of things, of which that name is always to be the mark.

---

[1] I. e. its general ideas, or generalisations, which Locke calls 'abstract ideas.'

[2] Bk. III. ch. iii. Here and elsewhere Locke regards *universality* as but accidental to our knowledge, the whole and utmost of which consists in ' perception of the agreement or disagreement of our *particular* ideas.'

(Bk. IV. ch. xvii. § 8.) He is always shy of the universal, disparages it as an instrument of discovery, and views common terms chiefly as means of relieving the memory, otherwise oppressed by the multiplicity of particular substances, and of their simple ideas or qualities.

[3] Nominal essence.

Hence it is, that we may often observe that, when any one sees a new thing of a kind that he knows not, he presently asks, what it is; meaning by that inquiry nothing but the name. As if the name carried with it the knowledge of the species, or the essence of it; whereof it is indeed used as the mark, and is generally supposed annexed to it.

8. But this *abstract idea*, being something in the mind, between the thing that exists, and the name that is given to it; it is in our ideas that both the rightness of our knowledge, and the propriety and intelligibleness of our speaking, consists. And hence it is that men are so forward to suppose, that the abstract ideas they have in their minds are such as agree to the things existing without them, to which they are referred; and are the same also to which the names they give them do by the use and propriety of that language belong. For without this double conformity of their ideas, they find they should both think amiss of things in themselves, and talk of them unintelligibly to others.

9. First, then, I say, that when the truth of our ideas is judged of by the conformity they have to the ideas which other men have, and commonly signify by the same name, they may be any of them false. But yet *simple ideas* are least of all liable to be so mistaken. Because a man, by his senses and every day's observation, may easily satisfy himself what the simple ideas are which their several names that are in common use stand for; they being but few in number, and such as, if he doubts or mistakes in, he may easily rectify by the objects they are to be found in. Therefore it is seldom that any one mistakes in his names of simple ideas, or applies the name red to the idea green [1], or the name sweet to the idea bitter: much less are men apt to confound the names of ideas belonging to different senses, and call a colour by the name of a taste, &c. Whereby it is evident that the simple ideas they call by any name are commonly the same that others have and mean when they use the same names [2].

---

[1] As in cases of colour blindness.
[2] Here Locke must have in view our simple ideas of the things of sense, for men are often at cross purposes

BOOK II.
⎯•⎯
CHAP.
XXXII.

Ideas of
mixed
Modes
most liable
to be false
in this
Sense.

10. Complex ideas are much more liable to be false in this respect; and the complex ideas of *mixed modes*, much more than those of substances; because in substances (especially those which the common and unborrowed names of any language are applied to) some remarkable sensible qualities, serving ordinarily to distinguish one sort from another, easily preserve those who take any care in the use of their words, from applying them to sorts of substances to which they do not at all belong. But in mixed modes we are much more uncertain; it being not so easy to determine of several actions, whether they are to be called *justice* or *cruelty*, *liberality* or *prodigality*. And so in referring our ideas to those of other men, called by the same names, ours may be false; and the idea in our minds, which we express by the word *justice*, may perhaps be that which ought to have another name[1].

Or at least
to be
thought
false.

11. But whether or no our ideas of mixed modes are more liable than any sort to be different from those of other men, which are marked by the same names, this at least is certain, That this sort of falsehood is much more familiarly attributed to our ideas of mixed modes than to any other. When a man is thought to have a false idea of *justice*, or *gratitude*, or *glory*, it is for no other reason, but that his agrees not with the ideas which each of those names are the signs of in other men.

And why.

12. The reason whereof seems to me to be this: That the abstract ideas of mixed modes, being men's voluntary combinations of such a precise collection of simple ideas, and so the essence of each species being made by men alone, whereof we have no other sensible standard[2] existing anywhere but the name itself, or the definition of that name; we having nothing else to refer these our ideas of mixed modes to, as a standard[2] to which we would conform them,

about their simple ideas of reflection, with the result of much merely verbal controversy in theology and philosophy.

[1] In fact, there are endless varieties of connotation annexed to some of the terms which signify 'mixed modes,'

there being no obvious standard by which to determine their meaning. Take the word 'religion,' for example.

[2] Is this true of *all* mixed modes? Is there no other 'standard' for any of them than either a 'sensible one,' or

but the ideas of those who are thought to use those names in
their most proper significations ; and, so as our ideas conform
or differ from *them*, they pass for true or false. And thus
much concerning the truth and falsehood of our ideas, in
reference to their names.

13. Secondly, as to the truth and falsehood of our ideas,
in reference to the real existence of things. When that is
made the standard of their truth, none of them can be termed
false but only our complex ideas of substances.

14. First, our simple ideas, being barely such perceptions
as God has fitted us to receive, and given power to external
objects to produce in us by established laws and ways, suitable
to his wisdom and goodness, though incomprehensible to us,
their truth consists in nothing else but in such appearances
as are produced in us, and must be suitable to those powers
he has placed in external objects or else they could not be
produced in us : and thus answering those powers, they are
what they should be, true ideas. Nor do they become liable
to any imputation of falsehood, if the mind (as in most men
I believe it does) judges these ideas to be in the things themselves. For God in his wisdom having set them as marks of
distinction in things, whereby we may be able to discern one
thing from another, and so choose any of them for our uses
as we have occasion ; it alters not the nature of our simple
idea, whether we think that the idea of blue be in the violet
itself, or in our mind only ; and only the power of producing
it by the texture of its parts, reflecting the particles of light
after a certain manner, to be in the violet itself. For that
texture in the object, by a regular and constant operation
producing the same idea of blue in us, it serves us to distinguish, by our eyes, that from any other thing ; whether that
distinguishing mark, as it is really in the violet, be only a
peculiar texture of parts, or else that very colour, the idea
whereof (which is in us) is the exact resemblance. And it

BOOK II.

CHAP.
XXXII.

As re-
ferred to
Real
Existence,
none of
our Ideas
can be
false but
those
of Sub-
stances.
First,
simple
Ideas in
this Sense
not false,
and why.

that constituted by the conventional
use of words ? Men are no doubt apt
to be satisfied with one or other of
these standards, without pushing the
inquiry deeper. But what of the eternal
and immutable ideas of morality, and
the ultimate ideas of mathematics and
physics ?

is equally from that appearance to be denominated blue, whether it be that real colour, or only a peculiar texture in it, that causes in us that idea : since the name, *blue*, notes properly nothing but that mark of distinction that is in a violet, discernible only by our eyes, whatever it consists in ; that being beyond our capacities distinctly to know, and perhaps would be of less use to us, if we had faculties to discern.

Though one Man's Idea of Blue should be different from another's.

15. Neither would it carry any imputation of falsehood to our simple ideas, if by the different structure of our organs it were so ordered, that *the same object should produce in several men's minds different ideas* at the same time ; v. g. if the idea that a violet produced in one man's mind by his eyes were the same that a marigold produced in another man's, and *vice versâ*. For, since this could never be known, because one man's mind could not pass into another man's body, to perceive what appearances were produced by those organs ; neither the ideas hereby, nor the names, would be at all confounded, or any falsehood be in either. For all things that had the texture of a violet, producing constantly the idea that he called blue, and those which had the texture of a marigold, producing constantly the idea which he as constantly called yellow, whatever those appearances were in his mind ; he would be able as regularly to distinguish things for his use by those appearances, and understand and signify those distinctions marked by the name blue and yellow, as if the appearances or ideas in his mind received from those two flowers were exactly the same with the ideas in other men's minds. I am nevertheless very apt to think that the sensible ideas produced by any object in different men's minds, are most commonly very near and undiscernibly alike. For which opinion, I think, there might be many reasons offered : but that being besides my present business, I shall not trouble my reader with them ; but only mind him [1], that the contrary supposition, if it could be proved, is of little use, either for the improvement of our knowledge, or conveniency of life, and so we need not trouble ourselves to examine it [2].

---

[1] 'Mind him,' i.e. ask him to take note.

[2] The subjective idea of colour, dependent on the individual organism, is not, he implies, necessarily the same

16. From what has been said concerning our simple ideas, I think it evident that our simple ideas can none of them be false in respect of things existing without us. For the truth of these appearances or perceptions in our minds consisting, as has been said, only in their being answerable to the powers in external objects to produce by our senses such appearances in us, and each of them being in the mind such as it is, suitable to the power that produced it, and which alone it represents, it cannot upon that account, or as referred to such a pattern, be false. Blue and yellow, bitter or sweet, can never be false ideas: these perceptions in the mind are just such as they are there, answering the powers appointed by God to produce them; and so are truly what they are, and are intended to be. Indeed the names may be misapplied, but that in this respect makes no falsehood in the ideas; as if a man ignorant in the English tongue should call purple scarlet[1].

17. Secondly, neither can our complex ideas of modes, in reference to the essence of anything really existing, be false; because whatever complex ideas I have of any mode, it hath no reference to any pattern existing, and made by nature; it is not supposed to contain in it any other ideas than what it hath; nor to represent anything but such a complication of ideas as it does[2]. Thus, when I have the idea of such an action of a man who forbears to afford himself such meat, drink, and clothing, and other conveniences of life, as his riches and estate will be sufficient to supply and his station requires, I have no false idea; but such an one as represents an action, either as I find or imagine it, and so is capable of neither truth nor falsehood. But when I give the name *frugality* or *virtue* to this action, then it may be called a false idea, if thereby it be supposed to agree with that idea to which, in propriety of speech, the name of frugality doth

in all men, as their ideas of size and situation are. This is illustrated by the phenomena of colour blindness. (Prof. Rutherford reports rare cases in which the defective sense of colour was limited to one eye, thus giving opportunity for comparison.)

[1] All simple ideas, i. e. all phenomena actually presented by substances, are true, for the same reason that they are all real and adequate. Cf. § 14, closely followed in § 15.

[2] What of the *simple modes* of space and duration? He seems to rank them with simple ideas. Cf. Bk. III. ch. iv. § 17; ix. § 19.

BOOK II.

CHAP.
XXXII.

Thirdly,
Ideas
of Sub-
stances
may be
false in
reference
to existing
things.

belong, or to be conformable to that law which is the standard of virtue and vice [1].

18. Thirdly, our complex ideas of substances, being all referred to patterns in things themselves, may be false. That they are all false, when looked upon as the representations of the unknown essences of things, is so evident that there needs nothing to be said of it. I shall therefore pass over that chimerical supposition [2], and consider them as collections of simple ideas in the mind, taken from combinations of simple ideas existing together constantly [3] in things, of which patterns they are the supposed copies; and in this reference of them to the existence of things, they are false ideas :— (1) When they put together simple ideas, which in the real existence of things have no union ; as when to the shape and size that exist together in a horse, is joined in the same complex idea the power of barking like a dog : which three ideas, however put together into one in the mind, were never united in nature ; and this, therefore, may be called a false idea of a horse. (2) Ideas of substances are, in this respect, also false, when, from any collection of simple ideas that do always exist together, there is separated, by a direct negation, any other simple idea which is constantly joined with them. Thus, if to extension, solidity, fusibility, the peculiar weightiness, and yellow colour of gold, any one join in his thoughts the negation of a greater degree of fixedness than is in lead or copper, he may be said to have a false complex idea, as well as when he joins to those other simple ones the idea of perfect absolute fixedness. For either way, the complex idea of gold being made up of such simple ones as have no union in nature, may be termed false. But, if he leave out of this his complex idea that of fixedness quite, without either actually joining to or separating it from the rest in his

---

[1] 'Mixed modes' cannot be false, he says, because they are formed by the individual, and do not refer to real existence. Yet he recognises the reference of some of them to 'that law which is the standard of virtue and vice,' the immutability and eternity of which he elsewhere acknowledges.

[2] Cf. ch. xxxi. § 6.

[3] 'taken,' i. e. by observing the particular substances in which they appear, correspondence with which constitutes their 'truth'; and 'existing together *constantly,*' so that they can be the subjects of universal propositions.

mind, it is, I think, to be looked on as an inadequate and imperfect idea, rather than a false one; since, though it contains not all the simple ideas that are united in nature, yet it puts none together but what do really exist together.

19. Though, in compliance with the ordinary way of speaking, I have shown in what sense and upon what ground our ideas may be sometimes called true or false; yet if we will look a little nearer into the matter, in all cases where any idea is called true or false, it is from some *judgment* that the mind makes, or is supposed to make, that is true or false. For truth or falsehood, being never without some affirmation or negation, express or tacit, it is not to be found but where signs are joined or separated, according to the agreement or disagreement of the things they stand for. The signs we chiefly use are either ideas or words; wherewith we make either mental or verbal propositions[1]. Truth lies in so joining or separating these representatives, as the things they stand for do in themselves agree or disagree; and falsehood in the contrary, as shall be more fully shown hereafter[2].

Truth or Falsehood always supposes Affirmation or Negation.

20. Any idea, then, which we have in our minds, whether conformable or not to the existence of things, or to any idea in the minds of other men, cannot properly for this alone be called false. For these representations, if they have nothing in them but what is really existing in things without, cannot be thought false, being exact representations of something: nor yet if they have anything in them differing from the reality of things, can they properly be said to be false representations, or ideas of things they do not represent. But the mistake and falsehood is:

Ideas in themselves neither true nor false.

21. First, when the mind having any idea, it *judges* and concludes it the same that is in other men's minds, signified by the same name; or that it is conformable to the ordinary received signification or definition of that word, when indeed it is not: which is the most usual mistake in mixed modes, though other ideas also are liable to it.

But are false— 1. When judged agreeable to another Man's Idea, without being so.

---

[1] Cf. Bk. IV. ch. xxi. § 4.   [2] Cf. Bk. IV. chh. v–viii.

Secondly,
When
judged
to agree
to real
Existence,
when they
do not.
Thirdly,
When
judged
adequate,
without
being so.

22. (2) When it having a complex idea made up of such a collection of simple ones as nature never puts together, it *judges* it to agree to a species of creatures really existing; as when it joins the weight of tin to the colour, fusibility, and fixedness of gold.

23. (3) When in its complex idea it has united a certain number of simple ideas that do really exist together in some sort of creatures, but has also left out others as much inseparable, it *judges* this to be a perfect complete idea of a sort of things which really it is not; v. g. having joined the ideas of substance, yellow, malleable, most heavy, and fusible, it takes that complex idea to be the complete idea of gold, when yet its peculiar fixedness, and solubility in *aqua regia*, are as inseparable from those other ideas, or qualities, of that body as they are one from another.

Fourthly,
When
judged to
represent
the real
Essence.

24. (4) The mistake is yet greater, when I *judge* that this complex idea contains in it the real essence of any body existing; when at least it contains but some few of those properties which flow from its real essence and constitution. I say only some few of those properties; for those properties consisting mostly in the active and passive powers it has in reference to other things, all that are vulgarly known of any one body, of which the complex idea of that kind of things is usually made, are but a very few, in comparison of what a man that has several ways tried and examined it knows of that one sort of things; and all that the most expert man knows are but a few, in comparison of what are really in that body, and depend on its internal or essential constitution [1]. The essence of a triangle lies in a very little compass, consists in a very few ideas: three lines including a space make up that essence: but the properties that flow from this essence are more than can be easily known or enumerated. So I imagine it is in substances; their real essences lie in a little compass, though the properties flowing from that internal constitution are endless.

[1] This is a return to the assumption, so often made in the *Essay*,—that the secondary qualities and other powers of bodies depend upon the primary constitution and relations or 'texture of the atoms, in which Locke finds their 'real essence.' (Cf. Bk. III. ch. vi. and the annotations.)

25. To conclude, a man having no notion of anything without him, but by the idea he has of it in his mind, (which idea
he has a power to call by what name he pleases,) he may
indeed make an idea neither answering the reason of things, Ideas,
nor agreeing to the idea commonly signified by other people's when called
words; but cannot make a wrong or false idea of a thing false.
which is no otherwise known to him but by the idea he has
of it: v. g. when I frame an idea of the legs, arms, and body
of a man, and join to this a horse's head and neck, I do not
make a false idea of anything; because it represents nothing
without me. But when I call it a *man* or *Tartar*, and imagine
it to represent some real being without me, or to be the same
idea that others call by the same name; in either of these
cases I may err. And upon this account it is that it comes
to be termed a false idea; though indeed the falsehood lies
not in the idea, but in that tacit mental proposition, wherein
a conformity and resemblance is attributed to it which it has
not. But yet, if, having framed such an idea in my mind,
without thinking either that existence, or the name *man* or
Tartar, belongs to it, I will call it *man* or *Tartar*, I may be
justly thought fantastical in the naming; but not erroneous
in my judgment; nor the idea any way false.

26. Upon the whole matter, I think that our ideas, as they More
are considered by the mind,—either in reference to the proper properly to be
signification of their names; or in reference to the reality called
of things,—may very fitly be called *right* or *wrong* ideas, wrong.
according as they agree or disagree to those patterns to which
they are referred. But if any one had rather call them true
or false, it is fit he use a liberty, which every one has, to call
things by those names he thinks best; though, in propriety of
speech, *truth* or *falsehood* will, I think, scarce agree to them,
but as they, some way or other, virtually contain in them
some mental proposition. The ideas that are in a man's
mind, simply considered, cannot be wrong; unless complex
ones, wherein inconsistent parts are jumbled together. All
other ideas are in themselves right, and the knowledge about
them right and true knowledge; but when we come to refer
them to anything, as to their patterns and archetypes, then

they are capable of being wrong, as far as they disagree with such archetypes[1].

[1] The ultimate ground of our faith in the absolute reality, yet inadequacy, of human *knowledge*, is foreign to this and the two preceding chapters. The fourth Book is concerned with it, especially chh. iv, ix, x, xi, and xiv–xx; but in the second Book complex ideas, and their simple elements, are considered apart from the reality of the substances of which simple ideas are assumed to be the presented appearances. The distinction between human ideas and their reality implies, that individual men may, and often do, form complex ideas of substances that are inconsistent with the real substances of which the universe consists, the absolute reality being different from what is apprehended as real by them —implies, in short, the possibility of human error.

[CHAPTER XXXIII.]

[OF THE ASSOCIATION OF IDEAS [1].]

[1. THERE is scarce any one that does not observe something that seems odd to him, and is in itself really extravagant, in the opinions, reasonings, and actions of other men. The

[1] This chapter was inserted in the *fourth* edition, but was probably written some years before. In a letter to Molyneux (April 26, 1695), Locke mentions his intention to 'make some additions to be put into your Latin translation, particularly concerning the *connection of ideas*, which has not that I know been hitherto considered, and has, I guess, a greater influence upon our minds than is usually taken notice of.' The chapter appears in the Latin version, in 1701, entitled, *De idearum consociatione*, as well as in the French and English versions the year before. Locke's statement in it, that the 'connection of ideas has not been hitherto considered,' implies ignorance of its repeated recognition by Hobbes, not to speak of a succession of earlier writers, beginning with Aristotle. In Hobbes's *Human Nature* (1650) we have a statement and illustration of the principle, 'That the cause of the coherence or consequence of one conception to another is their first coherence or consequence at that time when they are produced by sense.' (Ch. iv. 2.) So also in the *Leviathan*, ch. iii :—' Of the Consequence or Train of Imaginations.' A hundred years after Hobbes this principle was systematically applied by Hartley to explain human knowledge; and under the name of ' custom' it is the constructive element in Hume's *Inquiry*. In its later developments, through the phenomena of heredity and law of evolution, it has been offered as the supreme law of organised life and intelligence, which brings man with other animals wholly under physical causation. It is curious that Locke, midway chronologically between Hobbes and Hartley, introduces ' association' not, as they did, to explain human knowledge, but with the opposite intent of accounting for human errors. In his *Conduct of the Understanding* (f. 41) he inquires further into ' the remedies that ought to be applied,' having, he says, ' in the second book of my *Essay* treated of the association of ideas historically, as giving a view of the understanding in this as well as its several other ways of operating ;— association being as frequent a cause of error in us as perhaps anything else that can be named, and a disease of the mind as hard to be cured as any ; it being a very hard thing to convince anyone that things are not so, and naturally so, as they constantly appear to him.'

BOOK II.
CHAP.
XXXIII.

least flaw of this kind, if at all different from his own, every one is quick-sighted enough to espy in another, and will by the authority of reason forwardly condemn; though he be guilty of much greater unreasonableness in his own tenets and conduct, which he never perceives, and will very hardly, if at all, be convinced of.

Not wholly from Self-love.

2. This proceeds not wholly from self-love, though that has often a great hand in it. Men of fair minds, and not given up to the overweening of self-flattery, are frequently guilty of it; and in many cases one with amazement hears the arguings, and is astonished at the obstinacy of a worthy man, who yields not to the evidence of reason, though laid before him as clear as daylight.

Not from Education.

3. This sort of unreasonableness is usually imputed to education and prejudice, and for the most part truly enough, though that reaches not the bottom of the disease, nor shows distinctly enough whence it rises, or wherein it lies. Education is often rightly assigned for the cause, and prejudice is a good general name for the thing itself: but yet, I think, he ought to look a little further, who would trace this sort of madness to the root it springs from, and so explain it, as to show whence this flaw has its original in very sober and rational minds, and wherein it consists.

A Degree of Madness found in most Men.

4. I shall be pardoned for calling it by so harsh a name as madness, when it is considered that opposition to reason deserves that name, and is really madness; and there is scarce a man so free from it, but that if he should always, on all occasions, argue or do as in some cases he constantly does. would not be thought fitter for Bedlam than civil conversation. I do not here mean when he is under the power of an unruly passion, but in the steady calm course of his life. That which will yet more apologize for this harsh name, and ungrateful imputation on the greatest part of mankind, is, that, inquiring a little by the bye into the nature of madness, (b. ii. ch. xi. § 13,) I found it to spring from the very same root, and to depend on the very same cause we are here speaking of. This consideration of the thing itself, at a time when I thought not the least on the subject which I am now treating of, suggested it to me. And if this be a weakness to which all men are so

liable, if this be a taint which so universally infects mankind,
the greater care should be taken to lay it open under its due
name, thereby to excite the greater care in its prevention
and cure.

5. Some of our ideas have a *natural* correspondence and
connexion one with another: it is the office and excellency of
our reason to trace these, and hold them together in that
union and correspondence which is founded in their peculiar
beings. Besides this, there is another connexion of ideas
wholly owing to *chance* or *custom*. Ideas that in themselves
are not all of kin, come to be so united in some men's minds,
that it is very hard to separate them; they always keep in
company, and the one no sooner at any time comes into the
understanding, but its associate appears with it; and if they
are more than two which are thus united, the whole gang,
always inseparable, show themselves together [1].

6. This strong combination of ideas, not allied by nature [2],
the mind makes in itself either voluntarily or by chance; and
hence it comes in different men to be very different, according
to their different inclinations, education, interests, &c. *Custom*
settles habits of thinking in the understanding, as well as of
determining in the will, and of motions in the body: all which
seems to be but trains of motions in the animal spirits, which,
once set a going, continue in the same steps they have been
used to; which, by often treading, are worn into a smooth
path, and the motion in it becomes easy, and as it were
natural. As far as we can comprehend thinking, thus ideas
seem to be produced in our minds; or, if they are not, this
may serve to explain their following one another in an habitual
train, when once they are put into their track, as well as it

[1] So far from trying to explain reason, by means of 'association of ideas,' Locke here expressly contrasts the 'natural' or rational relations of things with that connexion among ideas which is gradually generated, by their accidental coexistences and sequences in the mental experience of individuals. 'Inseparable' association, in an individual experience, is thus distinguished from intrinsic necessity of reason, and also from objective causality.

[2] Again Locke opposes association of phenomena according to the reason that is in nature—what he elsewhere calls 'the visible agreement that is in the ideas themselves'—to those associations which issue from 'the prevailing custom of the individual mind joining them together.' See *Conduct of the Understanding*, § 41.

does to explain such motions of the body [1]. A musician used to any tune will find that, let it but once begin in his head, the ideas of the several notes of it will follow one another orderly in his understanding, without any care or attention, as regularly as his fingers move orderly over the keys of the organ to play out the tune he has begun, though his unattentive thoughts be elsewhere a wandering [2]. Whether the natural cause of these ideas, as well as of that regular dancing of his fingers be the motion of his animal spirits, I will not determine, how probable soever, by this instance, it appears to be so : but this may help us a little to conceive of intellectual habits, and of the tying together of ideas.

Some Antipathies an Effect of it.
7. That there are such associations of them made by custom, in the minds of most men, I think nobody will question, who has well considered himself or others ; and to this, perhaps, might be justly attributed most of the sympathies and antipathies observable in men, which work as strongly, and produce as regular effects as if they were natural ; and are therefore called so, though they at first had no other original but the accidental connexion of two ideas, which either the strength of the first impression, or future indulgence so united, that they always afterwards kept company together in that man's mind, as if they were but one idea [3]. I say most of the antipathies, I do not say all ; for some of them are truly natural, depend upon our original constitution, and are born with us ; but a great part of those which are counted natural, would have been known to be from unheeded, though perhaps

---

[1] Locke thus makes little of those physiological 'explanations' of the associations among our ideas that refer them to motions in the nerves, which have played so large a part in materialistic psychology since Hartley. The cause therein supposed to explain why ideas, when often united, are apt ever after to keep company, in the individual mind in which they were so united, is alleged to be certain motions in the nerves ; 'ideas' themselves being our *feeling* of those motions, and thus dependent for their order upon mechanical causes.

[2] So Hartley, *Observations on Man*, vol. i. p. 108, and Stewart's *Elements*, pt. i. ch. ii.—' Of Attention.'

[3] The connexions thus formed, by accidents in the history of the individual, and so in unreason, give rise to Bacon's idols of the human mind, which fail to correspond to the objective connexions in nature that express Ideas of the Divine Mind. The complex ideas of substances that possess *our* minds thus come to be at cross purposes with the substances themselves, as they exist in the intelligible system of nature.

early, impressions, or wanton fancies at first, which would
have been acknowledged the original of them, if they had
been warily observed. A grown person surfeiting with honey
no sooner hears the name of it, but his fancy immediately
carries sickness and qualms to his stomach, and he cannot
bear the very idea of it ; other ideas of dislike, and sickness,
and vomiting, presently accompany it, and he is disturbed ;
but he knows from whence to date this weakness, and can tell
how he got this indisposition. Had this happened to him by
an over-dose of honey when a child, all the same effects would
have followed ; but the cause would have been mistaken, and
the antipathy counted natural.

8. I mention this, not out of any great necessity there is *Influence*
in this present argument to distinguish nicely between natural *of association to be*
and acquired antipathies; but I take notice of it for another *watched
educating*
purpose, viz. that those who have children, or the charge of *young*
their education, would think it worth their while diligently to *children.*
watch, and carefully to prevent the undue connexion of ideas
in the minds of young people. This is the time most susceptible of lasting impressions ; and though those relating to the
health of the body are by discreet people minded and fenced
against, yet I am apt to doubt, that those which relate more
peculiarly to the mind, and terminate in the understanding or
passions, have been much less heeded than the thing deserves :
nay, those relating purely to the understanding, have, as I
suspect, been by most men wholly overlooked.

9. This wrong connexion in our minds of ideas in them- *Wrong
connexion*
selves loose and independent of one another, has such an *of ideas a*
influence, and is of so great force to set us awry in our actions, *great
Cause of*
as well moral as natural, passions, reasonings, and notions *Errors.*
themselves, that perhaps there is not any one thing that
deserves more to be looked after.

10. The ideas of goblins and sprites have really no more to *An
instance.*
do with darkness than light: yet let but a foolish maid
inculcate these often on the mind of a child, and raise them
there together, possibly he shall never be able to separate
them again so long as he lives, but darkness shall ever afterwards bring with it those frightful ideas, and they shall be so
joined, that he can no more bear the one than the other.

Another instance.

11. A man receives a sensible injury from another, thinks on the man and that action over and over, and by ruminating on them strongly, or much, in his mind, so cements those two ideas together, that he makes them almost one; never thinks on the man, but the pain and displeasure he suffered comes into his mind with it, so that he scarce distinguishes them, but has as much an aversion for the one as the other. Thus hatreds are often begotten from slight and innocent occasions, and quarrels propagated and continued in the world.

A third instance.

12. A man has suffered pain or sickness in any place; he saw his friend die in such a room : though these have in nature nothing to do one with another, yet when the idea of the place occurs to his mind, it brings (the impression being once made) that of the pain and displeasure with it : he confounds them in his mind, and can as little bear the one as the other.

Why Time cures some Disorders in the Mind, which Reason cannot cure.

13. When this combination is settled, and while it lasts, it is not in the power of reason to help us, and relieve us from the effects of it. Ideas in our minds, when they are there, will operate according to their natures and circumstances. And here we see the cause why time cures certain affections, which reason, though in the right, and allowed to be so, has not power over, nor is able against them to prevail with those who are apt to hearken to it in other cases. The death of a child that was the daily delight of its mother's eyes, and joy of her soul, rends from her heart the whole comfort of her life, and gives her all the torment imaginable : use the consolations of reason in this case, and you were[1] as good preach ease to one on the rack, and hope to allay, by rational discourses, the pain of his joints tearing asunder. Till time has by disuse separated the sense of that enjoyment and its loss, from the idea of the child returning to her memory, all representations, though ever so reasonable, are in vain ; and therefore some in whom the union between these ideas is never dissolved, spend their lives in mourning, and carry an incurable sorrow to their graves.

Another instance of the Effect of the Association of Ideas.

14. A friend of mine knew one perfectly cured of madness by a very harsh and offensive operation. The gentleman who was thus recovered, with great sense of gratitude and acknowledgment owned the cure all his life after, as the greatest

[1] *Sic.*

obligation he could have received ; but, whatever gratitude and reason suggested to him, he could never bear the sight of the operator : that image brought back with it the idea of that agony which he suffered from his hands, which was too mighty and intolerable for him to endure.

15. Many children, imputing the pain they endured at school to their books they were corrected for, so join those ideas together, that a book becomes their aversion, and they are never reconciled to the study and use of them all their lives after ; and thus reading becomes a torment to them, which otherwise possibly they might have made the great pleasure of their lives. There are rooms convenient enough, that some men cannot study in, and fashions of vessels, which, though ever so clean and commodious, they cannot drink out of, and that by reason of some accidental ideas which are annexed to them, and make them offensive ; and who is there that hath not observed some man to flag at the appearance, or in the company of some certain person not otherwise superior to him, but because, having once on some occasion got the ascendant, the idea of authority and distance goes along with that of the person, and he that has been thus subjected, is not able to separate them.

16. Instances of this kind are so plentiful everywhere, that if I add one more, it is only for the pleasant oddness of it. It is of a young gentleman, who, having learnt to dance, and that to great perfection, there happened to stand an old trunk in the room where he learnt. The idea of this remarkable piece of household stuff had so mixed itself with the turns and steps of all his dances, that though in that chamber he could dance excellently well, yet it was only whilst that trunk was there ; nor could he perform well in any other place, unless that or some such other trunk had its due position in the room. If this story shall be suspected to be dressed up with some comical circumstances, a little beyond precise nature, I answer for myself that I had it some years since from a very sober and worthy man, upon his own knowledge, as I report it ; and I dare say there are very few inquisitive persons who read this, who have not met with accounts, if not examples, of this nature, that may parallel, or at least justify this.

BOOK II.

CHAP.
XXXIII.

Influence
of Associa-
tion on
intellec-
tual
Habits.

17. Intellectual habits and defects this way contracted, are not less frequent and powerful, though less observed. Let the ideas of being and matter be strongly joined, either by education or much thought; whilst these are still combined in the mind, what notions, what reasonings, will there be about separate spirits? Let custom from the very childhood have joined figure and shape to the idea of God, and what absurdities will that mind be liable to about the Deity? Let the idea of infallibility be inseparably joined to any person, and these two constantly together possess the mind; and then one body in two places at once, shall unexamined be swallowed for a certain truth, by an implicit faith, whenever that imagined infallible person dictates and demands assent without inquiry [1].

Observ-
able in the
opposition
between
different
Sects of
philosophy
and of
religion.

18. Some such wrong and unnatural combinations of ideas will be found to establish the irreconcilable opposition between different sects of philosophy and religion; for we cannot imagine every one of their followers to impose wilfully on himself, and knowingly refuse truth offered by plain reason. Interest, though it does a great deal in the case, yet cannot be thought to work whole societies of men to so universal a perverseness, as that every one of them to a man should knowingly maintain falsehood: some at least must be allowed to do what all pretend to, i.e. to pursue truth sincerely; and therefore there must be something that blinds their understandings, and makes them not see the falsehood of what they embrace for real truth. That which thus captivates their reasons, and leads men of sincerity blindfold from common sense, will, when examined, be found to be what we are speaking of: some independent ideas, of no alliance to one another, are, by education, custom, and the constant din of their party, so coupled in their minds, that they always appear there together; and they can no more separate them in their thoughts than if they were but one idea, and they operate as if they were so. This gives sense to jargon, demonstration to absurdities, and consistency to nonsense, and is the foundation of the greatest,

[1] 'Cette remarque est importante et entièrement à mon gré et on la pourrait fortifier par une infinité d'exemples.' (*Nouveaux Essais.*)

I had almost said of all the errors in the world ; or, if it does
not reach so far, it is at least the most dangerous one,
since, so far as it obtains, it hinders men from seeing and
examining. When two things, in themselves disjoined, appear to the sight constantly united ; if the eye sees these
things riveted which are loose, where will you begin to
rectify the mistakes that follow in two ideas that they have
been accustomed so to join in their minds as to substitute
one for the other, and, as I am apt to think, often without
perceiving it themselves? This, whilst they are under the
deceit of it, makes them incapable of conviction, and they
applaud themselves as zealous champions for truth, when
indeed they are contending for error ; and the confusion of two
different ideas, which a customary connexion of them in their
minds hath to them made in effect but one, fills their heads
with false views, and their reasonings with false consequences.

19. Having thus given an account of the original, sorts,
and extent of our IDEAS, with several other considerations
about these (I know not whether I may say) instruments,
or materials of our knowledge, the method I at first proposed
to myself would now require that I should immediately
proceed to show, what use the understanding makes of them,
and what KNOWLEDGE we have by them. This was that
which, in the first general view I had of this subject, was
all that I thought I should have to do : but, upon a nearer
approach, I find that there is so close a connexion between
ideas and WORDS, and our abstract ideas and general words
have so constant a relation one to another, that it is impossible to speak clearly and distinctly of our knowledge,
which all consists in propositions, without considering, first,
the nature, use, and signification of Language ; which, therefore, must be the business of the next Book.

END OF VOLUME I.

A CATALOGUE OF SELECTED DOVER BOOKS
IN ALL FIELDS OF INTEREST

A CATALOG OF SELECTED DOVER BOOKS IN ALL FIELDS OF INTEREST

THE ART NOUVEAU STYLE, edited by Roberta Waddell. 579 rare photographs of works in jewelry, metalwork, glass, ceramics, textiles, architecture and furniture by 175 artists—Mucha, Seguy, Lalique, Tiffany, many others. 288pp. 8⅜ × 11¼. 23515-7 Pa. $8.95

AMERICAN COUNTRY HOUSES OF THE GILDED AGE (Sheldon's "Artistic Country-Seats"), A. Lewis. All of Sheldon's fascinating and historically important photographs and plans. New text by Arnold Lewis. Approx. 200 illustrations. 128pp. 9⅜ × 12¼. 24301-X Pa. $7.95

THE WAY WE LIVE NOW, Anthony Trollope. Trollope's late masterpiece, marks shift to bitter satire. Character Melmotte "his greatest villain." Reproduced from original edition with 40 illustrations. 416pp. 6⅛ × 9¼. 24360-5 Pa. $7.95

BENCHLEY LOST AND FOUND, Robert Benchley. Finest humor from early 30's, about pet peeves, child psychologists, post office and others. Mostly unavailable elsewhere. 73 illustrations by Peter Arno and others. 183pp. 5⅜ × 8½. 22410-4 Pa. $3.50

ISOMETRIC PERSPECTIVE DESIGNS AND HOW TO CREATE THEM, John Locke. Isometric perspective is the picture of an object adrift in imaginary space. 75 mindboggling designs. 52pp. 8¼ × 11. 24123-8 Pa. $2.50

PERSPECTIVE FOR ARTISTS, Rex Vicat Cole. Depth, perspective of sky and sea, shadows, much more, not usually covered. 391 diagrams, 81 reproductions of drawings and paintings. 279pp. 5⅜ × 8½. 22487-2 Pa. $4.00

MOVIE-STAR PORTRAITS OF THE FORTIES, edited by John Kobal. 163 glamor, studio photos of 106 stars of the 1940s: Rita Hayworth, Ava Gardner, Marlon Brando, Clark Gable, many more. 176pp. 8⅜ × 11¼. 23546-7 Pa. $6.95

STARS OF THE BROADWAY STAGE, 1940-1967, Fred Fehl. Marlon Brando, Uta Hagen, John Kerr, John Gielgud, Jessica Tandy in great shows—*South Pacific, Galileo, West Side Story*, more. 240 black-and-white photos. 144pp. 8⅜ × 11¼. 24398-2 Pa. $8.95

ILLUSTRATED DICTIONARY OF HISTORIC ARCHITECTURE, edited by Cyril M. Harris. Extraordinary compendium of clear, concise definitions for over 5000 important architectural terms complemented by over 2000 line drawings. 592pp. 7½ × 9⅜. 24444-X Pa. $14.95

THE EARLY WORK OF FRANK LLOYD WRIGHT, F.L. Wright. 207 rare photos of Oak Park period, first great buildings: Unity Temple, Dana house, Larkin factory. Complete photos of Wasmuth edition. New Introduction. 160pp. 8⅜ × 11¼. 24381-8 Pa. $7.50

LIVING MY LIFE, Emma Goldman. Candid, no holds barred account by foremost American anarchist: her own life, anarchist movement, famous contemporaries, ideas and their impact. 944pp. 5⅜ × 8½. 22543-7, 22544-5 Pa., Two-vol. set $13.00

UNDERSTANDING THERMODYNAMICS, H.C. Van Ness. Clear, lucid treatment of first and second laws of thermodynamics. Excellent supplement to basic textbook in undergraduate science or engineering class. 103pp. 5⅜ × 8. 63277-6 Pa. $3.50

SMOCKING: TECHNIQUE, PROJECTS, AND DESIGNS, Dianne Durand. Foremost smocking designer provides complete instructions on how to smock. Over 10 projects, over 100 illustrations. 56pp. 8¼ × 11. 23788-5 Pa. $2.00

AUDUBON'S BIRDS IN COLOR FOR DECOUPAGE, edited by Eleanor H. Rawlings. 24 sheets, 37 most decorative birds, full color, on one side of paper. Instructions, including work under glass. 56pp. 8¼ × 11. 23492-4 Pa. $3.50

THE COMPLETE BOOK OF SILK SCREEN PRINTING PRODUCTION, J.I. Biegeleisen. For commercial user, teacher in advanced classes, serious hobbyist. Most modern techniques, materials, equipment for optimal results. 124 illustrations. 253pp. 5⅝ × 8½. 21100-2 Pa. $4.50

A TREASURY OF ART NOUVEAU DESIGN AND ORNAMENT, edited by Carol Belanger Grafton. 577 designs for the practicing artist. Full-page, spots, borders, bookplates by Klimt, Bradley, others. 144pp. 8⅜ × 11¼. 24001-0 Pa. $5.00

ART NOUVEAU TYPOGRAPHIC ORNAMENTS, Dan X. Solo. Over 800 Art Nouveau florals, swirls, women, animals, borders, scrolls, wreaths, spots and dingbats, copyright-free. 100pp. 8⅛ × 11. 24366-4 Pa. $4.00

HAND SHADOWS TO BE THROWN UPON THE WALL, Henry Bursill. Wonderful Victorian novelty tells how to make flying birds, dog, goose, deer, and 14 others, each explained by a full-page illustration. 32pp. 6½ × 9¼. 21779-5 Pa. $1.50

AUDUBON'S BIRDS OF AMERICA COLORING BOOK, John James Audubon. Rendered for coloring by Paul Kennedy. 46 of Audubon's noted illustrations: red-winged black-bird, cardinal, etc. Original plates reproduced in full-color on the covers. Captions. 48pp. 8¼ × 11. 23049-X Pa. $2.25

SILK SCREEN TECHNIQUES, J.I. Biegeleisen, M.A. Cohn. Clear, practical, modern, economical. Minimal equipment (self-built), materials, easy methods. For amateur, hobbyist, 1st book. 141 illustrations. 185pp. 6⅛ × 9¼. 20433-2 Pa. $3.95

101 PATCHWORK PATTERNS, Ruby S. McKim. 101 beautiful, immediately useable patterns, full-size, modern and traditional. Also general information, estimating, quilt lore. 140 illustrations. 124pp. 7⅞ × 10¾. 20773-0 Pa. $3.50

READY-TO-USE FLORAL DESIGNS, Ed Sibbett, Jr. Over 100 floral designs (most in three sizes) of popular individual blossoms as well as bouquets, sprays, garlands. 64pp. 8¼ × 11. 23976-4 Pa. $2.95

AMERICAN WILD FLOWERS COLORING BOOK, Paul Kennedy. Planned coverage of 46 most important wildflowers, from Rickett's collection; instructive as well as entertaining. Color versions on covers. Captions. 48pp. 8¼ × 11.
20095-7 Pa. $2.25

CARVING DUCK DECOYS, Harry V. Shourds and Anthony Hillman. Detailed instructions and full-size templates for constructing 16 beautiful, marvelously practical decoys according to time-honored South Jersey method. 70pp. 9¼ × 12¼.
24083-5 Pa. $4.95

TRADITIONAL PATCHWORK PATTERNS, Carol Belanger Grafton. Cardboard cut-out pieces for use as templates to make 12 quilts: Buttercup, Ribbon Border, Tree of Paradise, nine more. Full instructions. 57pp. 8¼ × 11.
23015-5 Pa. $3.50

25 KITES THAT FLY, Leslie Hunt. Full, easy-to-follow instructions for kites made from inexpensive materials. Many novelties. 70 illustrations. 110pp. 5⅜ × 8½.
22550-X Pa. $1.95

PIANO TUNING, J. Cree Fischer. Clearest, best book for beginner, amateur. Simple repairs, raising dropped notes, tuning by easy method of flattened fifths. No previous skills needed. 4 illustrations. 201pp. 5⅜ × 8½. 23267-0 Pa. $3.50

EARLY AMERICAN IRON-ON TRANSFER PATTERNS, edited by Rita Weiss. 75 designs, borders, alphabets, from traditional American sources. 48pp. 8¼ × 11.
23162-3 Pa. $1.95

CROCHETING EDGINGS, edited by Rita Weiss. Over 100 of the best designs for these lovely trims for a host of household items. Complete instructions, illustrations. 48pp. 8¼ × 11. 24031-2 Pa. $2.00

FINGER PLAYS FOR NURSERY AND KINDERGARTEN, Emilie Poulsson. 18 finger plays with music (voice and piano); entertaining, instructive. Counting, nature lore, etc. Victorian classic. 53 illustrations. 80pp. 6½ × 9¼. 22588-7 Pa. $1.95

BOSTON THEN AND NOW, Peter Vanderwarker. Here in 59 side-by-side views are photographic documentations of the city's past and present. 119 photographs. Full captions. 122pp. 8¼ × 11. 24312-5 Pa. $6.95

CROCHETING BEDSPREADS, edited by Rita Weiss. 22 patterns, originally published in three instruction books 1939-41. 39 photos, 8 charts. Instructions. 48pp. 8¼ × 11. 23610-2 Pa. $2.00

HAWTHORNE ON PAINTING, Charles W. Hawthorne. Collected from notes taken by students at famous Cape Cod School; hundreds of direct, personal *apercus*, ideas, suggestions. 91pp. 5⅜ × 8½. 20653-X Pa. $2.50

THERMODYNAMICS, Enrico Fermi. A classic of modern science. Clear, organized treatment of systems, first and second laws, entropy, thermodynamic potentials, etc. Calculus required. 160pp. 5⅜ × 8½. 60361-X Pa. $4.00

TEN BOOKS ON ARCHITECTURE, Vitruvius. The most important book ever written on architecture. Early Roman aesthetics, technology, classical orders, site selection, all other aspects. Morgan translation. 331pp. 5⅜ × 8½. 20645-9 Pa. $5.50

THE CORNELL BREAD BOOK, Clive M. McCay and Jeanette B. McCay. Famed high-protein recipe incorporated into breads, rolls, buns, coffee cakes, pizza, pie crusts, more. Nearly 50 illustrations. 48pp. 8¼ × 11. 23995-0 Pa. $2.00

THE CRAFTSMAN'S HANDBOOK, Cennino Cennini. 15th-century handbook, school of Giotto, explains applying gold, silver leaf; gesso; fresco painting, grinding pigments, etc. 142pp. 6⅛ × 9¼. 20054-X Pa. $3.50

FRANK LLOYD WRIGHT'S FALLINGWATER, Donald Hoffmann. Full story of Wright's masterwork at Bear Run, Pa. 100 photographs of site, construction, and details of completed structure. 112pp. 9¼ × 10. 23671-4 Pa. $6.50

OVAL STAINED GLASS PATTERN BOOK, C. Eaton. 60 new designs framed in shape of an oval. Greater complexity, challenge with sinuous cats, birds, mandalas framed in antique shape. 64pp. 8¼ × 11. 24519-5 Pa. $3.50

KEYBOARD WORKS FOR SOLO INSTRUMENTS, G.F. Handel. 35 neglected works from Handel's vast oeuvre, originally jotted down as improvisations. Includes Eight Great Suites, others. New sequence. 174pp. 9⅜ × 12¼.
24338-9 Pa. $7.50

AMERICAN LEAGUE BASEBALL CARD CLASSICS, Bert Randolph Sugar. 82 stars from 1900s to 60s on facsimile cards. Ruth, Cobb, Mantle, Williams, plus advertising, info, no duplications. Perforated, detachable. 16pp. 8¼ × 11.
24286-2 Pa. $2.95

A TREASURY OF CHARTED DESIGNS FOR NEEDLEWORKERS, Georgia Gorham and Jeanne Warth. 141 charted designs: owl, cat with yarn, tulips, piano, spinning wheel, covered bridge, Victorian house and many others. 48pp. 8¼ × 11.
23558-0 Pa. $1.95

DANISH FLORAL CHARTED DESIGNS, Gerda Bengtsson. Exquisite collection of over 40 different florals: anemone, Iceland poppy, wild fruit, pansies, many others. 45 illustrations. 48pp. 8¼ × 11. 23957-8 Pa. $1.75

OLD PHILADELPHIA IN EARLY PHOTOGRAPHS 1839-1914, Robert F. Looney. 215 photographs: panoramas, street scenes, landmarks, President-elect Lincoln's visit, 1876 Centennial Exposition, much more. 230pp. 8⅜ × 11¾.
23345-6 Pa. $9.95

PRELUDE TO MATHEMATICS, W.W. Sawyer. Noted mathematician's lively, stimulating account of non-Euclidean geometry, matrices, determinants, group theory, other topics. Emphasis on novel, striking aspects. 224pp. 5⅜ × 8½.
24401-6 Pa. $4.50

ADVENTURES WITH A MICROSCOPE, Richard Headstrom. 59 adventures with clothing fibers, protozoa, ferns and lichens, roots and leaves, much more. 142 illustrations. 232pp. 5⅜ × 8½. 23471-1 Pa. $3.50

IDENTIFYING ANIMAL TRACKS: MAMMALS, BIRDS, AND OTHER ANIMALS OF THE EASTERN UNITED STATES, Richard Headstrom. For hunters, naturalists, scouts, nature-lovers. Diagrams of tracks, tips on identification. 128pp. 5⅜ × 8. 24442-3 Pa. $3.50

VICTORIAN FASHIONS AND COSTUMES FROM HARPER'S BAZAR, 1867-1898, edited by Stella Blum. Day costumes, evening wear, sports clothes, shoes, hats, other accessories in over 1,000 detailed engravings. 320pp. 9⅜ × 12¼.
22990-4 Pa. $9.95

EVERYDAY FASHIONS OF THE TWENTIES AS PICTURED IN SEARS AND OTHER CATALOGS, edited by Stella Blum. Actual dress of the Roaring Twenties, with text by Stella Blum. Over 750 illustrations, captions. 156pp. 9 × 12.
24134-3 Pa. $7.95

HALL OF FAME BASEBALL CARDS, edited by Bert Randolph Sugar. Cy Young, Ted Williams, Lou Gehrig, and many other Hall of Fame greats on 92 full-color, detachable reprints of early baseball cards. No duplication of cards with *Classic Baseball Cards*. 16pp. 8¼ × 11. 23624-2 Pa. $2.95

THE ART OF HAND LETTERING, Helm Wotzkow. Course in hand lettering, Roman, Gothic, Italic, Block, Script. Tools, proportions, optical aspects, individual variation. Very quality conscious. Hundreds of specimens. 320pp. 5⅜ × 8½.
21797-3 Pa. $4.95

DECORATIVE NAPKIN FOLDING FOR BEGINNERS, Lillian Oppenheimer and Natalie Epstein. 22 different napkin folds in the shape of a heart, clown's hat, love knot, etc. 63 drawings. 48pp. 8¼ × 11. 23797-4 Pa. $1.95

DECORATIVE LABELS FOR HOME CANNING, PRESERVING, AND OTHER HOUSEHOLD AND GIFT USES, Theodore Menten. 128 gummed, perforated labels, beautifully printed in 2 colors. 12 versions. Adhere to metal, glass, wood, ceramics. 24pp. 8¼ × 11. 23219-0 Pa. $2.95

EARLY AMERICAN STENCILS ON WALLS AND FURNITURE, Janet Waring. Thorough coverage of 19th-century folk art: techniques, artifacts, surviving specimens. 166 illustrations, 7 in color. 147pp. of text. 7⅞ × 10¾. 21906-2 Pa. $8.95

AMERICAN ANTIQUE WEATHERVANES, A.B. & W.T. Westervelt. Extensively illustrated 1883 catalog exhibiting over 550 copper weathervanes and finials. Excellent primary source by one of the principal manufacturers. 104pp. 6⅛ × 9¼. 24396-6 Pa. $3.95

ART STUDENTS' ANATOMY, Edmond J. Farris. Long favorite in art schools. Basic elements, common positions, actions. Full text, 158 illustrations. 159pp. 5⅜ × 8½. 20744-7 Pa. $3.50

BRIDGMAN'S LIFE DRAWING, George B. Bridgman. More than 500 drawings and text teach you to abstract the body into its major masses. Also specific areas of anatomy. 192pp. 6½ × 9¼. (EA) 22710-3 Pa. $4.50

COMPLETE PRELUDES AND ETUDES FOR SOLO PIANO, Frederic Chopin. All 26 Preludes, all 27 Etudes by greatest composer of piano music. Authoritative Paderewski edition. 224pp. 9 × 12. (Available in U.S. only) 24052-5 Pa. $6.95

PIANO MUSIC 1888-1905, Claude Debussy. Deux Arabesques, Suite Bergamesque, Masques, 1st series of Images, etc. 9 others, in corrected editions. 175pp. 9⅜ × 12¼. (ECE) 22771-5 Pa. $5.95

TEDDY BEAR IRON-ON TRANSFER PATTERNS, Ted Menten. 80 iron-on transfer patterns of male and female Teddys in a wide variety of activities, poses, sizes. 48pp. 8¼ × 11. 24596-9 Pa. $2.00

A PICTURE HISTORY OF THE BROOKLYN BRIDGE, M.J. Shapiro. Profusely illustrated account of greatest engineering achievement of 19th century. 167 rare photos & engravings recall construction, human drama. Extensive, detailed text. 122pp. 8¼ × 11. 24403-2 Pa. $7.95

NEW YORK IN THE THIRTIES, Berenice Abbott. Noted photographer's fascinating study shows new buildings that have become famous and old sights that have disappeared forever. 97 photographs. 97pp. 11⅜ × 10. 22967-X Pa. $6.50

MATHEMATICAL TABLES AND FORMULAS, Robert D. Carmichael and Edwin R. Smith. Logarithms, sines, tangents, trig functions, powers, roots, reciprocals, exponential and hyperbolic functions, formulas and theorems. 269pp. 5⅜ × 8½. 60111-0 Pa. $3.75

HANDBOOK OF MATHEMATICAL FUNCTIONS WITH FORMULAS, GRAPHS, AND MATHEMATICAL TABLES, edited by Milton Abramowitz and Irene A. Stegun. Vast compendium: 29 sets of tables, some to as high as 20 places. 1,046pp. 8 × 10½. 61272-4 Pa. $19.95

JAPANESE DESIGN MOTIFS, Matsuya Co. Mon, or heraldic designs. Over 4000 typical, beautiful designs: birds, animals, flowers, swords, fans, geometrics; all beautifully stylized. 213pp. 11⅜ × 8¼. 22874-6 Pa. $6.95

THE TALE OF BENJAMIN BUNNY, Beatrix Potter. Peter Rabbit's cousin coaxes him back into Mr. McGregor's garden for a whole new set of adventures. All 27 full-color illustrations. 59pp. 4¼ × 5½. (Available in U.S. only) 21102-9 Pa. $1.50

THE TALE OF PETER RABBIT AND OTHER FAVORITE STORIES BOXED SET, Beatrix Potter. Seven of Beatrix Potter's best-loved tales including Peter Rabbit in a specially designed, durable boxed set. 4¼ × 5½. Total of 447pp. 158 color illustrations. (Available in U.S. only) 23903-9 Pa. $10.50

PRACTICAL MENTAL MAGIC, Theodore Annemann. Nearly 200 astonishing feats of mental magic revealed in step-by-step detail. Complete advice on staging, patter, etc. Illustrated. 320pp. 5⅜ × 8½. 24426-1 Pa. $5.95

CELEBRATED CASES OF JUDGE DEE (DEE GOONG AN), translated by Robert Van Gulik. Authentic 18th-century Chinese detective novel; Dee and associates solve three interlocked cases. Led to van Gulik's own stories with same characters. Extensive introduction. 9 illustrations. 237pp. 5⅜ × 8½. 23337-5 Pa. $4.50

CUT & FOLD EXTRATERRESTRIAL INVADERS THAT FLY, M. Grater. Stage your own lilliputian space battles. By following the step-by-step instructions and explanatory diagrams you can launch 22 full-color fliers into space. 36pp. 8¼ × 11. 24478-4 Pa. $2.95

CUT & ASSEMBLE VICTORIAN HOUSES, Edmund V. Gillon, Jr. Printed in full color on heavy cardboard stock, 4 authentic Victorian houses in H-O scale: Italian-style Villa, Octagon, Second Empire, Stick Style. 48pp. 9¼ × 12¼. 23849-0 Pa. $3.95

BEST SCIENCE FICTION STORIES OF H.G. WELLS, H.G. Wells. Full novel *The Invisible Man,* plus 17 short stories: "The Crystal Egg," "Aepyornis Island," "The Strange Orchid," etc. 303pp. 5⅜ × 8½. (Available in U.S. only) 21531-8 Pa. $3.95

TRADEMARK DESIGNS OF THE WORLD, Yusaku Kamekura. A lavish collection of nearly 700 trademarks, the work of Wright, Loewy, Klee, Binder, hundreds of others. 160pp. 8¾ × 8. (Available in U.S. only) 24191-2 Pa. $5.00

THE ARTIST'S AND CRAFTSMAN'S GUIDE TO REDUCING, ENLARGING AND TRANSFERRING DESIGNS, Rita Weiss. Discover, reduce, enlarge, transfer designs from any objects to any craft project. 12pp. plus 16 sheets special graph paper. 8¼ × 11. 24142-4 Pa. $3.25

TREASURY OF JAPANESE DESIGNS AND MOTIFS FOR ARTISTS AND CRAFTSMEN, edited by Carol Belanger Grafton. Indispensable collection of 360 traditional Japanese designs and motifs redrawn in clean, crisp black-and-white, copyright-free illustrations. 96pp. 8¼ × 11. 24435-0 Pa. $3.95

THE RIME OF THE ANCIENT MARINER, Gustave Doré, S.T. Coleridge. Doré's finest work, 34 plates capture moods, subtleties of poem. Full text. 77pp. 9¼ × 12.
22305-1 Pa. $4.95

SONGS OF INNOCENCE, William Blake. The first and most popular of Blake's famous "Illuminated Books," in a facsimile edition reproducing all 31 brightly colored plates. Additional printed text of each poem. 64pp. 5¼ × 7.
22764-2 Pa. $3.00

AN INTRODUCTION TO INFORMATION THEORY, J.R. Pierce. Second (1980) edition of most impressive non-technical account available. Encoding, entropy, noisy channel, related areas, etc. 320pp. 5⅜ × 8½.
24061-4 Pa. $4.95

THE DIVINE PROPORTION: A STUDY IN MATHEMATICAL BEAUTY, H.E. Huntley. "Divine proportion" or "golden ratio" in poetry, Pascal's triangle, philosophy, psychology, music, mathematical figures, etc. Excellent bridge between science and art. 58 figures. 185pp. 5⅜ × 8½.
22254-3 Pa. $3.95

THE DOVER NEW YORK WALKING GUIDE: From the Battery to Wall Street, Mary J. Shapiro. Superb inexpensive guide to historic buildings and locales in lower Manhattan: Trinity Church, Bowling Green, more. Complete Text; maps. 36 illustrations. 48pp. 3⅞ × 9¼.
24225-0 Pa. $1.75

NEW YORK THEN AND NOW, Edward B. Watson, Edmund V. Gillon, Jr. 83 important Manhattan sites: on facing pages early photographs (1875-1925) and 1976 photos by Gillon. 172 illustrations. 171pp. 9¼ × 10.
23361-8 Pa. $7.95

HISTORIC COSTUME IN PICTURES, Braun & Schneider. Over 1450 costumed figures from dawn of civilization to end of 19th century. English captions. 125 plates. 256pp. 8⅜ × 11¼.
23150-X Pa. $7.50

VICTORIAN AND EDWARDIAN FASHION: A Photographic Survey, Alison Gernsheim. First fashion history completely illustrated by contemporary photographs. Full text plus 235 photos, 1840-1914, in which many celebrities appear. 240pp. 6½ × 9¼.
24205-6 Pa. $6.00

CHARTED CHRISTMAS DESIGNS FOR COUNTED CROSS-STITCH AND OTHER NEEDLECRAFTS, Lindberg Press. Charted designs for 45 beautiful needlecraft projects with many yuletide and wintertime motifs. 48pp. 8¼ × 11.
24356-7 Pa. $1.95

101 FOLK DESIGNS FOR COUNTED CROSS-STITCH AND OTHER NEEDLE-CRAFTS, Carter Houck. 101 authentic charted folk designs in a wide array of lovely representations with many suggestions for effective use. 48pp. 8¼ × 11.
24369-9 Pa. $1.95

FIVE ACRES AND INDEPENDENCE, Maurice G. Kains. Great back-to-the-land classic explains basics of self-sufficient farming. The one book to get. 95 illustrations. 397pp. 5⅜ × 8½.
20974-1 Pa. $4.95

A MODERN HERBAL, Margaret Grieve. Much the fullest, most exact, most useful compilation of herbal material. Gigantic alphabetical encyclopedia, from aconite to zedoary, gives botanical information, medical properties, folklore, economic uses, and much else. Indispensable to serious reader. 161 illustrations. 888pp. 6½ × 9¼. (Available in U.S. only)
22798-7, 22799-5 Pa., Two-vol. set $16.45

SOURCE BOOK OF MEDICAL HISTORY, edited by Logan Clendening, M.D. Original accounts ranging from Ancient Egypt and Greece to discovery of X-rays: Galen, Pasteur, Lavoisier, Harvey, Parkinson, others. 685pp. 5⅜ × 8½.
20621-1 Pa. $10.95

THE ROSE AND THE KEY, J.S. Lefanu. Superb mystery novel from Irish master. Dark doings among an ancient and aristocratic English family. Well-drawn characters; capital suspense. Introduction by N. Donaldson. 448pp. 5⅜ × 8½.
24377-X Pa. $6.95

SOUTH WIND, Norman Douglas. Witty, elegant novel of ideas set on languorous Mediterranean island of Nepenthe. Elegant prose, glittering epigrams, mordant satire. 1917 masterpiece. 416pp. 5⅜ × 8½. (Available in U.S. only)
24361-3 Pa. $5.95

RUSSELL'S CIVIL WAR PHOTOGRAPHS, Capt. A.J. Russell. 116 rare Civil War Photos: Bull Run, Virginia campaigns, bridges, railroads, Richmond, Lincoln's funeral car. Many never seen before. Captions. 128pp. 9⅜ × 12¼.
24283-8 Pa. $6.95

PHOTOGRAPHS BY MAN RAY: 105 Works, 1920-1934. Nudes, still lifes, landscapes, women's faces, celebrity portraits (Dali, Matisse, Picasso, others), rayographs. Reprinted from rare gravure edition. 128pp. 9⅜ × 12¼. (Available in U.S. only)
23842-3 Pa. $6.95

STAR NAMES: THEIR LORE AND MEANING, Richard H. Allen. Star names, the zodiac, constellations: folklore and literature associated with heavens. The basic book of its field, fascinating reading. 563pp. 5⅜ × 8½.
21079-0 Pa. $7.95

BURNHAM'S CELESTIAL HANDBOOK, Robert Burnham, Jr. Thorough guide to the stars beyond our solar system. Exhaustive treatment. Alphabetical by constellation: Andromeda to Cetus in Vol. 1; Chamaeleon to Orion in Vol. 2; and Pavo to Vulpecula in Vol. 3. Hundreds of illustrations. Index in Vol. 3. 2000pp. 6⅛ × 9¼.
23567-X, 23568-8, 23673-0 Pa. Three-vol. set $32.85

THE ART NOUVEAU STYLE BOOK OF ALPHONSE MUCHA, Alphonse Mucha. All 72 plates from *Documents Decoratifs* in original color. Stunning, essential work of Art Nouveau. 80pp. 9⅜ × 12¼.
24044-4 Pa. $7.95

DESIGNS BY ERTE; FASHION DRAWINGS AND ILLUSTRATIONS FROM "HARPER'S BAZAR," Erte. 310 fabulous line drawings and 14 *Harper's Bazar* covers, 8 in full color. Erte's exotic temptresses with tassels, fur muffs, long trains, coifs, more. 129pp. 9⅜ × 12¼.
23397-9 Pa. $6.95

HISTORY OF STRENGTH OF MATERIALS, Stephen P. Timoshenko. Excellent historical survey of the strength of materials with many references to the theories of elasticity and structure. 245 figures. 452pp. 5⅜ × 8½. 61187-6 Pa. $8.95

Prices subject to change without notice.

Available at your book dealer or write for free catalog to Dept. GI, Dover Publications, Inc., 31 East 2nd St. Mineola, N.Y. 11501. Dover publishes more than 175 books each year on science, elementary and advanced mathematics, biology, music, art, literary history, social sciences and other areas.